Brittany Ferries

from a cause to a brand 1973–2005

Compiled by Richard Kirkman

LAINSON
PUBLISHING

To

Alexis Gourvennec

Creator of the Cause

and

Christian Michielini

Creator of the Brand

CHRISTIAN MICHIELINI
DIRECTEUR GENERAL

ALEXIS GOURVENNEC
PRESIDENT DE BRITTANY FERRIES

First published 2020
Copyright © Lainson Publishing, Lainson Lodge, 32 Sussex Road, Southsea, PO5 3EX.
All rights reserved.
ISBN: 9781527263758
The rights of Lainson Publishing and Richard Kirkman are to be identified for this work in accordance
with the Copyright Act 1991.

Contents

Introduction

Farmer-members of the SICA gather at the Kerisnel produce market in Saint-Pol-de-Léon. *(Ferry Publications Library)*

The story of how Brittany Ferries grew from the bold early aspirations of Alexis Gourvennec and a small group of Breton farmers operating a simple one-ship freight service, to become a market-leading ferry Company is one of a remarkable transformation. Brittany Ferries is now a highly respected international brand with the highest of reputations for quality and service on a portfolio of routes linking Britain and Ireland with France and Spain.

The fledgling Company overcame a seemingly endless sequence of external obstacles that repeatedly threatened the very existence of the business, through the drive, passion and commitment of a tight-knit management and operations team. Initially treated with contempt by other ferry operators on the English Channel, who dismissively referred to the Company as "the cowboys in the wild west", Brittany Ferries rapidly expanded by building a network of services that avoided direct competition with other operators. Expansion was not, however, supported on both sides of the English Channel. There was single-minded enthusiasm amongst the Breton farming community and in the wider Brittany region, where the hoteliers, camp site owners, restaurateurs and shopkeepers all welcomed expansion and new ship investment. But opposition arose in Britain from port and naval authorities, trade unions, and city councils for a variety of vested interest reasons.

Brittany Ferries used the unarguable logic of geography as the key marketing strategy to sell services to the British, Irish and Spanish markets from the outset; these were the shortest and the only direct routes to where holidaymakers really wanted to go. The Company established a distinctive and innovative commercial management style and culture by recruiting from outside the traditional ferry industry and challenging convention. The Breton farmers' original ambition, to link Brittany to the UK vegetable market, was extended to embrace the wider aspiration of becoming the leading freight and passenger operator of ferry services on the western Channel, and the pioneer of cruise ferry services to Spain. A holiday company was established, which soon became the leading operator of motoring holidays from Britain to France, introducing the concept of the gîte. In so doing the Company not only transformed the way British and Irish families went on holiday, but also created a new tourism industry in Normandy and Brittany that helped inject significant revenues into the local economies.

The early years were characterised by a distinct lack of financial resources and the fleet reflected this often hand to mouth existence. But a great strength of the Company lay in the founders' ability to develop and utilise the strong relationships that existed between different institutions in Brittany and France to find and deliver sound financial solutions. This provided stable foundations for the Company and allowed it to expand through the building of a fleet of new ships. The construction of the *Bretagne* heralded a new era of bespoke ships, designed with Breton style and imagination to meet the

The ship that started it all. The *Kerisnel* in her simple early livery, with the initials BAI proudly displayed on her twin funnels. *(Ferry Publications Library)*

Company's specific and carefully considered requirements. This firm footing allowed Brittany Ferries to adopt a long-term perspective when faced with the emerging challenges of exchange rate volatility, the opening of the Channel Tunnel - which prompted severe reductions in cross-Channel ferry fares - and the loss of duty free income. In contrast, the shorter-term financial shareholder-led philosophy of competitors led to their gradual withdrawal from the market. During the period of this narrative, Brittany Ferries became the sole operator of services from the England and Ireland to France and Spain sector.

The Company rapidly became a true multi-national enterprise, with a strategic approach that gave each team the freedom to develop their own business sector. The

Brittany Ferries' success has been built on timely investment in bespoke tonnage. The *Pont Aven* catches the sunlight as she heads across the Bay of Biscay. *(Ferry Publications Library)*

Roscoff-based management began the project, provided the financing, the fleet, and the crews, and trained and developed them to deliver award-winning on board services. The UK, Irish and Spanish teams brought in the bulk of the business, so the southbound trade predominantly drove the brand and route strategies. As more and larger ships were added to the fleet and new routes were opened, so passenger and freight traffic was generated to support their introduction by filling the greatly increased capacities.

Alexis Gourvennec, who was frequently given the title of the unelected 'President of Brittany', was the creator of the original aspiration, and developed the strength of character to move the many mountains which stood in the way of success. Christian Michielini, known to many of the employees and crews as 'Micky', the professional, charismatic, sometimes idiosyncratic, Directeur Général, who straddled the trans-national teams and blended their skills, enabling them to excel in their respective sectors, whilst retaining the support of the Board for innovation and growth. This book is dedicated to their leadership.

Brittany Ferries continues to go from strength to strength with a new generation of management, many of whom have spent lengthy careers with the Company, driving the growth and development of the business. The philosophy of long-term investment in an innovative, quality fleet, established during the currency of this narrative, continues to set standards to which other operators can only strive

This book is not intended to be a full history of Brittany Ferries. Instead, it reflects the narrative of those who became addicted to the cause on the British and Irish side of the English Channel, and led the development of the brand to its market-leading position. The formidable challenges of the early years necessitated a buccaneering response, and this story is told in detail. As Brittany Ferries expanded and matured, so the professionalism of the Company developed, and the number of crises was reduced, but there was still a formidable sequence of external events to be overcome. The story follows the cycle from the establishment of a single vessel freight service, to the point where Brittany Ferries became the sole operator of services in the western Channel to both France and Spain.

This transformation would never have been achieved without the dedication of a large number of passionate, committed and loyal individuals who each embraced the cause and contributed to the ultimate success of the Company.

This is their story.

One

Founders' Vision

The morning of Thursday, 22nd June 1961 started unusually quietly in Morlaix, a small town in the Finistère department of Western Brittany. The streets were deserted and normal commercial business suspended, as access to the town was sealed off by police roadblocks. Many shops, cafes, and bars were closed. There was a feeling of being in a community under siege. As the day progressed, a large crowd began to gather in the Place Emile Souvestre at the heart of the town, arriving in a host of 'caravans' of tractors, filled to overflowing with farmers; some had travelled from as far distant as Tours, 400 kilometres away. Tensions were high, as 3,000 gendarmes and riot police – many armed with sten guns and tear gas grenades - guarded key road junctions and other strategic points close to the town. Morlaix was effectively cut-off from the rest of Brittany.

By late afternoon, the square outside the Mairie de Morlaix was filled with more than 1,000 farmers. Ten times this number were taking part in demonstrations elsewhere across the town. Several farmers carried pitchforks; one brandished a dead fox hung from a pole, inscribed 'Debré', the name of the French Prime Minister Michel Debré. Many were armed with clubs, others carried crude gibbets. Their colleagues blocked and disrupted road traffic elsewhere across the region, as part of a coordinated plan. Riot police used tear gas to disperse a group of demonstrators attempting to block the main highway near St Brieuc; two major highways were blocked in the Vendée. The farmers were all protesting with common cause, seeking the release from custody of two of their leaders.

25-year-old Alexis Gourvennec and 39-year-old Léon Marcel faced five charges of leading civil insurrection, having spent a fortnight in custody following their arrest at the start of the month. They stood accused of leading an assault on the sub-préfecture, disrupting traffic, stopping communications, degrading public buildings and general disorder. Their protest at falling market prices for farm products was strongly supported across the community. Access to the small Morlaix courtroom was strictly controlled, but around 150 farmers crammed the public gallery to offer vociferous support to the accused, forcing the judge to suspend the hearing for a time.

The Public Prosecutor demanded 'long suspended sentences' for the two men, speaking of the threat of civil war if violent acts of seizing public buildings went unpunished. Leading the pair's defence, René Floriot, a leading Parisian lawyer engaged by the farmers' trade unions, gave an elegant, detailed and political exposition of the farmers' grievances. Aware that the trial had attracted international attention, he exploited the opportunity and addressed a worldwide audience. Floriot began by outlining the farmers' increasing frustration at their exploitation by the middlemen who controlled access to the main produce markets; he highlighted the lack of government action in support of Breton farmers, which had been repeatedly promised since 1948. In relation to the case at hand, Floriot argued that Gourvennec and Marcel had not been present when the raid on the sub-préfecture took place, and their arrest had strong political overtones.

7

After a four-hour trial the three judges adjourned to consider their verdict. They took just 20 minutes to conclude the charges were 'not proven' and, to loud supportive approval from the gallery, dismissed the case. The two 'ruddy-faced' men were carried shoulder-high to the bandstand in the Place des Otages, where they addressed a mass gathering of some 5,000 farmers. Gourvennec told the crowd he had benefited from his stay in prison and was returning fitter and stronger to resume the cause. Breton farmers would no longer tolerate their status as second-class citizens; demonstrations would be intensified until the government recognised and responded to the depth of the problem. The trial had generated keen interest amongst the media, and news of the outcome and Floriot's exposition of the farmers' argument was published across the world.

The Brittany region was perceived in two ways at this time. Locally, it was seen as a region built for maritime trade from a tract of land projecting out into the Atlantic from mainland Europe. From a more easterly, Parisian, perspective, it was viewed as an economic cul-de-sac, increasingly isolated from the main markets of Europe; a position which had been reinforced by the centralist economic policies of the de Gaulle era. Historically, the innovations of the industrial revolution had largely by-passed the region, and young Bretons were increasingly forced to move away from home to seek employment. The creation of the European Economic Community (EEC) in 1957 moved the economic focal point of Europe even further eastwards towards the Rhine, increasing the sense of isolation amongst the Bretons. The region experienced a gradual exodus of workers from the traditional agricultural and fishing industries, a position worsened by general population decline.

Breton agriculture existed on a semi self-sufficient basis until just before the Second World War but was largely invisible to the rest of France, save for those Breton products, principally artichokes, cauliflowers, potato plants and salted butter, which had established wider popularity. Farms were typically very small, operating at a subsistence level, with the specialisation in artichokes and cauliflowers encouraged by the rich soil and mild coastal climate which enabled the growing of 'early' vegetables during the produce season.

The Bretons had taken the future into their own hands towards the end of the 1950s by creating their own organisation to regulate and organise the market for fruit and vegetables, as well as to defend the role of the vegetable producers. The Artichoke Committee was created during a period of poor sales in 1958, the first step towards a producer-led organisation. Gourvennec was active in establishing the Société d'Intérêt Collectif Agricole (SICA) of Saint-Pol-de-Léon on 20th January 1961 and became its president; this organisation's objective was to ensure healthy, fair, just and transparent relations between producers and the market. In November 1961, the shippers and producers of Brittany signed a convention to create a sales and distribution network, which was implemented across départements in the region. The principles of this organisation were based on transaction transparency, standardisation of produce, quality control and, importantly, solidarity in defending the price of their agricultural output.

Geographical remoteness from Paris and the rest of France also helped foster strong feelings of regional identity, and the Bretons remained proud of their 'Celtic' origins and traditions. Interest in militant independence-from-France movements was growing. Government offices were perceived as symbols of the French government colonisation of Brittany and deemed to be legitimate targets for separatists and agitators. Whilst the French prime minister Debré responded to the outcome of the Morlaix trial by taking to the radio to warn that the Government would not be swayed by violence or disorder, there was a growing acceptance in Paris that something needed to be done for the region.

This was not an argument about more subsidies for farmers. The Breton agricultural community valued their independence, and in the coming years Gourvennec promoted self-help to address the central issue of exploitation of the community by buyers and

shippers. In 1964 he persuaded the small farmers of Saint-Pol-de-Léon to create the Comité Économique Régional Agricole Fruits et Légumes de Bretagne (Cerafel), a co-operative venture designed to organise agricultural production and marketing along modern commercial lines, moving market power back from the buyers to the farmers. Together they would find new markets, launch new species, and develop advertising campaigns and branding to reach new consumers. This venture quickly proved successful.

The political structure in France differs significantly from that in the UK. The state, region, and commercial businesses in France are more mutually supportive than is normal practice in the UK; each sector is there to help the others, although not by subsidising incompetence. This is a theme that will resonate throughout this book. There was considerable faith within this structure that the French state would fulfil its role, and both the Breton people and the state were happy to support Gourvennec as the community leader. He was apolitical, not part of any of the groups seeking independence for Brittany from the rest of France. His strong charisma and drive helped him exert control and influence, and farmers were happy to back his judgement with their money.

Gourvennec, working with representatives of other economic interests in Brittany, lobbied the government to invest in infrastructure and education to help reduce the Breton feelings of regional isolation. These efforts paid off when the government published the 'Sixth State Plan' in October 1968, which outlined a plan to lower rail tariffs, build motorways along the northern and southern coasts of Brittany to connect to the French motorway network, install an automatic telephone system in the region to improve communication capability, and build a new deep water port at Roscoff to facilitate the export of vegetables. Funding for the four initiatives was confirmed by French president Charles de Gaulle during a visit to Quimper on 2nd February 1969.

This was a fitting reward for the ongoing efforts to increase industrialisation in Brittany, with a strong focus on light industries in the electronics and telecommunications sectors. The development of engineering skills had been catalysed by the building of two Citroën plants at Rennes, a Michelin tyre factory at Vannes, and a Renault foundry at Lorient. Brest benefited from investment in port facilities to bring a capability to handle tankers of up to 200,000-tonne capacity, to service a refinery with storage capacity for three to four million tonnes of oil. The plan envisaged further investment in the leading ship repair yard on the west coast. The region's education needs were addressed by the transfer of three technical colleges to Brittany, the establishment of a national telecommunications study centre at Lannion, and the opening of an Oceanological Centre at Brest.

Proposals for a deep water port at Roscoff to enable greater regional engagement in maritime trade and the export of agricultural produce had a long history. As Gourvennec recounted later in a meeting with Paul Burns, who was to become Managing Director of Brittany Ferries in the UK and Ireland, he remembered when, at the age of 16, his father and friends talked about the prospects of a direct shipping link to Britain to export vegetables; he recalled his father telling of his grandfather and friends discussing the

Loading onions the traditional way at Roscoff. *(Richard Kirkman collection)*

same thing. Gourvennec said, "there comes a time when you do it and stop talking about it, or you do not do it and stop talking about it, but in any event, you have to stop talking about it." It was now time to stop talking about it and decide. Government support for the construction of port facilities at Roscoff would provide the necessary infrastructure to facilitate a ferry service to ship agricultural produce direct to the UK.

There were sound reasons for such a direct route from across the English Channel from Brittany. It represented a good outlet for Breton agriculture. Whilst Brittany still suffered remoteness from its major domestic markets in Paris, London was physically closer to Roscoff than Roscoff was to the French capital. The UK was a long standing net importer of agricultural products, with nearly half of the nation's food requirements imported at that time. There were already established ferry services to Southampton from the Normandy ports of Cherbourg and Le Havre. However, attempts to export Breton produce via these routes often fell victim to prioritisation given to the local Norman farmers, whose produce was more readily available, without the comparatively lengthy trip across difficult roads in Brittany and Normandy, therefore arriving at the ports in fresher condition. Relationships between the Brittany and Normandy regions were not close. If any lorries had to be left behind when the ships sailed from Cherbourg and Le Havre, they would usually have originated from Brittany. Having and using a local port in Roscoff would overcome this problem and allow the Bretons to use the developing expertise of Cerafel to market and sell their fresher produce in the UK market.

There were strong historic traditions of selling Breton produce in the UK, based around the former railway shipping routes. French onion sellers, known as 'Johnnies', became a familiar sight across southern England as they cycled around the country selling their wares during the produce season. At the end of the season they returned home; many Johnnies drowned when the London & South Western Railway Company's (L&SWR) *Hilda* struck the Pierres des Portes rocks off St Malo during her passage from Southampton to St Malo on 18th November 1905.

Roscoff had previously enjoyed regular cargo services by sea to the southern English coast. The L&SWR had established a twice-weekly shipping route from Southampton to Roscoff, on 1st July 1909. This service, with limited passenger accommodation, continued until the outbreak of war in 1914, Weymouth became the preferred port for Roscoff services after the First World War with, for example, private operators, shipping 2,000 tons of broccoli for onward transit across the UK by rail between February and April 1927. This trade grew rapidly, reaching 20,000 tons annually by 1931, and traffic expanded to include supplies of early potatoes. But the Second World War put a stop to the exports, and the traffic did not resume with any consistency thereafter.

The existing harbour facilities at Roscoff were inaccessible at certain tides, lacked the space and structures neded to store perishable produce waiting to travel, and could only accept small vessels. Whilst these ships could be used to transport fruit and vegetables, they were frequently old cargo coasters, incapable of meeting the refrigerated transit requirements of highly perishable produce such as cauliflowers. Many loads were damaged in transit when left on the open deck. On arrival in the UK, dockers would often have to wait up to an hour for the air to clear before they could unload cargo from the ships' holds. This did little for the image of what was, by then, being marketed as a premium vegetable.

Brittany was already beginning to market its products in a professional manner. The 'Prince de Bretagne' brand, created in 1970 by Marc Gilon, gave local produce a clear identity and emphasised the regional heritage of vegetables grown by the six co-operative members of Cerafel along Brittany's northern coast. This single brand image was shared collectively across their network, with a marketing drive supported by media communication, retail promotional material, market research, common packaging and customer contact. Promotion was not limited to the French and British markets, but extended across Europe, Asia and North America.

The outlook looked increasingly positive from January 1973, when the UK and Ireland were set to join the EEC. The logic was simple. Brittany would soon find itself at the heart of a new western trade axis, running from Spain up the west coast of France, across the English Channel and along the growing UK motorway network to Birmingham and Glasgow, with 'landbridge' services connecting through Wales and across the Irish Sea to Ireland. Roscoff lay right at the centre of this axis. The major produce markets in the UK lay in much closer proximity to each other than those of mainland Europe, so could be serviced more efficiently. Gourvennec perceived great opportunities for the Breton agricultural sector through the export of early vegetables to this new market; he envisaged transforming demand for artichokes substantially from the 250 tonnes exported each year, whilst also being personally interested in a new market for his pork products.

There were other reasons a new ferry service from Roscoff could be highly beneficial

Above: **The new harbour facilities take shape at Roscoff.** *(Ferry Publications Library)*

Below: **Construction work in the port at Roscoff.** *(Ferry Publications Library)*

in assisting Brittany's much needed economic regeneration. The port would give British and Irish families quick and direct access to the heart of their favourite holiday region in France. The new service would bring significant tourism development, combining the attractive local culture, scenery, and beaches, with a pleasant, contrasting way of life, a perfect combination for British and Irish holidaymakers. This rural idyll lay in stark contrast to the established routes into France the via the short-sea English Channel ports, which required holidaymakers to drive through the far north of France to reach their holiday destinations in Brittany and west France; the industrial scenery in the Nord pas de Calais encouraged a fast drive south, and it was a bold holidaymaker who would endure the long drive from there to reach Brittany. As Ian Carruthers would later put it, it was like arriving in Middlesbrough when you want to holiday in Devon. Arrival on a direct service to Roscoff would encourage a different pace of travel, thereby greatly adding to the holiday and, from the Breton point of view, inputting more value to the local economy.

As the port in Roscoff began to take shape it became imperative to find an operator willing to serve the new facility. Brittany had been without a regular year-round direct ferry link to the UK since closure of the Southampton-St Malo route by British Railways in 1964. The closest services to the Brittany region were operated from Southampton, with Townsend Thoresen running three 'Viking' class vessels to Cherbourg and Le Havre, the latter in direct competition with P&O Normandy Ferries - a joint operation between the P&O subsidiary General Steam Navigation Company, operating the British-flagged *Dragon*, and the French Société Anonyme de Gérance et d'Armement (SAGA), operating the French-flagged *Leopard*. The two routes had grown to serve both the passenger and freight markets on a year-round basis following the demise of British Railways' services.

In early 1972, Gourvennec and Jean Guyomarc'h, president of the Morlaix Chamber of Commerce, began to approach shipping companies to gauge their interest in opening up a ferry route from Roscoff. They started with the established French ferry operators but were surprised by an overwhelmingly negative response. The same reaction followed their subsequent advances to British and other continent-based ferry operators. Politely received, they were told that a service from Roscoff would be expensive, with the largely seasonal export trade of Breton agricultural products being insufficient to justify a year-round operation. There was little prospect of profit, based on the Bretons' own projections of growth in freight traffic, even after taking into account the planned entry of the UK and Ireland into the EEC in 1973, for a service supporting a relatively undeveloped tourist market with little local hospitality infrastructure. Brittany had no industrial hinterland, was remote from the rest of France, and the Bretons were not even sure which English port would be best to serve with their proposed new service.

Only one company expressed interest but demanded financial guarantees from both the Chamber of Commerce and the farmers' organisations if minimum revenue thresholds were not achieved during a five-month operating season. Again, no profit was foreseen or projected from the exercise. The proposal was quickly turned down. Gourvennec and Guyomarc'h were undeterred; they believed that the economy was much simpler than the specialists perceived. They were persuaded that the geographical logic underpinning their ideas would determine success. Meanwhile, progress on building the port was rapid, with the linkspan already being put in place, and every prospect of the port being ready to receive business by the end of 1972, even if the provision of passenger facilities would not be completed. Having access to the port without a service was unthinkable and would destroy the credibility of those in the region who had lobbied so hard for investment in Roscoff. Would Paris ever listen to them again? Gourvennec's oft-quoted mantra that "where there's a will, there's a way" was about to be put to the test.

André Colin, president of the general council of Finistère, brought Gourvennec (in his capacity as President of the SICA of Saint-Pol-de-Léon), Guyomarc'h, Jean-Jacques Gouasdoué (a logistics specialist who founded Transports Frigorifiques Européens (TFE)), and other regional leaders together in the office of the Morlaix Chamber of Commerce, on 18th April 1972. Colin also invited Jean Hénaff to bring some shipping experience to the meeting. He was a former naval captain who then ran Transcoop, a co-operative of fishermen and canners on the south coast of Brittany. The group set out to find a solution to the problem of not being able to find a ferry operator and Colin looked to Hénaff to break the deadlock. The meeting opened with gloomy feedback on the discussions with potential ferry operators, but the discussion became more energetic when the possibility of establishing an independent shipping line was raised. Here was a means of testing the vision, determining once and for all whether a ferry service from Brittany would work.

Such an enterprise required capital, and Hénaff, as an individual, Gourvennec on behalf of the SICA and Guyomarc'h as president of the Morlaix Chamber of Commerce, each pledged FF5,000 to create a public limited company with FF15,000 capital.

The new Company, Bretagne Angleterre Irlande S.A., (BAI) reflected Gourvennec's determined Celtic agenda, and was registered at the Commercial Court of Brest on 29th April 1972, with Company Registration Number: 927 250 217. Hénaff assumed the presidency of the new enterprise, based on his professional knowledge of the costs of buying and operating a vessel.

A small team of around a dozen people soon assembled in the new BAI head office in rue Saint-Mathieu in Quimper. Collective enthusiasm overcame their relative inexperience, as the team faced a host of new challenges in establishing the Company in the freight market, acquiring year-round traffic to sustain the business, and developing a

The *Kerisnel* heads out to sea from Roscoff. *(Ferry Publications Library)*

tourist business; the most pressing task was to find a ro-ro vessel to operate the service, a project entrusted to Hénaff.

There was strong scepticism amongst shipbrokers that needed to be addressed. The three funding partners agreed that the initial priority should be the freight business; whilst the port facilities for freight were nearing completion, they were still a long way short of meeting tourist requirements. Early revenue was needed to offset the initial capital outlay. The export of produce was the main priority of the founding shareholders. Freight traffic took precedence. Passenger business could supplement freight income at a future date, so passenger marketing was deferred for twelve months.

Hénaff worked with a shipbroker to examine the market for freight ro-ro vessels and visited several shipyards to find a suitable second-hand ship. His interest focused on the *Lilac*, which had been constructed at the Astilleros & Construcciones S.A. yard in Vigo, Spain for the Topaz Shipping Corporation of Monrovia, on behalf of the Israeli Navy. Her keel had been laid down on 13th July 1970, and she was launched on 22nd April 1971. The *Lilac* was built as a tank carrier with a heavily reinforced deck plate, but she was was redundant for use in the already settled Arab-Israeli war and no longer required by her owners. The yard was having difficulty disposing of the vessel, as there was a limited market for small ro-ro freight ships that could take tanks. At 99.17 metres in length and 16.62 metres breadth, grossing 3,395 gross-tonnes and a service speed of 18 knots, she was very suitable for the proposed BAI service, and could carry twelve passengers and 540 lane-metres of freight traffic, equivalent to 45 commercial vehicles. But she came at a high price – FF18 million. This posed a significant capital requirement, far beyond initial expectations, which proved difficult to raise by conventional means; no bank wanted to commit to a speculative enterprise that professionals hinted was heading for rapid bankruptcy, operating from a port that other ferry companies felt had limited traffic potential. The shareholders were forced to look inwards to generate the resources needed to purchase the *Lilac*.

The SICA Saint-Pol-de-Léon had accumulated strong financial reserves in its first decade of operation, and Gourvennec was able to secure their support which, combined

The *Kerisnel* stands ready to receive her first load at Roscoff. *(Ferry Publications Library)*

with contributions from Cerafel and the Morlaix Chamber of Commerce, raised the capital of BAI to FF4.5 million. This commitment enabled Gourvennec to approach the Crédit Agricole bank to borrow the remainder of the money to complete the purchase of the *Lilac*. One of the first acts was to rename the vessel *Kerisnel*, after the produce auction market of the SICA Saint-Pol-de-Léon.

The *Kerisnel* required a few changes to prepare her for freight service. Accommodation had to be installed for the twelve drivers permitted to travel on each crossing, so demountable portacabins were welded to the deck to serve as dormitories, the canteen and a pantry. These facilities were basic and spartan, but matched the perception of the level of catering required by the small number of accompanying lorry drivers.

The Roscoff port works were now nearing completion, although no decision had been made as to the English destination for the new ferry service. Poole and Weymouth were contemplated, as they offered a comparatively short drive from the ports to the main English produce markets, but they would need long sea crossings from Roscoff. Plymouth offered a shorter sea crossing, enabling a round trip to be encompassed easily each day, but the port was much further away from the markets. Offsetting the negative of the

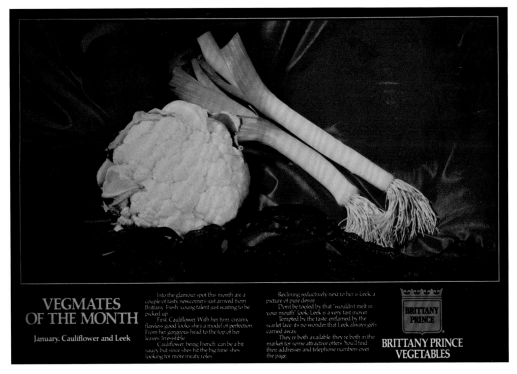

Prince de Bretagne vegetables were marketed as Brittany Prince in Britain. *(Rook Dunning)*

market distance was the fact that the UK motorway network was gradually extending towards the south west. BAI opted for the shorter sea crossing to Plymouth. The British Transport Docks Board (BTDB), the British government owned company which owned and operated Plymouth's Millbay Docks, shared the pessimism of the shipping 'experts' and demanded payment in advance for the required development of ferry facilities. The port needed dredging, and even a simple freight operation would require the installation of a 55-metre linkspan, plus the initial provision of 0.8 hectares of land for vehicle marshalling, with the potential to add a further two hectares of storage space if traffic grew; these works were contracted by BTDB to Thomas & Co for £400,000. However, the BTDB were enthusiastic enough to send a couple of staff by plane over Roscoff to view and photograph the new facilities; on returning to Plymouth they discovered that their camera had not been loaded with film...

Meanwhile, the freight traffic phase of the Roscoff port work was completed in September 1972 at a final cost of FF17 million, as construction continued on building the passenger terminal facilities.

BAI turned to an established partner of the Breton farmers for help in selling the new freight service. The SICA Saint-Pol-de-Léon employed the advertising agency Hautefeuille to market, advertise and promote their vegetable products across Europe under the Prince de Bretagne banner, which eventually became the tenth largest fruit and vegetable brand in the world. Hautefeuille's advice was sought on how to sell produce more extensively in the UK. The agency recommended Derek Brightwell, who was the former Marketing Director of Bovril, and worked for Foote, Cone and Belding (FCB). He had established a positive working relationship with Simon Bryan and Michael Constantinidi, who, coincidentally, had just resigned from Bovril's advertising agency SH Benson. Brightwell proposed to Bryan and Constantinidi that they join him in forming a new agency, with the 'Brittany Prince' produce account as their first client. Thus Bryan, Constantinidi & Brightwell (BCB) was formed. The new agency began the energetic promotion of Brittany-grown artichokes, cauliflowers and potatoes across the UK, with a distinctive brand style built around the colours of vegetables. Brightwell established a close and effective working relationship with Gilon, the director of external trade relations for the SICA Saint-Pol-de-Léon, and later head of Brittany Ferries. When the idea of a ferry service was first mooted in Brittany, it was natural that trusted partner BCB should be approached and asked for advice and help. It was to be the start of an enduring relationship that was to last for 26 years.

Brightwell proposed a rebranding of the ferry service to help improve visibility. Bretagne Angleterre Irlande and BAI were difficult names to communicate to a British audience and did little to give a sense of the route focus or the regional identity of the proposed service. He strongly proposed simplification of the brand name. The anglicised 'Brittany Ferries', which Brightwell recommended, was far more sympathetic to the target customer's ear and immediately created strong geographical associations with the region. The Board agreed, and henceforth 'Brittany Ferries' was used instead of BAI as the brand to promote and administer the Company, although BAI was retained as the name of the holding Company.

The forthcoming opening the new service was observed with interest by local road hauliers in Brittany. A British company 'Transfruit' had established an operation at Saint-Pol-de-Léon railway station in 1967, initially by car using the Société Nationale des Chemins de fer Français (SNCF) Dunkirk-Dover service, then from 1968 with lorries on the P&O Normandy Ferries and Townsend Thoresen routes from Cherbourg and Le Havre to Southampton. In 1968 Transfruit appointed Danzas, in Paris, as their agent to help expand Transfruit services southwards into France. Danzas was already active in Brittany through their subsidiary Denrées, which specialised in the small provincial agencies in large agricultural production areas. One such agency was in Saint-Pol-de-Léon, and the company established a second office in Saint-Méloir-des-Ondes near St Malo. The director of Denrée was a man named Christian Michielini. The Transfruit-Danzas partnership was approached by Hervé Mesguen, who had built a successful produce haulage business in Brittany. Commercial logic brought the three companies together, and TDM was formed. Mesguen sourced vehicles, and understood the local market, Danzas helped with the commercial aspects of the business and customs formalities, and Transfruit managed operations in the UK. The partnership could offer highly competitive journey times and deliver produce to market in far better condition than offered by traditional methods of shipment. By 1970, 50% of shipments from Brittany to the UK were being handled by TDM. It was obvious to TDM that new ferry route would challenge this business so TDM were keen to be active in the establishment and use of the service. Mesguen and Michielini together interviewed a potential employee named Alain Sibiril, to be appointed as the TDM representative in Plymouth; he had studied English at university and spent a year living in the UK. His appointment, based in Plymouth, helped give TDM an edge in establishing their operation alongside the planned ferry service.

Having now got to a stage when it was clear that Brittany Ferries would be operating from Roscoff to Plymouth, Gourvennec travelled to Plymouth on 6th November 1972 to meet with Mike Bartlett, a Partner at the Law Firm, Bond Pearce & Co. Gourvennec asked Bartlett to Incorporate a new British Company, BAI (UK) Limited, as soon as possible. The new Company would be required to enable BAI S.A to trade in the UK. BAI (UK) Limited was Incorporated on Tuesday 7th November 1972, Company Number 1080495. Brittany Ferries now had a British Company.

The *Kerisnel* was soon ready for service and began to provide income with a one-month charter to provide vessel-refit cover for P&O Normandy Ferries, between Southampton and Le Havre. She left Le Havre for the first time as a Brittany Ferries vessel on 13th November 1972, under the command of the Breton captain Ernest Lainé and

Crowds throng down the linkspan for the inaugural arrival
of the *Kerisnel*. *(Ferry Publications Library)*

chief officer Gérard Le Saux, who, like
many of the crew, had joined the company
from P&O Normandy Ferries, where they
were previously employed on the *Leopard*.
They were joined on the crossing by a
handful of BAI employees. Weather
conditions were sufficiently poor to deter
most vessels from sailing that day, but this
was a challenge to be overcome by the
Kerisnel's crew; the new Company did not
want to encourage the critics with a
cancelled sailing, despite there being a
solitary freight vehicle on board.
Approaching the English coast in a
strengthening wind, the *Kerisnel* changed
course and was hit by a wave that
swamped the bridge and caused her to
heel dramatically. There was a loud crash
from the car deck and the crew went down
to find their single freight vehicle cargo
lying toppled amidst broken bottles of
vintage cognac. It was an inauspicious
beginning, but the voyage was fulfilled.

Her charter completed, the *Kerisnel*
returned to the new deep water port at
Roscoff on 18th December 1972 for her
christening ceremony. A large crowd
assembled from early in the morning to
watch her arrival. Freshly painted, with an all-white hull split by a single thin horizontal
blue band from bow to stern and the initials BAI proudly displayed on her twin funnels,
the *Kerisnel* stood bright on a clear, crisp morning, dwarfing any vessel previously seen in
the port.

Gourvennec's wife Annie performed an emotional naming ceremony. The Breton
dream of many generations was finally coming true. This was a community event,
bringing everyone together to celebrate their investment; everyone had an interest in her
success. Curiosity was assuaged by two 'open days' and huge numbers took advantage to
inspect what visitors saw from the outset as 'their' vessel, the *Kerisnel*. They treated her
as their own, and it was to become something of a Sunday tradition to inspect the vessel
when she lay over on the berth after unloading operations had been completed. Access
to the vessel was encouraged by the crew, further strengthening the *Kerisnel's* links with
the local community.

The *Kerisnel* left Roscoff at midnight on 20th December 1972, under Capt. Lainé and
an entirely Breton crew on a trial voyage to Plymouth. A survey at the time suggested
that 78% of French seafarers were of Breton origin, and few had the opportunity to work
comparatively regular hours so close to home, so Brittany Ferries proved to be a highly
popular employer, and seafaring positions were much sought after. A handful of
shareholders joined the *Kerisnel* on this crossing, including the SICA Saint-Pol-de-Léon
Secretary General Henri Jacob, who was keen to feel part of the new enterprise. The
shareholders were desperate for the new service to survive as they had already invested
so much in the project; talk turned to finding the funds needed to procure another vessel
and meet the perceived demand for a passenger service to bring a further boost to the
local economy. A celebratory meal was held at the Holiday Inn in Plymouth to mark the
occasion. Her successful round trip completed, the *Kerisnel* stood ready to begin

operations and fulfil the dreams of the Breton people. This completed the first step of the cause, so long advocated by Gourvennec and his forefathers.

The *Kerisnel* spent the Christmas and New Year period in Roscoff, before a crowd of more than 3,000 gathered on the pier on the evening of 2nd January 1973 to witness the loading of her first commercial departure to Plymouth. The excitement was palpable as the Breton, French, and British flags flew, to musical accompaniment from the Bagad de Lan Bihoué. The first freight customer was 28-year-old Jean Claude Rolland with a cargo of apples, bound for the Cornwall wholesale market in Redruth. Paul Quéméner took an articulated lorry loaded with Mesguen's first shipment of cauliflowers to London for Transfruits. The ship's full load comprised of four lorries loaded with cauliflowers, three with apples, one with lettuce, one carrying paper for Senior Service cigarettes, three empty vehicles and one car, a green Citroën Ami 6. This was the first passenger vehicle to cross from Roscoff to Plymouth and carried Alain Sibiril, who was heading across to set up a branch of Mesguen in Plymouth. Little did he realise this was to be a 40-year endeavour. A spokesman stating that Brittany Ferries hoped to carry around 150,000 tonnes of cargo in their first year of operation.

The *Kerisnel* sailed on time at 23:00 with her regular crew supplemented by 13 passengers. On arrival in Millbay Docks, Plymouth at 07:00 the following morning, she was greeted by the newly recruited local team under the direction of Nick Burnel, who had been appointed as the company's first manager in England; his role encompassed the operational aspects of the new service, managing the turnaround activity for each arrival from Roscoff. The *Kerisnel* sailed for Roscoff at 11:00 with four empty trailers and one loaded lorry and just one accompanying driver.

Burnel and his team worked from temporary offices in very primitive conditions housed in a former air raid shelter on the Quay at Millbay Docks. The Plymouth staff were selected by Burnel, who had been recruited by the Roscoff team in October 1972 to establish the Plymouth operation. He brought in Armand le Bras, who had extensive experience from his time with P&O Normandy Ferries in Le Havre, as Commercial Manager, and his son Bernard. He also recruited Josee Dyer to support the commercial direction of the UK Company. Millbay Docks was not well laid out to accommodate ferry traffic and the whole operation had an experimental air. The BTDB struggled to accommodate the new service and had a conflict of interest with the government owned Sealink ferry company, which operated services from Newhaven to Dieppe, and was, at that time, considering re-opening the passenger route from Weymouth to Cherbourg for the 1974 summer season. Established cross-Channel ferry operators further east continued to view the new operation with disdain. What kind of threat could a 12 lorry driver freight-only service at the geographical periphery of England and France pose to their own well established operations?

The first arrival in Plymouth received widespread publicity and was reported in the Coventry Evening Telegraph under the heading '£5.5m Market Ferry Service': -

'A £5,500,000 enterprise between south west England and Brittany began operating yesterday when lorries hauling vegetables were landed at Millbay Docks, Plymouth, from the French ferry ship *Kerisnel*. The voyage by Brittany Ferries' new ship was the first of regular daily sailings across the 95 miles of channel between Roscoff in Brittany and Plymouth'.

[*Coventry Evening Telegraph 4th January 1973*]

The UK, Denmark, and Ireland joined the original six members in the EEC on 1st January 1973. As Gourvennec later noted, the Company was a day late in serving the new expanded Community. Much of the argument in favour for those countries joining the EEC had been based on the long-term political and economic benefits which would accrue from new trading relationships with other member countries. But it was to take

Brittany ferries NAVIRE : Nº DE VOYAGE 001

BRITFERRY PLMTH
BAIROS A 74360F

FREIGHT MANIFEST OF MV KER SNEL SAILING FROM ROSCOFF TO
PLYMOUTH 2/1/73 AT 11 .

1 000489 PPD FVA 6952 QE 29 7347 QN 29   14500
   PAPETERIES DE MAUDIT QUIMPERLE   SENIOR SERVICES
      20 PALETTES PAPIERS A CIGARETTES/ PADDLES OF PAPER 8738

2 000497   FVA 2024 QA 29   8595 QK 29   815EEEE 8120
   L HARIDON   RAW AND CO
   1000 COLIS POMMES/ PACKAGES APPLES   19596

3 000495   FVA 7946 QR 29   8120
   L HARIDON/ ROW AND CO
   1000 CARTONS POMMES/ PACKAGES APPLES   19600

4 000496   FVA 8086 QS 29   562 QN 29   8120
   L HARIDON ROW AND CO
   000 CARTONS POMMES/ PACKAGES APPLES   19600-

5 000494 COL FVA)-, 869 K   15000
          LAN 869 K
   TRANSFRUIT LONDON/ TRANSFRUIT LONDON
   V DE/EMPTY

6 000487   RC ALV 270 B   1500
   BA ROSCOFF/BAI ROSCOFFEEEEE PLYMOUTH   9000

7 00048 COL FVR 8549 QJ 29
   MESGUEN ST POL/ TRANSFRUIT LONDON
   960 PLATEAUX DE LA TUES/ LOADING PLATFORMS LETTUCE 2880

8 000479 COL FVR 7088 OT 29   9208
   SEVERE ST POL/OK LONDON
   230 CAGOTS CHOUXFLEURS/ PECKSNIFF OF CAULIFLOWERS 9000

9 000480 COL FVR 3 56 QP 29   11000
   MESGUEN ST POL/ TRANSFRUITS)LONDON
   574 CAGOTS CHOUXFLEURS/PECKSNIFF CAULIFLOWZERS   14350

10 000478   CA   56L LM 29
   SIBIR L ROSCOFF/SIBIRIL ROSCOFF
   VOITURE/CAR

11 000490 COL RT 188 GN 29   13000
             6002 QL 29
   GROUPAGE/ TRANSPORTS COMPAGNY
   698 CAGOTS CHOUXFLEURS/ PECKSNIFF CAULIFLOWERS
   7 CARTONS VIS ET ECROUS/ CASES OF SCREWS ANS
   NUTS   18 10
                                         18 04

2 000493 COL RT 2560 QA 29   13 000
            307 XM 29
   GROUPAGE/PERISABLES PLUMMOUTH
   656 CAGOTS CHAUXFLEURS/ PACKSNIFF CAULIFLOWERS 17000

13 000468 CA   4083 QP 29   1250
                BAI ROSCOFF / BA PLYMOUTH
LIGNES D ERREURS : 4
END OF ITEMS : 3

BAIROS A 74360F
BRITFERRY PLMTHM

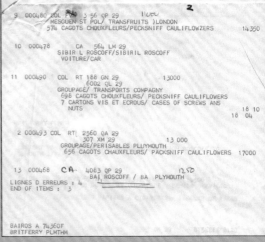

BRITTANY FERRIES

Nº 000481 R

COMMERCIAL VEHICLE MOVEMENT ORDER
ORDRE DE MOUVEMENT DE VÉHICULES COMMERCIAUX
(Not negotiable) (Non négociable)

B.A.I. Direction générale : 31 rue de Douarnenez, 29000 QUIMPER
S.A. au capital de 5 000 000 F. R.C. MORLAIX 72 B 21

Service Exploitation

ROSCOFF
GARE MARITIME
Tél. (98) 69.71.56
(98) 69.76.10

PLYMOUTH
MILLBAY DOKS PLI 3 EF
Tél. (0752) 21540

TELEX   TELEX BRITFERRY 45380

NAVIRE KERISNEL

Please receive the following for Shipment
Veuillez recevoir les Véhicules suivants pour expédition

FROM ROSCOFF to Plymouth   SAILING ON
DE   A   DATE DE VOYAGE 2-1-73

BON A EXPORTER
L'AGENT DES DOUANES

DATE 2.1.73

Vehicle Type	Number	Tare Weight of Vehicle	Nbr. and Kind of Packages	Description of the Goods Said to contain	Gross Weight of Goods
RIGID	8529 QJ29		960 Plateaux de Laitues		2880
10 litres					

No. IMP 0011

B.A.I. - BRITTANY FERRIES

Vessel: KERISNEL   Date: 03/01/73
Vehicle No.: 8529 QJ 29
Type FVR   Length: 15 M
Payment (Agents): PPD Transfruit
C.V.M.O. No. 000489

Freight Supervisor

Signature

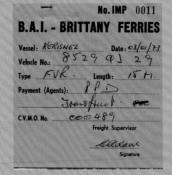

This page: **Documentation from the *Kerisnel*'s first sailing from Roscoff to Plymouth.** *(Alain Sibiril collection)*

five years for tariff levels to be regularised across the EEC, and in the early stages of membership UK tariffs were still imposed on imports from EEC countries. The Reading Evening Post noted on 20th February that membership of the EEC would bring an expansion to the cross-Channel market, highlighting the new route from Roscoff, which it observed had already proved particularly beneficial to French exporters of vegetables. Traffic volumes from France were given a further boost when import duties into the UK were reduced, as planned, by 20% from 1st April 1973.

Brittany Ferries' initial plans envisaged three return crossings on the route each week, increasing to five during the peak produce season, but the *Kerisnel* was soon carrying out

b.a.i. u.k. ltd
brittany ferries
millbay docks plymouth pl1 3ef
tel. (0752) 21840·20057 telex: britferry plmth 45380

Above: **Brittany Ferries letterhead**.

Right: **Freight agents'
accommodation at Plymouth.**
(Alain Sibiril)

a daily rotation. Traffic was initially modest, despite the Breton enthusiasm for the new line. Many hauliers in France were unwilling to commit themselves to the service or transfer their business from other ferry operators until they were convinced that the new Roscoff-Plymouth route was going to be a permanent fixture. A one vessel service was always vulnerable to disruption, so it was wise for them to maintain business elsewhere as insurance against breakdown, bad weather or other service interruptions. Other ferry operators, although holding the new Brittany Ferries service in contempt, were, nonetheless sufficiently aware of its presence, to actively and widely publicise any shortcomings, delays, or problems of which they became aware. Hauliers needed confidence in the farmers' capabilities as ship operators before they could make big traffic commitments, which made Gourvennec and his colleagues all the more determined to make the venture a success. The *Kerisnel* continued to operate regardless of weather conditions to prove a point, even if loads were small, often crossing in sea conditions that would be unthinkable in the modern era. There was a strong customer focus from the beginning, with crews demonstrating flexibility in scheduling, waiting for loads if they were advised that a vehicle was arriving late into the departure port. There was also pressure from hauliers, who frequently demanded that the *Kerisnel* sail in challenging sea conditions as, once committed to support the route, they had no practical alternative to using the service.

By the end of the first quarter of operation Brittany Ferries had carried 17,000 tonnes of traffic, compared to the original target of 40,000 tonnes. Besides local cabbages and cauliflowers, the *Kerisnel* had carried fruit from across south west France, cognac, cigarettes and Spanish oranges, together with some industrial exports from Brittany. Traffic continued to diversify, but it was largely one way traffic to the UK, leaving an empty return leg to be filled. French hauliers found return loads difficult to acquire. The Bretons were not used to importing anything from the UK, had few contacts in the import market, and found established transportation habits hard to break.

The BAI Board was keen to provide capacity to meet aspirations for a passenger service by operating a multi-purpose vessel from the 1974 season. An order was placed with the French shipyard Société Nouvelle des Ateliers & Chantiers of La Rochelle-Pallice, for a new passenger and freight-carrying vessel capable of carrying 40 freight vehicles and 80 passengers. The vessel was to be named *Penn-Ar-Bed* after the Breton translation of Finistère, or 'Land's End' in English. The proposals to establish a passenger service were encouraged by the number of passengers who sought to join the *Kerisnel* at Plymouth and Roscoff and had to be turned away, even in the earliest days of the freight-only service. Although the prime purpose in establishing Brittany Ferries had been the export of agricultural products, it was evident that passenger income would be needed to balance and underpin the finances of the Company, in line with other successful cross-Channel ferry operations. There was no doubting the potential of the market because of Brittany's long standing popularity with adventurous British tourists. And a thriving passenger business would bring wealth to the wider region. There was a precedent set further east in the English Channel, where Thoresen Car Ferries (later renamed Townsend Thoresen) had established their successful multi-purpose ro-ro services from

A staple of the first season of operation – a well loaded trailer of cauliflowers on the quay at Millbay Docks. *(Alain Sibiril)*

The *Poseidon* operated for Vedettes Armoricaines to provide the first passenger service between Roscoff and Plymouth. *(Ferry Publications Library)*

Southampton to Cherbourg and Le Havre as early as 1964, after British Railways withdrew from the market. The formula of operating vessels capable of carrying both passenger and freight traffic was clearly the right one to follow.

Plans to introduce a second vessel to the Plymouth-Roscoff route were made public as early as March 1973. The Observer noted on 25th March: -

'If you live in Devon, holidaying abroad should be easier from December, when Brittany Ferries start taking passengers and cars on their service between Plymouth and Roscoff. Sailings will be daily, take six hours, and there will be accommodation for 250 passengers and 70 cars.'

In the short-term, activities at Roscoff were being watched closely by a shipowner named Mr Le Bris, who ran Vedettes Armoricaines, a shipping company offering excursion sailings from Brest to the Île d'Ouessant. Le Bris approached Gourvennec with a proposition for the two organisations to work together; he had chartered the *Poseidon*, a Stena Line passenger ship, and Brittany Ferries had the *Kerisnel* – why could the two vessels not run in tandem? The concept interested Gourvennec, as it allowed the passenger market to be tested in advance of Brittany Ferries' second vessel being delivered. The 1,358 gross-tonne 66.5-metre-long 805-passenger capacity *Poseidon* was built by Ulstein M/V A/S in Norway in 1964 to a Knud E. Hansen design, and was the second vessel operated by the emerging Stena Line. She was designed as a daytime sailing vessel. The *Poseidon* operated several excursions for French schoolchildren between St Malo and Jersey before an agreement was concluded with Gourvennec, and the *Poseidon* began running in parallel with the *Kerisnel* from 15th May 1973, slightly later than planned due to delays in resolving the contractual arrangements. The *Poseidon* operated from Roscoff to the Trinity Pier in Millbay Docks, Plymouth.

It did not take long for relationships between the two companies to come under strain. The *Kerisnel* maintained her planned freight schedule, but the *Poseidon* was operated more like an excursion vessel, often lingering in port to await the arrival of sufficient passengers to justify a departure. The *Poseidon* did not sail at all on occasions if there was insufficient traffic to warrant a crossing. By the time her operating season finished on 15th September, the *Poseidon* had averaged carryings of 120 passengers per day through the summer, but her presence had given Brittany Ferries some valuable experience of the potential for a passenger business. There was clearly a demand and, following the *Poseidon* being withdrawn at the end of the summer, a significant number of potential passengers were still being turned away from the freight-only *Kerisnel*.

There was an increase in freight capacity and competition on the western Channel

The upper deck of the *Kerisnel* during a quiet crossing. *(Ferry Publications Library)*

routes from June 1973 when the *Antelope* began operating from Poole to Cherbourg for a new company called Truckline. This freight-only service was an initiative promoted by Peter Allsebrook, and was financed by Banque Worms, Hambros, TNT, Bill Cottell, and Frank Allen, owner of a large Hampshire-based international haulage business. Poole Harbour Commissioners invested in reclaiming land to build a terminal facility in their port and installed a 22-metre linkspan with a side-loading ramp designed specifically to attract the car export business. The *Antelope* was joined later in the year by the *Dauphin de Cherbourg*, but the two vessels quickly proved inadequate for the service as the growth of the company was encouragingly rapid.

The *Penn-Ar-Bed* was launched at the Société Nouvelle des Ateliers & Chantiers shipyard at La Rochelle-Pallice on 17th May 1973. Her passenger complement was upped to 150 as understanding of the potential market grew, then increased again to 320 at the end of the *Poseidon's* operating season, both changes occurring whilst the new vessel was under construction. The Company's plans envisaged the *Kerisnel* being converted to carry passenger traffic during her winter refit, so that the two vessels could offer a balanced service for the 1974 season. Completion of the *Penn-Ar-Bed* was delayed by strikes at the shipyard during the autumn, but growing optimism was justified by advance interest in the passenger service. This could prove to be a significant second source of income.

The cost of the *Penn-Ar-Bed* rose to FF30 million, requiring an increase in capital, largely sourced from the SICA Saint-Pol-de-Léon and, as BAI had no capital reserves, from further bank borrowings. The harsh reality of the capital sums involved in shipping and the attendant risks of bankruptcy were difficult lessons for the farmer-shareholders. The situation also highlighted the lack of progress in attracting new shareholders to bring capital into the business, a task that had been entrusted to Hénaff.

At the end of the first year of operation, the balance sheet showed a loss of FF7 million

The launch of the *Penn-Ar-Bed* on 17th May 1973 at the Société Nouvelle des Ateliers & Chantiers shipyard at La Rochelle-Pallice. The vessel had an inbuilt list that had to be corrected before she entered service. *(Ferry Publications Library)*

against revenues of FF7 million. This outcome could have tipped the fledgling Brittany Ferries into bankruptcy, but the shareholders demonstrated their determination to continue by committing more funds to support the Company. This was a long-term project; the shareholders were not going to be blown off course by the burden of short-term set up, launch and initial operating costs. There were also external events that had impacted these financial results, with oil price rises, increased costs in consequence, and a sustained period of bad weather during the winter of 1973-74 which all depressed performance, but the company transported 5,932 freight vehicles in the year, with numbers growing steadily month by month. The results were sufficiently below expectation to cause plans to convert the *Kerisnel* to passenger operation to be put on hold, and an alternative use was sought for her for the 1974 season.

Forward prospects looked better. More and more companies were sampling the freight service, particularly those sceptical hauliers who had been reluctant to commit traffic in the early days. Passengers continued to be turned away from the freight-only operation, and Plymouth's comparative isolation from the rest of Britain was being tackled by the

The *Penn-Ar-Bed* is outfitted in a revised Company livery with two tone blue and orange strips on her white hull and a new logo on the funnels. *(Ferry Publications Library)*

gradual extension of the M5 motorway westwards towards Exeter. The Clevedon and Mendip hills section of the M5 opened in January 1973, followed by the Bridgwater by-pass in December that year, with the Taunton by-pass to be completed in April 1974. Traffic could only grow as Plymouth became more accessible.

Bookings for the new Brittany Ferries passenger service opened to the public in November 1973, announced by a simple typeset advertisement in regional newspapers. One such advert in the Liverpool Echo on 21st November encouraged passengers to: -

'Cross to the Continent on the new luxury car ferry Penn-Ar-Bed from Plymouth ferryport to Roscoff in Brittany and you are well on your way to Spain and Portugal. Special rates for 36-HOUR AND 60-HOUR RETURN EXCURSIONS. Passports not required.

Bookings open from November – for more information on fares and reduced rates for group travel, see your local travel agent, or contact:

Brittany Ferries, Plymouth Ferryport, Plymouth. Telephone Plymouth 21840, 20057.

Further strikes at the La Rochelle-Pallice shipyard delayed the arrival of *Penn-Ar-Bed*, and she did not undertake sea trials until mid-January 1974. There was time to display her to the public at an open day in Roscoff, before Capt. Lainé took command of her first departure for Plymouth, shortly before midnight on 24th January 1974. Paul Quéméner, who was an owner-driver working for Mesguen, had the distinction of following his crossing on the first voyage of the *Kerisnel*, with passage on the inaugural trip of the *Penn-Ar-Bed*.

The timing of the launch of the passenger service was inauspicious. An oil supply crisis had begun in October 1973, when members of the Organisation of Petroleum Exporting Countries (OPEC) proclaimed an embargo on countries which had supported Israel during the Yom Kippur war, including the UK but not France. The oil price rose four-fold, from $3 to $12 per barrel by the end of the embargo in March 1974. This was compounded by a sequence of strikes in the UK, including one by coal miners, which paralysed the economy and led to a three-day working week, with electricity also rationed to three days each week in order to conserve fuel stocks. Prime Minister Edward Heath called a general election and lost his majority, and a minority Labour government took power. The period of reduced working hours came to an end on 7th March 1974, fortunately in time for the main holiday season.

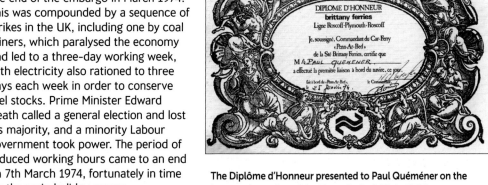

The Diplôme d'Honneur presented to Paul Quéméner on the inaugural crossing of the *Penn-Ar-Bed*. *(Alain Sibiril)*

The arrival of the *Penn-Ar-Bed* and the decision not to operate a two-ship service meant that the *Kerisnel* was no longer required for the Plymouth-Roscoff route. She was transferred to Ouest Ferries, a new BAI subsidiary which was to open a service between St Nazaire and Vigo. The inspiration of Hénaff, this route was introduced to transport new cars from the Citroën factory in Rennes for export to the Spanish market through Galicia, the Celtic region in north west Spain.

The *Penn-Ar-Bed* had modest public spaces including a shop, cafeteria and an information counter, which reflected the ad hoc expansion of her passenger capacity during the building phase. The shop could easily be identified by the long queues of passengers waiting to be served. Alcohol, tobacco and perfumes were displayed on shelves behind a counter where a stewardess processed sales. These were early days in the development of the duty-free business, and passengers often sought the captain's advice on the correct tobacco or whisky to purchase. On board cabin accommodation was limited and primitive by modern standards, with wire sprung beds supporting thin mattresses, underneath a very low deck head. The Bureaux de Change was a vital feature; in the days before the widespread acceptance of credit cards, anyone travelling long distances by car needed considerable quantities of cash to buy fuel en route. British travellers, under Government currency regulations, were restricted to taking £25 sterling per person with them when leaving the country.

Promotional work for the new passenger service was supported by the French Government Tourist Office (FGTO), who placed a series of half page 'Make a beeline to Brittany' adverts in UK newspapers. They noted that "This brand new car ferry has a bar, restaurant, promenade deck, cabins and duty-free shops. There are daily sailings in each direction and passengers get their first night's camping free!". Taking a swipe at prevailing conditions in Britain, they encouraged passengers to "Take your car with you as France has no petrol shortages".

The service was still highly personal, with the vessel often held to wait for late freight drivers, even if this delayed passengers. This was important if freight customer loyalty was to be retained, especially when limited traffic was available and sailings were infrequent. Freight business was still proving difficult to attract. The Sunday Telegraph reported a typical instance. "There is too much rigidity, on both sides", explained a Devon export agent. During the 1974 paper shortage, I found a supermarket in Brest, that wanted to order one million toilet rolls, and I knew of a Midlands firm that, by luck, could meet the order. "Quick", I said, "rush a million rolls to Brest by ferry via Roscoff." They thought about it and came back with the answer. "Sorry, we only deal through our agent in Paris". By the summer of 1974 the *Penn-Ar-Bed* was operating at full capacity in both directions, often leaving passengers and cars behind on the quay. Reservations and booking procedures were not state of the art.

Not all the *Penn-Ar-Bed's* crossings were as smooth as in the brochures, but her ability to keep going became a hallmark of the Company. One of the earliest crossings, in severe weather, generated headlines on both sides of the channel. '12 metre waves and a Force 11 storm, a painful crossing for the *Penn-Ar-Bed*' reported Ouest France. 'Eight hours of nightmare', 'Night of terror', headlined the Western Evening News in Plymouth, continuing 'all the passengers were praised by the crew, and the Captain confirmed that he had taken all measures for their safety'. The Captain noted 'I have a good boat and an excellent crew...'.

The SICA Saint-Pol-de-Léon still retained a large majority of the shares within Brittany Ferries and was pressured to continue financial support, despite initial expectations that this call on resources would gradually be reduced by an influx of new shareholders. The expanded shareholder base failed to materialise. On 26th June 1974 Brittany Ferries

Above: **The duty free shop on the *Penn-Ar-Bed*.** *(Ferry Publications Library)*

Left: **The bar on the *Penn-Ar-Bed*.** *(Ferry Publications Library)*

withdrew from the Ouest Ferries venture, which was proving to be financially unsuccessful. The combination of these two failures resulted in the termination of Hénaff's position as president and Gourvennec took over the role. With Hénaff gone there was no longer any reason for Brittany Ferries to stay in Quimper, and the team moved to temporary offices in the midst of the new Terminal construction site at Roscoff.

The opening of the passenger service required Brittany Ferries to establish a stronger presence in the UK market. With the limited budgets of a small operation, Brittany Ferries was not in a position to compete with the advertising coverage of larger ferry and holiday companies in the respective markets. Support from the FGTO was especially welcome. From the earliest promotional initiatives, Le Bras led the team and realised that creativity in brochure style, sales, advertising and public relations had to be the hallmark of the enterprise. Advertising, brochure design, production and distribution to Travel Agents were all ably managed by BCB. Sales strategies and direct selling to Travel Agents, and

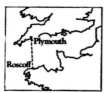

Advertising support from the FGTO added weight to the Company's presence in mainstream media.
(Richard Kirkman collection)

Caravanning and Camping Holiday Companies, including Canvas Holidays and Eurocamp, were managed by Dyer.

Public Relations in particular, had a major role to play in the Company's success, as carefully planned campaigns could achieve significant media coverage for comparatively modest outlay. Toby Oliver was recruited to bring specialist public relations and communications expertise to the Company. Oliver had a background in local journalism with the Kentish Express in Ashford, before working for Welbeck Public Relations, a subsidiary of FCB. Oliver was recruited to work on public relations initiatives for the Brittany Prince vegetable brand, but he was given the choice of working on a pitch to secure the account for a brand of port (an ultimately unsuccessful bid) or Brittany Ferries when the business expanded to cover the new account from 1974; he chose Brittany Ferries over alcohol and thus began a productive long-term relationship. Whilst the early relationships were established with Welbeck, it was felt that more could be achieved by using a smaller, nimbler public relations agency for whom Brittany Ferries would be the primary account. This led to the establishment of Toby Oliver and Partners, whose investors included Brittany Ferries and Brightwell. The new agency worked from the BCB offices in Burnsall Street, London.

From the very beginning the emphasis in public relations and marketing was to be on destination-led messaging, rather than focusing on ships, in contrast to the established convention amongst other cross-Channel ferry operators. The new public relations arm was named 'The Brittany Information Bureau', based on the promotion of the region of Brittany and the best way of getting there being Brittany Ferries - the insider's way to the region. A second Brittany Information Bureau later opened in Dublin staffed by Roddy Guiney and Caroline Bourke under the direction of the UK office.

Whilst an advertiser directly controls the message within an advert, the success and impact of a public relations campaign is controlled by journalists. The former invites an element of scepticism in the reader, but good journalistic copy is more believable and the best way to get a message across when budgets are more limited. There was always the risk that a journalist would encounter challenging weather during a ferry crossing, or miserably cold conditions on arrival on holiday, but most could be relied upon to deliver an objective message and give the Brittany Ferries name credibility by placing the story on the right pages.

The relationship between the Brittany Ferries management team and the Brittany Information Bureau was very strong, so there was never a lack of things to write about. Oliver came with a comprehensive list of contacts in the media, which ensured that the message could always achieve the right coverage. The major press features on ferry companies at the start of the booking season were a prime target and it became an annual objective to be prominent on these pages. This depended on the cultivation of relationships and encouragement to journalists to sample the product. Having an allied account with Bermuda Tourism also helped!

The role of public relations as a weapon in the marketing armoury grew as the Company expanded. The later addition of holiday products to the portfolio brought a new range of promotional opportunities for press releases and trips, allowing Brittany Ferries to control all aspects of the journalistic experience. The dramatic improvement in the on board catering offer as the service expanded opened up multiple chances to promote the Company in a positive way to distinguished it from competitors. These unique features allowed Brittany Ferries to stand out from other ferry and holiday companies by the integration of the 'French' experience, but also gave a useful 'hook' to journalists that allowed them to write on topics outside the norm.

With limited financial resources and still just operating a one ship service, the Brittany Ferries team needed creative initiatives to establish the Company brand more widely in the UK. A significant helping hand came from across the Channel. Gourvennec knew Jacques Goddet, the head of the Tour de France organisation, and in a remarkable coup extended an invitation to the race organisers to involve Brittany Ferries in one of the 1974 race-stages by holding it in the UK. A plan unfolded whereby the race would begin in Brest and call at Saint-Pol-de-Léon before reaching Roscoff and cross to Plymouth on the *Penn-Ar-Bed*. A race-stage would follow on closed roads around Plymouth, before the return crossing to Roscoff in readiness for the race to resume from Morlaix. This would be the first Tour de France race-stage ever held in Britain. Brittany Ferries agreed a comparatively modest FF600,000 contribution to the race organisers in exchange for the immeasurable publicity that the event would generate on both sides of the Channel.

It was an ideal moment to launch the Company to a wider audience. Over four days from 27th June 1974, television, radio and sports pages were filled with artichokes, cauliflowers and ferries, as the Tour caravan passed from Brittany to England and back again. The Tour was known locally as the 'artichoke race' in recognition of the efforts of Brittany Ferries in bringing the pageant to the UK. The Daily Mirror, sponsor of a trophy for the Plymouth race-stage, published articles advising readers on 'How to cook 'Chokes''. Every opportunity was taken to generate publicity. The corporate logo appeared on race jerseys, T shirts and bikes. In one of his first events for Brittany Ferries, Oliver recalled sitting in a trailer being hauled by a tractor around the A38 Plympton by-pass where the race-stage took place on a closed road, chucking artichokes to the crowds whilst they waited for the cyclists to pass; with hindsight, a rather dangerous way for spectators to be introduced to an exotic vegetable...

Burnel moved on from Brittany Ferries in the late summer of 1974, and was replaced in Plymouth by Le Bras. The strength of the passenger market became increasingly clear as the summer progressed, and attention turned to the question of how to accommodate the continuing growth in passengers. There was no obvious advantage in operating the now spare but still freight-only *Kerisnel* opposite the *Penn-Ar-Bed,* and the costs of converting her to a multi-purpose vessel were deemed excessive. What was needed was a larger, more efficient, ro-ro vessel with passenger and freight capability, even if this required further speculative heavy financial investment; this was a significant challenge to the Company and its shareholders, given the frequent short-term cash flow problems. Gourvennec and his team began to consider their options.

The first step was to dispose of the *Kerisnel*, and she was sold in October 1974 to Cie. Generale Maritime Marseilles, who renamed her *La Durance*. Her departure forced Brittany Ferries to charter the 3,390GT freighter *Valérie* to cover the *Penn-Ar-Bed's* annual refit during the same month, but the cash generated by the *Kerisnel* sale helped the Company's financial position and removed a liability from the books. The *Valérie* proved an unsatisfactory substitute for the *Penn-Ar-Bed* as her lack of passenger capacity stalled the growing passenger business, but this further confirmed that an expanding future for the Company lay in the operation of multi-purpose vessels.

Above: **The *Penn-Ar-Bed* during her first season of operation.** *(Ferry Publications Library)*

Right: **Brittany Information Bureau letterhead**

Far right: **The Tour de France route 1974.** *(Cyclisme Magazine)*

In the 1974 season Brittany Ferries carried 91,500 passengers, 12,483 cars, and the 9,648 freight vehicles represented a 75% rise in traffic from 1973. Turnover tripled to FF21 million on what was still a one ship service.

The new year was accompanied by the lifting of a potential threat to the young Company, when the UK government cancelled construction work on the Channel Tunnel on 20th January 1975, citing uncertainty about the country's membership of the EEC, a doubling of the project cost estimates, and general uncertainty in the economy. Some construction work had begun in 1974, with boring machines on both sides of the English Channel driving short tunnel lengths as part of a twin government-funded project to create two rail tunnels for car shuttles. The French government was unhappy with the British decision. With the UK also adapting legislation to its new membership of the EEC, the rules on free movement of goods and people were gradually easing. All this was positive news for ferry operators.

Provision of a second vessel became Brittany Ferries' priority for the 1975 season. Maurice Chollet, the Company's first Chief Financial Officer, understood that this would bring the right degree of flexibility and back up to the existing operation, whilst generating the possibility of future profit. Capacity needed to expand to create economies of scale and protect the growing volumes of traffic from competition. But there was insufficient business in the west to justify adding a second vessel to the Plymouth-Roscoff roster. A new route was needed. Sealink re-opened their seasonal Weymouth-Cherbourg passenger link in April 1974, supplementing their existing services to the Channel Islands from the port, and Cherbourg now enjoyed regular services from Southampton, Poole and Weymouth. Potential predators were getting closer to Brittany.

The early success and expansion of Brittany Ferries into the passenger business led to

The *La Duchesse de Bretagne* operated short-lived services to St Malo for Jersey Lines in the 1967 and 1968 seasons. *(Ferry Publications Library)*

the Company being courted by several established operators, including P&O's Normandy Ferries, who offered to buy a shareholding, enter into a form of joint operation, or even to buy out the founding shareholders. One financial offer of four times the original capital was received. Whilst there was a temptation to reward the confidence of early investors by taking profits through a sale, Gourvennec and the Board were not minded to consider any of these offers. They decided they were still in this project for the long-term. A new owner or external shareholder in Brittany Ferries would inevitably not share the original passion, motivations or Celtic identity of the agricultural community, which had driven their determination to overcome the challenges in getting the Company off the ground. The sense of a 'cause' would be lost, so these opportunistic approaches were rebuffed.

The growing volumes of traffic through Roscoff were also evident to the people of St Malo; the port had been the main destination for rail/sea passengers travelling to Brittany for a century, but had not seen a year-round cross-Channel ferry service since the last departure of the *St Patrick* on British Railways' Southampton service on 27th September 1964. French Line had run a limited summer service from Southampton with the *Lisieux* in 1965 but soon closed the operation, and Jersey Lines' attempts to establish a business to both the Channel Islands and St Malo from Plymouth, Torquay, Weymouth and Southampton with the *La Duchesse de Bretagne* in 1967 and 1968, also faltered. The British Railways route had been loss-making for a long time, with cars loaded onto the *St Patrick* by crane, and no possibility of carrying vehicular freight as there was no linkspan in St. Malo. The port also suffered from a severe tidal range, which heavily restricted the hours of operation. Lock gates also constrained access to St Malo, making a modern, frequent ro-ro service both difficult to operate and expensive to accommodate.

The Malouins began to consider whether it would be possible to install a linkspan in the port to tap into the growing interest in ro-ro traffic. These ambitions coincided with Brittany Ferries' aspirations to protect their investment in Roscoff by expanding their route structure. St Malo represented a logical expansion of services, enlarging the hinterland, securing the 'west' within Brittany Ferries' control and maintaining the geographical focus on the Brittany region. There was a compelling argument that any approach from the St Malo authorities to use their port had to be accommodated to prevent other ferry operators plugging the gap; such a competitive development would pose an existential threat to the Company and prevent future expansion. Gourvennec and Jacob began discussions with the port authorities to find a solution to their mutual interests.

More capital would be needed if Brittany Ferries were to expand to a second Channel route, and when Gourvennec and Jacob's presented their ideas to the Board their ambitions did not find favour with other shareholders. There were concerns that expansion was taking place too rapidly, with the capital costs of a second vessel being incurred before there was sufficient income to achieve returns on the initial investment. There were clear risks to this venture and shareholders were reluctant to dig deeper into their pockets, especially following repeated calls on their financial resources to cover trading losses and fleet investment. Gourvennec reluctantly approached the Parisian Ministries for help, but they were not interested in helping, as their interest was focused on the problems of the larger nationalised French ferry operations on the shorter cross-Channel routes further east.

The negotiations with the St Malo authorities dragged on. Mr Blin, President of the St Malo Chamber of Commerce, was sceptical about Brittany Ferries' ability to finance the project. This prompted Gourvennec to take the lead and sign an agreement committing the Company to source funding and secure a second vessel in time to launch a service from St Malo as soon as a linkspan could be installed. The parties agreed to give themselves two years to fulfil their mutual obligations and set a deadline of the end of 1976 to avoid advertising a service with neither ship nor linkspan. This took the pressure off Brittany Ferries' shareholders and gave time to plan for expansion in the knowledge that there was a secure agreement with the port. The decision to open a route from St Malo was greeted internally with general enthusiasm. The St Malo authorities for their part turned to Marine Development (Glasgow) Ltd under the direction of John Rose for the design of the linkspan, and the installation was part overseen by Mike Hendry, who was later to become owner of Cenargo. Meanwhile Brittany Ferries faced a more immediate capacity problem for the 1975 season as the *Penn-Ar-Bed* was proving too small to satisfy growing demand. Then, suddenly, everything began to change.

TT-Line of Lübeck, Germany, had provided ferry services between Travemünde in Schleswig-Holstein and Trelleborg in southern Sweden since 1962. At the launch of their new vessel *Nils Holgersson* at Rendsburg on 26th October 1974, TT-Line announced that their spare ship *Gösta Berling* would be deployed on a new route across the English Channel in 1975. There were no immediate plans for where the ship would be based or the route on which she would be deployed, and TT-Line began to explore their options. Discussions were held in Roscoff on the possibilities of a joint venture between TT-Line and Brittany Ferries on the Plymouth-Roscoff route. Like other approaches at the time, little progress was made in taking the idea forward; the German proposal was felt to be predatory, another attempt to exploit the success of the young Company and, like the earlier takeover approaches, was doomed to failure. TT-Line went away to consider other opportunities.

Gourvennec realised that, with Brittany Ferries' ambitions to move towards a two-ship fleet, there was a clear need to bring in professional expertise to manage the increasingly complex business. The shareholders were farmers, not transport professionals, and the scale of the operation was moving away from their field of expertise. Large capital investment needed to be managed in an appropriate manner. Whilst the enterprise had developed well with local management, future phases of expansion would require a fresh approach, preferable from someone who could challenge convention by not being other shipping background. There was no desire to replicate the approach of the mainstream ferry competitors. Gourvennec knew the individual he wanted for the new post of Directeur Général of Brittany Ferries, and had been wooing him repeatedly for some time. The appointment in January 1975 of 40-year-old Christian Michielini proved to be an inspired turning point for the Company.

Two

Introducing Professional Management

Christian Michielini with his long serving secretary Marie-Jo Véron. *(FerryPublications Library)*

Born in Paris in April 1934, the son of a Venetian father and a Basque mother, Christian Michielini followed his stepfather into the freight forwarding business and succeeded him as head of the Denrée subsidiary of Danzas in the late 1950s. The company was located in the Halles Centrales, the fresh food market in the heart of Paris, and undertook international freight forwarding, with a particular focus on the distribution of, amongst other items, cured meats and cheeses from Italy, cheeses from Holland, and gruyère from Denmark. By the time Michielini left at the end of 1973, Denrée had moved to a large new warehouse in Thiais, south of Paris, and expanded to a fleet of 70 vehicles operating regular freight services between France and Italy, the Benelux countries, and Great Britain. Michielini then spent a short time as an associate to Pinto, an import specialist, but felt that the opportunity to join Brittany Ferries was too good to turn down, despite being offered triple the salary elsewhere. He felt that Brittany was a good place to bring up his family and relished the battles that he knew lay ahead. Michielini's knowledge and experience of international food transport made him an ideal candidate for the new role of Directeur Général; he could speak the same commercial language as Brittany Ferries' shareholders and brought a wealth of experience to the role. He was a familiar figure in Brittany from his work in establishing TDM, which had been a customer from the very first sailings.

Michielini was appointed as a director of BAI alongside Alexis Gourvennec as chairman, and Maurice Chollet as finance director. The role of Directeur Général focused on strategic and internal management issues for the Company, and formed an effective partnership with the chairman, which freed Gourvennec to handle relationships with the shareholders and banks and manage his own farming interests. Michielini moved into a red caravan adjacent to the cattle lairage at the port in Roscoff whilst work continued on building the new passenger terminal.

With the passenger service now fully established, Brittany Ferries had the confidence to commission their first colour brochure from BCB for the 1975 season in the UK market. This 16-page publication offered a different approach to other ferry brochures in the market by being destination rather than ship-led and strongly promoted 'Brittany Ferries to the French West Country' with features on the *Penn-Ar-Bed* and a collage of images of

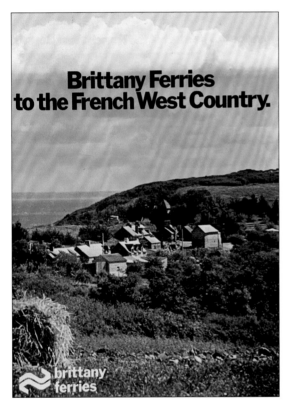

Above: **Life on board the *Penn-Ar-Bed* as depicted in the 1975 brochure.** *(Ferry Publications Library)*

Left: **1975 brochure cover.** *(Ferry Publications Library)*

Brittany. Whilst not the main focus of the brochure, the *Penn-Ar-Bed* was described as a 'little piece of Brittany... carrying 200 cars and a lot of happy people. When you drive into Roscoff, you'll have already experienced a few hours of the atmosphere and friendliness of Brittany, before you've even got there.'

The geographical logic underpinning the proposition was explained through a series of figurative maps, in which the Plymouth-Roscoff route lay at the heart of journeys from Glasgow and Fishguard through the Atlantic Arc to the Spanish border. Reader understanding of the new service was enhanced by a series of suggested holiday itineraries through western France. Prospective passengers were encouraged to 'East, drink and be Breton', seek 'Sea, sand and seclusion' and 'Learn to enjoy the car again'. Prices were presented in a separate stitched-in document.

The early vessel acquisition transactions had been conducted by Jean Hénaff with

Asmarine, the Paris office of the international shipbrokers Clarksons. The initial introduction had been made by Bob Kirton of Townsend Thoresen, who suggested to his contacts at the shipbrokers that the new Roscoff company might be looking for help. One of Michielini's first tasks was to establish a relationship with the shipbroker, as he wanted to understand the process of ship acquisition by meeting the people doing the work. Having been approached by Clarksons, Michielini arranged to meet and have lunch with one of their London-based brokers. The team comprised of Neil Brine, who undertook ship chartering, and Jim Mason, who dealt with vessel sales and purchases. Michielini walked to Bill Bently's restaurant in Bishopsgate, London, in the company of Mason and the two immediately established a strong relationship. They were to meet on almost a fortnightly basis for the next two decades. Mason was invited to Roscoff to meet the team in their temporary accommodation and was taken to meet Gourvennec at the SICA

Above and right: **More views from on board the *Penn-Ar-Bed*.** *(Ferry Publications Library)*

offices in Saint-Pol-de-Léon. The message from the Chairman was clear, even in translation. "We want to do this; you find the ships and we'll find the money."

Meanwhile TT-Line's plans were becoming clearer. In January 1975 the company announced that the *Gösta Berling*, which had been renamed the *Mary Poppins*, would re-open the route from Southampton to St Malo from 29th May 1975, initially operating six return crossings each week. The 110-metre long vessel would offer accommodation for 850 passengers and 120 cars, with a standard and quality of facilities far in excess of anything then contemplated by Brittany Ferries. TT-Line planned to replace the *Mary Poppins* with the freshly named *Oliver Twist* (formerly the *Nils Holgersson (2)*) from 1976, if the route proved successful. TT-Line had not been the only company expressing an interest in serving St Malo from Southampton; British Railways also considered the option of re-opening their old route, but were hindered by the bureaucracy of a government owned enterprise, and it was the German proposal that proceeded more quickly.

News of the planned opening of the route was not well received in Roscoff. Gourvennec felt betrayed by Blin, feeling that their 1974 agreement had been broken. Blin defended the St Malo decision, pointing out that the port was required to be open to all vessels regardless of flag, and Brittany Ferries had no right of exclusivity in use of the port. TT-Line would overcome the handicap of not having a linkspan by accessing the port through the lock gates. He argued that St Malo needed a ferry service and it was wise for them to take the one on offer rather than wait for a speculative future venture from Brittany Ferries with, as yet, no defined route or vessel.

Gourvennec was aware that TT-Line had every right to operate this route under maritime law and EEC regulations. But it felt like a big injustice. The market for direct services to Brittany would never have been tested without the huge financial risk undertaken by the Breton farmers. TT-Line, like all the other established companies, had expressed no interest in helping the community get their service to the UK off the ground. Now they were looking to resurrect the Southampton-St Malo route, but only after the potential for services to and from the region had been demonstrated. As he later put it, "it's too easy now to come and claim a share of the cake that nobody wanted."

The issues were widened by TT-Line's decision to register the *Mary Poppins* under the Cypriot flag and sail with a mostly Filipino crew; a position that was quickly exploited to bring the French maritime unions into the argument. This was pitched as a life or death challenge for Brittany Ferries; if TT-Line was allowed to establish the service, the Company would be left serving a small isolated market in the far west, and would die, asphyxiated, unprotected and remote from the main traffic flows.

Gourvennec was not alone in his concerns. The arrival of a German competitor troubled other established operators on the western Channel, particularly P&O Normandy

Below: **TT-Line 1975 brochure cover and schedule.** *(Richard Kirkman collection)*

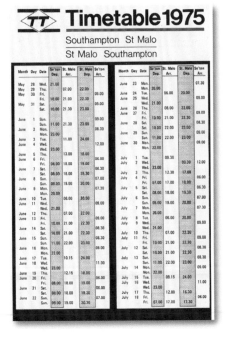

An international group of trade union protesters march through the streets of St Malo. *(Ferry Publications Library)*

Ferries, Sealink and Townsend Thoresen. Seamen's unions on both sides of the Channel joined forces with dockers to protest at this threat to the established order. Michael Traber, managing director of TT-Line, attempted to defuse the situation by meeting with the trade unions and proposing that the *Mary Poppins* be crewed by an equal mix of German, English and French seafarers, with the vessel registered under the German flag. However, the trade unions had no interest in concessions and Traber returned to Germany all the more determined to press ahead with his plans.

There was insufficient trade for two operators from St Malo, and Gourvennec was not inclined to share the business with anyone. He and his team were determined that the *Mary Poppins* would not operate on the western Channel. Gourvennec embarked on a tour of the government ministries in Paris with Michielini, Alfred Gauthier, Henri Jacob, and Jacques de Menou. "We have been pioneers opening up this region of Brittany and we demand that our company is given a monopoly of this western traffic", he told the French government. But the response was consistent; TT-Line was planning to operate entirely within the law and could not be stopped.

Resistance gathered momentum as seafaring unions garnered support, entreating members to be ready for action against TT-Line. Officers from the *Penn-Ar-Bed* lobbied Yvon Bourges, the French Minister of Armed Forces, who was also mayor of Dinard. The Breton deputies took advantage of a meeting of the National Assembly and questioned Mr Cavaillé, the Secretary of State for Transport. By mid-May the walls of Brittany were covered with hostile posters – 'TT-Line, go home!', 'Corsairs yes, pirates, no!', 'The raptors are coming, Bretons what are you waiting for?', 'One occupation, that's enough!'. The tensions rose.

In the meantime, it was the turn of the Brittany Ferries' Plymouth office to be the scene of protest. On 22nd March angry egg producers from across Britain sealed off the gates at Millbay Docks s to protest against the import of eggs, which they claimed were subsidised by the French government. Scuffles broke out when police refused the protesters access to the docks, and a group of around 40 gained access to the terminal building after charging the dock gates. The protesters claimed victory when a lorry load of 17 tons of French eggs was unable to be discharged and returned to Roscoff.

Meanwhile, planning for the 1975 season continued, and in April Brittany Ferries secured a six-month charter of the *Falster*. A 2,424 gross-tonne vessel, which had been completed in January 1975 by Trondheims Mekaniske Verksted in Norway and designed for service in the Baltic, she was 109.7 metres long, 16.5 metres in breadth and operated at a service speed of 19 knots. She could carry 250 cars, but just 345 passengers, making this a difficult commercial ratio of car to passenger business to balance. But the charter of the *Falster* came with an option to purchase her if she proved to be a successful proposition on the route. The vessel was renamed *Prince de Bretagne* - in another passing reference to vegetables - and her arrival allowed the Plymouth-Roscoff service to be upped to twice-daily departures during the summer season. The *Penn-Ar-Bed* took the 23:00 overnight departure daily from Plymouth, returning from Roscoff at 12:00 the next day. The *Prince de Bretagne's* daily roster saw her leave Roscoff at 23:00, returning the following day from Plymouth at 11:00.

In May the *Mary Poppins* sailed to the Pool of London to promote the TT-Line Southampton-St Malo service, before heading round the coast to Southampton to inaugurate the route. But her arrival in Southampton was delayed as dockers refused to allow her to berth, throwing mooring ropes back into the water. Seafarers on British ferry services from Southampton went on strike in protest at the perceived threat to jobs posed by the interloper.

Meanwhile Gourvennec worked hard to get the message across to the Malouins, who were still keen to exploit the opportunities presented by a regular service from England. Arguments between Brittany Ferries and TT-Line on flags, crewing and entitlement seemed irrelevant to those who just wanted the route to open. An angry Blin was quoted as saying: "I see that the Roscovites arrived in number to make the law or rather the "outlaw" and that's quite abnormal. I think the government will take the necessary measures to ensure the freedom of persons and property is guaranteed and that free movement is respected. It's shameful."

Gourvennec faced a hostile audience at the casino in St Malo on the afternoon of 28th May. He gave a speech outlining the history of Brittany Ferries, painting a picture of a Company built on the determination and risk-taking of a few Breton farmers, and testifying to its success, speaking of the promising future that the Company could help bring to Brittany. Here was a project for the whole region, not just Finistère. This was not just a Breton argument. French and British maritime trade unions lined up fully behind the protests, fighting against the *Mary Poppins'* Cypriot flag of convenience and the continued use of Filipino crew on board. Growing industrial action forced the mass suspension of all cross-Channel services, from Weymouth and Cherbourg in the west to Dover and Dunkirk in the east, with Townsend Thoresen and Sealink crews refusing to work, in sympathy with their French colleagues. The protesters' strategy at St Malo was simple; stop the *Mary Poppins* berthing in the port. The harbour entrance was blocked by a flotilla of vessels, led by the *Penn-Ar-Bed,* and a steel cable was stretched between the banks of the access channel to the lock.

The inaugural departure of *Mary Poppins* from Southampton at 23:00 on Wednesday 28th May was cancelled after intending passengers found access to the ship blocked by protesting dockers. But news of the cancelled sailing was slow to travel to France in the pre-internet era; thousands of farmers from nord-Finistère converged on St Malo on the morning of Thursday 29th May for the *Mary Poppins'* scheduled arrival at 07:00. Cars were requisitioned to bring villagers to the port from across the region.

Gourvennec, Michielini, Chollet, and Gauthier joined a large crowd assembled on the Quay who were brandishing banners, shouting slogans and singing songs. Everyone watched and waited. Spirits were high and drew on the fortitude of the Bretons and their memories of the War – one German invasion was quite enough, they argued... Gourvennec briefed journalists: "If the problem does not find a solution within a reasonable time, we light the fire elsewhere. We do not lose a battle like that twice." The CRS riot squad stood-by in significant numbers but observed developments passively.

The *Mary Poppins* arrives in London for a publicity visit prior to heading for Southampton to open the TT-Line route to St Malo. (*Ferry Publications Library*)

Gourvennec later revealed that his actions had the full support of the French government, including Prime Minister Jacques Chirac, who gave him a four-day window during which he promised the CRS would not intervene. After that he could not guarantee holding back.

There was still no sign of the *Mary Poppins* as 29th May drew to a close. Her return crossing from St Malo to Southampton at 22:00 had already been cancelled. Friday morning brought a fresh band of protesters armed with clubs, slingshots, pitchforks, and even shotguns, to welcome the vessel. There were rumours that some separatist activists were ready to use explosives to block the lock gates. But another day passed with little action, with Gourvennec highly active and prominent in raising the spirits of the protesting group. They remained ready and waiting. The timetable showed *Mary Poppins* leaving Southampton at 10:00 and arriving in St Malo at 21:00, returning an hour later. But this second planned sailing was also cancelled. Another night passed, but the following morning came news that the *Mary Poppins* was finally on her way, having left Southampton on the evening of Friday 30th May.

The *Mary Poppins* was first spotted on the horizon by the crowds in St Malo at about

09:30 on the Saturday morning. Tension mounted as she slowed to approach the port. At first it seemed as if the *Mary Poppins* would attempt to breach the blockade, but she then slowed to a stop. Her Master hailed the demonstrators and asked them to allow his ship to berth; they refused. He repeated the question and received the same response. The protesters held their breath. The Master had exerted his rights under maritime law and been rebuffed. The *Mary Poppins* re-started her engines and slowly turned away to sail back to Southampton, to the accompaniment of huge cheers from the quayside.

The *Mary Poppins'* passengers disembarked on their return to Southampton and the rest of the season's sailings were cancelled, with the vessel withdrawn and sent to open up a short lived route between Travemünde and Copenhagen. Gourvennec and his fellow protesters on both sides of the English Channel had won, however illegal their protest. People power had overcome the rule of law.

Michielini told to a journalist from Radio Station France 3 "I was coming from a

The *Penn-Ar-Bed* on the berth at Roscoff, as the *Prince de Bretagne* sails for Plymouth. *(Ferry Publications Library)*

respectable Swiss Company, and I was not expecting do a port occupation. We blocked the harbour. We did a true maritime war. I have well educated myself to Gourvennec's methods, I used to be in the commando units. Sometimes, the end justifies the means. We should not confuse ourselves. It was essential. We should be dead if we had not defended St Malo."

The outcome presented Brittany Ferries with a dilemma. They were now highly unpopular in St Malo, a port which found itself deprived of the planned service and the benefits it would bring to the community. Brittany Ferries' monopoly of routes to Brittany needed to be protected; other operators might well seek to fill the void if St Malo did not receive a service quickly, and if these were British or French operators, they would be difficult to protest against. Brittany Ferries was forced to accelerate plans to serve the port.

With just two ships available to the Company the short-term options were limited, but the *Penn-Ar-Bed* was utilised to operate a trial service from Plymouth to St Malo, operating three return crossings each week from mid-August until early October 1975. It was very much a stop gap effort and made little commercial sense, forcing customers to make a 'dog-leg' transit of the channel, with most passengers driving west to Plymouth to return east by sea to St Malo. The lessons from this short season were clear; if a St Malo route was to be a commercial success, the English home port for the service needed to be further east than Plymouth.

Michielini was now finding his feet in the organisation and had witnessed a baptism of fire at St Malo. He needed help if Brittany Ferries were to realise their full potential. The Bretons had demonstrated their ability to conceive of the service, provide funding to source and sustain the fleet, and recruit the local manpower needed to supply and operate it. But the Company still relied on French nationals supported by BCB and their partners to generate business from the UK. There was a growing realisation that this approach was unsustainable if the Company was to make inroads into UK-originating traffic. Over 85% of the cross-Channel passenger business came from the UK, and there were insufficient French freight hauliers to fill the vessels in both directions. The future required a fuller understanding of the UK market to generate inbound traffic if plans to develop beyond the Plymouth-Roscoff route were to succeed. This was not going to come from an office populated solely by French nationals. The first step was to find a seasoned professional manager for the UK operation, preferably, like Michielini, from a non-shipping background, to bring a fresh outlook and approach.

Michielini turned to Derek Brightwell for help – did he know of anyone who might fit the bill? Brittany Ferries' shareholders trusted Brightwell's judgement following his revitalisation of the 'Prince de Bretagne' vegetable account, and BCB's subsequent creation and development of the Brittany Ferries brand; his colleague Michael Constantinidi knew of the right candidate.

Paul Burns was born in County Donegal, in the Republic of Ireland, and therefore had an appropriate Celtic background, preferred by Gourvennec. He had set up Hertz Rent a Car in Ireland, was transferred to the London office, and built a successful career with Hertz, rising by 1972 to the position of Vice President, Organisation Development, Hertz of Europe. At this stage he been approached by Constantinidi, on behalf of Trust House Forte (THF) hotels; the two hotel companies had just merged but had no sales department or reservations system. Burns' experience of the Hertz reservations systems made him an ideal candidate and he became sales director for THF Hotels and six months later for THF Travel, which comprised Millbank Travel, Sovereign Travel and Swan Hellenic Cruise Line. It was time for Constantinidi to make another approach to Burns.

Burns was contacted during a business trip to Hong Kong in early May 1975 and expressed interest in the opportunity. The call led to a series of meetings with Brightwell and Michielini, with enthusiasm on both sides about the potential appointment. They outlined the philosophy devised by BCB to promote the new operation, and shared the geographical logic that underpinned the entire proposition; the success of the Plymouth-Roscoff route and future ideas for St Malo hinged on the ease of access for British tourists to holiday areas of France, based on the proximity of the destination ports to Brittany, the Pays de Loire, Poitou-Charentes, Dordogne and Aquitaine. Unlike other ferry operators, with their focus on ships and wide route networks, destination-led marketing of a focused region would remain the strong unique selling proposition for Brittany Ferries. This approach fitted with the aspirations and interests of the Brittany Tourist Board, who had funds available to support the venture.

Later, Gourvennec outlined the background to the establishment of Brittany Ferries in a joint presentation with Michielini to Burns in Roscoff. He referred to the 400-year history of inter-trading amongst Celtic peoples along the western coasts of Europe, broken when the French directed the trade eastwards, and the English compelled Wales, Scotland and Ireland to look east to their new capital, London. The Bretons, Gourvennec insisted, were always the first to pay the geographical penalty of remoteness. Their aspiration had been to become independent of Normandy by going direct to or as close as possible, to Celtic Cornwall. His substantial body of research on the produce market assured him this was a viable long-term economic prospect.

To date, Brittany Ferries' success had been entirely French-driven. So, as potentially the first non-Breton senior management appointment outside France, Burns asked for assurances that he and his team would have the delegated responsibility, authority and full accountability for the profitable growth and development of the business in the UK.

The clean lines of the *Penn-Ar-Bed* are evident as she heads back to service from refit. *(FotoFlite)*

Gourvennec was strong in his response. For too long, the Bretons had been subjected to policies impacting on the region dictated by organisations based outside Brittany, without the people's interests at heart. He assured Burns that the Roscoff team would not be dictating how the UK business should be managed, and emphasised that the new role would report directly to Michielini. This confirmed to Burns that he would have the independence to be able to work with the BCB team and the UK employees of the Brittany Ferries to build a successful business.

Burns returned to London and agreed to join the Company from 1st July 1975, working initially on a 'cash-only' basis paid by the Company accountants, Touche Ross, until his contractual position could be ratified in his formal appointment as the Company's first UK General Manager. Gourvennec undertook to settle this with the Board, and made it clear this was his appointment, rather than Michielini's. It was to prove another inspired appointment, as Burns brought the original thinking, drive and commitment needed to make the business a success. He quickly established a strong working relationship with Michielini, giving them both the confidence that the wider vision could be realised. His arrival was a significant step for the Company, taking the UK operations outside day to day Breton management control for the first time. But it was necessary, because the Plymouth operation had focused on logistics, not sales; there was an urgent need to balance trade beyond produce exports from Roscoff and limited seafood and cattle exports from Plymouth. Burns' appointment acknowledged that the commercial aspects of the Company needed to be managed and led from the UK side of the Channel, by experts who could deliver market-driven knowledge, experience and a professional focus. Brittany Ferries had now recruited the services of an experienced businessman to help address these needs. One of Burns' early priorities would be to set up the permanent service from England to St Malo.

Paul Burns speaking at the AA Travel annual conference in 1979. *(Paul Burns collection)*

The Plymouth management team and office staff welcomed and responded positively to the appointments of Michielini and Burns, and the general direction to develop Brittany Ferries' business in the UK.

Burns brought a refreshing and robust honesty to the role, reflected well in his later response to a passenger complaint, following a breakdown of the *Quiberon*: -

'We regard it as the height of arrogance to describe the apologies which we made as being 'empty'. Your arrogant self-righteousness and your bitter and twisted verbiage we find to be as irritating and repugnant as you find our efforts to bring you back to England subsequent to the breakdown of our ship.

It is obvious that any further apologies would be utterly wasted so none will be offered and if you feel as a consequence of what happened you will never travel with us again, that is a decision which would bring us immeasurable comfort and relief. Compensation is the furthest thought from our mind.' The correspondence was published in Private Eye.

The Plymouth office remained managed by Armand Le Bras, supported by Josee Dyer as sales manager; she was a Breton, who was born and grew up in Morlaix, before moving to work and learn English in Bournemouth, where she met and married an English engineer. Dyer now lived locally in Plymouth and was recruited to the team as a native French speaker with considerable sales experience in the UK travel industry. She responded quickly to the newly established independence of the team, and was given responsibility for development of the passenger business in the UK. Dyer soon determined and implemented a coherent sales policy for the Company.

The principal task facing the Company was to promote the Plymouth-Roscoff route, particularly to the UK travel trade, which for many years had been selling and booking ferry crossings to France by focusing largely on the short-sea cross-Channel routes, particularly the Dover-Calais service. Ferry routes further west across the Channel were a more complicated sale, with comparatively infrequent crossings and more complex on board accommodation requirements. At that time, companies such as Canvas Holidays and Eurocamp had grown large volumes of cross-Channel business on the traditional ferry routes. Dyer was given the task of securing a portion of this business for Brittany Ferries. She vigorously took on the role and bookings from the travel trade started to grow substantially from early 1975.

The challenges facing Brittany Ferries to raise visibility of the name and awareness of services were addressed by manning stands and booths at the main travel and leisure exhibitions, including The Holiday Show, The Camping and Caravanning Show, and The Boat Shows in London and Southampton. Working with BCB, and particularly exploiting public relations opportunities with Toby Oliver, Dyer was able to achieve prominent coverage and promotions in both the local and national press. She also succeeded in attracting prominent personalities to visit the Brittany Ferries stands at the shows and arranged for these individuals to travel with Brittany Ferries to Roscoff, with press and television photographers recording them boarding the ferry. By the end of 1975, Brittany Ferries had begun to achieve national brand recognition.

Jerry Lock, with Bill Dudley acting as his deputy, managed the freight services. In 1975, most freight traffic was still inbound to the UK, originating from the Roscoff area, although the volume of UK-sourced traffic was increasing, primarily from freight operators located in the west and south of the country. There was considerable interest in the UK business community at the commercial opportunities presented by the new Brittany Ferries route. In August 1975, for example, farmers in Devon saw the attraction of selling milk to creameries near Roscoff, which offered them 41p a gallon for their product, compared to the 23p they could obtain in the UK. The milk was used in the manufacture of butter, which was then re-exported to Britain.

Burns found himself in a Company where Michielini had already begun to make things happen for the Board, guiding and managing their expectations, and determining which of their many aspirations were practical. Michielini became the link between Gourvennec, the Board of Directors and the operational Company. His respected professional background in Danzas allowed him to speak with authority. Michielini's commitment to the cause was total and he strongly shared the corporate ambitions to take on competitors directly.

Marc Gilon was appointed the head of Brittany Ferries by the SICA de Saint-Pol-de-Léon and the Economic Committee, with the express purpose of driving the sale of produce through increased exports. He was a graduate in agronomy and business law from the Paris Chamber of Commerce and joined Cerafel in 1970. Appointed director of external trade relations, Gilon helped create the Prince de Bretagne brand. Everything began with the vegetables and derived from the strength of the brand. Even the ships' new orange logo came from the distinctive colours of vegetables. Gilon wished to be seen as the driver of the marketing strategy, but this exposed tensions between his interests and those of Michielini who was running the day to day Company. At the Board it was often difficult to anticipate which way an issue would be decided. Gilon was influential because the shareholders depended on him to sell their vegetables, but Gourvennec was highly supportive of Michielini and depended on his wide practical knowledge and experience to help make the right decisions.

BCB were retained to continue to drive the marketing and sales effort of Brittany Ferries, in addition to their promotion of vegetables for Prince de Bretagne. Their relationship with the Company was working well, and Michielini and Burns decided against the recruitment of a substantial marketing and sales team; it was more cost effective to utilise the strength of BCB's marketing knowledge and the quality of the public relations work of Oliver than set up an internal team for the same tasks.

Local relationships with the community in Plymouth were often fraught when Burns arrived. The attitude of the Local Authority was often considered by the Brittany Ferries team to be somewhat pompous, almost as if Plymouth City Council believed they had a financial stake in the Company. The town clerk, Forbes Watson, who was personally both positive and supportive of Brittany Ferries, was compelled by his council members to protest, sometimes publicly, if the service was interrupted when a ship was taken out of service for refit or other operational reasons. But the City Council provided little in the way of either financial support or business for the Company. The BTDB Port Manager in Plymouth, Marcus Watt, also sometimes behaved towards Brittany Ferries in ways which seemed beholden to the City Council, and did not shy away from being critical of the Company. This still reflected a more general antipathy of the BTDB towards Brittany Ferries at that time.

Once Burns' formal appointment was confirmed on 18th November 1975, he began

Left: **Promoting the Company – Josee Dyer meets Prince Phillip at the 1976 Boat Show.** *(Lindsay Clarke)*

Above: **Josee Dyer (L) is joined by Dominique Gigante of Gîtes de France to present a holiday competition prize with tv personality Terry Wogan.** *(Lindsay Clarke)*

the important task of strengthening the management team. If Brittany Ferries was to fulfil aspirations to expand eastwards it needed substantial additional resource to put these plans into effect. He turned to a former colleague from Hertz who had moved on from the company to join the Heron Corporation. Ian Carruthers was a former Merchant Navy officer, who had been recruited by David Longden to join the Hertz car rental business in Edinburgh. He rapidly rose through the organisation before moving on to the Heron Corporation, working in their truck rental business. Carruthers arranged through his contacts for a company car for Burns and the pair agreed to fly from London to Scotland together for Burns to pick up the vehicle on 21st November. Burns told Carruthers about the new venture during the flight. By the end of their meeting Carruthers was sufficiently interested in the opportunity to agree to drive down to Plymouth to inspect the ship and have a look at the operation. Burns returned to London before driving to the Holiday Inn in Plymouth, which was to be his home for more than two years.

It was a long drive from Edinburgh to Plymouth in the days before completion of the motorway network, and when Carruthers arrived to view the *Penn-Ar-Bed,* he discovered that the inbound sailing from Roscoff had been cancelled, as there was insufficient traffic to justify the departure. An angry Burns told Carruthers he should not join this crowd, "we cannot run a ferry service without operating a ferry." A bemused Carruthers returned to Scotland without seeing the ship, but with a promise from Burns that he would get back to him when he had made more headway with making the Company more professional.

In late February 1976 Burns again made contact with Carruthers and asked him to join Brittany Ferries to help start the new route to St Malo. Carruthers was enjoying success with the Heron truck rental business and had recently encouraged Longden, his former boss from Hertz, to join him at the company. There were some suspicions about what he knew about the future of Heron when he announced he was moving on. Burns offered an acceptable financial and relocation package and Carruthers was hooked. He neatly fitted Gourvennec's preference for another member of the Celtic management team in England. Carruthers met Burns again on 25th February and Michielini agreed Burns' recommendation to appoint Carruthers' to strengthen the management team the following day.

The two-vessel fleet was proving inadequate to meet demand and cover the increasing costs of the operation, especially with the anticipated opening of the new route to St Malo. The chartered *Prince de Bretagne* had proved unsatisfactory during the 1975 season, primarily due to her limited passenger accommodation, so Brittany Ferries did not take up their purchase option. Instead the Company returned to Trondheims Mekaniske Verksted in Trondheim to explore options for the construction of a vessel similar to the *Prince de Bretagne,* but one capable of carrying more passengers to meet the planned expansion of the Plymouth-Roscoff route. Mason introduced Michielini to the Norwegians as 'the man with no money', but he soon gained their confidence. The outcome was the decision to invest in a new ship to be built in Bergen and fitted out in Trondheim, but she was not to be launched until 20th June 1976 and was not to enter service for Brittany Ferries until 24th May 1977.

In the meantime, the Company was readying itself for the opening of a St Malo service in 1976, with the urgent need to fix the English port for the route and find a vessel to operate it.

Three
A second British port

One of the key lessons from the brief Plymouth-St Malo operation of 1975 was that a 'dog-leg' route across the Channel did not hold much geographic logic; a service to St Malo from an English port lying much further east than Plymouth was more desirable. At that time Brittany Ferries employed Morvan Fils as their port agent in St Malo. The family-owned agency had been active in the city since 1896 and specialised in commercial shipping links between St Malo, the Channel Islands and England. Christian Morvan had been one of the leading local advocates seeking to encourage Brittany Ferries to come to St Malo; he was vice president of the Chamber of Commerce and a member of the port Board. Morvan set about helping to find a solution to the opportunity. Taking the characteristics of an efficient St Malo service – a round trip crossing from England in 24 hours, with two-hour turnarounds at each destination port, suggested that the maximum passage time would be ten hours - Morvan traced an arc from St Malo to work out how far a vessel averaging 18 knots could travel in ten hours; discounting Plymouth, this line included ports between Weymouth in the west and Portsmouth in the east. Of these, Southampton was too far away from the open sea to maintain a regular 24-hour cycle of operation, Weymouth and Poole had potential conflicts with competition from, and port berth occupancy by, existing operators, and Portsmouth was undeveloped as a ferry port. Portsmouth, however, had the distinct geographical and commercial benefits of the shortest road transit to London.

Portsmouth was, like Plymouth, a major naval port, and was the operating base of Royal Navy ships, ranging from aircraft carriers to submarines. It was not certain that a regularly scheduled ferry service would be permitted from the port.

Morvan was also the agent for freight services in St Malo, including those operated by a shipping company owned by Jack Norman; he had established the Commodore and Condor shipping companies to operate freight and passenger services from the Channel Islands to St Malo. Commodore also ran a lift-on lift-off freight service from Southampton to the Channel Islands, operated jointly with British Railways, and was an importer of international produce to the Camber dock in Old Portsmouth. Norman had also opened up services from the Albert Johnson Quay on the north side of Portsmouth naval dockyard in December 1967. This quay was capable of handling two vessels simultaneously, but the facilities came under pressure as Commodore grew their business to the Channel Islands and the jointly operated British Railways lift-on-lift-off service started from the site in 1972. The northern boundary of the Albert Johnson Quay was extended by two acres by Portsmouth City Council, as the site owners and Norman's landlord, in 1975. They granted a 66-year lease of the Albert Johnson Quay to Norman in 1974, and he was in the process of moving his entire operation from the Camber dock to take advantage of the new site's access to the M275 motorway, which was due to open to the nearby Rudmore roundabout in March 1976. When approached about the new venture, Norman believed he could accommodate an evening arrival and departure of a passenger ferry from St Malo at the Albert Johnson Quay. Discussions between Norman and Brittany Ferries began in August 1975; Norman proposed that he would build a linkspan on the Albert Johnson Quay and in return Brittany Ferries would pay a fee for each arriving and departing passenger passing over the facility. Norman also proposed that he should act as the port manager and agent for Brittany Ferries in the UK. The

Company's plans for a Portsmouth-based operation began to take shape.

Portsmouth City Council had not considered operating ferries from the mudflats north of Albert Johnson Quay, before they received the proposal from Norman, but the idea of so doing was quickly developed. After considering Norman's plans, the City Council responded that they owned the port and believed it would not be possible for him to operate and manage a ferry service. But they did say that the Council took the proposal seriously and were considering the proposition. The Council had only to agree to buy the mudflats, because they already controlled road access to the proposed site through their landholdings. There was an opportunity to build a new terminal on the site of a former gasworks lying close to the Albert Johnson Quay. Removal of the gasworks would enable the site to be extended over the Portsea Island General Cemetery, which dated back to 1830. This site was a rectangular plot running west from Commercial Road to the Portsmouth Harbour shoreline, with four tree-lined paths. Portsmouth City Council eventually decided to proceed with the project, but they were bound by government restrictions to construct the planned new port development for less than £1 million.

The requirement for significant capital investment in a ferry port to support an operation to St Malo for a young Company with a limited single-ship operation from

The French-built *Terje Vigen* was quickly identified by Jim Mason as being the right ship to open the Portsmouth-St Malo service. *(Ferry Publications Library)*

Plymouth carried a high risk of failure. Portsmouth City Council contacted Townsend Thoresen to gauge their interest in transferring their established services from Southampton to Portsmouth. At this time Townsend Thoresen had been operating in Southampton since 1964 and enjoyed a significantly higher profile and status than Brittany Ferries, being part of the dominant private sector cross-Channel operator. Townsend Thoresen were far too entrenched in Southampton to consider a wholesale move, but the company suggested that a limited seasonal operation might be contemplated if facilities were made available.

A contract was signed by Portsmouth City Council with Norman to support development of the linkspan; Norman provided annual revenue guarantees of £180,000, underwritten in a back-to-back agreement with Brittany Ferries. This indirect approach suited Christian Michielini, who preferred to work with a man he was familiar with, rather than directly with the City Council. The prime driver of this early development of the port, with the major year-round commitment, was Brittany Ferries.

With the *Prince de Bretagne* returned to her owners in October 1975, Brittany Ferries was again back to operating a one ship fleet. The newbuild vessel was a long way off completion; in the short-term another ship was needed to supplement the *Penn-Ar-Bed* for the summer season on the Plymouth-Roscoff route, with a larger vessel also required to open up the Portsmouth-St Malo route on a longer-term basis.

Jim Mason and Michielini enjoyed a very close working relationship from these early days, with the Directeur Général taking every opportunity to tap into the shipbroker's knowledge. Michielini would often ask Mason to head over to Roscoff at short notice for a discussion about the fleet. His presence on the ship from Plymouth would be detected by Capt. Lainé and taken as a sign that new tonnage was imminent, so Mason developed the diversionary tactic of asking the officers what kind of ship they would design. A talented artist, Mason would paint up their designs to distract them. His experiences at sea gave Mason an understanding of the conditions that the crew and passengers had to tolerate

The *Armorique* in Plymouth. *(Paul Burns collection)*

in bad weather and helped his appreciation of shipboard life. By now appointed as Brittany Ferry's shipbroker and agent, Mason began the search for a vessel for the Portsmouth-St Malo operation and a second vessel for Plymouth. He went over to Denmark to inspect the *Travemünde* but it turned out that the vessel was no longer available. The local Danish broker offered the *Gedser* as an alternative, but she was far too small for the proposed deployment. Frustrated, Mason spent the evening looking through the German reference book that was the ship 'bible' at the time and found the *Terje Vigen,* which was quickly selected as being highly suitable for the Portsmouth operation, with the *Bonanza* following later to boost the Plymouth fleet.

The *Terje Vigen* was built by Société Nouvelle des Ateliers et Chantiers in Le Havre in

1971 to sail between Oslo and Åarhus for DA-NO Linien, making her maiden voyage on 13th May 1972. Of 5,732 gross tonnage, she was 116.6 metres long and 19.2 metres in breadth, with a service speed of 20 knots; she could carry 700 passengers accommodated in 410 cabin berths and 200 reclining seats, and 170 cars. The *Terje Vigen* was one of several similar ferries, built to an innovative design by Knud. E Hansen, that made the most of external light by featuring big picture windows; she was an expensive vessel yet featured on board furniture from IKEA. The *Terje Vigen* was a good fit for the new Portsmouth operation with the right speed, capacity and accommodation for the route, and was duly acquired by Brittany Ferries in November 1975. She completed her Scandinavian service on 30th December 1975 and was sent to the Meyer Werft shipyard in Papenburg to undergo a substantial £1 million refit in readiness for her new role. Michielini and Burns flew in Brittany Ferries' Cessna 125 from Plymouth via Brest to Papenburg to visit the shipyard and inspect progress on the *Terje Vigen*. The plane reached northern Germany and flew into fog; there was just 40 litres of fuel left so the pilot landed wherever he could. After a safe but bumpy touchdown the plane and passengers were arrested and taken into custody by the German army because they had landed on a taxiway, not on the runway. There was no fuel left. The corporate culture was still to operate on a shoestring, taken too far on this occasion...

The proposals to develop the Portsmouth-St Malo service were not without opposition. As early as January 1976 the Transport and General Workers Union (TGWU) stated in meetings held with Paul Burns that 'Portsmouth-St Malo will not happen', based on their vested interest in trade union jobs in the port of Southampton. The TGWU were soon active in advising workers at other ports, including Plymouth, of the perceived threat to dockworker employment from the proposed new operation. There were rumours of industrial action against all ferry operators if the Brittany Ferries plans went ahead. These actions were threatened in an era when secondary picketing by trade unions was still lawful and widespread. Concerns quickly spread to the customs and immigration authorities and the Queen's Harbour Master (QHM) in Portsmouth. Nobody would enjoy

1976 Brochure and sailing times. *(Ferry Publications Library)*

industrial strife, and Norman was increasingly fearful of the impact that industrial action would have on the rest of his Portsmouth operations.

In the meantime, preparations continued for the new service. The forthcoming season was heralded with a trade promotion themed 'Two New Year-Round Routes By Public Demand'. Yet opposition to the plans for the new St Malo service continued to mount. In a period of just two days in March, Burns received robust and hostile representations against the new service, from the Southampton Immigration service, the Southampton Customs service, the Norman family, the TGWU in both Southampton and Plymouth,

Bill Rook and Richard Dunning. (Rook Dunning)

the National Union of Seamen (NUS), Plymouth City Council, BTDB, Portsmouth City Council, and Plymouth Chamber of Commerce all outlining their concerns about the consequences of Brittany Ferries attempting to open a Portsmouth-St Malo service. This resistance prompted an urgent Board meeting in Roscoff, when the financial impact of expansion was debated. There was pressure building from the French banks and from shareholders, fearful of losses if the dispute escalated in the UK and began to curtail services. For a time, it looked as if the Portsmouth-St Malo plans would be dropped, but eventually it was agreed that Alexis Gourvennec and Maurice Chollet would seek a solution to financial concerns, whilst Michielini and Burns would resolve the Portsmouth disputes. This injected a degree of urgency into the TGWU discussions and required Josee Dyer to create momentum behind the UK sales effort for the new route. It was felt that commercial pressure to begin the service from the freight and travel industry would counter trade union and other opposition.

The *Terje Vigen* emerged from the Papenburg shipyard as the *Armorique*, the ancient name of the area of Gaul between the Seine and the Loire, which included the Brittany peninsula. Her facilities now included a lounge – advertised as being fitted with colour television – a discotheque and two duty-free shops, plus a choice of two self-service restaurants and a nursery staffed by trained nurses. She was to prove a popular member of the fleet in a long career with Brittany Ferries.

The 1976 brochure was expanded to 24 pages, with a four-page paper insert detailing the timetables and tariffs. The brochure again adopted a largely pictorial style, with an emphasis on the départements of Brittany. 'Welcome to our world' was the cover headline. 'The world of Brittany Ferries' heralded the arrival of the *Armorique*, depicted across two pages in an unbranded white livery, and described as 'our pride and joy'. The Company was the 'direct answer to holidays in Brittany', with the region boasting 'an excellent system of fast trunk roads that take you to your destination without any of the heavy traffic problems common to the more traditional Channel ports'.

The Plymouth-St Malo route opened on 7th April and offered a daily service until 15th June, after which the route transferred to Portsmouth. Plymouth-Roscoff enjoyed a daily service throughout the year, with a second daily departure offered between 28th May

The *Bonanza,* a seasonal charter for the Plymouth-Roscoff route that was also deployed to St Malo. *(Bruce Peter collection)*

and 16th September. The adult fare was £9.40 single, with a 60-Hour return fare priced at £12.00. Cars were charged in three price bands – up to 12' 6" (£11.00 Low Season, £15.20 High Season single journey), up to 14' 0" (£15.50/£21.50), and up to 18' 0" (£19.50/£26.00), with a 'per foot' rate of £1.50/£2.00 thereafter. A two-berth cabin to St Malo was priced at £8 by night and £4 by day. For those sailing on Plymouth departures there was the option to hire a caravan, offered in conjunction with Martins Caravans of Exeter.

Speaking to the press in February 1976, Burns noted that bookings on the Plymouth-Roscoff route were already well up on the previous year and said "we had anticipated that a third vessel will be required by 1977 and we now have a new ship under construction, which will enter service next year. However, response to our 1976 advertising and promotional programme has been so great that we have made immediate arrangements to bring forward our plans for three cross-Channel sailings per day." He apologised for the delays that some travel agents have been experiencing with sailing confirmations, as the overwhelming demand had placed considerable strain on reservation staff. The Company responded by taking on more reservations staff and increasing the number of telephone lines. The brochure was reprinted with the new sailing times.

Advertising support for Brittany Ferries was strengthened early in the year with the addition of Rook Dunning to the roster alongside BCB. The two companies worked together on projects from adjacent offices. Bill Rook and Richard Dunning brought their unique and immense art and design expertise to generate a succession of groundbreaking advertisements and brochures for the Company over the next quarter century. Rook Dunning brought in the skills of the renowned travel photographer Barrie Smith to enhance the illustrative quality of their brochures and advertising material, and he developed a strong empathy with the distinctive style of the brand. They inherited the solid and chunky logo in Franklin Gothic condensed type, which was now widely used across printed material and advertising, as well as beginning to appear on the fleet. It was reminiscent of an inelegant industrial style, a little like a railway company logo and often dubbed the 'Polish Railways' logotype, with a representation of the interplay between the coastlines of Brittany and South West England in the earthy orange colour of

A publicity photo of Ian Carruthers in the Brittany Centre. *(Ian Carruthers collection)*

vegetables. This was not time for a change, but the new team began to contemplate how the logo might be improved.

The *Armorique* arrived in Plymouth on 4th March 1976 and undertook a number of freight sailings to Roscoff, prior to her first passenger sailing on the Roscoff route on 25th March. The new berth at Portsmouth was not going to be ready until June, so the *Armorique* remained in Plymouth and operated the early season Plymouth-St Malo link from 9th April until 15th June, sailing from Plymouth at 23:00 each evening, to arrive in St Malo at 08:00 next morning, returning at 11:45 each morning and arriving back in Plymouth at 17:45.

Summer seasonal support for the Plymouth-Roscoff route was provided by the *Bonanza,* which was chartered from Fred. Olsen to operate from 28th May to 16th September 1976. At 3,972 gross-tonnes, she was 94.7 metres long and 16.2 metres in beam with a service speed of 19 knots. Built by Ulstein Werft AS in Ulsteinvik, Norway in 1972, she could accommodate 500 passengers and 200 cars but was designed primarily for day crossings, with limited cabin capacity. Her facilities included two self-service restaurants and a duty-free shop. She made her maiden trip to Roscoff on the 16:00 crossing from Plymouth on 27th May. Her daily schedule saw her arrive in Roscoff at 23:30, returning the following morning at 09:30 to reach Plymouth at 14:30.

Ian Carruthers finally joined the company on 10th May 1976. He initially drove down to Plymouth to meet the team and learn more about the business. After a few days observing the operation, he travelled with Burns to Portsmouth to review what was needed to open the new service to St Malo. It was his first visit to the City, and he found the new port was a building site, overlooked by the modern brutalist architecture of the flats on Commercial Road, which faced away from the port. It was hardly an inspiring place to work, nor a welcoming sight at the start or end of a holiday. Carruthers settled into a local hotel and found his new office in Norman House, Kettering Terrace adjacent to both the port and the Albert Johnson Quay. The two agreed to divide their port management responsibilities between Plymouth and Portsmouth, Carruthers to establish and manage the new Portsmouth operation, with Burns to continue his management of Plymouth in addition to his overall General Manager role. Carruthers and his team prepared for the avalanche of activity needed to get the Portsmouth-St Malo service running.

The Portsmouth operation was still dominated by the Norman team, who held the contractual relationship with the City Council and acted in the capacity of Brittany Ferries' Agent at the port. It was quickly evident to Carruthers that the Company's interests were not being well represented by Norman's team, and he quickly sought delegated authority to make things happen. The implementation of the Agency agreement between Norman and Brittany Ferries was difficult from the outset as the interests of the two companies were very different. There was a conflict between Norman's ambitions for his Channel Island and International businesses, and Brittany Ferries' expansion plans for the St Malo route. The Norman family management style was out of tune with the emerging Brittany Ferries business culture, which challenged the conventional ways of working through the establishment of new, efficient, cost-conscious business practices. Norman's local operations team was weak and beholden to the trade unions, with the dockers exerting considerable influence over the manner in which their activities on the Albert Johnson Quay were conducted. If trade union demands were not met, then industrial action soon followed. The local trade union, under the direction of Tony Harding, were intimidating, but they were acting within the law as it then stood. They viewed their employer with disdain; ten dockers would be required for a ship turnaround, but usually only eight would turn up, with the other two running taxis as a side business. For this limited activity they were each paid £30,000 a year. There were clearly going to be battles ahead for Brittany Ferries, but for now there were bigger issues to be addressed.

The legal arrangements with Portsmouth City Council took some time to conclude, but eventually Norman signed a three-year contract. After signature there were less than 100 days left to build the linkspan, the supporting shore facilities and to open up the terminal. Sheet piling was erected around the site of the new berths and the resulting void was filled with sand extracted by a Dutch dredger. However, the sheet piling had a habit of falling over causing the sand to escape, leading to several setbacks during construction. Nevertheless, good progress was being made and the Brittany Ferries' Portsmouth team began to plan for the commencement of operations, which were now on target to commence in June. There was barely a month for Carruthers to establish himself, understand what needed to be done and implement a plan.

Meanwhile Townsend Thoresen were finally persuaded by the City Council to operate a trial ferry service from Portsmouth to Cherbourg. Their proposition involved transferring the *Viking I*, which had inaugurated sailings from Southampton to Cherbourg for Thoresen Car Ferries on 11th May 1964, to run a twice-daily return Portsmouth-Cherbourg service between 17th June and 12th September 1976. Whilst operating from Portsmouth offered a one hour reduction in crossing time to Cherbourg compared to sailing from Southampton, the company was still heavily invested in the port of Southampton and saw their new Portsmouth operation very much as an experiment. They sent Bob Kirton, operations manager at their Southampton base, to build-up their presence in Portsmouth. Townsend Thoresen brought a confident, aggressive attitude, using their experience to influence Portsmouth City Council to meet their needs. They were quick to endear themselves to the Portsmouth community and exploit the public relation opportunities at the port by renaming *Viking I* the *Viking Victory*.

The Portsmouth team was augmented by the recruitment of a group of enthusiastic individuals who would make their mark on the Company for many years to come, and whose growing commitment to the cause would help the operation surmount a multitude of hurdles. Ralph Joss, Graham Smith and Leonardo Ciccarone were amongst those recruited at this stage. Teresa Spencer joined and was to head the reservations team. The new team had little experience of what would be required for a passenger-based ship handling operation and there was no infrastructure in place to help them. Carruthers contracted Burns Security, a local security company, to provide men in uniform to give the operation an appearance of some credibility. They used a then innovative walkie-talkie radio system, but an initial mix-up with licences led to radio frequencies being shared with other ship and taxi operators, causing considerable confusion for all.

Ciccarone, who came from Bari in southern Italy, had worked at sea for Swedish Lloyd before coming ashore, and spoke several languages. After the service was established, he spent time in Spain generating freight business for the new route. In a sign of the immaturity of the Company at the time, his unguided enthusiasm often resulted in low value traffic materialising on peak sailings with dubious payment terms, but this was all part of the growing pains of the new service. Ciccarone became 'Mr. Brittany Ferries' as far as many distant regions were concerned.

The reservations team needed a comprehensive administration system to be able to track and record bookings, and in the pre-computer days the only one available was that which had been established in Plymouth. Reservations could be recorded only in one place as everything was done manually. A strategy emerged of bookings being handled by the relevant departure office. Carousels of manual paperwork were brought up by van from Plymouth to Portsmouth to be installed in Norman House as part of the change. The consequences of these carousels falling over in transit were too awful to contemplate...

Opening the Portsmouth office enabled Brittany Ferries to recruit a new team of young staff, many straight out of school, to work on taking reservations and then, as the business expanded, booking holidays, combined their roles with operational duties in the passenger terminal. Here was challenging and interesting work and an opportunity to grow careers in parallel with the expansion of the Company. The small and tight-knit team had few personal attachments and was happy to stay late to solve the many problems that arose; a great team spirit quickly evolved. The atmosphere was more like a 'start up' company and the lack of formal 'corporate' systems encouraged staff to use their initiative. Those who displayed this trait - or 'bossiness', as early employee Julie Burrows described it - thrived.

Burrows joined when there were just five reservations clerks, eventually moving on within the Company to take on the processing of bookings for the new holiday products. Responsibility was delegated right down through the team in a way that would be unthinkable today, but it was a necessary response to a rapidly growing business, seeking to do things differently, without the baggage of legacy systems and culture. The Company could not afford to bring in 'experts' because the scale of the business did not allow for it. But the loyalty of the freshly recruited team in both Plymouth and Portsmouth ensured that there was continuity, and the level of experience grew from the traumatic early years.

The passion of employees was matched by the glamour of the uniform, worn by all staff to bring homogeneity and style to the office. There was glamour in working for a French company and the uniform was very chic, projecting a distinctive image in the terminal, and even amongst staff travelling to work. Staff could also enjoy the benefits of visiting France at a time when this was less commonplace. Turnover was very low despite the multitude of challenges thrown at the Company at both UK ports in the early years. This was helped by a management style that favoured trust in employees, and encouraged continuity by enabling the team to grow with the business. Many of these

The information desk on the *Penn Ar Bed*. *(Ferry Publications Library)*

young early employees were to spend their entire working career with Brittany Ferries.

The first Portsmouth office was a short walk from the terminal at Norman House, where Brittany Ferries occupied the ground floor and had a shop entrance. As the business expanded, the Company came to occupy two separate floors; later, as the holiday products took off, a staircase was put in to connect the two so that nobody had to leave the office. Pressure on space mounted as the accounts team expanded, and Carruthers ended up sharing a portacabin at the rear of the building with the freight team. From this cramped start came the dream of a dedicated office, which eventually manifested itself in the building of the Brittany Centre, capable of absorbing all the Company's staff in the port.

In Plymouth, the early Brittany Ferries offices were in Stirling House close to the entrance to the port, where the accounts team were based under Jim Butler, before the team moved into the Associated British Ports (ABP) office, with a training centre added to one side as the Company became more professional and the demand for space grew. Butler soon identified the prime necessity of transforming the Company's already legacy administrative 'systems' that had been designed for low volume operations. He set about designing and installing a new ticket system, and cabin charts for each departure with integrated reference codes that linked documents for speedy retrieval from the manual filing system. The telephone system at Plymouth was primitive and needed to be replaced with a 'key and lamp' installation to create visibility for incoming calls.

Resistance to Brittany Ferries plans for Portsmouth was beginning to strengthen across a wide spectrum: the West Country police, fearful of the impact of road blockages if industrial action went ahead, Plymouth City Council, still fretting about the impact of the new Portsmouth route on the local business, the National Union of Railwaymen (NUR), who threatened strikes on rail services to Plymouth, Portsmouth and Southampton, the Southampton Branch of TGWU, who warned the Company to abandon any plans to carry freight to or from St. Malo, the Plymouth Branch of TGWU who feared that a successful Portsmouth to St Malo service might mean the closure of the Plymouth to Roscoff services, and the National Union of Seamen. Even Irish Continental Line, who had picked up rumours of a future interest in Brittany Ferries operating from Cork, joined in with a threat to block any future service from Cork to Roscoff.

Burns, defiantly, confirmed at a press conference in Portsmouth on 27th May that Brittany Ferries would commence sailings to St Malo when the new Portsmouth ferry port opened on 17th June 1976. This drew a vitriolic response from the Trade Unions, resulting in frequent and hastily convened meetings to try to assuage their concerns, but with Brittany Ferries strongly adhering to their position that they would not withdraw from the planned opening of the St Malo route. After many hours of robust and angry meetings, the Company conceded to a fallback position limiting the summer 1976 Portsmouth-St Malo route to be to a passenger-only service. This succeeded in providing further time for continuing discussions and negotiations on the Freight dispute and created certainty on the launch of the new route, as planned, for the summer season.

In the run up to opening the new St Malo service Derek Brightwell and Toby Oliver arranged for 80 guests, including Portsmouth City councillors, Immigration and Customs officials, and tour operators, to be flown in a BAC 111 from Southampton Airport to St Malo to view the port. The party was met at the airport on departure by Carruthers, who was given an envelope containing the group's tickets and itinerary by Brightwell's secretary with the news that he had been admitted to hospital, having suffered a suspected heart attack. As the group boarded the aircraft Carruthers was taken aside by an HM Customs official and advised that two of the councillors were believed to be carrying over £1,000 (the currency export limit was then £25) and would have to be removed from the flight. This caused delay to the departure and some embarrassment to the other councillors as their colleagues were led away to be charged. Nothing appeared to be straightforward at this stage...

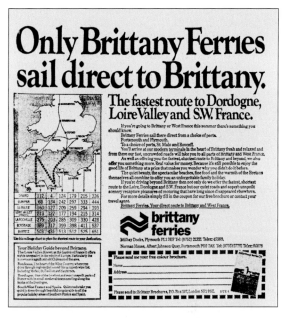

The strapline 'Only Brittany Ferries sail direct to Brittany' summed up the Company's unique selling proposition, but could cause difficulties when services were disrupted. *(Ferry Publications Library)*

The *Armorique* sailed from Portsmouth at 21:00 on the evening of 15th June with the Lord Mayor of Portsmouth as guest of honour on board. She arrived on schedule in St Malo the following morning for a day of celebration. The new ferry port of St Malo was formally opened at 08:00 on 17th June 1976, prior to the return departure of the *Armorique to* Portsmouth, at 09:00. She arrived back in Portsmouth at 18:00 for the formal opening of the new Portsmouth Continental Ferry Terminal, marked by bands, much pomp and further ceremony. But a small trade union demonstration by dock workers from Southampton outside the port gates greeted her arrival. The Lord Mayor of Portsmouth hosted a formal dinner in the Guildhall on the evening of 17th June. The *Armorique* left Portsmouth for St Malo on her maiden departure as a passenger and car-only service at 21:00 that evening, scheduled to sail overnight from Portsmouth, arriving in St Malo at 08:30 the following morning, and depart on her return crossing at 11:00 to arrive back in Portsmouth at 19:30. Brittany Ferries' second permanent route was now up and running.

Townsend Thoresen commenced their Portsmouth to Cherbourg route with the newly renamed *Viking Victory* on the same day. The *Viking Victory* departed at 08:00 from Portsmouth and returned from Cherbourg at 14:00, with extra sailings at 18:30, returning at 23:59 from Cherbourg, at peak weekends. She also operated as a passenger-only vessel to avoid any trade union conflict. The two companies' services were accommodated on the single linkspan at the new terminal.

Michielini, Burns and Carruthers hosted a celebration lunch with Portsmouth staff on 18th June. There was no respite in activity for the Company over the following weekend as the Company's new vessel was launched in Trondheim on 20th June. She was now named the *Cornouailles,* after the French name for Cornwall. Her design followed that of the *Prince de Bretagne*, but there were significant issues with the quality of her build. The Norwegian shipyard had a strong reputation for building offshore rigs and bulk tankers, but had little experience of building ferries and was seeking to enter the market. When the team, including Michielini, Burns and Jim Mason, assembled in freezing weather conditions in the shipyard on 24th June it was apparent that the *Cornouailles'* external skin was flawed, looking emaciated, with her structural ribs sticking out along the line of the hull. The shipyard had applied the wrong temperature to the welds, such that the ship's sides buckled. The bow door was a misfit and inoperable; the builders had never

Above: **A luxury cabin on 'A' deck of the *Armorique*.** *(Ferry Publications Library)*

Left: **The 'Le Corsair' tea shop aboard the *Armorique*.** *(Ferry Publications Library)*

built one before. Mason agreed to remain in Norway to try to resolve the problems; Michielini and Burns returned to their offices.

The *Armorique* had barely settled into her new schedule when, on 5th July 1976, she struck a rock in heavy fog when passing close to the Grand Jardins outside St Malo, whilst under the guidance of the local port pilots. There was some initial doubt as to whether the *Armorique* could reach the port safely given the state of the tide, as there was no lay-by berth at the time, but eventually she was able to berth safely. Fortunately, there were no passenger injuries. A subsequent inspection reported that the damage to the ship was much worse than originally feared, with the *Armorique's* variable pitch propeller severely damaged and her hull impacted. She was sent to Le Havre for repair but was destined to be out of service for three months.

The incident could scarcely have happened at a worse time, just at the start of the peak season with very strong levels of forward bookings in prospect for the remainder of the summer. Carruthers had returned home to Scotland to have a quiet weekend with his family. It was planned to be his first break since joining the Company. Michel Mériadec rang him at home to appraise him of the situation, and he flew straight back to Portsmouth. The accident tested the capabilities of the new Portsmouth team, who were faced with the full cancellation of services having barely got used to operating them. Resources were stretched, as passengers had to be rebooked on other services, refunds made, and complaints handled. Burns Security helped maintain a sense of order. The difficult decision was made to suspend further new bookings until 28th July to help ease the pressure.

It was quickly established in Roscoff that there was a problem with the Company's

The 'Iroise Bar' on the *Armorique*. *(Ferry Publications Library)*

insurance policy for the *Armorique*. This contract had been under negotiation for a long time, trying to get an appropriate level of insurance at the best price. The finally negotiated cover had been agreed on Friday 2nd July, but the contract documents had still not been completed, as the offices were closed over the weekend and the ship had grounded early on Monday morning. The *Armorique* was uninsured.

It was imperative to find a replacement vessel, with the upcoming school holiday period destined to provide so much of the Company's projected turnover for the year. Carruthers flew out to St Malo to help manage arrangements for stranded passengers, whilst Burns remained in Plymouth to arrange for the *Bonanza* to be transferred across to take over the service. But it quickly became apparent that the *Bonanza's* lack of cabins made her unsuitable for passengers on the long overnight crossings from Portsmouth.

There was also a daily race against the tide. The 21:00 departure from Portsmouth required a nine-hour passage to arrive in St Malo at 07:00 and berth in the port ahead of the falling tide. The harbour at St Malo ran dry at around 07:00 each morning and the ship had to lie in a specially-dug 'hole' until the tide rose to a level at which the ship could float and depart. The 16-knot *Bonanza* could not be relied upon to reach the port in time to be able to turn around and leave again, so sailings had to be cancelled every four days in order to return to schedule, as by now turnarounds had been reduced to as little as 30 minutes; she was cumulatively running an hour later with each crossing. There was little time to load supplies. On one memorable occasion the team in Portsmouth were regaled by the *Bonanza*'s Purser as they stood on the linkspan in Portsmouth, shouting that the ship had no bread for the upcoming crossing to St Malo. Carruthers and all the available team were forced to head off in all directions to find bakeries and gather up all the bread they could find. This was maybe the first time a ferry departure was a little late waiting for the bread.

Efforts to find a replacement vessel proved difficult at the peak of the summer season. So, another difficult decision was made to replace the *Bonanza* with the *Penn-Ar-Bed*, which was more limited in passenger capacity but better equipped, and had the speed needed to complete the overnight crossing in time to meet the tide restrictions in St Malo. The *Bonanza* remained on the Portsmouth-St Malo route until 15th July when the transfer was planned to take place. However, local TGWU members in Plymouth refused to let the *Penn-Ar-Bed* leave the port, in protest at the sacrifices being made on their Plymouth-Roscoff route to aid fellow trade union members in Portsmouth. The Plymouth dock workers believed that refusing to permit *Penn-Ar-Bed* to leave for Portsmouth would aid their fellow Trade Union members in Southampton. The *Penn-Ar-Bed* was delayed leaving Plymouth by some 15 hours until the TGWU would agree to her release. The Plymouth-Roscoff service was then operated by the *Bonanza*, halving the number of sailings and providing an inferior night service to that planned and advertised.

The *Penn-Ar-Bed* duly arrived in Portsmouth, but quickly generated much criticism from passengers for her lack of facilities - she had been christened the '*Penn-No-Bed*' by respected travel writer David Wickers in an article in the Sunday Times. With capacity for 300 passengers and 160 cars, the *Penn-Ar-Bed* did not compare well with the 700-passenger capacity and 170 cars of the *Armorique*. There was little option other than to restrict passage to one or two passengers per car, with the remainder travelling to Cherbourg on a later Townsend Thoresen sailing from Portsmouth, with an onward coach transfer arranged to St Malo to reunite them with their driver and vehicle. There was little resistance to this strategy amongst the predominantly male drivers, but when Carruthers stood on a table in the Portsmouth Terminal to explain these circumstances to a group of assembled passengers – there were no tannoy speakers in the building - one individual asked how cyclists would be treated; it was a two-day ride down the peninsular from Cherbourg to St Malo. This was a long way even for mopeds, many of whom were diverted to Weymouth for their return crossings. This problem could be overcome if cycles and mopeds remained with the *Penn-Ar-Bed* whilst their riders took the Cherbourg sailings and the connecting coach service. Carruthers arranged for the Portsmouth dockers to be instructed to load the cycles and mopeds on board the *Penn-Ar-Bed*.

On the first morning after the new cycle/moped plan had been implemented, Carruthers received an early call from the St Malo office, shortly after the arrival of the *Penn-Ar-Bed*. 'The people are here, but there are no bikes' he was told, despite the previous instruction to Portsmouth dockers to load the bikes onto the ship. Clearly this had not happened. Cyclists were compelled to spend 24 hours in St Malo awaiting their rides. Carruthers went down to the quay in Portsmouth that evening and berated the dockers for not loading the cycles, and insisted they be loaded for that night's St Malo sailing.

As Carruthers was about to head back to his hotel later that evening, long after the ship had gone, he overheard the customs and immigration staff complaining that they were unable to find their bikes. Curious, he thought... The following day there was another early call from St Malo. 'We have a problem, there are so many bikes, more bikes than people'. It was organised chaos; in their haste to obey orders, and with the *Penn-Ar-Bed* crew anxious to get away to beat the tide, the dockers had loaded every bike they could lay their hands on to avoid another debacle. No matter that many of them belonged to Portsmouth shore staff...

Every day brought similar stories of chaos, which continued until a larger vessel could be found for the service.

Some short-term relief came with the charter of the *Olau West* from Olau Line, which replaced the *Penn-Ar-Bed* on the Portsmouth-St Malo route from 5th August. She had been built at Schiffbau Gesellschaft Unterweser in Bremerhaven, Germany in 1964, and

The *Penn-Ar-Bed* approaching St Malo whilst covering for the *Armorique*. *(Ferry Publications Library)*

sold to Olau Line in 1970. A 3,061 gross-tonne vessel, she was 97.4 metres in length and 17.8 metres in breadth and had a service speed of 18 knots. The *Olau West* was substantial enough to accommodate 1,500 passengers and 165 cars but was far from ideal for the service and was chartered with some misgivings. However, she was the only ship that Mason could source at such short notice. The *Olau West* arrived in Le Havre without any stores or equipment. Carruthers gave the team a two-metre long telex printout with a list of catering equipment needed for the vessel and instructed them to go out and hire items from wherever they could. Their prompt response epitomised the flexibility required from all staff at that stage. The *Olau West* was rushed into service and the immediate capacity problem was resolved. The *Penn-Ar-Bed* returned to Plymouth.

But nothing was going right for Brittany Ferries. On 7th August, the *Olau West* ran aground close to the Mole des Noires at the outer entrance to the harbour, as she left St

Malo on just her second morning departure, with 600 passengers on board. She was quickly re-floated at 12:12 and it was deemed safe for her to continue the crossing to Portsmouth. But when the *Olau West* was inspected on arrival in Portsmouth, the damage proved to be much worse than anticipated, forcing her to be withdrawn from service and sent to Vlissingen, Netherlands for repair. Things had gone from bad to worse; the Portsmouth-St Malo route was left with no prospect of any service until the *Olau West* returned. All traffic was transferred to Townsend Thoresen sailings via Cherbourg until 19th August, with customers facing the long drive across the Cotentin peninsular.

Customer confidence could easily have been damaged by a second vessel grounding in St Malo in a matter of weeks. Carruthers faced the press and told them the *Olau West* had been withdrawn due to 'sand up its intakes', an explanation which fortunately sufficed for the gathered journalists. He omitted all mentions of striking granite or rocks. The team was getting plenty of operational experience and quickly learning how to turn adversity to public relations advantage.

When performance of *Olau West* was reviewed on her return to traffic she was deemed unsatisfactory for the long-term on grounds of both capacity and speed. She was withdrawn from service on 10th October and returned to her owners. The Portsmouth-St Malo route was again left without a ship, as the *Armorique* was still under repair. However, this gave a window of opportunity for the St Malo authorities to undertake the substantial works necessary to widen and deepen the approaches to the berth and install other navigational aids to permit the operation of a year-round service at most states of the tide. The new Terminal in Portsmouth was left without any cross-Channel ferry services as Townsend Thoresen had completed their seasonal operations on 12th September when their services returned to Southampton for the winter. Their first summer of operation from Portsmouth had proved successful, bolstered by traffic transferred from Brittany Ferries, and Townsend Thoresen announced their intention to return for the 1977 season.

The commencement of regular cross-Channel ferry traffic from Portsmouth was still viewed with suspicion by many. Capt. Ommanney, the Royal Navy port captain, who held the equivalent naval status as the captain of a vessel, saw his territory threatened and sought to prevent the movement of ferries interfering with the fleet. The Royal Navy was not minded or encouraged to take a positive approach, as their resources were being reduced and their power was diminishing. Proposals for new routes, more sailings and bigger ships sailing from the ferry port were countered by 'we haven't cleared that' as muscles were flexed.

Whilst operating the new Portsmouth-St Malo route in the summer of 1976, Burns and Carruthers agreed that pilotage at Portsmouth and at Plymouth was the next major issue that needed to be addressed. Each arrival and departure of a Brittany Ferries vessel at both ports incurred a pilotage charge of between £400 and £600. Added to the financial issue, was the question of the operational methods of the pilots. There were constant delays to both arrivals and departures, when the mandatory pilot did not make themselves available at the due time.

Townsend Thoresen Masters were permitted to hold pilotage licences for Portsmouth, but these were only available to British-registered vessels. Michielini approved Burns' proposal to approach Trinity House, as the UK pilotage licencing authority, to request that Brittany Ferries' Masters be treated equally with the same pilotage rights as those enjoyed by Townsend Thoresen when entering a British or French port. Extensive negotiations with Trinity House made no progress towards finding a solution. Meanwhile, as the negotiations dragged on, French Masters on Brittany Ferries' ships were making as many 'pilotage' visits to the ports as their British counterparts. It was recommended by Burns and Carruthers that the Company should continue to pick up and set down the pilots but cease paying the charges invoiced by the pilots. The Board agreed, and payment of the invoices stopped. The pilots continued to board and disembark the

Brittany Ferries ships on each arrival and departure, and invoice their charges; they were self-employed and Trinity House took a proportion of their wages. The stand-off led to Trinity House threatening to take action on behalf of the pilots against Brittany Ferries, with the possibility of bailiffs being instructed to arrest the *Armorique* on one of her arrivals in Portsmouth.

Brittany Ferries formally advised Trinity House that the unequal, nationalistic discrimination against the Company's French Masters would be made known to the press and television media, who would be invited to be present at any attempted arrest of a vessel; Trinity House would be identified as being the cause of any interruption to Brittany Ferries' services. An admiralty writ could not be served after 19:00, so there was a limited window for the action, given the published schedule. Carruthers offered to introduce anyone seeking to serve the writ to passengers so they could explain why the ship was unable to sail. The French embassy advised the UK government that any arrest of a French vessel on the contentious issue of pilotage would be seen as an unfriendly

The *Olau West* was chartered by Brittany Ferries in 1976. *(FotoFlite)*

act, and the granting of licences to British Masters at French ports would be reviewed if reciprocity was not granted. This had far more significant implications for the wider British ferry industry, as the number of British ships requiring access to French ports far outweighed the number of French vessels visiting the UK. British shipowners, notably Townsend Thoresen, changed their tack and began to lobby in favour of Trinity House licences being issued to non-British Masters.

No bailiffs arrived to pin an arrest warrant to the mast of the *Armorique*. Carruthers was able to rip up the cheque, kept handy in his pocket to hand over at the eleventh hour, if all else failed.

The Plymouth team found themselves in almost constant conflict with the BTDB because of the port's long-established agreement with the TGWU in relation to manning levels for dockers' attendance at each ship berthing in Plymouth. There was a similar agreement in place in Portsmouth that each vessel-berthing would be attended by ten dockers. At that time the cost was £200 per man or £2,000 per call; equivalent to £1.4millon each year. These agreements were originally established when cargo was loaded onto and removed from ships using manual labour assisted by cranes. Brittany Ferries was the first ferry company to operate multi-purpose ro-ro vessels at both Portsmouth and Plymouth and was, therefore, the first to berth ships which did not require dock labour. Dockers continued to operate as though Brittany Ferries required the same dock labour as before. They would continue to attend each arrival and departure, but did not become involved in any way in the berthing process, or the unloading and loading of the vessel, which was achieved by self-driven vehicles. If there was an empty vehicle requiring a tug movement they would haul it off or put it on the vessel, but that was an exceptional requirement. Burns was happy to confront the convener with 'or else what?' when they threatened to withdraw their labour. 'If you withdraw labour you lose the £2,000 and we are very happy' he said. 'We'll call all the dockers in every port in the UK out on strike...' was the not unexpected response from the dockers' representatives. Just one more problem that remained to be resolved...

The Portsmouth-St Malo operation could hardly have got off to a worse start, but at the end of the first summer season the results were encouraging. The route had attracted 75,000 passengers and 18,000 cars despite all the difficulties, and this level of passenger traffic justified ambitions to establish the route on a year-round basis. It proved that Brittany Ferries could manage expansion and develop new routes through adopting their innovative approach. The Company was already looking at the next stage of development; the possibility of opening and operating a joint venture service between Roscoff and Rosslare was considered in conjunction with Irish Continental Line in October. But the parties were unable to reach agreement on the arrangements and the idea lapsed. Yet the talks had rekindled an interest in the possibilities of operating an Irish service – after all, the parent company of Brittany Ferries was still named BAI.

Brittany Ferries' activities in Portsmouth were watched closely by interested parties in Southampton. Townsend Thoresen, Sealink and P&O Normandy Ferries were long-established operators in the port and were keen to ensure that Brittany Ferries, which they regarded as an upstart operator, should be made to fail as quickly as possible to avoid abstraction of their traffic. They were aware that there was limited availability of land in and around the developing Continental Ferry Terminal in Portsmouth and perceived that, if Brittany Ferries effectively established themselves, they could reap competitive advantages which could not be replicated in Southampton. Dockers in Southampton saw the obvious threat to their roles if Portsmouth was successful. Southampton had the container and cruise ship businesses, but the possible loss of the cross-Channel trade was seen as a dilution of trade union strength. Further, there was the possibility that, if traffic through Portsmouth grew, the attitude of the Royal Navy could prove increasingly obstructive as the expanding number of commercial vessel movements conflicted with the port's naval operations; operators who were established first in the port would benefit from 'grandfather' rights in such circumstances.

The Brittany Ferries' Portsmouth-St Malo service was still constrained by the agreement with trade unions to carry only passengers and their vehicles, but this was not sustainable in the longer-term. Off the record discussions were held with Townsend Thoresen on how this situation could be addressed, but the Southampton-based operator remained nervous about transferring freight traffic to Portsmouth and sensitive to disruption of its core operations. The company was also conflicted, having supported and encouraged the Southampton dockers' in their active attempts to block Brittany Ferries at Portsmouth.

Southampton was a highly unionised 'scheme port' under the National Dock Labour Scheme, where it was a criminal offence not to be registered as an employer, or to employ a non-registered docker. Even if a dock worker committed a serious criminal offence, it was almost impossible to either discipline or to dismiss them as the trade unions, primarily the TGWU and the NUR, controlled all recruitment. The system was rife with what were known as 'Spanish practices' with dockers promised a job for life, leading to inefficiencies and frequent strikes. It was little wonder that the Southampton Unions were concerned at developments in Portsmouth, as employment there lay outside the National Dock Labour Scheme.

The TGWU and the NUR sought an undertaking from Southampton ferry operators that they would not abandon the port even if Brittany Ferries managed to open a Portsmouth to St Malo freight service, but the Southampton operators were not prepared to give the requested assurances. The threat to the trade unions was clear and serious. But the Southampton ferry operators positioned themselves to oppose the opening of Portsmouth-St Malo for freight, so that the TGWU and the NUR regarded them positively relative to Brittany Ferries. The two trade unions told Brittany Ferries that they had the full backing and support of their employers in Southampton, including the ferry companies, and the port owners. This was seen by the dockers as being the time to demonstrate strong trade union power in the UK; the high profile and long-lasting Grunwick industrial dispute continued in north London, and saw daily mass picketing outside the film processing laboratory with frequent violent clashes between the police and demonstrators.

Burns held many meetings with TGWU leaders in Southampton and Plymouth throughout the summer of 1976 to attempt to agree terms and arrangements for carrying freight on the new Portsmouth-St Malo route. It seemed everyone from the BTDB in Plymouth, to the West Country Tourist Board, the Police, the AA, the Plymouth and Southampton Chambers of Commerce, and many more, were demonstrating their concerns about the possibilities of trade union industrial action, and to some extent sympathising with the concerns at the possibility of the Plymouth to Roscoff services being reduced if Portsmouth to St Malo was very successful. This had been avoided in the short-term by not carrying freight traffic during the summer which, given the fleet issues experienced during the season, turned out to be a blessing. But there would be insufficient passenger business to sustain the service on a daily basis during the leaner winter months.

These difficulties with naval authorities, port owners and trade unions were viewed with bemusement by the shareholders, directors, managers and staff of Brittany Ferries in Roscoff, where the Company was able manage and operate its business relatively unhindered; activities in the French ports had a strong gallic influence and they largely controlled the activities of the trade unions, and operated without external interference – why was this not the same in the UK? But there was no alternative to the confrontational approach because there was no money available for other courses of action. On occasions, Burns had to go to Barclays Bank in Plymouth with a bank draft – often days late – to get the wages and to pay for the bunkers to avoid ships being laid up, particularly in times of crisis. The operation was still running on a hand to mouth basis and the prospect of a long winter at Portsmouth with no freight traffic was unthinkable. Compromise was not an affordable option.

Meanwhile, Brittany Ferries had been hosting regular meetings between French exporters and British importers for some time, attempting to encourage the British palette to expand beyond the staple cabbage, potatoes and onions, and explore consumption of more exotic produce such as artichokes. Brittany Prince and BCB were at the forefront of these campaigns, and there was an increasing British interest in the importation of Breton produce. As the *Armorique* neared her return to service from repair, there was little option other than to engage in confrontation with the trade unions if this initiative was to succeed and produce exports grow to secure a future for freight traffic and, by implication, the Portsmouth-St Malo route.

This was a provocative challenge to the trade unions, who felt that even the transfer of a relatively small volume of freight traffic from Southampton had to be opposed. Other ferry operators viewed the potential of freight traffic at Portsmouth with alarm and did much to raise fears amongst the dockers community and other workers at Southampton. Truckline, the growing freight-only operator on the Poole-Cherbourg route, accused Brittany Ferries of unfair competition; in September the Regional Council of Brittany enabled a series of grants to the Chambers of Commerce of Morlaix and St Malo to assist Brittany Ferries. There was no equivalent offer to Basse Normandie for their Cherbourg-Poole service; this was deemed unfair and was challenged by Truckline. It seemed everyone, everywhere had an interest in creating difficult operating conditions for Brittany Ferries. "Stop Portsmouth to St Malo" was the unanimous call all along the south coast of England.

In the towns and cities along the central English Channel coast, it appeared that Brittany Ferries had become disruptive to the long-established and deeply rooted ways in which cross-Channel shipping had operated for more than a century. The ferry companies and their crews, almost exclusively British, port owners and operators and their employees, dock workers, customs officials, and the immigration officers all felt threatened by the ambitions of Brittany Ferries, who were trying to open ports and routes in order to achieve their ambitions in a manner that might diminish, transfer and negatively affect existing businesses. There was an increasing perception that the main beneficiaries of these changes would be the Breton agricultural industries, owned by the Brittany Ferries shareholders, and the regional tourism industry which would greatly gain from the increased numbers of British holidaymakers. In 1976, there was little benefit from these services to the towns and cities along the English Channel coast or, indeed, to the UK in general. The numbers of French tourists were unlikely to significantly increase in the short-term and British exporters were not going to grow substantially because of the marginal increase in freight capacity being offered by Brittany Ferries.

These perceptions were actively encouraged by competing ferry companies resulting in the establishment of a focus by the TGWU, the NUR and other Trade Union members, on stopping Brittany Ferries, almost at any cost.

The escalating number and length of meetings attended by Burns continued throughout October, whilst contingency plans were drawn up by the port authorities, British Rail, and the police to cover possible demonstrations and disruption to existing services. The French Trade Unions and the Marine Marchande in Paris were fully supportive of the Brittany Ferries' position. By mid-October, Michielini, Burns and Carruthers, supported by Gourvennec, devised a strategy whereby freight traffic on the Portsmouth-St Malo route would be initially restricted to five lorries and drivers per crossing, with drivers fully understanding the potential consequences of their passage and attempted entry into the UK. Channel Stevedores were primed and ready to handle the marshalling arrangements for freight traffic on the quay at Portsmouth.

When the *Armorique* arrived in Portsmouth at 19:30 on the evening of Monday 8th November with her first five freight vehicles - one Irish, one British and three French - the port was blockaded by a picket line of more than 200 aggressive, hostile dockers holding placards aloft demanding that the service be blocked. Most of the protesters were from Southampton and arrived in Portsmouth by bus; there was a strong suspicion amongst the Brittany Ferries team that the transport had been provided by the Southampton ferry operators. Outside the port, Commercial Road, the main access road into Portsmouth, was closed by police. The *Armorique's* bow door was opened at the berth, but the police advised that the lorries should not be discharged, so the lorries and drivers remained on board. At 21.30 Armorique departed for St Malo.

The following evening the *Armorique* returned with the same lorries on board, and the outcome was the same. This arrival and departure stand-off continued for a week, with the lorry owners being paid to leave their vehicles on the car deck in anticipation of eventually being able to get them into Portsmouth. Michielini was on board the

Armorique throughout the week. Burns and Carruthers and their shore team met the vessel each evening. They, and others, tried to negotiate with the dockers' leaders. Meanwhile, the Portsmouth-based dockers were keen to admit and handle the lorries in the port, sensing the potential employment advantages to themselves. This factor further deepened the antagonism of the Southampton dockers, whose numbers increased each evening. The process was rapidly mutating from being a demonstration to becoming a mob.

The Southampton dockers and growing numbers of other national dock workers were intractable. Ross McWhirter (of Guinness Book of Records fame), who was active in the Freedom Movement, met with Burns to push him towards legal action against the trade unions. Things changed on Monday 15th November when the *Armorique* went through the now familiar ritual of opening her bow door on arrival, but this time the first lorry emerged whilst police held back demonstrators at the port entrance. Gradually, all five lorries were discharged onto the quay. The *Armorique* returned to St Malo with no freight on board.

The following morning, the *Penn-Ar-Bed* arrived in Plymouth from Roscoff loaded with 24 lorries and 52 passengers, but dockers refused to handle her arrival in sympathy with their fellow trade union members blockading Portsmouth. The *Penn-Ar-Bed* sat outside the port throughout the day and tried again to berth in the evening, but was greeted with the same refusal by the next shift of Plymouth dockers. She returned to Roscoff with her freight. Passengers were advised to drive to St Malo and cross to Portsmouth on the *Armorique*. Both routes were now being boycotted for freight movements by the TGWU dockers, and there were further trade union threats to 'black' any haulier who used the Portsmouth-St Malo route. The BTDB rang Michielini and demanded that the *Armorique* be withdrawn from the Portsmouth route, but their approach received a strong rebuttal.

Meanwhile the *Armorique* continued to make the St Malo to Portsmouth crossings, empty. The five lorries discharged on 15th November left the port the following day after their drivers met with TGWU leaders and the police, and they were permitted to return to the *Armorique* for their return passage to St Malo on 18th November. Plymouth dockers felt betrayed by this concession by their Southampton trade union colleagues and, after extensive talks with Michielini and Burns, agreed to call off their industrial action in Plymouth on 19th November.

The arrival of the *Armorique* in Portsmouth with a further four lorries on 20th November was met with reinforced demonstrations, with all roads leading to the Ferry Terminal blocked and police reinforcements in attendance. The vehicles were not discharged, and another tense stand-off began. The pattern continued for the next few nights, but the mood turned very ugly on 23rd November. More than 100 protesters were faced with a barrier of 300 police, who attempted to prevent access to the quay. Police were knocked to the ground as the dockers surged forward and broke through, but order was eventually restored. When Burns arrived from Plymouth and drove into the port, his car was surrounded by angry dockers who tried to overturn it and set the vehicle alight. He was rescued from his car by police. Portsmouth dockers were assaulted and intimidated, their cars were vandalised and even set alight, and tyres were punctured. This anarchy could not go on for a prolonged period.

Discussions between Burns and Carruthers and the TGWU began in Norman House under the auspices of the independent Advisory, Conciliation and Arbitration Service (ACAS), on 22nd November. Burns attempted to bring other ferry operators into the negotiations; Sealink felt that, as a nationalised enterprise, they should not get involved, Townsend Thoresen ignored the approach. The negotiations were conducted by the British management team on behalf of Brittany Ferries, but there was a marked absence of support from Roscoff. The serious, increasingly acrimonious, publicity being generated by the disputes, which had now continued for many months, was being perceived in Roscoff as unhelpful to the Company. Whilst it was a Breton trait to confront conflict, the culmination of difficulties with trade unions, the Royal Navy, the police, the pilots, and the port authorities at Plymouth and Southampton caused the commitment of the Roscoff management team to waver.

The problems escalated, following a change in the attitude and behaviour of the port authorities in Portsmouth. The City Council was not enthusiastic about confrontation with the trade unions; the Port Manager increasingly believed more in the future of Townsend Thoresen services than he did in the future of Brittany Ferries. The Council let it be known that the determination of Brittany Ferries to operate a year-round St Malo service was threatening the development of the Portsmouth Ferry Terminal. The Royal Navy continued to see ferries as a nuisance with both Townsend Thoreson and Brittany Ferries being in conflict with the scope of their operations.

Against this negativity, positive movement in the trade union position was achieved on 28th November and agreement was finally reached two days later. The ACAS-brokered solution required Brittany Ferries not to operate a freight-only ship from Portsmouth in 1977, to sail only to St Malo from Portsmouth, to remain competitive on freight charges on the St Malo route so as not to undercut Southampton freight rates, and to pay Portsmouth dockers the same rate as their counterparts in Southampton. This was a face-saving exercise for the trade unions, who were aware that their continued violent actions were losing the support of their employers in Southampton, by damaging the image and reputation of the port. The way ahead was now clear to operate the *Armorique* as a passenger and freight vessel from Portsmouth to St Malo. Planning for the 1977 season could finally begin in earnest.

The achievement of this agreement by Burns and Carruthers was acclaimed by Michielini as perhaps the breakthrough which transformed Brittany Ferries from being seen as "the cowboys in the west" to becoming a significant ferry operator on the English Channel. The Southampton operators began to agree with this perception. Brittany Ferries was now a force to be reckoned with.

This was an important and hard-won victory for Brittany Ferries. Despite being less than three years old, the Company had demonstrated its determination to succeed, whether challenged by large established operators, trade unions or 'events'. The ability to carry freight through Portsmouth laid the foundations for the future success of operations for all companies at the Continental Ferry Port. As Southampton dockers had feared, it began the demise of the cross-Channel ferry trade from their port. Ironically the big winners were those Southampton-based ferry companies who had supported and encouraged their dockers to resist Brittany Ferries' freight service. They were unashamedly quick to begin transferring their passenger and freight operations to Portsmouth after Brittany Ferries had paved the way for them to do so.

The year proved successful across all routes for Brittany Ferries; in 1976 the Company carried 281,200 passengers, 48,261 cars, and 12,205 freight vehicles to achieve a turnover of FF60 million. There were well founded prospects for expansion, and a strong base on which to grow traffic on existing routes, which were now clear of industrial conflict. The Company was beginning to operate according to its strengths. Roscoff provided the financial backing and delivered the 'product', by way of increasing the quality of on board services. The UK arm of the Company provided the overall strategic input, a large part of which was defining the brand. The UK team, including BCB, Rook Dunning, the Brittany Information Bureau, and the Brittany Ferries management and staff, marketed and sold the product in the Company's biggest market, generating the sales revenue required to fund future planned growth. The UK also provided the shipbroking skills of Mason, to source, charter and negotiate, in conjunction with Michielini and Burns, the procurement and building of the right ships.

With the passenger business providing an increasing proportion of Company income, Brittany Ferries began to encounter a fundamental financial issue from which it would always be difficult to escape. The bulk of passenger and freight traffic on all cross-

Channel ferry routes originated in the UK, so sales revenue was primarily generated in pounds sterling, but operating costs were mainly incurred in French Francs. Not only did the UK team have to generate sufficient volumes of traffic each year to support the expanding business, but exchange rates had to remain favourable for Brittany Ferries to succeed; a good year's trade could be completely undermined by a weakening in the value of the pound sterling relative to the French franc. Conversely a strengthening British pound could transform financial performance. Either way the Company was powerless against changes beyond its control. Whilst this was a fundamental problem faced by all French-owned ferry operators on the English Channel, it was one from which competing British ferry companies were largely immune, as their revenues and costs were predominantly in the same currency.

Burns and Carruthers found their new roles becoming really interesting when they were able to apply their business acumen in developing a commercial strategy to find new business for the Company. The car-based package holiday business was in its infancy at this time, with established operators in Southampton and Dover beginning to carry increasing volumes of holiday traffic. Camping and caravanning operators were in the process of setting up increasingly sophisticated permanent pitch-sites in France, allowing a new generation of travellers to holiday without having to pack a tent in their car boot. But these pioneers were offering week-long holidays with weekend changeover days, so they were keen to secure capacity of Friday and Saturday sailings, but not on the quieter midweek crossings. Whilst Brittany Ferries' interest lay in carrying people who were going on a motoring holiday, especially those who were driving through France and Spain with caravans and trailers, the traffic needed to be balanced as far as possible throughout the week.

It proved very difficult to assess potential volumes and price them to put a coherent business plan together; the whole process used to drive Dyer wild. Persuading tour operators to change the established Friday and Saturday departures, was a task which she undertook with a mixture of excitement and frustration. Over time the operators began to amend their holiday dates, with better midweek ferry fares encouraging holidaymakers to change their travel plans.

The concept of pricing car deck traffic by length arose from this predicament; here was a common 'currency' that could be applied to all business in order to plan for booked traffic on board. There was no requirement for competitors to do this as they offered more frequent departures and consequently had less pressure on individual sailings. Brittany Ferries had one crossing out and one crossing back. Income per linear foot or metre was often poor but if traffic was turned away it would have to be replaced with individual travellers. That was a big problem with the *Penn-Ar-Bed*, with capacity for 300 passengers, 160 cars, two owners' cabins and 24 berths, and a frequently poor-quality of food in the restaurant.

With traffic growing and strong advance interest in the upcoming season, Brittany Ferries made plans to introduce additional sailings on both the Portsmouth-St Malo and Plymouth-Roscoff routes in 1977, and to maintain a twice-weekly schedule on the Plymouth-St Malo route. From 23rd May until 24th September 1977, the Portsmouth-St Malo route was set to enjoy two return crossings from Monday to Friday, with one return crossing on Saturdays and Sundays.

The 1977 brochure was launched by Dyer, Derek Brightwell and Michael Constantinidi at an open day on board the *Armorique* in Portsmouth on 19th December 1976. The new Company logo, in lower case lettering, featured as the title of the 'brittany ferries '77' brochure. The new brochure again featured largely pictorial content under the cover theme of 'Welcome back to our world'. The focus continued the philosophy of utilising creative destination photography to sell the holiday instead of the ships. Fourteen pages were devoted to extolling the virtues of Brittany as a destination, compared to just four about the ships and routes. This was the major difference in approach to the market from the young Company. Proudly stating that 'Only Brittany Ferries sail direct to Brittany' the copy highlighted the advantages of the choice of ports on both sides of the Channel, and the mix of day and night crossings. At this stage the text stated only that '...with Brittany Ferries your holiday begins the moment you arrive'. The quality of on board offer would have to wait a while to be delivered consistently enough to be a strong selling message. The vision of fast uncrowded roads, warm hospitality, and value for money, addressed the key distinguishing characteristics of a holiday in Brittany. But other holiday areas were not ignored, with a map to illustrate 'the fastest route to Brittany, Dordogne, Loire Valley and S.W. France'. This was accompanied by a laboriously compiled table of road distances to selected destinations from the main Channel ports, highlighting the mileage savings achievable by travelling directly to and through Brittany. 'A world of difference' was offered on board the *Armorique* and the *Cornouailles*; the latter was introduced as 'a brand-new custom-built ship', with both offering 'a high proportion of cabins and berths to ensure your crossing is as relaxing and enjoyable as possible. Our typical Breton hospitality shows itself the moment you drive on'. The Company was able to boast that the *Armorique* and the *Cornouailles* offered the highest ratio of berths to passengers on any English Channel ferry service.

The timetable and a reservations form were introduced as a paper insert inside the glossy brochure. The tariff was a simple split between Low Season and High Season fares, although the pricing strategy was updated to charge vehicles on a 'per foot' length basis - £1.50 per foot in the low season and £2 per foot between 17th June and 18th September. Passenger fares started from a year-round £12 one way crossing, with a 60-hour return available at £16. A double cabin on the Portsmouth-St Malo route could be taken for £14, with couchettes priced at £4 and Pullman seats at £2. The brochure featured a double page map to highlight the delights of 'Camping and caravanning in beautiful Brittany', drawing attention to the fact that there were over 750 campsites and 1,200 farms which offered great facilities in the Region. At this stage, passengers were left to their own resources to find out more about these holiday opportunities.

Butler's improvements to the reservations system led to a completely reorganised and simplified process with a new ticketing and accommodation allocation system. It remained a hugely labour-intensive activity and additional reservations staff were

employed in both Plymouth and Portsmouth to handle the growing business. Amongst the new intake was Sharon Alexander, who joined the company as a Reservations Clerk in December 1976, as part of a recruitment plan to improve the levels of the Reservations service. All new staff were trained and inducted by Dyer, who installed a high level of customer service awareness, which was going to be essential in the coming season to offset the negative legacy of disruption imposed on customers in 1976. Staff training was completed with just days to spare before the start of the new booking season.

The booking process was entirely manual, with passengers required to fill in their booking form and send it to the appropriate departure office for their sailing – at Millbay

1977 Brochure cover. *(Rook Dunning)*

Docks, Plymouth or Norman House in Portsmouth – as the records could only be kept in one place. Travel Agents had to record and submit the same data. At the reservations offices every departure had a chart which outlined the number of vehicle spaces, the number of passengers, and the on board accommodation; this was essentially the 'stock' that could be sold. Soft leaded pencils and erasers were much in vogue as reservations accumulated. The initial reservation was acknowledged by the issuing of an invoice that showed the calculated fare, which was sent back to the customer and required payment of a deposit to confirm the reservation. The final payment would be required 30 days before departure, which prompted a flurry of reminder letters to be sent out before each sailing, followed by a host of incoming cheques to be reconciled against the original reservations; credit cards were very much a rarity in the 1970s. Once the finance team had reconciled the cheque payment, or the client had called in and paid at a travel agent or one of the popular motoring organisations like the RAC or the AA (which had large travel agency interests at the time), the booking could be confirmed and the tickets issued. The process consumed massive amounts of paper, with booking slips held in carousels at the centre of the team's round tables, recording all the passenger, vehicle and accommodation bookings for each sailing. Looking back at the complexity of even this simple operation, it was a remarkable feat to be able to keep records and fill sailings without overbooking. At this stage everything was done by mail and limited telephone calls; sophisticated call centres were a thing of the future. The UK reservation system was replicated in Roscoff, with ghost booking allocations of space for French-originating business on each sailing.

A Freight reservations team was established in Portsmouth to cover all routes, with Carruthers taking on responsibility for UK freight business in addition to his operational duties at the port.

The new year brought time to consider more positive developments after the tumultuous events of 1976. The year started badly when winter weather brought operational difficulties, and the *Penn-Ar-Bed* was forced to run for shelter in hurricane-force winds on 14th January during her crossing from Plymouth to Roscoff. Several lorries on the car deck overturned as the ship pitched in extreme conditions. These were the joys of a year-round service proposition in the relatively open seas of the western Channel.

Discussions were held with Bernard Meyer of Meyer Werft in January 1977 to review possible enhancements to the *Penn-Ar-Bed,* and the shipyard agreed to work up proposals, which were presented to the Company at the beginning of August 1977. The month of February saw Michielini, Burns and Mason holding exploratory talks with Olau Line to consider opportunities to work together, following the charter of the *Olau West* in 1976. Many ideas were discussed at length, but the initiative came to naught.

With the trade union difficulties now largely resolved, and public perceptions of Brittany Ferries becoming increasingly positive, Gourvennec made a rare visit to the UK. Accompanied by Michielini, Burns and Carruthers, he held largely positive meetings with the port authorities and City officials in both Portsmouth and Plymouth. He believed that the time was now right to focus on the growth and building up of the Company by enhancing the product offer. He was welcomed to help cement the goodwill that was being established after the traumas of the previous year.

It was becoming clear to the UK management team that the quality of on board services was very variable and not in keeping with the projected image of the Company. This perspective was strongly supported by Dyer based on her direct experience of selling the service. This aspect was outside their control as it was manged from France, but there was a clear need to professionalise the operation and create a more appropriate ambience on board the fleet for British passengers. Michielini listened to these almost incessant demands to take action to overcome the negative press and customer comments being received about on board services. He responded by finding and

A reception on board the *Penn-Ar-Bed* with Armand Le Bras on the extreme left, Sharon Alexander in the striped top and Eddie Chapman (in trademark trilby hat), the BTDB General Manager at Millbay Docks. *(Paul Burns)*

employing Jacques le Rouzo, who joined Brittany Ferries in April 1977. Le Rouzo had extensive experience from his time with French Line including working on the classic liner *France*. Michielini gave him the brief of developing on board catering facilities to meet the needs of the British market, but with a French twist. His arrival was to be the start of a revolution in Brittany Ferries' shipboard standards. Le Rouzo visited Plymouth soon after his appointment, met with Burns, Carruthers and Dyer who laid on what might be described as a welcome ceremony. After an all day meeting, answering Le Rouzo's questions and offering his assurances, he spent three days visiting restaurants and food suppliers across Devon and Cornwall as part of his induction to the Company and introduction to the UK. He wanted to understand what standards needed to be achieved to ensure the complete satisfaction of the core passenger market. Le Rouzo went on to spend a further six weeks touring catering establishments in the UK, before returning to France to make his recommendations and implement his findings.

Michielini was highly resistant to employing seafarers from traditional French maritime employment sources, despite Brittany Ferries' popularity amongst the Breton seafaring community. He described bringing established seafarers into the Company as "like injecting yourself with a virus." The shipping industry had a tradition of corruption and dubious employment practices, as crew often shuffled between several jobs, and France was no exception to this. The Hotel Services department on French ships was often the position of last resort for officers displaced from more technical roles. Qualified deck and radio officers were highly competent in their roles but, as these traditional occupations disappeared, they frequently found themselves in the unaccustomed and ill-suited position of purser, facing up to passengers and trying to manage catering crew, for whose roles they had no experience and little respect. The situation in Roscoff was not helped by an equivalent lack of maritime expertise in the shore management team, as Brittany Ferries grappled with the issues of an expanding business. Le Rouzo set out to change this and transform the business. He began by establishing a comprehensive set of catering and accommodation standards to be applied across the fleet, and won enthusiastic support right across the Company, with particular support from Dyer, to implement the new standards.

The issues on which Brittany Ferries had focused considerable management time and effort - resolving the opposition to the Company in the UK with sometimes violent disputes, the need for the UK management team to focus on building the business in the UK, the relative ferry inexperience of the ship and shore management team in Roscoff, and the need to quickly upgrade the on board facility - all combined to compel a radical change in how the resources of Brittany Ferries were to be deployed. Key decisions were to be made at a periodic management meeting called and conducted by Michielini, and attended by the heads of all locations and departments, that redeployed responsibilities and authorities and led to plans to build on the strengths and resolve the weaknesses of the Company.

Michielini was to spend significant time and energy on developing the ship management resource based in Roscoff. He went on to recruit new management and build a sales team, qualified to develop the French passenger market and deliver northbound passenger traffic from Roscoff and St Malo. Working with Le Rouzo, he would deliver the resource to establish pace-setting standards of food and beverage products, high-quality customer services and much improved on board passenger and crew accommodation. He needed to work closely with Mason in planning how Brittany Ferries would find the right ships to meet the Company's growing traffic, whenever and wherever it would be needed and to retrofit the existing fleet to meet the new standards.

Burns and Carruthers presented a strategy to Michielini to transform the UK Company from being effective firefighters, supported as much as possible by BCB, to the establishment of policies and procedures covering the commercial, sales, marketing, pricing, and reservations structures required to substantially increase passenger sales revenues across a three-year period. Emphasis was placed on greatly increasing UK-originating southbound freight traffic to levels matching the more captive northbound business.

The impact of this Corporate restructure was to build an organisation geared to effectively plan, organise, lead and control the growth of the business on the established routes, and to explore what, if any, other route opportunities might exist. Teams on both sides of the Channel were now working to their knowledge and experience, with a clear emerging demarcation of their respective separate but integrated roles.

Michielini got to work with the Roscoff-based management team, implementing a

The *Cornouailles*, sporting a large Brittany Ferries logo on her bow, undertakes berthing trials at Plymouth. *(Ferry Publications Library)*

LUCHEON

LUNCHEON

the 9th of May 1977

by the naming ceremony of

M/F CORNOUAILLES

Bretagne Anglettere Irlande S.A.

Roscoff - France

Left: **The menu cover for the luncheon to mark the launch of the** *Cornouailles* **launch on 9th May 1977.** *(Paul Burns)*

Above: **The menu for the meal.** *(Paul Burns)*

Opposite page right: **The guest list for the meal.** *(Paul Burns)*

radical restructuring and strengthening of the organisation. With the assistance of Le Rouzo and Chollet, he began to build the shore-based and on board service expertise which was to establish Brittany Ferries as the English Channel's leading ferry brand, and become recognised as the service leader in the industry. Chollet used his financial acumen to provide the support to make these changes happen. Michielini met almost every ship arrival in Roscoff, went on board and spent time, some said an excessive amount of time, speaking with the captains, officers and crew, inculcating the need and the ambition to be the best ferry service on the Channel. He succeeded in engendering the support and enthusiasm from the shipboard crews to work with Le Rouzo to deliver whatever was needed. Michielini and Mason, with Burns in tow, travelled all over Scandinavia, meeting and establishing relationships with shipbuilders, ferry operators, and other shipbrokers. They put in place an understanding that Brittany Ferries was determined to grow in volume, in service levels and in its financial ability to transform the cross-Channel ferry business. Together they established Brittany Ferries as being a serious contender on the international stage.

In the UK, Burns, Carruthers, and Dyer, supported by their colleagues in BCB, including Brightwell, Constantinidi, Toby Oliver, Bill Rook, and Richard Dunning, set up a system of close and co-operative working to deliver the levels of passenger and freight traffic needed to deliver the sales and revenue volumes required to support the present and future fleet investment and on board services being made from Roscoff. Brittany Ferries was now set on a path to grow and succeed.

Several ferry and passenger ship operators from the UK transiting through the western Channel were finding it difficult to maintain their longer-distance ferry services. Southern Ferries announced their withdrawal from the Southampton-Pasajes (San Sebastián) route on 14th November 1975. The following spring, the withdrawal of Aznar Line's *Monte Granada* from their Southampton-Santander service left the route with just one vessel, the *Monte Toledo*. On 26th April 1977, Brittany Ferries offered a special rescue package for motorists who had planned to cross from Bilbao to Southampton, which allowed them

Mrs. Adresseavisen	Mr. Helouet	Mr. Siewers	Mr. Tricot
Mr. Adresseavisen	Mrs. Høiby	Mr. Sivertsen	Mr. TV-operatør man
Mr. Adenot	Mr. Høiby	Mr. Skrøder	Mrs. Tårland
Mrs. Anchér	Mr. Jacop	Mrs. Thorsvik	Mr. Tårland
Mr. Anchér	Mrs. Klingenberg	Mr. Thorsvik	Mr. Urvoy
Mr. Auffret	Mr. Klingenberg	Mr. Torsteinson	Mr. Vidal
Mr. Berthou	Mr. Laine		
Mr. Bouget	Mrs. Langnes		
Mr. Brightwell	Mr. Langnes		
Mr. Bruley	Mr. Lechat		
Mr. Burns	Mr. Le Bars		
Mr. Chappron	Miss Legoff		
Mr. Cholet	Mrs. Le Saux		
Mr. Claireaux	Mr. Le Saux		
Mrs. Colin	Mr. Leufstadius		
Mr. Dautriat	Mrs. Marstrand		
Mr. Delugin	Mr. Marstrand		
Mr. Dheret	Mr. Mason		
Mr. Dumont	Mr. Merrien		
Mr. Durand	Mr. Michielini		
Mrs. Enger	Mr. Persson		
Mr. Enger	Mrs. Pettersen		
Miss Eriksen	Mr. S. Pettersen		
Mr. Glad	Mr. K. O. Pettersen		
Mr. Goddet	Mr. Phillpot		
Mrs. Gourvennec	Mr. Prima		
Mr. Gourvennec	Mr. Sandberg		
Mrs. Grønn	Mrs. Schyberg		
Mr. Grønn	Mr. Schyberg		
Mr. Hansen	Mr. Scolan		

Madame Colin, Alexis Gourvennec and Christian Michielini at the blessing ceremony for the
Cornouailles. *(Ferry Publications Library)*

to rebook on Brittany Ferries' services, with a special hotel booking service through the Plymouth and Portsmouth offices for those who wished to stay in Brittany on their diverted journey. In the pre-satnav world, Brittany Ferries even provided detailed route maps to help ease the long journey. Burns, with Oliver, quickly pointed out to the media that Roscoff and St Malo were the closest channel ports to Spain. The rescue effort to repatriate passengers from Spain to the UK resonated and lingered with Burns.

Meanwhile, Michielini worked with Mason continued to review the provision and management of available and planned new ships. Although the *Cornouailles* had been launched on 20th June 1976, progress on fitting her out was proving very slow. Only Mason had been able to attend the launch, which occurred just as the Portsmouth-St Malo route was starting up. The long Norwegian winter of 1976/7 saw temperatures drop to -20°C, and welders were unable to work in the freezing temperatures. When Michielini, Mason and Burns visited the Trondheim shipyard to inspect the fitting out of the vessel on 31st March 1977, they were unimpressed with the standard of finish of the ship. The still skeletal outline of the vessel was worrying, the bow door still did not fit properly and one of the seats collapsed when sat on; the build quality was proving a nightmare. Mason was deputed to tell the Swedish shipbroker that Brittany Ferries would not be taking delivery of the ship. A formal complaint was made to the shipyard seeking financial compensation. A subsequent visit for the naming ceremony on 9th May was equally depressing. The morning inspection revealed that there were significant issues remaining with the bow door; it was still not correctly set and fitted, and had to be welded securely closed for the ship to be able to operate at all. The quality of construction of the hull further concerned the Brittany Ferries' team. Robust exchanges with the shipyard management marred the lunchtime naming ceremony, and it was a tense luncheon that followed. Michielini still refused to accept the ship, but eventually the parties agreed to get an independent expert opinion to resolve their dispute; the *Cornouailles* was now late in entering service. A new bow door was eventually fitted in Dunkirk as part of the settlement of the dispute,

Freight traffic discharges from the *Cornouailles* in Plymouth. *(Alain Sibiril)*

after the *Cornouailles* had been in service for three months.

A visitor open day on the *Cornouailles* planned in Plymouth for 22nd May was pushed back to the following day. The *Cornouailles* was resplendent in her white hull with a blue and orange horizontal stripe and sported the new Brittany Ferries logo on her funnels – a symbolic representation of the interaction between the coasts of Brittany and south west England. The vessel was open to inspection by journalists on 24th May, prior to entering service on the 22:00 departure to Roscoff that evening. But the following morning her maiden arrival in Roscoff was blocked from entering the port by a fleet of around 40 fishing trawlers. The skipper of the trawler *La Corse* had been fined £800 by a court in Plymouth on 23rd May for fishing with too fine a mesh whilst some 50 miles off the British coast. The French trawlermen demanded better French naval protection when fishing in international waters. The *Cornouailles* returned to Plymouth, having been unable to berth in Roscoff. She remained in Millbay Docks for three days with passengers using her as a floating hotel until the dispute was settled; the *Cornouailles* finally returned to Roscoff with the 22:15 departure from Plymouth on 27th May. One more memory to be recorded in the calendar of "events".

The arrival of the *Cornouailles* allowed frequencies on the Plymouth-Roscoff route to be increased, with up to three sailings daily at weekends from 27th May. The *Cornouailles* became dedicated to the Plymouth-Roscoff service with the *Armorique* allocated to the Portsmouth-St Malo route. The *Penn-Ar-Bed* offered an adventurous rotation which sustained the Plymouth-St Malo link on Mondays and Tuesdays, supplemented the *Armorique* on Portsmouth-St Malo on Wednesdays, Thursdays and Fridays, before sailing back from St Malo to Plymouth to offer the additional sailings to Roscoff on Fridays and Saturdays. These were very tight operational schedules to maintain, with the potential to export delays between routes.

Brittany Ferries' achievement in opening up freight traffic from Portsmouth, coupled with a successful first season at the port, encouraged Townsend Thoresen to re-open their Portsmouth-Cherbourg service in 1977 and transfer a second ship from Southampton. The *Viking Valiant* opened up a new Portsmouth-Le Havre route for both passengers and freight from 28th May. Carruthers organised and promoted an open day aboard the *Armorique* on 29th May to divert attention away from her new competitor in Portsmouth.

The additional Brittany Ferries St Malo service, now coupled with Townsend Thoresen's expansion plans, placed significant strain on the facilities in Portsmouth and the two operators lobbied the City Council to encourage them to build a second linkspan. The investment was eventually approved, and a second berth was provided from the 1978 season; the work also included an extension to the passenger terminal and resurfacing of the marshalling area to increase the space available for traffic.

In June 1977, Carruthers, Dyer and Burns worked with Oliver to organise a profitable publicity coup in Portsmouth. The Royal Navy had spent five years planning the Spithead Fleet Review to commemorate the Silver Jubilee of HM Queen Elizabeth, with a flotilla of vessels on display from aircraft carriers to inflatable dinghies. The scale of the review and the assembling of the Royal Navy fleet blocked access to Portsmouth Harbour for all vessels wishing to cross the English Channel. Brittany Ferries' response to being unable to sail to St Malo was nimble and quick, with the announcement of a cruise on the *Armorique* to view the assembled ships; effectively a Brittany Ferries Fleet Review, ahead of the Jubilee Fleet Review. Permission to do so was at first refused by the Royal Navy, but when the local port captain and officers were offered places on the *Armorique's* bridge, they saw a way to accommodate the request. It was an opportunity to offer 600 places on the *Armorique* at £100 per person, generating a very welcome £60,000. All places were quickly sold.

Capt. Lainé welcomed guests on board for a midnight champagne supper on 27th June, followed the next day by a continental breakfast in the cafeteria, before the

The 1977 Silver Jubilee Spithead Review with Brittany Ferries

Armorique left the Albert Johnson Quay at 09:30 on 28th June. She sailed slowly through the naval port and reached Spithead at 10:00 to transit slowly through the course of the assembled Review fleet, before taking her position at a specially authorised anchorage off Ryde Pier at 12:45. Authoritative commentary was provided from the bridge by David Jacobs, then one of the BBC's leading broadcasters. He was accompanied by Capt. D N O'Sullivan, Commanding Officer (designate) of *HMS London*. As the Queen received official guests at a luncheon on board *HMY Britannia*, those on the *Armorique* partook of a Grande Bouffe in the Salon Lounge. The Queen reviewed the fleet from 14:30 until 17:00, and then the Review area was re-opened, allowing the

Left: **Guests at the Fleet Review received a specially commissioned folder with the itinerary for the day.** *(Paul Burns)*

Opposite page right:**The itinerary for the *Armorique*'s tour of the Fleet Review vessels.** *(Paul Burns)*

Below:**Plan of the vessels at the Fleet Review.** *(Paul Burns)*

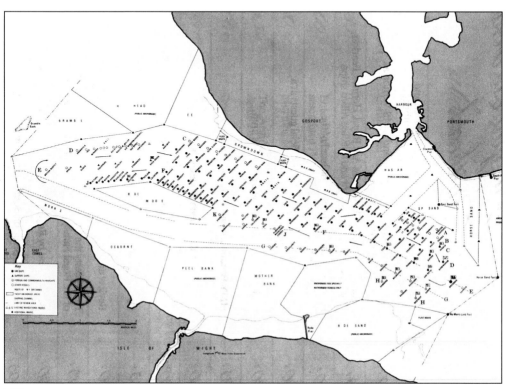

On behalf of Commandant E. Lainé and his crew, we welcome you aboard the M.V. Armorique

The 1977 Silver Jubilee Spithead Review. Your guide to events aboard the *Armorique* and at *Spithead*.

Midnight:	Champagne Supper.	*11·00:*	HMY Britannia with Her Majesty the Queen and members of the Royal Family sails for Spithead.
From 08·00 :	Continental Breakfast served in the Cafeteria.	*11·07:*	Royal Salute from HMS Dolphin and HMS Vernon as HMY Britannia passes.
09·30	The Armorique leaves Albert Johnson Quay.	*11·19:*	Royal Salute fired by HM Ships Ark Royal, Hermes, Fearless, Tiger, Glamorgan, Fife, Kent and selected Allied ships.
10·00 :	Enters Spithead and sails slowly through the assembled Fleets.	*11·30:*	HMY Britannia anchors at the head of the Review Lines.
11·00 :	Morning coffee served.	*12·30:*	Her Majesty the Queen receives official guests at a luncheon aboard HMY Britannia.
12·45:	The Armorique takes position in the Specially Authorised Anchorage.	*13·30:*	Review area closed and warning guns fired.
13·00:	Grand Buffet Luncheon served in the Salon/Lounge.	*14·25:*	HMY Britannia weighs anchor.
16·30:	Afternoon Tea served in the Cafeteria.	*14·30:*	Her Majesty the Queen Reviews the Fleet.
17·45:	The Armorique weighs anchor and returns slowly to Portsmouth offering a further opportunity to view the assembled ships.	*16·30:*	HMY Britannia anchors at head of Review Lines.
19·15:	Disembarkation from the Armorique.	*16·45:*	Fly Past by aircraft of the Fleet Air Arm.
		17·00:	Review area opens and guns fired.
	The Bars will remain open all day.	*20·15:*	Her Majesty the Queen, accompanied by other members of the Royal Family, dines aboard HMS Ark Royal.
	Commentator: David Jacobs, Esq.	*21·00:*	Beat Retreat by Royal Marines on Southsea Common,
	Naval Advisor: Captain D.N. O'Sullivan RN, Commanding Officer (Designate) HMS London.	*22·05:*	Firework Display on Southsea Common by City of Portsmouth.
		22·30	Fleet illuminated.

All times are approximate.

Armorique to weigh anchor at 17:45 and return her guests through the assembled vessels to disembark back at the Albert Johnson Quay at 19:15. A memorable day for all concerned and tremendous publicity for the Company.

But life in Brittany Ferries remained eventful. The next surprise occurred when the *Cornouailles* suffered a bow thruster failure, and had to be replaced by the *Penn-Ar-Bed* whilst she underwent repairs. Better news came from the *Armorique,* which operated flawlessly from Portsmouth with the troubles of 1976 now well behind her.

Over the winter of 1977-1978, there was one daily return sailing on each of the Portsmouth-St Malo and Plymouth-Roscoff routes. The *Penn-Ar-Bed* was sent to dry dock to allow her passenger areas to be upgraded, in the first project of the planned Michielini/Le Rouzo on board refurbishment programme. This increased her capacity from 300 to 420 passengers, expanded sleeping accommodation to 230 berths in two and four berth cabins with washbasins, and adding 154 reclining seats. She was to return to service in early 1978 with unchanged vehicle deck capacity for 160 cars. Her planned role for 1978 was again to supply additional capacity on the Portsmouth-St Malo route during the week, Plymouth-Roscoff at weekends, and join the two routes together with her weekly crossing from Plymouth to St Malo.

As the Portsmouth operation settled down to become less crisis-driven the opportunity was taken to strengthen the team. Butler became Finance Manager to take control of the increasing complexity of the UK finances. He worked closely with Chollet and gained his confidence to enable the introduction of systems for financial and budgetary control that could satisfy both the French team and the auditors. His role was to become increasingly important as the Company expanded its activities. Gordon Day became the freight representative for the UK. He had previously worked with Carruthers at both Hertz and Heron, and eventually rose to take on the increasingly important Freight Manager role. Jon Clarke joined the team as a reservations clerk, before moving into the freight office in Portsmouth. All three were to enjoy long careers with the

The 1977 Jubilee Spithead Review: The Disposition of the Fleet.

The fleet that Her Majesty will review includes representative ships from the Royal Navy, Commonwealth Navies, fellow member countries of N.A.T.O., C.T.O., the E.E.C. and certain British Mercantile organisations.

LINES A AND B contain fast patrol boats, representatives of the Corporation of Trinity House, as well as other lighthouse services and sail training ships.

LINE C is headed by the survey ship HMS Herald and consists of survey ships and craft of the Hydrographic Service which was founded in 1795 Other vessels include representatives of the Royal Maritime Auxiliary Service, The Fishing Fleet, Ministry of Agriculture, Fishery and Food and Department of Agriculture and Fisheries, Scotland.

LINE D is headed by the nuclear submarine HMS Superb and consists of nuclear and conventional submarines of the First, Second and Third Submarine Squadrons of the Submarine Flotilla. Following these are craft of the Royal Naval Hovercraft unit and frigates of the First Flotilla. Next are representatives of the Royal Corps of Transport, Sail Training Associations, Sea Cadet Corps, Royal National Lifeboat Institution, Her Majesty's Customs and Excise, the Post Office and a yacht from Gordonstoun School.

LINE E is headed by the 43,000 ton aircraft carrier HMS Ark Royal the flagship of the Commander-In-Chief Fleet. 846 feet long, t has a company of 2,570 and is capable of catapulting an 18 ton strike aircraft into the air at up to 160mph. It is followed by HMS Hermes, flag officer carriers, amphibious ships, the assault ship HMS Fearless, a command helicopter cruiser, guided missile destroyers and frigates of the Second Flotilla. The line continues with ships of the Royal Fleet Auxiliary Service and British merchant vessels

LINE F is composed of guided missile destroyers, including HMS London, whose name has appeared at nine Spithead Reviews. (The oldest ship's name present is HMS Valiant which first appeared in 1794 Following is Command Helicopter Cruiser HMS Blake, which carries four Sea King anti-submarine helicopters, ships of the First Flotilla which includes HMS Phoebe, a Leander Class frigate which featured as HMS 'Hero' in the BBC TV series 'Warship'

LINES G, H AND K consist of Commonwealth and foreign warships and British merchant vessels.

LINE J consists of mine counter measures vessels, the Fishery Protection Squadron, and the diving training ship HMS Reclaim This line is headed to the East by visiting warships.

Brittany Ferries.

The 5,371 ton Armorique is one of Brittany Ferries' fleet of modern comfortable ships which operate the only ferry service from Britain direct to Brittany.

Brittany Ferries sail from Portsmouth and Plymouth to exclusive ports in Brittany–historic St. Malo and picturesque Roscoff.

From these ports fast roads take you south to all the popular holiday regions of South West France including the Loire Valley, Dordogne and Aquitaine.

In recent years Brittany has become one of the most popular regions in France for British holidaymakers. Brittany Ferries, with its regular services has been in an ideal position to assist in this important development.

Company and contribute significantly to its future success.

The experience of the first five years of operation had demonstrated the Company's determination, resilience, and ability to overcome strong commercial, political and physical opposition. Its success was the ability in tapping into the growing business and to creating new markets, offering what was an increasingly attractive product. New employees were proving to be fully engaged, despite all the operational setbacks, and their commitment to the cause matched that of their Breton colleagues. Competitors were paying increasing attention to the Company's success. It was apparent to the UK management team that this element of success could attract a deeper-pocketed operator to break into the markets the Company had established. Steps had to be taken to consolidate Brittany Ferries' control of routes west of Cherbourg.

Brittany to Ireland had always been a prime target route amongst the Celtic aficionados in Brittany and was also an objective for their equally Celtic supporters in Ireland. Ireland was always considered to be one of the primary destinations along the

The *Armorique* shows off the new Brittany Ferries livery to advantage. *(FotoFlite)*

Atlantic arc to be served during the initial formation of BAI, so much so that it was incorporated into the holding company name. What had not yet been evaluated, or given serious consideration to date, was how difficult it would be to sustain services in a relatively small market with a stand-alone vessel committed solely to an Irish route. Sharing a vessel with the Plymouth-Roscoff route to meet peak demand from Ireland would dilute capacity on the established service and weaken Brittany Ferries' presence in the UK, if the Irish vessel was drawn from the existing fleet. This was a difficult problem to resolve, but the concept of opening a service to Ireland was still raised periodically, mainly to seek to satisfy the initial Celtic dream.

However, there were voices on the Board which were opposed to opening a route to Ireland. The possibility of a route to Cork was more aspirational than real, because the ferry terminal lay a significant distance up the river Lee at Tivoli, where there was just enough room to turn a ship to give access to the berth. This location could not service vessels larger than the *Armorique,* which could carry 700 passengers and 170 cars. Aubrey McElhatton, Chief Executive of the Irish Government owned ferry operator Irish

Continental Line, had already made plain his and his company's strong opposition to any service from Cork to Roscoff. But the Irish Travel Agents Association and the port of Cork Harbour Commissioners were very supportive of the idea.

Services between Ireland and France had been operated since May 1968 by Normandy Ferries-Irish Continental Line, a joint venture comprising Irish Shipping, the General Steam Navigation Company and the Société Anonyme de Gérance et Armament (SAGA). The *Dragon* and *Leopard* offered a link between Rosslare and Le Havre until October 1971, when Normandy Ferries pulled out of the venture to concentrate on its service from Southampton to Le Havre. There were no services in 1972, but Irish Shipping continued to pursue the idea and eventually reached agreement with Lion Ferry, the Norwegian Shipping Company Fearnley & Egar, and CIÉ (Córas Iompair Éireann) to form Irish Continental Line. The new company was to operate the *St Patrick*, recently built by Schichau Unterweser A.G. and jointly owned by Irish Shipping, Lion Ferry, and Fearnley & Egar. At 5,285 tonnes, the *St Patrick* could carry 1,040 passengers and boasted 555 berths, with vehicle decks to accommodate 200 cars or 30 freight vehicles. She made her maiden voyage from Rosslare to Le Havre on 2nd June 1973. The service operated three times each week, year-round, increasing to alternate days in July and August, and quickly proved popular with both holiday traffic and freight hauliers exploiting Irish entry into the EEC that year.

Burns visited Cork in July 1977 to meet with the Cork Harbour Commissioners and understand their views on a possible ferry service from Cork to Roscoff. They expressed support for such a service whilst cautioning him that any announcement of a plan to operate a service could trigger extensive and determined opposition from a significant number of objectors in Ireland. He took note of their advice but had some confidence in Brittany Ferries' ability to overcome opposition based on their track record to date.

The Irish route was not actively in consideration when Burns read in Lloyds List that the Swedish Lloyd ferry service from Southampton to Bilbao with the *Patricia*, and the Aznar Line route from Southampton to Santander with the *Monte Toledo,* were both ceasing operation in September 1977. The withdrawal of these two services would leave Spain without a direct ferry or passenger ship service from the UK. Burns felt that this might present an opportunity for Brittany Ferries. Having spent some time researching the types of service and ships which were offered by Swedish Lloyd and Aznar Line, Burns decided that it would be worthwhile to undertake further investigation to see if Brittany Ferries might be able to provide a replacement service whilst overcoming the operating difficulties which had compelled the two operators to withdraw.

Burns decided to "wing it" and, without consulting anyone in Brittany Ferries, drove on his own initiative from St Malo to northern Spain to meet with shipping agents in Bilbao and Santander. Later, he posed as a journalist in Bilbao to try to establish why the Swedish Lloyd service from Southampton could not continue. He met with the Bilbao port management team, who outlined their understanding of the reasons for the route closure. To Burns it was immediately apparent that ship handling practices at Bilbao were archaic, bound by old, outdated and costly practices. This was not the way that the Brittany Ferries did business. In contrast, the smaller port of Santander did not have these negative legacies.

On his return to Portsmouth via St Malo, Burns told Carruthers where he had been and his reasons for having gone there. The two discussed the possible project and how it could operate. Burns won Carruthers' support if he decided to take the proposal further. A week later, Burns met with Michielini and gently raised the subject of Santander. Michielini made no attempt to conceal his reaction and dismissed the idea of a Plymouth-Santander route as being totally crazy. He did not give reasons for his response, other than it was something he would not be prepared to raise in Roscoff. It was a non-starter.

Burns enlisted the services of BCB under a confidentiality agreement, with Michael Constantinidi taking a particular interest in researching the market and reporting back on his findings. Burns developed an outline proposal with BCB based on his determined belief that this opportunity was significant and had to be carefully considered. BCB were less positive, mainly due to their concerns at Brittany Ferries' ability to deliver what they agreed with Burns was a very substantial project. The proposal was designed to identify and find ways to overcome the weaknesses of previous attempts to provide a Spanish passenger and freight service, which hitherto had been based around sailings from Southampton, all day layovers in port and a 36-hour crossing time each way. The thinking had to be different; what advantage, for example, would a service from Plymouth be able to bring?

The 424 nautical mile route from Plymouth to Santander would be significantly shorter than the 550 nautical mile crossing from Southampton. The French government now allowed French-flagged ships to sail inside the island of Ouessant, close to Brittany's western coast, shaving the crossing length for a Brittany Ferries service by another 20 nautical miles. A sailing from Plymouth could reach Spain in 24 hours, saving passengers two nights on their round-trip holiday journey, and at the same time improving vessel productivity for Brittany Ferries. Further, if the vessel operated to Spain during the week, it could provide additional capacity from Plymouth to Roscoff at weekends, whilst it repositioned to offer a link between Roscoff and Ireland. Good arguments, if there was another opportunity to raise the matter with Michielini and persuade him to take it to Gourvennec and the Board. A big 'if' at the time.

Burns invited Michielini to dinner in a good restaurant in London, ordered a bottle of Michielini's preferred wine and set about creating an ambience to get a hearing for the Spanish route. Quite early in the evening, Michielini confessed that he had given the idea some thought and effectively wanted to be convinced. Burns did what he could to make a convincing case. By the end of the evening, Michielini agreed to consider how he could make an approach to Gourvennec.

One week later, Burns persuaded Michielini to fly with him to Santander. They first made a short tour of Santander and the port area, which Michielini liked. They did not meet with anyone in Santander. Next morning they drove on to the port of Bilbao, where they found all the required facilities in place, as Bilbao had been the port of choice for UK-Spain services for many years. Lunch was taken at the Royal Yacht Club – a very British experience in an area with strong British connections. Burns was concerned that Brittany Ferries could be dragged into the historic methods of operation, with the vessel hanging around in the port all day. He strongly believed that there was a need to do something different. Bilbao was well suited to the cruise ships that came in and laid over for ten hours to allow passengers to explore ashore, before sailing again. But none of the facilities were in place for rapid vessel turnarounds, and the port was far too engrained in traditional ways of working. Burns' emerging plan was for a turnaround period of just two hours to empty and refill the ship and get her back under way, a concept which was then unprecedented on a crossing of this length. The proposition was simple; 24 hours out, two hours lay over, 24 hours back, two hours lay over. Repeat.

Santander was the alternative destination port for the proposal, with good onward motorway connections from the city. Burns introduced Michielini to Modesto Piñeiro on the recommendation of a legal contact based in Barcelona. Piñeiro's main commercial interest was as a shipping agent in the port, but he was also the region's Member of Parliament. This was a very conservative part of Spain – it had been strong Franco territory during the civil war. The Royal Summer Palace was built there, and became a favourite holiday haunt of Franco. There was a small cruise terminal capable of being refurbished, but there were no linkspans or ro-ro facilities in the port, so these would have to be built. Pinheiro was well placed to make this happen.

BCB's initial research findings were relatively positive, and the net of Brittany Ferries personnel being appraised of the project was gradually widened. Chollet began to consider the financial implications; others went to Santander to review the operation.

Capt. Lainé expressed reservations at the practicality of the schedule with the *Armorique*, feeling that the prolonged intensity of the operation would put too much strain on the vessel, but his colleague Capt. Gervain felt that it could be made to work. Everyone was sworn not to bring the research activity to the attention of Gourvennec

A compelling plan was emerging for a service to Santander, but the Board still had to be won over. Appraised of the plans in early October 1977, Gourvennec was initially uninterested and not positive. He met with Michielini and Burns in Roscoff, and after much discussion and a barrage of persuasion, agreed to take the proposal to selected members of the Board to get off the record reactions. But on 15th October this carefully selected group soundly rejected the idea in a series of angry exchanges. The farming interests on the Board were understandably sceptical about getting involved in any ferry service that would not serve Brittany directly. They believed that the Southampton dockers would again take action, because the proposed route would be replacing what

The *Prince of Brittany*, with the funnel logo providing the only company identity; her arrival released the *Armorique* for new duties. *(Ferry Publications Library)*

had been an established route from Southampton for 70 years. They would again close down operations at Plymouth and Portsmouth. The degree of opposition was clear even without the translations; the table was thumped hard. What has Santander got to do with Brittany? Swedish Lloyd could not make it work... Why should they invest in this when the fledgling company was just getting on its feet after all the previous year's operational and financial problems and calls for money? Forget it, was the clear message. Burns took a lot of personal criticism, verging on abuse, from the Board and his position came close to being untenable. He returned to Plymouth feeling bruised and was tempted to abandon the idea.

Burns discussed the events that had taken place in Roscoff with Carruthers, who encouraged him to continue. He persuaded Michielini to approach Gourvennec to allow the project to continue. After further discussion, Gourvennec agreed to let Michielini, Burns and Chollet re-work the numbers. There were days of intense work over the following weeks. Burns strongly believed that the future was going to be a modern shipping service to an attractive port in Santander with onward road connections via a new autoroute. It was going to be a tough battle to get the route started.

The first formal presentation to the full Board took place on 5th November. The proposal was heavily rejected despite Gourvennec stressing the urgency of a decision. Brittany Ferries' dominance of the western Channel would be complete if this far-western gap was plugged. This time the arguments were less personal and less vehement. Michielini and Burns agreed to undertake one further re-working of the figures with Chollet, and present them again to the Board. There was, everyone agreed, one final opportunity to get approval at the next Board meeting on 16th November. The heavily reworked proposal was presented again by Gourvennec and Chollet; this time they heavily stressed the historic Celtic links between Brittany, Galicia and Ireland. There was no firm decision, rather there was a consensus and with a mixture of thanks and apologies to Burns, Gourvennec, at the end of the third Board meeting to discuss the new route, gave the go ahead. He closed the meeting by telling Michielini and Burns that "you need to make this work."

No time was wasted in publicising the new routes as the booking season was about to open. The Cork-Roscoff service was announced at a press conference in Cork on 23rd November. The following day both routes were announced at press conferences in London and Plymouth. Finally, the Plymouth route was launched in Spain with an announcement in Santander on 25th November. The new Spanish route would operate from 17th April until 26th October 1978, with the Irish route running from 26th May until 30th September. The confident Capt. Gervain was named as Master of the *Armorique* for the new services.

The proposed schedule was creative but challenging. The *Armorique* would operate the services on both the new routes, sailing from Plymouth to Santander at 08:00 each Monday, arriving at 09:00 and returning at 11:00 on Tuesday, to reach Plymouth at 10:00 on Wednesday. Her second trip to Spain left at 12:00 on Wednesdays, reaching Santander at 13:00 on Thursday to return at 15:00 and reach Plymouth at 14:00 on Friday. This gave her time to cross to Roscoff and prepare for a 23:30 Friday night sailing from Roscoff to Cork to arrive at 13:30 on Saturday, with a 15:30 return to Roscoff arriving at 07:30 on Sunday which allowed the *Armorique* to return to Plymouth in time to repeat the exercise. The schedule proved enduring. This was an ambitious intensive proposal with an 18-knot ship equipped with two engines, but the service was the best that could be offered with the available resources.

Passenger fares on the new Spanish service ranged from £26 to £40 single, with vehicles charged on a 'per foot' basis. The company offered 72,000 passenger places on the Santander service during 1978, and a further 26,000 on the Cork operation. Whilst Burns was aware that previous efforts to service the Spanish market had failed, he told the press that there were distinct advantages to the new operation from Plymouth, notably around the reduced 24-hour crossing time and the connectivity of Santander as the destination port in Spain. Burns noted that the port offered good access to autoroute links to the Costa del Sol, west towards Portugal and eastwards to the Pyrenees and the south of France. A new Spanish brochure was quickly released on the market in December.

In Ireland the new route was announced before any arrangements were in place with the authorities to accommodate it. Offices were secured in Grand Parade in Cork in January 1978, and staff interviews began, with Anne Upton and Trish Murphy selected to form the team. They began work on 15th February, manning the new office, taking telephone bookings and helping Burns establish the Brittany Ferries presence in Ireland. Beverley Scanlon transferred across from the Plymouth office to become the part time Cork office manager and train the team; she was later to marry and settle in Cork. Meanwhile Heads of Agreement were signed with Piñeiro in Santander to set up the Spanish operation.

But Cork was not without challenge. Irish Continental Line went to the High Court for an injunction, claiming they had agreed the prior right to use of the port for French services with the port authority, and this initial application was successful. A further application from Brittany Ferries to set aside this injunction was led by Peter Sutherland, then a junior counsel in Dublin; this was also successful, and a date was set for a formal hearing. The judge railed in anger at the waste of time – under the 1923 Shipping Act no port could refuse access. Was this Irish Continental Line stopping another shipping company from enjoying free access? He ruled in favour of Brittany Ferries and the Company was awarded costs.

In spite of losing their Court case, Irish Continental Line suggested to Michielini and Burns they would welcome a discussion on a possible joint arrangement between the two companies on services from Rosslare and Cork to Roscoff. Exploratory meetings were held. Meanwhile the Cork case went to appeal at the High Court in Dublin, with the case set to be heard later in the spring of 1978.

As the *Armorique* was now scheduled to operate to Santander and Cork, replacement tonnage was need on the Portsmouth-St Malo route, and Mason began a search. On 6th October 1977 the team inspected the *Prince of Fundy* with Mason at Grenå, Sweden. She had been built in 1970 by Schiffbau Gesellschaft Unterweser AG in Germany for Lion Ferry and used by them on the Portland, Maine-Yarmouth, Nova Scotia route from the USA to Canada until 1976, when she transferred to the Varberg-Grenå service for the 1977 season. She brought increased capacity for 1,000 passengers (300 higher than the *Armorique*) and 220 cars (50 higher) on the route. The *Prince of Fundy* offered 561 berths, 421 of which were in en suite cabins, with a further 132 in cabins with a washbasin, plus 150 reclining Pullman seats. Other facilities included a buffet restaurant, café, two bars, a disco, duty-free supermarket and television in the reclining seat areas. It was agreed that she would make an excellent ship for the Portsmouth-St Malo route and the charter party was signed on 4th November, prior to final approval for the Spain and Ireland expansion. The *Prince of Fundy* was to be renamed the *Prince of Brittany*. Burns highlighted to the media that, through the increased capacity offered by the *Prince of Brittany* and the refitted *Penn-Ar-Bed*, Brittany Ferries was now well placed to take advantage of the increasing demand for the Company's services.

Sealink was added to the list of former Southampton-based companies committing themselves to services from Portsmouth, with the inauguration of a new daily ro-ro service from Portsmouth to Guernsey and Jersey with the *Earl Godwin* on 8th November 1977. The vessel sailed overnight from Portsmouth, returning from the islands by day.

By the end of the 1977 season, Brittany Ferries' freight traffic had grown from 5,932 units in 1973 to 16,194 in 1977, of which 25% was French agricultural produce, and the company looked forward to further growth of an anticipated 17% to an expected 24,000 units in 1978. Passenger traffic had grown to reach 383,536 passengers in the same period. According to Carruthers, the Company soon expected to make a financial return on an annual turnover which was now running at £16 million. After the dramas of 1976 and a calmer year in 1977, Brittany Ferries braced itself for a year of dramatic expansion in 1978.

Four

Opening to Spain and Ireland

The opening up of new routes to serve Spain and Ireland required Brittany Ferries' promotional activities to be expanded to a new level. The brochure for the 1978 season reverted to the use of full-page photography to paint images of idyllic holiday destinations. Of the brochure's 24 colour pages, 20 were devoted to the promotion of destinations. BCB believed that if the reader could be hooked into wanting to be in each picture – walking through those woods, visiting that Loire chateau, playing on that beach – then an irresistible and compelling proposition would encourage them to book. The strong use of double- and single- page photography said more about the feeling of a holiday than any amount of copywriting could achieve, but the poetry of the accompanying captions reinforced the key messages: -

'If fruits de mer be the fruit of love, play on.
Indulge. And make the world, the wild romantic Breton world, your oyster',
'Gold-white your beach.
Wide to the blue inviting sea.
Open to the polished sky.
And you are there to see'

The 1978 brochure cover and Spanish brochure cover. *(Rook Dunning)*

The *Armorique* and *Cornouailles* were joined by the *Penn-Ar-Bed* in the fleet descriptions, with the latter returning to service 'after an extensive refit to increase and improve passenger accommodation'. Early editions of the brochure added a 'Stop Press' footnote to highlight that 'New Ship. Prince of Brittany. Enters service. Portsmouth-St Malo. April 1978. Accommodates 1,000 (581 comfortable berths) 220 cars'. The Spanish service was highlighted in the French brochure by a 'Stop Press' stamp. Photographs of ships' crew were featured for the first time, adopting various postures although one officer was depicted smoking in more tolerant times. Even passengers smoking in cabins were a feature of contemporary photographs. A central eight-page insert contained the harder sell of the Company's services, expanding the area served to 'Brittany and S.W. France – There's no simpler or short way'. A four-page spread gave a comprehensive overview of 'Your historical, eventful, sightseeing, coastal, country, camping, caravanning, gourmet guide to Brittany'.

Fares were restructured for the 1978 season by reducing the peak period by four weeks, so that it ran from 1st July to 3rd September, with 'low season' fares frozen from 1977. Passenger fares became seasonal, albeit there was only a £1 difference between Low and High Season rates. Vehicle fares to France were charged either by the metre or the foot, with the High season rate a rather precise £2.14 per foot. On the Santander service the passenger rate depended on the type of accommodation chosen, from £26 to £28 single for a Pullman reclining seat to £36 to £40 for a two-berth suite, dependent upon the season of travel. These were based on month of travel, with the off-season months of April, May and October, mid-season comprising of June and September, and the high season the peak months of July and August, introducing a three-tier tariff. Vehicles travelling to Santander were charged on a 'per foot' basis, with the seasonal rate also dependent on the number of passengers travelling, from free for four passengers in the spring and autumn to £5 per vehicle-foot for two adults in the peak.

The strapline 'Only Brittany Ferries sail direct to Brittany' was again used extensively in advertising to promote the French services. Advertisements went to some lengths to explain the background to the 'unique world of Brittany Ferries', outlining the development of services and noting that the routes 'opened up a vigorous exchange in trade, most notably the fine produce from Brittany itself – the Market Garden of France, which arrives daily in British shops fresh from Brittany Ferries'. Brittany Ferries offered 'hauliers and exporters a choice of sailings on year-round routes with excellent traffic-free road connections to all parts of Brittany, South West France and Spain'. Passengers were described as 'arriving fresh and relaxed to discover the diverse natural pleasures of Brittany and South West France'. The FGTO offered supporting advertisements encouraging holidaymakers to 'Find France in the quiet corners of picturesque Brittany'.

Ros Ambler joined the Brittany Information Bureau, bringing eight years' experience of public relations in the leisure and catering sectors. She was to make a significant impact on promotion of the Company, played an important role in brochure production, and was eventually made a director of BCB.

Now that the shipping of freight through Portsmouth was established, Brittany Ferries needed to find business to fill the *Armorique,* even though she could only take 16 lorries on each sailing. She hardly posed a material threat to the established ferry services from Southampton. Ian Carruthers drove the sales initiative in his capacity as Freight Manager. P&O Normandy Ferries' and Townsend Thoresen's competing services to France had the advantage of being part of wider route portfolios that could support dedicated freight sales teams to promote their group of services. But this was never likely to encourage anything other than rate cutting, and cross-route deals that tended to drive rates downwards. Customers were rarely interested in meeting a salesman who wanted to increase rates. Geography remained at the heart of the Brittany Ferries' commercial freight strategy, embracing the logic for hauliers of taking the most direct sea route to reach their French and Spanish destinations. The sales proposition was clear; Brittany Ferries could offer a better service and get the necessary permits to help hauliers with a bespoke, more personalised offer. But it was often an uphill task. Carruthers went to see one haulier in East London who had a big international freight business. His host said he was flexible and would 'go anywhere, if the money's right'. So Carruthers outlined all the benefits of the Plymouth-Roscoff service. 'I never go to East Germany, son' he replied. So much for the geographical strategy...

It was true that Roscoff in winter could sometimes feel like Rostock, because the place was frequently bleak and deserted. Brittany Ferries had to keep services running throughout the winter period because credibility would be forfeited if services stopped for anything longer than a short dry dock period to service the fleet. Freight traffic in particular would leach away to competitors. Other operators could call on their larger fleet resources to maintain continuity during refit periods and had alternative routes within their portfolios, but Brittany Ferries did not have the luxury of affording short-term charters.

Yet there was an enduring optimism in the Breton team that there was a cohort of people in Britain pining to spend the off-season in Brittany. This was a perspective that needed correction, but the strong local belief in the destination was a concept that could continue to be harnessed. From the UK viewpoint the geographical logic of Brittany Ferries' route structure was underpinned by destination-led promotion to educate off-season travellers about the attractions of Brittany; potential passengers needed to be given reasons to go to the region and ideas of what to do when they got there. The target market was easily identified as upper- and middle-class audiences who were inclined to try something different and had the disposable income to satisfy their desire. This group were already stalwarts of camping and mobile home holidays, travelling on inclusive packages with established operators like Canvas Holidays and Eurocamp. There was clearly a need to expand the range of products in the market, but they had to be very competitively priced and formulated in line with the vision of what a holiday should be. A limited range of specialist opportunities, including shark and salmon fishing, golf, and horse riding, were offered by the Company in both England and France in 1977, and this programme was expanded in early 1978 to target weekend breaks in the off-season. Paul Burns had developed a 'Go as You Please' product in his time at THF and felt that a similar package would work well in Brittany. He was to be proved right.

Christian Michielini was persuaded by the owner of Le Manoir du Cleuziou, near Louargat, that expanding the property as holiday accommodation and a camp site was a worthwhile venture, and Brittany Ferries entered a commercial agreement to assist with the development. It soon became evident that both parties had bitten off more than they could chew, and the operation frequently resembled the popular comedy Fawlty Towers. Michielini left Carruthers to sort out the mess. The only staff in the Company with experience of running hotel-like ventures were the ships' pursers, and for a while many of them found themselves rostered ashore to Le Manoir du Cleuziou to help unravel the problems.

In the winter of 1977/78, the *Armorique* undertook a cruise to Lisbon, Morocco and the Canary Islands to test the market for a cruise product, a concept which the Roscoff team were keen to promote. Like many of her successors and most cruise ferries, the *Armorique's* passenger accommodation was designed for the short duration trips of a maximum of two nights on which she was normally employed, and her cabins did not lend themselves to the storage of the volume of passenger clothing deemed appropriate for the cruise experience. The exercise was not repeated, although the later arrival of the *Bretagne* in the fleet tempted many in Roscoff to consider a further attempt at entering the cruise business. For now, the concept of a mini cruise to Santander was as far as these ambitions could be taken.

The first visit of the *Armorique* in Cork was planned for Friday 17th March 1978, St

Patrick's Day, to generate publicity in advance of the main operating season. Carruthers went over to Ireland to oversee the first arrival of the *Armorique*. The local team was unused to ship operation and preparations were behind schedule for this initial 'one-off' ship visit. Carruthers quickly discovered that, amongst other things, no crane had been arranged to set up the gangway to allow passengers to disembark or guests to board. He urgently began to put the necessary arrangements in place.

The *Armorique* left Roscoff for the route inauguration celebrations on the early evening of 16th March, with over 300 passengers on board. The large Breton contingent included six pipe bands, two folk groups, ceilidh groups, dancers, bell ringers and uilean pipers. There were civic representatives from Lorient, Clohard-Carnoet, Ploughastel, Treguier and Quistinic travelling to meet with their respective twin towns of Galway, Dunmore East, Westport, Killarney and Drumshanbo, and others seeking to establish 'twinning' links. The enthusiasm generated by this new opportunity was infectious; this was the manifestation of the Breton Celtic dream. Business interests were strongly

The reception before the Grande Bouffe on the first arrival of the *Armorique* in Cork. L to R: Paul Burns, Liam French, General Manager, Cork Harbour Commissioners, Alexis Gourvennec, The Taoiseach, Jack Lynch, Christian Michielini, Gene Fitzgerald, Irish Minister of Labour, and Paddy Crowley, Chairman of Cork Harbour Commissioners. *(Michielini family collection)*

represented in the party, which also included the President, Secretary and Treasurer of the Breton Breeders of Connemara ponies, together with some 60 journalists. The weather was dire for the crossing with the vessel pitching and rolling in a Force Nine gale, and waves reaching ten to twelve metres in height. There were few takers for the cafeteria on the 15-hour crossing. Everyone was relieved to dock in calmer waters at high tide at 09:30 on a cold St Patrick's morning. The *Armorique* passed the Tivoli Terminal and sailed all the way into the city centre of Cork, berthing at Custom House Quay.

The Breton bagadou announced the arrival of *Armorique* with an aubade, their welcome echoed back by Irish bands in kilts waiting on the quay. An assembly of dignitaries waited on the quay to watch the arrival; the bands manfully played on whilst the crew struggled to lift the gangway into position by hand, eventually resorting to a block and tackle. But the passenger ramp would not reach up to the ship's access door, and this issue could not be resolved until the tide fell by 12:30. The band faltered in the cold and the dignitaries shivered. This delay did not matter to the Bretons; the important point was that they had arrived. Eventually, a plethora of hearts and bigouden costumes from Plougastel and Quimper passed in procession off the ship with dancers and musicians behind floats and the orphéons towards the city centre, where a large crowd thronged the streets in welcome. It was a memorable St Patrick's Day parade for all.

The evening was a Celtic extravaganza, with flute, pipe, and drumming bands – the Celtic dream of a link from Cork to Roscoff was being realised. Passengers began to board at 18:00 for a dinner which attracted the great and the good, from the French ambassador and consular officials to the Lord Mayor of Cork, the Cork born Taoiseach (Irish Prime Minister), Cork elected Government Ministers, the Harbour Commissioners and others. Alexis Gourvennec was introduced to the gathering as 'the unelected

The *Armorique* on her berth at Tivoli, Cork. *(Port of Cork)*

president of Brittany'. He was accompanied by Michielini. Trish Murphy and Ann Upton from the local team told the press they were looking forward to a busy season. There were plenty of tensions behind the scenes; agreement was yet to be reached with the dockers and the port pilots, and the legal challenge to the service from Irish Continental Line remained unresolved. All these issues continued to make life difficult, but for now this was a night for celebration. The assembled guests settled down to enjoy a spectacular Grande Bouffe, with the very best of Brittany produce and seafood on offer.

Around 22:30 Capt. Lainé was called to the bridge by an ashen faced officer. He returned and asked Michielini and Burns to go with him to the bridge. "We have a problem..." he said, with some understatement.

The *Armorique* was not the only vessel to have struggled with sea conditions that day.

The super tanker *Amoco Cadiz* had left the Persian Gulf in early February under the experienced Capt. Bardari, heading for Rotterdam via the Cape of Good Hope, and loaded with 223,000 tonnes of crude oil. This was a routine voyage for the five-year-old ship, which was fitted with the latest navigational aids. At dawn on 16th March the *Amoco Cadiz* had progressed to a point around 30 miles off Ushant in the traffic separation lane and was rolling north eastwards in a heavy swell after a difficult crossing of the Bay of Biscay. The initial voyage plan was to head across the Channel to Lyme Bay, where the vessel was to transfer part of her cargo to a second tanker before proceeding up the English Channel to Rotterdam. At around 09:30 the *Amoco Cadiz* was forced to alter course to avoid a small tanker which was heading south in the wrong separation lane. This brought the *Amoco Cadiz* a mile closer to the French coast than planned. Suddenly her navigational problems were compounded when the *Amoco Cadiz* failed to respond to her rudder; she was out of control. Capt. Bardari reacted quickly, sending out warning messages by radio and stopping the engines. His engineers quickly discovered that a junction box had ruptured in the steering compartment, but this precipitated a sequence of equipment failures which, by late morning, resulted in the rudder blade being left to swing freely.

The *Amoco Cadiz* drifted towards the Brittany shore, but relief was available from the tug *Pacific* which was around an hour away and soon came alongside in support. The two

Left: **The bow section of the *Amoco Cadiz*.** *(Plymouth Herald)*

Right: **The clean-up operation under way on the Brittany beaches.** *(US Department of Commerce)*

vessels disputed whether the *Amoco Cadiz* required towing or whether this was a salvage operation, an argument with significant financial consequences for the *Amoco Cadiz's* owners if the latter proved to be the case. The *Pacific* managed to fix a towing line to the *Amoco Cadiz,* but the two vessels continued to dispute the contractual terms of the towing arrangements until the line parted at the tanker's bow. The *Amoco Cadiz* restored a single propeller to help keep her away from the shore, but this engine had to be stopped again for safety reasons when the *Pacific* came astern in an unsuccessful attempt to fix another line; the *Amoco Cadiz* was forced to drop her port anchor. Another line was secured but the two vessels failed to agree over the next action. Capt. Bardari wanted to use his engines to force the *Amoco Cadiz* forward, but he had the *Pacific* lying in a vulnerable position immediately in his wake; the *Pacific* wanted to pull him to starboard. The argument proved academic when at 21:04, the *Amoco Cadiz* struck the Men Goulven rocks a mile offshore, almost exactly at high water, the worst possible moment for subsequent salvage. Damage was severe, and it was immediately clear that the *Amoco Cadiz* would have to be abandoned; further distress messages were broadcast and the French emergency services responded quickly, lifting the crew off the stricken vessel by helicopter.

Whilst the *Armorique* was arriving in Cork on the morning of 17th March, the *Amoco Cadiz* was lying astride the Men Goulven rocks with her back broken just forward of the bridge, and was beginning to leak oil. By now, a slick some four miles long had reached the shores of Brittany at Portsall. There was a national oil pollution contingency plan (POLMAR) to deal with this kind of scenario, based on the lessons learned from the loss of the tanker *Torrey Canyon* off Cornwall on 18 March 1967. But the plan had not been updated since 1972 and had never been tested. The scale of the unfolding disaster was far greater than anything envisaged in the POLMAR plan.

As Michielini digested this news he rightly insisted that it should not spoil the evening's celebrations, and the team returned to the party. There was little else they could do.

The *Armorique* was not scheduled to leave Cork on her return crossing to Roscoff until 12:00 on Saturday 18th March, so Gourvennec and Michielini flew directly across to Morlaix to make their way to Roscoff in order to assess the situation. The outlook was bleak; the slick from the *Amoco Cadiz* had now trebled in size, there were limited barrages available to control it, and weather conditions precluded salvage action. Worse, the Spring equinox was approaching, peaking with the highest flood tides on Easter Sunday 26th March, and there was little point in beginning clean-up exercises until this had passed, as the rising tides would only wipe out any work done in the interim. The consequences for the fishing communities were dire; the seaweed harvesting season was due to begin on 15th April and tourism, already suffering from prolonged winter weather and an early Easter, now faced the prospect of widespread cancellations.

By the time Burns got back to Plymouth two days later there was chaos in the reservations office, as passengers made mass cancellations in response to the extensive media coverage of the disaster. Both the Plymouth-Roscoff and Cork-Roscoff routes were suffering badly, but Portsmouth-St Malo was, as yet, relatively unscathed. Burns flew across to Morlaix and thence to Roscoff. The stench of oil in the town was overpowering so, after a discussion about the financial consequences with Michielini and Maurice Chollet in the Brittany Hotel, the trio drove back inland to Morlaix.

Gourvennec, Michielini, Chollet and Burns met that evening in the Hôtel de L'Europe in Morlaix to consider their options. As the discussion continued long into the night, two well-dressed men were sitting nearby in the bar, seemingly listening-in to the conversation. Burns approached them to find out who they were, and what their interest was in the discussion. This proved to be a prescient move. The two were lawyers from the American legal firm Speiser & Krause, who had been working on litigation in relation to the loss of Turkish Airlines Flight 981, which had crashed in Ermenonville forest near Paris on 3rd March 1974, killing all 346 on board. They had travelled straight across to Brittany on hearing of the *Amoco Cadiz* grounding, to assess the situation and the potential legal opportunities for their firm. It was a fortuitous meeting of minds. Brittany Ferries had the local knowledge and contacts to guide Speiser & Krause to the right people to assess the impact of the disaster; they in turn could find ways to help the company weather the financial storm ahead and prepare the case for compensation.

By Good Friday 24th March the oil slick covered some 80 miles along the beaches from Portsall in the west to the Île de Bréhat off Paimpol in the east and stretched 18 miles out to sea. The west-facing Île de Batz off Roscoff was particularly badly hit. A thin layer of oil was seeping under the barriers up the Rivière de Morlaix almost as far as Morlaix itself. 'Operation Teaspoon', the clean-up operation, could not begin until Tuesday 28th March, after much of the remaining oil on the *Amoco Cadiz* had been deliberately forced out of her hull by the military authorities. Brittany was immediately supplied with resources to address the problem, with 5,800 military personnel committed to clean the beaches, supplemented by 3,000 civil volunteers and over 1,000 vehicles.

The *Amoco Cadiz* generated a huge amount of unwelcome publicity for Brittany's holiday businesses, with the media story evolving from the tanker sinking, through to the film of oil on the beaches, the devastating consequences for wildlife, and then the clean-up operation. The over-riding impression was of holiday beaches soaked in oil and ruined by the incident. With a brand so closely associated with the affected region, Brittany Ferries bore the brunt of the public backlash. The immediate flood of booking cancellations required customer money to be refunded without question, but the Company was soon within seven days of running out of cash. Chollet was concerned at the Company's ability to survive; there were good bookings for the summer on the St Malo and Santander routes, but there was no money in the short-term to keep the operation going.

Gourvennec approached the French government for support, Chollet dealt with the banks, whilst the UK management team team did their best to shore up the business and maintain the confidence of staff and suppliers. Butler arranged with Barclays Bank for an overnight deposit treatment for the funds which were coming into the current account, which were then made available on the London money market at rates which reached 19% at times, bringing a healthy six-figure annual income.

The news media continued to cover the oil spill in detail. A severe storm began to break up the oil slick a week after the *Amoco Cadiz* grounding, but it also covered the sea front areas with specks of oil. The clear up effort was now well under way and oil was being scooped up from the beaches and taken to designated disposal sites. At one point there were 569 railway tankers standing in the station area in Roscoff ready to receive oil waste; eight small tankers and dredging ships were chartered to remove spoil from the harbour. But when the Danish-registered *Henriette Bravo* sank in the Channel loaded with 2,800 tonnes of oiled weed, the authorities determined it inappropriate to continue clearance by sea. Roscoff was a vast basin of tar, with the sea flat and wave-free, like a black viscous lake.

As the month of April progressed there were continuing cancellations and refunds. The Company was close to going out of existence.

There was increasing anger across Brittany over the devastating impact on the tourism industry, with pressure applied on the authorities to permit clearance of oil using dispersants, which hitherto had not been used for environmental reasons. In response the FGTO launched a promotional campaign under the banner 'Operation Verité' and in early May brought a party of foreign journalists to view the clean-up operation on the beaches. Some sense of positivity was returning

Speiser & Krause became significant in assisting in the promotion of Brittany Ferries as one of the prime victims, alongside the fishing, lobster, oyster and shellfish industries, which had been wiped out by the spillage. It became almost impossible to sell Brittany produce of any description, as consumers feared contamination by oil pollution, irrespective of where in the region it came from. Burns went with Speiser & Krause to the Marine Marchande in Paris to assemble the case. This was a crisis that impacted right across the community; farmers were not going to be able to sell produce, fishermen were ruined, the ropemaker had lost his trade, milk producers were suffering, and tourism businesses faced disaster. A case was made to the French government to fund continuity whilst the bigger picture of compensation was resolved. The arrangements offered in return were straightforward – the government would provide funds to the Chamber of Commerce and they in turn would take the responsibility to distribute money to affected parties and protect local businesses, including Brittany Ferries, who got a major share. The company would sign over their rights to settlement to the French government in return for this support, with surplus funds returned at the end of the case. Spicer and Krause assembled the full list of a chain of suffering from bread suppliers to wine growers. They were acknowledged experts in handling this type of claim, set against the murky 'offshore' and international law issues of such an action in the maritime industry.

They knew that the most sympathetic court would be in the 26th district of Chicago, the most liberal in the USA, so the claim was lodged there. The aim was to recover a minimum settlement of $200 million with Brittany Ferries getting its fair share. It took 26 years for the case to be concluded, although an interim settlement was achieved in the mid-1980s.

More had to be done to compensate for the loss of business. A 'child goes free' offer was used to tempt passenger bookings and a Freight Drivers Club opened to boost loyalty amongst the freight community. Drivers were offered a £5 voucher for each single crossing, redeemable against future passenger travel, subject to a maximum value of £400. Carruthers said in his role as Freight Manager that "The international driver is the hub of what is often a big operation and just as manufacturers are paying more attention to him, we intend to do the same." "Our problem is shortage of capacity, not excess" responded an unsympathetic Keith Wickenden of Townsend Thoresen.

The Brittany tourism problem needed a British solution if the industry was to recover, as the French habitually do not go north for their annual holidays; preferring to head south to the sun. French northbound tourism was not the answer, but the cancellation of bookings continued despite all the communication and marketing efforts to present a positive image. British and Irish families were giving up their holidays in western France, as the media image remained one of the entire Brittany region under tar. The strong marketing slogan "Only Brittany Ferries sails direct to Brittany" looked hollow when nobody wanted to travel to Brittany. Local Breton concerns were more about the impact on produce exports, as most agricultural production was unaffected by the oil, although seafood exports were being wiped out. But the British and Irish -originating tourist business was the lifeblood and cash cow for Brittany Ferries. If something was not done to turn around the loss of bookings, there would not be a Brittany Ferries.

As is often the case when disaster strikes, the answer proved to be obvious. It was not possible to promote the Brittany beaches as an attractive proposition for holidaymakers from the UK and Ireland, but their hinterland was not tainted with the same contamination. The region had a plentiful supply of small cottages and farmhouses which could be used as holiday cottages, and which would resonate with lovers of the French lifestyle and countryside holidays. The concept of selling 'gîte' holidays was born. This built on the tentative steps that had already been taken in establishing a small range of Brittany Ferries package holidays in previous years.

Simple logic was used by the team to understand where the British tended to holiday in France. The quickest method was to look at where the major camping holiday specialists established their campsites, for whilst there was the whole of the country to choose from, they chose to concentrate in selected areas. Brittany Ferries undertook research which established that, of all those who spent more than three or four days in France, 70% did so in Western France, so it was clear that the route structure was serving the right destinations. The advertising message continued to reinforce this, and this strategy proved extremely successful.

Operational aspects of the new holiday products were run from St Malo for the practical reason that most of the holiday sites were in closer proximity to St Malo than to Roscoff. Paul Armandary was appointed to lead the French operation, and his team went out into the Breton countryside to inspect properties, assess their suitability for inclusion in the scheme and convey their verdict on whether the property made the grade. It was a good time to approach property owners – the biggest source of holiday beds in the region – as forward booking levels for other business were in freefall. The UK teams established the reservations systems and processes to underpin the operation, devised the first brochures and began to promote the products. The booking system was entirely manual and added a further level of complexity to the management of shipboard capacity.

The first products were promoted with a simple single-colour textual brochure from

May 1978, just two months after the *Amoco Cadiz* went aground. Customers had to have great faith in the descriptions and trust in Brittany Ferries to deliver the product. The initial choice of properties was variable, with five mice-ridden houses being a particularly memorable part of the portfolio, but the concept of gîte holidays was well received in the UK. The range was expanded to 80 sites within a year, and the inspection regime honed to exclude sub-standard properties. Every aspect of each property was rigorously inspected, from the quality of the bed sheets to the important provision of tea-making facilities. Company certification became a pre-requisite for inclusion within the brochure, and random inspections were maintained to ensure consistency of the product.

Brittany Ferries' holidays had a significant number of advantages in the marketplace, particularly in the 'dual language' nature of the enterprise. Customers could deal with a UK office to make their reservation, but if anything went wrong whilst they were away on holiday, they could contact the local office in St Malo (and later, Santander) for assistance. The offices had English-speaking staff who were familiar with the needs of customers and the nature of the properties, as they had negotiated most of the contractual arrangements and were talking regularly to hoteliers and gîte owners.

The holiday product started simply from an administrative perspective, with just 19 hotels around the ports in Brittany, before the rapid expansion into the gîte market. But the holiday business added more complexity to the booking process, more paperwork and writing, and with this came a drive for efficiency. Rolodex systems were introduced to hold tickets; options, confirmations, payments and travel were all colour-coded, so the status of any booking could be seen at a glance. It was to be some time before the whole process could be computer-driven, but this brought new problems as the systems would go down and there was potential for double bookings. But these errors were small in comparison to the volume of people being processed with comparative ease, and the importance of cash being generated by the new business.

Oliver launched and managed an extensive public relations drive and played a big role in creating visibility for these new products. Gîtes quickly acquired a cult status, becoming a very fashionable holiday product in the UK and Irish markets. This placed great pressure on accommodation resources, as competing holiday companies sought 'stock' for their own brochures. The UK team fought hard to encourage their French colleagues to address this growing demand and established close working relationships with Gîtes de France and the FGTO, particularly Dominique Gigante, who introduced contacts in France. It helped that Brittany Ferries was a French company, as the central organisations were keen to help their own. But there was a developing tension between Gîtes de France and Brittany Ferries as the former was making money on the back of special discounted Tour Operator rates (ITX rates) offered by the Company, and Gîtes de France resisted the growth of Brittany Ferries holiday products with which they were in competition, especially in Brittany where there was a strong local preference to offer properties through the ferry company. If anything went wrong with a booking, Breton property owners had easy access to Gourvennec to put things right.

Brochure production was a laborious exercise at this time. The descriptions of each gîte had to be typewritten and sent to the printer to be set in lead -setting. Proof copies would be sent back by courier for checking and there would be several iterations of this flow of marked-up paperwork before the final copy could be signed off for printing. The earliest gîte brochures were descriptive, requiring an element of creativity to distinguish each property; small drawings were later added which was a huge step forward, but property photography came much later. A pattern was established whereby the annual brochure production process would start early in July and take up all of the summer months, even though the brochure would not be printed until December. At the same time pricing had to be fixed for the forthcoming season up to 18 months ahead of departures, with little latitude for error or adjustment without an expensive wholesale withdrawal and reprint of the brochure.

Amidst all these difficulties, Brittany Ferries took delivery of the *Prince of Brittany* for the Portsmouth-St Malo route. When she arrived in Southampton, the *Prince of Brittany* underwent an inspection by the safety authorities, who withdrew her certification on the basis that a number of the metal doors that had been fitted for her service in Portland, Maine had been replaced by wooden doors. This change had been undertaken in France under the supervision of Bureau Veritas, with the full approval of the French safety authorities. An international stand-off commenced, as the two national authorities threatened to impose their standards on each other's fleets. Resolution came in the form of an agreement on mutual inspections and common application of standards. The *Prince of Brittany* finally arrived in Portsmouth on 15th April ready to take up the service, freeing the *Armorique* to transfer to Plymouth for her new routes.

The Santander service was launched at a special reception at a foggy Plymouth on Sunday 16th April. The Lord Mayor of Plymouth, Ramsey Thornton, presented Capt. Gervain with a framed print to mark the occasion, and Eddie Chapman, manager of Millbay Docks, handed him a commemorative piece of silver plate. The *Armorique* had undergone an extensive refurbishment at Falmouth for the new route, and her facilities now included a cinema showing the latest releases, and a children's playroom. BCB were involved in upgrading the décor on the *Armorique*, through one of their yacht designer contacts. Speaking on board the *Armorique*, Burns expressed great satisfaction with the level of advance passenger bookings for the route, which was already encouraging the Company to consider whether the service should be extended to operate year-round. A final decision would depend on the reaction of the freight community. It was becoming clear that the market was very different from the established cross-Channel routes; still predominantly British but with a higher proportion of passengers owning second homes on the Iberian Peninsula. These were people with both time and money at their disposal; the on board and shore services had to adapt to meet their needs.

The inaugural sailing of the *Armorique* on 17th April featured 38 vintage Rolls Royce and Bentley cars, owned by members of the Rolls Royce Enthusiasts Club, who were heading to a special rally in Gerona organised by the local tourist authority. They included Silver Ghosts from 1915 and 1924, the latter having been purchased by its owner for £36. The cars were valued and insured at £1.5 million. When the time came to load the *Armorique* the Club became very protective of their vehicles, demanding that a minimum of a one-metre space be left around their vehicles to prevent d possible damage during the crossing to Santander. As the departure time of 08:00 approached it became evident that not all other cars which had been booked could be accommodated on the car deck. Motorbikes were loaded into the back of an empty van to save space, but 24 cars were left behind, and two motorcyclists were forced to return up the linkspan when there was no room remaining for them. Angry passengers, some of whom had booked six months previously, remonstrated with staff on the quay and made their feelings plain to assembled media. Burns found himself standing on a table in the terminal addressing the disgruntled crowd. Toby Oliver had a press party with him travelling to Spain, and persuaded them that this 'little hitch' would be sorted. 'We did not foresee any problems like this' he said, 'it is a combination of overbooking by travel agents and the extra care we have had to take with this valuable cargo'. The *Armorique* sailed some 45 minutes late, leaving the stranded passengers with a two-day wait until the next departure. The Band of the Royal Marines continued playing throughout. "Rule Britannia" echoed around Millbay Docks and the press and TV crews were having a field day.

The new route was described as the 'easiest, most enjoyable way to Spain', the 'fastest, shortest ferry service yet to Spain' saving 'both time and money'. But the maiden voyage departure did not quite reflect the marketing claims. There was widespread coverage of the displaced passengers and cars on television, radio and in the press. Booking cancellations followed, as potential customers contemplated the consequences for their holiday of a missed sailing or a missed place on the car deck.

The *Armorique* berthed on schedule in Santander, Capt. Gervain had made up for the late departure from Plymouth. Michielini and Burns flew to Santander on the previous evening, so they could be part of the Spanish welcoming party, which included a Spanish military band playing music appropriate to the occasion. The *Armorique* berthed flawlessly, dressed overall, with her flags fluttering in a gentle breeze. The Captain came ashore to be welcomed and presented to the dignitaries. The linkspan was extended and put in place and the bow door began to open. But it failed to open fully and jammed. It was closed and failed to open on the second try. A 1915 Silver Ghost had been loaded first and was planned to be the first vehicle emerging onto the linkspan. Press and TV had been briefed and were positioned to capture the moment when the Silver Ghost would drive off, but nothing was moving.

The *Armorique's* crew appeared, dressed in bright orange overalls, and lowered themselves down the side of the *Armorique* and began using sledgehammers on the bow

Above: **The *Armorique*'s bow door finally opens in Santander.** *(Modesto Piñeiro collection)*

Top right: **Paul Burns and Christian Michielini watch the *Armorique* approach the linkspan in Santander with the first passenger arrival.** *(Modesto Piñeiro collection)*

Bottom right:**An expensive cargo of Rolls Royce cars discharged on the quay.** *(Modesto Piñeiro collection)*

door connections. The Band played on. After some fifteen minutes the crew were successful in getting the door to open. The opening movement was applauded by all on the quayside.

Everyone now awaited the emergence of the Silver Ghost but there was a further delay. The car had a flat battery and would not start. The Band played on whilst a tractor was sourced to unceremoniously tow the Silver Ghost up the linkspan. Rolls Royce after Rolls Royce then emerged, making up for the previous incidents. The dignitaries, invited guests, journalists and the TV crews happily retired to a VIP brunch at the Bahia Hotel.

The manner in which the *Armorique's* problems were overcome in Santander demonstrated the competence of the Piñeiro family and their company to manage the business in unexpected and adverse circumstances. Modesto Piñeiro Sr., his son Modesto Jr., and their team managed the new Brittany Ferries business and ensured that the Spanish management of the Company could reliably be entrusted to their family. Whilst Modesto Sr. died many years ago, Modesto Jr. became the new Modesto Sr. and his son, the new Modesto Jr, now manages the business. A dynasty in the making.

In an effort to raise media awareness of the improving situation on the holiday beaches, the Brittany Information Bureau commissioned an opinion poll on behalf of the region's Economic Committee to evaluate perceptions of the impact of the *Amoco Cadiz* disaster in the UK and Ireland. This also served to highlight the extent of the clean-up programme and the scale of the impact of the oil slicks on the beaches. The research revealed considerable misconceptions. Most people questioned thought that all of

Above: **Capt. Gervain welcomes guests to a reception on board the *Armorique* in Santander, flanked by the chairman of the Santander chamber of commerce and Modesto Piñeiro Sr.** *(Modesto Piñeiro collection)*

Top right: **Passengers disembark from the first arrival.** *(Modesto Piñeiro collection)*

Right: **The mayor of Plymouth is welcomed by Modesto Piñeiro Sr.** *(Modesto Piñeiro collection)*

Brittany's 1,100-kilometre coastline had been affected, rather than the 350 kilometres of the north west coast which had actually been impacted by the slick. Over 60% of those questioned did not appreciate that the clean-up operation would be complete by the summer holiday season. The poll highlighted that these perceptions came from television news images and newspaper reports, which had tended to give an exaggerated impression of the scale of the damage. The press release noted that 80% of British and Irish tourists to Brittany visited areas unaffected by the aftermath of the oil spill.

Gourvennec underwent an extensive tour of the Brittany beaches in his role as

President of the Economic Committee of Brittany, and released news that one-third of the clean-up had been completed. There was confidence that the areas of the affected Brittany coast would be largely clear of oil by the end of May. He deemed that the clean-up operation was progressing "extremely well." Areas south of St Mathieu and east of Paimpol were unaffected, beaches had been cleared between Paimpol and Trégastel, there was moderate pollution between Trégastel and Brignogan, and general pollution between Brignogan and St Mathieu.

More positively amidst the *Amoco Cadiz* gloom, Irish Continental Line's challenge to the Cork service was finally withdrawn on the steps of the High Court in Dublin on Tuesday 25th April. The Irish Continental Line Board was still of the opinion that there was an agreement in place, but decided, in the interests of Irish Tourism, that the case should not proceed to court. No damages or costs were paid by either party. Both companies intended to proceed with their independent plans and service advertising. Brittany Ferries publicly welcomed the announcement and saw the new Irish Continental Line position as a significant gesture towards the resolution of the differences between the two parties.

Vehicles load aboard the *Armorique* for the inaugural crossing from Cork to Roscoff. *(Port of Cork)*

The way was now clear for the Irish service to commence.

The inaugural Roscoff-Cork sailing left France on 26th May 1978, arriving in Cork at 13:30 the following day. The *Armorique* got stuck in the mud whilst turning outside Tivoli but soon freed herself. However, when the vessel finally berthed the stern door would not open, repeating the issues experienced in Santander. A local band was playing on the quay and faces were getting redder and redder as loud hammering noises emanated from inside the ship. Suddenly the door burst open, to the relief of those on board who thought they might be going back to Roscoff. The Lord Mayor of Cork was on hand to greet her arrival and was taken on board the *Armorique* by Capt. Gervain. The ship had brought around 200 passengers and 65 cars – only one of which was Irish – and returned with similar numbers. Bookings for the four-month season were said to be running at 85% of capacity, but this was far from the numbers turning up at the Tivoli Terminal.

Burns began a regular summer routine of flying with Brymon Airways from Plymouth to Cork every Saturday morning during the season to meet the incoming ship at around 14:00 and manage the discharge, load and departure at 17:00 before flying back to Plymouth.

The port of Tivoli continued to prove to be a difficult place to operate to because of the physical constraints on access. The *Armorique* consistently hit mud as she tried to turn in the port area, and the authorities were indifferent to requests to undertake the necessary dredging. This was no way to run a ferry service and Burns began to look for an alternative location.

The tasks of resolving the difficulties that arose in getting the new Cork service established, operating within the limited facilities of the port, resolving stevedoring disputes, and seeking approvals from the Cork Harbour Commissioners, were managed Sean Geary, who was then the Trade Development Officer of the port of Cork. Geary worked seamlessly with the Irish team to help overcome the many difficulties that were encountered.

More problems originated from B&I Line, who were concerned at abstraction of traffic from their traditional 'Landbridge' route from Rosslare to Pembroke Dock. This enabled continent-bound Irish passengers and freight to reach France by utilising their services to Wales and then taking other operators' cross-Channel routes; it was a significant business which was now under threat from the direct alternative to France. B&I Line took every opportunity to publicise problems arising on the Cork service to try and undermine it.

The team worked hard to assuage Irish concerns about the aftermath of the *Amoco Cadiz* disaster, with statements that there had not been any serious effect on forward bookings. Burns updated the press on the battle for compensation and observed that there were now few signs of oil spillage on the beaches. Local media were impressed by the Breton support for the new venture and their ambitions for the Celtic connection and all that this entailed in cultural and commercial links between Ireland and France. The outlook was positive, and talk turned to serving the emerging new ferry terminal at Ringaskiddy with a new and faster vessel, included the possibility of the crossing time being reduced by three hours to a twelve-hour passage.

Brittany Ferries were keen to promote the route as the fastest car ferry service for Irish holidaymakers heading to the continent. But Burns described the service as 'a necessary inconvenience of travel' when he outlined the way in which the new route would be promoted. 'If there was a bridge between Ireland and France, people would use it rather than the ferry itself' he said. Brittany Ferries would concentrate on selling the destination, rather than the ferry itself, on the basis that passengers were more interested in where they were going rather than their means of transportation, and it would be a waste of time to promote aspects of the crossing that people took for granted. In France the Company would concentrate on promoting the Celtic connection and the cultural similarities with Ireland, and in Ireland they would promote Brittany and the speed and directness of the crossing. He noted wrily that he had some 400 directors in the farming community to deal with, although they did not interfere with the day to day operation. Board meetings could be delayed for hours at a time whilst directors delivered the harvest, he observed. Local Irish media were impressed at the lean management structure of Brittany Ferries and suggested it could be a model for Government owned local ferry operators. Journalist Dick Brazil reported that he found the *Armorique* to be amongst the most impressive ships he had ever seen, although he was disappointed when the showing of 'Black Emmanuelle' was interrupted by a projector failure in the cinema...

The Bretons reciprocated Irish hospitality when the Lord Mayor of Cork travelled on the *Armorique* to Roscoff on 3rd June. A formal dinner was held in his honour at the Morlaix Hotel the following evening. Relationships between the two communities were strengthening, and the visit helped assuage Irish concerns about the state of the Brittany beaches.

Brittany Ferries was operating from a shared area alongside the B&I Line terminal at Tivoli. Graham Smith travelled over from Portsmouth to help manage the local operation. His pace of life dropped from two sailings per day to two sailings per week.

The horizons of Brittany Ferries were now not limited to services to France and Spain. Emboldened by the emerging success of the Cork and Santander routes, Michielini and Burns drove on from the first scheduled arrival in Cork to visit Warrenpoint in County Down, in Northern Ireland, on 29th May and consider a service across the Irish Sea to Heysham. The pair returned to Warrenpoint on 14th August to receive a proposal from the port, and also took the opportunity to inspect Greenore, which offered a 90-minute reduction in crossing time for a route across the Irish Sea. The proposal came to naught, albeit this is now a very successful route for Seatruck Ferries. A joint operation from Cork was also reviewed with Irish Continental Line, and proposals were put to Michielini for consideration, but Brittany Ferries had insufficient resources to support anything other than a weekly sailing at this time.

Boeing Jetfoils operated on a number of services across the Channel, but were not suited to the longer routes operated by Brittany Ferries. *(Miles Cowsill)*

An approach from Boeing to consider operation of a Jetfoil service was also treated seriously. The Boeing Jetfoil (Model 929) was designed for passenger comfort at high speeds, with three narrow struts fitted to the vessel creating a fraction of the wake that a ship of its size would normally make. The 27-metre long vessel was highly manoeuvrable and could accommodate 250 passengers at speeds of more than 45 knots. Michielini and Burns visited Dieppe on 24th July and travelled across to Newhaven on the Jetfoil that was in operation on that route. Their experience was not good. Nonetheless Michielini considered the opportunity to be worthy of further investigation, and talks continued between the parties. Michielini and Burns later flew to Seattle, at Boeing's expense, to view more craft in operation. As a result of that visit, Boeing produced an outline plan embracing a proposed two craft deployment for Brittany Ferries. The plan envisaged two craft based in Dieppe, with one offering three daily return crossings to Brighton based on a two-hour passage time, and the second operating from Dieppe to Portsmouth (in two hours thirty minutes), whence it would operate two round trips to Jersey (taking three hours ten minutes each) before returning to Dieppe. The service would run throughout the summer, with a more limited winter operation. The Portsmouth-Dieppe service was predicted to have a twenty per cent load factor, based on departure times from Dieppe at 05:30 returning from Portsmouth at 23:00, but the two other services were expected to trade more sucessfully. Alternative scenarios were produced which considered less intensive use of the craft, and the possibility of basing the craft in Portsmouth, with Brighton as a satellite location. The opportunity was not pursued, as there was scepticism that the craft would be capable of handling the sea conditions, and the scheduling would need to be ambitious in order to make a financial return, thereby placing significant strain on the vessels.

Meanwhile, Jetlink Ferries were looking to open a new Brighton-Dieppe Jetfoil service from May 1979 and Brittany Ferries was kept appraised of these developments. In November 1978, Jetlink Ferries announced that a Boeing Jetfoil 929-115 would be

The *Prince of Brittany* on passage to St Malo. *(Ferry Publications Library)*

employed on this service, carrying 285 passengers across in just over 90 minutes. The first craft was purchased by Associated Newspapers, who held a substantial part of the equity in the Company, as part of a £12 million deal.

The public relations support team had started life as the Brittany Information Bureau, covering the whole of the region of Brittany. This was very much in line with the initial relationship between BCB and the young Company. The team had developed strong skills in creative promotion of the services and the region but had also built unanticipated but much required strengths in handling crisis situations, based on their practical experience of the early years of Brittany Ferries. But with the expansion of services to Spain and Ireland the name appeared inappropriate, so it was changed to the Brittany Ferries Information Bureau (BFIB) in 1978. There was still a heavy involvement in the promotion of destinations despite the name change, as this remained consistent with the marketing philosophy established by BCB. The Bureau continued to help the Brittany Tourist Board and produced a tourist magazine for them for a time. The BFIB was able to add the promotion of northern Spain to the portfolio and worked hard to sell the destination and the mini-cruise voyage opportunities offered by the sailings from Plymouth.

One night a group of animal welfare activists came down to Plymouth and insisted that the ship should not sail in a Force Six gale because it would upset a lorry load of calves waiting to board. Capt. Gervain was Master of the *Armorique* for the Plymouth-Roscoff-Cork run. The activists chained themselves to the railings in the port and Capt. Gervain came down from the ship to talk to them. "What is the problem?' he asked. "The ship's rolling cannot be the problem as the calves are in the garage, they're not in the bar; the garage does not roll. If the calves are in the bar then we have a problem, and I sympathise with your position." The calves were permitted to board because he was right.

As the services settled back to their less intensive autumn schedules, the *Prince of Brittany* made her first commercial sailing from Plymouth to Santander, leaving on 4th October. This enabled the *Armorique* to be withdrawn and head to Falmouth for a major refit which was planned to take much of the autumn and early winter.

The year ended on a positive note when the services were described as good in a Which? Survey in the UK, with graded the vessels as clean, with good food and plenty of comfortable seating and sleeping facilities. Brittany Ferries shared this accolade with Belgian Marine, the SNCF, Hoverlloyd, Swedish Lloyd, Tor Line and Townsend Thoresen.

The Brittany Regional Tourist Committee judged the 1978 season to be "the worst that the Finistère hotel industry has ever known", with total visitors down by 50% up to June, 36% in July and 20% in August, with all coastal communities suffering a drastic fall,

The 1979 brochure featured another pictorial cover and a range of innovative holiday products. The text (opposite) sought to entice holidaymakers by educating them about the attractions of Brittany. The fleet began to have its own identity (page 108). *(Rook Dunning)*

irrespective of whether they had been affected by the oil spill on the beaches. But a full year of the Portsmouth-St Malo route enabled Brittany Ferries to record substantial growth in business to 525,700 passengers, 96,328 cars and 20,618 freight vehicles – all records by some margin, although substantially less than might have been anticipated without the misfortune of the *Amoco Cadiz*.

The 1979 brochure was the first to feature the new range of holidays and breaks. Following the successful format of previous years, it again comprised bold use of full-page colour images, this time suffixed by journalistic commentary. Betty Jones of *Woman's Weekly* was noted as saying: -

> "Most recent, and one of the most successful of all, was an idyllic week spent in a cottage in the heart of Southern Brittany, the pleasure of the stone-built, wood-furnished cottage in a totally rural setting made complete by the comforting assurance of modern heating, plumbing and kitchen equipment. The cottage was one of the 'gîtes rureaux' to be found in the country areas of France, built in the traditional style of the locality and intended for the use of holidaymakers in search of rural peace combined with a particular and very special local welcome. The Breton hospitality offered to us by the farmer's family who had built and owned our cottage was something to be prized well beyond the call of any normal landlord's duty."

14th January 1978

The quote was accompanied by photography of a typical gîte, opposite a page extolling the virtues of camping holidays. The holiday content was incorporated into the central 'insert' of the brochure and demonstrated the significant progress made in the

Your historical, eventful, sightseeing, coastal, country, holiday-staying, gourmet guide to Brittany.

Our history, customs and events.

Bretons are descended from the ancient Britons, the Celts. Jealous of their national individuality, they have always been religious and imaginative, living in a land of saints and legends.

Festivals, fervent and impressive, known as Pardons, are held on various Saints' days. There is an exciting variety of other less religious goings-on, too.

In Nantes, during March, a memorable carnival procession. Come April, fairs and horseraces in Rennes and Vannes; and the famous folk festival of Bleun-Brug will be on somewhere or other.

June and there's all the fun of the fair at Lannion. Into July, the Cowes-Dinard yacht race. Festivals, even one for bagpipes, fill in your August, with regattas, golf, ballet and bridge at La Baule.

A traditional Brittany head-dress.

Here, too, in Brittany are man-made marvels and wondrous phenomena.

Huge stone megaliths at Carnac, or the mediaeval Calvaries, carved to depict the Lord's Passion.

From monuments to cathedrals. Like, for example, St. Pol de Léon. To museums. Try Rennes with French paintings from the 14th century. Or Nantes, for local popular art. You're the sightseer. You choose. Don't miss out either on Mont St. Michel, standing splendid over shining expanse of sand.

These are the kinds of holiday happenings and sightseeing you can expect in Brittany.

Our beaches.

Brittany is seaside holidays like they used to be. So let's explore. On that northern stretch of coast, discover Dinard, boasting three fabulous beaches. Across the river, the safe sands and historic, ramparted city of St. Malo, famous arrival and departure point for Brittany Ferries.

Now move west, along a string of holiday havens. St-Cast, Sables d'Or and then Val André, the picturesque harbour, small rocky headland and wide-sweeping sands.

Such is the Emerald Coast. It ends at one of France's most stylish resorts, Perros-Guirec. And it's here, where the sunred rocks glow rose-pink, that the Armorican Corniche begins.

Now into North-West Brittany. On this spectacular coast is Brittany Ferries home port, picturesque Roscoff and the quiet wooded valleys and narrow estuaries of Les Abers.

Round the headland, South-West Brittany. La Cornouaille. Here the landscape could be Cornish, wild and rugged. Yet so in contrast to the quiet charm of nearby Audierne. Bénodet, too, is a worthy port of call before you enter the Golfe du Morbihan. A small land-locked sea, scattered with islands which shelter the white, wide beaches.

Now for the last word in style: La Baule, on a long curving bay. You've got golf, tennis, casino, and five-mile beach. All very South of France.

Brittany is everything to do with the sea.

Our countryside.

Brittany, inland. A land of moors. A country of the woods. Of dense forests, deep valleys and clear trout streams.

Our magic place which embraces such a Brittany is Huelgoat. In forests and grottoes, the heather-carpeted moorland, and deep still pools.

'Fruits de Mer' one of Brittany's Specialities.

Inland Brittany is dotted by a thousand chapels, a score of churches and nine cathedrals. Most famous of cathedral cities is Quimper, famed for its pottery.

For the foot-loose and fancy-free, Brittany is full of atmosphere, fantasy and fortress.

Such as the multi-towered Fougères, standing proud and magnificent on the border between Brittany and France. Castles such as Vitré, 14th century. Strongholds such as Kerjean, and Josselin, high and defiant above its ancient town.

Brittany, within, is mediaeval, winding streets and half-timbered houses. There's Vannes, one-time Celtic capital. There's the delights of Dinan and the Gauguin-loved peace of Pont-Aven.

Brittany inland is another place to Brittany by the sea. But every bit as beautiful. And unexpected.

Our holiday places.

Brittany is coastline and beaches and peaceful countryside: a land not surprisingly offering a wide variety of accommodation for every sort of holiday-maker.

There are gîtes. In France that includes places like a cottage, a farmhouse, maybe a flat. The ideal choice if you like being independent, comfortable and not having to spend a fortune.

There are villas. Cooking, eating when you wish to. Furnished villas in their hundreds. At all prices, all sizes, and all areas.

Hotels, too, of course. The Logis de France Association lists some 3,500 with rooms from 25F to 125F a night. All French hotels are graded, from one-star acceptable to five-star de luxe, but even one-star means standards must be kept. You'll find Brittany hotels give you a warm welcome, offer traditional cooking, are clean, comfortable and remarkable value.

Brittany, with so much to offer as a holiday land, has something very special for anyone wishing to taste the good, easy life of this magic country, and you've no need of a fortune either.

Our camping sites, 750 of them. All with a sense of style uniquely French: in their design, their setting and their facilities.

Camping on peninsula or farmland. Facing the Atlantic at Beg Meil, say, with its small sandy beach. Or you're in the country's heart. Wherever you decide to settle, you'll discover what it means to feel free, camping Breton style.

Camping sites are classified in four categories.

****Camps de Tourisme.
Constantly maintained, with well-equipped brick buildings. Other facilities are listed in first-class category.

***First-class.
Well-equipped with running water, flush toilets. Full washing facilities. Electric points and lights. Telephone. Shops. Sports facilities. Full-time warden.

**Second-class.
As above, but less well-equipped.

*Third-class.
Full washing facilities and flush toilets. Site accessible by car. Camp warden during day only.

Our food and drink.

Brittany, with all that sea, is for lovers of fish dishes. There's richly sauced lobster served with cream. The salmon, trout, oysters and a local delicacy, stuffed clams. Seafood, too, that's less exotic: shrimps, prawns, mussels and winkles. Meat includes veal and that special highly-flavoured Breton leg of mutton. Try the local cheeses and the excellent crêpes.

For food. For drink, you've got Muscadet, the ideal accompaniment to sea food. Most favourite spirit locally is Calvados. Anything for the children? Super fruit juices, and very popular, pomegranate syrup.

French like a superb start to any meal. 'Gouyen, an Pernod (If we please)'

Next, restaurants. 'Menu touristique' priced from 20F, for simplest meal. 'Menu gastronomique,' listing regional specialities, is more expensive. When it comes to paying, add 12% unless bill is marked "service compris" or "prix nets." Note, too, railway stations are good places for reasonably-priced meals.

On the following pages, discover for yourself what well-known travel writers have said about Brittany and her neighbours.

When it comes to ships, Brittany Ferries have a comfortable lead.

Prince of Brittany

This latest addition to the Brittany Ferries Fleet carries 1,000 passengers and 220 cars. There are 561 sleeping berths in 2, 3-and 4-berth cabins: many with shower and toilet, and 238 comfortable reclining seats. It is extremely well-appointed, with a help-yourself restaurant, a café, and a children's playroom. Two bar one with a disco, and duty-free facilities. Service speed 20 knots.

Armorique

Refurbished for 1979, this ship can take up to 700 passengers and 170 cars. There's now a new restaurant and self-service cafeteria. There are 420 berths, cabins are mainly two-berth. All cabins have their own wash-basin, and many have shower and toilet. Also available, 244 reclining seats. Other facilities include a cafe, lounge bar, cinema and colour television lounge. Children's playroom and duty-free shops. The Armorique's service speed is 20 knots.

Cornouailles

The custom-built Cornouailles can take up to 500 passengers, in 244 berths and 100 reclining seats, as well as 200 cars. It has a spacious help-yourself restaurant, seating 230, lounge-bar, duty-free shops, colour television and a service speed of 19 knots.

Penn ar Bed

The extensively refitted Penn ar Bed now carries 420 passengers, with 230 berths in 2- or 4-berth cabins. 154 reclining seats and space for 160 cars, as well as a help-yourself restaurant, colour television lounge, lounge bar and duty-free shops. Its service speed is 18.5 knots.

first year of developing the holiday product. The gîtes took centre stage, with an initial 47 locations on offer from as little as £32 for a week in the low season. Customers were also given opportunities to stay on choice of five farms, hire a self-drive cabin cruiser from £157 joining at Châteaulin on the river Aulne, or hire a horse-drawn roulette (caravan) from £130, with three different week-long tours from Quimperlé in South West Brittany.

Starting a holiday programme brought a whole new range of challenges to test the resilience of the Company's staff, who were becoming adept at rising to whatever was thrown at them. It took a while for gîte owners to appreciate the standards required to satisfy the UK market, but gradually the programme of inspections helped create higher levels of consistency. The roulottes were an unconventional product. Holidaymakers could freely head off once they got control of their caravan and its one horse-power, and received basic instructions on how to feed and water the horse from time to time. One group collected their roulotte and trotted off down the road deep into Brittany. Halfway through their holiday there was a telephone call to the Brittany Ferries team in St Malo. "I've got a problem. Uh, the horse is dead. It just keeled over" said the distressed caravanners. Finding a replacement horse and removing the deceased was all in a day's work for the St Malo team. One gîte burned down because the occupant ignored instructions and emptied the ashes from the fireplace outside the building, causing it to catch fire. On another occasion a family hired a cabin cruiser from Châteaulin; when they arrived to pick up the keys to their vessel they discovered one of their party was too wide to get through the cabin door of the cruiser. "What do we do now?" was their plaintive cry. Every day brought a whole new learning curve...

The core timetable featured twice-daily sailings at the peak on the Portsmouth-St Malo route, up to three sailings daily between Plymouth and Roscoff, a weekly sailing between Plymouth and St Malo, and, unusually, a low season one way route on Fridays between Portsmouth and Roscoff, leaving at 10:30 and arriving at 22:00. Passenger rates increased to £13 (low season) or £14 high season) single, whilst car rates were now fully metric, from £5.50 to £8 per metre.

The Spanish and Irish routes were featured in separate brochures. The season began much earlier, with the first arrival in Cork on 10th February and the first departure from Plymouth to Santander on 19th February.

The year opened with a flurry of presentations to the travel trade and the travel press, a pattern which was to become a staple of winter activity. On the morning of 3rd January some 50 Northern Ireland travel agents were hosted at the Europa Hotel in Belfast; after lunch it was the turn of 20 key freight operators to have Brittany Ferries' 1979 plans outlined. The following day 70 Irish travel agents were hosted at the Shelbourne Hotel in Dublin, followed by 30 freight operators. Cork was the venue on 5th January for 40 local agents at the Imperial Hotel, with 20 southern Ireland freight operators following. Press events were also held in Belfast, Dublin and Cork.

Sharon Alexander was appointed Reservations Supervisor in Plymouth in 1979, overseeing the upgrade of the telephone systems and the integration of the Portsmouth-based Holiday booking systems into the ferry booking systems.

The *Armorique* spent her lengthy autumn and winter period at the Falmouth Ship Repair yard being fitted with new Sperry Gyrofin stabilisers. At the same time, she underwent a major refurbishment of her passenger facilities, including the installation of a new à la carte restaurant, together with an upgrade to her cabin accommodation. It was intended that the *Armorique* return to service to inaugurate the new year-round Santander and Cork season on 10th February 1979, but instead she found herself trapped by a strike at the shipyard. As the work could not be completed, the *Prince of Brittany* was temporarily transferred to the Santander service, with the *Armorique's* return eventually delayed until April.

A small company with limited budgets always faced the challenge of making the brand stand out in a crowded advertising marketplace. The Tour de France experience

Above: **The *Breizh-Izel* leads the *Armorique* at Cork on 1st July 1979.** *(Ferry Publications Library)*

Right: **Spanish mini-cruise and holiday brochure 1979** *(Rook Dunning)*

Below: **The *Munster* had an eventful summer on charter to Brittany Ferries.** *(Miles Cowsill)*

Above:**The *Regina* is seen at Portsmouth during her charter to Brittany Ferries** *(Ferry Publications Library)*

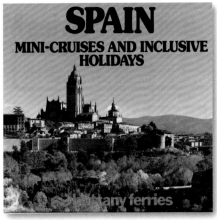

illustrated that modest outlays in sponsorship could yield big promotional dividends if exploited in the right way. A further opportunity arose in 1979. One of the bigger freight customers at the time was Frank Allen, who was one of the early investors in the Truckline service. He was a close friend of the yachtsman Chay Blyth, and effected an introduction which led to a meeting between Burns and Blyth to discuss a sponsorship proposal on 11th February 1979. Blyth outlined his plans to achieve a unique yachting 'treble' with a new yacht designed to be the world's fastest ocean-going trimaran. He aimed to win the 'Royal Western/Observer Transatlantic Race' in 1981, the 'Round Britain & Ireland Race' in 1982 and the 'Route du Rhum', also in 1982.

Blyth came with a strong pedigree in yachting and racing. He had rowed the Atlantic with Capt. John Ridgway in an open dory in 1966, and was awarded the British Empire Medal for his exploits. He followed this in 1969-70 by single-handedly sailing the yacht *British Steel* around the world westwards against the prevailing winds, for which he was made a Commander of the British Empire. His *Great Britain II,* crewed by paratroopers, had won the elapsed time prize for the fastest yacht overall in the first Round the Word yacht race in 1973/74, and his *Great Britain IV* won the Round Britain race in 1978.

Blyth went away to work up a proposal. He returned in December 1979 with the design of a trimaran developed in conjunction with John Shuttleworth, which maximised speed and minimised 'frills' as a pure racing machine. The 60-foot yacht would take eight months to design, build and launch.

Blyth was smart enough to recognise the promotional potential for Brittany Ferries. The Observer/Europe One Transatlantic Race was scheduled to start from Plymouth on Saturday 6th June 1981 with a restricted entry list of 100 of the world's fastest yachts. The Race had Anglo-French sponsorship, so Brittany Ferries was a perfect sponsor for him. There would be ample opportunity in the build-up to the race to highlight the importance of Brittany Ferries to Plymouth on a local, national and international stage. The Round Britain & Ireland Race was to follow from 10th July 1982 and could carry the promotional message around the British and Irish coasts. The Route du Rhum was to start in St Malo in November 1982 and cross to Guadeloupe in what was a predominantly French long distance race, which could generate significant publicity in France. Blyth planned to exhibit the yacht at International Boat Shows and secure a high profile personality to name the vessel.

The proposal was to name the yacht *Brittany Ferries GB* and enter the three races under that name. Blyth would contribute £30,000 from his own resources to the campaign and sought a further £75,000 from Brittany Ferries for sponsorship. The opportunity was too good to resist. The final package from all sponsors was worth up to £150,000 and the venture was launched by Brittany Ferries at a press conference in London on 19th December 1980. Blyth emphasised that this was an all-British boat, despite the sponsor's identity. The deal would enable Blyth to sail with Robert James in the three races. The new trimaran was to be similar in size to *Lionheart*, the British 12-metre challenger for the Americas Cup, but with only just over a quarter of *Lionheart's* displacement she had the ability to sail twice as fast. Blyth went away to oversee construction of *Brittany Ferries GB*. This was the start of a long and successful sponsorship partnership with Blyth, which was easily to achieve the objective of raising the company's profile.

Meanwhile, Brittany Ferries began to open up the 'Real Spain' through a programme of mini-cruises and inclusive holidays on the Santander route launched in March 1979. This included coach tours with hotel accommodation, self-catering apartment holidays and bed and breakfast offers, with prices similar to those charged by previous operators on the route in 1976. The five, eight- and ten-night coach tours ranged in price from £87 to £190, including the Channel crossing with cabin berth and full board accommodation in Spain. The self-catering apartments were some 50m from the beach at Zarauz near San Sebastián, with a seven-day holiday starting from £86 per person in March. Motoring packages included five- and ten-night tours with bed and breakfast accommodation for between £79 and £176.

For the 1979 season it was planned that the Plymouth-Roscoff route would be covered by the *Cornouailles,* with the *Prince of Brittany* and the *Penn-Ar-Bed* allocated to the Portsmouth-St Malo service, whilst the *Penn-Ar-Bed* operated the linking Plymouth-St Malo route. Growing freight traffic encouraged the Company to supplement the fleet by chartering the 1971-built *Normandia* to provide additional capacity across all Channel routes, whilst also offering some sailings from Roscoff to Cork. The 105.3-metre long vessel could carry 480 lane-metres of freight, but was only to spend a single season with Brittany Ferries.

In mid-June the *Cornouailles* broke down with engine problems and had to be withdrawn for repairs, forcing a charter of the *Munster* from B&I Line for a 20-day period. The 1,000 passenger and 220 car capacity *Munster* arrived in Plymouth from Roscoff on 4th July. She had barely settled into her new service pattern when the Company's operational problems were compounded as both the *Penn-Ar-Bed* and the *Prince of Brittany* suffered similar engine issues within a short space of time, forcing both to be withdrawn from service. All three affected vessels had been refitted in the same shipyard at Brest, and attention focused on the engine bearings that had been fitted during their winter overhauls.

The charter of the *Munster* was extended following the *Prince of Brittany's* problems, but the standards on board the Irish vessel were significantly below those which were expected by Brittany Ferries' customers. Letters of apology were issued to passengers for the quality of on board accommodation and the Company came very close to suing B&I Line for the state of their vessel. The *Penn-Ar-Bed* recovered sufficiently to re-open the Portsmouth-St Malo service on 19th July. Jim Mason looked hard for another vessel approaching the peak of the season, eventually finding the 1972-built Swedish vessel *Regina,* which was available to cover the period until the *Prince of Brittany* returned from repair. She was capable of carrying 1,000 passengers in addition to 170 cars, so had the capacity to assist, and was chartered for the short period from 6th September until 1st October. The *Munster* arrived in Portsmouth on 8th August, to release the *Cornouailles* to return to Plymouth for the remainder of the summer. On her first crossing to St Malo she ran briefly ran aground in exactly the same way as the *Armorique* had previously, but fortunately she was able to resume her schedule, as the damage was slight.

Irish bookings were stronger than anticipated and the *Cornouailles* was able to replace the *Penn-Ar-Bed* on the Cork-Roscoff service during the peak season from August to offer much needed increased capacity. Meanwhile, discussions continued with B&I Line on a possible joint venture on Irish services.

A row over the size of mesh permissible in fishing nets escalated in September, as fishermen in Roscoff hurled a consignment of crayfish and lobsters from Brixham into the dock, overturned a lorry and fouled British fish imports with diesel oil to prevent them being sold. This followed the arrest of two Breton crayfish boats in Milford Haven for infringing British fishing regulations. 200 fishermen occupied the *Cornouailles* and prevented vehicles boarding the evening departure to Plymouth on 26th September, and the following day's departures were cancelled, leaving around 100 cars stranded on the quay in Roscoff. The fishermen would only permit women and children to board the vessel. The dispute was eventually resolved following meetings between Michielini and the protesters. The British stance on fishing regulations was taken to the European Court of Justice by the European Commission.

The new conservative UK government announced the abolition of exchange controls in October 1979. These had originally been introduced at the outbreak of war in 1939 to prevent an exodus of capital from the UK and formalised in 1947 in the Exchange Control Act. The maximum sum of money that could be taken abroad was limited to £25, although these restrictions were often flouted. The Thatcher government determined that there should be no constraints on the use of the pound, freeing holidaymakers to take as much money with them as they desired. Continental holidays were becoming easier.

In late October 1979 Rangers Football Club played a second round European Cup Winners' Cup match against Valencia in Spain. There were significant concerns about the behaviour of supporters, at a time when football hooliganism was rampant, but the Supporters Association guaranteed that if Brittany Ferries carried fans there would be no problems. The opposite proved to be the case; one of the fans jumped over the side of the *Armorique*, and passengers on board were subjected to outrageous behaviour from the fans. The Captain radioed ahead to Santander and requested assistance so there was a line of the Guardia Civil waiting for them on arrival in Santander. Carruthers was travelling on board and told them they would not be coming back with Brittany Ferries; their return journey was hereby cancelled. The fans responded by saying they would just come back and storm the ship. Carruthers marshalled several of the burliest deck crew to meet the fans and introduce them to some of the obstacles they might face. They were quickly discouraged. But from this action emerged a policy that football groups would not knowingly be accepted on board Brittany Ferries' ships again.

By the year end Brittany Ferries was able to record increases in business across the passenger, car and freight markets, despite all the issues experienced in the early summer. Passenger traffic had grown to 618,912 passengers, car traffic had broken through the 100,000 celing for the first time to reach 117,248, and the number of freight vehicles reached a new record of 25,156. Michielini commented, "Some said that this Company was a foolish gamble, managed by a band of idiots. I think that the figures we are making are demonstrating the contrary"

At the start of the new decade Brittany Ferries faced increasing competition for space at the Portsmouth Continental Ferry Terminal. Townsend Thoresen services had expanded to offer four sailings each day to Cherbourg and one to Le Havre in the peak, now using the *Viking Valiant* and *Viking Venturer*. Sealink added to congestion at the port in the evenings with their nightly sailing to the Channel Islands with the *Earl William*. Over at Southampton, the P&O Normandy Ferries' services were rebranded as P&O Ferries to bring some cohesion to the shipping group's interests; the *Dragon* and *Leopard* continued to offer twice-daily services to Le Havre. At Poole, Truckline had introduced the purpose-built *Coutances* and *Purbeck*, which were later supplemented by the *Tourlaville* to offer four-sailing daily in each direction to Cherbourg. Sealink maintained a seasonal service from Weymouth to Cherbourg with the elderly turbine steamer *Maid of Kent*. An intensive price war developed during 1980 between Townsend Thoresen, Sealink and P&O Ferries across all cross-channel services. A doubling of the price of oil between 1979 and 1980 saw the price rise to $28 a barrel, and was accompanied by reductions in supply from Saudi Arabia and post-revolution Iran. Domestic fuel shortages led to queues at petrol stations, and Brittany Ferries' costs were hit hard. But sterling strengthened against the Franc by over 10% during the summer season, bringing welcome exchange rate relief to the annual results.

Brittany Ferries' fares for the 1980 season were announced in December 1979, with many being pegged at their 1979 levels. A price freeze on many sailings was achieved by introducing four new tariff bands. The off-season, standard, off-peak and peak structure allowed off-season fares to be held at 1979 levels until the end of April 1980, outside the Easter period. The new off-peak fare applied to midweek day sailings during the peak season of 10th July to 31st August and was the same as the standard tariff applied at Easter, May to July, and September to December. Although the average fare increase applied across all channel sailings between May and December was 16%, Brittany Ferries noted that this was below the national annual inflation rate at the time. But there was a welcome announcement of further increases in capacity with the addition of two vessels to the fleet. The Plymouth-Roscoff route would acquire a second ship, with up to four sailings offered daily at the peak, increasing capacity by 50%. And the *Prince of Brittany* would be supplemented by a new 1,200 passenger capacity vessel on the Portsmouth-St Malo route from June to September, with two sailings a day each way with capacity of 4,400 passenger spaces every day.

Burns sought to make capital from the price war and noted that "the only benefit to the travelling public of the present supposed ferry price war has been to make people carefully check the actual cost getting to their holiday destination in Europe. As a result of careful scrutiny people are discovering that Brittany Ferries' routes can be substantially cheaper for holidaymakers making for Brittany and West France when land costs and time are considered. They are also discovering that Brittany Ferries increases in prices for 1980 are less than any other ferry company on the western Channel."

The 1980 French brochure was the first full-colour production of timetables and tariffs, and the pioneer of fare and sailing information in a grid format. Fares were presented in four coloured seasons – off-season, standard, off-peak and peak – allowing the Company to offer greater flexibility of pricing, but also to exploit the income potential of the busiest sailings, when the car rate to France rose from £8 per metre in 1979 to £10 per metre in 1980. The brochure still featured a destination-led approach, with photographs of the fleet featured for the first time. Evocative double page spreads of 'The tranquil beauty of rural France: the rustling woods, lush meadows & castles' and '... fairs, fêtes and country crafts: there are, too, the pleasures of the table', presented an appealing prospect. The range of holidays had expanded considerably, with options for 'Go as you please' touring holidays with hotel bookings, some linking together the French and Spanish route, a much-expanded range of gîtes, Brittany Breaks, golfing holidays, self-catering cottages, and a coach tour to Mont St Michel. The staple horse-drawn roulette and self-drive cabin-cruisers were also featured. The Spanish brochure described a crossing on the *Armorique* to Spain as 'holiday-going in style' and featured 'comfortable cabins', bars, the children's play area, duty-free shopping opportunities and

French and Spanish services brochures and French market brochure covers. *(Rook Dunning/Paul Burns)*

a sumptuous buffet.

The Plymouth-Santander route was closed from 4th to 28th January whilst the *Armorique* underwent her annual refit, with one weekly sailing until 25th February and two sailings each week thereafter. Off-peak sailings were heavily promoted by a 'Car goes free' offer if four people were travelling in the car. Caravan traffic was also encouraged between January and May and October and December at rates up to 50% below the 1979 fare.

The Irish Travel Agents' and freight companies' roadshows were repeated at the start of the year, with visits to Belfast, Dublin, Cork, Limerick, and Galway. The Irish Continental Line challenge to the Cork operation had rankled Michielini and he was keen to look at Irish options to strike back. There were still ambitions to consider routes from Ireland to the UK, with further visits by Michielini and Burns to Rosslare, Dublin, Dun Laoghaire, Greenore, and Warrenpoint in early February 1980. A Warrenpoint proposal was previously provisionally approved by the Board, but the assassination of Lord Mountbatten in Carlingford Lough in August 1979 and the deteriorating political environment in Northern Ireland led to a decision to put a hold on the option.

Michielini and Burns spent time together to jointly agree a strategy for the opening of possible new routes and further expansion of the fleet. Their thoughts encompassed the urgent acquisition of a freight vessel with capacity for seventy drivers, to address demand for driver-accompanied traffic, to be followed by a ship capable of carrying over 1,000 passengers and 250 cars for the Spanish and Irish routes, for delivery by not later than May 1981. The fleet plans envisaged a new build vessel with a service speed of 24 knots for the Portsmouth-St Malo route, to enter service in April 1982, with a sister vessel following in April 1983. Finally, a newbuild would be required for Spanish services by not later than March 1983.

The plan looked at the possibility of a Portsmouth-Dieppe route being opened as soon as 1982, offering a year-round passenger and freight service in a joint operation with

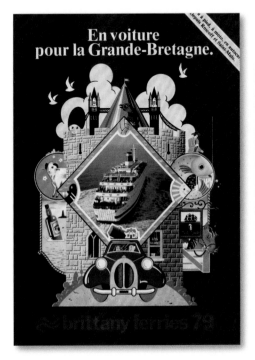

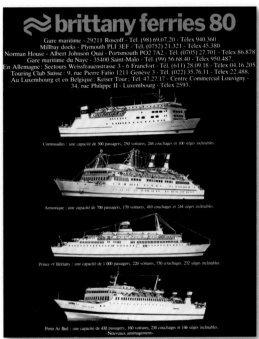

Paul Burns at the 1980 Belfast Road Show with Laureen Castles of Castles Travel, Lurgan Co. Armagh, and Wesley Pentland, owner of Wesley Pentland Travel, Belfast, who was Chairman of the UK Chapter of ITT (Institute of Travel and Tourism) and was later elected as President of ABTA (Association of British Travel Agents). *(Paul Burns)*

Schiaffino, who were then operating a freight service between Dover and Ostend, and were anxious to have a partner in their expansion strategy. A Portsmouth-Caen route was, by Michielini, enthusiastically considered possible from 1982, but this would be being a seasonal passenger service with a year-round freight operation, in a joint operation with the Caennaise. Weekly seasonal services were examined as being worthy of consideration to operate from 1981 on new routes linking Plymouth with Oporto, and Roscoff with Dublin. To accommodate these proposals, Plymouth, Roscoff, Portsmouth and St Malo would each require the construction of linkspans capable of handling 142-metre long, 24-metre-beam vessels. Dredging would be required at St Malo to handle the larger vessel from 1982, and port facilities at Ringaskiddy needed to be in place to handle a transfer of services from the Tivoli Terminal in Cork by 15th May 1981. It was an ambitious plan but reflected the team's growing confidence in their ability to plan and develop an expanding network of activities in the western Channel. Much of the examination was fanciful and was aimed at exploring ways of avoiding other operators encroaching on what Brittany Ferries regarded as its territory but also to ensure that there were no realistic opportunities missed by the Company.

On 28th February the new operating partner for the *Prince of Brittany* on the Portsmouth-St Malo route was revealed as *Viking 6,* a 5,071-tonne vessel with capacity for 1,200 passengers and 215 cars, which was to be renamed the *Goelo* after the region in the north east of Brittany. She was to be chartered from Viking Line from mid-June until mid-September 1980. The *Goelo* had accommodation for 609 passengers in a combination of cabins and sleeperettes, and her facilities included two bars, a cafeteria and restaurant, and a duty-free supermarket and gift shop. She was a big step forward in standards of cabin accommodation on the English Channel, having previously been employed in the Alaskan cruise market. The *Goelo's* major disadvantage was a low deck height, which precluded her carrying significant volumes of freight traffic. Mason was having a busy time, as the Italian freight vessel *Faraday* was also chartered to offer additional freight capacity on the Portsmouth-St Malo route for the 1980 season. The *Faraday* could carry 1,230 lane-metres of freight and twelve passengers. The *Prince of Brittany* was proving to be a very useful asset, so she was purchased from her Swedish owners for $8 million and re-registered in Morlaix under the French flag.

The *Armorique* returned to Cork to re-launch the Irish service on 16th March, accompanied by Breton bands and a large contingent of press. St Patrick's Day was celebrated in the now accustomed manner and the festivities concluded with another Grande Bouffe hosted by Gourvennec and Michielini on board the vessel. This time there was to be no late night drama.

Mason scoured the market to find a freight ship to meet the immediate need to expand capacity on the Roscoff, Santander and Cork services. He found the ten-year-old

Iniochos Express in Greece, and Michielini and Burns flew with him to Piraeus to inspect her on 3rd March. The ship was all that was readily available, and was badly needed to expand freight capacity, so a charter arrangement was agreed. She had been built by the Taikoo Dockyard & Engineering Company in Hong Kong for the Union Steamship Company of Wellington, New Zealand, and was 111.6 metres in length, 17.07 metres in bean and could carry twelve passengers and 65 freight vehicles at a service speed of 16.5 knots. The *Iniochos Express* was renamed *Breizh-Izel,* the Breton name for Lower Brittany, and sailed from Greece for Roscoff, arriving there on 26th March. She then headed to Plymouth to take up her inaugural sailing.

When the *Breizh-Izel* started loading for her first crossing from Plymouth to Roscoff, traffic had to be reversed on the vessel, as she was only fitted with stern doors. Stevedores reversed the trailers with their tractor units down the ramp, to load the vessel in the conventional manner, but one misjudged his angles and hit the funnel housing with his trailer; the entire structure collapsed into a heap of bricks and mortar, revealing the funnel behind. The mortar had been painted to look like steel but the funnel casing was now found to be of more primitive construction. There was no way the ship could sail. A team was sourced to shift the bricks before the engineers could begin to work out how to

**The elegant lines of the *Goelo.* (John Hendy)*

build a new funnel housing. Only then could the *Breizh-Izel* start her duties. But to add to the woes it was discovered that *Breizh-Izel* was riddled with blue asbestos, so this also had to be made safe before the ship could enter service.

The company's shareholder base had now expanded to include the Comité Économique de Fruits et Légumes de Bretagne, La SICA de St-Pol-de-Léon, Les Caisses de Mutuelles Assurances Agricoles de Landernau, La Chambre de Commerce et d'Industrie de Morlaix, La Chambre de Commerce et d'Industrie de St Malo, La Chambre Regionale de Commerce et d'Industrie de Rennes, La Chambre d'Agriculture du Finistère de Quimper and La Chambre d'Agriculture d'Ille-et-Vilaine de Rennes.

By now the management team was beginning to feel they had been tested in every way possible. They had faced industrial action and riots ashore and afloat, ship groundings, oil spills, breakdowns... the list was endless; each situation had been overcome and the Company had become stronger, more cohesive and gained experience the hard way. The original Breton cause was now embraced by colleagues on both sides of the English Channel, for adversity created a common purpose. But fate was always ready to provide further tests.

The *Breizh-Izel* was forced to return back to Santander on 7th July following a credible warning that there was a bomb on board the vessel. The Master asked for help from other merchant vessels to escort her back to the Spanish port, but in the event the alert proved to be a false alarm.

On Monday 14th July 1980 the *Armorique* left Plymouth on her regular voyage to Santander with 700 passengers and 170 cars on board. Around 90 nautical miles into the journey a fault developed in one of her engines, which had to shut down. The *Armorique* continued through the Bay of Biscay on one engine and arrived very late in Santander the next day. Her return journey left late on Tuesday 15th July and she limped back towards Plymouth on her remaining engine. It was evident that the next rotation to Spain would run extremely late or have to be cancelled.

Looking astern from the bridge of the *Goelo*. *(John Hendy)*

The team in Plymouth stepped in to help. A replacement vessel was out of the question at such short notice and it was unclear when the engine problem could be rectified. But costs would escalate quickly if passengers had to be accommodated in hotels or compensated for lengthy overland journeys across France. Chartered aircraft were a suitable option to take limited numbers of passengers in each direction; those prepared to leave their car keys with office staff could fly and be reunited with their vehicles later when the service resumed. Three chartered aircraft were offered, with the capability of being in Santander by 09:00 on Thursday 17th July.

Passengers began arriving at Millbay Docks from as early as 07:00 on the morning of 16th July for the scheduled 12:00 departure to Santander, but the *Armorique* was not expected to arrive from Spain until around 18:00 that evening and would require immediate attention to her faulty engine. Staff assembled at the port gates to advise passengers that they should leave their cars and keys; they would be accommodated in local hotels overnight prior to transferring to join flights to Santander. Burns contacted the General Manager at Exeter Airport and Group Captain Phillips at RAF St Mawgan. He agreed with the Airports' management to get approval for landing, servicing and take off for the chartered aircraft beginning the airlift the following morning. This unwelcome news was received stoically; most passengers were happy that there was a pro-active plan in place to get them to Spain as quickly as possible. These outward flights could return with stranded passengers from Santander, providing a neat, if expensive, partial solution to the problem.

Burns asked the staff for volunteers to base themselves at Exeter Airport and at RAF St Mawgan, managing departing and arriving passengers and managing the buses which were chartered to transfer passengers to and from the airports.

The first flights left early on the morning of Thursday 17th July and headed south, before returning with passengers from Santander, with time to complete a second

The *Breizh-Izel* was to spend nine years with Brittany Ferries and subsidiary companies. She was the only vessel in the fleet without variable pitch propellors, so required great skill from her crews when manoeuvring. *(FotoFlite)*

rotation that day. The operation was running smoothly, and repairs to the *Armorique* were effected quickly to allow her to resume sailing from Plymouth. Meanwhile the last flight with Vickers Viscount G-ARBY was being refuelled in Santander for the final time. Her return flight to Exeter with 58 passengers and four crew left at 19:33 local time. The recovery operation was nearly complete. Burns and many of the staff were in the Terminal offices at Millbay Docks, waiting for the final landing to complete and to get home after a tough day. This was exclusively a Plymouth rescue effort.

The flight of G-ARBY was given a clear run to Exeter Airport, approaching the runway from the south. As the flight began to make its descent towards the airport, all four engines cut out whilst still some eight miles out from the runway, turning the Viscount into a glider. It was evident to Capt. Whittaker that they would not make it to the runway, so he issued a May Day call and looked for somewhere to crash land. Luckily it was still daylight on a drizzly, grey evening and he was able to select a site and bring the aircraft down as gently as he could. The Viscount came down near Wiggaton, around a mile and a half from Ottery St Mary, at 20:53. The first that the Brittany Ferries' team knew of the incident was when it was shown as a newsflash on local television programmes. Initial reports received by Burns from the volunteer staff at Exeter Airport suggested that the aircraft had crashed and that many passengers had been killed. He immediately got in his car and drove rapidly to Exeter Airport, a worrying experience in an era without mobile phones. On arrival at Exeter Airport he met with the team, and received the welcome news that the Viscount's fuselage had remained intact and there were no casualties, apart from a flock of sheep which had found itself directly in the path of the approaching aircraft. Capt. Whittaker had executed a textbook crash landing. Getting everyone home now became a big priority.

A later inquiry into the incident by the Air Accident Investigation Branch could not explain how the aircraft had run out of fuel, but suggested that the aircraft's port fuel gauge was unserviceable, and that Capt. Whittaker should have undertaken a dipstick measurement of the fuel tanks prior to departure from Santander. It was evident that little, if any, fuel had been loaded during the refuelling exercise in Spain, leading to much speculation as to why this might have been the case, including widespread rumours of fraud. Whatever the reason, the luck of the passengers and the Company had held; a major disaster with untold consequences for the future of Brittany Ferries had been averted.

Having recovered from the shock of the crash landing, the Company now faced a new challenge. On 13th August French fishermen began a blockade of Channel ports in protest at high fuel costs, falling wholesale prices for fish, and shipowners' plans to reduce crews and salaries to cut expenditure. French police advised home-bound tourists to travel to the Belgian ports of Ostend and Zeebrugge, where Townsend Thoresen and Sealink transferred their short-sea operations to beat the blockade. 15,000 passengers were trapped in France by the dispute and tempers flared at the height of the tourist season.

Attempts to beat the blockade by ferries at Cherbourg and St Malo had limited success and provoked the fishermen to intensify their blockade, extending it to prevent yachts leaving the country. The situation became increasingly desperate for holidaymakers running out of money at the end of their holiday. But is also led to wholesale refunds for those unable to leave Britain; the situation became increasingly desperate for Brittany Ferries. Sympathy for the strikers was in short supply. By 19th August all French channel ports except Roscoff were blockaded, and a five-sailing schedule was planned from Portsmouth and Plymouth to serve the port. Meanwhile, angry lorry drivers blocked all roads into Cherbourg with rotting food in retaliation for the blockade. Townsend Thoresen's *Viking Victory* spent over a day at sea trying to reach St Malo as an alternative to berthing in Cherbourg but found the port closed.

Fishermen in Brittany rarely went on strike to block ports because the pressure on them from local farmers was too strong; the export of produce was the number one priority for everyone in the region. But on this occasion, they belatedly joined the protest and brought 50 vessels to blockade the berth in Roscoff. The *Cornouailles* was prevented from leaving the port by the blockade on 20th August. Fighting broke out between holidaymakers and strikers on the quay, as the former attempted to slip the moorings of the blockading trawlers, believing that the *Penn-Ar-Bed* was trying to enter the harbour to berth. The *Penn-Ar-Bed* was able to land some 50 passengers using a lifeboat on a nearby beach, but the company was not prepared to provoke the fishermen by breaking the blockade. Around 500 passengers remained stranded on the *Penn-Ar-Bed* lying off the port.

With no sea-access available to French Channel ports, and Belgian ferry ports besieged by stranded passengers from across northern France, the team decided the only option open to them was to offer additional capacity to Santander. The *Armorique, Prince of Brittany* and *Goelo* were transferred to operate sailings from Plymouth to Santander, departing at 90-minute intervals on 20th August. They were followed south the following day by the *Penn-Ar-Bed*. Now Britany Ferries faced substantial extra fuel and crew costs at the same time as they were required to refund bookings. The Company was running out of money; this was another existential crisis. Unlike other ferry operators, Brittany Ferries did not have alternative Channel ports to sail to, nor was it able to fall back on financial support from non-affected routes within a group portfolio.

Gourvennec went from Morlaix to Roscoff to speak to the fishermen's leaders but faced a robust response because all Channel ports were on strike and the fishermen did not want to break ranks with their colleagues. The chairman indicated that he would be back in one hour with six muck spreaders and, if the trawlers remained, they would never fish again as they would be covered in excrement. True to his word, he returned with the muck spreaders ready and loaded. The fishermen were given one hour to clear the berth. They knew Gourvennec was serious, and were on their way within minutes, lifting the blockade of Roscoff and allowing the *Cornouailles* to sail on 21st August with 200 cars and 500 stranded passengers on board. The fishermen agreed that the *Cornouailles* could make a return crossing, but also made it clear that the port would be closed again later. But by the end of the week support for the national dispute was waning, and the fishermen agreed to withdraw their blockade of holiday traffic. Burns observed to the press that "the St Malo fishermen met and decided not to take further action for the moment. At Roscoff the fishermen have actually left the port and we don't anticipate that they're going to return." They did not return largely because Gourvennec left the muck spreaders on the quayside ready to be used again if required. Gourvennec's robust action stopped Brittany Ferries being closed down, as bills were going unpaid and there were no fuel bunkers remaining for the fleet, without which the Company would not be able to sail.

Whilst welcome news, this development left Brittany Ferries in a quandary as the majority of the fleet was now heading back from Spain, displaced from their normal routes and schedules. Strikebound passengers expected sailings to resume immediately and were unhappy when told that their ship was sailing back from Spain at the speed of a bicycle. Consideration was given to flying passengers back from Santander to Plymouth with chartered Brymon Airways planes, as the scheduled service was not going to be able to resume in full until early September. Fortunately, Brittany Ferries was building a loyal clientele, becoming accustomed to journey disruption whether it be for engine problems, ships running aground or strikes, and they began to boast to each other of their involvement in the different 'campaigns'. But there was also a developing paranoia in the Company that their positive efforts to build a successful business were constantly being sabotaged by forces outside their control.

One permanent casualty of the Fishermen's blockade was the Brighton Marina-Dieppe Jetfoil service, which closed at the end of August 1980.

In the midst of the fishermen's blockade, Brittany Ferries faced a further problem. The dispute with Trinity House pilots had not been finally resolved, and payment was still being demanded for all French ships berthing in Portsmouth despite the Masters' pilotage experience and competence, and the lack of any similar charges for British ships in France. The 1979 Merchant Shipping Act allowed for the granting of pilotage licences to EEC nationals, but the UK Department of Trade declined to implement this until it had the consent of all interested parties – which included other shipping companies and the resident pilots, all of whom had a vested interest in resisting the change. In an attempt to force the issue, Brittany Ferries refused to pay pilotage dues in Portsmouth for the *Prince of Brittany* and Trinity House served a writ on the vessel over an unpaid bill of £12,564. The writ was due to expire on 26th August, with the threat of the ship being seized if the sum remained unpaid. Carruthers was prepared with a cheque, in the knowledge that the situation would escalate rapidly if the writ was enacted with sanctions likely to be placed

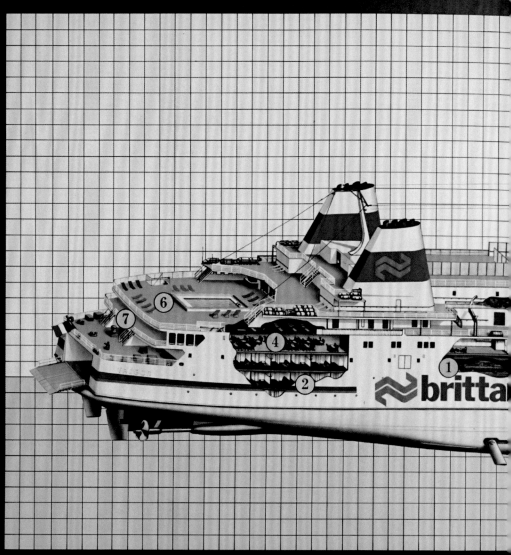

BRITTANY FERRIES NEW
MORE SAILINGS–MORE CA

Brittany Ferries are introducing a new ship on the England-Spain service in 1981.
The 11,500 ton Tregor, the largest car ferry ever to operate year-round to Spain, joins our fleet and will be operating from Plymouth to Santander starting in May. During the summer months, the Tregor, with a service speed of 21 knots, will be sailing from Plymouth on Mondays and Wednesdays, returning from Santander on Tuesdays and Thursdays. For the winter, spring and autumn, and weekend sailings this summer, your ship will be the popular fully-stabilized Armorique.

1 300 cars carried: the largest capacity to Spain ever.

2 Over 900 sleeping berths in 2, 3, and 4-berth cabins, all with private shower/W.C.

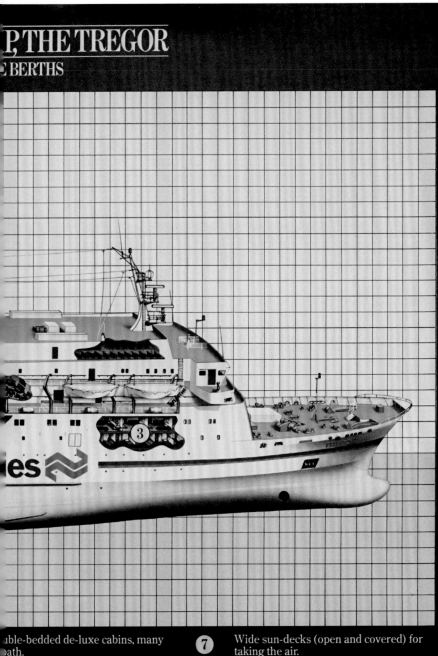

P, THE TREGOR
BERTHS

The proposed double page brochure spread of the *Trégor* in Brittany Ferries' livery *(Rook Dunning)*

ble-bedded de-luxe cabins, many ath.

⑦ Wide sun-decks (open and covered) for taking the air.

ous restaurants and coffee shop oom to relax.

⑧ Air-conditioned cinema showing feature films.

ars, disco, spacious lounges, drinks y-free prices.

⑨ Fully-stabilized for an easy-going, enjoyable voyage.

ming pool, sunbathing area and bar.

on British ships in French ports. Burns told the press that British civil servants and vested interests were "frustrating the intention of Parliament". He noted that the Company was losing £150,000 a year because of a practice which contravened EEC regulations. The British authorities had far more to lose from French reciprocal action, particularly as their stance had little international validity. The writ lapsed and the sum remained unpaid.

Capt. Lainé, who had previously been Master of the *Leopard* before joining Brittany Ferries, was invited to sit the pilotage examination. As he sat before the Board, they asked how many acts of pilotage he had undertaken into Portsmouth. He sat and pondered. The question was repeated but he remained silent. "Do you understand the question? he was finally asked to the frustration of the panel. "Yes" he replied, "I am just doing the calculation. I think the answer is 2,422." The Board requirement was twelve...

The financial problems generated by the fishermen's dispute compounded the issues caused by rising fuel prices. Costs were rising whilst revenue was being refunded at the peak of the season. Finances were stretched by the additional charter cost of vessels to serve the expanding services to Ireland and Spain. The fragile Company could not sustain finance charges, which by now had reached ten per cent of turnover. Each month-end required significant financial wizardry by Maurice Chollet, Jim Butler and his team to balance the books and pay the staff. Brittany Ferries could not continue to rely on elderly inadequate chartered tonnage, especially with several of the existing charters coming to their natural end. Trading losses mounted to £1 million, despite an 18% rise in business and the growing success of the holiday business. With annual inflation in the UK standing at 18% and unemployment at two million, the prospects for the 1981 season were bleak.

But with strong forward interest and continued traffic growth, and in line with the agreed strategic direction, attention turned to accommodating further expansion of the Santander and Ireland services. Plans to grow the Plymouth-Santander service to three departures each week for the 1981 season were signed off by the Board on 10th October, based on the agreement between Michielini and Burns in Dublin. Mason was despatched to find a larger vessel for the Plymouth fleet. This prospect required further investment in facilities in Cork and Plymouth, and negotiations began with both authorities in late October. Michielini and Burns met with the BTDB in Plymouth and discussed provision of a new linkspan together with changes to the port layout to accommodate traffic from the potential new vessel. Mason identified the *Bolero* as a potential solution to the capacity issue and Michielini and Burns flew out to Hamburg on 8th November to visit the ship. The *Bolero* was built in 1973 by Dubegion-Normandie S.A. Prairie au doc, of Nantes as a sister to the ill-fated *Scandinavian Star*, and a near sister to Southern Ferries' *Eagle*. She was 141.2 metres in length, with a beam of 21.9 metres, and could carry 1,600 passengers in 800 cabins, with deck capacity for 245 vehicles and 22 freight units. Her service speed was 18 knots. The *Bolero* operated as the *Prince of Fundy II* in the summers of 1973 to 1976 between Portland, Maine, and Yarmouth, Nova Scotia. During the winters she operated for Commodore Cruise Lines, before transferring to Scandinavian services. Michielini, Burns and Mason were pleased with the vessel and agreed a charter party with owners Fred. Olsen on 9th November. The respective lawyers went away to draw up the full contractual details.

It was agreed that the *Bolero* would be renamed the *Trégor* after one of the nine provinces of Brittany. Michielini asked Mason to prepare an artist's impression of the vessel in Brittany Ferries livery, and this was sent to Rook Dunning for the 1981 brochure. There was no time to waste, given the volume of work needed ashore to accommodate the *Trégor*, and publicity had to be generated to ensure that potential customers were aware of the expanded services. Negotiations on the necessary investment began with the authorities in Cork on 13th November. The new ship was included in presentations to the Irish Travel Trade on 14th November and incorporated into the 1981 brochure by BCB; this brochure was finalised on 4th December. Burns set in train brochure production to permit publication in time to meet the prime post-Christmas booking period. Assurances from the team in Roscoff were sufficient to give him the confidence to proceed prior to full Board approval. Mock ups of the *Trégor* in Brittany Ferries' livery and internal designs were prepared by Constantinidi and Rook Dunning. The plans were made public with a press release in the UK on 14th December 1980, promoting 'dramatically increased capacity' in the new season's expanded schedules. The *Trégor* could accommodate 900 passengers in berths in en suite cabins, with a further 104 in a sleeperette section. Other facilities included a swimming pool, cinema, large restaurant, large coffee shop, spacious sun decks, two bars, a duty-free supermarket and a perfume and gift shop. Burns observed that "the ship was designed as a cruise vessel and she has recently been operating off the east coast of America and in the West Indies." The expansion of the service would be accompanied by the biggest ever programme of motoring, coach and mini-cruise holidays in Spain. The Times reported on 15th December of a doubling of services to Spain with the introduction of the 11,500 tonne ship from May 1981. In Plymouth, the BTDB accelerated plans to complete shore investment to support the *Trégor,* working closely with Marine Developments Ltd, and the linkspan works were confirmed on 17th December. All was proceeding well for the new acquisition.

Maintaining the pace of change, discussions also continued with interested parties in Dublin on a service from Roscoff to Dun Laoghaire slated to commence in the 1982 season.

On 20th December the *Trégor* charter proposal was taken for approval at the regular Brittany Ferries Board meeting. Gourvennec advised Michielini of the outcome – the proposal had been rejected by the Board and the charter was not approved. There was no explanation behind the Board action but, perhaps mindful of the Company's recent financial difficulties following the summer blockades and the reluctance of the supporting banks to provide further finance beyond existing commitments, the Board elected to continue with the *Armorique* and frustrate growing demand on the Spanish service. For the first time they decided not to back a carefully considered and costed expansion plan, despite the extensive works by third parties which had been put in place to support it. At Plymouth, the BTDB were investing over £1.1 million in a linkspan and facilities to accommodate the expanded service and the new ship, *Trégor*. Steel had been ordered in Cork to support the upgrade at Ringaskiddy; arrangements were being made in Santander. The Company had to disentangle itself from all these agreements. Fred. Olsen threatened to sue over the failed charter. The 1981 brochure featuring the *Trégor* had to be pulped, hastily recast and reprinted, with schedules based on the *Armorique*

Burns believed that he had been given approval to negotiate and put in place the necessary contracts, brochures, announcements, works and staffing to accommodate the ship. Having been told by telephone that it was all cancelled and everything had to be undone, he felt he had no option other than to accept blame with the port owners, the marketing and sales team and resign from Brittany Ferries. Gourvennec and Michielini refused to accept his resignation and tried to persuade him to change his decision, but to no avail.

Burns communicated the Company's decision to the authorities in Plymouth and Cork, and to Modesto Piñiero in Santander. He apologised to each of them, and implied he had misunderstood the state of play in Roscoff and told them was leaving Brittany Ferries. In the last week of 1980, Burns cleared his desk in Plymouth, said his farewell to the staff at a dinner and returned to London. He formally confirmed his departure from the Company on 7th January 1981 and left two days later.

Brittany Ferries plans for the 1981 season and beyond now faced a significant recast.

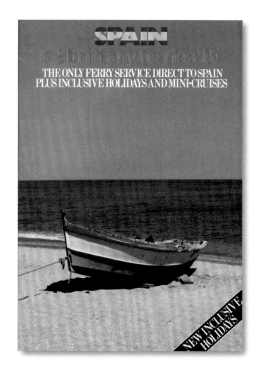

Five

Towards a sound financial footing

rittany Ferries was fortunate that there was a capable candidate ready to assume the role of General Manager for the UK & Ireland in the absence of Paul Burns, and Ian Carruthers was quickly appointed to the position in January 1981. His responsibilities were refined to encompass all the Company's activities outside France, but the first task was to undertake a complete rethink of the strategy for the 1981 season. The re-planning of schedules, updating of pricing and the revamping of brochures to remove all trace of the *Trégor* across the portfolio had already fallen to Carruthers, and he returned on the last flight from France on Christmas Eve 1980, with agreement reached on a revised strategy. Derek Brightwell and Michael Constantinidi of BCB were instrumental in a rapid turnaround of a new brochure design, which quickly went into production at a crucial time in the booking season.

In early January Carruthers took a call from Brightwell. "We've got the brochures ready, but the printer says that unless he's paid up front, he's not willing to push the button." News of the Company's financial difficulties had spread, but without a brochure the Company was finished. It was the key element of the sales armoury in the pre-internet days; without a document on the shelves there was no visibility or credibility in the eyes of travel agents or the travelling public. Carruthers approached Jim Butler and asked how much money there was in the bank – publishing the brochure had to be the number one priority, whatever other demands there were on cash. He said "I need you to send me the money - you just have to trust me, I know what I'm doing. You have to do this". The printer was paid up front, but never did any work for the Company again. The latest crisis was over.

An already substantial task became more difficult when Christian Michielini fell ill in January 1981, and the ongoing management of unravelling arrangements for the *Trégor* fell solely to Carruthers in his new role. There was a difficult balance between the programme of change required to sustain the business and the need to maintain public confidence in the future of Brittany Ferries. P&O Ferries made an offer to manage the UK sales and marketing effort for the Company around this time, but their approach was rejected.

The Company adopted a new strapline for the 1981 season. 'Only Brittany Ferries sail direct to Brittany', which during the Fishermen's dispute had on occasion drawn the response "Ah, but when?", was updated to become 'The short cut to Brittany, South & West France and Spain'. Already

Toby Oliver, Rob James, Christian Michielini, Chay Blyth, Ian Carruthers and David Owen at the naming ceremony for *Brittany Ferries GB* at Tower Bridge. *(Ian Carruthers collection)*

127

brittany ferries

WELCOME ABOARD

Captain F. Gervain, the officers and crew of the M.V. Armorique welcome you aboard for a grandstand view of the start and early stages of The Observer/Europe 1 Transatlantic Race 1981 organized by the Royal Western Yacht Club of England.

The fully stabilized 5,731-ton Armorique is designed to carry 700 passengers and 170 cars, and has a speed of 20 knots.

M.V. ARMORIQUE

PROGRAMME

Friday 5th June
20.00-21.30
Boarding. Drinks and refreshments available in cabins. The ship's bars will be open. Early morning calls may be requested at the information desk on A deck.

Saturday 6th June
07.30-09.30
Continental breakfast served in the cafeteria and Le Biscaye restaurant.
09.00
Final boarding.
09.45
The Armorique sails for authorized position by starting line.
12.00
Start of race by Vice Admiral Sir William Pillar K.C.B., Chief of Fleet Support.
12.30-15.30
Grand Buffet luncheon served in Reclining Seat Lounge.
17.30
Return to Plymouth. Disembarkation.

COMMENTATOR: GEOFFREY HALES – WINNER 1976 HANDICAP RACE

ALL TIMES ARE APPROXIMATE

Above: **Programme of events on the *Armorique* to mark the start of the 1981 Observer Transatlantic race.** *(Paul Burns)*

Below: *Brittany Ferries GB* **logo.** *(Ian Carruthers collection)*

advertisements were able to state that Brittany Ferries offered 'the biggest choice of Inclusive Holidays in France and Spain. From Go As You Please Motoring Holidays in hotels and paradores, Gîtes, Apartments, to Mini-Cruises and many more'. The key focus was on the saving of time, trouble and money by landing closer to the holiday destination and saving hundreds of miles of unnecessary driving time, and cutting the cost of petrol, meals and hotels en route. 'The short cut south' became the new brand suffix.

The *Prince of Brittany* was chartered to Irish Continental Line at the start of the 1981 season, covering for the *St Patrick* on the Ireland-France routes, and the *Breizh-Izel* followed her later in the summer to sail between Rosslare, Cherbourg and Roscoff in a joint freight operation between the two companies.

The sponsorship arrangements with Chay Blyth were now beginning to generate publicity. The initial deal envisaged Blyth being able to keep the boat under his ownership after competing in a specified number of races, but as costs rose, particularly when it was discovered that the vessel was too large to fit under a bridge near the yacht-builder's yard, Brittany Ferries agreed to share in the proceeds of a future sale. There was considerable competition amongst crane-owners to secure the contract to lift the trimaran over the River Looe road bridge in February 1981.

Publicity for the transatlantic voyage began when Blyth sailed the *Brittany Ferries GB* under Tower Bridge in London for her naming on 14th May. The ceremony was conducted by David Owen, the former Foreign Secretary and founder of the Social Democratic Party. The positive news continued as the race yachts began to assemble in Millbay Docks in Plymouth for a week of qualifying cruise races before the formal start of the two-handed Observer two-handed transatlantic race to Newport, Rhode Island on 6th June 1981. 103 boats started the Race and British hopes were split between Blyth and Rob James in *Brittany Ferries GB,* and Robin Knox-Johnston and Billy King-Harman in *Sea Falcon.* They faced a strong challenge from the French, who included Eric Tabarly with his foiler trimaran *Paul Ricard,* Marc Pajot in *Elf Aquitaine,* Loic Caradec in *Royale* and Oliver de Kersauson in *Jacques Ribourel,* at 78 feet the biggest boat in the race, and the Canadians Mike Birch and Walter Greene in *Tele-7-Jours.* The *Armorique* was employed to host guests to observe the start of the Race, which occurred in strong 30 knot winds. Almost immediately a succession of incidents forced several yachts to retire. These gales continued for several days, and more competitors suffered in what many experienced skippers said was amongst the worst conditions they had ever encountered in racing.

Chay Blyth waves to the *Quiberon* whilst on trials with *Brittany Ferries GB. (Ian Carruthers collection)*

By the second day Blyth and James were in the lead, some 130 miles west of the Scilly Isles and making fast progress. Five days later *Brittany Ferries GB* had opened up a 100-mile lead over the second yacht *Tele-7-Jours.* Soon the papers were beginning to contemplate a record crossing of the Atlantic, with just over 1,000 miles to go on 16th June, and the existing record of 17 days 23 hours 12 minutes well within reach. But the following day winds lightened to 10 knots and progress slowed. The increased speculation and tension served to increase the visibility of the yacht's sponsor. By 19th June *Brittany Ferries GB* had increased her lead, with less than 250 miles to go to the finish line.

Carruthers and Oliver flew out to Rhode Island to greet her arrival. *Brittany Ferries GB* arrived in Newport at 00:50 GMT on 20th June, setting a new crossing record of 14 days

13 hours and 54 minutes, 140 miles ahead of the second yacht *Elf Aquitaine.* The *Gauloise IV* was third and Knox-Johnston and King-Harman fourth in *Sea Falcon.* There was a huge media gathering to witness Blyth's arrival, with in excess of 200 journalists and photographers present in scrum-like conditions. Carruthers vividly recalls a public relations representative from Möet et Chandon jumping onto *Brittany Ferries GB* clutching a magnum of champagne to secure a prominent position in photographs, despite having contributed nothing to the crossing. 'Victory Ahoy for British voyager' was the banner headline above a photograph of *Brittany Ferries GB* in the Observer as the newspaper recorded Blyth's win, capping a succession of positive reports for the sponsor, which included a front-page picture of the yacht. The Observer public relations team was then headed by Barbara Binder, who was subsequently to join the Brittany Ferries Information Bureau.

Brittany Ferries' investment in sponsorship was more than justified by the coverage received, helped by the race record. But there was a lesson in Blyth's success. The marina was packed for the arrival of *Brittany Ferries GB,* with journalists keen to record the event. As subsequent vessels arrived, the number of journalists tailed off quickly, so by the time the stragglers arrived they were having to tie-up their own yacht to the quay. It was an important experience; the real winners in the publicity stakes were the race sponsors and the yacht that came first. Only the sponsors were guaranteed publicity from their investment.

Brittany Ferries GB subsequently finished a narrow second in the Round Britain Race in July 1982 but was outside the podium places in the Route du Rhum that year after the self-steering mechanism failed and the yacht began sailing round in circles. The sponsorship came to an end when the level of insurance became unaffordable.

The perils of individual vessel sponsorship were illustrated in 1980, when *Brittany Ferries France,* a yacht sponsored by the French arm of the Company, ran into difficulties whilst returning home after competing in the single-handed transatlantic race. She sent out a May Day signal at around 15:00 on 28th July 1980 from a position some 360 miles north east of the Azores, and this message was picked up by commercial airliners passing overhead. A USAF C-130 plane, which was crossing on the Atlantic on a routine training flight, was diverted to assist. Fortunately, it had a team of specialist divers on board, who specialised in the recovery of astronauts from space capsules landing in water. The yacht was found capsized at around 20:30, with the crew of four clinging to the hull; two of the medically trained divers parachuted to assist and found one crew member with head injuries and another with a fractured leg. Life rafts were dropped on the scene as the C-130 guided the Greek ship *Nisses Myconos* to pick up the injured. The *Queen Elizabeth 2* was also in the area and alerted in case the injuries proved to be serious, but she was stood down although the ship's doctor provided assistance over the radio. The men were picked up by the *Nisses Myconos* at 02:00 the next morning.

Blyth embarked on a journey to recreate the original Clipper route with *Brittany Ferries GB* in a venture televised by the BBC. All went well until Carruthers received a satellite phone call from a distant voice, clearly in distress in tumultuous weather conditions. "I'm having trouble with my mast – can you help arrange for a replacement to be delivered to my next port so I can round Cape Horn?" asked Blyth. Amidst the many day to day issues affecting Brittany Ferries, finding a replacement mast was an unwelcome, somewhat out of the ordinary and difficult task. He rang the yacht's insurers, who refused to cover a trip round Cape Horn, so the trip ended, and the vessel eventually came home to be sold to Beefeater. The yacht later capsized and was sunk in mid-Atlantic in a 'monstrous gale' whilst on a delivery voyage to New York on 28th October 1983.

In 1981, Alexis Gourvennec was elected as Chairman of Crédit Agricole de Finistère, then the second largest to Paris of the banks that constituted the Crédit Agricole co-operative.

There was still a strong desire to consider opening a route to a port further east than St Malo, in order to strengthen the Company's market position. In a change from the strategy that initially considered a route from Dieppe more important, Gourvennec and Michielini opened discussions with the city of Caen about the opening of a new route from Portsmouth, which it was believed could open as early as 1983 and deliver up to an estimated 500,000 extra passengers, perhaps rising to as many as 1.5 million within five years. Caen was a new destination port, without direct competition, which made it a much more attractive proposition than Dieppe. When the discussions became public, there was a strong response from the ports of Le Havre and Cherbourg, but Gourvennec was philosophical. "the government will give some money for the new port at Caen, and some money for new roads from Cherbourg, so everyone will be happy" he was reported as saying.

Opening up Brittany Ferries' operations further east along the French coast had been a long-held ambition of Michielini. His background in Danzas gave him a wider perspective than many of his Breton colleagues. This viewpoint was strongly supported by the UK team, who were keen to take the fight more directly to Townsend Thoresen, Sealink, and P&O Ferries. But the company was still essentially a Breton operation, financed through the region, the agricultural shareholders and the local départements who had comparatively little interest in, or understanding of, the need to expand beyond their home territory.

For Michielini, expansion was a pre-requisite to building a firm foundation for the company across Brittany and Normandy and resisting any incursion by British-based competitors. His interest in Caen as a destination dated back to 1977, when he had made his first visit to inspect the port facilities with Burns. Sailing to the city of Caen itself involved a time-consuming slow passage along the Caen canal from the coast at Ouistreham, but placing the port at the canal mouth would solve this problem. Caen lay midway between Cherbourg and Le Havre, with increasingly easy access to the autoroute which was opening up as the French road network expanded, thereby creating better and quicker access to the prime holiday areas of France further south. Ouistreham lay closer to the main Alpine ski resorts than any other cross-Channel port. And it was a shorter drive from the potential port site to Brittany, than the equivalent journey from Cherbourg.

The Caen authorities approached Townsend Thoresen to gauge their interest in opening up a new route, but the established operator declined, expressing the opinion that north easterly winds would make berthing difficult at Ouistreham. In reality, a service to Caen would bisect their existing route options from Southampton and Portsmouth to Cherbourg and Le Havre, so would more likely abstract traffic from their established business rather than gain business from competitors, whilst incurring all the attendant costs of additional tonnage and a new port operation. It would only work for Townsend Thoresen as a service to block other operators, but they were confident enough in their own operation to see this as an unecessary development. They remained content to reject the idea.

The commercial reasons that discouraged Townsend Thoresen from progressing the Caen option attracted Brittany Ferries to the proposition. A route from Portsmouth to Caen could take traffic away from Cherbourg and Le Havre, undermining the Townsend Thoresen, P&O Ferries, Sealink and Truckline services. The only serious alternative for a new route to Normandy was to Dieppe, which had originally been the prime candidate. Dieppe was the home of the Sealink service from Newhaven and the former Jetfoil link from Brighton, but the port in the heart of the town was cramped and Michielini preferred to progress the Caen option; useful contacts were established in the Calvados département, particularly with René Garrec, who was close to Michel d'Ornano, then president of the Lower Normandy region.

Garrec remained a strong supporter of the project and continued to lobby behind the scenes to make the proposition a reality. The Calvados region was already popular with visitors to the classic casino resorts on the northern French coast, home to the historic towns of Caen and Bayeux, and the site of the historic Normandy beaches, but the département considered it suffered commercially due to the lack of direct access to a ferry service from England. The local economy was not in good shape with the loss of many traditional industries, but the tourism business had under-developed potential. Existing cross-Channel routes encouraged tourists to by-pass Calvados and head directly to the main holiday areas further west and south. This geographical isolation was likely to be further exacerbated if the embryonic ideas for a Channel Tunnel were to come to fruition. Garrec persuaded d'Ornano and Paul Spriet, the new president of the Caen Chamber of Commerce, of the merits of the ferry project. The Chamber of Commerce became convinced of the need to open up Ouistreham as a gateway to the region, and was sympathetic to Brittany Ferries being the preferred operator.

Equally supportive was the UK team, for the task of making a financial success of a route to Ouistreham would fall to them. There were never any doubts in Portsmouth that the route could be successful, as the logic of geography, which had been so tellingly applied in establishing existing Brittany Ferries routes, was even more pertinent in the Ouistreham case. Gut instinct and an innate sense of the market drove this thinking. A glance at the map explained the rationality of the proposal. The port of Le Havre was positioned on the north bank of the Seine, so those travelling to the holiday areas of France first had to head east to cross the river by the Tancarville bridge, before returning west. The Cotentin peninsula placed Cherbourg more distant from Brittany than Ouistreham, and the growing French autoroute network would bring the main route along the Channel coast within easy reach of the city of Caen. Journey times on the largely parallel routes from Portsmouth to Ouistreham and Le Havre would be similar, so shorter road distances to onward destinations gave Ouistreham the advantage. Whilst Cherbourg enjoyed a shorter crossing to the English coast, this was not necessarily an advantage on overnight crossings, where the ability to take a cabin to get some sleep was an integral part of a longer holiday journey. And the Normandy beaches lay within easy reach... The plans for a Ouistreham service continued to be developed.

Meanwhile, Townsend Thoresen increasingly focused their western Channel services on Portsmouth, and the port facilities and storage capacity were becoming highly constrained and unsuitable. In the summer, the morning Southampton-Cherbourg sailing was transferred to depart from Portsmouth, increasing the company's high season departures to five each day. Any further expansion of Brittany Ferries' operations would be thwarted if more services were attracted to the port and the level of congestion grew. So, the first step to enact the Ouistreham plan was to secure the opportunity to use Portsmouth as the English base. There were still only two linkspans in the port and an additional service could not be accommodated without the provision of another linkspan and the creation of significantly more land for vehicle marshalling and storage. The growth in traffic experienced in the 1980 and 1981 seasons encouraged the Board to support the aspirations of the UK team to enter into a contract for a long-term expansion plan with the City of Portsmouth. An agreement was finalised whereby the City Council would invest in what became known as 'Phase Three' of the port Masterplan, which comprised substantial reclamation work on the north side of the existing port to provide the necessary infrastructure to support the new route to Ouistreham. Brittany Ferries would get a new linkspan and 4.3 acres of storage capacity to accommodate their expanded traffic; in return the Company agreed to doubling the annual port dues payable to the port to £600,000 when the works were completed. Portsmouth City Council went ahead with their plans to reclaim additional land from the northern mudflats and placed an order for the linkspan. The works were scheduled for completion in 1983, when the new service to Ouistreham was expected to commence.

Despite its financial difficulties Brittany Ferries was still generating positive news in the media, particularly for the Plymouth-Santander service. A contemporary newspaper successfully highlighted the key selling points as it reported: -

> "The French-owned Brittany Ferries is now the only roll-on roll-off car ferry link between Britain and Spain, and much of its success is due to the uncomplicated shore to ship transfer in your heavy-laden car at both Plymouth and Santander. At both ports there is but one terminal, exclusive to the company, so even the traveller who needs a ball of string and a compass to find his way round the honeycomb of docks at Dover and Southampton has nothing to fear.
>
> The key to the success of Brittany Ferries in attracting young families to Spain is the 12-hour cut in the 36-hour voyage which now extinct passages from Southampton took. That 24-hour trip from Plymouth means better use of the ship and more civilised departure and arrival times. In high season from March 19 to October 27, the *Armorique* leaves Plymouth at 8 AM on Mondays and 11:30 AM on Wednesdays, and Santander at similar times on Tuesdays and Thursdays, after a two-hour passenger turnaround. In winter there is a once-weekly service departing Plymouth on a Wednesday and Santander the next day. A purpose-built ferry purchased by Brittany Ferries in 1976, the *Armorique* takes 700 passengers and 165 cars, and unlike previous competitors from Southampton rarely has trouble filling.
>
> With your compulsory red triangles in case of breakdown neatly stacked beneath the travelling cot in the boot, the drive from Millbay docks Plymouth to the terminal on Calle de Antonio Lopez, opposite the cathedral at Santander, is a pleasure. There are no long queues of cars at either end for embarkation or customs.
>
> After driving onto the car deck, it is wise to take everything you need with you to your cabin because there is the complication of summoning a member of the crew to escort you should you wish to return to the vehicle during the voyage. A steward takes you to your cabin which is air conditioned and either two or four berth. All have their own washbasin and many a shower and a lavatory. With the children safely ensconced with a hostess and a pile of toys and games in the playroom, there is time to enjoy the three sundecks and the duty-free bars as if it were properly the first day of holiday. There is a discotheque and the cinema featuring three up-to-date films except for the first performance which is for those children in the early afternoon who have tired of the playroom. For compulsive shoppers there is a duty-free supermarket and a separate gift shop. For lunch you may help yourself in the cafeteria but at night there is excellent five course menu in the French restaurant which will cost about £8 a head. Children are not allowed.
>
> That civilised departure and arrival schedules mean that you're woken in time for an English or continental breakfast an hour before you dock. It all amounts to an excellent time saving start to a family holiday in Spain with your car and without the irritations of a trek through France. The car fare is calculated on the number of passengers in it. But as a price guide the return fare in high season for family with two children travelling in a Cortina and occupying a luxury four berth cabin will be £369.90 this summer. That more than covers the cost of petrol through France, but it can mean the difference between taking a touring holiday in Spain with young children or not."
>
> *Michael Horsnell, The Times 17th January 1981*

One lesson from the fallout from the *Trégor* cancellation was that additional management resource was needed to support the drive for growth from the UK if plans for further expansion were to be realised. The structure was just too lean. Carruthers moved quickly to find support, returning to one his colleagues at Hertz and Heron. David Longden had initially recruited Carruthers into the Hertz organisation and now Carruthers outlined a proposition similar to that which had tempted him to Brittany Ferries – this could be a really interesting role, or a disaster, but well worth the gamble. The two had previously looked to set up a truck rental business together but had been unable to secure the necessary capital. Here was an opportunity to build something together. Longden was hooked.

Their shared Hertz background was very important. Like their former colleague Burns, the pair shared the values that they had been taught during their time with the vehicle rental company. Hertz developed a particular kind of person, usually very well educated or with a practical rounded education grounded in discipline-led organisations. The company gave responsibility at a young age, so that managers felt they were running their own business, and gave them the management tools and training to be successful. The decline of Hertz began during the first oil crisis of 1973, when the business had to focus on much smaller cars than the 'gas guzzlers' to which people had become accustomed. American experts brought in to analyse the European operation felt it should close everything but the largest of operations. Avis profited from the opportunity that this presented, as did many other regional hire companies, including Salford Van Hire and Enterprise. This was another lesson learned. It was a bad decision and Carruthers and Longden were flabbergasted at the short sightedness of it all. They concluded that economies are cyclical and businesses required a long-term perspective to be successful; it was necessary to take advantage of better times to be ready and able to ride out the inevitable future difficulties, a philosophy which matched the perspective adopted by Brittany Ferries' shareholders from the outset.

Working at Hertz involved overcoming frequent problems; vehicle quality was very poor at this time, cars were unreliable and they frequently broke down. There were never enough vehicles available for customers arriving in hordes off flights at the Scottish airports where Carruthers and Longden cut their managerial teeth; further experience that readied them for life with Brittany Ferries.

Hertz had a primitive punch-card computer, one of the very earliest IBM machines, which worked with mixed success. But the organisation taught the need to take emotion out of business, yet never lose that sense of emotion; crucially it preached the value of management information. Brittany Ferries' budgeting processes came as a shock to Burns, Carruthers and Longden, with the whole company budget on a sheet of A4 paper outlined in pencil. There was no significant revenue budgeting, no measurement of statistics, no revenue analysis per passenger, per car, or per freight unit. It was totally amateur compared to Hertz. Carruthers and Longden set about instilling the discipline to set objectives and standards to work towards, and began evolving the management tools needed to measure corporate performance. This was a huge change for the time, even if it seems an obvious step from a more modern perspective.

Longden's decision to join Brittany Ferries was the start of highly successful partnership, which was to help drive the Company to a dominant position on the western Channel. The two had complementary strengths and worked closely together, often disguising the closeness of their working relationship to the benefit of the Company in a 'hard-man soft-man' routine. Longden moved to Plymouth, taking over responsibility for operations at the port and controlling the marketing activity of the Company in the UK and Ireland. There was thus a clear split of responsibility between the two colleagues. Their background created the foundation for the development of a corporate culture and began to encompass a UK 'cause' to which the team could feel bound to. There were no fancy mission statements; it was simply seen to be important to win in all aspects of business life. And in a Company that was still 'David' in a battle against several 'Goliaths' this was a grand objective which began to instil a pride in what everyone was trying to achieve. This was assisted by avoiding a blame culture; if things went wrong the energy was put into making them right, a need to solve the problem rather than search for the guilty. This approach extended through to budgets, within which money was freely moved around between different functions for the common good.

The financial year 1980-81 ended with an increase in Company losses to £2.4 million following the heavy levels of borrowing needed to support the acquisition of the *Prince of Brittany* and the *Breizh-Izel*, and the continued impact of the ongoing price war on Channel crossings driven by the short-sea routes, although a strengthening pound helped limit the deficit. There had been marginal growth in passenger carryings to 735,745, but the number of cars shipped fell to 137,608, and freight volumes dropped slightly to 25,421. Whilst the St Malo and Roscoff routes were largely remote from the main ferry fare battlegrounds further east, the routes had to remain price competitive; geographical advantages can only sustain a reasonable level of price premium. The immediate outlook was not good; annual inflation in Britain was running at 18% and more than two million people were unemployed. 1981 had been a summer of discontent across Britain, with riots breaking out in Toxteth on 5th July which quickly spread to many other cities across the country.

The *Prince of Brittany* arrives at Portsmouth early in her career with the company. *(John Hendy)*

The *Goelo* completed her final Portsmouth-St Malo crossing on 28th August, and was returned to her owners at the end of her two-year charter period. But the policy of sending Mason to scour the market to find appropriate replacement second-hand vessels at the right price was proving an increasingly difficult proposition. The disparate collection of ships operated by Brittany Ferries barely merited the description of a 'fleet', and Carruthers and Longden well understood the need to improve their quality to deliver a 'sellable' service proposition. A ferry typically has a commercial life well in excess of 25 years but will lose or make money on a daily and annual basis. This long-term investment had to be reconciled with the shorter term fluctuations inherent in annual commercial returns.

Gourvennec and Michielini were initially resistant to ideas of expansion and fleet investment at a time when the Company was losing money and the market outlook was so poor. It was not clear how improvements and changes to the fleet could be funded. But Maurice Chollet was supportive of the strategy, and used his financial acumen to help create a growing realisation that Brittany Ferries would be in peril if it failed to continue to invest. The Company had to plan beyond the mere survival tactics that had characterised the story to date, and invest heavily to secure the future. The shareholders again faced the prospect of digging deep to continue their support for Brittany Ferries, but their reticence amidst poor financial results suggested this approach was not a sustainable long-term strategy.

Whilst it ran against regional instincts, Gourvennec looked to the French government for help and opened up discussions with the Marine Marchande in Paris. A continued independent French ferry operation on the English Channel was clearly a good thing, protecting French jobs and bringing tourism benefits across the country. The response was positive, but support was offered at a significant price. The region should pay its share of any rescue plan, and the government insisted that Brittany Ferries must

The *Goelo* heads to St Malo on her morning sailing from Portsmouth. *(FotoFlite)*

abandon the St Malo routes as a pre-condition of state help. This prospect was untenable to the Bretons, who could not understand how central government could dictate such draconian terms. This government response mobilised Breton resources behind a new regionally-based rescue plan for Brittany Ferries.

Chollet had been working on a such plan for over a year. Brittany Ferries could demonstrate a good track record of generating income but was burdened by high cost of borrowing funds needed to charter vessels for the fleet, even though these were at commercial market rates. The Company could not by itself raise the large amounts of investment capital required to facilitate further expansion. Corporate performance had been buffeted by ship breakdowns, accidents, fishermen's strikes, port blockades, and dockers' disputes, demonstrating both its resilience and its fragility. No bank was prepared to lend on the necessary scale against such a track record.

Gourvennec brought together the presidents of the four Breton départements, the president of the Brittany Region and Louis le Pensec, the government Minister of the Sea, to find a way forward. There was common agreement that Brittany Ferries must remain a Breton enterprise; it was unthinkable that it could be sold to another ferry operator. The French government was still keen to find a solution to support Gourvennec because he was seen as a political operative, even though there was still a strong Breton separatist movement at the time. The outcome was an elegant and very French financial solution.

The structure of supportive relationships between region, state and commercial business was significantly more developed in France than in the UK. When President François Mitterrand came to power in 1981, he enacted a policy of giving the French Regions more control over their activities as part of a programme of decentralisation of state power. The concept of the Société d'Économie Mixte (SEM) was born. The SEM was a public limited company, in which a public body such as a local authority held between 51% and 85% of the capital, and was entitled to at least one representative and half of the votes on the company board. The SEM was able to carry out development operations, construction or operation of public services of an industrial or commercial nature, or other activities of general interest. However, it was not allowed to operate in an anti-competitive manner.

If a SEM were established to borrow money and purchase vessels at market rates, it could own and charter back the Brittany Ferries fleet whilst providing both capital and financial credibility for the Company. In return, Brittany Ferries could fund the interest on capital loaned to the SEM by paying agreed market-rate charter fees over a fixed duration, thereby reducing the annual finance costs for the Company, but also providing certainty of income for the SEM. The outcome was the creation of the Société Anonyme Bretonne d'Économie Mixte d'Équipement Naval (Sabemen). The founding shareholders of Sabemen were the Brittany Region, the Brittany départements, the Pays de Loire Region, and Brittany Ferries. The initial shareholding of Brittany Ferries in Sabemen was modest, but the new arrangement allowed the Company to maintain its independence whilst having access to the capital sums needed to invest and move forward. Brittany Ferries shareholders would receive a portion of their initial investment back in cash, but the Company could now fund improvement and expansion plans, provided their business plan demonstrated the ability to make payments in return. As Gourvennec put it at the time "In agriculture, you can be a farmer without owning the land, and you can own land without being a farmer. There is no shame to that. So let's apply this rule of farming to maritime transport."

The partnership bound Brittany Ferries closely to Sabemen, particularly to its regional shareholders. Sabemen now had the power to guide the strategic direction of the Company by determining the fleet composition, operating arrangements and general traffic conditions that it had to meet. The SEM required strong financial reporting and forecasting and was permitted two observers (censeurs) on the management board of the Company. The main private shareholder in Sabemen remained Brittany Ferries. The vessel rent payable to Sabemen included rents charged by the lessor, amortisation of ship-related investments (including upgrades) and any exchange rate differentials if a vessel was financed in a foreign currency. Sabemen was therefore able to balance its budget until the ships were disposed of.

This was a pivotal moment for the Company. The new relationship with Sabemen enabled corporate strategy to switch from seeking survival and living a 'hand to mouth' existence with an eye on annual financial performance, to an operation that had the luxury of taking the long-term view. This was a profound change and one which distinguished Brittany Ferries from its main ferry competitors who, as private companies, remained subjected to the demands of the short-term vision and financial whims of private shareholders. There was considerable nervousness about the new arrangements amongst the management team, as many felt that the Company's independence was being sacrificed. But Gourvennec maintained that as long as the Company paid charter fees to Sabemen on time it would be left alone to determine its destiny. He was to be proved right.

The new financial arrangements drew much criticism from other ferry companies, who found their attempts to see off their diminutive competitor were proving increasingly unsuccessful. They now argued that Brittany Ferries was receiving illegal state subsidies, a stance which they repeatedly maintained for as long as they remained in competition. Toby Oliver grew accustomed to fielding these questions from journalists and strongly defending the independence of the company from state support. But the story would not go away. There was a cultural gulf between approaches to state and regional relationships with industry in the UK and France, with substantial misunderstanding in Britain of the French position. There were now three contrasting business models amongst cross-channel operators; private companies (Townsend Thoresen and P&O Ferries) operating ferries as a stand-alone commercial enterprise with an eye on annual profits; nationalised businesses (Sealink in the UK and SNCF in France) initially seeing ferries as an extension of, and integrated with, connecting rail services, but now increasingly challenged by the growth of vehicle traffic; and the social enterprise model now being pioneered by Brittany Ferries.

The rescue package was ratified by the Breton Regional Council in February 1982 and ownership of the *Armorique*, *Cornouailles* and *Prince of Brittany* was transferred to Sabemen; they were immediately chartered back to Brittany Ferries, which benefited from an £8.5 million cash injection. The Company now had the solid financial backing that would permit it for the first time to be able to make the right fleet decisions and invest appropriately in the business. This quickly manifested itself in the decision to build the Brittany Centre as a base for the Company and its holiday business in Portsmouth, with work starting early in 1982.

The creation of Sabemen also allowed Brittany Ferries to address the year-long hold on expansion on the Plymouth-Santander route created by the absence of the *Trégor*. In winter 1981-82 authority was given to look for a ship for the route from the following spring. With access to substantial capital resource in place, Mason could begin the search for a transformative cruise ferry to add to the fleet as a statement of the Company's new intent and direction. The drive for this vessel came from the UK team, as they had proved increasingly able to demonstrate their skills in attracting traffic to support the business model. Michielini relied on Carruthers and Longden and their team to justify the expansion, and Sabemen, shareholders and creditors had sufficient confidence in their abilities to back their judgement. It was becoming clear that Brittany Ferries was moving in the right direction for the long-term, and any short-term issues were there to be overcome.

The logic outlined by the UK team was simple. Brittany Ferries had grown by focusing on destination-led advertising and had created the concepts of Holiday France and Holiday Spain to help sell their services. A modern cruise ferry would be a tangible manifestation of these ideas, and a focus for improvements in quality in the on board product. The fleet of *Penn-Ar-Bed*, *Cornouailles*, *Prince of Brittany* and *Armorique* had been acquired incrementally as the need arose and opportunity presented itself, but they represented an old and inappropriate image for the brand that the UK team was trying to create. When the last vehicles were tightly squeezed onto cramped and busy car decks, passengers were on occasions forced to climb out of their sunroofs to leave their car, and there was no room for freight in the peak season for what was trying to be a balanced multi-purpose business. Freight capacity had to be available year-round if winter business was to be retained. More vehicle deck space was fundamental to future growth.

Sabemen brought financial credibility and gave Mason the opportunity to look beyond traditional sources of supply for cross-Channel tonnage and find vessels that matched the perceived quality of the brand. The cross-Channel experience did not feature anything that could be said to be approaching a 'cruise ferry' standard, although this concept was developing rapidly in Scandinavia and the Baltic. Here, comparatively large vessels were employed on the longer sea crossings from Sweden to Finland and Germany, which were of similar duration to the routes operated by Brittany Ferries. The Silja Line and Viking Line products were proving sufficiently attractive to build a substantial passenger market around the quality of hotel services and on board shopping opportunities. These companies were developing a true 'cruise' experience in their ferry products and the team aspired to match a standard where the ships were becoming a destination in themselves. But the Scandinavian business was also different to that on the western Channel, as there was significantly less 'point to point' traffic; it was very much a

The *Nils Dacke* in her TT-Line Saga Linjen guise. *(Ferry Publications Library)*

mini-cruise market. Mason began an extensive search of the Scandinavian market.

Attention focused on the *Nils Dacke*, which had been built in 1975 for the Malmö-Travemünde route and changed hands several times before being acquired by TT-Line as part of their purchase of Saga Linjen. The ship could sail at 22.5 knots, thereby enabling a potential two-hour reduction in peak crossing times on the Spanish route. The 7,950 gross-tonne, 129.0-metre-long ship had a beam of 21.1 metres and could carry 1,140 passengers accommodated in 757 berths in 280 cabins. Her car deck accommodated 252 cars, although her freight capacity was restricted. She could replace the *Armorique* on the Irish and Spanish services, allowing her to transfer back to her original Portsmouth-St Malo route. But the *Breizh-Izel* would have to work in tandem with the new acquisition to top-up freight capacity to Santander. The proposition made sense, and the *Nils Dacke* was long-term-chartered from TT-Line by Sabemen, with an option to purchase her at a later date. A guarantee of FF24 million was given to Sabemen by the Brittany region to help finance loans for the vessel, which totalled FF80 million. Continuing the policy of using local names for the fleet, she was renamed the *Quiberon*, after the peninsula and town in the south of Brittany. The *Quiberon* came with complete with a Swedish captain, mandated by her owners, who was required to work alongside a Brittany Ferries captain, although this led to friction and an occasional lack of clarity as to who was in charge. One advantage of retaining the Swedish flag on the vessel was that gaming could be carried out on board, in contrast to the ban on these activities on French-flagged ships. There was a significant potential source of income from the casino.

The *Quiberon* underwent a major refurbishment and extensive refit at the Jos. L Meyer Yard in Papenburg, where spare space on her upper car deck (Deck 5) was converted to cabin accommodation to give her a cruise ferry configuration. Her main passenger facilities were located on Deck 6, where she featured an à la carte restaurant (Le Sinagot), a self-service restaurant (Les Îles), Le Ponant Café, and the tearoom Le Moulin Mer, together with two gift shops. Two small cinemas could be found on deck 5, together with a kiosk and perfume shop. Brittany Ferries was not well equipped to handle a major reconfiguration and upgrade of passenger facilities on this scale, and the task was delegated to a contact of Le Rouzo from Brest. Carruthers and Longden felt that the result was disappointingly inconsistent with their desired new image for Brittany Ferries, with dark and dingy interiors reflecting the existing approaches of other operators across the English Channel. It was evident that a new direction would be needed for future acquisitions. But for now, the *Quiberon* was a huge step forward in quality and capacity.

With fleet issues being addressed, attention turned to investing in a more professional approach to handling reservations. Butler was already using a very early personal

1982 brochures for the French and Spanish holiday markets. *(Rook Dunning)*

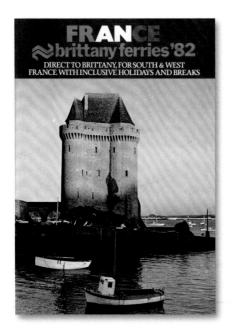
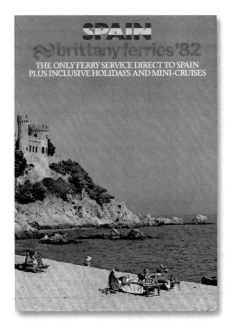

computer to model pricing and revenue scenarios as an aid to budgeting and forecasting. The systems in France were geared up to their local interests of ship crewing and finance. What was needed was an holistic system that could revolutionise the booking process and handle all the complex issues of holiday inventory. Most ferry companies on the English Channel operated high frequency, and high volume routes, where the need to manage and optimise inventory on individual sailings was a low priority. With a comparatively limited sailing frequency it was essential that Brittany Ferries optimised financial return from each departure, and this was challenging with a manual system operating across four ports. Carruthers and Longden looked to their Hertz background, which emphasised the importance of good systems and processes. Brittany Ferries was to be a pioneer in the development of call centres and computerised passenger reservations systems in the ferry industry.

Butler had the confidence of Chollet to develop commercial systems to encompass reservations, ship inventory, ticketing, deposit-handling, payments, tour operator accounts, receivables, supplier information and billing; the two were to become life-long friends. He was tasked with finding a company that could develop a bespoke system that could be rolled out across Brittany Ferries, and found a small developer who fitted the bill. Computer equipment was sourced from Irish Continental Line and installed in a new computer centre in the Plymouth office; it was to become the largest computer system in south west England. Full implementation of system capability took time. There were inevitable cross-Channel tensions which had to be managed until the UK was given full control of the system. Initially the new reservation system was used only for bookings originating in the UK, but eventually the full multi-national capability was exploited.

A complex system required professional internal management, capable of understanding and setting the requirements for software developers, and overseeing implementation of the system with the vision to expand and exploit it in the future. Mick Mott brought a wealth of experience to this task and much needed organisation to the system. The first holiday product transferred from the use of primitive 'T' cards to the world of computing was the gîte stock. Butler spent a considerable time specifying all of the wide range of sales products, with the accounting records and information summaries that were necessary for an efficient business. The scheme was intended to be a pilot, but the value was quickly recognised and everyone wanted to be part of it; the result was a process of continuous development.

Expanded capacity and a reservations system required business to justify it and the team set about finding more passengers and freight to fill the vessels. Freight traffic was difficult to attract when sailings and capacity were limited, but the new capacity allowed for the provision of guaranteed space for freight vehicles, with a very short cut-off time. This helped counter some of the 'turn up and go' advantages of the short-sea routes. But the main revenues would continue to come from the passenger business, which was still very seasonal, with a concentration during school holidays and the summer. The main problem was to create the desire for passengers to choose to travel with Brittany Ferries by increasing name recognition.

The market was very different to the present day. There was no easy access to customers through the internet and social media. As increasing numbers of Britons began to venture abroad for their holidays, the growth area in French holidays was in camping and pre-erected tents, although the purchase of overseas property for holiday use was also increasing. The car was a significantly more important component of the family holiday. Low cost airlines were still a thing of the future, and there were limited ranges of family package holidays to the 'Costas'. Motorists were historically attracted to the short-sea routes across the English Channel, partly because the Brittany Ferries alternative was new and relatively unknown. But none of this substantial business was travelling to the Calais hinterland for their holidays. The answer kept coming back to promoting France and the holiday destinations, with the fleet as a means to an end, as

The *Prince of Brittany* arriving at Portsmouth. *(John Hendy)*

the quality of vessels did not yet justify a focus on their merits. This strategy remained at variance with the established approach of other ferry operators, who saw the sea crossing as the focus of their 'offer', despite the frequently more widely variable standard of their fleets.

Over 100 new sites were added to the portfolio of self-catering properties in 1982, bringing the total to 450. The Company also introduced a simplified pricing structure on a per person basis inclusive of a vehicle return fare; prices started at £44 per person for a week in a party of four people during the low season, inclusive of ferry crossing.

The spring of 1982 was dominated by the Argentinian invasion of the Falkland Islands, which began on 2nd April and prompted a heavy military response from the UK. A task force was assembled to relieve these remote communities in the South Atlantic, which included the sending of a fleet of naval and civilian vessels to relieve the islands. Whilst Brittany Ferries was not affected, Townsend Thoresen provided three ships to the Falklands task force, including the Portsmouth-based *Europic Ferry*. Passenger sailings continued unchanged across the Channel, but there was a nervousness amongst the British public, especially in the naval cities of Plymouth and Portsmouth. The task force sailed south from Portsmouth, and the conflict continued for three months before the Argentinian forces surrendered on 14th June.

Brittany Ferries faced its own internal problems in the Spring with seasonal strikes by French seamen. All Portsmouth-St Malo services were cancelled for a week in March in the light of potential industrial disruption. Passengers were advised to travel on other routes operated by P&O Ferries and Townsend Thoresen. A pattern was emerging whereby Brittany Ferries' seafaring unions would make unreasonable demands at the start of each summer to force concessions from the Company in order to avoid disruption at the peak of the season. This situation could not be allowed to continue.

Phil Bowditch joined Brittany Ferries as Portsmouth Operations Manager in early April. He arranged to travel overnight from Portsmouth to St Malo on the *Prince of Brittany* to rendezvous with Carruthers in France and drive across to Roscoff to meet the team. Waking in the middle of night, he found the ship silent and without lights. Quickly dressing and heading out on deck, he found the vessel being towed towards Cherbourg by a tug. A fire in the engine room, caused by a ruptured fuel line, had been extinguished by the crew but the *Prince of Brittany's* engines were out of use. Carruthers drove up to Cherbourg to meet Bowditch and help the recovery effort; the two later returned to Portsmouth with Townsend Thoresen. Carruthers then faced a series of hostile media interviews about the incident, which was deemed of sufficient importance to feature on Radio 4.

The *Prince of Brittany* was to be out of service for some six weeks for extensive repairs. Passengers were offered alternative crossings from Weymouth to Cherbourg and Sealink's *Ailsa Princess* provided short-term cover before the *Viking 1* was chartered from Sally Line between 13th April and 10th May to bring the necessary capacity to the route whilst the *Prince of Brittany* underwent repair.

The *Prince of Brittany* was supplemented on the Portsmouth-St Malo service from 20th May by the *Armorique*, which operated the night crossing from St Malo and daytime return sailing, with the *Prince of Brittany* offering the night sailing from Portsmouth, returning by day.

The *Quiberon* completed her refit at Papenburg on 20th May and sailed to Plymouth to take up the Spain and Ireland roster. Although designed for work in the less challenging environment of the Southern Baltic, she proved to be ideal for conditions in the Bay of Biscay, and quickly became a popular vessel. The *Quiberon* established new quality standards for ferries serving Ireland, and her size prompted a move from the established terminal at Tivoli docks to the facilities at Ringaskiddy, some 15 kilometres down the river from Cork. The arrival of the *Quiberon* was accompanied by the signing of a new ten-year

Formula 1 world champion Alan Jones joins Gordon Day, Ian Carruthers, Modesto Piñeiro Jr and Toby Oliver to promote Spanish freight services at a trade show in Harrogate. *(Ian Carruthers)*

Prince Charles is welcomed on board the *Prince of Brittany* by Ian
Carruthers and Christian Michielini. King Constantine of Greece and Capt.
Cisque look on. *(Ian Carruthers collection)*

agreement with the BTDB in Plymouth, which gave Brittany Ferries exclusive use of Millbay Docks, with investment in port facilities by the authority. This long-term arrangement suited both parties and more than compensated the BTDB for their disappointment with the *Trégor*. With the future direction of the Plymouth services now secure, attention moved to considering the next stages for development of the Portsmouth routes.

The summer proved relatively uneventful until, at the end of the season, the *Armorique* ran aground in fog outside St Malo on 18th September 1982. She was taken out of service for repair in Le Havre and the laid up *Penn-Ar-Bed* substituted.

By the autumn of 1982, the company was well on the road to financial recovery and able to exploit the public relations opportunities arising from the raising of the Henry VIII warship *Mary Rose* in the Solent on 11th October. Carruthers persuaded Michielini to take the *Prince of Brittany* out of service for two days to be chartered by the Mary Rose Trust as host vessel for VIPs witnessing the event. The raising of the vessel was also broadcast live on BBC television. Le Rouzo arranged for the Company's best chefs to be on board to feed the 400 guests of the Trust and British Petroleum, one of the main sponsors. Also amongst the VIP guests on board were Prince Charles, King Constantine of Greece, Lord Mountbatten of Romsey and the Earl of Marchwood.

Mindful that these prestige guests might need special hospitality, Carruthers asked the organisers how they should be handled, and they shrugged, "well it's your ship, you should look after them; no matter what we do we're bound to offend somebody. If you would not mind, could you look after them?" Carruthers said "Really? Well we've got a small officers suite..." So he became the host for a memorable lunch with everyone around the table in relaxed mood, a bemused captain dining with Prince Charles and King Constantine and a detective sitting quietly observing events from the corner of the suite. A television relayed what was happening outside in the Solent as a mammoth crane readied to lift the wreck from the sea bed. Prince Charles said, "I can't have a big lunch because I'm going to go dive." Instead of lunch, he was given a bottle of Chateau d'Yquem and some foie gras as a gift and Prince Charles went off to get changed. As the group watched events unfolding outside, they heard the nation being told that Prince Charles was coming out of the side of a Brittany Ferries ship ready to dive on the wreck. This was a seal of approval for the Company; the publicity was priceless.

In October the *Prince of Brittany* undertook a further visit to the heart of Cork as part of a special trip from Le Havre. She berthed at the North Custom House Quay before heading on to Swansea and returning to Le Havre.

The 1982 season ended with further growth recorded to reach 749,386 passengers, but the difficult trading conditions were evident in slight falls in passenger vehicles (to 136,612) and freight units (to 24,230). However, the pound sterling was trading well against the French Franc, hitting a peak of FF12 before slipping back slightly in the autumn. This helped provide a further boost to corporate finances.

The start of 1983 marked the tenth anniversary of the first sailing from Roscoff. The company could boast remarkable progress from a single vessel freight-only operation to a fleet of six ships now operating across four routes, with strong financial backing for the first time in its history. Continuous growth in passenger traffic had been achieved as the

Above: **Jim Butler.** *(Jim Butler)*

Top right: **Expansion works at Portsmouth under way.** *(Portsmouth Port)*

Right: **The new Brittany Centre in Portsmouth.** *(Miles Cowsill)*

Company expanded. Brittany Ferries celebrated by opening the Brittany Centre, as the new home of all Portsmouth operations. It was conveniently located in Wharf Road, just outside the entrance to the continental ferry terminal, and was a visible statement of Brittany Ferries' presence for everyone travelling through the port. The building housed the teams responsible for the development, management and administration of all the Company's holiday products, the brochure production teams, the general management team and, initially, the administration and commercial management of freight traffic. Anne Titcombe joined the Company and was to provide invaluable support for Ian Carruthers over the coming years.

The BTDB were aware that facilities in Plymouth were inadequate for the expanding ferry business, and built a new terminal with office space allocated to Brittany Ferries on the top floor. Jim Butler designed the accommodation for the management team,

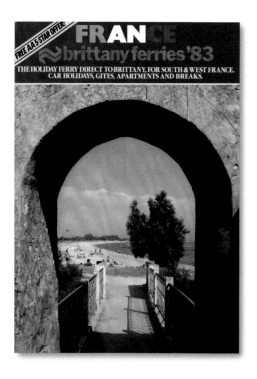

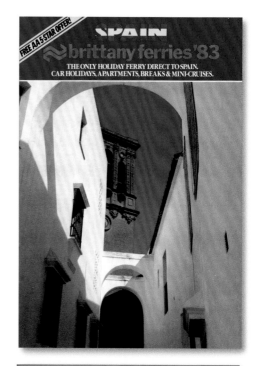

France and Spain brochure covers for the 1983 season, and the first dedicated Gites brochure. *(Rook Dunning)*

accounts department, the reservations team and the mainframe computer.

Trading conditions were still very difficult, with UK unemployment reaching 3.2 million in February. Brittany Ferries announced a virtual price freeze for vehicles during the coming summer season, with passenger fares rising by 50p to £23.50 single.

The 1983 season saw publication of the Company's first dedicated gîte holiday brochure, a 64-page production with colour covers and a predominantly black and white interior. Properties were listed with a description of the setting and facilities, but it was something of a leap of faith for the customer to choose their holiday accommodation from the limited textual description, although this was no different to the standard for other brochures at the time.

The new computer-based reservations system was employed for the 1983 season, and it was soon evident that Brittany Ferries had a substantial lead on competitors in this area. This encouraged the team to drive further development to stay ahead. This first season was a significant test for the new system, as the Company established links between the Plymouth and Portsmouth offices to enable them to coordinate activities for the first time to handle all telephone calls and reservation processes. At the height of the January booking rush, the Company had the capacity to process 5,000 calls each day, and the system slowed under the pressure. This coincided with the first television adverts designed to raise the profile of Brittany Ferries, which proved difficult for all concerned. This was a very positive problem to have, but lessons were learned and more resilience was built into the system for subsequent years.

More than £1 million was spent during the Spring upgrading facilities on the *Armorique*, the *Prince of Brittany* and the *Quiberon*. The *Armorique* covered the *Quiberon's* duties on the Plymouth roster whilst she was away at refit. It was to be an eventful exchange.

As the *Armorique* headed on her outward journey from Roscoff to Cork at around 05:00 on 2nd April 1983, fire was detected in a linen cupboard forward on deck 5 by three Irish schoolchildren. The vessel was around 20 miles north of the Isles of Scilly, with 680 passengers on board at the time. The blaze lasted for about an hour before being out by the *Armorique's* crew, but the ship's generators were put out of action. Royal Navy Sea King helicopters were scrambled from Culdrose and RAF Brawdy, after the captain radioed that the fire had broken out; lifeboats were launched from St. Mary's on the Isles of Scilly, St. Ives, Sennen and Penlee, and Irish Continental Line's *St Killian* was amongst nearby ships that went to aid the *Armorique*. Some of the injured were airlifted to the St. Clare Hospital in Penzance by helicopter. The *Armorique* was eventually escorted to Mount's Bay by the St. Mary's lifeboat and the *St. Killian,* arriving there early in the afternoon.

Sadly, one passenger died, whilst eleven were admitted to hospital and 67 were seen and subsequently discharged from the hospital emergency department, largely suffering from the effects of smoke inhalation. A further 50 crew went ashore for medical examination. The fatality was a Frenchman, Jean Lamay, a schoolteacher who was leading a Breton school party and was found asphyxiated in his cabin having been overcome by smoke when he returned to collect his shoes, ignoring announcements not to return to passenger accommodation. More than 66 cabins were found to have been damaged by smoke from the fire. The public coroner's inquest was held in Penzance, even though the *Armorique* was on passage from France to Ireland, as the body was landed in St Mounts Bay.

The *Armorique* eventually returned to Roscoff and was taken out of service for a week of repairs. She returned to service on 9th April. Brittany Ferries later filed a complaint with the public prosecutor of Morlaix against unknown parties, believing that the fire "cannot be attributed in any case to a technical failure of any kind whatsoever". Michielini noted that investigators had observed several failed fire attempts in different places on the *Armorique*. The subsequent investigation was led by the French authorities as the vessel was French-registered, but the UK supported with evidence and assistance. It transpired that a group of French schoolchildren had been sold cigarette lighters by a lorry driver on board, and the fire had been lit in the linen cupboard as a prank, following several previous attempts to start a blaze.

At the start of 1983, the Jersey States government solicited applications from operators for a service to compete against the established Sealink operation from Portsmouth and Weymouth. Sealink was the successor organisation to the railway companies that had developed daily links with the Channel Islands from Southampton and Weymouth in the nineteenth century. Now operating ro-ro services to Guernsey and Jersey from both Portsmouth and Weymouth, Sealink was earmarked for privatisation from parent company British Rail in the early 1980s, a process that was to lead to its eventual acquisition by Sea Containers in July 1984. The railway monopoly of passenger services had never faced a significant competitive challenge, but Commodore Shipping and Huelin Renouf still offered freight container services from Portsmouth. Commodore Shipping and Sealink had jointly operated a lift-on lift-off venture for a short period, before Sealink switched to full roll-on roll-off operation from Portsmouth in late 1978. Sealink now employed the *Earl Granville* on a daily night-out, day-back schedule from Portsmouth, and the *Earl Godwin* on shorter daytime crossings from the rail-linked port of Weymouth, whence a seasonal service to Cherbourg was also offered with the *Earl Harold*. Michielini's interest in the Channel Islands had been kindled by the earlier discussions with Boeing Jetfoil, but the Jersey States proposition prompted Carruthers to think about the opportunities that a Channel Islands service might offer.

The Portsmouth stevedoring contract switched from Channel Stevedores to Mainland Market Deliveries (MMD) after dockers refused to handle additional Brittany Ferries sailings during the 1983 summer season. The displaced dockers hauled a container to block the linkspan as the *Prince of Brittany* attempted to berth on 21st June, and used a fork lift truck to push a portacabin through a fence. Police eventually restored order and

Above: **The buffet restaurant on the *Quiberon* marked a step forward in the quality of on board catering.** *(Miles Cowsill)*

Left: **Passengers wrap up well on the open deck of the *Quiberon*.** *(Miles Cowsill)*

passengers disembarked the vessel an hour behind schedule. Channel Stevedores threatened legal action against Brittany Ferries for breach of contract.

Passenger volumes broke through the 750,000 level for the first time in 1983, reaching 755,316, and there was a slight recovery in the number of passenger vehicles to 140,413, and freight units to 24,302.

On 31st December 1983, Townsend Thoresen finally closed their Southampton passenger operation and transferred all their western Channel passenger services to Portsmouth. The Solent port had been the company's home since the start of the Thoresen Car Ferries operation in 1964. Townsend Thoresen began to make their mark in Portsmouth when 'Viking House' was built as their new office on a former car park at the entrance to Wharf Road from the Rudmore roundabout. Henceforth Brittany Ferries faced serious competition concentrated directly on the doorstep.

Six

On to Caen and Cherbourg

With Brittany Ferries' finances now on a much sounder footing, and plans for the Ouistreham route continuing to progress well behind the scenes, the UK team sought to update the corporate identity to bring a more modern feel to the public image. The Brittany Ferries logo had remained unchanged since the arrival of the *Armorique* in 1976, but was now looking outdated. The 'earthy orange' symbol deployed in a Franklin gothic condensed font was solid and chunky, but seemed more industrial than elegant, justifying the often-used analogy of being the 'Polish Railways' logo; the lower case 'brittany ferries' lacked the impact of a fresh, modern design. BCB began to work with Rook Dunning to develop a new logo for the 1984 season. A broad consensus emerged that a new Egyptian face with a slab serif introduced solidity and a sense of tradition, even though this was a slightly unusual font to employ at this time. The proposal was a strong visual device and worked in multiple environments; it looked good on an A4 letterhead but could be equally well employed on the hull of a vessel; this was a serious constraint in shipping logo design, when the practical considerations of how the device might be applied by a painter hanging from a crane trying to write letters twelve feet high on the side of a ship, were taken into account. The proposal adopted a two tone 'wave' logo above the name, with a new strapline 'The Holiday Fleet'. The identity retained the earth and sea stripe along each vessel's white hull, which was reflected in the colours of the new logo.

It fell to Ian Carruthers to convince Christian Michielini that this new direction was both appropriate and essential. There was considerable initial scepticism in France at the ideas of their British colleagues, but the team was eventually won over. There then began the long process of applying the new identity across the company; there was no desire in France to effect a rapid changeover to the new style, so the application had to wait until the next time each vessel was due to be repainted. The roll-out was hindered by a lack of instruction to painters at the shipyards; the use of stencils resulted in the funnel logo being applied back-to-front on several vessels. When this was drawn to Michielini's attention he shrugged and opined that no-one would notice, and he was proved right. Vessels were left in this state until

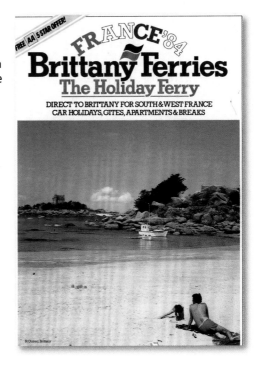

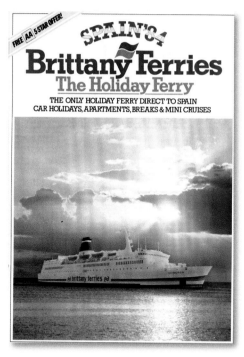

Brochures for the France (page 149), Spain, and Gîte products sporting a new logo for the 1984 season. *(Rook Dunning)*

their next repainting and the discrepancy went unremarked. Several iterations of orange and red colours were applied before a final colour evolved. The new font was used across promotional material to bring a common identity to the product, although brochures and some advertising appeared with both identities for a while.

As the quality of on board product began to improve, so the space used to promote the ships and their facilities took more prominence in the 1984 brochure. On board images of the *Armorique*, *Prince of Brittany* and *Quiberon* were used to support the prospect of a delightful taste of France from the moment passengers came on board vessels in the fleet. But the primary content was still destination- and product-led. From Relais and Châteaux Hotels to Le Manoir du Cleuziou, Seaside Hotels to Car Touring Holidays, there was something for everyone as the holiday products matured to offer ever more comprehensive coverage of the market. The brochure emphasised that, as the 'Number One' car ferry operator to France, Brittany Ferries was sailing with a more civilised fleet from the most convenient holiday ports in the UK to two exclusive ports in Brittany, many miles closer to the destination. This experience represented a beautiful start to a holiday.

Passenger fares increased marginally on French routes in 1984, from £23 to £23.50 single, with relatively minor changes on vehicle rates and cabin charges held on night crossings. It was a year of consolidation. Free AA Five Star cover was offered on all 'C' and 'D' tariff sailings, and with more 'C' tariff departures, the Company was able to claim that it was offering more low-priced summer sailings than before. The summer schedules replicated those of previous years, with the *Breizh-Izel* offering additional freight capacity on the Plymouth-Santander route during the summer months in support of the *Quiberon*. The Sunday Times observed that, in a survey of 20 Channel ferry services, the Portsmouth-St Malo route offered the cheapest ticket cost per mile, being less than one-third of the equivalent Dover-Calais rate.

With plans in place to expand the Portsmouth operation, focus switched back to the Plymouth-Roscoff route, where growing demand was putting increasing strain on the *Cornouailles*. After another exhaustive search, Mason identified the *Gelting Nord* as her potential replacement for the 1984 season. One of four sisters built by Meyer Werft in the 1970s, the vessel started life as the *Apollo,* operating for Viking Line between Kapellskär in Sweden, and Mariehamn and Nädendan in Finland, before being sold to Nordisk Færgefart and renamed *Gelting Nord*. She was 108.7 metres in length, 17.2 metres in breadth, and could carry 1,200 passengers and 260 cars at 18.5 knots. Brittany Ferries had some limited experience of operating her sister, *Viking 1,* during the disruption to service caused by the *Prince of Brittany* fire in 1982. Another of her sisters operated for Sealink from Portsmouth to the Channel Islands as the *Earl Granville,* the acquisition of which had been the last vessel transaction undertaken by Mason before he left Clarkson's to set up as an independent brokerage. So, he was very familiar with the vessel design

The *Bénodet* on passage between Plymouth and Roscoff during her first season. *(FotoFlite)*

and its capabilities.

The *Gelting Nord* entered service on 30th April as the *Bénodet,* named after the resort in southern Brittany, following a £3 million refit. The *Bénodet's* improved accommodation and increased capacity was a significant step up from the *Cornouailles,* allowing her to be released from service and chartered to SNCF for a two-year period to serve their Newhaven-Dieppe route. The *Bénodet* had a successful first season and was sent to St Malo for further refit work in the autumn. The *Penn-Ar-Bed*, which had been laid up since her period covering for the *Armorique* on the Portsmouth-St Malo route, was brought back into service on the winter Plymouth-Roscoff service when the *Cornouailles* headed for Newhaven in January.

The British government initiated the process to transfer Sealink from British Rail to the private sector, and the bid invitation drew the ire of trade unions, prompting a two-day strike in protest at the move by British seafarers. This brought a short-term dividend on 31st May, with Brittany Ferries' services unaffected. The privatisation process continued nonetheless, and the operation was rebranded as Sealink British Ferries when it was sold to Sea Containers in July 1984.

P&O Ferries also found their services disrupted by industrial disputes at Southampton, and for a time transferred the *Dragon* to operate from Portsmouth, with management of each movement handled by Brittany Ferries under contract on their behalf. At this stage Brittany Ferries had expansion plans and limited money, whilst P&O Ferries had money but no plans. Discussions were held between the two companies to consider if there was an Anglo-French solution to their respective issues; plans were drawn up for a schedule where 'Brown' Ferries and 'Blue' Ferries were timetabled to work in partnership in a similar fashion to the way P&O Ferries had operated with French and British ships in their fleet. From the Brittany Ferries perspective this was a 'back stop' solution if it did not prove possible to open the Ouistreham route by any other means, and the discussions eventually came to naught. But Carruthers sent a summary bill for the temporary handling arrangements in Portsmouth. When this was queried by P&O Ferries with a request for a full breakdown of costs incurred, Michielini retorted "tell them we're not in the plumbing business." The bill was paid.

New four-day wine tours for the serious wine lover were offered to Bordeaux, Medoc or the Loire in the autumn of 1984. The trip via St Malo took participants to visit châteaux in the wine growing regions, with the opportunity to buy wine at producers' prices. As an incentive, wine purchases did not have to be paid for until the return to Portsmouth, whilst Brittany Ferries arranged for the initial payment, customs clearance and duty payments. However, purchases were restricted to just twelve cases of wine per passenger!

In Ireland, Beverley Scanlon left Brittany Ferries in 1983, and was replaced as the Company's manager for Ireland by the internal promotion of Ann Upton. Upton married Denis Murphy in 1986; he was instrumental in establishing the Swansea-Cork Ferries operation and became the company's first chairman.

Talks with the city of Caen about opening the Portsmouth-Ouistreham service continued, but there was still widespread resistance to the project. The Breton shareholders struggled to understand why their Company needed to expand beyond the core business in the home region of Brittany. This step would move the operation away from the agricultural interests of the founding shareholders and require a substantial capital injection to execute. With each step eastwards, the interests of the original shareholders were being diluted and it was unclear how far east management ambitions would take the Company. Dieppe? Boulogne? Calais? The changed focus would also potentially detract from the existing services to St Malo and Roscoff.

The French government and many elected representatives on the Regional Council of Normandy also expressed their disquiet, but many of these voices had a vested interest. The clamour was led by the Cherbourg authorities, who feared that a pincer movement between services from Portsmouth to St Malo and Ouistreham could throttle the established Truckline freight service from Poole. Projections of a loss of 20% of freight business and a revenue deficit of FF5 million were circulated. Approval for the new Ouistreham route was not immediately forthcoming from Paris, and there was tension in the discussions as the government sought to retain a strong degree of involvement and control over Brittany Ferries' expansion plans.

Gourvennec faced up to the Calvados authorities when they received this government rejection. He observed that this was only to be expected, as the government had opposed plans to establish the early services from both Roscoff and St Malo, when their economic analysis suggested that the routes would not be successful. Brittany Ferries had proved otherwise in each case. On the contrary, he argued, government approval would have been a cause for concern... Gourvennec's lobbying worked, and regional plans began to be drawn up for the new route. The Calvados authorities were invited to inspect the UK operation to see how the route from Ouistreham would be managed; the authorities were particularly impressed by the reservations system, which convinced them that the new route could be handled professionally, with a high degree of relevant competence and a sound understanding of the market.

Meanwhile, the French government was also concerned at the growing strength of British-led competition, which threatened the continuation of French-flagged ferry services on the Channel. Both Brittany Ferries and Truckline were vulnerable to attack from Townsend Thoresen and Sealink British Ferries. If the two French operators could be

A well loaded *Quiberon* heads to sea from Ouistreham later in her career with company. The vessel was purchased by Brittany Ferries in December 1984. *(Miles Cowsill)*

encouraged to work together then perhaps there might be a solution. This was easier said than done, as there was considerable animosity between the two companies fuelled by the potential of the Portsmouth-Ouistreham route, and they were both competing hard against each other in the freight sector. But, approval for Ouistreham would strengthen Brittany Ferries' hand against British competitors.

Truckline had commenced cross-channel operations in June 1973, when they initiated their 64 nautical mile freight-only route from Poole to Cherbourg, the shortest crossing of the English Channel west of the Dover Straits. The Truckline business was established on three basic principles from the outset; it was to be an Anglo-French operation, it would be a freight-only route, and it would offer a high-quality service from one unencumbered port to another unencumbered port. All these principles had been sustained over the subsequent decade. Some 2,324 freight units were carried in the first year, and the Company gradually expanded. Financial difficulties encountered in the late 1970s were resolved by introducing French investors, and the business was able to introduce two new freight-only vessels in 1978, the *Coutances* and the *Purbeck*. By 1983 Truckline was carrying 65,000 freight units annually on the Poole-Cherbourg route, and in 1984 a second linkspan was installed at Poole and the port storage area expanded by 40 acres. This was a substantial business and had a dominant position in the freight market in the western Channel. There were no immediate prospects of a joint operation.

The new Portsmouth-Ouistreham route was formally launched to the media on 7th October 1984. Described as the first new cross-Channel route for some years, the Company emphasised that the route would open up access to Paris and the South of

The *Trégastel* at sea. *(Ferry Publications Library)*

France, particularly for those travelling from West London, the Midlands, and the West Country. Carruthers noted at the press conference that the new route had the backing of the French Minister of the Sea and would open the full potential of Normandy to the British holidaymaker. Trade reaction was very positive from the outset, as the new route would ease access to Lower Normandy, expand consumer choice in the western Channel and provide a strong challenge to other established operators, who were not renowned for their quality.

The option to purchase the *Quiberon* was exercised in December 1984, and she was bought for FF97.3 million supported by public aid of FF8.4 million. In the same month Townsend Thoresen responded to the Ouistreham challenge with the announcement that they would 'jumboise' the *Viking Valiant* and *Viking Venturer* to expand freight capability on the Portsmouth-Le Havre route. This would be achieved by adding a new bow section

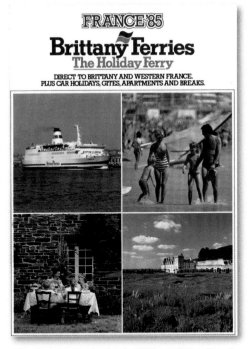

Two distinctive styles for the 1985 portfolio of brochures, with greater emphasis on the quality of the *Quiberon* in the Spanish brochure. *(Rook Dunning)*

to each vessel, lifting off the superstructure, and inserting an additional vehicle deck above the hull. The project was very freight-driven and little enhancement work was proposed to the vessels' passenger accommodation. But their operation would require the installation of new double deck linkspan facilities at both Portsmouth and Le Havre to enable the two levels of vehicle deck to be loaded on the vessel at the same time, improving the efficiency of turnarounds and substantially increasing the volume of freight that could be handled on each crossing. The work would be undertaken in early 1986, with both vessels returning to service before the Portsmouth-Ouistreham route opened.

On 3rd December, P&O Ferries acknowledged that their Southampton-Le Havre services could not compete with the shorter crossings from Portsmouth, and announced the move their operations to the Continental Ferry Terminal. It was to prove a short lived independent operation, as P&O Ferries was purchased by Townsend Thoresen for £12.5 million on 4th January 1985, and the British-registered *Dragon* and French-registered *Leopard* were absorbed into their established Portsmouth operation. The two vessels received upgraded passenger facilities and improvements to their propulsion units to enable them to sustain the more intensive crossing schedules from Portsmouth. The 1985 season saw the *Dragon* and *Leopard* allocated to the Portsmouth-Le Havre route, with the *Viking Valiant* and *Viking Venturer* switching to cover the Portsmouth-Cherbourg service.

Brittany Ferries experienced a small drop in tourist carryings in 1984, with passenger volumes falling by 3.2% to 731,422 and vehicles by 4.8% to 133,711, but freight traffic continued to grow with a rise of 11.8% to 27,162 units. With the pound sterling holding steady at an exchange rate of above FF11 throughout the year and prospects for the 1985 season of continued stability, corporate income was at the highest levels since Brittany Ferries had been established. Nonetheless, fares for the 1985 season had to remain competitive with the short-sea sector and increasing local competition from

Townsend Thoresen, so passenger and vehicle fares were reduced by up to twelve per cent in the high season and five per cent in low season. Thus, a family of two adults and two children saw a £20 reduction in their fare for the summer return journey to St Malo or Roscoff.

Holiday products were a key feature of Brittany Ferries' plans for the 1985 season; campers and caravanners were incentivised with the offer of a free overnight pitch at sites near Roscoff and St Malo when travelling on day crossings between Sunday and Thursday. This 'added value' approach avoided excessive discounting of off-peak sailings yet provided an attractive offer. Over 200 hotels were now featured in the 'Go as you please' programme, 90% of which were available in July and August.

Prices on the Plymouth-Santander route and the northern Spain holiday programme were raised by 5%, with the attraction of motoring breaks to the parador at Fuente Dé, the picturesque Comillas and the coastal resort of Rubadesella, as well as the established destinations of Santillana del Mar, San Sebastián and San Vicente de la Barquera. Carruthers said "the growing strength of our holiday products and allied programmes has enabled us to make our fare structure more competitive. We would like to see our ferry-only reservations grow again and I believe that our highly competitive fares stance in 1985 will help us achieve this objective. With the new larger ship on the Plymouth-Roscoff route, and the increase in holiday products on offer, we are confident that Brittany Ferries will consolidate their position as the number one tour operator to operate in both France and Spain".

The *Prince of Brittany* was refurbished during the winter period with attention to her cabins, increased seating provision in the cafeteria and a new reclining seat area.

The transfer of the *Bénodet* to a new venture in the Channel Islands in 1985 (chapter 7) created an opportunity to secure a further improvement in tonnage for the Plymouth-Roscoff route. Mason was sent to source the right ship and found the *Njegos*, then operating in Italy between Bari and Bar. She had been built in 1971 by Schiffau-Gesellschaft Unterweser in Bremerhaven and formerly operated as the *Travemünde* between Gedser and Travemünde. The 3,999 gross-tonne vessel offered capacity for 1,200 passengers and 370 cars, and at 20.5 knots offered greater operational resilience than the *Bénodet*. She offered 260 berths, predominantly in two-berth cabins, and reclining seat accommodation for 400 passengers. On board facilities included a 300-seat self-service coffee shop, a 200-seat restaurant, a children's playroom, bar, duty-free supermarket and a gift shop. The *Njegos* was renamed the *Trégastel*, after the commune in the Côtes-d'Armor department in Brittany. Her arrival would bring a doubling of capacity on the Plymouth-Roscoff route in just two years.

The *Trégastel* was sent to the Meyer Werft shipyard at Papenburg for a £750,000 refurbishment programme prior to her delivery, which included the fitting of a new reclining seat area. Carruthers flew over to the yard with Michielini to see how the work was progressing. The pair arrived in the captain's cabin to find the chief engineer and captain in earnest conversation with the shipyard team, debating the colour of the curtains to be used in the reclining seat lounge. Both individuals were seriously underqualified to make a judgement, yet the Company required them to make the decision, with untold lasting consequences for the ambience and appearance of the vessel. Michielini and Carruthers agreed that this method of approval had to stop. It was a wholly unprofessional approach and ran counter to all the work being undertaken to create and build a strong brand image for Brittany Ferries. A fresh approach was needed for future vessels, starting with the new ship for the Portsmouth-Ouistreham route.

The Normandy region was ready to facilitate quick implementation of the plans for the Portsmouth-Ouistreham route. A £25 million investment in building the port facilities at Ouistreham was announced in January 1985, having been ratified by the French government in the face of predictably stiff opposition from both Le Havre and Cherbourg. Gourvennec and Michielini, supported by Chollet, worked with the regional authorities to develop a new financial model to facilitate the developments based on their Sabemen experience. This became the inspiration for a new mixed economy company, the Société d'Équipement Naval du Calvados (Senacal), which was constituted on 10th June 1985 under the direction of Garrec. As with the Breton model, the new SEM would acquire the vessels required for the route and charter them back to Brittany Ferries at full commercial market rates. The primary shareholders of Senacal were to be the Basse Normandie region, the Calvados département, Brittany Ferries, the City of Caen and the Caen Chamber of Commerce.

This new development was a clear threat to existing operators, and British competitors were quick to suggest again that Brittany Ferries was receiving illegal subsidies. The concept of a ferry service providing secondary benefits to a wider community thereby

The *Trégastel* arrives in Plymouth to complete her maiden voyage from Roscoff. *(Ferry Publications Library)*

justifying regional investment over the long-term was one that seemed alien to the British psyche. There was no way in which an equivalent funding and financing model could be applied in the UK, even if such mechanisms were available, because the benefits of holiday traffic were largely in one direction, namely into France. The success of the SEM model depended on sustained confidence within the French shareholders of the ability of the UK team to continue to generate business as the route portfolio expanded. Rumours were spread in the British media about the nature of Brittany Ferries' funding, prompting the Company to contemplate a legal response, but this was not taken further to avoid exacerbating the issue.

Meanwhile, as 1985 progressed it became clear that Truckline was encountering severe financial difficulties. The company was no longer investing in its services and began to lose momentum against the expansion plans of Brittany Ferries and other operators in the western Channel. The sister freight vessels *Coutances* and *Purbeck* could carry 46 trailers but were proving too small to compete effectively in a growing market. Poole Harbour required significant dredging to accommodate the passage of any larger vessels. Shareholder Worms & Cie. began to look for a way to sell their interest in Truckline. Here was a rare opportunity to expand through the purchase of a competitor and strengthen the Company's grip on the western Channel freight business. Carruthers implored Michielini to lobby Gourvennec to buy Truckline whilst the opportunity was available and before anyone else got involved. But there was no money available from shareholders for a purchase of this scale, and this kind of transaction did not qualify for SEM support.

It took some time to convince Michielini of the merits of a deal and he in turn met strong resistance from his French colleagues. Gourvennec was eventually persuaded of the strategic value of the investment, and suggested that the SICA Saint-Pol-de -Léon

Left: **David Longden, Capt. Ivan Claireaux, Maria Hammett and Christian Michielini toast the arrival of the** *Trégastel* **at Plymouth.** *(Paul Burns)*

Right: **One of the lounge areas outside the passenger reception on the** *Trégastel*. *(Ferry Publications Library)*

might be able to help with their resources. Relationships between Gourvennec and Pierre Legras, a prominent spokesman for the Normandy region and chairman of Truckline, were strained from previous disputes about SEM funding, but eventually agreement was reached and the transaction was announced on 3rd July 1985. The acquisition proved a master stroke, restoring the credibility of Brittany Ferries, which had been accused of welcoming freight traffic during the winter months before discarding it in favour of the passenger business during the summer. The authorities in Cherbourg were sceptical about the consequences of the venture, believing that even a combined Truckline and Brittany Ferries would struggle in the face of competition from Townsend Thoresen, especially following the stretching of their vessels. Michielini and Carruthers gave a presentation on the way ahead; there was keenness to invest as the Cherbourg authorities felt they were losing out against the two SEMs. They were pacified when told of developing plans for a passenger service on the Poole route.

Brittany Ferries was visibly moving up several gears to become a major player in the market; in a short space of time it had announced the forthcoming opening of the

Portsmouth-Ouistreham route, the start of a new Channel Islands service, and now the purchase of Truckline. The ugly duckling was turning into a swan.

Acquiring Truckline enabled Brittany Ferries at a stroke to eliminate one of its main competitors in Normandy, increase fleet capacity and become the leading freight operator on the Western Channel. This was an entirely consistent development, as the addition of the new operation to the portfolio continued the long-established corporate strategy of stepping incrementally eastwards – first Roscoff, then St Malo and now Cherbourg, with Ouistreham (Caen) to follow. Each new route built on but protected the existing structure and made it increasingly difficult for any competitor to penetrate the power base of the Company.

A strong established name in the freight market, Truckline became the brand name for Brittany Ferries' freight services, with the distinctive yellow brand identity retained on the Poole fleet.

Poole's success in the freight market was based on fast clearance through the port formalities – it was marketed as the clearway port. A haulier could be guaranteed to be on the

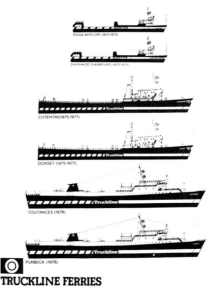

We are expanding

thanks to

your support

TRUCKLINE FERRIES
Telephone   Poole 71100   Telex 417144

Truckline advertisement showing the growth of their fleet. *(Ian Carruthers collection)*

The Truckline workhorse *Purbeck* with another well-loaded freight crossing. *(FotoFlite)*

road within an hour of landing at the port, whereas they could face substantial delays at competing ports further east. At this time the ports were full of handling, clearing and ships' agents, with plenty of people seeking to take a cut from the opportunities presented by international freight transport. Freight movements were generally slow, as bureaucracy intervened to extract the relevant taxes and charges. There was a huge parasitic industry still living off the back of the ferry operators, until electronic systems could be put in place to streamline the processes. This became another objective for the Company.

Shortly after the Truckline takeover Brittany Ferries announced the injection of £3.5 million to expand and improve the Poole-Cherbourg service. The *Coutances* and *Purbeck* were to be stretched by 15.5 metres, with deck capacity increased to handle 63 trailers. A contract for the transformation was awarded to Ateliers et Chantiers in La Rochelle, with the work to take place over a five-month period from January 1986. The Poole Harbour Authorities agreed to dredge the harbour to facilitate the passage of the larger ships. The *Coutances* left for the stretching work in January and returned at the end of March, when the *Purbeck* left to receive the same treatment.

The Truckline team worked from portacabins in Poole, reflecting a lack of investment by the company's previous owners, and signifying an absence of confidence in the longevity of the operation. The Poole Harbour Commissioners were unwilling to invest in a terminal to accommodate passengers as they also lacked confidence in the survival of the project. Carruthers wanted to create a central reservations office for all Brittany Ferries freight services, and persuaded Michielini that investing in a new terminal and office building at Poole that could accommodate staff transferred from Portsmouth, would be a significant statement about Brittany Ferries' intentions for Truckline. The office was built and opened in an heroic 120 days. British Channel Island Ferries (BCIF) reservations were moved to the new office under the management of Liz Rodgers, with the remainder of the accommodation used for the Group's freight business and a small team handling inbound French holiday business to a selection of around 150 classic English pubs with accommodation. Rodgers was another example of those who dedicated their career to Brittany Ferries; she had spent time as Carruthers' secretary and, as her experience grew, she took increasingly important roles in the Company.

With funding from Senacal in place, attention turned to finding a suitable vessel for the new Portsmouth-Ouistreham service. Mason was on a business visit to the Netherlands with Panos Marangopoulos (who had supplied the *Breizh-Izel*) to view a potential acquisition from Stoomvart Maatschappijby Zeeland (SMZ). It transpired that the ship, which had been on the sale list for two years, had just been sold, so the trip seemed to be a waste of time. However, the local broker said that the *Prinses Beatrix* had just been made available. She had a perfect configuration for the Portsmouth-Ouistreham route, and Mason knew instantly that she was the right acquisition. He rang Michielini and left a message to tell him to look up the vessel in the industry 'bible' and let him know his thoughts as quickly as possible. Michielini looked up the ship. There were two vessels named *Prinses Beatrix* in the book; he saw the first one, a woefully inadequate vessel, but did not turn the page to see the SMZ ship. He impolitely returned the call and suggested his time was being wasted, but when the right vessel was pointed out, Michielini immediately asked for the plans to be sent over. These were despatched to his house in Devon and Mason headed over from Rotterdam to go through them with Michielini in his dining room. This was another opportunity too good to miss, and an offer was quickly made.

The *Prinses Beatrix* was purpose-built in 1978 for the SMZ Hoek of Holland-Harwich route. A two-class vessel, she was 131 metres long and 22.6 metres in beam and could carry 1,500 passengers by night and 1,000 by day, together with 320 cars at a speed of 21 knots. She was already operating on a long overnight crossing, with a daytime return, so was highly suitable for the characteristics of the new Ouistreham route. The *Prinses*

Beatrix was formally acquired from SMZ on 1st October 1985 for FF101.8 million (supported by public aid of FF10.1 million), following negotiation of the deal by Michielini, Longden and Mason. It suited both parties to delay the transfer, so the *Prinses Beatrix* was immediately chartered back under bareboat arrangements to SMZ until her replacement, the new *Koningin Beatrix*, could enter service. After the deal had been struck, Stena Line made a counter, better offer for the *Prinses Beatrix*, but SMZ did the honourable thing and held to the price already struck. The *Koningin Beatrix* was delivered late, which forced Brittany Ferries to slightly delay the start of the Ouistreham service, but this allowed for better preparation.

The forthcoming opening up of the Ouistreham route was a major step forward for Brittany Ferries, and required a substantial sales effort to educate the travel trade and potential customers about the benefits of the new service. But the Ouistreham name was

The *Prinses Beatrix* in her SMZ Sealink Harwich-Hoek of Holland guise. *(FotoFlite)*

unfamiliar and henceforth the focus had to be on Caen, as the City was a much more readily identifiable destination for the British market. Portsmouth-Caen therefore became the name for the new service.

The Company opened an office on one of the industrial estates in Caen to host all the planning meetings for the new route; there was a huge amount of work to be completed before the route could open on the planned date in June 1986. The French arrangements and facilities in the port of Ouistreham were the preserve of Michielini and his team; Michel Mériadec moved from St Malo to take charge of the local development. The UK team handled the expansion at Portsmouth and set about generating traffic for the new route.

The sales effort in the UK began in autumn 1985, even before the first brochures were published. If the route was to stand any chance of success in its inaugural season it was imperative that it was featured by tour operators in their 1986 brochures, even though the port was in the early stages of construction and the ship's identity had yet to be revealed. The acquisition of the *Prinses Beatrix* could not be publicised as she was still operating from the Hoek of Holland to Harwich, and SMZ had yet to negotiate the impending changes to the service with their crews. Somehow the travel trade had to be given the confidence that the Caen service would materialise and deliver on all the promises about standards and quality.

The answer was to utilise the *Armorique* for a special sailing from Portsmouth to Caen in September 1985, taking key travel trade and tour operator personnel all the way up the canal from Ouistreham to visit the city. There were no port facilities in place to be viewed as the vessel passed Ouistreham; the area earmarked for the linkspan and marshalling area was still the site of the Canadian war memorial, and a gypsy camp lay behind this. The memorial had yet to be relocated, with due solemnity and respect, to a more prominent position on the roundabout at the entrance to the port. Tour operators were told that the route was definitely going to happen; the immediate future and success of the service depended on their confidence, because featuring a new route in a brochure

The *Armorique* visits Caen in September 1985 with a full complement of travel trade personnel on board. *(Ferry Publications Library)*

when there are no facilities in place takes a degree of optimism.

It was a mark of Brittany Ferries' standing with the UK travel trade that the Company was trusted to fulfil its promises and the Portsmouth-Caen route was featured in all the relevant brochures for the 1986 season. Bookings were quickly generated for a route that only existed on paper, albeit with substantial infrastructure under construction. It was hugely important to get the route off to a good start.

The UK team never wavered in their enthusiasm for the project, believing that Portsmouth-Caen would become the defining route for the Company. The service needed an identity that would distinguish it from the competition. Brittany Ferries was already established as the 'Holiday Fleet'; what else could be said? Derek Brightwell, Bill Rook and Richard Dunning looked at ways of giving the route a strong identity and identified the concept of the 'By-pass to Holiday France', as a key distinguishing factor. The new route would operate to a purpose-built port remote from the industrial areas that characterised other French ports east of St Malo. The proposition became to take the by-pass; by-pass busy Calais, by-pass industrial Le Havre, by-pass it all and come straight to the attractive part of Normandy. It was a winning formula. Few anticipated that within two years it would become the busiest route on the channel outside Calais, carrying over one million passengers each year.

The actions taken to manage pricing in advance of the 1985 summer season helped business recover from the falls of 1984, with growth of 19.5% in passengers to 873,728, and 13.9% in vehicles to 152,312, and a mammoth 211.8% growth in freight to reach 84,694 units, the latter boosted by the Truckline acquisition. In a single year, Brittany Ferries had been transformed into a significant player in the cross-Channel freight market and prospects for the 1986 season looked good.

Yet, amidst these positive developments for Brittany Ferries, the British and French governments requested the submission of proposals for a fixed link tunnel under the Channel in April 1985. This was the outcome of a process agreed by Margaret Thatcher and François Mitterrand in 1981 to examine the potential for a privately funded project,

The *Armorique* arriving at St Malo on a morning sailing from the UK. *(Miles Cowsill)*

one that was as much about creating activity in the construction sector for a vanity project as it was about meeting any perceived lack of capacity. The ferry industry reacted to the news from their different perspectives. Townsend Thoresen predicted that fares would fall and marginal services around the English coast from Portsmouth to Felixstowe would close. Sealink British Ferries countered that the Tunnel would wipe out short-sea services, but regional routes away from direct competition from the link would prosper. Brittany Ferries expressed the view that "we don't think a fixed link will affect the western Channel much." Potential bidders went away to prepare their proposals against a remarkably short submission deadline of 31st October 1985.

It was still the practice to lay-up ships during the winter period in St Malo, as there was insufficient business to sustain their continued off-season operation. The UK team tried several ideas to try and generate revenue. The *Armorique* would make a perfect hotel for short breaks if she were moored alongside the quay in St Malo, but the ship would still need to be heated, with all facilities open to create a welcoming environment, which created insurmountable costs. Car cruising was another concept developed by the team. The *Armorique* could be utilised to sail to the Channel Islands and pick up hire cars at the end of the season, before returning to the UK. She would then sail with passengers for the Iberian coast and North Africa, replicating the former P&O service. Passengers would have access to the hire cars on the car deck and be able to head ashore at each port for a day exploring the locality. But, as with the cruise service tried previously, cabin facilities on the *Armorique* were designed for a maximum of one or two nights use and the idea was not taken forward. The team kept looking for new ideas.

The Cherbourg authorities supported Brittany Ferries' acquisition of Truckline having been offered the prospect of a passenger service on the Poole-Cherbourg route. Introducing this operation from the 1986 summer season would place pressure on Sealink British Ferries' established service from Weymouth to Cherbourg, whilst tapping into latent demand from the affluent hinterland of Poole and Bournemouth. The plan envisaged the *Coutances* and *Purbeck* continuing to operate as freight-only vessels, with the surplus *Cornouailles* offering additional twice-daily seasonal freight capacity whilst

Sealink's *Transcontainer 1* passes the aircraft carrier HMS *Invincible* as she enters Portsmouth Harbour on 14th August 1985 during the short lived service from Dieppe handled by Brittany Ferries. *(John Hendy)*

simultaneously testing the passenger market potential with a summer service carrying a maximum of 300 passengers on each sailing. However, standards of accommodation on the *Cornouailles* could not match the quality of those now being enjoyed by passengers on Brittany Ferries' other routes. Branding this as a Brittany Ferries operation could unrealistically raise expectations about the product offer on the Poole-Cherbourg route, whilst potentially dragging down the image of the parent Company. Simpler standards prompted a simple solution.

Regular travellers in France were already highly familiar with the 'Les Routiers' brand. Established in Paris in 1934, it started as a published guide to the best independent restaurants and accommodation for French road travellers. A 'Les Routiers' plaque on a building signified that the establishment was well-managed, clean and hospitable, with good food and excellent service at a reasonable price. The brand expanded to encompass a wide range of traditional hotels, guest houses, bed & breakfast establishments, restaurants, bars, bistros and cafés, all of which offered a high standard of cuisine, served by friendly staff and value for money, delivered in an establishment that was passionate about maintaining excellent standards across the business.

The inspired solution to the Truckline problem was to rebrand the passenger service 'Les Routiers', thereby establishing a precise mental image of what could be expected. The on board product was simple and unpretentious because all passengers got a meal in the same way as in a Les Routiers restaurant. All aspects of the service reflected the same simplicity, whether in a meal on board, or in a cup of coffee or a beer. The concept was an immediate and easily marketable success, helping also to establish and promote the Les Routiers brand in the UK. The route was given its own brochure in a simple distinctive style, with the Les Routiers logo on the cover; it became the 'Insider's way to France' helping establish the image of something special and different.

In a further foray into the freight market, Brittany Ferries became the handling agents for a short lived service operated from March 1985 by the French arm of Sealink from Dieppe to Portsmouth utilising the freighter *Transcontainer 1*. Traffic levels did not meet expectations on what was a 'dog-leg' service across the Channel, and the service closed in October.

The competition to design and construct the Channel Tunnel reached a crescendo on 31st October, when the entries were submitted. One of the four short listed bidders was the Channel Expressway proposal, developed by Sea Containers despite their recent acquisition of Sealink British Ferries, which envisaged a drive through road tunnel with separate rail tracks. Although public opinion strongly favoured any drive through proposal, the winning entry was a more conventional twin rail tunnel submitted by the Channel Tunnel Group/France-Manche. Their success was announced at a joint meeting between the British and French premiers in Lille on 20th January 1986. The project comprised two rail tunnels and a central service tunnel, linking shuttle terminals at Cheriton and Coquelles. Road traffic would be carried on drive through rail vehicle shuttles between the two terminals, with half the tunnel capacity purchased by British Rail and SNCF for through train services between London and Paris. This gave Eurotunnel, the new Anglo-French operating concession holder, a significant guarantee of future income.

The ferry industry mounted a strong campaign against the tunnel under the 'Flexilink' banner, much to the bemusement of continental authorities. The main short-sea ferry operators were British -based private sector companies, who combined resources for an intensive media campaign which was continued over the next two years. But British and French government support for the venture was not swayed by the Flexilink campaign, and formal approval for construction was given by both governments in 1987. Ferry operators now had six years to contemplate their response to the planned completion and opening of the Channel Tunnel in 1993. The huge future increase in capacity in the Dover Straits sector that the tunnel would facilitate posed an existential threat to the ferry industry right across the English Channel. But with geography remaining at the heart of the Brittany Ferries proposition, the Company was less concerned at the development than some of its rivals.

The message from Carruthers to the Roscoff team was clear. Brittany Ferries was in a fortunate position in the western Channel; as the Company added capacity and opened new routes, more passengers and freight vehicles arrived at the ports to fill the vessels. Further capacity yielded more people, and more freight; it was evident that the Company was doing something right. The focus on destination advertising was working, despite being at variance with the ship-led approaches of other ferry operators; it was the holiday destination that created the need for the cross-Channel crossing, not the other way round. The destination was the key to success. This was how the Channel Tunnel would be resisted, so the message remained consistent and simple. France and Spain are great places to go on holiday and Brittany Ferries is the best way to get there. And if you

The Brittany Ferries parrot became a memorable icon for the Company. *(Rook Dunning)*

sail with the Company, your French or Spanish holiday will start the moment you board the vessel. But Brittany Ferries' advertising continued to focus on being destination-led, as fleet quality had not matured sufficiently to be the focus for promotional activity.

As Brittany Ferries' route expansion plans unfolded there was an increasing need to expand brand awareness by building better name recognition. Two new routes launched in the portfolio in the same year was a big challenge, but the problem remained that Brittany Ferries was a less familiar brand than their long-established competitors, who benefited from the visibility created by larger advertising budgets supporting wider route structures and the opportunity to cross-sell between routes. BCB were asked to look at how this problem could be overcome. Carruthers and Longden were convinced that the Brittany Ferries campaigns had to be more minimalist than those produced by the major international advertising agencies of their competitors, yet be distinctive enough to be unforgettable. The BCB proposal was to invest in television advertising, but to do so in way that was fresh and memorable, otherwise the campaign would be a waste of resources. Working closely with Rook Dunning, a multitude of ideas were considered. Finally it was decided to bring a talking parrot to the television screens and radio in 1986. This would meet the brief in being both different and difficult to forget, but was a radical change from the brand image that had hitherto been created.

The concept was a tough sell to the team in Roscoff, whose perception of both France and Brittany Ferries was at odds with the image of a talking parrot; their personal world of Dior and Chanel contrasted with the rural idyll of 2CVs and unspoiled landscapes being promoted in Britain. The adverts went into production, with leading director Bryan Forbes at the helm and a voice-over provided by actor and comedian Kenneth Williams, performing at his most camp. Carruthers arrived at the BCB offices one day to find the stairway swamped by parrots waiting to audition for the part. The 'winning' parrot was Pierre, who came from Marwell Zoo. In the pre-digital manipulation era, the adverts had to be shot live, with the parrot mimicking words that were later added by voice-over. This was not the easiest effect to achieve. Pierre was fed peanuts interspersed with pebbles; each time he received a pebble the inedible object was spat out, thereby creating the mouth movement that was later edited to simulate speech. His repetition of 'Brittany Ferries' became an advertising cliché.

The sums of money involved in an advertising campaign were substantial, but this proved to be an outstanding investment. Carruthers and Longden knew that the adverts were a success when staff reported they had found themselves being mimicked by parrot voices as they travelled to work in uniform. The parrot played an unlikely but very significant role in putting the Brittany Ferries name on the map.

Less visible but equally effective were a string of radio advertisements featuring speaking cars. The campaign focused on getting name and destination recognition across the airwaves. 'Hello, I'm an Austin 1100, nice to meet you - you're a Ford Capri?'. 'Well it's nice here in Brittany Ferries' garage, isn't it? Where's your owner taking you?' The cars held conversations that culminated in linkage of Brittany Ferries and the destination. 'Very Brittany, very Brittany Ferries'. The message was again not about the ships but the destination and the holiday experience.

In early January 1986, the *Cornouailles* returned from her SNCF charter to cover the

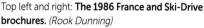

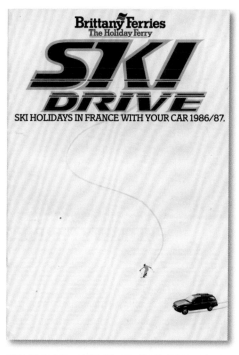

Top left and right: **The 1986 France and Ski-Drive brochures.** *(Rook Dunning)*

Right: **The 1986 advertising campaign.** *(Rook Dunning)*

Poole-Cherbourg freight operation with the *Breizh-Izel*, whilst the *Coutances* went away to be lengthened. The latter returned to Poole on 30th March to release the *Purbeck* to head for La Rochelle to receive the same treatment. The *Armorique* was chartered to SMZ between 25th March and 16th April to operate on the Harwich-Hoek of Holland route alongside the *Prinses Beatrix*, pending the delayed entry into service of the new *Koningin Beatrix*. For a time, therefore, both vessels operating on the Dutch route were owned by Brittany Ferries.

Several attempts were made to sell the *Cornouailles* at this stage. One scheme envisaged the vessel being purchased by an Iranian group with big plans for the ship; they knew exactly where they were going to put a mosque on board. The proposal was backed by the French Overseas Guarantee scheme for a while, but they eventually refused permission for the transaction. A separate Egyptian proposition also came close to being finalised when an offer was received for the $10 million asking price; but the Egyptians wanted the transaction to include an invoice for $14 million and Mason and the team smelt a rat. The *Cornouailles* remained a Brittany Ferries vessel.

Meanwhile, Townsend Thoresen announced that they would transfer the two remaining vessels in their 'Super Viking' fleet from Felixstowe to Portsmouth from spring 1986, to replace the *Dragon* and *Leopard*. The new configuration envisaged the *Viking Viscount* and *Viking Voyager* covering the Portsmouth-Cherbourg link, whilst their jumboised sisters *Viking Valiant* and *Viking Venturer,* which would return from their stretching exercise sporting a distinct ungainly appearance, offered enhanced freight capacity to Le Havre. The withdrawal of the *Leopard* led to industrial disputes with her French crew, a situation resolved by placing the *Viking Voyager* under the French registry for her first season of operation on the Cherbourg route.

The start of 1986 saw Brittany Ferries begin a serious attempt to become the leading gîte provider in France. This business had traditionally been dominated by Gîtes de France, an organisation set up by the French government in the 1950s to encourage farmers to restore dilapidated farm buildings. The company operated from a central office in Paris and grew to market around 30,000 properties right across France. These were sold across Europe with an allocation of properties given to the office in London which could be booked directly by members of the Amis des Gîtes de France who, in

The proximity of the new facilities at Ouistreham to the open sea is evident as a coach leaves the *Armorique*. *(Ferry Publications Library)*

return for an annual fee of £3, received a handbook listing 1,500 properties. Unlike Gîtes de France, Brittany Ferries had the advantage of selling through 6,000 travel agents across Britain, and a reservation system adapted to accommodate the growth in gîte business and integrate it with the ferry reservation. Gîtes de France responded by upgrading its own system and offered special ferry rates with Sealink British Ferries and Sally Line instead of gîte-only arrangements. But Brittany Ferries retained the advantages of route geography and anticipated significant growth in the 1986 season with the opening of new geographical opportunities by the route from Portsmouth to Caen. The number of gîtes was increased from 600 to 700, with additional properties in the most popular destinations of Brittany and the Loire Valley. More properties were added in

Normandy in anticipation of the opening of the new route, as only 2% of Britons holidaying in France stayed in this area.

A new Ski-Drive brochure offering winter holidays was accompanied by a press release which attracted considerable attention when it stated that 'the programme offers a good standard of self-catering apartments, all within 200 kilometres of the slopes.'

Brittany Ferries took delivery of the *Prinses Beatrix* on 1st May 1986 and immediately sent her to dry dock in Rotterdam for a refit which included conversion to a one-class ship. Lessons were learned from the *Trégastel* experience, and a competition was initiated to re-design her interior, with leading design houses invited to present their ideas. Several British design teams went across to Roscoff to present their concepts; they commonly suggested black wood, dark finishes and tartan fabrics – features typical of other cross-Channel vessels of the time. In contrast, a French designer painted a poetic picture of how the vessel should recreate images of the sea at her bow, with the land featuring at the stern; the internal décor ought to reflect the motion of the waves. The reviewing panel was blown away by these ideas from Bernard Bidault of Architectes Ingénieurs Associés (AIA), a company well known for their work in hospitals, in this, their first foray into the marine environment. The presentation marked the start of an enduring and productive partnership which embraced not just the on board design but extended to terminal and building works as well. The AIA designs on *Duc de Normandie* included a French-style patisserie with café furniture and rustic signage, a Brasserie restaurant, and a cafeteria resembling a French motorway service station. The aim was to bring a taste of Breton life from the moment passengers boarded the vessel; the décor was aligned with trends in the most modern cruise ship and Scandinavian cruise ferry design.

Brittany Ferries' existing cadre of engineers were insufficiently experienced to undertake major project work on this scale, so Michielini looked for an experienced naval architect to support delivery of the upgrade works; Bureau Veritas recommended Michel Maraval from the shipyard at La Rochelle as project manager. Although his parents ran a farm at Fontainebleau, Maraval was a mechanical and naval engineer, a graduate of the Nantes Central School, the Nantes Institute of Administration and Harvard. He joined Brittany Ferries in 1985, and his passion for marine design was to help define the Company's brand in the coming years and laid the foundations for his eventual rise to become Directeur Général of the Company. He immediately made his mark on the *Prinses Beatrix,* which emerged from Rotterdam renamed the *Duc de Normandie*, the Norman title of William the Conqueror.

The *Armorique* undertook two further special sailings for the travel trade to Caen at the beginning of June 1986 in the run up to the opening of the facilities at Ouistreham. All was set fair for the next major step in the expansion of Brittany Ferries.

Shortly before the *Duc de Normandie* made her inaugural arrival in Portsmouth on 5th June 1986, Carruthers received a call in his office from the QHM to ask why the vessel had not taken on a pilot as she approached the port. He responded that the captain was well qualified and held a pilotage licence based on his many previous visits to the port. The QHM replied that the *Duc de Normandie* was not named on his certificate. "Surely we can rectify that when the ship arrives", said Carruthers. But again, the QHM said the *Duc de Normandie* would not be allowed into the port. Carruthers asked where the QHM had got the information on certification from, would it perhaps be from representatives of Townsend Thoresen, who just happened to be on the pilotage committee? The problem was quickly resolved but illustrated the lengths to which competitors would go to try and impede Brittany Ferries whenever possible.

The first sailing of the *Duc de Normandie* from Portsmouth to Caen left on the evening on 5th June 1986 to arrive symbolically in Normandy on 6th June, the anniversary of D Day. Forty veterans were invited to accompany the first sailing in an emotional return to the beaches. Royal Engineers' Captain Sidney Clarke recalled that "this is rather different from 42 years ago. We were under constant attack. There was smoke everywhere. You could not tell if it was day or night".

The *Duc de Normandie* represented a revolution in standards, inaugurating a new generation of vessels. For the first time the interior of a Brittany Ferries vessel had been designed with passenger aesthetics and wellbeing in mind; she represented a triumph of AIA design. The restaurants, public areas, retail facilities, integrated bakery, all featured décor designed to bring an immediate taste of France to the British traveller. The Claude Monet salon featured a Calvados still; the wine bar had a cider press. Everything was designed to give a coordinated impression of French life. Carruthers noted that the new Portsmouth-Caen route would particularly benefit tourist to Normandy, as well as those wanting to travel on quickly to Paris and the south of France. He observed that the main

The first arrival of the *Duc de Normandie* in Portsmouth. *(Ferry Publications Library)*

A13 autoroute to Paris started in Caen, thereby providing fast driving links to the French capital, and the new port was also the nearest English Channel gateway to the Loire Valley.

Longden recalled: -

"Some of the cabins on the *Duc de Normandie* were fairly near to the ship's propeller shafts which, without the benefit of modern-day laser alignment, constantly vibrated. Whenever you moved anything in the cabins bits of folded up paper and scrunched up cigarette packets would fall out; as soon as they were removed, there was another vibration. Invariably these were the cabins allocated to staff travel but they soon realised that the best option was to get as close to the showers and toilets as possible - and don't touch any of those bits of paper. Every time you travelled, you'd find a new noise that needed plugging..."

These cabins were always the last to be sold, and pursers were instructed to give complainants a full refund of their accommodation charges with that statement that the noise only occurred at certain levels of power output and they must have been unlucky. Maraval later attempted to solve the problem by reprofiling the stern of the vessel, but the new configuration made little difference

For the Portsmouth team the opening of the new route represented a dramatic change of pace, shifting gear from the twice-daily sailings to St Malo to competing head on with Townsend Thoresen with the additional daily sailings to Caen. The *Duc de Normandie*

Top left: **The *Duc de Normandie* arrives in Ouistreham on her inaugural crossing from Portsmouth.** *(Miles Cowsill)*

Bottom left: **The cafeteria area on the *Duc de Normandie*.** *(Miles Cowsill)*

Right: **Plenty of seating available on the open deck at the stern of the *Duc de Normandie*.** *(Miles Cowsill)*

operated three crossings each day during the summer, with no Monday afternoon sailing from Portsmouth so that her schedule placed the weekend sailings in a consistent configuration to meet the peaks in outbound and return traffic. Demand for the new service from both passenger and freight businesses was overwhelming, with the *Coutances*, *Purbeck* and *Prince of Brittany* all being transferred to offer additional sailings to support the Portsmouth-Caen route. From mid-September the autumn/winter schedule was eased to offer one round trip each day, leaving Portsmouth at 08:30 and Caen at 23:00.

The opening of the service offered the opportunity to forge more formal links between the civic authorities and communities of Portsmouth and Caen which led to a joint agreement being signed on 5th June 1987 at the Guildhall in Portsmouth. The two cities declared that they would undertake to foster exchanges and meetings between their respective citizens in all fields of endeavour, including commerce and social pursuits. A second ceremony was held in the Hotel de Ville, Caen the following day. Since then the Lord Mayor of Portsmouth has made an annual visit to Caen to lay wreaths at the D Day commemoration ceremonies.

A week after the opening of the Portsmouth-Caen route, the *Cornouailles* formally opened the Les Routiers passenger service between Poole and Cherbourg on 14th June 1986, offering up to four single crossings each day. The Mayor of Poole was hosted by his counterpart in Cherbourg at a special lunch as a full complement of passengers

Aboard the *Duc de Normandie*

Top left: **A two berth luxury cabin.** *(Miles Cowsill)*

Bottom Left: **The L'Alambic bar at the stern of D deck.** *(Miles Cowsill)*

Right: **The La Brioche Doree tea room on D Deck.** *(Miles Cowsill)*

disembarked. Carruthers hinted at a growing relationship with the port of Poole, stating that the Company was looking to introduce a service to the Channel Islands from the port. He paid tribute to the team that had completed the £4 million scheme in just 187 days. The new route was an overwhelming success, helped by a 'Beware of Tourists' campaign in local media, which drew attention to the presence of the new route in a highly creative way.

The new Portsmouth-Caen service opened up the potential to consider new areas for the holiday business much further east than the existing portfolio. Carruthers and Longden went to visit Josee Dyer, who by now had left Brittany Ferries and moved to Paris with her husband. The Dyers had built Albion, a company specialising in helping large corporations establish a presence in France. The two outlined their ambitions for a programme of apartment-based short break holidays of three-, four- and seven-night duration. Dyer agreed to source the necessary apartments and found a range with suitable car parking near the centre of Paris, each of which was also conveniently located for visits to the popular tourist destinations of Versailles and Fontainebleau. A special brochure was produced to promote the Parisian opportunity, with breaks starting from £62 per person, including a car. Press trips were arranged, and journalists reported enthusiastically about the new product. But the idea of a city break by car did not take off – the last thing people wanted on a break in Paris was a car - and the programme of holidays lasted just one season. Another valuable lesson.

The jumboised *Viking Venturer* entered service for Townsend Thoresen on the Portsmouth-Le Havre route on 26th June, with sister vessel *Viking Valiant* following on

The Honfleur restaurant on D deck of the *Duc de Normandie* showcased the new standards of cuisine offered by Brittany Ferries. *(Miles Cowsill)*

3rd July; their thrice-daily crossings brought a significant uplift to the freight-carrying capability of the route. Townsend Thoresen was fighting back against Truckline and the opening of the Caen route.

Later in the year in a twist of fortune, Townsend Thoresen found itself facing a takeover bid by the P&O Group; the two had complementary property portfolios and many synergies in their shipping interests. In a reversal of previous changes, Townsend Thoresen was acquired by the P&O Group on 5th December 1986, with the £345 million deal confirmed on 19th January 1987. The P&O Group assumed full management of the Townsend Thoresen ferry networks from the end of February 1987.

By the end of October Brittany Ferries was able to announce that they had broken through the one million passenger level for the first time in the previous twelve months. Freight demand was growing rapidly, with over 100,000 units carried to France and

Spain, consolidating the Company as the number one freight carrier on the western Channel. With two new routes firmly established on the eastern flank, management attention turned to the problem of accommodating increasing demand on the Plymouth-Santander service, which was beginning to exceed the capacity offered by the *Quiberon*. Consideration was given to stretching the *Quiberon*, but Michielini was more ambitious. With financing more readily available through the SEM, there were opportunities to consider a more radical solution. Thus, the *Bretagne* project was born.

But there remained some serious internal problems to be addressed. The annual strike pattern amongst Brittany Ferries' seafarers, was highly disruptive to both passengers and freight customers, and could not continue if Brittany Ferries was to remain a credible cross-Channel operator. The industrial relations atmosphere was changing, particularly in

The *Cornouailles* opened the Poole-Cherbourg service in 1986. *(Miles Cowsill)*

the UK, where government reforms were tilting the balance of power towards company management, encouraging more bullish attempts to curb the perceived excesses of trade union power. This was to become one of the most challenging social conflicts in the history of Brittany Ferries.

In December 1986, services were disrupted by a further day of action by ships' crews working in the Hotel Services division, who sought equality of holiday entitlement with more senior staff, and job guarantees to match those enjoyed by other seafarers. The Hotel Services staff were largely employed on a seasonal basis and recruited under the French Maritime Labour Code, which was an expensive social scheme for the Company. Very few staff chose to return every year, making the process of recruitment and training both laborious and costly, whilst failing to deliver the consistency of quality needed in the on board product. This particular industrial action, coming on the back of the regular series of spring strikes, prompted a strong reaction. Michielini knew precisely when to strike back.

Brittany Ferries' insurance arrangements required crew on board at all times in order to take a ship out to sea from the tidal berths in Roscoff and St Malo if the need arose. Vessels were permitted to remain on their berth in Plymouth or Portsmouth, but still needed to be manned for security purposes. The crew recognised these requirements and shared the manning duties amongst themselves during strike periods so that everyone ended up losing the same amount of pay. Michielini believed that any trade union battle had to be fought on the Company's terms at a convenient moment, with strikers feeling the pain in their pocket. He discussed a way forward with Carruthers,

The double-deck loading capability of P&O European Ferries' stretched 'Super-Viking' class offered signiificant advantages over the single deck of the *Duc de Normandie*. A port shuttle bus awaits foot passengers at Portsmouth.
(Miles Cowsill)

seeking to establish how the fleet could be berthed without needing to be manned. The two agreed that a prime opportunity presented itself over the Christmas season.

Carruthers was concerned that passengers could find themselves stranded if there were no contingency plans in place during a possible shutdown. He approached Bob Kirton of Townsend Thoresen for help in moving passengers and freight if Brittany Ferries was unable to carry them; would Townsend Thoresen be able to accept them? Brittany Ferries held the ticket money but needed help in accommodating the traffic... The two companies already had reciprocal arrangements in place to cover disruption to services, and the positive response helped clear the way for action. This allowed smooth arrangements to be in place for customers. The plans could now be enacted.

Brittany Ferries announced that the fleet would be laid up as usual over the 1986 festive period. The fleet was then moored on safe berths in port or inside the locks at St Malo, and the crews went home for the festive season. They then received a letter from the Company instructing them not to return after the Christmas break. There was uproar; the trade unions demanded to know what was going on. But Michielini held the line. No crews would be allowed back to sea until they would give a guarantee that passengers and freight customers would not be held to ransom again. Blackmail would not be tolerated. Brittany Ferries made it clear that the Company would wait as long as it took for crews to return, even if the business was forced to close.

There was strong support for the Company from passengers and freight customers, who understood the need for the action. Some 400 passengers found their return holiday journeys disrupted and were offered alternative crossings with Townsend Thoresen. The stand-off with the trade unions dragged on into 1987 and lasted for twelve days before settlement could be reached and the crews started to return to work. The final agreement was comprehensive and addressed a number of long standing issues on all sides; there would be no recruitment of foreign seamen, and an additional 13th month of salary for crews, but they would be entitled to twelve fewer days of leave. When the crews did return there was a festering anger, encouraged by trade union leaders. Michielini wisely made it clear that Brittany Ferries' stance was not anti-union, but if trade unions took action in May the Company would respond in January. There was a need for common sense to prevail; much as Brittany Ferries might like to rid itself of trade unions, they served a purpose and doing away with them was not on the agenda.

One unintended consequence was that the trade union leaders came under sustained threat from their colleagues and neighbours, who began to appreciate that the future of Brittany Ferries, and many jobs in the region, was being put at risk by their actions. The crews enjoyed some of the best jobs in Brittany, with some 2,000 employed directly and indirectly by Brittany Ferries, many of whom were young employees who would find few job opportunities elsewhere. The position of the trade union leaders became untenable and many left the Company.

The 1986 season proved to be a defining step forward for Brittany Ferries. The addition of a partial year's carryings on the Portsmouth-Caen route and the opening of the Poole-Cherbourg passenger service helped passenger volumes grow by a healthy 34.8% to hit 1,117,886 passengers. Vehicle carryings recorded a 61.1% rise to reach 245,352, and there was growth of 15.9% in freight traffic to 98,176 units. The confidence placed by the Company in the ability of the UK team to generate traffic for the new route was amply rewarded, easily demonstrating that if additional capacity was available it could be filled. Investment in the *Duc de Normandie* showed the Company's ability to raise on board standards and create the highest quality service of any fleet on the English Channel. This gave substantial credibility to Gourvennec and Michielini in their relationships with the SEMs, making future investment a much easier proposition. Brittany Ferries looked forward to a full year of operation for the Portsmouth-Caen route in 1987 and could begin to contemplate building a bespoke flagship that embodied all of the positive characteristics that the Company stood for.

Seven

A Channel Islands venture

As the contracted port works in Portsmouth to accommodate the Caen service neared completion in 1983, Brittany Ferries was a long way from opening the new route, as the plans were not fully developed, there was no vessel earmarked for the service, and the port facilities at Ouistreham were some way from approval. But Brittany Ferries was committed to paying an enhanced level of port dues with the potential for a £300,000 annual deficit in the finances, as the St Malo route traffic only incurred annual dues of £300,000. This was a sum that the Company could ill-afford. There had to be some way of plugging the gap until the Caen service started. At the same time the Company was still looking to dispose of the *Penn-Ar-Bed,* which was only operating an intermittent basis. Could she be part of a solution?

The States of Jersey's desire to introduce competition on their mainland shipping services prompted thought of a solution to the port dues problem. Two other interested parties, Mike Hendry of Cenargo, and Peter Morton of Merchant Ferries, held discussions with Ian Carruthers, and the trio focused on the opportunities for the *Penn-Ar-Bed* to be utilised on a Channel Islands service. If Cenargo purchased the *Penn-Ar-Bed* and operated her from Portsmouth on a service managed by Brittany Ferries, the port charges at Portsmouth would absorb a significant proportion of the excess £300,000 that the Company would have to be paying to Portsmouth City Council anyway. The financial problem would be minimised, and the *Penn-Ar-Bed* would have a new home. But she was inadequate for the long overnight crossings from Portsmouth to the Channel Islands and could not compete with the established Sealink product. The parties agreed not to progress the idea at this time, and plans to start a possible service from 1984 were put on hold.

Then Carruthers was approached by Colin Carter, who was working on behalf of Roger Bale of Sealab Securities, a company which had significant financial interests in a variety of Channel Island businesses. Bale was chairman of Huelin Renouf, a long-established freight carrier to the Islands, which operated a lift-on-lift-off container service from Portsmouth, and had extensive distribution interests in both Guernsey and Jersey. A meeting was convened in Jersey and the participants quickly widened to include MMD, then Sealink's biggest freight customer on their Channel island services, who operated in Portsmouth from a large warehouse at Flathouse Quay, which lay just to the south of the Albert Johnson Quay. MMD brought the potential for a substantial amount of freight traffic, with the added opportunity to undermine Sealink's business. Freight rates on ferry services to the Channel Islands were significantly higher than on cross-Channel ferry services, in part because of the Sealink monopoly, but also because it was a market of finite size. There was general agreement that there was scope to take a proposal forward, especially if Brittany Ferries could source a more appropriate ship than the *Penn-Ar-Bed.* The idea of Channel Island Ferries was born, and the three parties established the company, splitting the shareholding between them.

Brittany Ferries' participation in the concept was sold to Christian Michielini on the basis that there was no risk of any significant capital requirement. All the Company had to do was charter a ship and ensure that Channel Island Ferries generated enough income to cover the additional £300,000 annual harbour dues commitment to Portsmouth City Council. Brittany Ferries' only input was to cover the difference, if any, between the dues and £300,000, but it was committed to this pay sum anyway, so would benefit even if the payments fell short. At the same time, a competitor to Sealink would help curb any expansive aspirations they might have on the western Channel. Michielini approved the plan, provided it did not require capital from the core Brittany Ferries operations. He wanted the investment to be made through the UK Company under Carruthers' control.

Initial plans were paused when utilisation of the *Penn-Ar-Bed* was questioned by the UK Department of Transport, who required a reduction in her freight-carrying capacity if

The *Earl Granville*, sister of the *Corbière*, arrives at Portsmouth from Guernsey in June 1984, sporting her pre-privatisation Sealink livery. *(Richard Kirkman)*

she was to sail under the British flag. The proposed launch of Channel Island Ferries services was put back to the 1985 season, and thoughts turned to alternative fleet deployments that could support ambitions to establish the service, without detracting from existing fleet operations. The shareholders approved the decision to proceed, and began the lengthy process of preparing plans for the new operation.

Meanwhile the established Sealink operation was part of the group of former British Rail shipping interests that was going through the process of transfer from the public to private sector. Sealink was sold to Sea Containers on 19th July 1984 for £66 million, and the new company would trade as Sealink British Ferries. After 142 years of operation, interrupted only by wartime occupation of Guernsey and Jersey, the integrated link between mainland railway companies and ferry services to the Channel Islands had been severed.

Initial uncertainty about Sealink British Ferries future plans for the services after privatisation, and speculation about service cutbacks on a loss-making operation, gave added impetus to encourage Channel Island Ferries to fill the gap. The company announced their new service on 8th August 1984. Services would operate on a year-round basis from Portsmouth, with a commitment to offer a strong passenger and freight service using a ship capable of carrying up to 500 passengers, manned by British officers and crew. The identity of the proposed vessel was not revealed, but the new company intended to commence operations in April 1985. The announcement was reported as being 'greeted with enthusiasm and considerable backing from all the official bodies controlling ferries into and out of the islands' and gave 'residents the security of their own freight and passenger lifeline'. A Channel Island company with an island-based shareholding played well with Island communities, in contrast to the former nationalised operator going through the uncertainties of transition to the private sector.

In early October, Sealink British Ferries announced a £5 million investment in the *Earl Granville* and *Earl William* to launch a new upmarket two-ship operation from Portsmouth to the Channel Islands, to be marketed as the 'Starliner' service. The vessels would receive major internal refits to provide quality overnight facilities for just 400 passengers, all accommodated in cabins. On daytime crossings the vessels would operate with a maximum of 800 passengers, with a Cherbourg call added to the daily rotation. Weymouth services would become seasonal daytime-only sailings, with *Earl Harold* and *Earl Godwin*.

The new Channel Island Ferries schedule was fitted around berth availability at Portsmouth, sailing from Jersey at 19:30, and Guernsey at 22:15 to arrive in Portsmouth at 08:00 the following morning, berthing at the Brittany Ferries linkspan, before departing again at 10:00 - the reverse of the Sealink British Ferries winter schedule. However, the changes to the Sealink British Ferries schedules to incorporate a Cherbourg call on daytime crossings meant that Channel Island Ferries could offer competitive journey times for passengers in each direction to the Islands. Sealink British Ferries retained the advantage of freight capacity, particularly the key overnight crossing from Portsmouth which enabled 'next day' delivery in Guernsey and Jersey, and brought Island produce to the mainland in time for the London morning markets.

Channel Island Ferries chose to match Sealink British Ferries' 1984 standard return fare of £56 for the 1985 season and offered overnight two-berth cabins for £14, but their competitor's fare structure was very different. The Portsmouth route, aiming at an upmarket clientele, would charge a single fare of £59, which included a buffet dinner, en suite luxury cabin with television, and a full English breakfast. In comparison the return air fare from Southampton was around £68. The peak return fare via Weymouth was fixed at £58.

The search for a suitable vessel for the new service settled on a charter of the *Bénodet* from Brittany Ferries, which put further pressure on the Sealink British Ferries operation. The *Bénodet* offered significantly more capacity than the original proposals had envisaged and, as a sister of the *Earl Granville*, she could readily match her competitor's operation and service. Further, she would fit comfortably into the notoriously restrictive Channel Island ports. After completing her 1984 season on the Plymouth-Roscoff service, the *Bénodet* was sent to St. Malo for a £1.15 million refit and overhaul. She was renamed the *Corbière*, after the iconic lighthouse in Jersey, and re-registered in Nassau in the Bahamas.

The *Corbière* could carry 250 cars, with berths for 230 passengers and an additional 170 reclining seats. The new operation would create 106 jobs for British officers and crew, and up to 140 shore roles, 48 of which would be in the islands and 92 in Portsmouth, where the management team were based on the ground floor of Norman House, directly beneath Sealink's local office. Targets of 140,000 passengers and 16,000 freight vehicles were set for the first year of operation, representing a 20% share of the sea market. In the new, post-privatisation era, Channel Island Ferries was able to offer through rail/sea fares from the outset, connecting with British Rail services to Portsmouth Harbour.

The intention was to offer a contrasting service to that of Sealink British Ferries. Channel Island Ferries was free to operate on a 'low cost' basis with no legacy of the restrictions and the costs inherent in the more traditionally manned, unionised and British-flagged competitor. Although there was an aspiration to employ French crews on the new service, there were difficulties engaging them on Brittany Ferries' terms and conditions, so British crews were employed instead. Capt. Doug Wilkinson, a former deck officer with Union Castle joined the company from Cenargo as Senior Master and became responsible for recruiting and training the two crews, who were to work on a two-weeks-on, two-weeks-off basis. Denholm Ship Management were engaged to manage the provision of crew, even though they hadn't run a ferry service before. But previous ferry experience was not what the company was looking for. Like Brittany Ferries, a fresh approach was needed to distinguish the new operation from Sealink British Ferries. Brittany Ferries was able to offer their French professional expertise to advise on the provision and supply of duty-free goods and the creation of catering menus. The best of

The *Corbière* leaving Portsmouth in first season. *(Richard Kirkman)*

both worlds was emerging.

The new working arrangements suited Brittany Ferries well. Channel Island Ferries would pay for use of Brittany Ferries' systems, which could be adapted quickly to get the new company up and running , and there were now charter revenues from the *Corbière*. Ken Waite was recruited from a career with P&O Normandy Ferries to help drive the passenger business, and Phil Bowditch transferred across from Brittany Ferries to manage the important freight traffic. Barbara Binder was brought on board to handle public relations, whilst BCB and Rook Dunning handled advertising and creative material, with Peter Lusher taking a prominent role. Passenger reservations were initially handled by a section of the existing team at the Brittany Centre, with calls switched through to the unit from a dedicated line. Denholm Ship Management were able to source engineers and deck officers but knew little about passenger service, so the Portsmouth management team ended up undertaking many of the mundane tasks needed to establish the new company. This led to some entertaining exchanges.

One of the early tasks was to replace the Brittany Ferries hardware on the *Corbière* with Channel Island Ferries branded stores to help establish the identity of the new company. Plates on board the *Bénodet* were name-stamped Brittany Ferries so it was important to procure Channel Island Ferries plates. Tenderers were invited to a meeting at the Brittany Centre and asked if their equipment could handle the conditions they would be exposed to at sea. "What happens if they fall? - presumably they are unbreakable?" one salesman was asked. "Of course," they replied, and dropped one to prove their point. It broke. He tried again with the same result, until the office floor lay deep in broken china... but he got the order in the end.

The new service needed to be different, innovative and efficient. One way of demonstrating this was to use duvets in cabins – revolutionary for the time, but capable of speeding up the process of making up cabins on ship turnrounds, as well as demonstrating a new approach. The order was placed and the duvets and covers arrived, but when tested it was found that the two didn't quite fit - there was always a bit of duvet sticking out from the cover. This was a consequence of the rush involved in getting off the ground, with the team mucking in to get the job done because the in-house experience was not available. But all was in place as the launch date approached.

Channel Island Ferries brochure cover 1985
(Richard Kirkman collection)

The different approach of Channel Island Ferries was marketed as 'The Better Way' using a simple folded brochure. A public open day aboard *Corbière* in Jersey attracted 8,000 visitors, prior to her inaugural departure from St Helier on 27th March. Terence

The *Corbière* dressed overall on her first arrival in St Helier on 23rd March 1985. *(Dave Hocquard)*

Terence Alexander inaugurates Channel Island Ferries first sailing in St Helier on 27th March 1985. The Rolls Royce came from Roger Bale's private collection. *(Ferry Publications Library)*

Alexander, who played the father-in-law in the popular BBC television series Bergerac, officiated at the inauguration ceremony, before driving his trademark white Rolls Royce on board the 19:45 departure to Portsmouth via Guernsey. On arrival in Portsmouth at 08:15 the following morning, *Corbière* was met by the Lord Mayor, John Marshall, his Lady Mayoress Louisa Taylor, and Chay Blyth, for a champagne breakfast in the carvery restaurant, before the *Corbière* took passengers south with her first 10:00 departure, an excusable 40 minutes late. The *Corbière* arrived back in Jersey on schedule at 17:45.

Sealink British Ferries' ambitions to launch the 'Starliner' operation at the end of March were thwarted by a national shipyard strike in Denmark, giving Channel Island

The *Corbière* arrives in Portsmouth for the first time on the morning of 28th March 1985. *(Ferry Publications Library)*

Ferries the bonus of a full month operating against the stand in vessel *Ailsa Princess*. By the end of June, Channel Island Ferries had carried 85% of the passenger traffic and 80% of passenger vehicles on the Portsmouth-Channel Islands route. Sealink British Ferries retained a higher proportion of the freight business, but rates were dropping as competition intensified, and shareholder MMD was switching much of its traffic to Channel Island Ferries.

A third brochure reprint was delivered in July, and Channel Island Ferries began to make inroads into the trade car shipments that supported the Islands' extensive car hire businesses. By the end of August, Channel Island Ferries had carried 68,000 passengers, attracting 83% of the Portsmouth-Jersey market. Sealink British Ferries countered with a claim of 80% share of the freight market, but faced mounting losses on the services, with a budgeted £3 million profit for the year now projected to be a £7 million loss. There was clearly only sufficient business to sustain one profitable operator. Sealink British Ferries announced radically revised plans for the 1986 season, with the two-ship Portsmouth service retained and fares significantly reduced, moving away from the fully inclusive price structure on the *Earl Granville* and *Earl*

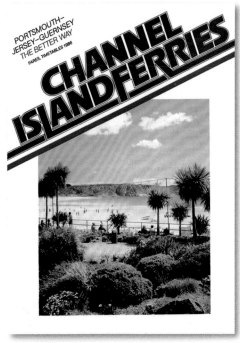

Channel Island Ferries brochure 1986. *(Richard Kirkman collection)*

William. The Weymouth service was reduced to a single vessel operation using the *Earl Harold*.

In Autumn 1985 the *Corbière* went to Rotterdam for refit and improvements to her passenger areas; the *Cornouailles* was chartered from Brittany Ferries in the interim, operating with a French crew and Channel Island Ferries' catering team.

In December, Channel Island Ferries announced similar schedules for 1986, but with the daily operation brought forward to 6th May, and a new standby return fare of £28. The company was well on course to meet the target of 130,000 passengers for the first full year, expecting to carry 100,000 by the end of 1985.

But 1986 proved to be a difficult year. It became increasingly evident that the sea passenger market to Guernsey and Jersey was in freefall; there was a drop of 38% in the number of Jersey arrivals by sea from Portsmouth between 1984 and 1985, despite the enhanced capacity on offer through the tripling of the fleet dedicated to the route. Things got worse in 1986 as air competition bit more deeply into the sea trade. The freight business was stable but finite, as the Islands' imports and exports were relatively static. By May, senior representatives of Channel Island Ferries and Sealink British Ferries were meeting together to consider the way forward. Attempts by Sealink British Ferries to offer financial inducements to persuade Channel Island Ferries to withdraw from the market were rejected. The pressure on both companies increased through the summer months. Joint talks moved on to consider the potential consolidation of services, and the two sides eventually agreed a merger of their operations. The new joint venture was announced on Tuesday 30th September 1986. A new company, to trade as BCIF, was established to ensure the long-term viability of sea services in the face of the increasing air competition and mounting losses. The new BCIF team was populated by Channel Island Ferries personnel, strengthened by a small number of former Sealink British Ferries staff. BCIF was registered in Jersey, with shareholding split evenly between Channel Island Ferries

British Channel Island Ferries brochure 1987.
(Richard Kirkman collection)

and Sealink British Ferries.

BCIF intended to start operations from Portsmouth the following day, utilising the *Corbière* and the *Earl Granville* on charter from their parent companies, with a winter sailing schedule of day and night sailings to both Islands. The Weymouth route would operate with the *Earl Harold* from 15th May to 26th September 1987, thereby accommodating 70% of the passenger traffic on this route. The loss-making Cherbourg calls would cease immediately, leaving Sealink British Ferries' *Earl William* surplus to requirements.

In parallel with the public announcement, Sealink British Ferries advised their trade unions that they were withdrawing their Channel Islands services from Portsmouth and Weymouth with immediate effect, and all staff employed on these routes would be made redundant from Saturday 4th October. The rapid implementation of the plan forced a quick and angry response from the unions. Officers and crew went on immediate strike, with sit-ins on the *Earl William* in St. Peter Port, the *Earl Godwin* in Weymouth, the *Earl Granville* in Cherbourg and the *Earl Harold* when she arrived in Portsmouth, having been diverted from Weymouth as the *Earl Godwin* blocked her intended berth. The strike spread to other Sealink British Ferries routes, to add to the growing financial pressures on the company.

Guernsey and Jersey were reduced to being served by a single-ship operation, having enjoyed a five-vessel summer season. The *Corbière* could easily handle passenger traffic volumes, but vital freight capacity was severely reduced. With the *Earl William* blocking the linkspan in St. Peter Port, Guernsey was served by disembarking passengers directly on the quay, with car traffic diverted to Jersey and shipped back to Guernsey using Torbay Seaways' side-loader vessel the *Devoniun II*. The Guernsey Harbour Master, fearful that local dockers would strike in sympathy with the Sealink crews, eventually stopped foot passengers from landing. BCIF gave notice that they would suspend the service to Guernsey if the blockade continued, and the new company withdrew their service for five days from 13th October, before agreement was reached with the trade unions; the *Earl William* then sailed to Weymouth to join the rest of the strikebound fleet. Sealink British Ferries was unable to reach any accord with the unions that would allow the *Earl Granville* and the *Earl Harold* to join the BCIF joint venture on the terms agreed with Channel Island Ferries.

Meanwhile, fast craft passenger-only operator Condor took advantage of the limited capacity now available and deployed the hydrofoil *Condor 7* to provide an alternative service for affected travellers from Jersey and Guernsey to Weymouth. The service carried 18,000 passengers in 18 days of operation, convincing Condor that a regular schedule would be a viable proposition for the 1987 season.

Frustrated at the lack of progress with the joint venture, and facing growing public concerns at the lack of capacity, Channel Island Ferries took out a High Court injunction against Sealink British Ferries, suing them for failure to provide two vessels on bareboat charter to BCIF. In court, Sealink British Ferries' Queens' Counsel claimed that the strike had prevented Sealink British Ferries from fulfilling their obligations and argued that, when the dispute was settled in mid-October, the agreement with the National Union of

Marine, Aviation and Shipping Transport Officers (NUMAST) put it out of their power to provide the two vessels on the agreed terms.

In a landmark interpretation of force majeure clauses, the judge held that the settlement between Sealink British Ferries and the unions represented 'a completely new causative event in their disablement from performing the joint venture agreement', and that Sealink British Ferries' entry into that settlement agreement, 'far from being an act beyond their control, represented a genuine choice on their part'. He noted that the strike could well have been easier to settle if Sealink British Ferries had avoided the 'tragic miscalculation' represented by their 'brutal' introduction of the agreement without prior consultation. He considered that it would be the 'most unjust if Channel Island Ferries had had to bear the brunt of Sealink British Ferries' improvidence in this regard'. Sealink British Ferries' finance director was told by the judge that his evidence was unbecoming of the financial director of a public company, and there was evidence that the company's lawyer had attempted to forge Carruthers' signature on documents.

Judgement in favour of Channel Island Ferries was upheld in the Court of Appeal, and Channel Island Ferries compulsorily purchased Sealink British Ferries' 50% interest in BCIF in January 1988. Sealink British Ferries was banned from operating direct services to the Channel Islands for a minimum period of twelve months, to give BCIF a free hand. Further, the authorities in Jersey banned Sealink British Ferries from using St Helier for twelve months.

Legal wrangling between the two companies continued until 1991, with Sealink British Ferries claiming repayment of loans made at the time of the proposed merger and BCIF counterclaiming for financial losses during the period of disrupted services. By the time judgement was made in favour of BCIF, legal fees had outweighed the sums in dispute. The *Earl Granville* remained with Sealink British Ferries and opened a seasonal Portsmouth-Cherbourg service for the 1987 season.

A period of intense and bitter competition ended, leaving BCIF with a near monopoly, with the emerging Condor operation and Torbay Seaways as future seasonal competition. Channel Island Ferries had wildly exceeded the expectations for the new service, but BCIF now faced the considerable challenge of providing a credible service for 1987. The collapse of the joint venture left their service proposals in tatters, with two of the three planned vessels no longer available to the company. The *Corbière* continued to maintain her old schedule, with a 10:00 daytime sailing from Portsmouth to Guernsey (16:30-18:00), then Jersey (19:45-22:00) before an overnight return crossing, arriving in Portsmouth at the slightly earlier time of 07:00, but there was to be no second passenger vessel for the route in 1987. The *Breizh-Izel* was chartered from Brittany Ferries to offer additional freight capacity, sailing night-out, day-back from Portsmouth.

The Weymouth service was scheduled to start from 15th April 1987, with an overnight departure and daytime return crossing to balance the Portsmouth operation, but finding a suitable vessel proved difficult. Carruthers and Jim Mason went with the Denholm team to Greece to inspect Marlines' *Baroness M;* she had recently been operating in British waters for P&O Ferries as the *Lion,* so it was felt that little work would be needed to introduce her to service. A charter was secured, and she was renamed the *Portelet,* with Capt. Colin Perkins appointed as her Senior Master. The *Baroness M* had benefited from an extensive refit in Greece in 1985, during which 96 four berth en suite cabins had been added by Panos Marangopoulos, her owner. He agreed to paint the new BCIF logo on the *Portelet's* hull before she left from Greece. She arrived in Weymouth on 5th April to be stored, before heading to Portsmouth to cover the *Corbière's* four-day refit in Southampton. It was immediately apparent that the Greek painters had painted 'British Channel Island Ferries' at a highly irregular angle on the hull so that it sloped dramatically; it had to be repainted. Carruthers was furious.

The *Corbière* returned from refit sporting her new correctly-applied corporate identity with the word 'British' appearing above the old Channel Island Ferries logo on her hull.

The *Corbière* and the *Portelet* now offered combined daily peak capacity for 2,190 passengers, substantially below the 3,800 offered by both operators in summer 1986.

The *Portelet* returned to Weymouth on 15th April ready to commence service that evening, but a Department of Transport inspection identified a number of issues; the fittings were unsafe, the fire doors had plastic handles and the sprinkler system was inadequate in her new aft cabins. There followed two days without any sailings from Weymouth, and the inspectors only permitted the *Portelet* to sail on the third day with a reduced passenger certificate, pending completion of the necessary remedial works. Carruthers' anger grew. He went with Mason to meet Marangopoulos in Paris and demanded compensation. The humbled Greek shipowner agreed to pay £20,000. But he, in turn, threatened to sue Bureau Veritas, who had overseen the conversion work; they

The *Portelet* turns sharply for the berth as she arrives in St Peter Port, Guernsey. *(Miles Cowsill)*

could not defend the actions of their local manager in Greece, and paid up.

The *Cornouailles* was chartered by Channel Island Ferries on behalf of BCIF to sail in tandem with the *Portelet* and offer additional capacity for the Easter period. Remedial works on the *Portelet* were then completed after the busy period, whilst the *Cornouailles* maintained the service. It was an inauspicious start, drawing heavy criticism despite the problems that the company had encountered in providing any form of service at all. The *Portelet* returned to establish a pattern of night sailings at 22:45 from Weymouth, arriving in Guernsey (06:45-07:15) then on to Jersey (09:15-10:30), before offering a daytime return crossing to Guernsey (12:30-13:00) and Weymouth, where she arrived at 18:00. This seasonal service operated until 27th September, with the *Portelet* laid up in Weymouth for the winter, after carrying some 138,000 passengers and 28,000 cars in her first season.

Meanwhile, invigorated by the success of their short notice autumn 1986 operation,

Condor signed an agreement to operate a seasonal summer service from Weymouth to the Guernsey and Jersey between 10th April and 17th October 1987, using the hydrofoils *Condor 5* and *Condor 7*. The service started from St Malo and ran via Jersey and Guernsey to and from Weymouth. Condor carried 46,200 passengers in their first full season of operation on the UK route.

David Donhue was brought into BCIF as Managing Director, bringing with him a wealth of experience from his time with Townsend Thoresen. BCIF changed their Portsmouth schedule from 3rd January 1988 to operate overnight from Portsmouth to the Islands with the *Corbière*, departing at 21:30 and sailing direct to Jersey (07:00-09:00), returning via Guernsey (11:00-12:30) to arrive back in Portsmouth at 19:00. This provided a better schedule for freight customers, with overnight deliveries to the Islands counterbalanced by access to the UK produce markets facilitated by the daytime return crossing. The Weymouth schedule reverted to a daytime 13:00 departure to Guernsey (17:30-18:30), and on to Jersey (20:30-22:00) before returning overnight to Weymouth for 06:45 the following morning. The *Portelet* was re-chartered by BCIF and commenced her summer season of Weymouth sailings on 6th April, but services were disrupted by a strike by the NUS from 4th May, with the *Breizh-Izel* brought in from Brittany Ferries to maintain the freight service; the industrial action was short lived and crews returned to work from 6th May.

By now, Brittany Ferries' initial objective of offsetting port charges at Portsmouth through operation of the Channel Islands service had been more than fulfilled, and BCIF was now contributing to problems of port congestion. BCIF services had to be moved away from the port to allow the parent company to achieve ambitions to expand the Portsmouth-Caen route. On 19th August 1988, BCIF announced that all their services would be transferred to Poole from 2nd January 1989, reducing the passage time by up to two hours and narrowing the journey differential with Condor. Whilst true for the Portsmouth route, Poole departures represented a lengthening of crossing times for passengers relative to Weymouth. The seasonal vessel charter needed to support a service from Weymouth was no longer deemed economic, leaving the port clear for Condor. A freight-only service was contemplated from Portsmouth, but full consolidation of operations at Poole was considered the best option.

The reduction from two ships to one was implemented by chartering the 8,987-tonne *Scirocco* from Cenargo to replace the *Corbière* for the 1989 season. As the renamed *Rozel,* she would be the largest vessel ever to operate to the islands, with capacity for 1,300 passengers and 296 cars, cabin accommodation for 671 passengers, and seating for a further 982. The *Corbière* was returned to Brittany Ferries for the Poole-Cherbourg service, and the *Portelet* was sent back to Marlines on completion of her Weymouth season. In December Channel Island Ferries purchased the *Cornouailles* from Brittany Ferries, financing the acquisition through the balance sheet. She was chartered to BCIF to replace the *Breizh-Izel*, offering winter freight capacity and a summer daytime passenger service from Poole, with an overnight return crossing from the Channel Islands.

The move from Portsmouth to Poole was not well received by the freight community,

British Channel Island Ferries brochure 1988.
(Richard Kirkman collection)

who had established shore infrastructure to support Portsmouth services, and valued the easy access offered by the port to both the motorway network and London. In October, Channel Island Ferries shareholder MMD approached Commodore Shipping with a view to establishing a joint ro-ro freight service from Portsmouth to Guernsey and Jersey; these discussions expanded to consider closer integration between the two companies. A new joint company, C&M Shipping, was formed in Guernsey, and discussions were held with Sealink British Ferries, who also had an interest in the commercial opportunities presented by BCIF's departure from Portsmouth. Plans were quickly formulated to replace the BCIF Portsmouth freight capacity.

Emboldened by BCIF's withdrawal from Weymouth and their own 59% year on year growth to 73,500 passengers from the port in 1988, Condor announced plans for a £5 million investment in the *Condor 9,* a 450-passenger 35-knot vessel to be built by Aluminium Shipbuilders in Portchester, with delivery scheduled for April 1990. This would

In need of a repaint, the *Breizh-Izel* arrives in Portsmouth with a well-loaded BCIF freight sailing from the Channel Islands. *(Miles Cowsill)*

be the largest catamaran of its type in the world.

The *Corbière* brought the last BCIF sailing into Portsmouth on 2nd January 1989 and sailed light to Poole in readiness to operate the company's first departure from the port at 21:30 on the same day. The *Rozel* made her maiden voyage on 21st February with the 21:30 sailing from Poole, after the *Corbière* had arrived from the Islands with her final passenger sailing for BCIF. The *Rozel* sailed straight into some of the worst storms of the winter, but quickly proved her worth. The *Corbière* continued to operate for BCIF in freight-only mode, until the arrival of the *Cornouailles* on 10th May which was now renamed the *Havelet* after a refit at Brest. The *Havelet* offered a morning freight-only sailing from Poole and an overnight return until 25th May, when sailings were timetabled for passengers until the end of September.

The new C&M Shipping freight service from Portsmouth commenced from 3rd January 1989 with the *Earl Godwin* in freight-only mode, managed under contract by Sealink British Ferries. On 20th March the *Pride of Portsmouth* replaced the *Earl Godwin* under a three-year charter to Mainland Transport (Holdings) Ltd, owner of MMD. The links between Commodore and MMD were consolidated from 1st August when Commodore took full control of the MMD Group. At Weymouth the seasonal Condor service began on 10 April with the arrival of the *Condor 7.*

The Elizabeth Harbour was opened in St. Helier by the Queen in May in anticipation of the arrival of the larger vessel; the Harbour could handle vessels up to 130 metres in length, which now matched the facilities at St. Peter Port in Guernsey, thereby increasing the permissible length of vessels on the Channel Island routes.

At around 11:45 on 26th September 1989, the *Rozel* struck rocks on the inside of the Castle Cornet breakwater in St Peter Port harbour when arriving from Jersey. She was some 40 to 50 yards from the Lighthouse at the time, and lost three blades from her port propeller whilst also damaging her port rudder. The *Rozel* headed to Falmouth for repair, where it was determined that she would require a new propeller boss and a new rudder stock. The *Armorique* was brought out of lay-up and arrived from St Malo to take up the service under charter on 28th September, before she in turn was replaced by a further loan of the *Reine Mathilde* from 9th October. The *Reine Mathilde* had a difficult time on the route and suffered damage on a number of occasions during gales, being pinned against La Collette Marina wall in St. Helier on 28th November whilst trying to berth in 55 mile per hour winds, highlighting the vulnerability of the Elizabeth Harbour to any prevailing southwesterly wind; she left for her refit on 13th December. The *Armorique* returned to assist but she also encountered challenging conditions, with one crossing delayed 48 hours by storms, giving day trippers a much-extended break.

The switch to Poole initially proved a success for BCIF, with a 20% rise in carryings to 499,022 passengers in 1989. Condor was also growing, and carried 85,191 passengers, giving the fledgling operation a significant 17% market share by the year end. BCIF marketed a 'French Connection' service in conjunction with Brittany Ferries and Emeraude Ferries to offer a Poole-Jersey, Jersey-St. Malo, St. Malo-Portsmouth round trip for the 1990 season.

BCIF saw the *Rozel* return to traffic after her extensive repair on 2nd January 1990. In the spring, Humber Ship Repairers secured a £2 million contract to upgrade the *Havelet* with a large new sun deck, restaurant, bar, a new Pullman lounge and improvements to the cafeteria. The work commenced on 2nd April for completion in early May. The *Corbière* returned on charter to stand in for the *Havelet* during her refit, and BCIF also chartered the *L Taurus* to offer additional freight capacity. Condor re-introduced their cross-Channel service from 2nd April 1990 and announced the arrival of Britain's first wave-piercing catamaran from 1st June.

The newly enlarged Commodore Group gained access to the wharfage, warehousing and road haulage operation of MMD, and the introduction of the ro-ro operation from Portsmouth proved successful. Commodore withdrew from the lift-on lift-off container business to operate solely with ro-ro services from August 1990. BCIF fought back by purchasing their Poole freight competitor, Torbay Seaways Freightliner, together with the *L Taurus* on 10th April 1990. The vessel made her last journey for her former owner on 15th June, and was renamed the *Sylbe* to be employed on an intermittent freight service to the Islands under the banner 'Channel Island Freight'. BCIF made inroads into road haulage operations by investing in a fleet of curtain sided trailers to Island road-specifications, building on the previous experience of Channel Island Ferries in this market.

Although the *Condor 9* was much delayed from her anticipated April delivery, Condor announced plans to move into the vehicle market with a new car-carrying wave-piercing catamaran for the 1992 season. BCIF Chairman Carter responded that "these things (catamarans) are not yet proven and 1992 is a long way off." The *Condor 9* finally entered service on 17th August but soon encountered problems in rough seas and was withdrawn from service for the rest of the season after just three days of operation, pending the fitment of a new ride control system.

The start of the 1991 season proved slow to pick up, with the Gulf War having an impact upon bookings, but Condor began to take a more significant proportion of the sea business, carrying 125,000 passengers during the year. Such levels of abstracted business in both the passenger and freight markets could not be ignored. Channel Island Ferries tried to exercise their right to purchase the *Rozel* at the end of her charter, but the Cenargo asking price was rejected as unrealistic, even though the deal could be financed. BCIF announced in late summer 1991 that would charter the smaller *Reine Mathilde* for the next two years from Marine Invest, who had purchased her from Brittany Ferries. The vessel would be renamed the *Beauport*. Whilst this was seen as a stopgap move for the company pending a longer-term decision, it marked a turning point. As if to

The *Rozel* brought substantial capacity to the services from Poole, but she proved too large for economic operation. She is seen here in St Helier, Jersey. *(Miles Cowsill)*

reinforce this, Jersey harbour Master Capt. Roy Bullen expressed his belief that the future for passenger transportation by sea lay with wave-piercing catamarans not larger superferries.

With the conflicts of interest from their relationship with Commodore proving incompatible with a shareholding in Channel Island Ferries, MMD sold their shares to the remaining shareholders and Brittany Ferries' interest was increased to 49%.

The *Rozel* made her last sailings to the Channel Islands in January 1992 and the *Beauport* entered service in February after a £1 million refit. The *Beauport* offered passenger-friendly facilities but was not well equipped to sustain the freight business. Meanwhile, Commodore's business was healthy enough to consider plans for new ro-ro tonnage, and the company entered discussions with a broad range of shipyards and finance houses in May. After considering proposals from 19 shipyards, Commodore placed an order with Royal Schelde in October for a new £18 million freight vessel capable of carrying 94 x 12-metre units for delivery in May 1995.

Condor enjoyed another successful year in 1992, with 25% growth in passenger carryings to reach 20,000 in July, and a 10,000 year on year passenger increase in the first five months of operation. To maintain the momentum and add to the pressure on BCIF, on 24th August managing director David Norman announced plans to introduce two car-carrying wave-piercing catamarans to compete directly with BCIF from spring 1993. On the same day, TNT Shipping and Development took a 50% financial stake in Condor, with Australian Chris Butcher becoming executive chairman. The bigger financial and technical resources now open to the company helped facilitate the order for the 580-passenger, 84-car-carrying *Condor 10* from Incat in Tasmania.

The original BCIF business case had been predicated on a monopoly of services to the Islands, but the company now faced strong competition on two fronts. The move to Poole

The *Armorique* operating for BCIF to cover for the stricken *Rozel. (Robert Le Maistre)*

had hit the core freight business, exacerbated by Commodore Shipping's new focus on ro-ro and their takeover of MMD. The intermittent freight service with the *Sylbe* dwindled and she was laid up in Poole before being sold in spring 1993. Meanwhile Condor's upcoming investment in two car-carrying catamarans would further impact on passenger and vehicle carryings. Condor was able to offer competitive journey times of 2hrs 15mins from Weymouth to Guernsey and 3hrs from Weymouth to Jersey, substantially quicker than BCIF from Poole. The financial stress on BCIF mounted when Condor announced a fare-freeze for 1993. Both rival operations had comparatively low overheads relative to BCIF'S multi-purpose ferries, and Condor was able to secure summer profits without maintaining a winter passenger service, as there was no Service Level Agreement with the States' governments requiring them to operate year-round. Commodore was unencumbered by any obligations to the passenger business and could concentrate on being a dedicated low cost freight operation. At the end of the season and facing another downturn in carryings, BCIF announced a reduction in services for the 1993 season.

At the 1993 BCIF Annual General Meeting Carruthers observed that the policy of the island governments was short-sighted. "As far as we know Jersey has the smallest port in northern Europe and only allows vessels up to 130 metres. They don't build ships of 130 metres anymore; they are much larger" he said. The company expressed strong disappointment at the decision of the island governments to give permission for Condor to operate their car-carrying wave piercer in 1993. Despite this, BCIF bookings for the forthcoming season looked good.

In the event, Condor's search for a second vessel for cross-channel operation proved too difficult. The *Condor 10* commenced service on 31st March, but Condor chose not to operate a second fast craft in 1993 blaming delays to the delivery of the second craft, and also scrapped plans to operate a car-carrying service between the Channel Islands and St Malo. BCIF re-introduced the *Havelet* as a passenger vessel from 27th May to offer

The *Cornouailles* enjoyed a new lease of life as the *Havelet* for BCIF, seen arriving in St Peter Port, Guernsey. *(Miles Cowsill)*

a twice-daily passenger service from Poole alongside the *Beauport*, until 19th September. An intense price war between BCIF and Condor escalated through the summer season, forcing rates downwards, with each offering special fares for short stay passengers with cars in an attempt to grow market share.

Towards the end of the summer rumours about the future of BCIF began to circulate in the Channel Islands, but Donhue denied there was any risk to the business; he observed that BCIF was developing a long-term strategy for the remainder of the decade with a number of replacement vessels being examined by the company. By the end of the season BCIF was facing a £3 million loss and competition from Condor extending through the winter months. BCIF announced that the charter of the *Beauport* would not be renewed and that, in further retrenchment, the company would operate passenger services with just the *Havelet* in 1994, supported in the freight market by a new charter of the *Purbeck*, which had been purchased by Channel Island Ferries from Brittany Ferries when she was surplus to requirements following the arrival of the *Barfleur*. The

Beauport undertook her final sailing for BCIF on 31st October and the *Purbeck* commenced duties the following day.

The pincer attack from Condor and Commodore was hitting BCIF's profitability, although company cash flow was still strong, but these financial problems coincided with difficult trading conditions for Brittany Ferries. Bale offered to invest more in BCIF, but this input could not be matched by Brittany Ferries. There was only room for one operator on the Channel Island routes, and the Channel Island Ferries board considered a deal was best done whilst the company was strong and before the BCIF cash was exhausted during the winter period. Holyman had the ability to provide substantial continued financial support to Condor and was determined to demonstrate that the future lay in the operation of fast craft.

The *Reine Mathilde*, renamed the *Beauport*, was another Brittany Ferries vessel deployed on BCIF service, here in St Peter Port, Guernsey. *(Miles Cowsill)*

Carruthers opened discussions with Condor Chairman Butcher, and eventually sale terms were agreed; not even Donhue was aware of the proposal at this time. The deal required investment by Condor and Commodore to provide sufficient cash to enable all BCIF shareholders to be reimbursed in full. All redundancy costs and legacy port commitments would be financed by the two companies, with Condor assuming a short-term charter of the *Havelet*, and Commodore taking a longer-term charter of the *Purbeck*. On 7th January 1994 Carter advised shareholders that BCIF would cease operating passenger and freight services from 22nd January. Simultaneously Condor announced the purchase of the passenger business, with Commodore buying the freight operation.

Condor agreed to retain all the seafaring staff, although the takeover resulted in 150 redundancies in the Channel Islands and a similar number in Poole. All mainland passenger sailings were transferred to Weymouth and freight sailings were concentrated at Portsmouth. The *Havelet* made her last sailing under BCIF management from Poole on

20th January, leaving the Channel Islands without any passenger service until 7th February, when the *Condor 10* returned to service.

The *Havelet* made her final sailing for Condor under the charter arrangement on 29th October 1996 and was then laid up in Weymouth. Later in September 1998, when Condor was fighting to retain States' approval to retain monopoly operation of the island services following a period of poor performance and a tender challenge from P&O European Ferries and Hoverspeed, Carruthers was approached by Condor and asked if the *Havelet* could be sold to act as a year-round conventional vessel for their Channel Island services. The speed with which Condor needed to conclude the transaction – it had to be completed in an afternoon - helped secure a favourable price for Channel Island Ferries and a good profit was made on the sale. The money was to prove useful when Brittany Ferries needed cash the following year.

The *Purbeck* charter was completed in 1995 and the vessel returned to Channel Island Ferries. The still active management company then employed her on a succession of charters to Sally Line, Irish Ferries, Truckline, Gaelic Ferries, Falcon Seafreight, Brittany Ferries (for the Portsmouth-Caen service), Commodore Shipping and Tranz Rail in New Zealand. She was eventually sold to Toll NZ Consolidated Ltd on 8th March 2006.

Channel Island Ferries made a significant contribution to Brittany Ferries from fulfilling the initial objective of saving port dues payments, to purchasing two ships and chartering vessels. Significant income was provided through profits on operations and the sale of vessels, but also from the use of reservations and other computer systems and the provision of all duty-free products for sale on board through Brittany Ferries. The Channel Islands venture proved that the team could build an independent new business from scratch and take on and beat a long-established operator by approaching service provision from the perspective of doing things differently. In the end, the sale of the company was a pragmatic solution, and Carruthers was proud that none of the shareholders lost money in consequence.

Brittany Ferries returned to the Channel Islands in a joint venture with the Columbia Threadneedle European Sustainable Infrastructure Fund, which purchased the Condor business in March 2020.

The *Beauport* encountering heavy seas as she passes Corbière lighthouse on 30th August 1992. *(Dave Hocquard)*

Eight

Bretagne –
the game changer

Artist's impression of the *Bretagne* used for pre-launch publicity purposes in brochures. *(Rook Dunning)*

The growth in traffic experienced following the acquisition of Truckline, the opening of the Portsmouth-Caen service, and the introduction of a passenger vessel to the Poole-Cherbourg route in 1986, coupled with the sound financial backing available from the SEMs, brought Brittany Ferries to the unaccustomed position of being able to contemplate the implementation of a unconstrained fleet strategy. The *Duc de Normandie*, which now incorporated many of the bespoke features required to create an attractive on board experience to support the brand, had been particularly well received. Borrowing ideas from the Baltic and Scandinavian markets, where the cruise ferry product was most advanced, her holistic design, theming and light interior finishes pointed the way forward. Now the promise of the advertising message in the main markets could be delivered on board. Brittany Ferries could begin to become a tangible brand across all aspects of its relationship with customers.

This opportunity was supported by the UK team, who encouraged the Company's movement away from the reliance on elderly second-hand tonnage, adapted to meet passenger needs, which had kept Brittany Ferries growing during the early years. The corporate expertise in generating income lay in the UK, with a robust sales track record, based on the strength of the brand in the UK market, that demonstrated that any capacity that was made available would be filled with traffic. Expansion of the route

195

structure to St Malo, Santander, Caen and Cherbourg had all, in turn, met with success, and justified confidence in the UK team and their strategic recommendations. Now was the time to begin to deliver the right fleet to match the expanded route structure. The team backed Christian Michielini's judgement that Brittany Ferries needed to move beyond stretching existing ships and think in terms of developing its own bespoke fleet. Sabemen was ready to back this view with investment.

For the first time Brittany Ferries could contemplate building a bespoke vessel to meet the needs and requirements of a route and its customers. Such a project would be a strong statement of intent, the first purpose-built cruise ferry on the English Channel, and a sign of growing confidence in the face of the future challenge from the Channel

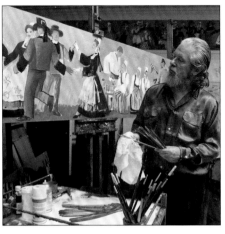

Top left: **The *Bretagne* under construction in the Chantiers de l'Atlantique shipyard in Saint-Nazaire.** *(Ferry Publications Library)*

Bottom left: **The *Bretagne* undertakes sea trials, with her full livery not yet applied.** (*Ferry Publications Library*)

Top right: **Alexander Goudie at work.** *(Lachlan Goudie)*

Opposite page: **An artist's impression of the reception area on the *Bretagne*.** (*Ferry Publications Library*)

Tunnel. The project would bring together professional expertise from across the Company to deliver a collective vision, a focus for all the improvement initiatives that were helping drive the business forward.

Michel Maraval's creative work on the *Duc de Normandie* gave the Company the confidence to go and build their own vessel. His experience had taught him the flaws of designing a vessel without considering the way in which it will eventually be managed and operated. He envisaged a fully inclusive process from the start, involving key personnel from across the Company at all stages from inception to final delivery, with experts in navigation, engineering and Hotel Services brought in throughout the life of the project to ensure the design met their operational needs. The final product would represent this collective involvement and, crucially, would be 'owned' by everyone from their association with the process of decision making at every stage of the project.

All thse ideas came together in the initial concept for a vessel capable of carrying an ambitious 2,000 passengers and 600 cars on the Plymouth-Santander route. The project envisaged the ship being named the *Bretagne* from the outset.

The positive reaction to the *Duc de Normandie* encouraged Brittany Ferries to explore more professional support from Finland, and early discussions were held with Wärtsilä, who were the design force behind many of the successful Baltic ferries of the early 1980s. This interest in potential new tonnage attracted an approach by the engineering consultancy Elomatic, based in Turku, whose managing director had previously worked for Wärtsilä. The consultancy began work on a design. The proposed new vessel would differ from her Scandinavian and Baltic sisters; their trade was very passenger-oriented

and featured comparatively small vehicle decks relative to the areas devoted to passenger circulation and accommodation areas on the vessel. The *Bretagne* needed to incorporate comparable high-quality in the public areas of the ship, whilst featuring much higher capacity vehicle decks, with the capability of achieving rapid loading and discharge when in port. Further, the new vessel needed to able to withstand the rigours of the passage across the Bay of Biscay, whilst providing comfortable travelling conditions whenever possible.

Board approval was given to take forward the concept into the design phase, and discussions began with a range of shipyards based on an initial invitation to tender for the project. There were significant internal pressures to award the contract to a French shipyard as a means of supporting the national shipbuilding industry, but this was still a price-sensitive decision. The most interesting and competitive proposals were received from tenders submitted by Van der Giessen de Noord in the Netherlands, and British Shipbuilders of Govan, with the lowest bid coming from the latter that quoted a price of

FF437 million for construction of the vessel.

The negotiations edged towards an agreement with the Scottish bidders, although the vessel would have to be British-registered if it was to receive state support from the UK government, so the benefits of French registration would be lost. But Sabemen had provided financing for Brittany Ferries' investments since 1982 and had difficulty in contemplating support for an investment outside France. Then the Chantiers de l'Atlantique shipyard in Saint-Nazaire expressed an interest in building the *Bretagne*. Chantiers de l'Atlantique had been nationalised in 1986/7 and the shipyard's output was subsidised by the state; French President Jacques Chirac was keen for this prestigious new build order to be awarded to this French company.

The Chantiers de l'Atlantique shipyard was then in the midst of constructing the *Sovereign of the Seas* to be delivered to Royal Caribbean Cruise Line at the end of 1987,

Left: **Alexis Gourvennec officiates at the naming ceremony of the *Bretagne*.** *(Ferry Publications Library)*

Top right: **The *Bretagne* is guided into Roscoff for the first time by Capt. Ivan Claireaux.** *(Paul Burns)*

Bottom right: **Madame Bourges performs the naming of the *Bretagne*.** *(Ferry Publications Library)*

but would then have the capacity to build another vessel in the shipyard. The French government put pressure on Brittany Ferries to accept the Chantiers de l'Atlantique proposal through the Industry Minister Alain Madelin, but the price was significantly higher than the Scottish deal, and delivery dates were much longer. State support was offered, then withdrawn after exploratory discussions with the EC in Brussels. There were also cultural problems with the Saint-Nazaire shipyard, which was not accustomed to a client with very specific ideas on design and the manner of delivery.

Gourvennec insisted that the contract would go to Scotland unless Chantiers de l'Atlantique could build the vessel at the FF437 million Govan tender price. This stalemate dragged out over several months but, after further government intervention, agreement was eventually reached to build the vessel in Saint-Nazaire at the Scottish price. The award of the contract was announced on 8th May 1987, prompting an immediate row between Britain and France over the decision to reject the Govan bid. British Industry minister Giles Shaw demanded an EC inquiry into the decision to ensure that the French government had not breached Community rules, which then limited the amount of state aid for any single order to 28% of the cost price. Shaw expressed surprise and disappointment at the decision to place the order in France and suggested that this meant that either Brittany Ferries had accepted a less advantageous offer than the Govan

The *Bretagne* arrives in Plymouth for the first time accompanied by a tugboat salute. *(Ferry Publications Library)*

deal, or the French had broken EC rules. British Shipbuilders pointed out that they had carried out detailed contractual negotiations with Brittany Ferries about the order and that the French shipyard had only entered the bidding process early in the year after the tenders were submitted. But the protests came to naught and the final contract was signed on 9th June 1987, with completion timed to allow the *Bretagne* to enter service for the 1989 summer season.

Finance for the *Bretagne* was arranged through an Economic Interest Grouping (EIG). This was a financial vehicle established to optimise tax organisation that was typically used for substantial industrial assets. The EIG took out financial loans to purchase the *Bretagne* and then leased the vessel to Sabemen, which in turn sub-leased her to Brittany

Ferries on a back-to-back 20-year charter. The *Bretagne* was owned by the EIG. A guarantee of FF270 million was given by the Brittany and Pays de Loire regions to help finance the *Bretagne*; the total finance package reached FF295 million. A similar financial vehicle was later to be used in the acquisition of the *Normandie* and the *Barfleur*.

The UK Labour party spokesman Gordon Brown accused the French government of being guilty of sharp practice, or at worst a dangerous deception. A formal British complaint to the EC quickly followed, but in July the Commission opened procedures against both France and Britain, as each country had offered levels of state support to the contract in excess of that submitted by the Dutch government in support of the Van

The reception area on the *Bretagne* is a focal point at the heart of the ship; Alexander Goudie's work is strongly featured. *(Ferry Publications Library)*

der Giessen de Noord bid, and above the maximum 28% cent level provided for within the EU Directive. In January 1998 the Commission noted that the French government had provided FF40 million in aid to Brittany Ferries and a 28% production aid directly to Chantiers de l'Atlantique. The French authorities refused to reduce their support to the Dutch level but were given two months to regularise the situation. In March, the Commission ordered the French government to withdraw subsidies to the shipyard as the level of aid made available in support of the order contravened the EEC's 6th directive and had to be trimmed. Britain's Department of Trade and Industry noted that the result was that Chantiers de l'Atlantique was set to suffer a significant loss, since they had decided to proceed with building the *Bretagne* in advance of the Commissioners' decision.

Meanwhile, the new build team assembled in Saint-Nazaire at the start of 1987. The

Brittany Ferries contingent included Fleet Director Commandant Jean Raymond Thomas, the Technical Directors Raymond Le Tarnec and Michel Denecker, Jacques Le Rouzo as director of Hotel Services, and the Masters Ivan Claireaux and Joseph Hardouin. Many Chantiers de l'Atlantique employees were from the Chantiers Dubigeon shipyard in Nantes, which had closed several months previously; this workforce brought substantial practical ferry construction experience. Their first task was to agree in Breton the translation of the draft 500-page English construction contract into the French language...

The shipyard team visited the Brittany Ferries operations in Roscoff, Plymouth,

Left: **The reception desk on the *Bretagne* is similar in style to a plush hotel.** *(Ferry Publications Library)*

Top right: **Cabin accommodation for families featuring pull down bunks.** *(Ferry Publications Library)*

Bottom right: **Timeless quality in the restaurant.** *(Ferry Publications Library)*

Santander and Cork and travelled between these ports by sea to get a full understanding of the environment in which the *Bretagne* would be operating. Their findings were incorporated into the resultant design, which featured a robust forward hull form to permit a high cruising speed in the typical extremes of Bay of Biscay weather, and an automatic mooring system capable of handling strong winds in port areas. The vessel's low meta-centric height, coupled with the installation of anti-roll stabilisers, was to prove highly effective in setting new standards of passenger comfort. Four Wärtsilä engines were installed under licence, designed to give the *Bretagne* an operating speed of 21 knots, and enable delivery of a 24-hour passage time from Plymouth to Santander, with power available to recover the service in the event of bad weather. Rates of fuel consumption were designed to match those achieved on the *Quiberon*, but the 80% higher carrying capacity of the *Bretagne* made her a significantly more efficient vessel. It was clear why a new vessel was more attractive than a project to stretch her older stable mate. Interior design of the *Bretagne* was led by Bernard Bidault and the Nantes-based

AIA, who had so impressed during the *Duc de Normandie* conversion.

The loss of Townsend Thoresen's *Herald of Free Enterprise* at Zeebrugge on 6th March 1987 occurred as the plans were evolving. The outcome of the inquiry into the tragedy and the changes in safety standards that were mandated as a result, were to influence the subsequent design of the *Bretagne*.

From the outset, the *Bretagne* was designed to be a pioneering ship. She incorporated a 'safe return to port' capability, which featured a diesel fuel tank located in the funnel capable of restarting the ship's engines in the event of a generator fire or engine room blackout. The *Bretagne* could thus easily reach a port of safety wherever an incident might occur in the Bay of Biscay. Learning lessons from the fire on the *Prince of Brittany*, the *Bretagne* was equipped with three generators, each physically isolated by steel partitions, with dual fuel circuits. An engine could therefore continue to operate, by being enabled through independent electrical switchboards which permitted electrical distribution, even if the other ships' engines had been lost to fire. An 'addressable' fire detection system (similar to that fitted on the *Sovereign of the Seas*) immediately identified the precise location of any fire on board, rather than having a group of alarms in a broad area, allowing action to be taken directly from the bridge instead of requiring crew to be sent to identify the source of an alarm.

On the car deck, the *Bretagne* was fitted with smoke, flame and heat detectors; the sprinkler system would start automatically if all three were detected simultaneously. With up to 600 cars on the vessel's garage decks this overcame a big potential source of problems. This was a truly innovative development and not then mandated by the Safety of Life at Sea (SOLAS) regulations, making it difficult to reach agreement with the safety authorities, as there were no relevant controls to be measured against. The garage deck scupper systems on the *Bretagne* were four times the size mandated by SOLAS regulations.

The *Bretagne* was the first English Channel passenger vessel to be fitted with passenger evacuation slides. Their rapid deployment enhanced evacuation safety and took over from the traditional process of launching lifeboats and life rafts. Her navigation bridge incorporated wraparound windows, a safety control centre and navigation equipment situated alongside the propulsion and rudder controls, in a design that set design standards still in place today. The *Bretagne* was the first ferry to deploy a system of separated rudder helms, which placed a rudder in the axis of the ship when the corresponding rudder was placed astern, thus increasing torque and enhancing manoeuvring capability. The oversized rudders increased drag and reduced speed, but this was compensated for by greatly improved vessel manoeuvring.

In a further unusual and innovative touch, art lover and aesthete Michielini delegated the entire internal decoration of the vessel to the Scottish artist Alexander Goudie, who was married to a Breton girl, and a was renowned lover of Brittany. He built a substantial portfolio of paintings of the region in a style reminiscent of the Breton artist Mathurin Méheut (known for his work on the SS *Normandie*) and the Pont Aven school. Goudie's Celtic background was important, as it freely opened up access to local culture and allowed him to be accepted into the community. He was given free rein to deliver his vision of Brittany across all areas of the vessel, from restaurants to bars, cabins to reception areas, right down to the colours of carpets, blinds and curtains. Goudie supervised the outfitting with his son Lachlan, who quickly became very bored, so Jim Mason took him to one side and the pair spent time drawing together. Each room was given a Breton theme, and Goudie's work invited passengers to embrace the landscapes, markets, fishing ports, and personalities of Brittany through a series of paintings and lithographs in cabins and public areas. The varied works included the region's buildings, countryside, holiday beaches, seascapes and culinary delights as well as the colourful traditions of the Breton way of life. His pièce de résistance was a mural of dancers and musicians dressed in regional costume as the centrepiece in the main reception area of the *Bretagne*. The new vessel would be an unparalleled floating art gallery.

Construction work on the *Bretagne* was delayed at the Saint-Nazaire shipyard. The vessel was due to be launched in October 1988, but this date was postponed until 5th January 1989, and this second date also fell by the wayside. The tensions rose in the shipyard and Mason was sent over with Oliver Weiss, a member of the legal team, to resolve the delivery issues; Mason optimistically took three days of clothing, expecting a protracted debate. The shipyard owners and Brittany Ferries' management team held frequent meetings in the 'Grill' to try and resolve the difficult problems they were facing. The stress was palpable, and Mason broke the ice by sketching a poster of Michielini as a 'wanted' man. There were questions over the levels of manpower being committed by the shipyard to the job, so Mason extended his stay and spent a fortnight counting workers on and off the ship to ensure they were meeting their contractual requirements.

The *Bretagne* was finally launched on 4th February 1989. She undertook her sea trials

Left: **The *Bretagne* on her first sailing to Santander.** *(Miles Cowsill)*

Top right: **Arriving in Cork during her first season of operation.** *(Miles Cowsill)*

Bottom right: **The spacious main car deck of the *Bretagne*.** *(Miles Cowsill)*

at the end of May during which she reached an impressive top speed of 25 knots. But her delivery was further delayed by six weeks following a strike by metalworkers at the shipyard. On 9th July, the day prior to planned handover, the work was still unfinished and Christian Michielini walked out of a meeting with the shipyard management, refusing to accept the vessel. After an intensive effort to get the vessel completed, agreement was finally reached at 14:45 on 10th July after another tense stand-off, and the vessel was formally handed over to Brittany Ferries. Capt. Hardouin had just five hours to prepare his vessel to receive 1,500 guests on board, including 350 former employees of the Chantiers de l'Atlantique, and sail from the shipyard.

The *Bretagne* left St Nazaire at 21:00 on 10th July bound for Roscoff. Settling in on board, Michielini attempted to take a bath in the Owners Cabin - one he had long promised himself - but found to his embarrassment that the taps had not been connected. The *Bretagne* arrived in Roscoff on the morning of 12th July to the sound of Breton bagpipes amidst a crowded quayside welcome. First aboard were Alexis Gourvennec and the shareholders, then the company's shore staff, and finally residents of the Léon region. Guests were welcomed by Gourvennec and, after a religious ceremony, the *Bretagne* was named by Madame Bourges. The champagne bottle refused to break on the hull, despite four attempts, as the patriotic red, white and blue ribbon was caught by wind drag each time it was released. It broke first time when Mason arranged for the ribbon to be replaced by a cord. Official speeches, a bagadou concert, and a display of aerobatics followed, before guests settled down to enjoy a Grande Bouffe of breton lobster, sea bream, salmon, veal, rib of beef, parma ham, terrine of sweetbreads, duck aiguillettes, ham and pineapple, timbale of asparagus mousse, fondant vegetables, mixed salads, a cheese platter and a trolley of desserts, accompanied by wines from Chateau de L'Oiselinière and Domaine de Terrebrune.

The introduction of the *Bretagne* marked another landmark in the evolution of Brittany Ferries. For the first time the Company was able to match the marketing proposition of the 'Holiday Ferry' with a distinctive product that delivered the promise of a unique French on board experience. The *Bretagne* was truly a game changer, dramatically different from her competitors, embodying all the strengths of a coherent design and destination-matched style. Passengers were travelling to France because they embraced the French lifestyle and everything that this entailed. Authentic French gastronomy could now be enjoyed by passengers during the crossing; the holiday could truly begin the moment they stepped on board the vessel. The French experience was being brought closer to Britain.

Brittany Ferries had an option to build two more vessels to the *Bretagne's* design; these would have provided considerable homogeneity across the fleet and created significant efficiencies in stores provision and easier inter-availability of vessels between routes. The vessels would also have been hot properties in the charter market if they could not be deployed on the western Channel. But the pound sterling slipped from FF11.0 to FF9.5 between spring 1989 and spring 1990 hitting income, and the banks were nervous about the Company's ability to manage big ships, even though these were considerably easier to operate. The options could not be taken up, much to the regret of the management team.

Nine

Preparing for the Bretagne

A s Brittany Ferries recovered from the crew lock-out of early 1987, it was evident that there were still significant problems in delivering a consistent on board experience to match the promise of the advertising message and the quality of the brand image being nurtured by the UK team. The Company was falling short. Although 85% of the passengers on board were British, many crew members still did not speak English as it was not a requirement of their recruitment through the French merchant navy system. Officers worked within a strict hierarchical structure, and often struggled to appreciate the British psyche. Brittany Ferries' competitors employed largely British crews and tailored their on board offer to an anglicised palette, as that was where their maritime traditions lay. Here was a way in which Brittany Ferries could distinguish itself, by extending the French on board experience now being delivered on the *Duc de Normandie* across the rest of the fleet. A step change in quality would allow the holiday to truly begin on board the fleet.

Positive lessons were learned from the frustrations of the Hotel Services crew which had led to the persistent periods of industrial action, and the gross inefficiencies inherent in the manner of their recruitment, employment, management and retention. The strikes proved pivotal in helping transform Brittany Ferries' on board experience.

The solution to the problems of delivery of a consistent quality of on board service could only lie in France, whence shipboard operations were managed. Christian Michielini's attempts to professionalise service delivery had to overcome resistance from the Brittany Ferries Board, many members of which had a vision limited to potatoes,

The *Duc de Normandie*. *(Richard Kirkman)*

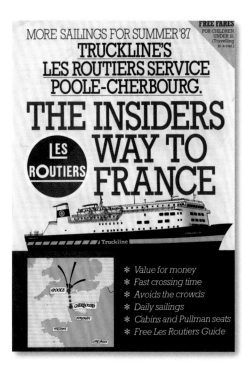

The 1987 France brochure , Les Routiers brochure for the Poole-Cherbourg service , Spain brochure and Gîtes brochure. *(Rook Dunning)*

artichokes and cauliflowers. But the argument was eventually won in 1987. The result was the creation of a new subsidiary of Brittany Ferries, the Société De Services De Restauration et D'Hotellerie, or Serestel, a hotel services company bringing together all aspects of on board service delivery. Serestel had an inspirational leader in Jacques le Rouzo, who had Michielini's full backing to make whatever changes were needed to transform the organisation.

The new structure allowed the restrictions of the French Maritime Labour Code to be by-passed by employing staff directly through the Serestel company, producing a financial saving of around FF20 million in the first year alone. Serestel became a framework to join up the previously disparate group of on board functions led from France; Hotel Services, restaurants, shops and all on board facilities, together with the shore infrastructure that supported them, could now be managed by a specialist team, free to recruit the leading exponents of each aspect of on board service. The integration of these functions enabled a review of operational logistics to deliver a holistic transformation of service quality. The professionalism of each of the trades across the passenger service sector could be acknowledged and developed for the first time. Freedom from the constraints of the French Maritime Labour Code enabled internal promotion to be gained by capability and qualification, rather than through the long-established maritime tradition of seniority. Serestel could define and deliver a consistent service quality across the fleet. But this transformation would take time, as it needed to encompass the complete spectrum of Hotel Service activity.

The first step towards raising on board standards required a wholesale reappraisal of all aspects of service delivery to plan for delivery of a seamless integrated product. This 'root and branch' transformation was difficult for other ferry companies to replicate, because the new system embraced the entire product offer experienced by passengers

delivered through one common organisational structure. Serestel could do this because all aspects of the service came within its bailiwick, unlike British competitors who frequently sub-contracted key elements of their service to outside parties. Inspiration for the new Serestel team came from an extensive programme of visits to leading institutions across the world to seek ideas that might support service improvements or define a product style. Serestel borrowed and refined ideas on presentation and service provided they improved the on board product.

Brittany Ferries' clientele was becoming increasingly diverse as the Company expanded, particularly in the second half of the 1980s with the opening of the Portsmouth-Caen route. To the veteran Francophile traveller were being added an increasing number of families on summer holidays and breaks, and many passengers travelling to France for the first time. Each group had different budgets and quality expectations, so was looking for a variety of catering propositions to satisfy their needs. The establishment of Serestel opened up the opportunity to provide a diversified range of catering offers to deliver the required level of choice needed to satisfy the market. Serestel would cater for all tastes, from the high-end gastronomic table

The Brittany Ferries parrot makes a public appearance on the cover of the 1987 Big Breaks brochure. *(Rook Dunning)*

to fast food self-service, with the added temptation of tea rooms and freshly prepared pastries; something to suit all tastes and pockets. Serge Hinault was recruited as the first Pastry Chef in 1987, and an in-house pastry and dessert production unit was established in Roscoff to deliver a consistent high-quality product. A second unit was to follow later at Ouistreham. Gone were the synthetic desserts characteristic of the traditional cross-Channel market and perpetuated by competitors. In came the irresistible temptation of fresh French patisserie.

The creation of outstanding on board restaurants was based on much more than the consistent serving of the highest quality food prepared from the freshest ingredients by highly trained chefs. All details of the restaurant, from the customer reception to the internal ambience, the quality of lighting, the minutiae of table presentation, and the style of menu design were each planned in great detail. The delivery of each course to the right diner at the right time with the minimum of questions was the result of extensive training of waiters to ensure they understood their customers' requirements and paid attention to their choices, even though there might be dozens of tables to serve. Such standards could only be sustained by planning service delivery from the ground up. This re-engineering of the entire on board product delivery mechanism, coupled with changes to the shore operation needed to support the process, was a slow and meticulous process. Coupled with the planned changes to the fleet, Serestel was laying the foundations for a transformation of the service, and the holistic extension of the brand beyond brochures and advertising, allowing the 'Holiday France' proposition to be extended on board. Now, Brittany Ferries was increasingly in control of all aspects of the holiday. The bar was being raised.

For the 1987 season the *Duc de Normandie* continued her winter schedule of a one round trip daily service between Portsmouth and Caen, with the schedule switched to operate overnight from Portsmouth at 23:30 (fitted onto the berth after the departure of the St Malo sailing at 21:00), with a 16:30 return from Ouistreham designed to optimise attractiveness for freight carryings. Her frequency was upped to three-daily-crossings at mid-season weekends from April to November and a full thrice-daily crossing schedule during the peak summer. The Portsmouth-St Malo route operated daily, with day-out (09:30), night-back (21:15) schedules from Portsmouth during the winter, reverting to night-out (21:00), day-back (10:45) during the mid-season and twice-daily (09:30/21:00 from Portsmouth, 10:45/21:15 from St Malo) during the peak summer season. The Plymouth-Roscoff service was reduced to a weekly sailing in winter, operating overnight (23:30) from Plymouth on Fridays and returning overnight (23:30) on Saturdays, with six departures offered each week during the mid-season and eleven departures weekly at the peak. The *Bretagne* maintained two departures each week between Plymouth and Santander, fitting in her weekend Roscoff and Cork rotation from mid-May to mid-September.

The 1987 brochure continued the use of creative destination photography with a striking image of Mont St Michel on the cover. Copy and images focused on the rural French idyll, with full-page photography of open roads winding through French countryside. Just four of the 60 pages promoted the fleet and their on board facilities; the destination was still the prime focus of the content. BCIF was cross-promoted with its own page in the brochure. Separate brochures were produced for the gîte market, in which 950 properties were advertised, Cabin Cruiser Holidays, the Big Book of Breaks, 'Velo' cycling holidays in the Western Loire, and Ski-Drive holidays in the French Alps. The distinctive parrot continued to make an appearance in the Big Breaks brochure.

Whilst the Les Routiers Poole-Cherbourg service featured in the main brochure, it also had its own colourful four-page A4 leaflet advertising 'The Insiders way to France'. The start of the Poole-Cherbourg operating season was brought forward to 1st June with sailing frequencies increased, building on the success of the route in the first season. Although advertised as a 'no frills, value for money approach' service, pricing on the route was identical to that offered on the Portsmouth-Caen service. On board accommodation was described as 'clean and comfortable' with the Les Routiers restaurant featuring an 'appetising, well-cooked and simply presented' menu.

The 'ByPass' was the focus of the 1987 advertising campaign. 'How to sail to France avoiding the dire straits' introduced the theme, whilst the banner headline announced 'the new Calais, Cherbourg, Le Havre, Dieppe ByPass'. The Portsmouth-Caen route was described as 'the new Holiday Route for a clear run into all of Holiday France'. Promotion of the Poole-Cherbourg route was undertaken independently through the Les Routiers brand, and the service was not featured on the main brand advertising map; it was, after all, heading to one of the ports which the Portsmouth-Caen service was by-passing.

With a new vessel on order, the *Duc de Normandie* setting new quality standards for English Channel services, and Serestel beginning to make an impact, the corporate strapline was updated from 'The Holiday Ferry' to 'The Holiday Fleet' to provide a more accurate reflection of the on board experience.

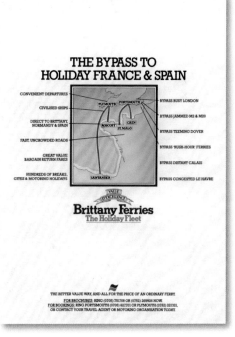

ByPass advertising. *(Rook Dunning)*

1987 started positively with the pound beginning to recover against the French Franc, starting a rise from around FF9.4 to FF11.0 within two years, but there followed a disaster which shook the ferry industry to the core. On 6th March, Townsend Thoresen's *Herald of Free Enterprise* capsized whilst leaving Zeebrugge during a routine evening sailing to Dover. The clam shell bow doors on the vessel had inadvertently been left open as the ship left the quay, and water flooded straight onto the vehicle deck, causing the vessel to roll and finally fall onto her side. 193 passengers and crew lost their lives in horrific circumstances, the worst peacetime loss of life in a maritime accident since 1919.

The traumatic disaster was a wake-up call for safety standards in the ferry industry, particularly when the subsequent inquiry drew attention to cultural factors behind the accident that were embedded within the management style of Townsend Thoresen. All companies readily re-appraised operational procedures to ensure that there could be no repetition of the circumstances. Many subsequent improvements were made to the design of ro-ro vessels, including the fitting of watertight doors, the addition of indicators showing the position of the vessel's bow doors where not previously provided, and the banning of undivided decks.

Whilst Brittany Ferries did not employ any vessels with clam shell door designs, the impact on customer confidence was severe, and in the short-term the reservations team had the difficult task of reassuring callers of the inherent safety of the Company's operations. Ian Carruthers sought to emphasise that "like everybody, we have validated our procedures, but we have rigid controls before sailing, like pre-flight cockpit checks. Ferries are not designed to put to sea with the doors open. It is such a fundamental thing, just as jumbo jets are not designed to land without wheels. When the DC-10 had a serious problem, it was never suggested that all aircraft were unsound. Our Chief Officer, the second in command, is responsible for the doors. In addition to our set procedures our doors have sensors which pick up any movement at sea."

DINER

Salade de jambon fumé aux noisettes

Filet de saumon à l'ose lle

Toast de chèvre chaud

Assiette gourmande

Poui ly fumé Michel Redde 1983
cuvée Majorum

Château Mouton baronne Philippe 1979
grand cru classé du Médoc

Trégastel celebration menu. *(Ian Carruthers collection)*

In May the *Trégastel* returned following a major refit, during which a new fin-stabiliser system was fitted to replace the previous system. Passenger facilities were improved, with a new bar area designed by Bernard Bidault presenting a 'French village square' atmosphere. Seating and the duty-free shopping facilities were also upgraded. David Longden stated that the work was "in line with our policy to create the most comfortable and stylish on board passenger facilities to be found on Channel ferries." Her return was celebrated with a special dinner on board.

Brittany Ferries' strong position in Plymouth was consolidated by the signing a new ten-year agreement with ABP which gave the Company sole-user status for passenger

Swansea-Cork Ferries' *Celtic Pride* provided useful additional capacity on the Irish service; she is seen here in Cork. She came with a Polish crew. *(Ferry Publications Library)*

services from Millbay Docks to France and Spain. The port authority installed another deep water linkspan in anticipation of the arrival of larger vessels and, building on the general improvements in passenger facilities and expansion of marshalling areas, plans were advanced for a new terminal to handle the growth in traffic anticipated from the new vessel. Carruthers noted that the new berth was "critical to our plans" and that the Company hoped to be in a position to announce its fleet expansion plans shortly.

The formal announcement of the signing of the construction contract for the *Bretagne* was made on 10th June 1987. Her arrival in spring 1989 would almost double passenger capacity on the Santander and Roscoff routes from Plymouth and dramatically increase freight space on the routes, with guaranteed year-round capacity for up to 62 freight units.

Traffic on the Portsmouth-Caen route continued to grow healthily, with the *Duc de Normandie* heavily booked with passenger business throughout the summer; the *Purbeck* was transferred from Poole to add much needed freight capacity at Portsmouth and release pressure on the *Duc de Normandie*. The freighter *Miseva* was chartered in May to operate until 25th June on the Portsmouth-Caen route. Demand from Ireland was also proving strong, and the *Celtic Pride* was chartered from Swansea-Cork Ferries to offer additional midweek Cork-Roscoff sailings during the peak season. The 1972-built 7,800GT vessel was 128.8 metres in length and 19.5 metres in beam; she could carry 1,000 passengers, and 146 cars or 20 freight vehicles, with capacity of 420 cabin berths. The *Celtic Pride* was a welcome addition in capacity to support expansion from Ireland.

The autumn was marked by the 'Great Storm', which brought hurricane conditions to the English Channel on the night of 15th-16th October. Toby Oliver was returning from Caen to Portsmouth aboard the *Duc de Normandie* accompanying a small exclusive press party made up of Elisabeth de Stroumillo, the travel editor of the Daily Telegraph, Ivor Herbert, the travel writer for the Mail on Sunday, and Desmond Balmer, the travel editor of The Observer. The group had been in Brittany and Normandy judging the finalists in the Brittany Ferries restaurant competition; passengers had written reviews of restaurants visited on holiday and the judging panel went to visit six short listed establishments to award prizes. A booklet containing the reviews was made available on board the fleet the following year. After visiting the last restaurant in Bayeux the party noted that the wind was getting up. Once on board the *Duc de Normandie,* the Captain announced that a rough crossing lay ahead, but the vessel had to sail as it would be unsafe to remain alongside the berth. A 'rough crossing' proved to be a bit of an understatement... When the *Duc de Normandie* eventually arrived in Portsmouth just about every item of glass and crockery had been smashed, and furniture was scattered to all corners of the vessel. But neither Oliver nor the cream of British travel writers had been seasick!

One consequence of the loss of the *Herald of Free Enterprise* was that the P&O Group could not continue to operate their Townsend Thoresen brand with the fleet's distinctive orange hulls. Although P&O had barely assumed management responsibility for the services at the time of the disaster, the brand was tainted. The company announced on 21st October that the operation would henceforth be known and branded as P&O European Ferries (combining the P&O brand with the name of the holding company of Townsend Thoresen), with the fleet switching from the interim livery of a pale blue funnel and orange hull to a new dark blue and white vessel livery.

Work started during October on extending the M40 motorway from Oxford northwards to Birmingham, which promised significant improvements in journey times for passengers travelling from the Midlands and North via the A34 and M27 through to Portsmouth and Poole. The competitive position of both ports relative to the short-sea routes would be enhanced as a consequence. However, this improvement was soon counterbalanced by the start of construction work on the Channel Tunnel on 15th December, with a planned opening date of 1993. The long-anticipated threat was to become a reality.

Limited competition for the Iberian freight business started in 1987 with the intermittent operations of Vasco Shipping Line, which started a weekly service from Poole to Viana de Costelo in Portugal, utilising the small freighter *Thomas Wehr*. This vessel was later replaced by the even smaller *Flipper* and *Seafowl*, and the service struggled to achieve any form of consistency. It was to cease trading in 1989.

The 1987 season saw further growth across Brittany Ferries with new records again set across all three markets, but tourist growth was rather less than might have been anticipated given the performance of the previous year and a full season of operation of the Portsmouth-Caen route. The year was described as the nadir in British travel to France. Passenger volumes rose by 6.0% to 1,248,952, vehicles by 4.8% to 257,190 and freight units by 15.2% to 113,113, the first time that the 100,000 level had been breached in the freight sector. The additional freight capacity provided on the Portsmouth-Caen route proved highly beneficial, and with many summer sailings of the

Duc de Normandie operating full and turning away traffic, it was clear that additional capacity would be needed if the route's longer-term potential was to be realised. Plans were announced for second ship on the Portsmouth-Caen route in 1988, to run opposite to the *Duc de Normandie* from 19th May to 11th September. The *Cornouailles* had enjoyed another successful season on the Les Routiers Poole-Cherbourg service, and her 1988 operating season was extended to run from 27th May to 11th September, with two return sailings on four days each week and one on the remaining three.

Jim Mason secured the bareboat charter of the 6,642 gross-tonne *Gotland* to facilitate the necessary increase in capacity on the Portsmouth-Caen route. The *Gotland* was built in 1973 for *Stena Line*, but was sold shortly after launch to *Rederi A.B Gotland* and then chartered out to TT-Line and Moby Lines. At 123.8 metres in length and 20.5 metres beam, she could carry 1,670 passengers and 300 cars, offering similar capacity to the *Duc de Normandie*. Her interiors were distinctively Scandinavian, with designer furniture and an emphasis on bright orange fittings. Proposals to rename her the *Lisieux* were not

A charter of the *Gotland* enabled the Caen service to expand to three daily sailings in 1988. *(Miles Cowsill)*

implemented. The *Gotland* was operated with British officers, Irish deck and engine crew and Breton hospitality staff, all managed by Denholm Ship Management. The charter facilitated the expansion of the Portsmouth-Caen service to three return sailings each day during the peak season, matching the frequency offered by P&O European Ferries on their competing Portsmouth-Le Havre route.

The promotional theme for the 1988 season was 'Value d'Excellence', offered across the ferry fare structure and in the Holiday products. Brittany Ferries was able to state that 85% of sailings in 1988 would be offered in lower price bands than 1987. Lead-in adult prices on the Portsmouth-Caen and Poole-Cherbourg routes were £14 single, with cars priced from £34; for the Portsmouth-St Malo the prices were from £18 (passengers) and £38 (vehicles) single, whilst from Plymouth-Roscoff they were from £17 (passengers) and £34 (vehicles) single. With special 60-Hour and Five- and Ten-Day return fares available, these prices were below those offered on the short-sea routes from Dover and Folkestone. The Plymouth-Santander route offered a free car passage when three passengers travelled together with the vehicle outside the main season.

The 'Holiday Fleet' strapline was at the heart of the brochures, which positioned Brittany Ferries as 'The uncommonly civilised way to Holiday France and Spain'. It outlined the reasons why the Company helped 'leave behind all the reasons why people often *need* a holiday after crossing the Channel', without the 'Cash and Calais' day trippers, the excited coachloads of schoolchildren, the frantic scrum in the bar and the Wembley atmosphere in the Duty Free. The 'By-pass to Holiday France & Spain' theme was retained in advertising, with clear maps showing the geographical logic of the route structure flanked by the advantages of western Channel sailings with Brittany Ferries. The concept was extended in similar style to embrace 'The By-pass to Holidays in France & Spain' and The By-pass to Thousands of Inclusive Holidays in France & Spain' with the map replaced by a brochure cover.

Stephen Tuckwell, a former worldwide head of advertising for British Airways was brought in to strengthen the BCB team in April 1988, and was to play a significant role in the development of the corporate brand over the coming years.

The start of the year was dominated in the cross-Channel ferry industry by the start of a long running industrial dispute in Dover between P&O European Ferries and the NUS and NUMAST trade unions over ship manning levels and employment terms and conditions. P&O European Ferries sought to make cost savings of £6 million per year on the running costs of the Dover fleet, as part of their strategy of facing up to the challenge of the Channel Tunnel. The dispute started in early February and led to eleven ships being laid up in Rotterdam, Vlissingen and Chatham as crews went on extended strike. Although agreement was reached with the officers' union, the dispute with the seafarers was protracted and 2,300 were served with redundancy notices. A change in legislation now prevented both secondary picketing and sympathy strikes, and permitted P&O European

The French and Gîtes brochures for the 1988 season. *(Rook Dunning)*

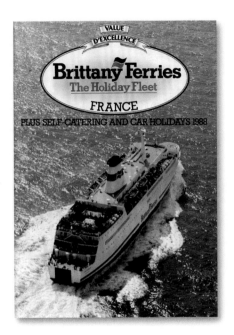

Ferries' services from Portsmouth to operate normally, but some traffic transferred from the short-sea sector to bring a short-term bonus to Brittany Ferries. The *Gotland* was brought into service during mid-March, two months ahead of her planned introduction date, to support the Portsmouth-Caen route. She concentrated on carrying the large volumes of school groups that had transferred from the Dover-Calais route. This had the advantage of concentrating this traffic on a single vessel, allowing the *Duc de Normandie* to focus on carrying the motorist business and avoid more-lucrative traffic sharing space with hordes of excitable schoolchildren.

There was no prospect of Brittany Ferries' crews being involved in any sympathetic industrial action as there was a no-strike agreement in place and all western Channel operations continued as normal. With passenger bookings for the peak season running 30% ahead of their 1987 level, even before the impact of the NUS strike at Dover was felt, the *Prince of Brittany* was added to the Portsmouth-Caen route roster to bring

The *Connacht* required substantial heavy cleaning to bring her up to Brittany Ferries' standards before she emerged as the *Duchesse Anne. (Miles Cowsill)*

further capacity, with the *Armorique* transferring to cover the *Prince of Brittany's* planned duties on the Portsmouth-St Malo service. By May, growth on the Caen route was sufficient to justify the utilisation of the *Breizh-Izel* to deliver further freight capacity, bringing a four-ship service to the route. Looking further ahead, there was an emerging need to boost capacity on the Portsmouth-St Malo service, and Mason was despatched to scour the market to find an appropriate vessel.

Bookings received a further boost when the independent Holiday Which? magazine ranked Brittany Ferries' holiday products amongst the most popular with their readers in a report which generally suggested that Tour Operators' standards were dropping.

Brittany Ferries was open to carrying all kinds of freight and Freight Manager Gordon Day went to Blackpool to secure a special contract with pigeon fanciers from the north of England. This group would load their prize birds into specially adapted lorries and have them shipped to continental destinations to be released simultaneously, allowing them to race each other home. On one occasion several trucks were lined up on the quay at Poole waiting to head for Lyon to be released. One of the dockers pulled a lever whilst inspecting the vehicle and inadvertently released 2,000 pigeons into the sky; they immediately headed for home. No-one knew which birds had been released and which had gone on to France, and there was some embarrassment explaining the predicament. The fanciers were surprised to see their prize birds returning before they should have been released...

On 30th March 1988 Sealink British Ferries re-opened their Portsmouth-Cherbourg route, with a twice-weekly extension to Guernsey using the otherwise redundant *Earl Granville*.

The following month the result of Mason's search became clear when Brittany Ferries announced the purchase of the *Connacht* for the Portsmouth-St Malo route. The *Connacht* was completed in 1979 at the Verolme Dockyard in Cork for B&I Line's Cork-Pembroke Dock service and she opened the route in May that year. This service was not a great commercial success and the company was forced to undertake a series of financial restructurings that led to the 7,000 gross-tonne *Connacht* being surplus to requirements and available for sale. She could offer capacity for 1,350 passengers and 316 cars and was capable of delivering a service speed of 20 knots, making her an ideal configuration for the St Malo route. Her capacity would represent a significant step up from the 1,000 passenger, 200 car carryings of the *Prince of Brittany*. The purchase was completed by Sabemen in October and was followed by a substantial programme of conversion and refurbishment to bring her up to Brittany Ferries' standards, prior to her planned entry into service in May 1989. Coupled with the future arrival of the *Bretagne*, the acquisition represented another significant expansion in fleet capacity.

This was not the end of Brittany Ferries' ambitions. Bolstered by growth in freight traffic of 40% over 1987 carryings, Michielini and his team began to consider an order for a new freight vessel for the Poole-Cherbourg service. The demand from all sectors on the Portsmouth-Caen service was exceeding all expectations and it was clear that something needed to be done to overcome the need to provide the right capacity and avoid having to concentrate so many small vessels on the route. A second large multi-purpose vessel was needed, with substantial freight capacity topped by high-quality passenger facilities. The combination of the two projects could potentially taking fleet investment to over £100 million, but they would be an attractive proposition for shipyards. The message from the UK team was clear; we can fill these vessels when they arrive.

As the P&O industrial dispute at Dover moved towards resolution ahead of the peak season, the *Prince of Brittany* and *Breizh-Izel* left the Portsmouth-Caen route, but the freight vessel *Gabrielle Wehr* was chartered to offer additional summer capacity alongside the *Duc de Normandie* and *Gotland*. The 1978-built 7,365GT vessel was 141.3 metres long and 17.4 metres in beam and offered 1,148 lane-metres capacity for freight.

The arrival of the *Connacht* on the Portsmouth-St Malo route from the 1989 season would allow the *Prince of Brittany* to be released to support the Portsmouth-Caen route on a more permanent basis, and permit the *Gotland* to complete her service with the Company, as planned on 11th September 1988. The *Connacht* was delivered on 3rd October and sent straight to the Meyer Werft Yard at Papenburg for a ten-week £2.5 million refit, improving her accommodation to reach the standard of the *Duc de Normandie* and repairing and upgrading her engines. The vessel was in a poor state of repair after her Irish ownership, and the eventual cost of the refurbishment proved to be twice the price of the original estimate. Cabin accommodation was restored on 'C' deck, having only been removed by B&I Line the previous year. The cafeteria was rebuilt with high-tech equipment and 250 new seats, in preparation for a new upgraded menu to be introduced when she entered service in April 1989. A new 70-seat Viennoisserie followed the successful pattern established on the *Duc de Normandie* in serving croissants and pastries. The *Connacht* was renamed *Duchesse Anne*, after Anne of Brittany, the only woman to have been queen consort of France twice, between 1491 and 1498, and 1499 and 1514. She was a strong supporter of Brittany in the fight against the rest of France, and became a symbol of Breton patriotism.

At Portsmouth, Brittany Ferries paid for guaranteed slot times on the berths in their name, which had allowed Channel Island Ferries and now BCIF to pay lower port charges on the back of the parent Company. When Brittany Ferries applied for additional slots to permit their second vessel arrival each evening during the 1989 season, the Port Authority declined the request. The new timings could have easily been accommodated if the slot times allocated to P&O European Ferries were varied slightly, but Port Manager Tony George declined to make the change. This created significant anger at Brittany Ferries and BCIF, and Carruthers outlined to George why this was a mistake. With three daily departures to Caen and two to St Malo plus the Channel Islands departure, something had to give. BCIF gave advance notice in August of their intention to transfer their services to operate from Poole with effect from January 1989, thereby releasing space and slot times at Portsmouth for Brittany Ferries' own use, but allowing BCIF to be accommodated in another Brittany Ferries-dominated port, from where their reservations team were already managed. Carruthers later discovered that P&O European Ferries did not make any payment to the port authority for their guaranteed slot times, which added to Brittany Ferries' frustration with the approach of the Portsmouth port management.

The Company reservations system had been developed incrementally from the very early days of paper-based systems to become a computer-based ferry booking system onto which the various holiday products were gradually being grafted. This piecemeal development proved both complex and inefficient as the business grew, but was the only way to incrementally match business development with a system that was always lagging slightly behind in capability. Brittany Ferries was amongst the first companies to attempt to integrate ferry and holiday reservation bookings into a single system. The development was undertaken in-house in Plymouth, and the system was offered to French colleagues as a way of managing inbound holiday business to Britain. Incremental development could only take the Company so far, and Carruthers and Longden were desperate for better management information to allow the business to be run more efficiently; eventually Michielini was persuaded that investment in an entirely new system was justified and urgent.

After going through a tender process, the investment in a new £3.5 million reservations system was announced, which was trailed as the most modern in Britain. The new system was sourced from SD-Scicon running on DEC hardware, and provided a fully integrated ferry travel, inclusive holiday, and freight reservation service, coupled with the sales accounting 'back-office' that would support the Company in its continued planned expansion. Passenger call times would be improved by between 25% and 30%, reducing the time taken to confirm a ferry booking to two minutes, and an inclusive holiday to three minutes. Carruthers observed that no other travel operator would have anything like the sophistication or efficiency of the new technology when it went live in autumn 1989, ready for the 1990 booking season. P&O European Ferries was already some two years behind in the development of its own 'Dolphin' reservations system, which had no capability for handling holiday products.

Carruthers stated that this investment would not only benefit the Company but the travel trade and general public as well. It would reduce operating costs and therefore improve profitability, offer a faster service and help to hold prices. The new system would spearhead the campaign to establish Brittany Ferries as the only real alternative to the Channel Tunnel.

The early development of the system proved tortuous. Brittany Ferries was already the operator of the largest computer system in south west England, but the developers soon realised that there was insufficient computing power available to handle the proposed configuration. The software simply could not be made to work, and the developers' contract was terminated. Alternative developers were sourced, but software costs rocketed. It looked as if the project was becoming unaffordable. Then, fortuitously, the cost of new hardware began to fall at broadly the same rate as the software costs were rising, so the two halves of the equation balanced each other out and the project became deliverable again.

The time taken to develop the system was well spent. When the new software went live it worked and became a major tool to streamline the booking process whilst providing a wealth of management information. For the first time the team could analyse traffic gaps in the business and seek to fill them without detracting from core business income. A review of passenger business on the Portsmouth-Caen service, for example, highlighted that there was a big gap in volumes between those taking the Five-Day return and passengers purchasing a full return fare. Clearly the full fare was a deterrent to those travelling for holidays of around a week abroad, so a Ten-Day return fare was introduced as an experiment, and it quickly proved popular, providing additional traffic whilst not detracting significantly from the established volumes of business that purchased the full return fare product.

As the business grew so did the management structure and it became evident that each port needed a general manager to support the introduction of new ships, the computerisation of the operation and the development of port infrastructure. Maria Hammett was appointed to the role in Plymouth, Chris Jennings filled the position in Portsmouth and Gina Gardner handled the operation in Poole. Each played a substantial role in the success of their ports in the coming years. With the fleet rapidly expanded, the business growing, and there was a need to install and program new telephone systems, migrate to computer-based bookings, the focus reservations on the Plymouth office, Sharon Alexander was promoted to the position of Contact Centre Manager, the position she still holds in 2020 after 43 years' service with the Company.

There were further positive developments. The impact of Serestel in increasing the quality of the on board product was acknowledged by Egon Ronay in his 'Just a Bite' guide, published at the end of 1988, which included a section on cross-Channel ferry services. The guide was geared towards those looking for restaurants which offer good value for money meals at reasonable prices. The publication quoted the purser of the *Trégastel* on a Plymouth-Roscoff sailing as saying 'She's not a bad old ship, but you can't turn a grandmother into a virgin'. Nonetheless the inspector's experience was described as "a pleasantly memorable one... contributed to by the food, service, ambience and glorious weather." The *Cornouailles* on Poole-Cherbourg was praised for an 'excellent value' menu; the meal was freshly cooked and tasty with a full litre of red wine per table. In contrast the inspector despaired at P&O European Ferries' *Viking Venturer*; he was "almost at a loss to describe how dreadful the lunch (in the Carvery) was... with utterly disgraceful quality and presentation of the food." Unsurprisingly therefore, P&O European Ferries services from Portsmouth were described as being amongst the worst the inspectors had ever travelled on. Brittany Ferries was praised as the carrier offering the best quality food and restaurant facilities on the Channel and topped the league table for all aspects of the crossing. This was an excellent outcome, given that the inspectors did not travel on the flagship Portsmouth services, and demonstrated just how far the quality of the on board product had progressed under the stewardship of Le Rouzo and management of Serestel. Oliver noted that typical French cuisine was served on board all Brittany Ferries' ships, with prices starting at only £6 per person for a four-course meal.

The growth in business in 1988 corrected some of the slowdown that had been experienced in 1987. Autumn business was sufficiently strong for the Portsmouth-Caen schedules to be expanded beyond the single round trip service, with the *Trégastel* brought across to support the *Duc de Normandie* on the route. The *Cornouailles* switched

Brochures and 'Superfleet' advertising for the 1989 season. *(Rook Dunning)*

to the Plymouth-Roscoff service before talking up on a long-term charter to Channel Island Ferries for BCIF use from November 1988.

The addition of chartered tonnage on the Portsmouth-Caen route and the impact of the NUS strike on P&O European Ferries' services at Dover helped boost traffic figures. Brittany Ferries experienced dramatic growth of 36.0% in passengers to 1,698,207, in vehicles of 52.5% to 392,220, and in freight of 33.9% to reach 151,429. In the main summer season between June and September the average growth on all English Channel services in the passenger market was 4.2% and 8.7% for vehicles, but Brittany Ferries could demonstrate growth of 39.6% and 50.6% respectively. It was a bad year for P&O European Ferries from Portsmouth on the back of the company's problems in Dover, with a drop of 125,000 passengers to Cherbourg and Le Havre during July and August leading to an overall fall of 21% in both passengers and vehicles during the year. The Portsmouth-Caen service was beginning to bite into their business.

There was an early launch for the 1989 programme. The new season promised the upgrade of the fleet across all six routes, with the arrival of the *Bretagne* and the *Duchesse Anne* as part of what was now described as the £70 million 'Superfleet' programme. The *Bretagne* would bring new standards to the Plymouth-Santander, Plymouth-Roscoff and Cork-Roscoff routes; the *Duchesse Anne* would enhance the Portsmouth-St Malo service and the *Reine Mathilde* would partner the *Duc de Normandie* to offer three sailings each day during the summer on the fastest growing route on the Channel from Portsmouth to Caen. This flagship route would have daily capacity for 4,000 passengers and 900 cars. There would be a dramatic increase in capacity on the Les Routiers Poole-Cherbourg service, where demand had consistently outstripped supply, with the introduction of the *Corbière* (to be replaced by the *Trégastel* later in the season) increasing the number of passengers on each sailing from 300 to 800. These radical changes needed to be supported by an aggressive fare strategy to ensure their success.

A stylistic image of the *Bretagne* graced the cover of the 1989 'Sailings, Fares & Special Offers' brochure which introduced 'Superfleet, the most significant development in ferry travel for a decade... the same price as an ordinary ferry and remarkable value'. The Holidays & Breaks brochure contained a fold out page with an A3 image of the *Bretagne*. The 'Value d'Excellence' theme was extended to include 'Holidays', 'Fleet', 'Hotels', 'Spain', 'Motoring', 'Breaks' and 'Short Breaks', all suffixed 'd'Excellence'. Public fares showed many reductions for the 1989 season, and promotional material used tables of fares to demonstrate the scale of price reductions and comparisons with equivalent crossings on the short-sea sector. Fare cuts of 11% to 13% against 1988 charges were outlined for the typical family of two adults, two children and a car, and the 10-Day return fares on selected sailings were shown to be some £36 below the short-sea equivalent fare. A family of two adults, two children under 13 and a car could make a return crossing on the Portsmouth-Caen route for as little as £93 for a Five-Day return fare. A wide range of price reductions could also be found across the full range of holiday products. The team was fighting hard to expand market share and grow the business in a difficult market.

Prices were held at £69 for the Spanish mini-cruise, which for the 1989 season would bring the incentive of travel aboard the *Bretagne*. The offer included the return foot passenger crossing and all meals with a four-course lunch and dinner with wine, and a complimentary bottle of spirits. An optional tour to Santillana del Mar was available out of season.

Longden was determined that discounting of fares was only ever the final option in the marketing strategy; far better to 'add value' to the core proposition and hold public fare levels whenever possible. This approach was illustrated by offers put to the Camping and Caravanning community for the new season. Daytime crossings to France were always more difficult to sell than overnight, and some 60% of the capacity available sailed by day. The Company negotiated arrangements with local campsites near each of the arrival ports to be able to promote a 'first night free' offer, which enabled campers travelling on day crossings to enjoy their first night in France at Brittany Ferries' expense. 'Le Camping Complet' packages offered four sites in Brittany and Normandy. 'Go as you please' offers extended the stay to between six and 14-nights accommodation at over 100 sites in Brittany, Normandy and the Western Loire.

The gîte programme was expanded to cover some 1,250 properties across France, with coverage expanded to Burgundy, the Rhone valley, Languedoc Rousillon, the Midi Pyrenees and Provence. The 372-page 1989 brochure illustrated and described each property. Prices started from £55 for adults and £12 for a child, for a seven-night stay with ferry crossing. Apartment holidays were expanded to embrace Aquitaine alongside

The *Reine Mathilde* docks at No 4 berth at Portsmouth in her first season in her new guise. *(John Hendy)*

Brittany, Normandy, Western Loire, Poitou-Charentes and Provence. The holiday portfolio also grew, with four new seaside apartment resorts at Ile de Re, Royan and Seignosse Le Penon in France, and Laredo in Spain. 'A La carte' motoring tours were offered in France, Switzerland and Italy, and the range of motoring break destinations and car tours was expanded. Coupled with the mix of 'Flexible France', 'Go As You Please', 'Welcome to France', 'Relais and Châteaux Hotels', 'Welcome to Spain', 'Parador and Pousada Touring Holidays', 'Seaside Holidays' and 'Cabin Cruiser Holidays', Brittany Ferries' position as the leading provider of continental holidays for motorists was being further enhanced. Free copies of the AA's 'Discover France' and the Daily Telegraph's 'France Without Tears' and Spain's 'Hidden Country' were offered as booking incentives.

Hugh Bruton joined the team in Ireland and was to hold roles in reservations and as a

Freight agent before becoming Operations Manager and eventually General Manager for the Irish services.

A combination of poor domestic weather in the summer of 1988 and, seemingly, a desire to return to old haunts, prompted a resurgence of bookings at the start of the 1989 season. Carruthers suggested that the quality of food and accommodation eventually had to bring British visitors back to France, and the more pro-active approach of the FGTO in supporting marketing initiatives to promote their country added to the more positive feeling. There were still concerns that duty-free sales would be withdrawn in 1992, and this blow to revenues was likely to be followed by the opening of the Channel Tunnel in 1993. But, more generally, ferry companies were gearing up to face these challenges head on, with substantial investment in new tonnage on the short-sea routes coupled with reconfiguration of existing vessels to reinvent the on board retail experience.

The success of Brittany Ferries on the Caen and Santander routes had not gone unnoticed by other operators, and Sealink British Ferries considered opening a route to Spain as part of chairman James Sherwood's belief in the future strength of peripheral routes relative to the short-sea sector and the Channel Tunnel. But the standards being set by the arrival of the *Bretagne* on the Plymouth-Santander route placed a high bar on the vessel configuration required to provide credible competition, and the plans came to naught.

Although the *Gotland* was laid up at the end of her operating season, Mason worked hard to find work for her until the end of her charter, and she was sub-chartered successively to SNCF for the Newhaven-Dieppe route, Irish Continental Line and lastly, Belfast Car Ferries before being returned to her owners at the end of her year with the Company.

The *Prince of Brittany* was withdrawn from the Portsmouth-St Malo route on 30th December to be given a major overhaul and refit at the Meyer Werft shipyard in Papenburg, Germany in preparation for her new role. She was sold to Senacal towards the end of 1988 and re-registered in Caen. Symbolic of her new ownership (for whom her name was unsuitable) and changed route deployment, the vessel underwent a sex change and was renamed the *Reine Mathilde*, after the wife of William the Conqueror, who was both Queen of England and Duchess of Normandy. She returned to traffic under the command of Capt. Bertrand Apperry in mid-February, fitted with a new fin-stabiliser system and boasting cabin accommodation for 539 passengers and further accommodation in 228 Pullman reclining seats. The *Reine Mathilde* now complimented the *Duc de Normandie,* which had just been voted the most elegant ferry on the Channel, to provide balanced capacity on the Portsmouth-Caen route.

The newly named and freshly refitted *Duchesse Anne* spent time on charter to Crown Line covering the Harwich-Hoek of Holland route at the start of 1989, before joining the Portsmouth-St Malo service on 13th February. Described under the heading 'Superfleet sets sail' in The Observer, the correspondent noted that there were no signs of Channel Tunnel nerves in Brittany Ferries as the first of the new 'superfleet' vessels was introduced to service. The *Duchesse Anne* had been made "as French as possible" said Carruthers. Coupled with the upgrade of the *Prince of Brittany* and the introduction of the *Bretagne* later in the year, there was a clear strategy to ensure that passengers were kept away from the Channel Tunnel by the introduction of better facilities.

The *Celtic Pride* made her final sailing for the Company in January and was returned to Swansea-Cork Ferries. The *Armorique* re-opened the Plymouth-Santander service from 15th January whilst the *Quiberon* covered the refit of the *Duc de Normandie* on the Portsmouth-Caen route. BCIF returned the *Corbière* from charter and she transferred to the Poole-Cherbourg service from 26th May.

The *Breizh-Izel* was sold to the Marelite Marine Co. Ltd, of Limassol, Cyprus in 1989 and converted to a passenger vessel and renamed the *Duchess M.* The negotiation of the contract between Michielini and Panos Marangopoulos was a fiery exchange, conducted initially in Michielini's office and then at a barbeque at his house. The clash of Basque/Italian and Greek culture generated much argument, with Mason trying to keep control of the outcome. At one point as tempers rose, he threatened to put the Bill of Sale on the barbeque, but this failed to calm the discussion, so he carried out his threat. Michielini and Marangopoulos were mortified, as this was as a substantial legal document that took a significant time to produce, and were only slightly mollified when Mason revealed it was a copy of the original. Shortly before the transaction was completed, an inspection of the vessel revealed that a large set of tools had been removed from the engine room; their absence was obvious from the painted outlines of the tools on the bulkhead. Marangopoulos demanded that they be returned before the deal could go ahead, so they had to be recovered from store in Roscoff.

Sometime later, Bruno Michielini was in the Roscoff office on a Friday afternoon when his father suggested he listen in to a phone call. He asked Marie-Jo Véron to call Marangopoulos in Athens, and pressed the loudspeaker button so that everyone could hear. "Hello Panos," he began, "How are you my friend? Are you ready to pay me for the ship I sold you, you remember?" Marangopoulos replied "Hello Christian, how are you my good friend? It is so nice you're calling me, I was just thinking of you. Tell me, when do you go to see me in Athens with Christine? It would be such a pleasure ..." he went on. "OK Panos" replied Michielini "but remember you have to pay for the boat I sold you, remember? When will you do that?" Marangopoulos' Greek accent became stronger. "No problem, Christian, I told you already you can trust me, we are friends ... when you go to Greece with Christine, you know you can come when you want to my place, I have a swimming pool, a very nice house you know and this is by the sea, and ..." The conversation was going nowhere. "OK that's all very fine Panos, but you give me your money first! And after I go to Greece..."

"Oh Christian" replied Marangopoulos, "Monday I will tell my lawyer to arrange that, no problem you know we are such good friends ... you didn't tell me when you go to my place with Christine, you know if she wants to ride, I know the best places to ride around my place, I can arrange very good horses for you both, and you know we will go sailing, I know she likes sailing and you too ...."

"That's OK, Panos, for sure I'll go, you're very kind, BUT YOU GIVE ME YOUR MONEY FIRST!"

This conversation went on this way until they - more or less - agreed on the payment. From that day on, it was clear to Bruno why they nicknamed his father 'The Greek of the Channel'.

The management of Serestel was strengthened by the appointment of Jean-Michel Giguet as director, and he quickly adapted to Brittany Ferries scale of operation and helped maintain the momentum of change in on board services.

Early in 1989 the French government opened discussions with Brittany Ferries on the possible acquisition of the SNCF Armement Navale, the ferry arm of the nationalised state railway, which then operated the Newhaven-Dieppe route in partnership with Sealink British Ferries under the Sealink Dieppe Ferries brand. The operation was offered in its entirety for a knockdown price, but with the proviso that the route be taken over together with its vessels and labour force. Michielini was not keen; he was well aware of the union problems that plagued the route and was unwilling to undermine the hard-earned improvements in industrial relations that had been achieved in Brittany Ferries. Nonetheless he asked Carruthers to prepare a paper to evaluate the potential of the opportunity. Carruthers' work quickly concluded that there were no benefits from taking over the operation; what value could Brittany Ferries add? The union problems were intractable, the quality standards were low, and the carefully constructed Brittany Ferries brand would be tainted by any association with the failing route. It was another valuable lesson in the management art of knowing when not to do something. Michielini concluded that taking on these services would be suicidal for the Company. Carruthers was convinced that any Brittany Ferries brand-expansion must come further south, potentially between France and Corsica, but he was warned that Mediterranean unions were in a different league to their counterparts on the Channel.

By March, Carruthers was able to announce a big surge in bookings and enquiries for the 1989 season, with a 59% rise on the previous year. He noted that "the current strength of the pound against the franc and France represents one of the best holiday experiences available." Company research suggested that British holidaymakers were turning against misleading introductory prices for air packages and reacting strongly to the previous summer's extensive flight delays by rediscovering the quality and value for

The *Duchesse Anne* leaving St Malo on her morning sailing to Portsmouth. *(Miles Cowsill)*

money of French motoring. Quality was identified as one of the most important factors in choosing a holiday.

One response to the difficulties of 1987-8 was to look for new ways of generating revenue. Brittany Ferries could compete directly with P&O European Ferries in the Western Channel for the full fare 'brochure price' business and was active in selling to the Tour Operator and Group Travel sectors, as well as having a substantial holiday business in its own right. The Company was less interested in promotional traffic, which formed a significant proportion of P&O European Ferries' business delivering high volumes but at very low rates. With three main pillars to income the Company was stable, but a fourth would enhance stability. With four legs on a stool, one can be taken away, but the stool still stands; with three legs the stool is vulnerable to any loss. Carruthers was keen to find this fourth leg.

Liz Rodgers and Julie Burrows promote the services with the aid of the parrot. *(Toby Oliver)*

P&O European Ferries had a very active 'shareholder' business which provided a substantial proportion of loyal good-yielding traffic. The scheme had originally been developed by Townsend Thoresen as a way of selling shares without giving any shareholder a sufficiently large stake in the business to threaten the ownership structure. Shareholders were incentivised by discounts on ferry travel across the Townsend Thoresen route portfolio, with reductions of between 20% and 40% on full fare travel offered on the Southampton, then Portsmouth, services, dependent on the number of shares purchased; these rights had transferred to P&O European Ferries with the company takeover. The shareholders now comprised some 124,000 individuals, well over half of whom were frequent travellers; almost two-thirds of them lived within the Portsmouth catchment area. Brittany Ferries could access the names of shareholders from the database in Edinburgh at a price, but providing them with an appropriate attractive offer was a near impossible task against their existing discounted offer. How else could regular travellers be attracted to Brittany Ferries?

Carruthers looked at alternative arrangements and, following a chance meeting with an executive from the Halifax Building Society at a newspaper conference in Berlin, sought to reach an agreement with the Society, which at that time had millions of members. If they could provide funding for a new vessel or some similar project, maybe there was a way in which there could be a discount scheme for Society members which would entitle them to reduced fare travel on Brittany Ferries? But the deal became too complicated to administer. Similar reciprocal deals were even contemplated with the Channel Tunnel, which was talking in terms of having its own loyalty scheme at the time, but these ideas also came to naught.

One particular group of regular travellers whose interests were not well supported by ferry companies were those who owned properties in France. Not only were these frequent cross-Channel travellers, but they were loyal to local, convenient ferry services, wanting to spend the maximum amount of time at their residences, rather than undertaking a long drive from a remote port. They often extended the use of their properties to their families and friends, who were an equally attractive target market. Large numbers of individuals had properties in Normandy and Brittany or used the western Channel ports to access destinations further south.

The French Property Owners Club (FPOC) was launched in late May 1989, offering members a 30% discount on standard passenger and vehicle single fares, and 10% savings on Five-Day return tickets, to bona fide owners of French properties, who had to provide written evidence to the Company of their property ownership in France. These concessions were extended to family and friends using the members' properties on production of a voucher. The annual membership fee was fixed at £15, with a one-off joining fee of £25. A family of four could save £74 on a peak season Portsmouth-Caen sailing just by joining the Club. Membership was initially artificially limited, creating a scarcity that encouraged non-members to join a waiting list of individuals keen to join up.

This scarcity value added to the mystique; there is nothing more attractive than a Club you have to wait to be able to join.

As Brittany Ferries had a sophisticated reservation system, travel patterns of FPOC members could be analysed in detail, and it became evident that they were, on average, travelling 4.3 times a year. This knowledge could be supplemented with an understanding of the duration of each holiday, the fare paid and the likely on board spend, to yield information on the value of each FPOC member. Thus, the number of members in the Club could be gradually expanded in the full knowledge of the likely impact on traffic volumes and revenues, which could be easily budgeted for. Marketing effort was switched to supporting estate agents selling properties in France, who were given incentives for their customers to receive a credit for their property inspection crossing against future bookings with Brittany Ferries if they subsequently made a purchase. FPOC became a prestigious badge, symbolic of property ownership, with access to a community of like-minded regular travellers who would meet on their regular Brittany Ferries crossings. The opportunity to become an FPOC member also encouraged P&O European Ferries' shareholders to sell their shares and become loyal Brittany Ferries customers.

The FPOC scheme was soon expanded to embrace opportunities for members to rent out their properties to other customers through the Brittany Ferries reservation systems. Many were naïve about the process of letting property, so the Company's local team from St Malo were able to visit them at their property and explain the process, based on their own experience in handling the gîte products, and advise on correct property presentation to satisfy the discerning Brittany Ferries customer. They were given advice on how to find the necessary local resource to maintain their properties to the required standard, and act as reception agents for arriving guests. The result was 'The French Collection', a brochure dedicated to British-owned holiday properties, where rentees had to travel with Brittany Ferries. Some owners preferred to operate independently and paid to feature in the brochure; in this scenario guests dealt directly with the owner but were offered a special deal for their ferry crossing. So FPOC brought the double benefit of additional traffic and greater capacity in the holiday portfolio. The French saying of wanting 'the butter and the price of the butter' was never truer.

The team in St Malo developed a system whereby all Brittany Ferries suppliers in the holiday sector were paid promptly and automatically without an invoice having to be presented for payment. If the booking was in the system and the customer travelled, then the payment was made. The Company would take on the task of communicating when property rental bookings had been made and could also advise when payment would be forthcoming. This system worked extremely well, saving significant administration and strengthened the bond between Brittany Ferries and its suppliers.

The conversations with the Halifax Building Society in Berlin also led Carruthers to overhaul another aspect of the business. Brittany Ferries had a substantial marketing budget, a large proportion of which was spent on press and magazine advertising. But it was not clear whether the Company was getting value for money, particularly in media buying, where advertising space varies considerably in price, dependent upon the page and position on the page, in a newspaper or magazine. Carruthers was introduced to a company that undertook media audits staffed by professional auditors who would to take an independent look at media invoices and 'spots' achieved across the advertising spend, and evaluate them against rates achieved by a pool of anonymous advertisers who worked within the same market sector. Thus performance could be measured against a group of peers. BCB had a good media buying operation, but this process trained a spotlight on their work and Brittany Ferries moved from being slightly behind average in rates achieved, to a position well ahead of the majority of the peer group in under twelve months. Far from resenting the work, the media team looked forward to the assessment of their performance. The relationship became so strong that payments to the agency were tied to Company performance, with a bonus paid in the good years. The agency was treated as an employee rather than a consultant and their team was brought into management meetings to fully understood what was going on in the business. In return, they behaved like employees, with a loyalty to the business. It was important that BCB, Rook Dunning, and Oliver had other clients to manage alongside Brittany Ferries so that they could stretch their creativity.

Film processing laboratories were added to the fleet during the spring to enable passengers to get their holiday photos developed and printed during the crossing in this pre-digital era. The service was priced at £6.20 for 24 exposures including a free album, and £7.20 for 36 prints. Meanwhile Longden was quoted as saying that the Company wanted to make the crossing "as pleasant and entertaining as possible for even our youngest passengers" as he launched a major refurbishment of children's play areas as

The *Normandie Shipper* sporting the Truckline livery as she adds valuable additional summer freight capacity on the Portsmouth-Caen route. *(FotoFlite)*

they were equipped with toys, games and video screens.

The facilities in Santander saw only limited use and were used as a coal berth when the Brittany Ferries vessels were elsewhere. Changes were needed in anticipation of the arrival of the *Bretagne*, but the Spanish port appeared reluctant to proceed quickly enough to be ready in time. Carruthers engaged a local architect in Portsmouth to speed the process and took sample plans down to Santander to share with the port authorities. Eventually the work started and a new berth was built, to be followed by an impressive terminal building, capable of accommodating all the Brittany Ferries team including those managing the holiday products.

The facilities at Santander closed for a period of three months to enable the development works to take place, with the *Quiberon* temporarily transferred to a coal yard on the other side of the city. The pragmatic and simplest way to process outbound traffic through the customs and immigration formalities was to continue to require passengers to check-in at the old terminal and then take the entire shipload of vehicles in a convoy across the city to the coal yard. One day the Chief Officer reported that he had a big problem; as he counted the number of vehicles boarding the *Quiberon,* he found there were far too many cars relative to the manifest. The mystery was soon solved; local drivers in Santander, intrigued by the passage of such a huge procession of traffic through the streets, had joined it to see what was happening and stayed with the flow even as the convoy boarded the ship. Disentangling booked traffic from inquisitive locals on the car deck proved to be a nightmare...

The *Bretagne* is dressed overall as she arrives in Plymouth for the first time. *(Ferry Publications Library)*

One couple hoping to head from Plymouth to Santander made national headlines in late June when they found that their 24-hour crossing to Spain had been reduced to just six minutes. Having boarded the Tamar Ferry to Torpoint in error and settled down to enjoy their crossing, the pair just had time to return to Millbay Docks to catch the *Quiberon* before she departed. The couple declined to be identified.

Meeting the increasing freight traffic on the Portsmouth-Caen and Poole-Cherbourg routes continued to stretch resources and encouraged the search for additional tonnage to avoid frustrating demand. An additional dedicated freight ship was needed to release freight capacity on the multi-purpose fleet and ensure that passenger vehicle traffic could be optimised at peak periods. The ro-ro freight vessel *Normandie Shipper* was secured on charter for three years from May 1989 and started her Portsmouth-Caen operations on 26th May. The vessel was built in Holland in 1973 as the *Union Wellington*. She was 142.3 metres long and 18.6 metres in beam and could carry 1,050 lane-metres of freight traffic (equivalent to 68 12-metre trailers) with 36 drivers at a speed of 18 knots. Her arrival allowed the *Coutances* to return from Portsmouth to join her sister vessel the *Purbeck* on the Poole-Cherbourg link.

The *Armorique* began her final season on the Portsmouth-St Malo link on 26th May and Mason began to look for a suitable ship to partner the *Duchesse Anne* from the 1990 season.

After 25 years of using 'Viking' names for the fleet on the cross-Channel services from Southampton and Portsmouth, P&O European Ferries renamed their ships to strengthen connections with their local area of operation. The *Viking Venturer* became the *Pride of Hampshire*, whilst sister vessel *Viking Valiant* was renamed *Pride of Le Havre*; the *Viking Voyager* and *Viking Viscount* became the *Pride of Cherbourg* and *Pride of Winchester*

Captain : J. HARDOUIN

Inauguration of M/V "BRETAGNE"

Plymouth, 14 July 1989

DINER - BUFFET

Homard breton en Bellevue

Cascade de fruits de mer

Saumon mariné à l'ancienne - Saumon glacé en chaud-froid

Jambon de Parme - Terrine de ris de veau

Aiguillettes de canard - Jambon à l'ananas

Carré de veau en gelée - Train de côtes de bœuf

Timbale de mousse d'asperges

Fondant de légumes - Salades composées

Plateau de fromages

Table des desserts

Muscadet sur lie " Château de l'Oiselinière "
Château La Tour de By 1983

Above: **Menu for *Bretagne* dinner.** *(Ferry Publications Library)*

Top right: **Menu cover for the *Bretagne* celebrations.** *(Rook Dunning)*

Middle right: **Preparing the grande bouffe for the *Bretagne*'s visit to Plymouth.** *(Ian Carruthers)*

Right: **Celebratory champagne bottle.** *(Paul Burns)*

respectively. With the criticisms of Egon Ronay still resonating, some £4 million spent on refurbishing the quartet during their winter refits at Falmouth. The fleet was re-registered in Portsmouth and the freighter *Gabrielle Wehr* chartered for the season to enhance freight capacity. Their Portsmouth office building was renamed Peninsular House as a sign of transition to new management. The company appointed Dick Martin as Managing Director, to follow the short but productive tenure of company chairman Peter Ford.

None of these changes could detract from the major event of 1989, as Brittany Ferries introduced the *Bretagne* into traffic.

The *Bretagne* stayed in Roscoff for two days after her naming ceremony, before crossing to Plymouth, where several hundred children lined Plymouth Hoe for her arrival to undertake a press trip on Bastille day, 14th July. Carruthers pointed out that the ship boasted a passenger certificate for 2,030 passengers accommodated in 367 en suite cabins with 1,146 berths (more than at the Savoy Hotel in London), and 454 club seats in

The *Bretagne* going astern at Plymouth. *(Miles Cowsill)*

five lounges. Many cabins had additional luxuries including a video television, hairdryers and a trouser press. The on board facilities had been created specifically to offer passengers a level of comfort and style previously associated only with cruise ships. With two cinemas, a choice of restaurants and bars, a cabaret bar and a duty-free shopping mall, hairdressing salon, children's entertainment room and sundeck space equivalent to eleven tennis courts, there was something for everyone. All freight drivers were provided with their own cabins and accommodation. Carruthers drew attention to the low noise levels and lack of vibration on the vessel from engines that could drive the ship at 21 knots and stop her dead within 480 metres. Dual stabilisation has been built into her design, whilst she had capacity for 580 cars on two decks. The main car deck could hold 61 trailers of 12.2 metres in height. The *Bretagne* set standards that other ferry operators on the English Channel would find impossible to surpass for a considerable period of time.

*O*n behalf of Commandant Ivan Claireaux, his officers and crew, welcome aboard Brittany Ferries new flagship mv Bretagne.

The ship, which has cost over £55 million and taken over two and a half years to complete, represents the very latest in high technology ferry design. Nothing has been spared in constructing a vessel that establishes completely new standards in both luxury and efficiency – standards that other ferry companies will find virtually impossible to surpass for a considerable time to come.

The elegant interior of the Bretagne and vast range of on board facilities have been created specifically to offer passengers a level of comfort and style normally associated only with cruise ships.

All our cabins are air conditioned and have, of course, private shower and WC facilities. And some cabins have additional touches of luxury such as televisions, radios, hairdryers and even trouser presses.

In fact, there are more beds on the Bretagne than are to be found at London's famous Savoy Hotel!

Original paintings, murals and friezes by the renowned Scottish artist Alexander Goudie grace many of the walls around the ship. These all reflect both the ship and the artist's Breton connections.

Amongst the many other impressive facilities aboard this ship are two spacious cinemas, a rather chic duty free shopping mall and a choice of restaurants and bars. And for those who enjoy simply basking in the sun, our vast sundecks are equal in size to no less than 11 tennis courts. And what better way to end the day than to visit the cabaret bar, where there is excellent live entertainment every evening.

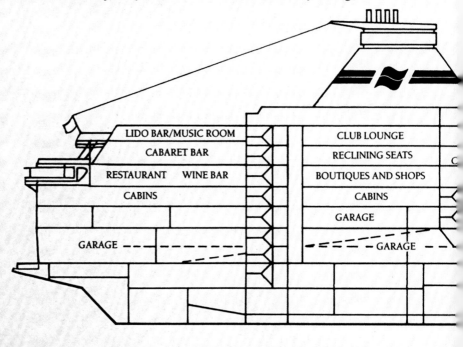

The arrival was planned in meticulous detail by the Brittany Ferries Information Bureau under Toby Oliver.

At 08:00 helicopters took off from the Long Room in Plymouth with film crews and a photographer to record the *Bretagne's* arrival. The vessel arrived at 09:00 and was greeted by tugs, a marine band and skydivers; local schools participated in a balloon race. After a press conference for local media on board the *Bretagne*, she left the

Children are naturally very important to us, too. They have their own specially designed entertainment room and video games area, with a charming playroom for the very young.

Not only does the Bretagne provide passengers with impressive service on board it also offers incomparable comfort at sea.

Vibration and noise levels more than compare with the most advanced cruise liners while a dual stabilizer system keeps movement to an absolute minimum.

The Bretagne has a remarkably high level of environmentally-friendly features. All waste water is retained in storage tanks rather than discharged into the sea and powerful compactors deal effectively with all garbage; a bilge water treatment plant also helps avoid pollution of any kind.

It is a significant fact that Bretagne's fuel consumption is the same as her predecessor on the route but her commercial capacity is 80% greater. Waste heat from the main engines exhaust gas is used for general heating and also to power the de-salination plant which produces on board drinking water. And the electricity output on board the ship is seven megawatts, sufficient to supply a town of 45,000 inhabitants.

Safety equipment on board more than meets the very strictest safety regulations and the ship features the most advanced radar equipment available.

Bretagne truly is a ship for the 1990's and Brittany Ferries is confident that all who sail on her will have a uniquely enjoyable and memorable crossing.

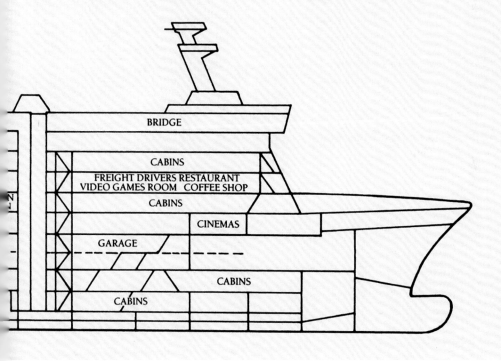

Bretagne description. *(Toby Oliver)*

linkspan between 11:30 and 15:00, with a live outside broadcast on BBC Radio Devon. Guests arrived for the evening reception by 17:00, accompanied by the Royal Marines band playing on the quay, and were taken to their cabins.

Guests were presented with a commemorative scroll signed by Commandant Ivan Claireaux which stated: –

'As Commandant of Brittany Ferries' new flagship *Bretagne*, it is my privilege and pleasure to welcome you aboard this impressive vessel.

Today marks the culmination of over two years close co-operation and effort between the company, its backers and the shipbuilders. The result, as you will see, has been to produce a cruise style ship that launches an entirely new era of ferry development.

We at Brittany Ferries are immensely proud of the *Bretagne* which we believe establishes new standards of on board service, luxury and comfort; standards that other companies can only strive to achieve as we enter the 1990s.

We hope you have an enjoyable time on board and look forward to you travelling with us on the *Bretagne* again in the near future.'

They also received a Goudie print and a booklet about his work.

The *Bretagne* left for the three-hour passage to Torbay at 18:00, and guests enjoyed a spectacular buffet dinner: –

Homard breton en Bellevue

Cascade de fruits de mer

Saumon marine à l'ancienne – Saumon glacé en chaud-froid

Jambon de Parme – Terrine de ris de veau

Aiguillettes de canard – Jambon à l'ananas

Carré de veau en gelée – Train de côtes de boeuf

Timbale de mousse d'asperges

Fondant de légumes – Salades composées

Plateau de fromages

Table des desserts

All this was washed down with Muscadet sur lie "Chateau de l'Oiselinière" and Château La Tour de By 1983. The speeches were hosted by Oliver, before a cabaret with dancers, a band and a duet encouraged everyone to party well into the night. The vessel returned to Plymouth at 08:30 the following morning and the crew had 24 hours to prepare for her maiden departure to Santander on Sunday 16th July 1989 with 1,100 passengers coming on board.

The introduction of the *Bretagne* allowed the *Quiberon* to transfer to the Plymouth-Roscoff route. The *Bretagne* had an immediate impact and was soon sailing full, giving an early indication that even larger tonnage would be required in the future if demand was not to be further frustrated. The *Bretagne* experienced gearbox problems on several occasions during her maiden season and on 3rd August was forced to put into Roscoff for repair whilst on passage from Plymouth to Santander, leaving passengers with a 900-mile overland journey. Delays during the peak season were exacerbated by the tight turnarounds scheduled for each port, as her additional carrying capacity placed pressure on port facilities, with up to 80% more business to discharge and load than had previously been carried on the *Quiberon*.

Meanwhile Sealink British Ferries investigated the potential for the introduction of fast craft on their Western Channel services. The *Earl Granville* suffered serious damage when hitting rocks whilst approaching Cherbourg from Portsmouth at 05:00 on 19th August with 700 passengers on board. A 15-metre gash was torn in her hull rupturing all the tanks in her double bottom and allowing seawater into fuel tanks and around the engines. The service was covered by the Isle of Man Steam Packet Company elderly vessel *Mona's Queen*, which fortunately had been on chartered to follow the French yacht *La Poste* at the start of the round the world yacht race on 2nd September. She took up duties on the Cherbourg route from 4th September and was replaced by the larger *St Patrick II* from

15th September until the end October, when the service was suspended for the winter.

The *Reine Mathilde* left the Portsmouth-Caen Service at the end of September 1989, leaving the *Duc de Normandie* as the sole passenger vessel on the link through the autumn and winter, with the *Trégastel* transferring from Poole to operate in a freight role, having made a very favourable impression on the Truckline service during the second half of the summer. The *Armorique* completed her season on the Portsmouth-St Malo route on 18th September and then undertook two spells of charter to support BCIF. The *Duchesse Anne* continued the service until mid-November, when she headed off for her

A warm summer's evening on the *Bretagne* as Pippa Grive, Christian Michielini, Julie Burrows, Ian Carruthers, Toby Oliver and Tracey Simons are entertained on the maiden crossing. *(Toby Oliver)*

refit, leaving the route closed for the winter. The Plymouth-Roscoff service was reduced to a largely freight-only winter operation from the end of October utilising the *Quiberon*, with the *Bretagne* operating a single weekend return passenger crossing.

The success of the *Bretagne* design prompted consideration of a new third-generation freight vessel for the Truckline fleet, as one of the two-vessel options available to the Company. The team were enthusiastic, and ideas were drawn up for a vessel with accommodation for up to 120 drivers and space for 140 twelve-metre trailers that could enter service early in 1991. However, the plans came to naught as banks were nervous at the speed of the Company's expansion and funds could not be raised. With the benefit of hindsight this was deemed the wrong decision.

Trading conditions for both passenger and freight business on the western Channel were much improved in 1989, and Brittany Ferries holiday sales grew by 50%, as the air package holiday market showed a marked decline in popularity. The difficulties of the

1987 season were now well behind the Company, with new records set for the passenger business in 1989. Overall passenger carryings broke the two million level for the first time, with 24.7% growth to reach 2,117,938 passengers. Vehicle carryings grew by 34.5% to 527,396. After the five-fold increase in volumes between 1984 and 1988, freight traffic slipped slightly by 2.9% to 147,309 units in 1989. The Plymouth-Roscoff route grew by 20% to reach almost 400,000 passengers. But the pound slipped from around FF11.0 at the start of the year to around FF9.8 at the year end, so the Company's financial position did not improve in proportion to the increase in carryings.

Although P&O European Ferries carryings on the western Channel improved from their low point of 1988, with a 16% growth in passengers and 32% growth in vehicles, Brittany Ferries' traffic was now carrying more than double their volumes of 1,185,245 passengers and 303,306 vehicles during the year. With the prospect of a full year's operation of the *Bretagne* in 1990, Brittany Ferries was poised to consolidate its position as the market leader. Thoughts turned to how the model of investment in the *Bretagne* could be replicated across other routes in the upcoming decade.

Ten

Enter the Barfleur and Normandie

Cross-Channel ferry operators faced two significant challenges at the start of the new decade; the EC was seeking to withdraw duty-free sales concessions on internal Community routes from 1st January 1993, and construction work continued on the Channel Tunnel, which was now scheduled to open in 1994. The Duty Free Confederation began a campaign to draw public attention to the impact on ferry services of proposals to abolish duty-free revenues, which generally made up around 18% of income for UK ferry companies. Brittany Ferries was less reliant on this source of income than other operators, but abolition was still likely to have a significant impact on the business. Construction work on the British side of the Channel Tunnel service tunnel began on 15th December 1987, followed by the start of work in France on 28th February 1988. The two sides linked up for the first time on 1st December 1990, with the northern running tunnel meeting on 22nd May 1991, and the southern tunnel joining together on 28th June 1991.

As construction work on the Channel Tunnel progressed, the Brittany Ferries team devised their own plans to meet the forthcoming challenge. The new strategy built on work undertaken by the Atlantic Arc regions to develop their road networks, and the central government support offered to build and promote new tourism initiatives. The resulting 'Horizon 1995' plan envisaged future growth of 70% in traffic across all ferry routes west of the River Seine by 1995. Nine public arguments were developed to underpin the corporate position to counter the threat of the Channel Tunnel: -

• The geographical advantages of travelling by the western Channel routes were unchanged. Two out of three Brittany Ferries' passengers would need to make a detour in their travel plans to use the tunnel.

• The popularity of motoring holidays on the French Atlantic Arc was growing twice as fast as holidays in other regions, in a trend that showed no sign of letting up.

• Motorway congestion was increasing around Paris and London, but the motorway network was being opened up, with new routes being developed away from the capitals.

• The time advantage of the Channel Tunnel was marginal in the overall journey for those heading to the west of France compared to more direct Brittany Ferries crossings.

• The western Channel crossings offered the advantage of overnight sea travel and reduced driving time. The rising costs of building the Channel Tunnel would force the tunnel operator to match ferry prices, otherwise shareholders would continue to lose money.

• Research suggested that around 25% to 30% of cross-Channel passengers feared the claustrophobia of the Channel Tunnel, or had concerns about security issues.

• The choice of short-sea ferry operators and routes was likely to be reduced, particularly if they were faced by price challenges.

• The cruise ferry option provided by Brittany Ferries offered a civilised alternative to the Channel Tunnel.

• Air operators would be concerned by abstraction of the foot passenger business

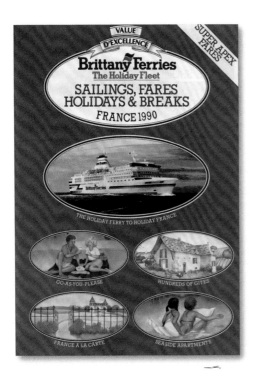

1990 Ireland brochure cover, UK sailings and fares brochure and the 1990 Truckline brochure. (*Rook Dunning*)

by the new Eurostar train services, but this was not a market that Brittany Ferries sought to serve.

The position was very different for P&O European Ferries. The Group comprised of three principal subsidiary operations based in Dover, Portsmouth and Felixstowe (which included a Northern Ireland service), that were nominally independent but for practical purposes directed by the Dover operation that contributed the bulk of profits. These constituent companies shared a common marketing strategy, sales teams, and reservation system, all managed from Dover. The Channel Tunnel posed an existential threat to the short-sea operation, and actions were taken to safeguard the business by using the construction period to build a plausible alternative. The first step had addressed the manning and working arrangements on the Dover fleet and resulted in the prolonged strike of 1988. P&O European Ferries inherited two new 'Chunnel Beater' bespoke-designed vessels, *Pride of Dover* and *Pride of Calais* from Townsend Thoresen, and now embarked on a £235 million fleet investment programme on the short-sea routes. The Dover-Calais fleet soon comprised five passenger vessels which, with slicker shore operations, allowed a 'Channel Shuttle' service to be promoted. The quality of on board services was enhanced with the introduction of Club Class lounges and branded restaurants to offer a distinctive alternative to the simplicity of the Channel Tunnel offer. Services were rationalised, with closure of the Dover-Zeebrugge passenger operation at the end of 1991, and withdrawal from Dover-Boulogne in 1993.

The short-sea services offered a contrasting business to the services operated on the western Channel. The Dover-Calais route appealed to those who wanted to combine a short duration sea crossing with a longer overland drive to reach their destination. The services were frequent, with up to 25 departures from Dover each day; complex

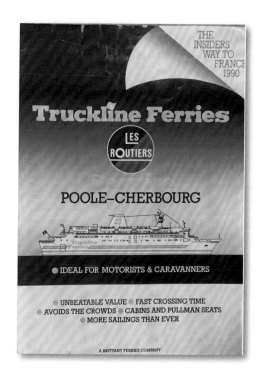

Top and above: **ByPass advertising campaign.**
(Rook Dunning)

reservations were not required on what was essentially a 'turn up and go' service. The short-sea sector attracted a wide range of socio-economic groups, travelling from across the UK to a wide range of European countries. The business was less seasonal than the western Channel routes, with only 40% cent of annual traffic travelling between June and September. There was a heavy emphasis on the group and coach businesses (40% of the total), but little comparative focus on inclusive holidays (3.5% of the total). P&O European Ferries did not offer package holiday products in its own right, relying on a relationship with Bridge Travel to satisfy this sector. The day excursion and promotional business, which formed a third of overall carryings, was significantly more important to the short-sea business. P&O European Ferries was therefore very active in promoting cheap excursion opportunities – 'France for £1' – in national newspapers, and these were offered across all continental routes. This policy was justified by its impact on driving the duty-free retail business, which provided 31% of annual revenue; just 25% of total income came from passenger and vehicle fares.

These business characteristics influenced the pricing approach of P&O European Ferries. The Dover-Calais service needed a constant supply of passengers to drive profits from duty-free sales, growing the market in advance of the Channel Tunnel opening so that the impact of any future loss of business could be minimised. The marketing strategy

The *Duchess Anne* at Roscoff. *(John Hendy)*

for P&O European Ferries' services across all Channel routes was focused on, and driven by, the interests of the short-sea sector. In the absence of the Channel Tunnel, P&O European Ferries' short-term strategy sought to increase volume and market share on the short-sea routes by growing the market, through a policy of heavy discounting and price-undercutting of rivals' businesses. This drove the overall cross-Channel ferry market fare structure and, through P&O European Ferries' western Channel services, was to have the greatest impact on Brittany Ferries

Following a successful 1989 season for both companies, Brittany Ferries and P&O European Ferries made plans to expand their operations in 1990.

Brittany Ferries' 1990 programme featured increased capacity, further upgrades to the fleet, a price freeze on many sailings, and expansion of the inclusive holiday products to France and Spain. The strategy sought to draw traffic away from 'poor-quality charter flight-based packages' as well as gain market share from other ferry operators. Summer season business benefited from extension of the 'Les Routiers' Poole-Cherbourg service to four departures each day from mid-May until the end of September, whilst the Portsmouth-St Malo route became year-round again from mid-February, with an extended two sailings each day summer schedule. The *Bretagne's* first full season on the Plymouth-Santander service was certain to enhance carryings on that route. Fleet upgrade work would be focused on the *Quiberon*, the *Duc de Normandie,* and the *Reine Mathilde*. Many prices in the low season were reduced on the Santander service, whilst fares were frozen on Channel services during the shoulder season. Overall fares were increased by a below-inflation six per cent to place more pressure on competitors.

In the holiday portfolio, the gîte programme was expanded by 20% to embrace 1,300 exclusive properties, including a selection of villas in the south of France. New chambre d'hôte short break holidays were added, offering bed and breakfast accommodation in French homes predominantly in Brittany, Normandy and the Loire valley. The broad range of motoring holidays grew to embrace Go As You Please hotels throughout France, Switzerland, northern Italy and the heartland of Spain. The Flexible France programme expanded to cover the south of France for the first time, featuring Logis and Auberges de France hotels, as well as more up market Relais and Châteaux properties. The 'à la carte' tour product extended into Spain and Portugal, with a range of paradors and pousadas brought into the portfolio.

The Portsmouth-St Malo season had been extended through to the end of 1989, with a short gap for the refit season, before the *Armorique* re-opened the service on 12th February and the *Duchesse Anne* took over from 26th February. The *Armorique* became the seasonal vessel on the route and operated from 24th May until 2nd October. The *Trégastel* transferred from Poole to cover for the *Duc de Normandie* refit on the Portsmouth-Caen route from 7th January to 11th February. The 1990 schedules for Caen were then covered by the *Duc de Normandie*, the *Reine Mathilde* and the *Normandie Shipper*. The Plymouth-Roscoff service became year-round again from 3rd January, with the *Quiberon* becoming the mainstay on the route. The *Duchesse Anne* debuted on the Plymouth-Roscoff service when she stood in for the *Quiberon* whilst she in turn covered the *Bretagne*'s refit and her own until 25th February. The Roscoff-Cork service re-opened on 16th March, with the *Quiberon* maintaining the service until 11th May, when the

The *Trégastel* seen shortly before taking up Truckline operations. *(Miles Cowsill)*

Bretagne took over for the summer season.

Before taking up the Irish service, the *Quiberon* underwent a £1 million refit, which included the installation of a new restaurant, a patisserie, a larger bar, a redesigned duty-free shopping area complete with Cave du Vin, a refurbished coffee shop and lounges, and the addition of two cinemas. The design work was again undertaken by Bernard Bidault, building on the success of his work on the *Bretagne*, to provide a feeling of space and relaxation. David Longden observed that "Brittany Ferries continues to stamp its authority on the ferry scene by setting standards which other operators have to strive to achieve if they are to compete successfully. The new *Quiberon* takes these standards a step higher and this, coupled with our unbeatable range of value for money inclusive holidays to France and Spain, underpins Brittany Ferries' leading position on the western Channel."

239

The Truckline passenger service from Poole was scheduled to begin on 18th May, with the *Trégastel* taking up the 07:30 sailing and the *Corbière* the 17:30 rotation. With up to four passenger sailings each day, and two passenger ships and two freight ships allocated to the route, Truckline planned to operate up to 16 sailings each day at the peak. And with forward bookings a healthy 238% up on the previous year, there were strong prospects for the route. Meanwhile, the *Purbeck* received fin stabilisers during her refit.

P&O European Ferries' Portsmouth-Cherbourg service was closed during the winter, but the *Pride of Cherbourg* re-opened the link on 14th March with an extended early season timetable. The *Pride of Winchester* joined her from 12th April, with the two vessels operating an intensive service through the season. The Portsmouth-Le Havre route was maintained by the *Pride of Le Havre* and *Pride of Hampshire* on a thrice-daily service through the year. Meanwhile, Sealink British Ferries announced their withdrawal from their routes to Cherbourg from both Portsmouth and Weymouth at the end of January, although the company took bookings right up to the time of the announcement.

The *Duc de Normandie* returned from refit with her car deck gleaming after a full repaint, albeit with some of the paint more recently applied than had been planned. The height of the mezzanine deck was quite low for car passengers leaving their vehicles, and on this occasion the first sailing was very busy and the deck fully utilised. One car went up on the mezzanine and its very tall driver parked up and squeezed out of the vehicle. As he stood up, he bumped his head on the ceiling and walked off, leaving his wig firmly attached to the tacky paint. He was oblivious of his distress until much later, but was no doubt adequately compensated.

The introduction of the *Bretagne* contributed to Brittany Ferries being awarded 'Best Ferry Company' in the 1990 Observer Travel Awards, voted for by some 11,000 readers. The award was collected by Longden at a ceremony in London on 27th March. The newspaper noted that the award was well deserved for the Company's investment in new ships and for maintaining standards of catering and passenger service ahead of its rivals. France was a big winner in the awards being voted the favourite country, with specialist operator Vacances Franco-Britanniques (VFB) receiving the best small specialist tour operator award, and Paris being the favourite weekend destination. Later in the year, Brittany Ferries was to win the Ivor Herbert Car Ferry award in the Mail on Sunday for the Portsmouth-Caen route.

In March, shareholders in Sea Containers voted to accept a takeover bid by Stena Line for the Sealink British Ferries business. The Hoverspeed operation remained within Sea Containers' ownership and the group announced their intention to open a new high speed service from Portsmouth to Cherbourg on 14th June, with three daily return crossings using the wave-piercing catamaran *Christopher Columbus*. A second craft was planned for the service from August to increase the number of daily crossings to five in each direction. Then being built by InCat in Tasmania, the two 74-metre long aluminium craft were capable of carrying 450 passengers and 84 cars, at 37 knots, potentially cutting the crossing time from Portsmouth to Cherbourg to 2 hours 45 minutes. These 'SeaCats' posed a new challenge for the established western Channel operators. Although Condor had long been operating catamarans on services to the Channel Islands, the Hoverspeed vessels were being built to a different order of magnitude.

Ian Carruthers and Longden quickly concluded that the SeaCat was not a major threat to their established business. The vessels offered speed, but those looking for the shortest possible crossing generally headed for the short-sea routes, so business was most likely to be abstracted from there. Like all craft approaching Portsmouth, the SeaCat was speed restricted through the port approaches, so could not take full advantage of pace for the full length of the crossing. Further, the speed created a timetable that led to a considerable number of 'off-peak' crossing times. Who wanted to travel at speed in the middle of the night? The carrying capacity of the SeaCat was limited relative to the scale of vessels now being operated by Brittany Ferries, and their aluminium structure precluded the carriage of freight traffic. The on board offer would be comparatively spartan and passengers would find themselves confined to seating for much of the crossing and, as the vessels' ride-keeping qualities were as yet unproven, they would not be able to operate in anything above moderate sea conditions. The drive for speed was seen to be a niche market; far better to let others lose money to determine whether or not there was truly a business opportunity.

Further fresh competition was proposed by British Iberian Line, who in autumn 1989 announced their intention to open a new service from Poole to Bilbao from 28th April 1990, with a twice-weekly 26-hour crossing. The company was jointly owned by Forward Marine Services and Seaways S.A. The vessel was later revealed to be the 1968-built *Maiden Castle* (formerly the *Patra Express* and *St George*) which could carry 1,000 passengers and offered three classes of accommodation; first, cabin and tourist. On board facilities were planned to include a cinema, casino, disco, first class restaurant, self-service cafeteria and a choice of duty-free bars. Single fares were advertised from £95 to £118 per person. The threat was short lived as it quickly became apparent that the *Patra Express* had actually been sold for cruise operations in Florida; the company's staff found they were not being paid and quickly walked out. British Iberian Line announced at the end of March that their service would be freight-only, still with a twice-weekly schedule, with the passenger service to follow later. British Iberian was then rumoured to have secured a charter of the *Earl William* from Sealink Stena Line, but this was refuted by her owners. The company closed down at the end of May 1990 having failed to operate any sailings and leaving a trail of debts, with many customers holding worthless tickets. Managing Director Geoffrey Benstead later faced criminal proceedings for obtaining money under false pretences, and was eventually sentenced to 15 months in prison.

A small fire broke out in the engine room of the *Reine Mathilde* as she crossed from Caen to Portsmouth on 9th April. The blaze was brought under control within 40 minutes, and there was no danger to the 600 passengers on board, although the ship was in darkness for a few minutes whilst the emergency generator was started. However, a 66-year-old man died of a heart attack despite the efforts of the ship's doctor and another doctor travelling as a passenger; although it was unclear whether the death was related to the incident. One crew member was overcome by smoke as he helped other crew members to extinguish the flames. The two were brought ashore by a coastguard helicopter. 120 schoolchildren returning from trips to France were hailed as heroes for helping to distribute blankets to other passengers during the alarm.

The Lee on Solent coastguard reported that the *Reine Mathilde* was stranded some 13 miles off Bembridge, Isle of Wight. Alerted to the problem, Carruthers rang the QHM at 03:00 to ask for tug assistance to bring the *Reine Mathilde* into port, but there was a demand for a 'no cure, no pay' salvage agreement to be signed before any help could be provided; the tug crew demanded £3,000 per man for their work. Carruthers signed under protest, arguing that the vessel was safely anchored and did not need salvage. The QHM viewed this as a purely financial issue, despite the fact that a passenger had died. Eventually, the *Reine Mathilde* was brought into Portsmouth under tow by the naval tug *Powerful* and berthed at No 1 berth, before later being towed across to Le Havre for repairs. Capt. Patrick Dheret and his crew were highly praised by passengers for their handling of the incident. Carruthers later fended off criticism that the ship's fire alarm was not sounded by stating that "it is easy to press a button and make bells ring. It is the consequences of those bells ringing that you have to deal with". Passengers had heard bilingual safety announcements as they boarded the vessel, and the captain was noted as retaining full control of the incident without creating any unnecessary alarm. A French inquiry was launched into the fire.

The *Trégastel* was brought in to cover for the *Reine Mathilde* until the time came for her own refit, when the *Armorique* took over. Repairs to the *Reine Mathilde* were expected to take six weeks but the damage proved to be more extensive than was originally estimated and she was unable to return to service until July. With the *Trégastel* required on the Portsmouth-Caen route, the Poole-Cherbourg season was forced to open with just the *Corbière*, with excess traffic transferred to Portsmouth and Plymouth. The Company's attempts to secure a charter from Sealink Stena Line of the *Earl William* were rebuffed. The *Trégastel* did not return to the Poole-Cherbourg route until 7th July.

Three unsavoury incidents with groups of bikers took place in the cabaret bar during one crossing of the *Bretagne* from Plymouth to Santander. The bar had to be closed during the passage, and the Spanish authorities refused to let the group enter Spain on arrival in Santander. They were returned to the *Bretagne* despite the protests of the Master. Forced to carry the group back to Plymouth, he faced up to the bikers supported by several burly crew members. The captain told them "You have to come back on my

Above: **The port facilities at Plymouth in June 1990, seen from the *Bretagne*.** *(Richard Kirkman)*

Left: **The terminal at Santander, June 1990.** *(Richard Kirkman)*

ship. I don't want to carry you, but I have to abide by the authorities. I've already advised the authorities in Britain about the problem. I have instructed the crew that if there are any problems on the crossing they are to break your bikes and put them in the sea...". There were no issues on the return sailing to Plymouth.

Following this, Brittany Ferries elected to ban male passengers travelling with motorbikes more than four years old. This was not well received by Hells Angels groups and other members of the biking community, but was more generally applauded by the majority of passengers. The ban was extended to all-male groups of more than twelve persons and enacted from June to December 1990. In response to press comment, Toby Oliver noted that the offensive behaviour was not caused by alcohol, and to close the bars would deprive well-behaved passengers from having a drink.

Inbound holiday business from summer 1990 was facilitated through the 'Bed & Breakfast Nationwide' guide, which had been established by two Colchester-based housewives in 1988. The pair created a guidebook when they identified a need for recommended accommodation from their own Bed & Breakfast visitors, and the contract with Brittany Ferries allowed them to expand their operation significantly.

Although the success of the *Bretagne* project had not immediately been followed through with a new vessel order for Truckline, there was growing confidence in the Company which led to discussions with shipyards on the possibilities of further new additions to the fleet. The Board was determined to have the new fleet fully in place before the Channel Tunnel opened in 1994 so that passengers could experience the geographical and quality advantages offered by Brittany Ferries' sailings in advance of the alternative new crossing being available.

Another high-quality vessel was also needed to operate alongside the *Duc de Normandie* and consolidate the Company's growing competitive advantage on the Portsmouth-Caen route. Freight traffic was constrained by the single-deck loading operation of the *Duc de Normandie,* which limited the number of vehicles that could be discharged and loaded during each port turnaround. P&O European Ferries' 'Super-Vikings' on the Portsmouth-Le Havre route were able to load simultaneously on two decks, through bespoke double deck linkspan facilities at each port. The future for Brittany Ferries lay in being able to match this efficiency and increase the volumes of traffic that could be loaded, remaining competitive in the freight market whilst retaining the optimal utilisation of the fleet on the route with a thrice-daily-crossing schedule. The SEM Senacal was now in robust financial health and enthusiastic to invest further in developing the fleet. Alexis Gourvennec and Christian Michielini led discussions on how a new vessel could be financed, based on the formula that had been established with the *Duc de Normandie*. This investment would need to include significant enhancements in the port facilities at Portsmouth and Ouistreham to build the necessary double deck linkspans to accommodate the new vessel.

Similar capacity constraints frustrated traffic growth on the Poole-Cherbourg route, where there was less requirement for more freight capacity but an inefficient service offer that required a multi-purpose vessel to supplement the freight ships on the route. A much larger vessel, albeit one constrained by the access limitations at Poole, could deliver significant economies if it allowed smaller, less efficient ships to be withdrawn. Port facilities would also require significant investment in Poole and Cherbourg to handle double deck loading of the vessel. The Cherbourg authorities viewed the success of the two existing SEMs with some envy, but now that the Truckline service was owned by Brittany Ferries realised that a similar financial model could be made to work for them. The time was right to take these ideas further, for the *Bretagne* demonstrated that Brittany Ferries had the technical capabilities to deliver a high-quality on board service. Options to improve capacity by stretching the *Duc de Normandie* or the *Quiberon* were also considered, but new tonnage was seen as the most effective plan.

The outcome of the discussions between Gourvennec, Michielini, Maurice Chollet and the Cherbourg authorities was the establishment in Saint-Lô in April 1991 of a third SEM, the Société d'Équipement Naval de la Manche (Senamanche), with a shareholding split between the Basse Normandie region, the Calvados département, and Brittany Ferries. This used the same funding approach as Sabemen and Senacal. With financial backing in place, discussions continued with shipyards for what was now a potential two-ship order based on the involvement of two SEMs. This time no French shipyards were able to deliver the order to the required tight timescales and price. Discussions were opened with a number of shipyards, before serious negotiations began in Scandinavia.

Thus, Brittany Ferries announced an order for two vessels for their English Channel routes on 17th May. The contract for the first vessel, later to be named the *Normandie*, was signed in May with the Masa shipyard of Turku, Finland. The *Normandie*, destined for the Portsmouth-Caen route would have capacity for 2,120 passengers and 600 cars, with a gross tonnage of around 27,000 tonnes. The contract price for this vessel was FF769.6 million, supported by public aid of FF40.0 million. Capt. Bertrand Apperry was appointed as the vessel's Senior Master and Landsman for the project, and was to split his time between Roscoff and Turku during the construction phase. He was supported by Chief Engineer Michel Lasvaladas and Project Manager Ilka Seppa from the Masa shipyard.

The original concept was for a sister vessel to be built to the same design, but the Masa shipyard was committed to other projects and unable to complete two vessels simultaneously, so a smaller design was developed in the hope that other builders might be able to take on the work. This design would be more appropriate for the physical constraints of Poole harbour. One Norwegian shipyard offered to build the smaller vessel, but when Michielini, Jim Mason and Michel Maraval went to inspect the facility it was evident that the dry dock was too small to accommodate a vessel of the proposed size, so they withdrew from the discussions. Later conversations with the Masa shipyard revealed that they had been approached by the same Norwegian shipyard to build a hull which, it transpired, was the Brittany Ferries design, in anticipation of the vessel being fitted out in Norway. Conversations turned to whether the Turku shipyard had the capacity for the job; whilst space was not readily available at Turku, there was a slot available at the Masa Helsinki shipyard.

The second vessel was designed to fulfil the brief for the Poole-Cherbourg route by combining extensive passenger facilities with a large and discreet freight-carrying capacity. She would have capacity for 1,200 passengers and be able to carry 270 cars and 70 freight vehicles, or 118 freight vehicles on freight-only sailings. The contract price for the second vessel, later named the *Barfleur* after the Cotentin harbour, was FF495.1 million, supported by public aid of FF40.0 million. The *Barfleur* was specifically designed to fit the constraints of Poole Harbour's narrow approach channel, as even with a 5.8 metre draught at low tide there was only two metres of water under her hull (although the channel was later dredged to deepen the channel). She would be the largest ship to regularly use the port. As planned, the new ship would be 18,000 gross-tonnes.

The construction contract for the *Barfleur* was signed by Senamanche with the Masa Helsinki shipyard on 20th September, with construction planned to start in March 1991. Overseeing her design and construction were the *Barfleur's* new Senior Master, Capt. Claude Lenoir, who divided his time between the shipyard and Roscoff, and ship's architect Maraval.

Both vessels were contracted for delivery in Spring 1992 and designed to meet the full requirements of the SOLAS 90 safety regulations. The combined investment was equivalent to £130 million. The arrival of the two vessels, well in advance of the Channel Tunnel's opening date, was again designed to position Brittany Ferries as the only clear alternative to the Channel Tunnel.

Maraval was heavily involved in the design of both vessels. He had enhanced both his and the Company's reputation by representing Brittany Ferries at the Passenger Shipping Association in London as the trade body considered the ramifications of the SOLAS 90 regulations following the *Herald of Free Enterprise* disaster.

The announcement of the *Normandie* contract came just as Carruthers was negotiating with the Portsmouth Port management team to resolve the capacity problems arising from the original 'exclusive use' clauses, and persuade them to invest in a new double deck linkspan needed to accommodate the vessel. He was confident of securing an early settlement, but needed to avoid revealing why there was an urgency to the discussions. Michielini was asked to hold back on any announcement to allow the negotiations to be concluded favourably. But news of the contract broke as Carruthers went to meet Port Manager Tony George to continue the discussions; George was reading Lloyd's List as Carruthers entered the room. "Where are you going to park this ship?" asked the smiling Port Manager. There was no room for manoeuvre and Brittany Ferries were forced to take out a loan from Barclays Bank to finance the provision of a double deck linkspan; the only concession the Port team would make was to guarantee that they would never offer another company better terms on port charges, without offering equivalent terms to Brittany Ferries first. This guarantee was soon broken, although it would take several years for this to become apparent.

Not all of the issues with P&O European Ferries were competitive. The two companies shared common concerns about the cost and flexibility of the stevedoring operation at Portsmouth. Carruthers was well advanced with plans to transform shore operations at the port by addressing the restrictive practices of the local stevedores when he approached Dick Martin with the idea of creating a new company to handle port operations in Portsmouth. There was common enthusiasm to address the issue, and this led to the formation of the jointly owned company Portsmouth Handling Services Limited.

Paul Hincke researched and implemented the procurement of a £300,000 fleet of TugMaster tractor units to marshal unaccompanied freight vehicles, and placed them in store at a farm in Hampshire, ready to take up duties. Then notice was given to Channel Stevedores. The existing stevedores reacted strongly to the change, using a forklift truck to try and move a freight portacabin into the sea. Carruthers obtained an injunction against Commodore, as the ultimate owners of Channel Stevedores, to stop further action, but the port authority was forced to put concrete blocks at the gate to Albert

A proud Ian Carruthers anticipates the arrival of the *Normandie* and *Barfleur* into the fleet. *(Ferry Publications Library)*

Johnson Quay which linked to the Continental Ferry Port, to stop them gaining access to the quay with their vehicles.

The terms and conditions for the new operation were very different to those that the stevedores had enjoyed previously. It was common knowledge that stevedores earned more than a Brittany Ferries Chief Officer, whilst they were often still holding down a second job in Portsmouth. Henceforth their wages would reflect the skills of the stevedores, but with salaries pitched as equivalent to an international lorry driver – then around £19,000 per year. And there would be no second jobs.

Joint meetings were held between Brittany Ferries, P&O European Ferries and the dockers in Peninsular House; the trade union representatives said that nobody would apply for jobs with the new company. Carruthers responded that 74% of job applications to the new company were from existing stevedores. Angered at the loss of the contract, Jack Norman headed over to Roscoff to complain to Gourvennec; Carruthers threatened to resign if the meeting went ahead. Norman came away empty-handed and then tried to sue Brittany Ferries. But the plan was implemented. This was an innovative and ground-breaking development, which was later replicated in Caen. Brittany Ferries and P&O European Ferries now had control of a vital resource and could manage the operation efficiently between them. The Portsmouth stevedoring operation soon became the best team on the south coast under the guidance of Bob Siddall.

Hoverspeed received extensive press coverage when the catamaran *Hoverspeed Great Britain* won the Hales Trophy for the fastest crossing of the Atlantic Ocean, after cutting almost three hours off the *United States'* record, which had stood since 1952. This record still stands in 2020. *Hoverspeed Great Britain* was due to enter service from Portsmouth to Cherbourg in early July, but the introductory date was delayed when the British and French authorities inspected the vessel and insisted on further insulation being fitted between the car decks and passenger areas before she could be issued with a passenger certificate. The timetable gave a crossing time of two hours 30 minutes compared to the conventional crossing time of four hours 15 minutes. On 6th July the *Hoverspeed Great*

The *Purbeck* heads out from Poole Harbour for Cherbourg in April 1990. *(John Hendy)*

Britain was hit and damaged by the Commodore freight vessel *Island Commodore* when entering Portsmouth Harbour, and the start of services was further delayed. Hoverspeed were forced to charter the *Earl Granville* as an interim measure from 19th July. The *Hoverspeed Great Britain* finally entered service with the 08:30 departure from Portsmouth to Cherbourg on 14th August, operating with a reduced passenger certificate for only 280 passengers and 17 crew. The craft had a difficult start, being out of service from 1st to 10th September with water jet problems, and then from 16th September until 13th October for further repairs. Carruthers and Longden's scepticism about the abilities and attractiveness of the new craft was fully justified.

In July the newly formed Sealink Stena Line announced their intention to inaugurate a new Southampton-Cherbourg service from the 1991 season, utilising the 1982-built *St Nicholas* from their Harwich-Hoek of Holland route. The 149.0-metre-long and 28.0 metre beam vessel had capacity for 2,200 passengers and 700 cars, and would be renamed *Stena Normandy* for the Southampton service.

There was still pressure on peak summer freight capacity on the Portsmouth-Caen route, so the freighter *Skarvøy* was chartered to run alongside the *Normandie Shipper* from mid-June until mid-September; she had capacity for twelve passengers and 695 lane-metres of freight or 58 trailers. Freight traffic on the western Channel was booming and P&O European Ferries chartered the freighter *St Magnus* to operate alongside their freighter *Gabrielle Wehr* on their Portsmouth-Le Havre route until 27th September. The *Pride of Cherbourg* and *Pride of Winchester* extended the Portsmouth-Cherbourg service until Christmas, with the former offering refit cover over the winter.

The *Armorique* damaged a propeller whilst docking at St Malo on 6th September, leaving her with one serviceable engine for the remainder of her season until 1st October, pending a complete repair at her planned refit. Her St Malo schedule was now unsustainable in this condition, so the difficult decision was made to confine her to operate between Portsmouth and Cherbourg with a lengthy six to seven-hour passage, forcing traffic travelling down the Cotentin peninsular by road to St Malo.

The UK's Conservative-led government had long been split over whether sterling should enter the European Exchange Rate Mechanism (ERM), the EEC's system for linking the values of currencies, but Prime Minister Margaret Thatcher eventually agreed that sterling should join the ERM on 8th October. The immediate impact was the first fall in interest rates for a year and a rise in London share prices. The ERM tied the value of currencies to the German mark, with the pound set at an initial rate of DM2.95 with a lower floor level of DM2.773 that would trigger government intervention. The ERM was intended to bring stability to European markets and encourage trade as an eventual precursor to the creation of a single European currency. But UK inflation was running at three times the level in Germany, interest rates were higher at 15%, and labour productivity was much lower than France and Germany, indicating the comparative health of the economy at the time.

The *Coutances* was sent on charter to the French government from 23rd September to help convey troops to support the Gulf war, sailing via the Suez Canal to Yanbu, Saudi Arabia under Capt. Le Fur. The *Havelet* was transferred to Truckline to cover for the *Coutances,* and the *Corbière* returned to BCIF until the *Coutances* returned. Following her repair, the *Armorique* was also chartered to the French government on 27th December to carry troops and equipment from Toulon to Yanbu, leaving France in January 1991.

Meanwhile, the St Malo authorities announced their planned investment in new facilities to allow larger vessels to use the port, with the work to be completed by 1992.

1990 was another successful year for Brittany Ferries, with continued growth in passenger traffic and a recovery in the freight sector. Passenger carryings reached 2,638,847, a rise of 24.6%, vehicle traffic rose by 19.1% to hit 627,887 and freight volumes saw 3.0% growth to reach 151,452. Turnover reached FF1.7 billion. Despite all the issues with the transfer of the *Trégastel* away from the route during the early season, the Poole-Cherbourg service experienced a 98% rise in passenger traffic during the year. P&O European Ferries saw their passenger traffic grow by 15.4% to 1,368,435, with vehicle traffic rising by 23.7% to 375,727 cars. Brittany Ferries was beginning to dominate traffic in the western Channel sector, and was now carrying 15% of all cross-Channel ferry traffic.

The combined capital of the three SEMs Sabemen, Senacal and Senamanche, increased to FF 375 million at the start of 1991 to finance the building of the *Normandie* and the *Barfleur* on top of the existing investment in the *Bretagne*. This was deemed essential to accommodate the growth in traffic being experienced by Brittany Ferries. Gourvennec was confident enough to state that the Channel Tunnel "doesn't scare us" and would not stop this expansion.

The *Bretagne* underwent a lengthy refit in Brest, and she re-opened the Plymouth-

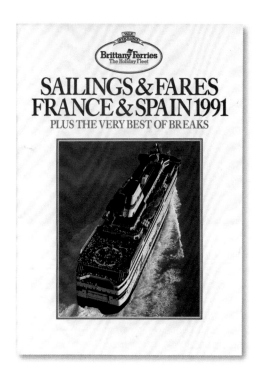

The 1991 Sailings & Fares brochure , Gîte Holidays brochure, the Ski-Drive brochure for the 1990-91 season and the Holidays & Breaks brochure for the 1991 season. *(Rook Dunning)*

Santander link on 9th January 1991, operating one sailing weekly until 13th March with the rest of her time on the Plymouth-Roscoff service. The *Duchesse Anne* joined her at refit from 30th December. The *Quiberon* returned to support the Santander roster to help provide three sailings each week on the route from 15th March in tandem with the *Bretagne,* following another agreement to take the *Celtic Pride* from Swansea-Cork Ferries for the low season Roscoff-Cork service. The Plymouth-Santander service reverted to twice-weekly with the *Bretagne* during the peak season whilst the *Quiberon* served Plymouth-Roscoff, as the *Celtic Pride* was fully employed on her normal duties between Swansea and Cork. The Spanish traffic was growing at such a rate that Michielini worked with Mason to investigate options to replace the *Bretagne* with a larger vessel.

The *Normandie Shipper* was refitted at Le Havre for a month from 22nd December, and the *Duc de Normandie* followed her to the shipyard for overhaul on 3rd February and was replaced by the *Duchesse Anne*. When the *Duc de Normandie* returned from refit, the *Duchesse Anne* re-opened the Portsmouth-St Malo service on 7th March, with the *Armorique* joining her from 22nd May to 1st October after her trip to the Middle East. The Poole-Cherbourg service was re-opened by the *Corbière* on 3rd May and she was joined by the *Trégastel* from 24th May until 22nd September.

The *Hoverspeed Great Britain* finished her maiden season of Portsmouth-Cherbourg sailings on 6th January 1991 and was sent to Cherbourg for refit. But on 17th January Hoverspeed announced permanent closure of the route, transferring the *Hoverspeed Great Britain* to the eastern Channel to support their short-sea operation.

The M40 motorway opened throughout between London and Birmingham via Oxford on 16th January, considerably improving the accessibility of Portsmouth and Poole from the Midlands and the North.

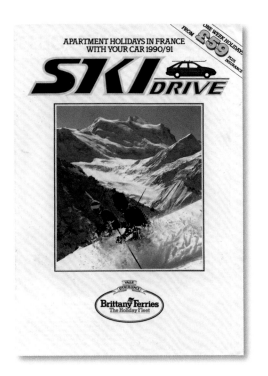

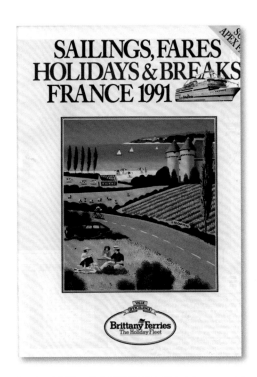

The *Stena Normandy* undertook berthing trials at Southampton on 20th January before returning to Harwich for a refit and to operate to the Hoek of Holland until the arrival of her replacement, the *Stena Britannica*. She arrived back in Southampton on 21st June ready to commence her new service to Cherbourg on 28th June. Her new schedule saw departures at 10:30 and 23:59 from Southampton on Tuesdays, Fridays and Sundays, with an inward sailing at 18:30 from Cherbourg. On Mondays, Thursdays and Saturdays the departures from Southampton were at 16:00, with sailings from Cherbourg at 09:30 and 23:59. On Wednesdays the vessel left Southampton at 16:00 and returned at 23:59. There was one daily round trip from 23rd September. Sealink Stena Line immediately declared a price war by reducing fares on selected Cherbourg sailings by 50%, but this did not provoke a response from the established operators.

In the early part of 1991 Michielini was approached during a meeting in France and asked if Brittany Ferries would be interested in joining a consortium seeking to bid for the South West television franchise in the UK. There were precedents for ferry operators taking a stake in local media, with Townsend Thoresen previously having a shareholding in the Southern Television franchise in Southampton. Michielini was intrigued and asked Carruthers to join

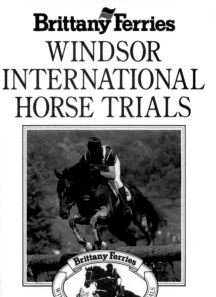

Brittany Ferries sponsored Windsor International Horse Trials programme. *(Paul Burns)*

Christine Michielini, Toby Oliver and Christian Michielini enjoy the horse jumping extravaganza with Princess Anne.
(Toby Oliver collection)

him at a meeting at the Great Eastern Hotel in London. As the pair entered the room it was being swept by Stephen Redfarn, later appointed as Chief Executive of the company, who was ensuring there were no hidden microphones listening to the conversation. The meeting was joined by representatives from Associated Newspapers and South West Water. The former already owned the Western Morning Herald in Plymouth amongst other media interests, whilst the latter was still recovering from the Camelford water pollution scandal. Brittany Ferries were seen as a positive local partner who could add local credibility to a bid for the television franchise and could 'warehouse' a share for Associated Newspapers. Michielini had contacts in FR3 in France who, he felt, could add both expertise and a European dimension to the bid. The initial investment to facilitate the bid was around £200,000, with a further £600,000 required if this proved to be successful. Michielini instructed Carruthers to use the UK marketing budget for this investment, and left him to take control of the proposal.

News of the bid became public in mid-May 1991, when John Banham, director general of the Confederation of British Industry was named as chairman if the franchise bid was successful. Associated Newspapers and South West Water each held a 20% stake in the bid, Brittany Ferries held 15% and Trilion 10%. A second contester entering the bidding was TeleWest Ltd, who were advised by Lazard Brothers and Touche Ross, and included television personality Angela Rippon as a non-executive director. The incumbent operator Television South West (TSW) also re-bid for the franchise.

When the results of the bidding process were revealed in October 1991, the Westcountry Television bid of £7.8 million was announced as the winning bid, TSW were deemed to have overbid at £16.1 million and TeleWest failed to qualify with a £7.3 million proposal. This was not the best of times for Brittany Ferries to find cash to invest in a peripheral business, but this proved to be a sound opportunity, and within four years was to yield a dramatic return on the investment. Michielini again insisted the funds to support Westcountry Television come from the UK marketing budget.

News of the success broke as Carruthers and Longden were in Spain, negotiating to become the official sea carrier for the Seville Expo, to be held in 1992. The talks progressed well, and news of the outcome of the bid was a cause for celebration, so the pair enjoyed an appropriately memorable meal together. But then the Expo team broke the news that they would not, after all, have a preferred sea carrier, choosing instead to focus their promotional efforts on air transport links to Seville. And TSW immediately appealed against the conclusion of the franchise bid process, so it was a chastened duo that returned to Britain. The TSW appeal was ultimately unsuccessful.

The franchise introduced Carruthers and Longden to a different world, populated by a breed of individuals anxious to make money. Every Board meeting discussed the remuneration of executives, who aimed to extract as much money as possible from the franchise before moving on. Salaries at all levels were huge compared to those in Brittany Ferries. Westcountry Television built a large structure on the outskirts of Plymouth to host their studio, and sub-contracted technical delivery of their output obligations to Harlech Television. The company was required to produce ten hours of television programming each week, which largely comprised a regional news programme with a single live presenter reading from an innovative, fully automated studio full of Sony equipment. 85% of revenue came from outside the region, but the business was able to generate income of around £25-30 million and annual profits of around £18 million. Carruthers and Longden were directors of the company, with Stephen Shaw acting as their alternate.

It was several years after the Chay Blyth experience before Brittany Ferries considered a further substantial sponsorship opportunity, although a relationship with the Bournemouth Symphony Orchestra proved very productive in raising corporate profile amongst a key target audience. Brittany Ferries sponsored horse trotting racing at Lingfield on 22nd July 1990 with the 'Prix Brittany Ferries', when a special edition of Paris-Turf was printed for English race-goers.

The Royal Windsor Horse Trials was a highlight of the equestrian calendar, which was sponsored by Polly Peck until 1990. When the sponsoring company collapsed at the end of that year, Michielini, who had a keen interest in the breeding and showing of horses, was approached to ascertain whether Brittany Ferries would be interested in taking over the sponsorship from 1991. The approach inferred that Princess Anne, as President of the Trials, would look favourably on the Company's involvement. Michielini asked Carruthers to incorporate the cost within the UK advertising budget, and a sponsorship package was negotiated with the organisers. Overall event sponsorship fitted well with the lessons learned from the relationship with Blyth in Rhode Island.

The horse trials community was a key target customer market for Brittany Ferries, and Carruthers and Toby Oliver set about ensuring value from the Company's association with the Windsor event. All the jumps on the course were made up to be elements of the Brittany Ferries experience, the centrepiece being a water jump into a lake in which a large model ferry was moored strategically so as to appear in all the press photography of the event. Oliver persuaded Channel 4 to broadcast the trials, and was seconded to the Horse Trials Committee, which met monthly with Princess Anne in attendance. A strong field of 234 entrants sought to take part, and the Princess Royal described the trials as an "essential proving ground for the sterner stuff of Badminton and Burghley".

The annual event proved a great opportunity to entertain passenger and freight customers, as well as the equestrian and travel media. Lunch was provided each day in a large marquee, prepared by chefs and served by stewards from the ships' crew. Guests were impressed to hear that they were being served a standard on board menu, rather than anything specially prepared for the occasion.

The Royal Windsor Horse Trials were subsequently twinned with the equivalent Company-sponsored event at Le Lion-d'Angers in the Loire Valley, providing further business and promotional opportunities. Brittany Ferries offered a £25,000 bonus to any rider who could win the triple crown of three-day events, including the trials at Windsor and autumn events at Blenheim and Le Lion-d'Angers in the same year. The sponsorship represented a productive investment, yielding unrivalled brand coverage for the cost, and continued until 1995.

Long standing rumours were confirmed in July 1991 when it became clear that P&O European Ferries were in discussion with Vapores Suardíaz about a joint venture to operate a twice-weekly ferry service from Portsmouth to Bilbao. Whilst this could pose a threat to the Plymouth-Santander operation, the service would be unable to compete on journey times with the established route, and required substantial fleet investment to match the quality of the *Bretagne*. The news accelerated Brittany Ferries' plans to find a replacement for the *Bretagne*, which was now operating at capacity. Meanwhile, P&O

The *Barfleur* under construction. *(Ferry Publications Library)*

European Ferries restructured their fleet by selling and bareboat leasing back the vessels. The *Pride of Hampshire* was sold to Investment Company BMBF (no 15), with the *Pride of Cherbourg*, *Pride of Le Havre* and *Pride of Winchester* sold to Howell Shipping Ltd.

When Michielini and Mason went to inspect construction progress on the *Barfleur* during the early summer they were very disappointed with the quality of the welding being undertaken at the Helsinki shipyard. There were unwelcome echoes from the *Cornouailles* experience in Trondheim. Mason drew this to the attention of Martin Saarikangas, the co-founder of the Masa Yards, who had rescued them from the bankruptcy of Wärtsilä. Saarikangas agreed that the standard was not acceptable and vowed to put things right. He asked Mason and Michielini to return the next day and tell the welders directly of their concerns, which they duly did. Saarikangas then took hold of a set of welding gear and proceeded to demonstrate the minimum standard he expected from his welders, despite it being many years since he had previously performed a weld. The output standards improved significantly thereafter.

The *Barfleur* was floated out in Helsinki on 27/28th July, with the *Normandie* following in Turku on 5th October. Carruthers said "when the tunnel eventually comes into service, continental freight will be faced with two clear alternatives – to use the tunnel or Brittany Ferries' western Channel services. The arrival of our two new Superferries next year gives us a head start on competition. It means that we can offer passengers attractive departure times direct to the main holiday areas of France and Spain, on ships setting such high standards that people will find it hard to make the decision to go down the tube when it eventually comes into service."

As the *Barfleur* underwent sea trials it became evident that she was suffering from severe deadweight problems. This came as a big shock to everyone associated with the project. Saarikangas reacted quickly to come up with an answer to the issue. The

The *Normandie* under construction. *(Ferry Publications Library)*

Barfleur's original design had incorporated the future ability to stretch the vessel by inserting up to three nine-metre sections to provide additional capacity as traffic growth dictated. He determined that the only practical solution was to 'stretch' her now, by adding one of these sections and increase her length by nine metres to 157 metres, but this would delay her entry into service. It represented a pragmatic outcome to the deadweight problem, and the parties agreed that the alterations to the design be provided at cost. The new section would add cabin accommodation for a further 200 people, enlarge the public areas of the vessel and increase the vessel's carrying capacity by an additional twelve trailers to 130 units. The additional cost represented good value for the extra capacity. The work began on 22nd December.

The delayed introductory date could not be hidden, with the potential to be highly embarrassing for all, but the Public Relations team was ready to put a positive spin on the change. To raised eyebrows from professionals in the industry, Carruthers was quoted as saying "During 1991 our carryings grew a further 19% on this route and we have decided after negotiation with the Masa Kværner shipyard in Finland to increase the capacity of the ship. This will increase the number of cabins with facilities, public areas and car/truck capacity substantially. We have agreed with Masa that our ship will now be delivered on 27th March 1992." The press reported this verbatim and the crisis was over, although there remained much speculation amongst the trade about what had actually happened.

With the arrival of two new vessels imminent, steps were taken to trim the fleet by disposing of vessels deemed surplus to requirements after the summer season. The *Corbière* made her final crossing from Cherbourg to Poole on 22nd September 1991 and was sold to Oy Eckerölinjens A.B., who chartered her to Estonian New Line, where she was renamed the *Linda 1*. The *Trégastel* completed her scheduled duties on the Cherbourg route on 29th September, with the *Reine Mathilde* finishing the following day. The *Trégastel* covered the *Quiberon* on the Plymouth-Roscoff route for ten days from 7th October, whilst she in turn covered for the *Bretagne,* whilst she underwent gearbox modifications; the *Trégastel* then moved into freight-only mode on the Portsmouth-Caen route prior to being handed over to P&O Scottish Ferries early in 1992, to operate as the *St Clair* on services from Aberdeen to Lerwick. The *Reine Mathilde* was sold to the Nassau-based company Marine Invest in 1991, for a planned chartered for a Cuban operation, but this fell through and she was soon chartered back to BCIF to replace the *Rozel*; she was renamed the *Beauport* to operate from Poole to the Channel Islands during the 1992 and 1993 seasons.

The *Armorique* completed her Portsmouth-St Malo season on 30th September and then undertook a charter for British Gas before being donated for a charity cruise to Cherbourg on behalf of the National Society for the Prevention of Cruelty to Children. She performed a selection of other charter work before returning to the Portsmouth-St Malo route to replace the *Duchesse Anne* until 30th December, when the route closed for the winter.

Brittany Ferries could reflect on a business that grew by 2.8% in 1991 to reach 2,712,000 passengers, with an additional 450,000 passengers travelling on BCIF services. Cross-Channel traffic accounted for 2,490,000 of this total, with the remainder travelling to Santander and Cork. Vehicle traffic continued to make more spectacular progress, rising by 14.8% to reach 720,799 vehicles, whilst freight traffic crept upwards by 2.3% to record 154,899 units. This performance resulted in a net profit of FF41.6 million compared to FF32.2 million in 1989-90, a rise of 29.2%, with turnover increasing to FF1.83 billion from FF1.69 billion (up 8.3%). Passenger and vehicle income grew by 12.7% to reach FF1.26 billion, freight revenue totalled FF 357 million, whilst holiday income grew by 7.6% to FF170 million.

Truckline was still the brand for all Brittany Ferries' freight operations and now boasted carryings of 50% of the freight traffic west of Dover, and the Company expected the impending arrival of the *Barfleur* to boost Poole-Cherbourg freight traffic by 20% in 1992 from the 80,000 freight units in 1990-91. Gordon Day noted that the Poole-Cherbourg route was proving increasingly attractive for the carriage of fresh foods, electrical goods and 'just in time' car parts from Spain and Portugal, and this trend was anticipated to increase further with the relaxation of EC trade barriers following the creation of the single market in 1993. Truckline became the first freight operator on the western Channel to receive full BS5750 quality assurance accreditation for its ro-ro freight marketing, reservations and handling services at Poole, Portsmouth and Plymouth at the end of 1991. This matched the achievement of the Port of Poole.

By 1992 Truckline was able to demonstrate how a computerised reservation system lay at the heart of the business, driving the efficiency of the landside operation and playing an important role in the safe and rapid loading of ferries. Truckline originally utilised a system based on personal computers, which was eventually upgraded to a mainframe system whilst retaining the existing software with several important enhancements. Jeremy Ledger, Truckline's systems manager, said that there were immediate benefits for operators from this approach in that there was no need for further staff training. The enhanced system gave reservations staff immediate access to a wide range of information, including space availability for booking on each sailing right across the portfolio of Truckline freight routes. The software also allowed staff to offer alternative routes and sailings if a requested sailing was fully booked. In the event that a customer could not be accommodated on their first choice of route, the system made an automatic note of the customer's requirements so they could be contacted if space became available. Special programs also enabled reservation staff to complete the necessary formalities for hazardous cargo, wide or heavy loads. The system was extended in 1991 to cover all aspects of port operations, from booking through ticketing, to the loading of ships. Efficiency was improved by linking directly to port authorities, HM Customs and the Special Branch team, to improve the recording of all relevant port information.

On arrival of a freight vehicle at the weighbridge in each port, the computer confirmed the reservation, logged and dated the time of arrival, and recorded the vehicle weight for the ship's manifest. Once logged into the system, drivers were required to report to the Truckline office, where they were issued with a computer-generated ticket incorporating boarding pass, cabin ticket, meal voucher and exit authority from the destination port. This process was slick and could be completed within a two-minute timescale for each vehicle. The tickets outlined descriptions of the loads being carried, including their weight, and any special comments or instructions for the ships loading officer. The ship could therefore be loaded efficiently by deck, with the loading officer automatically receiving full information of vehicle lengths, widths and weight. Berni Smith, Truckline's freight reservations manager, observed that the new system "made a great difference to the speed and efficiency with which we can do our jobs, with instant access to all the information we need while the system keeps automatic tabs on the progress and status of every booking or inquiry." Truckline made further developments to the system to allow reservation staff access to bookings across all routes and eventually allowed customers to the system directly from their own offices.

Brittany Ferries was now also the dominant operator in the cross-Channel ferry passenger and vehicle market west of Dover, with a 52% share of the passenger business, and 54% of the car market. The average yearly growth over the preceding five years had been 23% for cars, and ten per cent for freight units, and turnover had grown to £170 million, increasing by 16% each year. The fleet of twelve ships sailed 765,600 nautical miles annually, equivalent to circumnavigating the world every ten days. In the summer season between June and September, Brittany Ferries carried an average of 709 passengers and 181 cars on each sailing, by far the highest figure of any operator on the English Channel.

The *Stena Normandy* carried 250,000 passengers during her first season on the Southampton–Cherbourg route and Sealink Stena Line expressed their confidence in the volume of winter traffic being carried. The *Stena Traveller* was added to the roster to provide additional freight capacity for the service.

In the 1991 season the number of bed-nights booked through Brittany Ferries Holidays hit one million for the first time, with more than 20% of passengers booking an inclusive holiday or tour, and business more than tripling through the preceding decade. The British market represented the vast majority of these bookings. For the 1992 season, the Brittany Ferries Holidays operation offered a portfolio of over 20 choices of product, from gîtes to Relais and Châteaux hotels, EuroDisney to golfing holidays, and camping accommodation in France, Spain, Portugal and Switzerland. More than 2,500 individual establishments were represented, including over 1,000 hotels and 1,370 gîtes. A turnover of £17 million positioned Brittany Ferries as the leading overseas motoring holiday operator in the British market, yet it was also given the highest quality marks in the ferry holiday sector by the consumer magazine Which? Holidays were promoted through the two million circulation 48-page Ferry brochure, the 164-page Holiday brochure and 340-page 'Gîtes, Apartments, Cottages, Villas' brochure, both of which had a circulation of 1.6 million copies, and a range of more specialist brochure covering diverse interests such a skiing and golf. Annual promotional expenditure of £6 million made Brittany Ferries the sixth largest-spending French brand in the British market.

Whilst the number of French tourists choosing to travel to England was much smaller, it still represented a market of approaching 300,000 passengers and 20,000 vehicles, a volume which had also more than tripled in the preceding five years. A further 20,000 French passengers headed for Cork. The 'Voyage Aux Iles' brochure had a circulation of 600,000 copies and featured a wide choice of accommodation, including bed and breakfast, hotels, camp sites and cottage holidays.

The large camping holiday providers were an important part of the income mix, but from time to time they tried to muscle in on Brittany Ferries' own holiday business, as the Company was the only cross-Channel ferry operator to have a significant volume of holiday traffic in its own right. The operators also demanded dramatic reductions in rates. My Tours wanted to get into the French market by starting a camping business with the objective of establishing a portfolio of around 5,000 pitches within 18 months. They demanded the very best rate offer from Brittany Ferries, then, when they had been given an appropriately keen rate, demanded a further discount. Their approach was rejected. The response was always robust in these circumstances. Brittany Ferries had made a conscious decision not to enter the camping holiday business, even though all the elements were already at its disposal, including a sophisticated reservations system, that would make it comparatively easy for them to do so. Running a campsite would be an easy addition to the holiday portfolio. Conversely, it would be impossible for the camping holiday companies to enter the cross-Channel ferry business. The reality was that the tour operators needed Brittany Ferries more than Brittany Ferries needed the tour operators.

The *Duc de Normandie* left for Brest on 6th January 1992 for a major £3 million refit during which all her public areas were refurbished, a new cinema complex was added, and the duty-free shopping area was revitalised. The top deck reclining seat lounge was renewed and re-equipped with seats designed to be equivalent to those in First Class on long haul flights. These changes brought her facilities in line with those being completed during construction of the *Normandie*.

Some £26 million was spent to prepare for the arrival of the two new vessels. The introduction of the *Barfleur* in Poole prompted work to install a double deck linkspan both there and in Cherbourg. At Portsmouth, a new double deck linkspan had to be built, with an extension to Berth 4 to accommodate the *Normandie*. Work started in January 1992 and caused some upheaval to schedules for a period. A similar linkspan was needed at Ouistreham, where a second berth was also to be added, together with significant dredging to enable the vessels to be able to access the port in all weather conditions. New facilities were also planned for St Malo in anticipation of a replacement vessel for the Santander route enabling the transfer of the *Bretagne* to serve the port from 1993. Tidal problems had hitherto restricted the size of ship that could berth in the port and the availability of a new deep water linkspan would enable the Company to operate the *Bretagne* on the Portsmouth route.

The investment also included a new £10 million computer reservation system, which was in the process of being installed.

The *Armorique* operated the Portsmouth-Caen service on a limited one round trip daily basis, whilst work began on the installation of a new linkspan to facilitate double deck loading at Portsmouth. She was joined by the *Quiberon* from 21st March until the

Duc de Normandie returned from her refit on 10th April, with the two operating in tandem prior to the planned introduction of the *Normandie* in May. The *Bretagne* and *Quiberon* operated the Plymouth-Roscoff service throughout the winter, with the former covering the Plymouth-Santander operation year-round. The *Bretagne* was still suffering from repeated mechanical problems and was withdrawn for a period from February to be sent to Brest for repair; she returned to service at the end of March. The *Havelet* (ex *Cornouailles*) was chartered from BCIF from 23rd February to provide freight capacity on the Plymouth roster in the absence of the *Bretagne*.

The decision to stretch the *Barfleur* forced her planned January date on the Poole-Cherbourg route to be put back. The *Normandie Shipper* operated on the route whilst the *Purbeck* was transferred to cover Portsmouth-Caen. The *Duchesse Anne* also helped out on the freight service in January, before heading for refit. On her return she re-

Ian Carruthers and David Longden appreciate the scale of the *Barfleur's* propellors in the Masa shipyard. *(Kvaerner Masa Yards)*

opened the St Malo service from 1st to 21st March, operating to Poole because of the linkspan works at Portsmouth. The *Armorique* joined her from 20th May. The *Quiberon* left the Roscoff service on 17th March for Caen with the *Duc de Normandie* replacing her.

The instigation for new additions to the fleet continued to be driven by the UK team. Michielini trusted their judgement and his faith was justified by the continued demonstration of the ability to grow business to fill the capacity on offer. The strategy was demand driven. Michielini would approach Maurice Chollet to review the financial consequences of a proposal and the pair would then combine to convince Gourvennec of its merits. A carefully presented, rational case would meet with his approval. The mantra was simple - if it made sense it would be done. With new capacity coming for the Poole-Cherbourg and Portsmouth-Caen routes, attention turned to how the increasing levels of traffic on the Portsmouth-St Malo and Plymouth-Santander routes could be accommodated in the future. Traffic volumes on the Plymouth-Santander route were stretching the capabilities of the *Bretagne*, but if she was replaced by a larger-capacity vessel to Spain she would make an excellent ship for the Portsmouth-St Malo service. In early 1992 the partners in Sabemen (now owners of the *Armorique, Bretagne, Duchesse Anne,* and *Quiberon*) voted to double their capital investment in the SEM with a view to acquiring a new vessel in 1993 and take advantage of the port improvements being planned to accommodate larger vessels in St Malo. Mason began another search.

Carruthers noted that reservations for the 1992 season were running ten per cent ahead of 1991 and observed that the travelling public would soon have the choice to

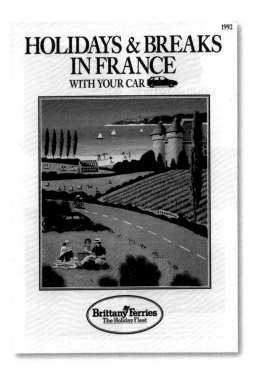

1992 Holidays & Breaks brochure and the Ski-Drive brochure 1991/92. *(Rook Dunning)*

"take their car on the back of a train through a claustrophobic tunnel to arrive miles away from France's main holiday areas, or alternatively travel in style and comfort on Brittany Ferries. Three years ago, the Company had one of the oldest fleets on the channel, and now it had the youngest and most modern, with new generation ships providing cruise ship standards." An extra floor was added to the Brittany Centre in Portsmouth to accommodate the additional reservations staff needed to handle bookings generated by the impending arrival of the *Normandie* and *Barfleur*.

The chartered *Havelet* was hit by a freak wave whilst some four hours into a passage from Cork to Roscoff on 22nd March. Capt. Howard Roberts made bilingual announcements and ordered passengers to emergency stations as the vessel rolled 30 degrees to port and two freight vehicles broke free, causing damage to other vehicles and rupturing the fuel tank of a lorry. As the ship sustained a heavy list, the crew foamed-down the car deck to reduce the risk of any fire spreading. Other ships were put on standby to assist as a precaution, but in the event were not needed. The *Havelet* returned to Ireland and was examined by an official from the Irish marine department, who found no signs that the vessel was unsound. Carruthers said the ship had left in Force Seven conditions after a forecast that winds would drop to Force Five. One passenger who sustained a badly twisted ankle and two others who suffered cuts and bruises were taken to Cork hospital whilst other passengers were accommodated in a local hotel. The passengers were quickly joined in the hotel by a lawyer, who sensed an opportunity and began to demand compensation from Brittany Ferries on their behalf. Carruthers described him as an 'ambulance chaser' and was sued for libel, but was successfully able to defend the case. The *Havelet* set sail for Roscoff again on 23rd March, but courted

Two roundels to promote the introduction of the *Normandie* and the *Barfleur*. *(Rook Dunning)*

controversy when Irish authorities claimed that she had not been given permission to sail after the mandatory inspection. A Brittany Ferries spokesman expressed surprise and confusion at the dispute over the ship's departure and, in a late-night television interview, Carruthers took issue with the Irish Minister of the Sea and the misinformation that he had been fed.

The investigation into the *Havelet* incident was subsequently carried out under Section 728 of the Irish Merchant Shipping Act, 1894. The report noted that the vessel took a very heavy roll to port in gale force conditions. The consequent damage sustained by cargo lashings and attachments culminated in all vehicles shifting to the port side. The report found that the loading and operation of the *Havelet* and subsequent emergency procedures were conducted fully in accordance with all the relevant legislation and codes of practice. There were, however, some instances where passengers were not properly shown the correct method of donning lifejackets. A number of additional general recommendations were made in the interest of ferry safety.

Ferry safety was a highly sensitive issue at this time. The loss of 193 lives on the *Herald of Free Enterprise* in 1987 had been followed by the tragedies of the *Scandinavian Star* in 1990, in which 158 died, and the *Moby Prince* in 1991, with a further 141 casualties. Ferry services were increasingly under scrutiny. Michielini noted that, whilst there was much emphasis on ship design and technological improvements to improve safety standards, systems ultimately involved people, and the most fundamental improvements came from repeated high-quality training of staff. This matched the views of Det Norske Veritas, who estimated that only 20% of accidents were due to technical defects or deficiencies, compared to 80% due to human failure. Moreover, two-thirds of human errors were committed by management, not operational staff. Det Norske Veritas developed an audit procedure to monitor the involvement of shore-based company executives and officers with those on board. Michielini was noted for his close relationships with shipboard personnel, and he led from the front on this issue. Brittany Ferries was the first French company to adopt the procedure and obtained its certificate of accreditation in June 1991 after an 18-month process. The documentation compiled by Fleet Director Jean Thomas stretched to nine volumes.

The *Barfleur*, resplendent in her yellow and grey Truckline livery, successfully completed her second set of sea trials in early March. Although issues with her deadweight and stability regularly came to the fore in press enquiries, Oliver was adamant that "there have been no constructional problems at all with the vessel." Her bespoke design allowed specifically for the constraints of Poole Harbour, and a £3 million work programme was completed at Poole to facilitate her arrival, included dredging of the approach channel to a depth of 6.6 metres, and widening it to accommodate ships of up to 165 metres in length. This required the removal of 750,000 cubic metres of sand and silt, which was carried out by Rohde Nielses A/S of Copenhagen using the bucket dredger *Ajax* and the trailer suction dredger *Viking R*. The extracted sand was sold to Bournemouth Council. The only remaining issue was any possible interaction with the chains of the Sandbanks-Studland chain ferry at the entrance to the harbour, but this lay

The *Barfleur* makes a fine sight during her inaugural crossing to Poole in the stretched guise that overcame her initial deadweight problems. *(Ferry Publications Library)*

outside the control of the Poole Harbour Commissioners and would have required an Act of Parliament to change arrangements. Vessels were subsequently to come close to hitting the chain on several occasions.

The *Barfleur* arrived in Poole for the first time under the command of Capt. Claude Lenoir on 4th April and was a focal point for the opening ceremony of the new double deck linkspan on Berth 3, which was unveiled by Gourvennec. The post lunch entertainment on board was provided by Janet Brown, a Margaret Thatcher impersonator. As she joined the party at the end of the meal, Michielini went on bended knee to kiss her hand, convinced she was actually the prime minister. Prince Edward took the opportunity to inspect the *Barfleur* and lunch on board in Poole on 7th April. The *Barfleur* made her first commercial crossing to Cherbourg service with a freight-only departure on 14th April, followed by her first passenger sailing the next day. She was then the biggest ship ever to berth in Poole, and her arrival allowed the formerly seasonal passenger service to be extended year-round. Longden expressed confidence that the Company's strong belief in the shortest, quickest on the western Channel would be swiftly justified.

The configuration of the *Barfleur* reflected her design as a freight vessel with excellent passenger facilities. The lower freight deck on Decks 1 and 2 (known as the basement) could accommodate 14 lorries. It was accessible by a lift from the main freight deck, capable of handling two vehicles simultaneously. The main freight deck on Decks 3 and 4 was accessed via a clamshell bow door and a combined stern door/ramp. Deck 5 hosted the main car deck which utilised the upper ramp in port, reached via a garage door to

Dick Reed (Chairman of Poole Harbour Commissioners) greets Alexis Gourvennec at the opening of the new linkspan in Poole. *(Ferry Publications Library)*

the bow and gates to the stern. Further 120-car capacity was available on the hoistable car decks on Deck 6; out of season these could be raised to permit loading of freight on Deck 5. Passenger facilities were concentrated on Deck 7, although there were reclining seat areas and cabins on Decks 5 and 6. The 'Turquoise' restaurant and 'Drivers Club' freight driver's restaurant lay at the bow of the ship. Moving aft, passengers could enjoy a duty-free shop and 'La Boutique' with the Information Desk, Bureau de Change and luggage room found mid-ships. Further astern lay the 'Les Dunes' restaurant and 'Le Kiosque' shop, 'L'Arc en Ciel' patisserie and a seating area. Facilities on this deck were completed by a children's playroom hosted by an entertainer during the summer months, and the 'Les Alizes' bar, which often featured live entertainment. Deck 8 featured further passenger cabins and the *Barfleur's* bridge, whilst Deck 9 was used as a sun deck.

The *Barfleur* operated alone on the Poole-Cherbourg route from May, with two round trips daily in the summer season, berthing stern to the ramp in Poole and bow first in Cherbourg. During the winter season from October to May she worked in tandem with the *Coutances* to provide three crossings daily from each port. On Mondays, both vessels remained in port for one 'sailing' to allow for maintenance activities and crew training. This also ensured that they remained on the same port schedule each week. The frequency was increased to four crossings daily during the peak season. The Poole Harbour Commissioners were hopeful that Brittany Ferries would consider switching the St Malo service from Portsmouth to Poole, or open a second service to France to take advantage of the shorter crossing times from the port.

From the start of services in 1986, traffic on the Poole-Cherbourg route had grown from 46,000 to 430,000 passengers over the five-month season, with freight traffic rising from 67,000 to 80,000 freight vehicles. Day expected Truckline to carry over 50% of all freight shipments west of Dover in 1992. The *Barfleur* replaced three ships on the route, and soon came under significant capacity pressure at peak periods. It was clear that a second ship would be needed for the 1993 season if the growth potential of the route was not to be frustrated.

Although marketed as a 'Les Routiers' service, there was nothing inferior abut the standards of passenger accommodation on board the *Barfleur*. *(Ferry Publications Library)*

Meanwhile, the *Normandie* was nearing completion at the Masa-Turku shipyard. She was launched on 5th October 1991 and moved to the fitting out basin for the final stages of her build. The *Normandie* undertook successful sea trials off Finland in wintry conditions in March and was handed over to Brittany Ferries at the shipyard on 5th May 1992. Michielini was bullish about the Company's prospects, stating that the investment in the *Barfleur* and *Normandie* would attract business as traffic making for the Channel Tunnel was increasingly slowed down by the heavy congestion of motorways around London and Paris. "For people going to the west and south of France from anywhere other than the south east of England, there will be no point in using the tunnel", he said. Noting that the number of passengers crossing the Channel with Brittany Ferries had risen from 526,000 in 1979 to 2.7 million in 1991, he predicted that volumes would reach 3.5 million by the end of 1994. Michielini observed that Brittany Ferries' profits rose by 29% in 1991 and would have been £8 million higher if the Company had employed British seafarers.

The Company proudly boasted that the £80 million *Normandie* featured the latest in high technology ferry design. Vibration and noise levels compared with the most advanced cruise liners, whilst a dual stabiliser system kept movement to an absolutely minimum. Safety equipment, including a double skinned hull was designed to exceed the strictest regulations then in force, and the ship featured advanced position monitoring equipment, similar to aircraft automatic landing systems, which allowed it to berth in any visibility conditions. The interior of the 10-deck *Normandie* and its range of on board facilities had been created specifically to offer guests a level of comfort, style and space normally associated with cruise ships. Aboard the new flagship were two cinema lounges, the duty-free shopping mall, a choice of restaurants and bars, children's video and entertainment area, playroom for the very young and a fully equipped hospital. All cabins were air conditioned and had private shower and toilet facilities and lounges were equipped with reclining seats similar to those found in business class sections of long haul airlines.

Ian Carruthers entertains Prince Edward on board the *Barfleur* as David Longden and Capt. Lenoir look on. *(Ian Carruthers collection)*

The *Normandie* sailed from Finland through the Baltic and into the North Sea, and was named at Beatrixhaven, Holland in a ceremony led by a Breton priest in the presence of the ship's godmother, Madame Garrec of Caen, on 14th May. Industrial action prevented the ceremony taking place in Caen as originally planned. The *Normandie* then sailed to Ouistreham for berthing trials. Large crowds gathered as Capt. Apperry brought his new vessel into Portsmouth for the first time on Saturday 16th May, arriving at 09:30 to undertake more berthing trials. She then moved to the naval berth at the South Railway Jetty to allow VIPs to board for a sailing to the Needles, her departure being accompanied by the Royal Marines beating retreat. She anchored off Cowes for guests to enjoy a firework display before returning to Portsmouth the following morning. The *Normandie* returned to Caen with her inaugural 08:00 sailing on 18th May, replacing the

Reine Mathilde and instantly providing a 40% increase in capacity on the route.

The QHM determined that the port of Portsmouth should be closed for 30 minutes for each movement of the *Normandie*, as she was treated as being equivalent to an aircraft carrier (as she was then larger than any vessel in the UK naval fleet) and required an admiralty tug to be on standby for each movement at a cost to Brittany Ferries of £1,000 each day. *HMS Chatham* was forced to give way to the *Normandie* as she left Portsmouth on her inaugural crossing. These regulations were not relaxed until 22nd June.

The *Normandie* was well received, from her name, evoking a glamorous and leisurely journey across the Atlantic, to the style and quality of her outfitting, which resembled an

Capt. Bertrand Apperry, Madame Garrec and Father Olivier Pellen at the blessing of the *Normandie* in Rotterdam.
(Ferry Publications Library)

hotel. She was seen to be brighter and more spacious than her competitors and delivered the concept that the holiday began as soon as you boarded. The vessel featured two cinemas, a fully equipped hospital, a shopping mall and a variety of restaurants. Chief Purser Josette Vignat summed up the mood by saying "we want people to treat it like a small cruise ship, it should really be a good part of the holiday." The Times, under the heading "Floating hotel makes its first crossing' noted that the 'marketing men had two summers to persuade the public that it beats half an hour in a tunnel.' The arrival of the *Normandie* heralded a new stage of the 'ruthless competition between Channel ferry companies, spurred by the Channel Tunnel.'

With the introduction of the *Barfleur* and now the *Normandie*, the average age of the Brittany Ferries fleet was just 9.4 years, making it the youngest of any ferry operator on the English Channel. This reflected the fact the Company had made significantly greater capital investment than any other cross-channel operator to meet the impending challenge of the Channel Tunnel. With less than two years to go to the opening, P&O European Ferries were still operating the comparatively elderly 'Super-Vikings' from Portsmouth, retaining their inadequate and inferior passenger accommodation.

Every effort was made to publicise the arrival of the *Normandie*, especially to those who were travelling on the P&O European Ferries Portsmouth fleet. One approach utilised the giant billboard adjacent to the Brittany Centre in Wharf Road, Portsmouth. A large graphic depicting the *Normandie* was built on the board, with lighting fitted to each of the cabin windows, so that the ship could be made to appear to be lit up at night. The

The *Normandie* is welcomed to Portsmouth on her inaugural visit by a traditional tug salute. *(Miles Cowsill)*

poster was topped by the statement 'Ooh la la...' and made a striking impact. It was visible to everyone using the Continental Ferry Terminal, as well as those passing on Commercial Road, the main route out of the City. But it drew the ire of Lord Sterling, Chairman of the P&O Group, who referred to Brittany Ferries as a 'paper tiger' when he saw it on a visit to the port. The advertising was clearly working.

The arrival of two new ferries provided a canvas for Serestel to enhance further the quality of on board service. Maraval's inclusive planning processes had allowed the perspective of the in-house service-provider to be incorporated within the design of both vessels. The crew recruitment pool was expanded to embrace seasonal hotel staff, with an emphasis on sourcing local staff from Brittany and Normandy. The growing reputation of Brittany Ferries in France and the professionalism of the recruitment and training processes encouraged more younger seasonal and permanent staff to dedicate their

Above: **The Information Area on board the** *Normandie* **creates a subtle feeling of spaciousness.** *(Ferry Publications Library).*

Below: **The Terrace Restaurant on the** *Normandie* **epitomises just how far standards of quality have progressed since the start of the Company.** *(Ferry Publications Library)*

Above: **The atrium stairwell linking the Information Area to the main passenger facilities on Deck 7.** *(Ferry Publications Library)*

Below: **Cabin accommodation on the *Normandie* matches cruise ship standards.** *(Ferry Publications Library)*

Above: **The *Normandie* arrives at Ouistreham with the *Normandie Shipper* already on her berth.** *(Ferry Publications Library)*

Below: **The *Normandie* is overtaken by the *Duc de Normandie* in Portsmouth Harbour during a press trip.** *(Miles Cowsill)*

hospitality and tourism careers to the Company. The slogan "Let yourself be transported; you will travel differently" was used to bring in recruits. Training courses initially developed with local hotels and catering schools in Brittany were extended to Lower Normandy. Serestel enabled Brittany Ferries to break away fully from the constraints of the traditional maritime employment code and offer the potential for fulfilling careers based on merit rather than seniority.

On 20th May the *Armorique* transferred to cover the Portsmouth-St Malo service for her final season; she operated a Portsmouth-Cherbourg-Poole-Cherbourg-Poole-St Malo schedule. At Poole the *Coutances* backed up the *Barfleur*, whilst the *Purbeck* did the

Above: **Commemorative logo for the** *Normandie* **inaugural celebrations.** *(Rook Dunning)*

Top right: **Menu cover for the** *Normandie* **inauguration.** *(Ian Carruthers collection)*

Right: **Programme of events for the Normandie inauguration.** *(Ian Carruthers collection)*

Below: **Menu for the inauguration dinner.** *(Ian Carruthers collection)*

DINNER

Cassolette de St-Jacques et langoustines aux truffes

Homard au vin de Pauillac

Plateau de fromages

Concerto aux fruits

Pouilly fumé Michel Redde
Château Mouton Baronne Philippe 1983

Chef des cuisines Y RIVOALLAN

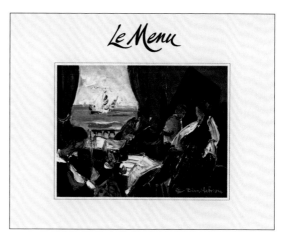

THE INAUGURAL CRUISE OF BRITTANY FERRIES M.V NORMANDIE
MAY 16-17 1992

PROGRAMME

Saturday May 16

16.30-18.30
Please feel free to wander round the ship at your leisure. Light refreshments will be available in "Le Pays d Auge" Viennoisserie and "Le Derby" bar.

17 00
Band of HM Royal Marines, Commander in Chief, Naval Home Command, will beat retreat on the quay

17.30
Ship departs for cruise to the Needles, weather permitting.

19 15-20 00
RECEPTION
This will be held in "Le Derby" bar.
Dress. Dinner Jackets.

20 00
Ship anchors off Cowes.

20.15
DINNER
Dinner will be served in "Riva Bella" and "Le Deauville" restaurants.
Please note a table plan will be on display outside both restaurants.

22.45
FIREWORKS DISPLAY
Please make your way on deck to watch the spectacular fireworks display taking place over Cowes.

23 00
CABARET
Relive the 60's and 70's in "Le Derby" bar dancing to the sounds of the most famous group of all time The Beatles courtesy of the Bootleg Beatles.
For those who want to go at a slower pace, enjoy the relaxing atmosphere of the Piano bar in "Le Deauville" restaurant.

24 00
MIDNIGHT MOVIE
Take a break from dancing and choose between two superb films to be screened in the cinemas.

Sunday May 17

07.30-09 00
BREAKFAST
The ship will have berthed back in Portsmouth in the early morning and breakfast will be served in the "Riva Bella" and "Le Deauville" restaurants.

08 30-09 30
DISEMBARKATION

same in Plymouth for the *Quiberon*, including a weekly trip to Spain on Saturdays from June.

Stena Sealink Line attempted to improve their carryings from Southampton by copying the short-sea strategy of aggressive price cutting during the summer, but these actions drew no response from either Brittany Ferries or P&O European Ferries. The *Stena Traveller* joined their Southampton fleet as a freighter from 15th April on a 28-week charter to determine if there was sufficient freight traffic to justify her retention.

The *Quiberon* hit the national media

headlines on 17th July after fire broke out in her main engine room. The vessel left Plymouth for Roscoff with 1,124 passengers, 94 crew and 243 cars on board, and was some 60 miles off the French coast when the fire began just after 11:15. The blaze was extinguished within an hour. Capt. Pierre Michel sent out a Mayday message and three Royal Navy search and rescue helicopters were scrambled from the Royal Naval Air Station at Culdrose in Cornwall. French marine firefighters were helicoptered in from Brest to help fight the fire. The minehunter *HMS Brecon* was also sent to assist the *Quiberon*, and an RAF Nimrod aircraft headed for the scene. In the event none of this support was needed. Passengers were asked to go to muster stations on the upper decks and the lifeboats were swung out, but a spokesman noted that there was no question of the ship being evacuated, with the Mayday call being a routine requirement in these circumstances. Two French naval tugs were sent from Brest to bring back the disabled ship to Roscoff, some 60 miles away. Weather conditions were fortunately bright and sunny, with a Force Five wind. The *Quiberon* was sent to Brest for repairs after discharging in Roscoff. Passengers praised the captain and his crew for their handling of the emergency. The cause of the fire was believed to be a ruptured pipe, which caused fuel to ignite when it came into contact with a hot pipe.

Sadly, Alain Etienne, a 28-year-old French crewman, died when he was asphyxiated by fumes whilst trying to put out the fire.

The incident happened at the start of the busiest weekend of the year as the summer holidays began, and resulted in the immediate halving of the Plymouth-Roscoff schedule. Michielini and Carruthers were both on holiday at the time, and Longden took a call from the BBC at home asking for comment before he knew that anything was wrong with the ship. Longden took charge in Plymouth and Carruthers flew back to Roscoff from the south of France on the Company plane, picking up a set of clothes in Cannes en route. Michielini was uncontactable. The Brittany Ferries Information Bureau split the team between Plymouth and Roscoff to try and help control the media attention. Carruthers face a hostile press conference in Roscoff. "How does the Captain feel about losing one of his crew?" was one of the insensitive questions on offer.

A charter of the *Munster* was considered to provide additional capacity, but too much work was needed to bring her up to Brittany Ferries' standards, so the Roscoff traffic was transferred to the Cherbourg and Caen routes. The *Armorique* switched from Portsmouth-St Malo to the Poole-Cherbourg route to offer enhanced frequency, with passengers compensated by cash payments and overnight accommodation for those who had booked cabins, and the *Coutances* moved from Plymouth to Poole to supplement the *Purbeck's* freight capacity. The cost of repairing the *Quiberon* was high, and the insurers considered writing her off at one stage. Re-cabling the vessel proved to be an immensely difficult task and sailings did not return to normal until 28th August, when the *Quiberon* resumed service.

Growing interest in battlefield tours was supported by the introduction of Brittany Ferries cassette tapes narrated by broadcaster Keith Howell and designed to be played through the car radio whilst touring the Normandy beaches. The tapes were produced with significant input from Sir Michael Grey, who enthusiastically supported the project. Sir Michael was Chairman of the Airborne Assault Normandy Trust, which sought to preserve the history of the 6th Airborne Division in Normandy, and played a leading role in the creation of the museum at Pegasus Bridge and the restoration of the site of the Merville Battery. The tours outlined the story of each of the key battles and took drivers to the locations of conflict, where veterans recounted what happened there. The first 'Pegasus Trail' tour covered the operations of the British 6th Airborne Division on D Day, and this was followed by the 'British D Day Tour' of the Gold, Juno and Sword beach landing sites of the British and Canadian forces. Both tours started from Ouistreham, and ended at the military cemetery at Ranville, and the Museum of the Battle of Normandy at Bayeux, respectively. The tapes were sold for a symbolic £19.44 through the Reservations

Pegasus Trail pack cover. *(Rook Dunning)*

Offices, on board the vessels and at each terminal, with all proceeds going to the Airborne Assault Normandy Trust. The project proved enduringly popular, and in later years the cassettes were replaced by compact discs, with the original material reworked into the new format.

On 9th July 1992 the District Council of Vizcaya and the Department of Commerce, Consumption and Tourism of the Basque Government announced that they had reached agreement with Ferries Golfo de Vizcaya (then a joint venture between P&O European Ferries and Vapores Suardíaz), for the initiation of a twice-weekly ferry service between Bilbao and Portsmouth. The agreement would ensure that preference would be given to candidates from Vizcaya and the Basque Country in recruiting crew, and to local companies for goods and catering services on the vessel. Ferries Golfo de

A far cry from the *Kerisnel* - the elegant lines of the *Normandie* at full speed. *(FotoFlite)*

FLEET D'EXCELLENCE

Luxury and style are the key words for cross-Channel travel in 1992.
Brittany Ferries has lead the way with a major upgrading of existing vessels and the
introduction of two brand new superferries, making the company's fleet the youngest
and most modern on the Channel routes.

The beautiful new Normandie is Brittany Ferries flagship
and offers cross-Channel passengers of the '90s the same qualities that made its
'30s transatlantic namesake so famous. space, comfort and elegance. It is currently
the largest ship operating between the UK and France.

The Normandie s ten decks offer passengers everything from cinemas,
restaurants and tea and coffee shops to a fully equipped hospital. For children there is
a play centre and a video games room, and shoppers can browse at their leisure in the
ship s duty free shopping mall.

The luxury flagship has space for 680 cars, no fewer than 220 cabins
with 780 berths, over 400 Pullman recliners and total seating in the restaurant, coffee
shop and bars for over 700 people.

Brittany Ferries philosophy of excellence is apparent throughout the company's
vessels, from the design of the ships down to the finest details of the cabins and the
decor of the bars. Special paintings have even been commissioned for each public
room on the Normandie.

The Normandie operates on the popular Portsmouth to Caen service
while the second new ship, the capacious Barfleur is slightly smaller at 20,500 tons
but displays the company's commitment to excellence in every respect.
It is currently operating between Poole and Cherbourg on Brittany Ferries
Truckline passenger service.

Advertisements from the 1992 campaign. *(Rook Dunning)*

Vizcaya would also open Tourist Information Offices in each of its ports. The two
authorities undertook to purchase travel vouchers to be distributed amongst low-income
groups as part of a social and cultural policy. Some 26,000 vouchers were to be
purchased for Pta 911.8 million between March 1993 and March 1996. The agreement
further stipulated that if the venture traded profitably the profit would be deducted from
the monthly payments from the authorities. Conversely in a loss-making situation the
authorities would pay Ferries Golfo de Vizcaya the difference between the partial sums of
the payments and the global sum agreed. The agreement allowed for the authorities to
receive ten per cent of any future profit from the route after the initial three-year period.
Carruthers expressed concern that the Spanish market was insufficient to sustain two
operators, and observed that the unusual funding arrangements were to be subjected to
close scrutiny.

The *Armorique* was chartered by British Steel to start the Round the World yacht race
from Southampton on 26th September. The charter required significant alterations to be
made to her accommodation for over 500 VIPs at the event. The *Quiberon* maintained
the Plymouth-Roscoff service until 14th November, when the route was incorporated into
the *Bretagne*'s Plymouth-Santander winter schedules. The *Duchesse Anne* operated alone
on the Poole-Cherbourg route until 30th December, with the *Armorique* standing in to
cover her duties on the Portsmouth-St Malo route.

On 7th September, 38 English football fans were refused travel from Plymouth as they
tried to head to Santander for a friendly game in Spain. Four known hooligans, who were
identified by police officers at the Millbay Terminal, were turned back. Any travellers
wearing scarves or football colours, and all men intending to stay within a 150-mile
radius of Santander were also refused passage. The Company justified the decision on the
basis that "we are a family-friendly company and intend to protect the majority of our

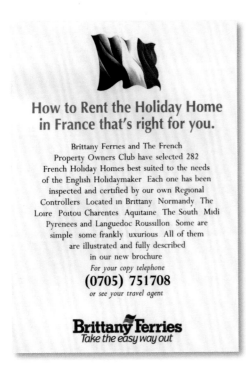

passengers. This was done in conjunction with the police." Whilst the decision drew predictable outrage from affected supporters, it was received well by other passengers.

As the month of September progressed, the UK government found it increasingly difficult to control sterling currency exchange rates. Under the ERM, member nations' currencies were meant to fluctuate within specific relative ranges, with the nations holding stronger currencies required to sell them and support those with weaker currencies in order to maintain the exchange rate system. The pound was one of the weaker currencies in the ERM and struggled to remain within its designated trading range. The UK government took action to place upward pressure on the pound, raising interest rates from 10% to 12% and then 15% on 16th September. But the move did not stop selling of the currency. By the end of the day the UK was forced to exit the ERM. The pound fell against the French Franc from FF9.7 to FF8.5, an effective and immediate cataclysmic drop of 14% in Brittany Ferries' UK income. The pound later fell to an exchange rate below FF8.0 and was to remain at this level for much of 1995 and 1996.

Whilst a low value pound was good news for exporters, sterling's withdrawal from the ERM had an immediate impact on revenues and yields for all cross-Channel operators and made continental holidays significantly less attractive to the British market. For French operators with revenues in sterling and cost in francs this was the worst possible development; an immediate drop in the value of most ticket sales combined with suppression of future growth and the possibility of a downturn on traffic. It was the perfect storm. All this came at a time when the Company had just completed a FF2 billion fleet investment programme, the justification for which had been predicated on a fine balance of exchange rates. The change came right at the end of the financial year, so the 1991-2 results were largely unaffected. But Brittany Ferries was to face increasing losses for the next four years, entering one of the most difficult periods since the Company's formation.

In a reaction to the falling value of the pound P&O European Ferries and Sealink Stena Line led an initiative to raise freight rates through a surcharge on tariffs for all cross-Channel ferry routes from November 1992; identical surcharges applying the same method of calculation were implemented by SeaFrance, Brittany Ferries and North Sea Ferries from the same date. Although implemented for only a short period, the European Commission judged there to the operation of a cartel, and subsequently fined each of the companies involved. Brittany Ferries was deemed a minor player in the collusion and was fined 60,000 ECU.

On 9th December 1992 the *Duchesse Anne* was in collision with the French dredger *Le Timac* as she approached St Malo from Portsmouth. The dredger was sunk and one of her seven-man crew killed. None of the 99 passengers on the *Duchesse Anne* was injured. The *Duchesse Anne* was taken out of service and sent to Brest for repair with the

Armorique brought in to cover her absence. The *Armorique* made her final sailing for Brittany Ferries on 30th December with the 21:30 from Portsmouth to St Malo. She was then de-stored and laid up at Bassin Vauban in St Malo prior to being put up for sale.

1992 was a difficult year for all operators on the western Channel. In the year ending September 1992 Group turnover rose to FF1,342 million and the Company made a net profit of FF22.1 million. Brittany Ferries saw passenger volumes fall by 2.7% to 2,639,803 and there was a small drop in vehicle traffic of 1.3% to 711,291 cars. Freight traffic continued to rise, with a further 8.7% increase in units carried. In spite of the severity of the recession, freight carryings grew to more than 168,000 units carried during 1992, compared to 154,000 units in the same period in 1991. In the first six months of operation of the *Normandie*, freight traffic on the Portsmouth-Caen route grew by 14%; the introduction of the *Barfleur* to the Poole-Cherbourg service resulted in an 8% rise in business. Day noted that the factors behind the success were having good routes, the right frequency and a year-round offer of freight capacity for customers.

P&O European Ferries experienced a 1% decline in passenger volumes during the 1992 season, coupled with a 4% drop in vehicles and a two per cent fall in freight carryings. Whilst the pound sterling's exchange rate had been relatively stable against the French franc at around 9.8FF/£1 for much of 1991/2 it had fallen to FF8.3 by the end of 1992. With substantial investment in two new ships during the year and Mason coming close to finding a replacement ship for the *Bretagne* on the Plymouth-Santander service, the short to medium-term prospects again looked bleak. But there was some limited respite on the horizon.

The abolition of duty-free sales for journeys made entirely within the EU was originally agreed by the European Commission in 1991, on the grounds that cut-price sales to cross-border travellers was an anomaly within a single market. The date for abolition was set as 1st January 1993 to coincide with the start of the new single market. As the deadline loomed, the duty-free sector lobbied heavily for a reversal of the decision, which required a unanimous vote of all EU member states. The approach proved successful, with the ferry industry (and other transport operations) granted an extra six and a half years to adjust their trading arrangements and prepare for the loss of revenue. The new abolition date became 30th June 1999. Restrictions on sales were also amended from 1st January 1993, to allow passengers to purchase duty-free goods for personal use without limit, and systematic border checks on purchases were withdrawn, providing a boost for on board revenues. Brittany Ferries had long recognised the drawbacks of building a business on fiscal anomalies, and was much less dependent on income from duty-free sales than competing ferry companies. The postponement of abolition was useful but not something that would transform the business. However, the decision allowed those ferry companies with a heavy dependence on profits from duty-free sales to perpetuate and expand this activity, with a greater incentive for travellers to buy higher quantities of product. The strategy of charging low fares to attract high-spending passengers could continue for a further extended period. This was a useful financial boost against the background of the decline in the value of sterling.

More immediately for Brittany Ferries, there was a desire to capitalise on the weaknesses of the competition in the western Channel and continue to develop the fleet. The SEMS were comfortable that the UK team could continue to generate the volumes of traffic needed to underpin expansion and were ready to continue their investment. The Spanish route was the next priority, for the *Bretagne* had demonstrated the business that could be generated by cruise ferry operation on the service. More capacity was now needed if the proposed P&O European Ferries service was to be thwarted. Mason began another search.

Eleven

Securing the Val de Loire

The 1987-built *Nils Holgersson* had short employment with TT-LIne on the Travemünde-Trelleborg route for which she was constructed. *(Ferry Publications Library)*

The search for a vessel capable of providing a capacity upgrade to the *Bretagne* yet be capable of handling the sea conditions of the Bay of Biscay quickly focused on another Scandinavian vessel in the form of the *Nils Holgersson*. She was built by the Schichau Seebeckwerft AG shipyard in Bremerhaven and delivered for service on TT-Line's Travemünde-Trelleborg route in February 1987. Traffic on that route declined dramatically between 1989 and 1992, and the *Nils Holgersson* was sold to SweFerry in February 1992. She remained operating on the route until 21st December 1992, but was put up for sale in a desperate attempt by SweFerry to stave off bankruptcy. Christian Michielini and Jim Mason moved fast to secure a rare opportunity to enhance the fleet with a large, high-quality vessel. The *Nils Holgersson* was inspected in early January 1993 and the £40 million purchase was announced publicly on 2nd February. The new acquisition was to be deployed on the Roscoff, Cork and Santander routes, allowing the *Bretagne* to transfer away to boost capacity on the Portsmouth-St Malo service and take advantage of the new enhanced facilities in the French port. The *Nils Holgersson* offered a modest increase in passenger capacity over the *Bretagne,* but incorporated more cabins and a bigger car deck. The 31,360 gross-tonne vessel was 161.5 metres in length and 32 metres in beam and could carry 2,280 passengers and 570 cars.

Prior to her entry into service, the *Nils Holgersson* underwent a short overhaul at the

Flender Werft shipyard at Lübeck in Germany, before she departed on 15th January as the renamed *Val de Loire* for the Ankommer INMA shipyard in La Spezia, Italy, for more extensive works; this included the complete reconstruction of her bow to improve her ability to sustain the Plymouth-Santander service in all weathers. Her accommodation was rebuilt to convert what had primarily been utilised as a 'day' ferry into one offering high standards of overnight accommodation. Michielini and Mason travelled to inspect the works in Italy and went out for dinner in La Spezia during their visit. They found themselves sitting in a restaurant recently fitted out with seats removed from the vessel during the refit. Michielini was not amused...

The *Val de Loire* was re-equipped with new Commodore Class cabins and a dedicated lounge on Deck 10; the main passenger facilities were located on Decks 7 (the Panoramic

Left: **Major changes were made to the superstructure of the *Val de Loire*.** *(Ian Carruthers)*

Top right: **The bow of the *Val de Loire* was reinforced to handle sea conditions in the Bay of Biscay.** *(Ian Carruthers)*

Right: **Undergoing a name change – the *Nils Holgersson* becomes the *Val de Loire*.** *(Ian Carruthers)*

Lounge, duty-free shop and self-service restaurant 'La Magdalena'), 8 (the à la carte restaurant 'Le Temps de Vivre', the bistro 'Le Café du Port', the tea shop 'Le Grand Large', and the piano bar 'Le Layon'), and 9 (the beauty centre, a photo shop and the bar 'Le Relais'). On Deck 1 could be found a Swimming Pool – a first for a cruise ferry - a Night Club, two Cinemas, and a Children Playroom.

The *Val de Loire* was given a maritime theme throughout the vessel, making liberal use of detailed models of 20th century Atlantic Ocean liners, with items of appropriate memorabilia, including sextants, searchlights, compasses and telescopes. More original artwork by Alexander Goudie and other artists was used to enhance the vessel. The 'Le Temps de Vivre' restaurant was decorated with watercolour paintings of the Loire Valley to help create a calming atmosphere, whilst 'Le Cafe du Port' and 'Le Grand Large' used images of fishing from Roscoff, with special stained-glass murals. The Commodore Class cabins were each named after different wines from the Loire Valley, with an appropriate complimentary bottle offered to occupants on Spanish sailings.

The refurbishment cost totalled £70 million making the acquisition cost of the *Val de Loire* some £120 million. Consideration was given to acquiring the *Val de Loire's* two sisters to enable a complete fleet renewal, but the additional need for appropriate refurbishment was too expensive a proposition. The *Val de Loire* was a further significant

The *Val de Loire* in the shipyard in La Spezia. *(Ferry Publications Library)*

piece of the 'Superfleet' jigsaw, coming on top of the investment in the *Bretagne*, *Normandie,* and *Barfleur*. P&O European Ferries was being left behind in the western Channel market.

1993 promised to be a year of further new ships and new routes, with the *Bretagne* deployed on an experimental Portsmouth-Santander winter service, and the *Duchesse Anne* utilised on two new summer routes linking St Malo with Poole and Cork, facilitated by the arrival of the *Val de Loire* in Plymouth.

The *Bretagne* opened the Portsmouth-Santander winter service on 28th January testing the potential for a route departing from closer than Plymouth to the large London and south east England market. There was some scepticism about the likely financial success of the route, because the longer passage could not be compensated for by any increase in fares for low season business. But proximity to a larger passenger market gave the service the best chance of success. The port of Portsmouth also opened access

1993 Holidays & Breaks brochure cover and Gîte Holidays brochure. *(Rook Dunning)*

to a substantially larger freight market than available through Plymouth in the winter, and this proved to be decisive in agreeing to the experiment. The complex summer operational schedule could only be operated from Plymouth, so the Portsmouth option was only ever likely to be a winter opportunity. With a crossing time of between 28 and 33 hours, the new route proved popular, especially for the mini-cruise business which provided a good income from on board spend.

The *Bretagne* sailed from Portsmouth to Caen and Santander until 16th March, when she transferred to Plymouth to open the Roscoff/Cork/Santander rotation from 17th March until the arrival of the *Val de Loire* on 16th June. The lack of a passenger service on the Plymouth-Roscoff route during the winter was not well received and there were strong local protests, but Brittany Ferries maintained that the loss-making operation was not sustainable during a lean period. The route was to be closed again from 15th November 1993, but the *Val de Loire*, *Quiberon* and *Bretagne* were used during the summer to offer up to three daily sailings to Roscoff.

The *Duc de Normandie* underwent overhaul from 28th January, then was laid up until she returned to the Portsmouth-Caen link from 15th March. The *Quiberon* sailed in freight-only mode on the route from 29th January until 14th March, with the *Normandie* and *Bretagne* covering the passenger sailings. The *Coutances* returned from Roscoff on 15th March to take up the *Quiberon's* Portsmouth-Caen freight sailing roster. The *Barfleur* refitted from 1st February with the *Duchesse Anne* covering her Poole-Cherbourg duties. The *Normandie Shipper* remained on the Poole-Cherbourg link for the remainder of the year.

The *Armorique* was chartered to BCIF between 2nd and 20th February to cover their refit programme. The *Duchesse Anne* opened her Portsmouth-St Malo season on 18th

The highly successful 'A few words about...' campaign. *(Rook Dunning)*

The campaign also featured single page press advertisements. *(Rook Dunning)*

The open road, Brittany Ferries style... *(Rook Dunning)*

March, with the *Quiberon* re-opening Plymouth-Roscoff the following day. The *Duchesse Anne* remained on the Portsmouth-St Malo service until the *Bretagne* returned to debut on the route, then she transferred to offer an expanded service on the Plymouth-Roscoff-Cork roster; she also initiated a new Cork-St Malo route from 21st June 1993, supporting the aspirations of the Poole Harbour Commissioners to expand services from the port.

The 1993 holidays programme was expanded to take advantage of the opening of the Portsmouth-Santander and Cork-St Malo routes, and the arrival of the *Val de Loire*. A new car inclusive fare offered major savings for travellers to France and overall fares were increased by an inflation-beating 2%. Modest price increases of 3% were applied to the Holiday products, and customers could take advantage of a new Privilege Card, which offered a 15% reduction on hotel restaurant bills. Fares on the Santander services were reduced by up to 30% in the shoulder season to place pressure on the new P&O European Ferries Bilbao service. The average price decrease was four per cent and single fares now started at £63 for passengers and £121 for cars. Special half-price fares were offered for the first child (4-13) on each booking, with additional children free, except during the high season, when return tickets started at £22.

Launching the programme, David Longden revealed that Brittany Ferries planned "to offer the only real alternative to the Dover Straits Shuttle, whether above or below the sea." The Company's strong position was based on a number of factors including the "unique on board style and guest comfort, value for money and above all geography, with the only direct services to the holiday areas of Brittany, Normandy and Spain." He drew attention to Brittany Ferries' investment plan and noted that with delays to the Channel Tunnel meaning it was "not so likely to appear above the parapet before the end of 1993, so we have even more time to convince holidaymakers of the advantages we offer."

Extensive research was commissioned in spring 1993 to evaluate consumer perceptions of the cost of ferry travel on longer routes and to build a better understanding of the right Brittany Ferries passenger market proposition after the opening of the Channel Tunnel. The HPI Research survey report challenged the commonly held assumption that longer crossings must inevitably cost more. The survey found that in 88% of cases where two adults travelled with a car to France before 14th July and after 24th August, they would cross more cheaply with Brittany Ferries than on any Dover-Calais service between 05:30 and 00:45. In the peak season, the Brittany Ferries sailings were cheaper in more than two-thirds of cases than any fare available on Dover-Calais services between 08:30 and 18:30. Researchers questioned consumers' perceptions of ferry fares and found a consistent under-estimation of costs on the short-sea routes, and an equivalent over-estimation of costs on the western Channel services. Ian Carruthers observed that motoring holiday operators had promoted the myth that shorter crossings must be cheaper, by including them in package holiday prices and charging a premium for other routes. "Our routes also avoid the tedious and costly drive from Calais to reach the main holiday areas of France," he said. The lessons from this research helped inform a new £1 million advertising campaign in 1993.

The 1993 campaign introduced a distinctive range of advertisements on the theme of 'A few words about...', which was to become one of the Brittany Ferries' most innovative and memorable campaigns. Evocative images were combined with witty text to attack the myths about different aspects of a French holiday in a positive way. 'A few words about French plumbing...' used an image of a colourful luxury bath to address concerns about the standards of French toilets and bathrooms. "Do you remember, years, ago, the music hall jokes about plumbing in France?" it asked. "What was so funny was that most of them were true." Explaining that French hotels were now amongst the finest and most civilised in Europe, the advertisement asked readers to "lay back in your bath and consider: making a booking. The 'A few words about French bedtime manners...'

advertisement depicted a freshly laundered luxury bed and described how the French took beds very seriously, and that these were good places to wake with "sun streaming across your bed as the smell of freshly made coffee and croissants drifts across." Similarly, the 'A few words about the typical French Gourmet...' advert used an image of a typical French child to extol the delightful family values that could be found dining in local communities across the country. 'A few words about French roads' used an image of a deserted road with beautiful beaches on either side to highlight the contrast with congestion on British roads. The strapline 'take the easy way out' accompanied the Brittany Ferries logo, and each advertisement included a photo of a 2CV car to add a stereotypical 'Frenchness'.

The campaign was sufficiently successful to encourage the French regions to consider participating in jointly funded promotional campaigns, with advertisements that would retain the look and feel of a Brittany Ferries advert but promote the individual regions as destinations in their own right. This would double the impact of the campaign to the benefit of both parties. Carruthers and Derek Brightwell toured the French regions to solicit their support, with Brightwell offering to be their consultant to secure the best deals. Each region was made to feel that they were in charge of the campaign, but all the adverts had a common feel so they appeared part of a much larger promotion and fed off each other. The combination worked well, and eventually the regional contributions outweighed Brittany Ferries' own budgets for these campaigns. This approach also raised the profile of Brittany Ferries with the regions, as the Company was still largely unknown outside the English Channel départements.

Some 500 protesting fishermen gathered in Roscoff on the evening of 21st February and threatened to wreck the harbour if they were not allowed to discharge the *Quiberon* in their own way. The vessel had arrived outside the port carrying 20 refrigerated lorries holding 300 tonnes of fish, and was only permitted to dock after extensive negotiations. The British lorry drivers refused to disembark, fearing threatened by violence by the protesters, and the destruction of their loads. The *Quiberon* left Roscoff with her full complement of vehicles still remaining on board, and headed for Cherbourg, where the drivers disembarked and went on their way unhindered. Meanwhile, the protesting fishermen wrecked a fish warehouse in the town, setting fire to freezers and pouring toxic chemicals onto the frozen fish, causing £300,000 of damage. Elsewhere, they caused damage estimated at £2 million to the national fish market at Rungis, near Paris. Their anger was prompted by currency devaluations, and the increasing presence of Russian fishing boats, which were creating a glut in the fish market and lowering wholesale prices. On 3rd March, 70 fishermen waited in Cherbourg to ambush lorries disembarking from the *Duchesse Anne*. They destroyed 27,000 fish on one British vehicle, dumping many in the sea and pouring dye on the rest. This was something of an 'own goal' as it later transpired that the fish had been caught by French fishermen and were being imported for consumption in France.

In a copy-cat action, a group of British fishermen blockaded the entrance to Millbay docks in Plymouth with a flotilla of more than 150 boats on the morning of 26th March, forcing the *Quiberon* to abandon her attempts to berth and head for Poole after a 2½ hour stand-off, leaving hundreds of passengers stranded on the quay. The action was in protest at foreign imports and restrictions on fishing rights and was eventually called off at 18:30.

With the opening of the Channel Tunnel now just a year away, and Brittany Ferries' fleet strategy now largely in place, there was renewed confidence about the future, despite continued difficult trading conditions. There had been heavy investment in port facilities in both Ouistreham and Cherbourg. In late May the authorities in Cherbourg announced their intention to build a new £6 million passenger terminal in the port for completion by 1994. Meanwhile, Michielini observed that "thanks to us, between Manchester and Barcelona, road hauliers will always save money and their drivers will have to respect the break." He expected that the real threat would come from fierce competition between the ferry companies, rather than the Channel Tunnel.

As the start date for the Ferries Golfo de Vizcaya Portsmouth-Bilbao route approached, P&O European Ferries, in whose name the new service would operate, secured the charter of the cruise ferry *Olympia* from Viking Line to open up their new service. The *Olympia* was built in 1986 by Oy Wärtsilä Ab, of Åbo in Finland, and was capable of carrying 2,500 passengers and 580 cars, with cabin accommodation for all passengers. She sailed from the Baltic on 6th April for a short overhaul in Southampton, prior to emerging as the *Pride of Bilbao* in time for her inaugural voyage from Portsmouth to Bilbao on 28th April. The inaugural weekly schedule for the 1993 season comprised of two round trips from Portsmouth, sailing on Sundays and Wednesdays at 09:00, and returning from Bilbao on Mondays and Thursdays at 16:30. Learning from the efficiency that underpinned Brittany Ferries' Santander operation, a single round trip was fitted in between Portsmouth and Cherbourg at weekends to offer additional peak time capacity on the route.

Brittany Ferries reacted strongly to the new competition, arguing that the ticket purchasing system agreed with the Basque authorities did not comply with EU competition rules. Carruthers said "my company is not afraid of competition but wants to be able to operate on fair terms. We can't compete with P&O and the Basque government combined." Pointing out that the subsidy was worth £5 million over three years, he stated he was also worried about the ability of the Spanish sea passenger market to absorb the additional capacity being offered by P&O European Ferries and the impact of support payments over the winter months. "If somebody can compete with you in the clear knowledge that they are receiving a subsidy which can pay for the winter deficit it is unfair to a company which operates a year-round service." He noted that Brittany Ferries had invested heavily on their route to Spain since P&O previously pulled out in 1976, and stated that if the subsidy was not withdrawn it could place a question over Brittany Ferries' ability to operate to Spain through the winter. P&O European Ferries' Dick Martin responded that "the Basque government are customers like everybody else. It has an interest in the service and wants it to be successful. It is quite possible that the Basque government will buy tickets if it thinks that it is the right thing to do." Brittany Ferries wrote to the European Commission, who quickly undertook to examine the alleged subsidy.

The European Commission required the Spanish authorities and all other interested parties to comment before the end of October, to allow them to determine whether the subsidy broke European fair trading rules. Carruthers welcomed the intervention, whilst noting that Brittany Ferries car carryings were some 50% higher than those of their rival since the start of the P&O European Ferries service in April. The continued focus on car-based holiday traffic yielded results very much in line with expectations for Brittany Ferries, whereas P&O European Ferries were concentrating on the cheaper promotion-driven mini-cruise market in pursuit of duty-free and on board sales revenues.

In April 1994 the European Commission ruled that Ferries Golfo de Vizcaya was being supported by the Basque authorities on terms that were not widely available in the market, thereby eliminating an element of risk for the company. The first agreement was repealed, and the European Commission required all moneys received by Ferries Golfo de Vizcaya to be returned, together with interest from the date of granting the aid. Carruthers welcomed the ruling and observed that the two companies could now compete on a level playing field.

Meanwhile, the investment in quality continued to reap dividends. Brittany Ferries was awarded five star ratings by the AA for excellent standards of service and facilities on both the *Normandie* and the *Bretagne,* making it the only company on the English Channel to receive this highest accolade for ferries. The Company won praise for the quality of on board self-service restaurants, winning four out of the six category awards;

the *Barfleur*'s Turquoise Restaurant was voted the outright winner for maintaining high standards and offering a good display of hot and cold food and freshly baked pastries in a bright and welcoming décor. Freight Director Gordon Day noted that the Turquoise Restaurant was adjacent to Truckline's Drivers Club, which shared the same galley, standards and range of good food, offering freight drivers the opportunity to share the same catering experience. The plaudits continued when Brittany Ferries was voted one of the top ten Tour Operator companies in a survey by Which? magazine.

The *Val de Loire* left La Spezia in late May and sailed to Santander under the command of Capt. Christian Selosse, ready for berthing trials in the port on 2nd June. She sailed

A day for celebration as the *Val de Loire* and *Bretagne* pass for the first time at Plymouth. *(Ferry Publications Library)*

from Santander the following day on a private crossing to Plymouth for VIPs and the travel trade, arriving in Devon on 4th June. Following further receptions in both Plymouth and Roscoff, the *Val de Loire* entered service between Plymouth and Santander on 7th June, making her first visit to Cork on 12th June. Her arrival allowed the *Bretagne* to transfer to the Portsmouth-St Malo route, as planned, from 14th June. The displaced *Duchesse Anne* then moved to cover the Plymouth-Roscoff service alongside the *Quiberon*, allowing Brittany Ferries to offer up to three daily departures on the route; the *Duchesse Anne* also covered the Roscoff-Cork route and opened up the new seasonal weekly Cork-St Malo service on 21st June.

The Irish services were now doubled in frequency, with the *Val de Loire* leaving Roscoff at midnight each Friday night, returning from Cork at 15:30 on Saturdays. The *Duchesse Anne* offered a second sailing from Cork to Roscoff, leaving Roscoff at 09:30 on Sundays and returning from Cork at 16:00 on Tuesdays. Carruthers observed that passenger demand had far outstripped supply on the Cork-Roscoff service, and these new arrangements would remedy that situation. For the *Duchesse Anne* this was a return to her birthplace, having been built in Cork in 1978.

The introduction of the *Val de Loire* was accompanied by a strong holiday programme to strengthen Brittany Ferries' position in the inclusive holiday market. A range of such holidays were offered in Santander, with durations from two- to seven-nights including the crossing to and from Spain. The 'Santander Strollers' provided accommodation in three-star hotels and started from £103 per person. For those taking their cars and

The *Val de Loire* offering a winter service on the Portsmouth-Caen route. *(Miles Cowsill)*

wanting to travel further afield to experience more of the 'real' Spain and beyond, Brittany Ferries had a selection of inclusive holidays linked to the Santander route. These comprised of a range of touring holidays providing accommodation in a wide choice of hotels, some of which were members of the famous Parador group. Included were many of Spain and Portugal's most opulent properties such as the 18th century Reconquista in Oviedo, the stunning Hotel Los Reyes Catolicos in Santiago de Compostela and the luxurious San Marcos in Léon. A full range of Spanish villas, apartments and country casas on the Atlantic and Mediterranean coasts were also offered with prices starting from £95 per person. Short breaks in Spain were also catered for through two inclusive Holidays; Spanish motoring breaks and freedom of breaks offered accommodation in appealing distant destinations within a reasonable driver suntanned air from £116 per person. For those seeking a very short break the Company offered mini cruises to Spain

Captain Christian Selosse on board the *Val de Loire.* *(Miles Cowsill)*

at £79 per person, which included the return cruise to Spain plus £45 of dining vouchers to be spent on board.

The transfer of the *Bretagne* to the Portsmouth-St Malo route proved highly successful, resulting in the quadrupling of traffic on the service following her introduction. A record 365,000 passengers were carried by the end of September, contributing strongly towards overall growth of 6% in car carryings across the Company during the financial year. Traffic was also sufficiently strong to sustain a year-round service on the Plymouth-Roscoff route, which was confirmed in September with the addition of three weekend round trips after the planned 15th November close down. This enhanced level of carryings encouraged the move, coupled with a strengthening pound and the relaxation of duty-free shopping allowances. The Cork-Roscoff and Cork-St Malo routes recorded a strong year, with carryings reportedly 55% ahead of the previous year, and the 100,000th passenger journey of the season recorded in early September. The success of FPOC, which now had now recruited 11,000 members in the first four years, was reinforced by the addition of a special brochure in which 400 members advertised their properties to the public.

The *Purbeck* was withdrawn in the autumn and laid up prior to a potential sale to Channel Island Ferries, whilst the *Coutances* remained on the Poole-Cherbourg route to operate alongside the *Barfleur.* The redundant *Armorique* was sold to the Chinese Government in early December for further operations in the Far East, sailing between Xiamen and Hong Kong as the *Min Nan*. She left St Malo for the last time on 18th December, bound for China.

Sealink Stena Line also proposed a fleet shuffling, with the *Stena Normandy* set to be replaced by the *Stena Saga* from March 1994, allowing her to return to the Harwich-Hoek of Holland route. Her replacement had inferior accommodation to the *Stena Normandy*, but would reduce operating costs on the route through lower leasing charges. The *Pride of Bilbao* was purchased by Irish Continental Line on 1st November for £IR56 million and re-registered in

The *Val de Loire* arrives in Cork for the first time with a press trip. *(Ferry Publications Library)*

Above: **Invitation to *Val de Loire* crossing from Santander.** *(Paul Burns)*

Top right: **Menu cover for gala dinner on the *Val de Loire*.** *(Paul Burns)*

Right: **Itinerary for crossing of *Val de Loire* from Santander** *(Paul Burns)*

Below: **Menu for gala dinner on the *Val de Loire*.** *(Paul Burns)*

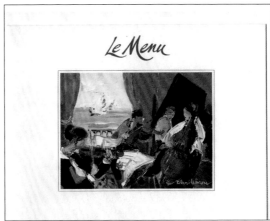

THE INAUGURAL CRUISE OF M.V. VAL DE LOIRE
SANTANDER-PLYMOUTH JUNE 2-4 1993.

PROGRAMME

WEDNESDAY JUNE 2

18.00
WELCOME ABOARD. PLEASE FEEL FREE TO WANDER AROUND THE SHIP AT YOUR LEISURE AND DISCOVER THE MANY FACILITIES FEATURED ON VAL DE LOIRE. LIGHT REFRESHMENTS WILL BE AVAILABLE IN LE LAYON PIANO BAR ON DECK 8. MUSIC BY "SOPHISTICATED LADIES".

19.30
RECEPTION
JOIN US IN LE RABELAIS BAR ON DECK 9 FOR PRE DINNER COCKTAILS.
MUSIC BY "ORIENT".
DRESS: LOUNGE SUITS

21.00
DINNER
DINNER WILL BE SERVED IN LE TEMPS DE VIVRE AND LE GRAND LARGE RESTAURANTS ON DECK 8.
YOUR TABLE NUMBER IS ON THE REVERSE SIDE OF YOUR SECURITY PASS AND TABLE PLANS WILL BE ON DISPLAY IN LE RABELAIS BAR AND OUTSIDE BOTH RESTAURANTS.

23.30
CABARET
MOVE BACK TO LE RABELAIS BAR FOR THE SPECTACULAR CABARET SHOW
DANCING WILL BE TO THE EXCITING SOUNDS OF "ORIENT".
FOR THOSE WHO WANT TO MOVE AT A SLOWER PACE, ENJOY THE RELAXING ATMOSPHERE OF
LE LAYON PIANO BAR OR SEE A LATEST RELEASE OR CLASSIC MOVIE SCREENED IN THE CINEMAS ON DECK 1.

THURSDAY JUNE 3

07.30-10.30
BREAKFAST
BREAKFAST WILL BE SERVED IN LE TEMPS DE VIVRE RESTAURANT ON DECK 8.

09.30
DEPARTURE
VAL DE LOIRE SAILS FROM SANTANDER AT THE START OF HER INAUGURAL CRUISE.
GO OUT ON DECK FOR THE LOVELY VIEW AS THE SHIP TURNS OUT OF THE HARBOUR ENTRANCE
AND HEADS INTO THE BAY OF BISCAY.

DURING THE CRUISE THERE WILL BE A WHOLE HOST OF ACTIVITIES TO ENJOY INCLUDING:

CLAY PIGEON SHOOTING, GOLF DRIVING PRACTICE, FUN FITNESS SESSIONS, WINE TASTING,
FLAMENCO DANCING DEMONSTRATION AND LESSONS, BRIDGE/ENGINE ROOM VISITS, 2 CINEMAS.
THE LADIES CAN ENJOY THE BEAUTY AND MAKE UP SALONS WHILE THE SWIMMING POOL AND SAUNAS
WILL BE OPEN FROM 08.00 UNTIL 20.00.
THEN OF COURSE THERE IS DUTY FREE SHOPPING!
LISTEN FOR ANNOUNCEMENTS PROVIDING DETAILS OF THESE VARIOUS ACTIVITIES.

12.00 – 15.00
LUNCH
LUNCH WILL BE AVAILABLE IN LE TEMPS DE VIVRE RESTAURANT ON DECK 8

16.00
TEA-TIME WITH MUSIC
ENJOY TRADITIONAL TEA-TIME IN LE RABELAIS BAR. MUSIC BY ORIENT.

18.30
COCKTAIL RECEPTION
JOIN US FOR DRINKS IN LE RABELAIS BAR ON DECK 9.

19.30
DINNER
DINNER WILL BE SERVED IN LE TEMPS DE VIVRE RESTAURANT.

21.30
ENTERTAINMENT
A SECOND CABARET SHOW WILL BE STAGED IN LE RABELAIS BAR. THEN LIVE MUSIC
WITH ORIENT. TWO MOVIES WILL BE SCREENED IN THE CINEMAS.

FRIDAY JUNE 4

07.00
BREAKFAST
SERVED IN LE TEMPS DE VIVRE, DECK 8.

08.30
ARRIVAL
VAL DE LOIRE ARRIVES IN PLYMOUTH. DISEMBARK.

Bermuda following the sale. The purchase of the vessel did not change her charter arrangements with P&O European Ferries, as the original contract with the bank of the Swedish-owned Rederi A.B Slite allowed for the charter to run until 2003. Irish Continental Line were able to achieve a 16% yield on the purchase price of the *Pride of Bilbao* at the daily dollar charter rate, and their shares rose by 16% following the purchase. For the 1994 season, the *Pride of Bilbao* was retimed to depart at 22:00 on Saturdays and Tuesdays from Portsmouth, returning from Bilbao at 12:00 on Mondays and Thursdays. This enabled the Cherbourg rotation to be optimised with a Friday night sailing from Portsmouth, returning on Saturday afternoon.

The success of the French Property Owners Club and the introduction of the *Val de Loire* to the Santander route encouraged the team to open a new Spain & Portugal Property Owners Club in the summer of 1993.

The *Barfleur* was withdrawn from service on the Poole-Cherbourg route at the end of November with major technical problems. Booked traffic was diverted to Portsmouth as there was no passenger vessel available to replace her on the Poole route. She returned to service at the start of 1994. The general overhaul of the Brittany Ferries fleet began in

The *Val de Loire* retained many of the fittings from her days in Scandinavian service.

Top left: 'Le Temps de Vivre' restaurant.

Bottom left: The reception area, complete with ship model.

Above: 'Le Grand Large' Tea Shop.

(All Miles Cowsill)

November 1993 with the *Quiberon*, which was replaced on the Plymouth-Roscoff link by the *Duc de Normandie*.

The first test run through the full length of the Channel Tunnel was conducted on 10th December as the operation geared up to a start of business in 1994.

The Christmas period was notable for delays to the *Bretagne*. Facing a Force Ten gale in the Bay of Biscay, she was forced to put into Lorient for shelter and arrived back in Plymouth on Boxing Day, after an unscheduled Christmas Day at sea. Her arrival back in port was covered by the BBC as a news item and featured on the national news broadcast. One well-dressed passenger, interviewed as he left the port, said the vessel's operation had been exemplary and the crew could not have done more to look after their passengers. What the television crew did not realise was that they had interviewed the ship's pianist, heading ashore on leave; more positive publicity...

Brittany Ferries reported a loss of FF12.3 million in 1993 on a turnover of FF1.389.6

million, despite passenger carryings increasing by 5.8% to 2.79 million, vehicle traffic by 4.8% to 74,551 and commercial vehicles by 4.8% to 177,023 during the year. Potential income was badly hit by deteriorating exchange rates, with the pound languishing around FF8.5 for much of the year, and there was to be a further gradual slide of the currency for the next two years. Not only did this situation cause severe problems for Brittany Ferries in balancing sterling income against French franc costs, but it also made France a less attractive destination for British travellers. Michielini was optimistic that the company would have a better year in 1994, as the British economy moved out of recession, but noted that Brittany Ferries was still at a disadvantage relative to their English Channel competitors in having to pay higher social charges through the employment of French crews.

P&O European Ferries carried 144,267 passengers and 28,801 vehicles on the Portsmouth-Bilbao route during the eight-month period of operation in 1993. This encouraged the opening of discussions with the ports of Bordeaux and La Rochelle about further new routes for the 1995 season. The company made a modest profit of £1.5 million on a turnover of £75.5 million. P&O European Ferries was not to return to profitability on its Portsmouth-based operation again until 2006, which would be under very different circumstances.

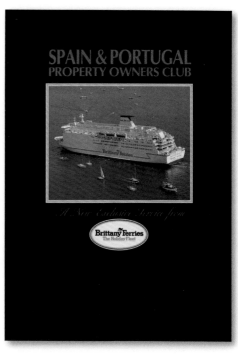

Spain & Portugal Property Owners Club brochure.
(Rook Dunning)

Brittany Ferries celebrated its 21st birthday in 1994 having achieved a market share of more than 50% on the western Channel and a business carrying almost three million passengers. The Company could reflect on having the youngest fleet on the English Channel, the largest ship (the *Normandie*), and having completed an investment plan of £350 million to upgrade the fleet, including acquiring the *Barfleur*, *Normandie* and *Val de Loire*. More routes were operated on the English Channel than any other operator, with a further two between Ireland and France. The ships sailed the equivalent of 35 circumnavigations of the globe each year. Each summer, the Company served three million meals and operated 'hotels' with nightly capacity for 6,200 guests; five and a half times the combined bed space of the Dorchester, the Savoy, and Claridges. Serestel was having a major impact on the quality of on board services, and pursers were now predominantly professionals recruited from the hotel sector to bring the 'floating hotel' concept to life. Over 1,000 passenger-facing staff, from pursers to musicians, were employed across the fleet; it was the only ferry company to employ a doctor an all its ships. Duty free sales were equivalent to a large supermarket, with 100 million cigarettes and 260,000 bottles of perfume sold each year. And it was the leading tour operator of motoring holidays to France and Spain, in a business with a £20 million turnover. The Company was lauded for being a catalyst in developing tourism to Brittany and Normandy, but had also played a major role in increasing the popularity of globe artichokes. To top it all, the Company hosted the French prime minster, Edouard Balladur, on board the *Bretagne* for the start of the Route du Rhum yacht race.

The *Quiberon* returned to service on 20th December, which allowed the *Duc de Normandie* to overhaul before undergoing a period of lay-up prior to returning to the Portsmouth-Caen service from 7th February 1994. This released the *Val de Loire* to

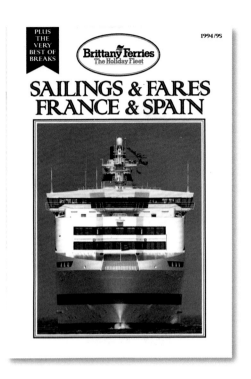

1994 Sailing & Fares brochure and Holidays & Breaks brochure. *(Rook Dunning)*

undergo her refit until 20th February with the *Normandie* following between 21st February and 6th March. The *Bretagne* was overhauled in early January before returning to service on 23rd January with both the Portsmouth-St Malo and Plymouth-Santander services closed in her absence. The end of Brittany Ferries involvement in the operation of Channel Island services was announced on 7th January and implemented on the 23rd of that month. The Brittany Ferries shareholding interest remained in Channel Island Ferries as a ship-owning company, managed from the UK operation; the *Purbeck* was retained on charter by Commodore, whilst the *Havelet* remained on charter to Condor, both with the owner's deck and engine crew. The *Purbeck* had proved to be a beneficial purchase by Channel Island Ferries, being financed by the bank, paid off, and refinanced twice during her ownership.

Protests by French fishermen, angry at a decline in wholesale prices which in their view was caused by the increasing volumes of fish imported into France, particularly from the former Soviet Union and Great Britain, continued to plague the cross-Channel ferry business. A lorry loaded with Scottish-caught fish bound for Spain was attacked by a crowd of around 100 fishermen as it left Roscoff on 1st February, and some 40,000lbs of fish was destroyed. This action drew a formal protest from Gillian Shepherd, the British Minister of Agriculture, to her French counterpart, Jean Ouech. Breton fishermen moved on to ransack the Paris fish market, before continuing to Boulogne and Calais to check the source of fish being landed, and venting their frustration on a local supermarket, when eight busloads of fishermen emptied all the freezers.

Research at the end of February suggested that Brittany Ferries held a 38% share of the total cross-channel car bookings being made for the 1994 season. The Company was also performing relatively strongly in the western Channel, winning a 62% share of a

The distinctive 'Flat out...' campaign. *(Rook Dunning)*

passenger market that was growing around 30% ahead of the previous year. The figures showed that Brittany Ferries' total passenger reservations through travel agents rose by 27%, with the St Malo and Santander routes proving particularly popular with the 'Range Rover set'. Brittany Ferries' reservations were substantially up despite the competitive market, and 64% of all Spanish ferry bookings completed through travel agents were on the Santander route. The research also suggested that Brittany Ferries was now the leading operator of inclusive motoring holidays in France, with a 16% share of the total market.

The first full year of operation for the *Bretagne* on the Portsmouth-St Malo route was proving immensely popular with customers, with a four-fold increase in advance reservations for the 1994 season. As the *Val de Loire* prepared to return to Plymouth to re-start the Santander service on 16th March, bookings for her season were reported to be 40% ahead of the same period in 1993. Longden drew attention to the fact that the 24-hour passage of the *Val de Loire* was significantly shorter than the 33-hour trip offered by the competition.

On 30th March the *Normandie* had a near-miss with a Cypriot-registered freighter whilst on passage from Caen to Portsmouth with 300 passengers on board. The Master took evasive action as the vessel cut across his bow and no injuries were sustained by passengers or crew members.

Elsewhere, the outlook for the 1994 Irish season was strong, with early bookings to Cork up by 40% on the new St Malo route and by 22% on the Roscoff service. Brittany Ferries was already carrying around a quarter of all French tourists to Ireland and numbers were predicted to grow following the failure of the French national football team to reach the 1994 world cup tournament in the USA. The 1994 Irish season got off to a

Driving flat-out direct to Holiday France.
(Or Spain)

Lights glitter in the distance. Closing fast. Is it a cruise-liner, is it a ferry? Nothing so ordinary. It's Brittany Ferries, one of a new generation of cruise-ferries that thinks it's a luxury hotel. It glides by. It's vast. You glimpse chic bars, elegant restaurants and lounges. And behind countless hushed cabin doors, discerning travellers are sped direct to the most convenient port for their holiday, bypassing busy ports miles out of their way. <u>And all for the price of an ordinary ferry.</u>

It's simply Brittany Ferries. The most modern fleet on the Channel. Where out of the ordinary service happens daily. And nightly. We have perfect sailings, great value fares and a range of marvellous holidays. For a brochure see your travel agent or ring (0752) 269926 or (0705) 751708.

difficult start on 2nd April. The *Val de Loire* was already some four hours late arriving in Cork, after encountering very heavy seas during a 19-hour crossing, but passengers were subjected to a further two-hour delay when the outer bow door suffered hydraulic failure. The ship was forced to leave the berth and return stern-first. Some 800 passengers had an extended wait on the quay prior to being able to board the vessel for her return trip to Roscoff, with few facilities open ashore and the port restaurant closed. But the ship was well received. The Irish Independent reported that: -

"The *Val de Loire* cost £70 million to build and the money shows. It resembles much more a luxury liner than a car and passenger ferry and even has suites comparable to those found on Caribbean cruisers. The décor of the public areas and bars, restaurants and lounges, rivals that of ships such as the *QE2*.

Impressive, too, is the cuisine on board. It is very French in accent and represents

Sealink Stena Line's *Stena Normandy* provided a short period of competition from Southampton to Cherbourg. *(Miles Cowsill)*

amazing value. Dinner, for around £15 a head, is positively Lucullan, beginning with a buffet table laden with the best sea food, charcuterie and salads, followed by entrees such as steaks, canard or veal, a challenging cheese board followed by typically French patisseries and desserts. There is a small buy excellent wine list with prices pitched only £1 above duty-free. The trip to France is a couple of hours short of a day and it offers first-timers an affordable taste of what going on a luxury cruise can be like."

The most challenging event of 1994 was the formal opening of the Channel Tunnel on 6th May. The first revenue-earning train ran through the Tunnel on 19th May, almost a year later than the planned opening date of 15th June 1993. A limited HGV-only service was then offered, with the first through freight train service following on 1st June. But the full 24-hour HGV service did not begin until 7th November. A short ten-day trial passenger car shuttle service was offered in early July, but regular car-carrying shuttle trains did not start operating until 29th September, missing the key summer traffic. A press run of the 'Eurostar' through passenger train service from London Waterloo to Paris Gare du Nord broke down prior to departure on 20th October, before the initial public service was initiated with just two trains in each direction from 14th November; these services were operated over existing domestic railway tracks between London Waterloo and the Channel Tunnel, significantly limiting the time advantages over air travel.

Although there was plenty of time for the ferry industry to prepare their response to the new competitor during the Channel Tunnel's construction phase, the commercial strategy of the fixed link was opaque until services began. A French report suggested that the main commercial losers would be Brittany Ferries and SNAT (the Société Nationale d' Armement Transmanche), the French arm of the Sealink operation. Some loss of traffic had been factored into the Brittany Ferries business plan, and there was an expectation that there might be some pressure on rates as the short-sea sector adjusted to the increase in competitive capacity being offered. However, the scale of price reductions prompted by the opening of the Channel Tunnel proved to be much greater than expected.

When the commercial rates were first mooted, the Eurotunnel team envisaged charging a return fare for car and occupants set at around the £300 mark, but prices soon collapsed, eventually being offered for as little as £30 for a return crossing. The strategy appeared to effect wide disruption in the ferry industry, wipe out as many routes as possible, and change the dynamics of cross-Channel travel. The Brittany Ferries team felt they were very much in Eurotunnel's sights, despite their remoteness from the operation. There was much frustration at the impact on the market and the reduction in consumer choice; the tunnel project was conceived to provide an opportunity to create jobs for the construction sector, rather than to meet any perceived shortfall in existing or planned capacity. It was a project to fund builders, not a project needed to meet demand. There was sufficient ferry capacity and route choice to take all the available road traffic, and the forthcoming introduction of Eurostar services from London to Paris and Brussels was primarily designed to abstract traffic from competing airlines on short-haul routes.

There were, however, restrictions on the freight traffic that could be carried through the Channel Tunnel, particularly in relation to hazardous cargo on both shuttle and through train services. Likewise, passenger ferries were severely restricted in the hazardous cargoes they were permitted to ship. UK Freight Director Gordon Day took the opportunity to sell the virtues of the *Coutances* and the *Normandie Shipper*, both of which could carry the majority of hazardous cargoes with their top deck configuration on the Poole-Cherbourg and Portsmouth-Caen routes respectively. He drew attention to the Company's reservation system which helped ensure compliance with the regulations and offered safe and efficient loading and handling from quay to quay.

Management of the Poole operation was strengthened by the appointment of Ken Waite as port manager, following the closure of BCIF. He brought 'grey hairs' to support what was still a young local team. Waite was later followed at Poole by another young recruit, Steve Warner, who was to spend 30 years with the Company, eventually rising to the position of UK and Ireland managing director before his untimely death in 2015.

Brittany Ferries' ninth route was launched on 14th May when the *Duchesse Anne* opened a new Poole-St Malo link with an eight-hour crossing time, offering four round trip sailings each week fitted into her schedules around her sailings to Cork. She operated outwards by day from Poole and returned overnight, dovetailing into the established service from Portsmouth and complementing the link to Cherbourg from the port. Bookings were reported to be 50% ahead year on year for the same period at the end of March. The *Duchesse Anne* was configured to carry 1,300 passengers and 280 cars, so brought ample capacity to the service. Day emphasised the accessibility of Poole from most of the UK and highlighted the fact that St Malo was the only French port on the

Channel from which freight drivers could legally cover the distance to the Spanish border in a single day.

The Times reviewed the 'value for money' offered by different cross-Channel operators in an article published on 8th April. The survey looked at 16 different routes and found that five of the six cheapest routes on a 'per mile' basis were operated by Brittany Ferries. Prices varied from the £0.53 charged per mile for a foot passenger on the Portsmouth-St Malo route to £1.82 for the same distance on a Stena Sealink crossing from Dover to Calais. For a car and five passengers the difference was even more stark - £2.62 charged per mile on the Portsmouth-St Malo route to £11.64 for the crossing from Dover to Calais. This served to reinforce the Brittany Ferries stance on the value proposition.

Three ships in the fleet were awarded the coveted AA Five Star accolade in the 1994 AA Guide to Ferries. The *Val de Loire* joined the *Normandie* and *Bretagne* in recognition of the highest levels of service and facilities, combined with excellent value. This was the second successive year that the *Normandie* and *Bretagne* had won the award. Longden expressed pride in being the only ferry company awarded the five star rating for services to Brittany, Normandy and Spain, combatively suggesting that these ships could be enjoyed "at prices which are often less than the Dover-Calais scrum."

P&O European Ferries had been searching for replacements for their 'Super Viking' fleet on the Le Havre route for some time, but their requirement for two identical vessels proved difficult. They were becoming increasingly desperate as they fell behind the fleet investment made by Brittany Ferries. The *Olau Britannia* and *Olau Hollandia* were employed on the Sheerness-Vlissingen service, but were too large for the available traffic on that route and Olau Line chose to close down the operation from May 1994, citing the impending opening of the Channel Tunnel and strong resistance amongst the German trade unions to any cost-saving proposals. This was an opportune moment for P&O European Ferries to step in with a charter. Chairman Graeme Dunlop was quoted as saying that "lack of capacity in recent years has meant that we have not been able to take full advantage of the market growth in the western Channel." But this was a last-minute deal as the Channel Tunnel opened, rather than the long planned strategic investments made by Brittany Ferries. There was little time to prepare the market for their introduction to service.

The two sister ships were delivered to Olau Line in 1989 (*Olau Hollandia*) and 1990 (*Olau Britannia*). Of 33,336 gross tonnage, 161 metres in length and 29 metres in beam, they were capable of carrying 1,716 passengers, all of whom could be accommodated in cabin berths, 575 cars or 118 trailers, at a top speed of 21.3 knots. P&O European Ferries secured the vessels under a five-year charter arrangement at a rate of $25,000 per day for each ship. Both vessels were delivered directly to Le Havre, where they underwent a short overhaul and repainting before entering service. The renamed *Pride of Portsmouth* operated a Ministry of Defence 'D Day' charter on 31st May, with her sister *Pride of Le Havre* starting on the Portsmouth-Cherbourg route on 4th June, as work to the linkspans in Le Havre had not been completed in time to accommodate them. The two vessels transferred to the Portsmouth-Le Havre service on 22nd June. Their arrival allowed the *Pride of Winchester* to be withdrawn from service on 8th July.

The debut of the new vessels was soured by a hostile reaction to P&O European Ferries' decision to retain some 58 Chinese staff, who had previously worked on board the ships for Olau Line on catering and non-maritime duties. Alexis Gourvennec wrote to the French transport minister Bernard Bosson in June, calling for the creation of a code of conduct for the control of use of a low wage seafarers by cross-Channel operators. The French minister try to set up a meeting between representatives of Britain, France, Belgium, Holland, and Germany to discuss the matter. However, the French Seamen's union the Confédération Française Démocratique du Travail (CFDT) were not prepared to wait for negotiations and took action at Cherbourg to stop D Day veterans leaving the

Pride of Portsmouth and *Pride of Winchester* on 3rd June. Passengers boarding both vessels were delayed for some nine hours following this industrial action. Further threats of industrial action at Cherbourg and a blockade of Calais forced P&O European Ferries' to dismiss the Chinese staff and replace them with British crew.

The arrival of the Olau twins represented a transformation of the P&O European Ferries capacity and the quality of service offered on board, and posed a significant challenge to Brittany Ferries, particularly to the ageing *Duc de Normandie* on the Portsmouth-Caen service. P&O European Ferries' Portsmouth-Cherbourg route also benefited from the enhanced capacity provided by the transfer of the old 'Super-Vikings' from the Le Havre route. But the configuration of the new vessels was not best suited to their new operation. The two vessels were designed to offer cabin accommodation on the lengthy overnight crossings of the Sheerness-Vlissingen route, with comparatively leisurely turnarounds in port. Employing them on a thrice-daily-crossing between Portsmouth and Le Havre with high volumes of freight traffic requiring rapid port turnarounds was likely to prove an operational challenge. The charter was a compromise reaction to the success of the Portsmouth-Caen route, and came at a high cost, which did little to enhance the economics of P&O European Ferries' western Channel operations.

Pressure on P&O European Ferries was kept up by Brittany Ferries in late June with a legal challenge to an advertising campaign in France to promote the upgraded Le Havre service, claiming that the campaign contravened French advertising standards.

The *Normandie* carried the largest consignment of military vehicles to Normandy since the D Day landings in 1994 as part of the 50th celebrations. Later in the summer she undertook a special chartered sailing from Portsmouth to Cherbourg to transport the cycling entourage of the Tour de France from the two stages of the Race that had been held in Britain - from Dover to Brighton and a series of stage races around Portsmouth. The Tour had used the Channel Tunnel for their outward journey.

The summer of 1994 saw a price war erupt on the short-sea crossings, which rippled further west, and it was evident that neither of the operators on the western Channel was enjoying financial success, despite the early flourish in bookings. Reports in the Sunday Telegraph that the *Normandie Shipper* and *Coutances* were available for sale as part of a rationalisation programme had to be hotly denied by Brittany Ferries.

The situation was not helped when the Company faced a further port blockade, as French and Spanish fishermen engaged in another tuna war. This followed a week of violent confrontations between French and Spanish tuna fishermen, after the French trawler *La Gabrielle* was seized by Spanish fishermen and towed into a Galician port in an attempt to prove that it was using oversized nets. The 1,700 passengers on board the *Val de Loire* found themselves heading for Roscoff instead of Santander after the Spanish port was blocked on 26th July, leaving a further 1,500 passengers stranded in Spain. The scene in the Santander terminal was described as 'hell'. Ramon del Vallé described how Brittany Ferries flew out a team from Plymouth laden with cash to give a full refund of tickets to those stranded in the port. The passengers were paid in the currency of their choice, and were offered a free ticket home across the English Channel on any Brittany Ferries route. Three coaches were secured to take foot passengers on the 685-mile journey to Roscoff. Exasperated by the action, Brittany Ferries lodged a £500,000 compensation claim against the Trawler Owners Association. Toby Oliver said the Company was lodging a protest to the authorities in Madrid and the Spanish ambassador in London. "This action by the fishermen is outrageous. Our passengers are innocent and are being treated in a cavalier and cynical fashion." he was quoted. The next departures of the *Val de Loire* were also forced to use Roscoff, and the fishermen's action was later extended to Bilbao and Gijon. Normal services from Plymouth finally resumed on 1st August when the blockade was lifted.

P&O European Ferries saw a 24% increase in traffic in August over the same period in

1993 following their enhanced capacity, but the operation suffered operational problems exacerbated by the tightly scheduled turnarounds in both Portsmouth and Le Havre. The company claimed to be optimistic about the success of their Spanish service and were said to be close to concluding negotiations with the Chamber of Commerce at Bordeaux to start a new operation to the port; the authorities in Bordeaux were worried by the decline of shipping traffic in the region and were anxious to establish a twice-weekly service to the UK.

At this time, Brittany Ferries also considered a new route to Bayonne to start from 1996, with a possible new ship taking 20 to 21 hours for the trip. Longden revealed that a feasibility study was being undertaken, particularly looking at port facilities. The route would complement existing services and be perfect for the Pyrenees and the south of France. He said it was "something the Company had been looking at for some time, in the light of P&O going on about Bordeaux." However, it would be necessary to price the route at the same fare level as Santander, although it was anticipated there would be price resistance from customers, who would expect rates to be lower for what was perceived as a shorter sea crossing. A service from Pauillac was also reviewed but ruled out, because the slow trip up the river Gironde would result in similar crossing times to Santander.

Brittany Ferries' banks were still concerned that there was no commercial back up plan if the introduction of the *Val de Loire* failed to yield the expected returns on the Santander service. Carruthers and Longden went with the Portuguese Tourist Authority to visit Viana do Castelo, just over the Spanish border in the Norte region of Portugal, to investigate the opportunities for a port within around a 26 hour passage time of Plymouth. The Iberian service could then comprise of one weekly sailing to Viana do Castelo and one to Santander, if the latter did not generate the required level of business. As around 28% of the traffic via Santander was known to be heading for Portugal, this could be another significant income stream, and Brittany Ferries could claim to be the only operator sailing to both Spain and Portugal. The port required the provision of new facilities and a linkspan, but this was not seen to be an insurmountable problem by the authorities. Carruthers and Longden spent time visiting hotels and posadas in the region to understand the nature of the market. They accumulated a series of gifts of local produce and wine from the hotels as they toured around, which steadily built up in the car. Their next stop was to be in A Coruña, but during the drive one of the packages leaked olive oil over Carruthers' tan suit. The packages were frustratingly dumped by the roadside. An hour later Carruthers went to get papers from his briefcase and realised that it had been thrown out of the car with the offending packages. So the car was turned round to head back; fortunately the briefcase was still sitting by the roadside... The visit to A Coruña was also productive with another potential destination and shorter crossing in prospect, but the Santander business carried on the *Val de Loire* held up well against expectations, and these alternatives were not required to be pursued further.

The *Val de Loire* joined the *Normandie* on the Portsmouth-Caen route from the late summer, with the *Bretagne* deployed to cover the winter Portsmouth-Santander and Portsmouth-St Malo routes.

Cross-Channel freight services became the focus of national attention on 23rd June, when Alan Clark MP launched a boycott of operators engaged in the live animal trade. The organisation Respect for Animals proposed that passengers boycott Brittany Ferries, P&O European Ferries and Stena Sealink in protest at their involvement in the trade, instead favouring services operated by Sally Line and Hoverspeed, which were unable to carry animals. Neither of these operators was seen as a direct threat to Brittany Ferries, and the company initially stated that it would continue to carry animals, as this was a legal trade, part of the Company's planned revenues, and an important business for farmers in the hinterland of English and French ports, particularly Plymouth and Roscoff. Sir Nicholas Hunt, director general of the Chamber of Shipping, felt that ferry companies were being unfairly singled out, noting that animals were checked by vets, who ensured that distressed animals were not permitted to travel. Livestock were given sea sickness tablets, put in air-conditioned areas on the vehicle deck, and regularly checked during the crossing to monitor their welfare. The trade was worth £160 million a year to ferry companies operating on the English Channel. Animal trade fell anyway during the summer as the European Commission imposed travel restrictions on livestock to prevent the spread of 'mad cow' disease from Britain.

The trade was particularly important to Brittany. The French had traditionally sourced livestock from the Netherlands, which necessitated a long overland journey. The establishment of Brittany Ferries helped cement strong links between West Country farmers and their counterparts in Brittany. The proximity of the two industries and the shorter transit time from farm to farm, even with a sea crossing, encouraged development of a trade in under-ten-day old milk calves. Lairage facilities were provided within ten miles of Plymouth and calves were inspected by a vet and certified prior to departure. The calves were often noisy during transit, but this was a natural feature of the life of young animals, rather than a sign of distress. On arrival in Brittany the calves were fattened for veal and their value rose dramatically. Carruthers noted that Brittany Ferries had lost more passengers than calves during their engagement in this trade.

Both Brittany Ferries and P&O European Ferries took the decision to stop the movement of live animals from August because of growing public concerns about the degree of animal suffering. Brittany Ferries' ban encompassed all export of live animals from 22nd August, except those for breeding or fattening north of the Loire Valley.

The controversy would not go away. P&O European Ferries and Sealink effected a total ban on movements on 1st October in response to continued public protests at the alleged cruelty of unregulated journeys, which saw some two million sheep and calves carried annually across the Channel. Brittany Ferries took a different path, continuing to carry livestock heading to be fattened on farms in Brittany, Normandy and Loire Valley, as these animals were not subjected to the conditions and long-distance journeys experienced elsewhere. The Company worked closely with the Royal Society for the Prevention of Cruelty to Animals (RSPCA) to ensure that this solution was acceptable. The RSPCA Director General visited Plymouth to inspect the arrangements and approved the plan whereby animals would spend no more than two hours in port prior to shipment, with port health authorities controlling the arrangements. Carruthers asked the main shippers to ensure their vehicles were in excellent condition to avoid any opportunity for criticism. The new arrangements were put in place.

Barely a fortnight into the new regime a newspaper reporter followed hauliers across the English Channel and revealed that many were flagrantly abusing the geographical restrictions; animals reportedly heading for northern France were being transported on much longer journeys further south, with some even reaching as far as Greece. Carruthers was incensed at the flagrant breach of the protocol and rang the chief executives of the two main livestock hauliers to advise them of an immediate ban on 4th November; this was well received by animal welfare groups, even though calves would now face a 24-hour overland journey from the Netherlands to maintain the trade in Brittany. Carruthers was determined to seek redress from those hauliers who had abused the system, and set in motion legal action to recover lost income. This took three years to conclude, but Brittany Ferries achieved a successful outcome. Meanwhile, the animal welfare groups moved on to make Shoreham port the focus for their protests, and there were violent clashes between protesters and police later in the year. In February 1995 campaigners protested at the carriage of empty livestock lorries from France to the UK and leafleted Millbay Docks, urging passengers to write to Carruthers and Neil MacFarlane, port superintendent, to get the trade stopped.

Portsmouth City Council announced their intention to use £7 million from the sale of property to fund expansion works and provide additional freight vehicle parking to meet expanding business needs at their port. This strategy was prompted by both Brittany Ferries and P&O European Ferries demanding that the City Council expand facilities. Port Manager Tony George claimed that this would probably be the last major investment the City would need to make in the ferry port in the twentieth century. He noted that pressure on space would increase if Sea Containers' plans to introduce a fast ferry service from Portsmouth with a 'super SeaCat' catamaran came to fruition during 1996. Work started on expanding the space available for trailer parking by eleven acres in August 1995.

In August 1994 Irish Ferries announced their intention to add to their existing Le Havre and Cherbourg services by offering a new route from Rosslare and Cork to Brest from 1995, a move which was supported by the Brest Chamber of Commerce and Industry. The route would offer a significantly shorter crossing time compared to the company's existing services, and compete directly with Brittany Ferries Cork-Roscoff route. Irish Ferries looked to outflank the port of Roscoff by sailing closer to the southern coast of Brittany, thereby tapping into demand for holidays on the French Atlantic coast and exploiting freight potential for hauliers in southern Brittany and as far south as Spain. The plan envisaged utilising the *St Killian II* and *St Patrick II* on the Brest service, but there was speculation that the *Pride of Bilbao*, owned by parent Irish Continental Line, could be used if P&O European Ferries did not to extend her charter. The crossing time of the May to mid-September service was anticipated to be 15 hours on twice-weekly sailings from Rosslare, and 15½ hours on a weekly sailing from Cork.

The new route required a linkspan to be constructed in Brest to accommodate the service, but progress stalled as the French authorities delayed authorisation of the investment, forcing Irish Ferries to appeal to the EU Competition Commissioner to unblock the delay. Irish Ferries suspected that Brittany Ferries might be lobbying to prevent the development, but this was categorically denied by Carruthers, who expressed his surprise that Irish Ferries had not considered sharing the facilities in Roscoff. From his perspective, Brittany Ferries had more important things to do than fight this once a week service and could make money by being a handling agent for the operation in Roscoff, as well as then having a full understanding of their competitor's traffic levels. Yet Gourvennec was keen to marshal local resources to prevent the construction of a linkspan in Brest, using similar tactics to those which had prevented the *Mary Poppins* reaching St Malo in 1975. Michielini strongly disagreed with the strategy, pointing out that it was illegal. This was the beginning of the end for the relationship between the two men.

With the clock ticking for the 1995 season, Irish Ferries' interest finally turned to Roscoff, where no investment would be needed. On 16th December 1994 the company reached agreement in principle with the Morlaix Chamber of Commerce – the port authority – to allow access to Roscoff from 27th May 1995. Irish Ferries went ahead with publicising their plans for the new route. However, in January 1995 the Morlaix Chamber of Commerce indicated its desire to suspend the negotiations, arguing that the company had published its schedules without prior agreement on slot times with the port. Irish Ferries again complained to the European Commission, citing that the port authority was trying to preserve the monopoly of Brittany Ferries' Cork services. The Commission concluded in May that the Morlaix Chamber of Commerce had abused its dominant position as the operator of Roscoff port by refusing access, and required the Chamber to grant access to the port by 10th June 1995. The *St Patrick II* arrived in Rosslare on her maiden sailing from Roscoff on 16th June, further legal arguments having delayed the start of the service from the planned and advertised date of 27th May.

The Irish Ferries service was to operate for just two seasons. A downturn in tourist numbers to France in 1995 and 1996 placed pressure on the service, and when a key flow of trade car traffic was lost Irish Ferries appealed to the Irish government for a subvention, using the argument that similar support had been given to Brittany Ferries by the French government in the past. But the Irish government believed that granting a subvention would open up requests to support operators on other routes that might be facing financial difficulties, and the application was refused. The service closed after the *St Patrick II* arrived in Rosslare on 8th September 1996 with her final sailing of the summer season.

The *Bretagne* offered an extended Portsmouth-Santander winter service from 20th November, with a departure from Portsmouth at 12:00 on Sundays, returning from Santander at 12:00 on Tuesdays, fitted in around two trips to St Malo leaving on Wednesdays and Fridays. The service operated until 12th March.

The *Armorique* laid up for sale in St Malo. *(Miles Cowsill)*

The *Duc De Normandie* completed her annual overhaul and was allocated to the Plymouth-Roscoff service to allow the *Quiberon* to be refitted, before laying over in January prior to covering for the *Val de Loire* refit in February. The *Duchesse Anne* was refitted at Le Havre in October, then laid up through the winter in St Malo until the end of March. The *Bretagne* was refitted in mid-January when the Portsmouth-St Malo and Portsmouth-Santander services were suspended until 3rd February 1994. The *Barfleur* was overhauled during the closure of the Poole-Cherbourg route to passengers in January.

On 12th December Michielini took the opportunity of a visit to Bayonne to announce the potential opening of a new route to there from Plymouth, as part of a three-legged service to Gijon in Asturias. He noted that the existing Spanish route was still getting good results, despite the opening of the competing service to Bilbao. The new route was conditional on the local communities sharing the risk of the project – potentially through investment in a SEM – particularly in sourcing a vessel for the service. Michielini warned that if P&O European Ferries concluded an agreement with the port of Bordeaux for a twice-weekly service to Pauillac that involved any kind of operating subsidy, Brittany Ferries would immediately request investigation by the European Commission. In the event neither route was to be enacted. The many hurdles of securing agreement for a two-destination route proved insurmountable.

At Christmas both the *Bretagne* and the *Val de Loire* visited Rouen on the now traditional Christmas Cruise. The latter had been due to visit Amsterdam, but bad weather prevented her heading to the Netherlands.

The year ended on a mixed note. Brittany Ferries had recorded a 5.8% increase in carryings across all routes, but the further fall in the value of sterling against the French Franc pushed the Company deeper into a trading loss. Passenger carryings broke through the three million level for the first and only time in the Company's history, reaching 3,022,198. Vehicle carryings also hit an all-time record at 738,194 cars, and freight volumes hit another record 192,451 units, a figure that was not to be surpassed until 2004. P&O European Ferries also carried record numbers of passengers and vehicles through Portsmouth in 1994; with some 1.66 million passengers and 456,790 vehicles. The *Pride of Bilbao* carried 199,843 passengers and 40,119 vehicles during her first full year of operation. P&O European Ferries carried a record 620 freight items across the Channel from Portsmouth on one day in November – 10% up on their previous best. The two freighters *Gabrielle Wehr* and *Thomas Wehr* were now being used to supplement the enhanced capacity offered by the former Olau ships. But P&O European Ferries also slipped to a loss of £1.6 million, despite turnover increasing by over 10% to £83.2 million. The increased costs consequent to the charter of the Olau vessels were beginning to become a burden.

Stena Sealink Line's Southampton-Cherbourg route achieved a 21% increase in passenger traffic and a 7% increase and freight units in the first eight months of 1994, with some 437,000 passengers compared to 359,990 in 1993. The *Stena Normandy* remained on the Southampton-Cherbourg route for the full 1994 season, despite expectations to the contrary. Stena Line looked to expand their operation with a new route to Brittany and a France-Ireland service possibly from Brest.

In January 1995, 'The Times' forecast that 1995 and 1996 would be the bloodiest years ever seen for ferry operators on the English Channel, predicting that either P&O European Ferries or Stena Line would be forced to reduce frequencies in the face of full operation of Eurotunnel's 'Le Shuttle' services. The latter was expected to push prices upwards for the season, whilst doubling the shuttle frequency from hourly to every 30 minutes to provide a capacity challenge. The overall cross-Channel market grew by 13% in 1994, but a high proportion of this was low value day trip traffic feeding the continued opportunities for on board revenues. Hoverspeed were reported to receive 40% of their annual revenue from this sector, P&O European Ferries 20% and Brittany Ferries 7%. This was an unsustainable business model and all operators were keen to avoid a repeat of the heavy price cutting of summer 1994.

The 1995 Ferry Guide featured a strong image of the *Normandie* on the cover, amongst a line-up of six brochures for the season, each using bold photography to good effect. The geographical advantages of the seven routes now offered from England to France and Spain were given due prominence, and the approach was backed up by a 'Let's make a B-line' campaign in national media. The fleet was becoming more prominent in advertising, with the on board ambience and experience of 'Café Society' providing a stark contrast to the Channel Tunnel offer.

One market that Brittany Ferries was well placed to attract was the Land Rover Discovery owner, as the height limit on Le Shuttle's double deck trains precluded them being carried, and Range Rover drivers were forced to use their air suspension on 'squat' mode to travel safely. Stories were encouraged in the national press to draw attention to

1994/1995 Ferry Guide and the 1995 'B-Line' advertising campaign. *(Rook Dunning)*

the numbers deserting the short-sea routes to head west and enjoy the overnight crossings to Caen and St Malo.

The gîte programme began to stratify into three price categories to reflect different levels of holiday product, with linen and towels provided in the more up market properties for the first time. Heating was an extra for, as product manager Julie Burrows stated, "price is all important so it would be wrong to penalise people who had to pay for heating in advance in case the weather turned out to be hot". Growth in the French gîte market had stuttered after 17 years of growth, as France faced more competition from emerging destinations, including Portugal, where prices were 20% lower.

The *Bretagne* was joined by the *Duc de Normandie* for the winter Portsmouth-St Malo service, with the latter providing a St Malo-Plymouth positioning trip to enable the Company to offer weekend sailings from Plymouth to Roscoff, thereby providing a year-round service again. The *Val de Loire* re-opened the Plymouth-Santander service on 17th March and the *Pride of Bilbao* re-started the Portsmouth-Bilbao service after overhaul on 26th March.

A 24-hour seamen's strike brought services to a halt on 23rd February as they protested at the use of Polish labour on a new freight service from Folkestone to Boulogne by Meridian, a British company. Brittany Ferries' services were suspended for the period of the dispute. Violent clashes broke out between strikers and riot police in Boulogne, but there was no similar action in Brittany. Services resumed the following day.

Brittany Ferries adjusted their Portsmouth-Caen schedules from 1st March to leave at 07:45, 14:30 (was 15:00) and 22:45 (was 23:30) from Portsmouth and 08:00, 16:15 (was 16:30) and 23:00 (was 23:59) from Caen. The bringing forward of the overnight sailing from Caen by 59 minutes but with the same arrival time, allowed passengers to enjoy an extra hour in bed. "That is the one that customers will notice" said Longden.

Ferries Golfo de Vizcaya became a wholly owned subsidiary of P&O European Ferries in 1994. The company still pursued financial support from the Basque region and in a new

agreement of 7th March 1995, the District Council of Vizcaya and Ferries Golfo de Vizcaya agreed that the former would purchase a further 46,500 vouchers between January 1995 and December 1998 for Pta985.5 million. The subsequent take up of these vouchers was poor; just 2,132 utilised the vouchers in 1996, 1,000 in 1997 and 400 in 1998. The scheme was quickly challenged by Brittany Ferries, who remained keen to compete on a level playing field, and their complaint was again upheld by the European Commission. They eventually ruled that the authorities had unlawfully implemented aid to Ferries Golfo de Vizcaya in breach of Community Treaties, and required that the sums of money be repaid by the company.

There was increasing nervousness in the ferry industry at the end of March, with bookings for self-drive motoring holidays down by 7% year on year. The heavy focus on cut-price 'booze cruise' tickets in the short-sea sector began to take its toll on the brochure price traffic. Longden was quoted as saying that "France won't break any records this year. It is getting increasingly difficult to persuade people to book a ferry crossing for £300 against a background of £1, £5, or £10 offers." Dominique Gigante of Gîtes de France protested about the pricing actions on the short-sea routes by saying that "They are bringing down the image of France as an elitist destination to the point where it becomes a one-stop place for shopping. They are hoping for a surge of summer business, but it isn't going to happen." Many operators offered discounts of up to 25% off the price of summer crossings booked in advance, which ran for several months throughout the winter.

P&O European Ferries boasted that bookings for the 1995 season were running 33% ahead of 1994 at the end of May, but the company still lagged behind in market share. By mid-June, things were becoming desperate and ferry companies slashed prices for summer crossings to France in an attempt to head off competition from the Channel Tunnel. P&O European Ferries announced a 20% reduction on its brochure prices for passengers booking crossings before the end of June; Brittany Ferries countered with a

CAFE SOCIETY
DIRECT TO HOLIDAY FRANCE AND SPAIN.

With Brittany Ferries, your holiday starts the moment you step aboard our award-winning, luxury cruise-ferries.

From our easily reached ports in the UK, we'll speed you direct to Holiday France and Spain.

You'll discover we're so much closer to all the most delightful holiday areas of France – Brittany, Normandy, the Loire Valley, Dordogne, Aquitaine and further south, Provence and the Mediterranean.

Our exciting brochures are packed with ideas and facts about our wide range of sailings and fares, holidays and breaks all offering excellent value, including some very special offers on fares for Caravan Club Members.

To make your reservation ring:
(01342) 316101

£100 return fare available for a car and up to five passengers on selected sailings every day until the end of September for people booking and paying by 30th June. Brittany Ferries claimed that £238 could be saved on return crossings from Portsmouth to Caen and £196 between Poole and Cherbourg, whilst with two passengers in a car on the Portsmouth Saint Malo return there was a saving of £190. Oliver said that "we did not want to get involved in an undignified price war but if our market share was being eroded we had to fight back."

The *Val de Loire* suffered a twelve-hour delay after being involved in a minor accident when leaving Ringaskiddy at 16:00 on 22nd April with 1,456 passengers on board. She was caught by a gust of wind whilst reversing off the berth and was blown on to a cattle ship berthed nearby. The two vessels touched gently but the *Val de Loire* was forced to wait in port until 04:00 the following morning whilst the authorities undertook the necessary safety investigations.

In a very early statement of intent for the 1996 season, Longden announced on 7th September that fares to Caen and Cherbourg for the 1996 season would mirror the ferry and tunnel fares from Dover to Calais. He stated that 'by tracking the Dover Straits fare we will play a part in creating a common cross-Channel fare. It will mean even better value for the passenger and more importantly will make the choice of route the most relevant factor in the passengers' decision. We are confident that the unique routes we operate to France will prove to be a huge attraction once the issue of price is common to all routes.' This initiative began from November 1995 and was applied to the whole of the 1996 season.

P&O European Ferries increased their business on both western Channel French routes over the summer 1995 period, but this improvement came at the expense of dramatically lowered average rates driven by the short-sea price war. Coupled with the company's substantial increase in costs following the charter of the two former 'Olau' ships for the Portsmouth-Le Havre route, this placed pressure on the profitability of the company. Off-peak high season fares for a car and passengers were offered for as little as £50 single. The fight between all companies in the cross-channel trade intensified as the year went on. At the end of the year Brittany Ferries reported a fall in French route traffic of 5% in passenger carryings and 15% drop in tourist vehicles by November, notably on the Portsmouth-Caen route which had faced the increased competition from the improved Portsmouth-Le Havre offer; the latter saw a 14.7% increase in passengers and 9.3% increase in tourist vehicles.

Whilst Brittany Ferries saw their share of traffic fall on the Portsmouth-Caen and Poole-Cherbourg routes, the strategy of holding rates and relying on the geographical advantages of the company's route structure outlined in strong advertising material minimised the damage. The Portsmouth-St Malo services saw record carryings during the summer, prompting the expansion of the 1995 winter service to five round trips each week with the *Duc de Normandie* and *Bretagne*. The *Duc de Normandie* replaced the *Quiberon* on the Plymouth-Roscoff service at weekends and operated a balancing St Malo-Plymouth sailing on Fridays and Mondays. The *Val de Loire* remained with the *Normandie* on the Portsmouth-Caen service through the winter, with the *Bretagne* covering Spain. Both the *Quiberon* and *Duchesse Anne* were to be laid up for the winter.

1995 had proved to be another difficult year for Brittany Ferries. Sterling fell to a rate of FF7.7 in against the French franc in the second quarter of the year, only recovering to FF7.9 by the year end. The combination of this new low level of exchange between the pound and French Franc and the impact of the opening of the Channel Tunnel, despite its initial operating difficulties, hit financial performance hard. Net losses in the year ending September 1995 reached FF80.3 million, as group turnover fell by over 11% to FF1,285 million. Passenger numbers were down by 4% to 2,779,418. Over 50,000 fewer cars were carried as the volume fell to 681,734, whilst freight traffic slipped to 185,807 units. The 'Franc fort' policy of the French government, allied to the price reduction on cross-

Channel fares being driven by the opening of Eurotunnel was causing significant damage to the Company. Gourvennec lobbied hard behind the scenes, protesting to the French government that they were behind so many of Brittany Ferries' problems; they had determined the exchange rate policy, the approach towards the eventual introduction of the Euro currency, and supported investment in the Channel Tunnel, totally undermining Brittany Ferries' efforts to compete strongly and develop a sound commercial business. Michielini placed pressure on Carruthers to sell the stake in West Country Television to help the Company finances, but he resisted as he did not feel that the time was right. Selling a partial share would yield significantly less than selling the whole company.

The overall French market suffered a 10% fall during the main summer holiday season, hit by the poor exchange rate of the pound, although nine million Britons visited the country during the year. But there was an increasing market focus on day trips, short breaks, EuroDisney and Paris. The FGTO increased their promotion budget for the British market by 40% for the 1996 season, seeking to fund stronger campaigns on television, on poster sites and through joint advertising with tour operators selling French products, including Brittany Ferries. One early trend for the new season was a rise in family holidays being taken outside the main school holiday periods to save around one-third on the peak season price. This was good news for ferry operators, and Longden was quoted as saying that "I don't think two weeks out of school affect's a child's education."

Brittany Ferries was not the only operator facing financial issues.

P&O European Ferries business grew to 1,686,000 passengers and 463,021 vehicles on their French routes, and 212,815 passengers and 41,715 vehicles on the Bilbao service. But this volume was achieved with a significant hit on the average rates achieved. With a full year of costs for their enhanced fleet, the company slumped to an £11.1 million loss after tax, £9.5 million worse than the more modest losses of 1994. Brightwell bought shares in P&O to allow him to attend annual company meetings and ask awkward questions about their operations in the western Channel on behalf of Brittany Ferries. It was evident that Chairman Lord Sterling had a deep affection for the Portsmouth services and was keen to see them survive despite being in an increasingly uncompetitive battle with Brittany Ferries. The P&O European Ferries services from Portsmouth were being commercially driven by the different interests of the Dover operation, with the local advertising and pricing strategy still required to be in harmony with that employed on the short-sea routes. Whilst the new ships brought the company closer in quality to P&O Cruises than the group's other ferry operations, no attempt was made to exploit the synergy with the Southampton-based business. P&O Cruises operated independently within the P&O Group and had little interested in its ferry sibling. And, unlike Brittany Ferries, there was no attempt on P&O European Ferries' services to provide a single company focus for the each aspect of the operation, with catering and retail activities supplied by Sutcliffe Catering (another P&O subsidiary), spas staffed by Steiner, and officers employed by an Isle of Man-based company. Different arrangements applied on other routes in the P&O European Ferries portfolio, so the brand had little on board synergy. Brittany Ferries treated contractors as employees so, for example, Oliver regularly attended management meetings so participated in, and was familiar with, all the Company's strategies.

With all ferry operators across the English Channel facing financial difficulties in the post-Tunnel world, it was clear that 1996 would be a year of significant change if the industry was to survive in the new era.

Twelve

Restructuring to survive

A view of the *Bretagne* and *Normandie* at Portsmouth, illustrating the well utilised freight storage capacity of the port. The proximity of the naval dockyard to the ferry terminal is apparent. *(Ian Carruthers collection)*

A s the difficult summer of 1995 unfolded, it became increasingly evident that the price war triggered by the full opening of the Channel Tunnel to passenger services had left Brittany Ferries in a highly exposed position. The Company was experiencing both a fall in traffic volumes and continued downward pressure on fares in both the passenger and freight markets. The sustained devaluation of sterling, which alone resulted in a FF120 million downturn in annual revenue during 1995, and the difference in social taxes paid on employees between Brittany Ferries and British ferry operators added another FF40 million charge to the Company's competitiveness. It was the almost perfect storm.

By the autumn, Alexis Gourvennec had spent several months seeking government assistance to support Brittany Ferries through their financial problems, with a sympathetic French Minister of Transport, Bernard Pons, in turn debating potential rescue plans with his ministerial colleagues. Gourvennec indicated that corporate losses were expected to worsen significantly by the end of 1995. As Brittany Ferries represented some 20% of the French merchant marine fleet, it was of national importance that support be given to facilitate a recovery. Gourvennec was clear that he did not want a subsidy. "I just want to be on equal terms with the English flags," he explained. The French press reported the seriousness of these discussions and suggested that the very

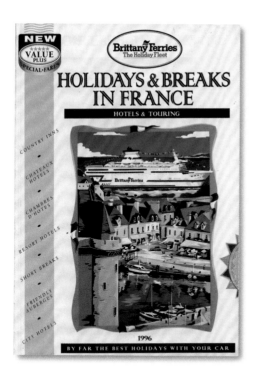

future of Brittany Ferries was at stake.

The scale of the difficulties created by these external events was evident in Brittany Ferries' financial performance. After the losses of 1995, budget projections for the 1996 season indicated a potential doubling of the annual deficit to FF169 million. The consequences were serious for the regions of Brittany and Lower Normandy as the interests of Brittany Ferries were now so inter-twined with the SEMs that a financial downturn put their income from fleet rent repayments in jeopardy. Gourvennec, Christian Michielini, Maurice Chollet and the SEMs combined to lobby the French State for support.

Meanwhile, the Brittany Ferries service pattern was unchanged for the 1996 season, with fares restructured to meet the continuing price challenge from the Channel Tunnel. The strategy of matching brochure fares on the Portsmouth-Caen and Poole-Cherbourg services with those offered on the short-sea cross-Channel routes was an approach eventually mirrored by P&O European Ferries to Le Havre and Cherbourg. This reduced most peak season fares but raised off-peak prices, with some rising by more than 50%. The rate for two people and a car on Poole-Cherbourg in June, for example, rose from £172 to £257. The fare structure was simplified; there were still single and standard return fares, but the single fare also applied to Five-Day returns (a lengthening of the duration of the former Three-Day returns); the Six-Day and Ten-Day return fares were abolished. There was a reduction in the number of tariff bands from five to four, removing the 'A' tariff description. Car rates now covered a car and driver, a car, driver and passenger, or a car, driver and up to eight passengers. New 'Value Plus' fares were introduced for an Eight-Day return trip if six nights' hotel accommodation was pre-booked through Brittany Ferries Holidays.

But it was not long before price cutting again characterised the holiday market. Drive France offered £50 off holidays as early as January, and Brittany Ferries were forced to respond with a free day crossing cabin offer for early bookings. 'Super APEX' fares were offered from Ireland, but early ferry bookings across the French route portfolio were

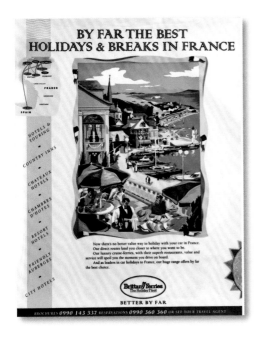

Left: 1996 Holidays & Breaks in France brochure and Ferry Guide *(Rook Dunning)*

Above and Below: Images from the 1996 advertising campaign. *(Rook Dunning)*

weak, as the price cutting of previous years discouraged passengers from making an early commitment. However, there were strong early bookings for the Plymouth-Santander service, bucking the trend elsewhere, on a route which seemed immune to the remote competition of the Channel Tunnel.

The 1996 brochures featured an artistic cover, with the images painstakingly cut from paper to create a striking colourful impact. The focus remained on holiday destinations, rather than the fleet, with just two of the 84 pages describing how 'Better holidays begin and end with Brittany Ferries'. Around this time, Bill Rook retired from Rook Dunning and Roger Cazemage, a senior Art Director from leading agency Saatchi & Saatchi, joined the company. Cazemage immediately became a very committed member of the team and was responsible for much of the quality work that followed.

The theme for the 1996 advertising campaign was 'By far the best... ', with the bold graphics from the brochures replicated in the national campaign, with the slogan 'Better be Far' added below the Company logo.

The year opened with speculation that Stena Line would introduce a £63 million High Speed Sea Service (HSS) vessel on a new Portsmouth-Cherbourg route in 1997. The new, large revolutionary craft were capable of carrying up to 1,520 passengers and 375 cars (or 120 cars and 50 freight units) at a speed of 40 knots. Significantly more substantial that the previous Hoverspeed SeaCats employed on the route, they offered an enticing combination of capacity and speed, but their fuel consumption made them very expensive to operate. The first HSS craft were introduced on Stena Line's Irish Sea services in spring 1996, with the Cherbourg service potentially to follow in the summer. The new Portsmouth port manager Martin Putman lobbied Stena Line hard, supported by the City Council, to bring one of their craft to the port. This approach brought strong protests from both Brittany Ferries and P&O European Ferries, who questioned why the City Council would seek to bring competition to the port's existing and long standing operators at a time when all services from Portsmouth were facing up to the difficult financial challenge of the Channel Tunnel.

Gourvennec's discussions with government paid off, when in mid-March Brittany Ferries was awarded a grant by the French government to cover crew social costs; this enabled the Company to match the level of charges paid by their competitors sailing under the British flag. The grant was worth some £40 million. Brittany Ferries paid social costs set at 43% of staff salaries to the French government at a cost to the company of over £10 million per year; the equivalent British charge was a 12% payment to government. The Times immediately suggested that 'targeting aid at ailing industries in order to preserve jobs is a flagrant breach of the Treaty of Rome ... a job saved in France is all too often a job lost in Britain. You do not have to be a Eurosceptic to find that unacceptable.' Channel Tunnel operator Le Shuttle challenged the grant, believing that the payment was a subsidy and thereby in breach of EU competition rules.

The French government had made their contribution, but in turn required Brittany Ferries and its funders to share the pain by restructuring the operation to help resolve the financial difficulties. The eventual agreement came in two forms. All the SEM shareholders, with the exception of Brittany Ferries, increased the capital holding in their respective SEM, which was passed back to the Company as a temporary three-year waiver of vessel rent accompanied by a 'better fortunes' mechanism to recover this sum as trading conditions improved. Brittany Ferries' proportion of the shares in each SEM was reduced accordingly, to reflect this new financial structure. The regional support through the SEMs totalled some FF246 million and was financed by an increase in SEM capital of a near-equivalent amount, effectively an injection of public capital of FF246 million into the Brittany Ferries Group in 1996.

This reduction in the short-term costs of the fleet enabled Brittany Ferries to undertake the internal financial restructuring measures necessary to bring into effect substantial organisational changes, whilst implementing a fleet renewal strategy to acquire a new vessel, then codenamed *Normandie 2*, to replace the ageing *Quiberon*. The three-year plan envisaged a return to profitability following these measures, although sustaining this performance in the longer-term was deemed uncertain as fluctuations in exchange rates, competitor strategies and the impact of the future loss of duty-free revenues were each likely to further impact the business. In addition to the changes in the SEM financial structure, the French government offered two tranches of financial support valued at FF70 million and FF80 million.

The financial solution required Brittany Ferries to implement a downsizing plan to reduce the Company's cost base. This plan required Brittany Ferries to withdraw from the recently opened Poole-St Malo and St Malo-Cork routes at the end of the 1996 season, and put the *Normandie Shipper* and *Coutances* up for sale. All other non-core assets were to be disposed of. Thus, over the period from 1995 to 1998, the fleet passenger capacity was reduced by 12% (1,375 passengers), cabin capacity fell by 9% (539 berths) and freight capacity dropped by 17% (1,480 lane-metres). Even by mid-2002, when it was anticipated that the *Quiberon* would be replaced by output of the *Normandie 2* project, it was envisaged that the fleet's overall capacity would be well below the Company's pre-restructuring capability.

Refinancing of vessels was another of the options exercised under the plan. The *Quiberon* was sold to the Trovil Shipping Company and immediately leased back, with rental payments spread over the period from 1995 to 2001. The financing period for the *Val de Loire* was extended by a further three years, after deferment of capital repayments on the loan from Crédit Agricole for the period 1995 to 1998; this resulted in additional interest costs from the bank, which were passed through Sabemen, the owning SEM, to Brittany Ferries. These two actions relieved financial pressure on the SEMs.

An initial redundancy programme for 24 office staff and 58 crew was implemented, which saved an additional annual total of FF19 million. Further cost-cutting measures included a wage freeze, abandonment of part of the 13th month payment arrangements, a 15% reduction in the advertising budget, and a re-organisation of land-based and other sub-contracted services.

These were difficult times for the UK team, many of whom had been employed by Brittany Ferries for much of their careers, which had seen them witness many challenging times. The cutbacks were a real test of their loyalty and commitment to the cause. There were still limited funds in the budget for annual wage rises, but management salaries were frozen, with the money allocated to increase other staff salaries. Carruthers went to some lengths to explain openly why this was the fairest way forward for all, and this salary strategy was accepted and helped cement the bond between Brittany Ferries and its UK employees. Later in the scheme, the management team received their share of the increases and other employees received less. But being open and honest about the policy paid dividends. Salaries in Brittany Ferries were never the highest but were seen to be fair and transparent. Graham Harrison created a set of management accounts that were shared across the entire management team so that everyone could have the same perspective on the Company's performance. All expense claims were listed in these accounts, so that the team could see how much their colleagues were claiming from the Company; Carruthers and Longden had a policy of approving all expenses to help cultivate trust amongst the team, which was self-policing through the open culture.

The most positive step of the plan was to commence a project to address one of the biggest capacity issues faced by the Company. The Portsmouth-Caen route suffered from an imbalance between the *Normandie* and the *Duc de Normandie*, which created daily fluctuations in capacity in each direction because of the three-crossing schedule; 65% of the total capacity was offered from Portsmouth to Caen one day and 35% the next, this being mirrored in the northbound direction. The restructuring plan envisaged replacing the *Duc de Normandie* with a new vessel of similar capacity to the *Normandie*, thereby permitting the *Duc de Normandie* to be transferred westwards to enhance capacity on the Plymouth-Roscoff route. This action would displace the *Duchess Anne* from the fleet.

The cumulative effect of all these measures was to produce overall financial savings of FF60 million in 1996 and a further FF50 million in 1997, reducing the Company's overall deficit by 60% in 1997 and eliminating it altogether in 1998. The team began the process of implementing the plan.

It came as no surprise that the French government elements of the restructuring plan were challenged by P&O European Ferries, who cited that this was State Aid to Brittany Ferries and therefore illegal, prompting the European Commission to initiate their investigatory procedures into the transaction. P&O's Lord Sterling argued that the value

The *Duchess Anne* arriving at St Malo from Cork. *(Miles Cowsill)*

of French government support to Brittany Ferries was estimated at around £15 million, with port dues paid in Calais by the P&O European Ferries' ships being effectively recycled along the coast to subsidise Brittany Ferries. The State Aid allegation was supported by the UK government, who pointed out that this support enabled Brittany Ferries to expand services in 1996, whilst Stena Line withdrew from the market and P&O European Ferries rationalised their operations. P&O European Ferries, the Chamber of Shipping and Ian Bruce, MP for Weymouth and Portland, supported the British national position.

In support of the restructuring plan, Associated British Ports pointed out that £8 million had been invested in improved facilities at Plymouth, of which £2.8 million had been funded by European Regional Development Fund grants. Over 300 jobs in the City were dependant on the ferry service, so the potential termination of services in the absence of a restructuring plan would be 'catastrophic' for both Plymouth and the surrounding region. Poole Harbour Commissioners observed that 450 local jobs were linked to Brittany Ferries' services, which accounted for half the turnover of the commercial port, which was likely to close if the ferry services ceased. The Commissioners had invested £15 million to help the development of Brittany Ferries' services from the port. The port authorities in Santander stated that Brittany Ferries represented some 20% of the trade through the port, which directly supported some 16% to 17% of the region's jobs.

The French regions expressed their strong concerns that the disappearance of Brittany

The *Duc de Normandie* heads out of Portsmouth for Caen on her 08.45 schedule. *(Miles Cowsill)*

Ferries would leave ferry services to Normandy in the hands of P&O European Ferries as a monopoly operator. They argued that Brittany Ferries had only become a viable commercial enterprise as a consequence of the successful implementation of the restructuring plan. The Company employed 1,741 workers in the Brittany and Lower Normandy regions, and Brittany Ferries' crew represented 20% of the French merchant navy, thereby helping sustain the pension fund. The French government noted that the 'business handicaps' that had created the financial crisis were all external events; Brittany Ferries had engaged in a genuine restructuring of its operation, from which it was emerging stronger and more competitive, with the target of operating without the further need for aid. It was clearly in the SEMs' interest to finance rent reductions through capital increases, as the alternative was to be forced to sell the fleet if the Company closed, which would realise a sub-optimal financial outcome for the regions. The French authorities pointed out that they wished to retain a credible competitive alternative in the central and western Channel, where Brittany Ferries' only serious competitor was P&O European Ferries.

The Commission eventually concluded that the initial payments of FF70 million and FF240 million to aid the restructuring programme were admissible and entirely in accordance with Community guidelines on State Aid for rescuing and restructuring firms in difficulty. It found that the FF80 million payment from the French government was not deemed necessary, as Brittany Ferries' recovery had been relatively rapid and this payment allowed the Company to take advantage of the extra funds and bring forward investments that were not considered to be part of the restructuring plan.

As part of the settlement, the UK team was given access to a £3 million budget for an advertising and marketing campaign to be delivered in conjunction with Maison de France. Such a windfall was difficult to spend effectively at short notice and the UK team concluded that it would be wasteful to spend more than half the sum. The French disagreed. Carruthers went over to France to argue his case and the money was not spent indiscriminately.

Consideration was also given to changing the name of the Company. Ferries at this time had a slightly down-market image, rather akin to bus travel, driven by the low-quality services that most passengers endured on the short-sea routes, whereas rebranding the Company as the more aspirational 'Seaways' or 'Lines' portrayed a more appropriate upmarket image, closer to luxury coach travel. A ferry could mean anything from the Sandbanks chain ferry through to the *Bretagne,* so the UK team tested the market to see how best Brittany Ferries could distinguish itself from competitors and reflect the quality standards now being offered on board in the brand. Market research was commissioned to seek customer feedback on the idea, with 'Brittany Seaways' being the preferred option of the British team. But the research decisively concluded that the reputation of the Company was already far too strong for any change to be considered – 'do so at your peril' was the primary and salutary feedback. The exercise was a valuable lesson in understanding the existing strength of the brand and the value of doing nothing.

The twentieth anniversary of the opening of ferry services from Portsmouth was celebrated in May. The port noted that fares were now cheaper than they had been when the *Armorique* and the *Viking Victory* began sailing in 1976. The operation was now worth £50 million annually to the city economy and since the opening date some 58,000 ship movements, 35 million passengers and eight million cars had passed through the port. The goodwill of the celebrations was marred by an ongoing disagreement between the incumbent ferry operators and the port over plans to raise charges. Although both Brittany Ferries and P&O European Ferries were clearly struggling in the marketplace, the port had made a profit of £4.7 million as recently as 1994 and was unwilling to make financial concessions.

On 20th June 1996 Brittany Ferries announced the implementation of the social plan to effect the cost savings necessary to underpin the restructuring plan. The Company's Works Council was informed of the intention to eliminate 5.5% of the seafarer and permanent shore staff positions representing 90 roles (66 seafarers and 24 shore staff) in total. Brittany Ferries also announced plans to release the *Duchesse Anne* at the end of the 1996 season. Michielini reported that "by all means of transport combined, the number of Britons travelling to France for holidays is falling by 25% to 28% compared to last summer," The French press again speculated about the Company's survival prospects.

The French government was still considering a plan to reduce port duties, which represented an annual charge of FF135 million for Brittany Ferries, through the creation of a solidarity fund. Money would transfer from the busier ports such as Calais, to ports with less traffic, such as Roscoff, to allow them to reduce their dues. The formula had two advantages: by benefiting all customers from the same port, it could not be construed as a subsidy or State Aid for Brittany Ferries; and it could be politically presented as a land-use planning measure by evening out the port tariffs across all French ports along the English Channel from Roscoff to Dunkirk. Brittany Ferries was the exclusive operator of ferry services from the ports of Roscoff, St Malo and Caen to the UK, but there was some benefit accruing to both Brittany Ferries and P&O European Ferries at Cherbourg; the scheme was carefully crafted by the French authorities to optimise the return for the local Company.

The *Normandie* was prevented from berthing at Ouistreham on the afternoon of 21st June when rioting French beef farmers blockaded the port. A group of farmers who were protesting about the collapse in beef prices triggered by the outbreak of British origin 'mad cow' disease drove tractors onto the linkspan and threatened to set light to any vehicles that attempted to disembark. The *Normandie* was forced to wait outside the port with 500 passengers on board for 13 hours, and was prevented from picking up a party of sick and disabled children who were waiting to return to Britain. Passengers were given free meals and accommodation on board. The *Normandie* finally docked at Ouistreham at 07:30 on 22nd June. Toby Oliver expressed the anger of many at the scene when he said "I can't emphasise enough how outraged we are that yet again our service has been disrupted and that the French authorities made no arrangements to allow us to go about our business." The farmers' 'mad cow' protests continued across France.

The *Duchesse Anne* relaunched the Poole-St Malo service on 1st July, with a four-sailing per week pattern, operating from St Malo overnight from Thursday to Sunday and returning from Poole on Friday to Monday mornings. Fares were offered from £111 for a car and driver for a Five-Day return.

There were many cultural differences between the way business is conducted in the UK and France. Regional power was stronger in France and central institutions found it harder to impose their will. This posed problems for the British team seeking to present a consistent French product to the UK market. Gîtes de France was especially troublesome. This was best presented to the market as a nationwide product, a one-stop shop available through Brittany Ferries regardless of where customers wanted to travel. But participation by each French region required their individual consent, as the central Gîtes de France organisation was unable to direct their involvement. The UK team spent many days going to general meetings and assemblies to present the case as to why they should work with Brittany Ferries, but there was always a proportion of the audience who were suspicious and did not want anything to do with it. Public understanding of, and exposure to, the Brittany Ferries brand was much stronger in the UK than in France, and outside the Brittany and Normandy regions it was often difficult to get the Company's voice heard. Carruthers often remarked to Michielini that nobody had heard of Brittany Ferries south of Rennes, yet the Company was a household name across the UK.

The downturn in holiday business and heavy levels of competition took its toll on the Gîtes de France operation. Their extensive stock of gîtes frequently suffered from a poor-quality image resulting from a continued lack of investment by many property owners, whilst sales volumes in the UK market were also hit by poor exchange rates for sterling against the franc, which made France less attractive to British holidaymakers. Gîtes de France holiday sales in the UK fell dramatically, from 100,000 customers in 1993 to around 20,000 in 1996. The organisation responded by cutting staff numbers from 40 to 15 in the same period, which reduced the level of service that customers could enjoy. Overall sales in the market were down 23%, with the self-catering sector falling by 40%. The Gîtes de France business needed to act differently to survive.

The French government reduced the period of national service conscription for 18-year-old males to ten months in 1992; around three-quarters of all young men went through this process at the time. Others gained business experience through an 'SME' scheme, whereby employment within specified enterprises counted as an alternative to national service. Brittany Ferries was an active supporter of this scheme, and some of the brightest and best recruits found themselves seconded to help the UK team. Xavier Schouller had joined the Portsmouth team in 1996, after completing a period working at the French Embassy on the SME exchange scheme. Like all other new recruits, he spent a year working on the quay as a Duty Manager to acquaint him with a full understanding of the operational aspects of the business, involving regular interaction with customers to appreciate their needs. Internal promotion within Brittany Ferries could only follow once this induction period had been completed. Schouller was promoted to run the Brittany Ferries holiday business, and was to play a substantial role in its expansion in the coming years.

Schouller took the first call that hinted at trouble ahead for Gîtes de France whilst working in the Portsmouth office. Schouller told Carruthers "I've had a funny phone call from France that it's all going belly up and we have to be in Gare du Nord tonight at eight o'clock." So the pair dropped everything and caught the train from London to Paris, travelling in great secrecy. On arrival, it was made clear that the general trend towards direct booking and the drift away from gîtes towards mobile home holidays was driving the Gîtes de France UK operation towards insolvency. Carruthers and Schouller were given a proposal and asked if Brittany Ferries could help with a rescue plan to enable the organisation to remain operational in the UK. There were difficult discussions with the organisation that held the commercial bond for Gîtes de France, as they felt that Brittany Ferries should bail the operation out. But Carruthers felt that Brittany Ferries was taking a big enough risk in offering guarantees that existing booked holidays would continue to be honoured; even this level of commitment required considerable trust from Michielini and Maurice Chollet that their British colleagues were doing the right thing. After much discussion, Brittany Ferries formed a 51:49 joint venture with Gîtes de France, which was made public at the end of August.

The new partnership, which took effect from 1 November 1996, aimed to develop and promote gîte holidays among the British and Irish markets. Brittany Ferries became the Gîtes de France brand's official distributor in the UK, marketing a new expanded portfolio of 1,200 properties, or about 7,000 additional beds on top of the original inventory already being sold by the Company. Michielini observed that these new arrangements would be "very profitable for both partners; this operation will also prove positive for Brittany Ferries' ferry business." For Gîtes de France, the agreement was expected to lead to an increase in the average annual occupancy rate for their portfolio of properties. "The target is twelve weeks of occupancy per lodging per year, from British clientele," Michielini continued. The focus would be particularly on western France, especially in Brittany, with a new range of high-end gîtes being offered, with rates of around FF1,800 per week.

The two companies started to work together to rebuild the Gîtes de France brand. The changeover was managed in such a way that existing Gîtes de France clients did not lose money, even though the parent company was effectively insolvent in the UK. All financial obligations were settled in full and Gîtes de France commercial problems were kept out of the public eye. Brittany Ferries now had a market-dominant portfolio of 2,000 gîtes, and promised to rejuvenate the market whilst cutting costs through the merger of the respective sales teams, the combining together of the individual databases, and the use of common property and ferry booking systems. The Gîtes de France operations in the UK moved to the offices in Plymouth, and the Brittany Ferries' reservations systems were used to host the holiday bookings from across Europe.

This solution was pragmatic rather than perfect; Carruthers and Longden would have preferred to remain in an arms-length relationship with Gîtes de France. As a ferry operator, the principal reason for remaining involved with the business was to be able to secure the ferry crossing elements of the traffic, and understand who the Gîtes de France customers were, and when and where they were travelling. Brittany Ferries had less interest in where these holiday clients were staying. But, Gîtes de France could be given an enticing ferry offer to present to their customers, with a strong recommendation to bind their travel arrangements to Brittany Ferries.

In the longer-term, the business interests of Brittany Ferries and Gîtes de France's portfolio of property owners differed, and the relationship gradually drifted apart, as the increasingly competitive online sales trends continued to pose problems. Brittany Ferries had to fill sailings across all days of the week and on departures at all times of day throughout the operating season. The gîte owner was far happier to take one £4,000 booking on a Saturday for a seven-night stay, rather than £1,000 a week for four weeks or £500 a week for eight weeks, but regular occupancy was of considerably greater interest to the ferry operator, especially if clients can be encouraged to travel during the middle of the week.

The majority of holiday homes for the French market were built in the UK and shipped out by sea. This was big volume traffic for cross-Channel ferry operators, with the added advantage that it could be carried on off-peak sailings as 'filler' traffic when space was available, albeit for which the charges had to be highly competitive. The trade was also a prime opportunity for fraud; every mobile home seemed to arrive in St Malo with reports of scratches that were not recorded when the unit was handed

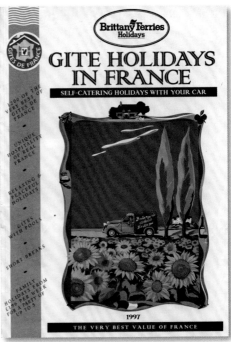

Gîte brochure incorporating Gîtes de France properties. (*Rook Dunning*)

over in Portsmouth. Financial claims mounted, as did the frustration with this high volume, low-rate, high-claim business. Eventually Carruthers and David Longden agreed that the only way to solve the problem was to accept no further liability for damages. Rock-bottom rates were still offered but in future no claims would be accepted. Each mobile home was accepted for shipment on the basis that it was shipped in perfect condition and checked by the hauliers' driver on arrival at the port, with no liability for any 'damage' when it arrived at destination. This became the standard basis for future shipments. There was little choice for hauliers other than to acquiesce to the new arrangements.

The mobile home transport business was also rife with tricks. Drivers would arrive with a mobile home on a trailer and report to the freight office to say it had been dropped off in the port ready for shipment. Harassed freight staff would then sign the docket to accept delivery, without having the time to cross-check where it had been parked in the marshalling area. The driver would return to his vehicle and drive away with the mobile home still loaded on the back. The owner would then submit a compensation claim, arguing that the docket had been signed by Brittany Ferries' staff to confirm that the mobile home had been delivered to the port, but nothing had been delivered to the destination. Eventually a host of mobile homes that disappeared under this scam were tracked down to a gypsy camp in the north of England and subsequently recovered. Technically they were now owned by Brittany Ferries as compensation had been paid, so they were shipped out to France and used as holiday homes for the various comité d'enterprise organisations in France.

The upheaval of 1996 was not unique to Brittany Ferries. P&O European Ferries considered a range of cutbacks to their services and initiated discussions with the Brittany Ferries team to explore joint options for more efficient operations. Protracted talks began in October to consider a possible merger between the two companies or some joint agreement on the structure of services and fares. These discussions were led by Carruthers, backed by the authority of Gourvennec and Michielini, and the two companies negotiated joint working arrangements, and produced budgets for a combined operation. Carruthers spent time in Brussels with Graeme Dunlop of P&O European Ferries, working in confidence to persuade the European Commission of the merits of the two companies working together to avoid further financial losses and retain jobs in the ferry industry. The European Commission had no objection to the proposal. Longden pledged that no routes would be cut, with the exception of Brittany Ferries' existing plans to rationalise the Poole-St Malo service, and said the two companies would be able to work together on Spanish routes, with the possibility of the opening a new service to Biarritz. He indicated that "fares would have to rise if the Company's future is going to be secured, but they won't be going up dramatically." The Times noted that fares had been reduced significantly in 1996, with a 21-Day return fare from Poole to Cherbourg or Portsmouth to Caen falling from £225 in the brochure to £138. Following approval from Brussels, attention turned to the British authorities' perspective on the merger, which was expected by the end of October 1996, in order to allow the 1997 brochures to be produced in advance of the main booking season.

The British government considered the situation for some three months and asked a host of complex questions, despite the evident urgency of the situation. They then declined to offer an opinion to the immense frustration of all parties. However, it was becoming increasingly evident as more information was shared between the parties, that there was a significant discrepancy between the commercial rates being achieved by the two companies. Brittany Ferries was achieving average passenger ticket rates 30% higher than an equivalent crossing with P&O European Ferries, and achieved average freight rates were some 20% higher. The mix of traffic on Brittany Ferries was far superior in yielding these outcomes, and P&O European Ferries' heavy dependence on the corporate strategy of using 'promotional' traffic to generate passenger volume and deliver on board sales revenues was severely exposed.

The figures were stark. P&O European Ferries had been making profits on their western Channel services during the period the 'Super Viking' vessels formed the mainstay of the Portsmouth operation. In their new guise, these were two large-capacity freight ships that had the ability to carry passengers. Financial losses on the local operation had begun to accumulate and grow as the company sought to revitalise their business and compete with the quality offered by Brittany Ferries through taking on the heavy charter costs of the *Pride of Le Havre* and *Pride of Portsmouth* from Olau Line, and the *Pride of Bilbao* from Irish Continental Line. The former pair were designed for lengthy overnight crossings and were totally inappropriate for utilisation on two six-hour daytime crossings and one overnight crossing each day. Brittany Ferries' divergent strategy had shown the way with the *Normandie*, which was a double deck freight vessel capable of carrying passengers in a considerable degree of comfort; a modern equivalent of the 'Super-Vikings'.

Michielini was brought into the debate and John Richards worked in Portsmouth on a variety of scenarios to evaluate the potential from the operation of a combined fleet. It was clear that Brittany Ferries could only 'draw or lose' from the arrangements; there was no margin for error with the state of the passenger and freight markets, and the right decision was to walk away from the proposal. But both sides now had a better understanding of how to manage their respective businesses, particularly P&O European Ferries, who now appreciated how far their rate structure lagged behind that achieved by Brittany Ferries.

The *Duchesse Anne* made her final sailing with Brittany Ferries on 30th September 1996 and was then withdrawn for sale. She was purchased by Jadrolinija P.O. of Rijeka, Croatia the following month, and later renamed the *Dubrovnik*.

The *Stena Normandy* made her last crossing for Stena Line on the Southampton-Cherbourg route on 30th November and was de-stored at Southampton prior to being withdrawn and sent to Falmouth for lay-up. Continued speculation that Stena Line would replace this service with an HSS vessel operating from Portsmouth to Cherbourg proved unfounded. The ambitions of the Portsmouth port authorities were thwarted, and the Channel Tunnel claimed another scalp.

The western Channel was not the only market where P&O European Ferries was looking to work more closely with a competitor. The price war bloodbath on the short-sea routes of the eastern Channel was forcing ferry operators to battle hard against each other, as well as the Channel Tunnel. The two largest operators, P&O European Ferries

The *Val de Loire* leaving Plymouth for Roscoff in June 1993. *(Miles Cowsill)*

and Stena Line, proposed a merger of their operations to allow them to compete more efficiently with their subterranean rival. Their rationalisation proposal also included absorbing the Newhaven-Dieppe route, midway between the eastern and western Channel routes, within the joint venture. The outcome would lead to substantially reduced capacity and create the potential for stabilisation of fares in the ferry sector, an outcome that would clearly benefit Brittany Ferries. The proposed merger was referred to the UK Monopolies & Mergers Commission on 28th November 1996 for examination.

The Commission observed that the opening of the Channel Tunnel had introduced substantial new capacity to both the freight and passenger markets. Ferry operators added to this excess capacity, in an effort to offer more sailings to compete against the frequency of Eurotunnel's Le Shuttle services. Whilst demand had grown strongly in both markets it fell far short of the additional capacity which had been provided in the sector across all operators. Against this background, fares and freight rates had fallen

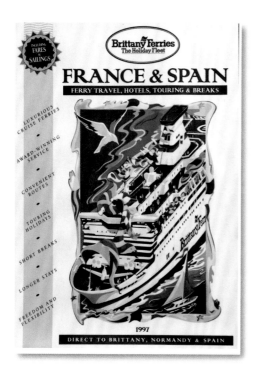
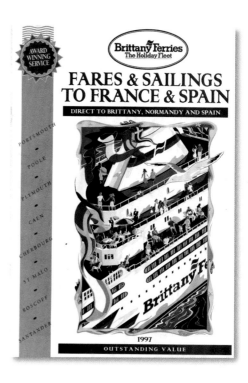

1997 'France and Spain' and 'Fares & Sailings' brochure covers. *(Rook Dunning)*

substantially from 1994 and the profits of all ferry operators on the short-sea routes were in decline, with some making losses for the first time in many years.

Brittany Ferries was one of several ferry companies to respond to the Commission. The Company welcomed a rationalisation of services on the short-sea routes and had no objections to the proposed merger if this led to an overall reduction in the considerable overcapacity in the sector that had arisen since the opening of the Channel Tunnel. Their submission noted that a combination of uneconomic pricing and promotions, combined with a liberal duty-free regime on the short-sea routes, had impacted on both volumes and pricing on the western Channel services. Brittany Ferries observed that it had withdrawn two ships from service, and that all companies operating on the western Channel had suffered considerable losses in the past two years. If the current situation was allowed to continue, with excess capacity and uneconomic operations on the part of Eurotunnel and the short-sea ferry operators, it would continue to impact on western Channel services, and further routes and services would need to be withdrawn as they would become uneconomic to operate. If, however, there was rationalisation of routes, a reduction in capacity and more economic pricing - if only to the point where companies broke even - the situation on the Western Channel routes would stabilise.

Brittany Ferries argued that the joint venture should be limited to apply to the short-sea routes as an independent business, without any form of commercial link with any of the remaining ferry operations of either P&O European Ferries or Stena Line. Their submission expressed concerns that P&O European Ferries' Portsmouth operation could benefit from a future synergy with the combined operation, and this would open up unfair competition. The Portsmouth operation must stand-alone, independent of the former parent company, as a condition of the merger, supported by appropriate criteria. Otherwise P&O European Ferries and Stena Line would be in a dominant position, accounting for nearly half of the total passenger and car market to and from continental Europe, and other companies might not be in a position to compete effectively. The Commissioners retired to consider the submissions.

On 18th November 1996 a fire was observed on a freight shuttle service as it entered the Channel Tunnel from France. In accordance with operational procedures, the driver attempted to take the train through to the UK terminal where the fire could be extinguished. But the locomotive and freight-passenger coach were rapidly enveloped in thick smoke and the locomotive lost power, forcing the train to stop at 21:58, some 19 kilometres into the tunnel. Passengers and crew were evacuated into the adjacent service tunnel, sustaining only minor injuries. The fire was not extinguished until 11:15 the following morning and inspection revealed that about 500 metres of tunnel had been badly damaged by the fire. With just one track available, the freight shuttle was suspended, and passenger services were seriously reduced. The Channel Tunnel was not fully re-opened until 15th May 1997.

In mid-November, the shareholders of West Country Television received an irresistible offer from United News & Media (trading as Carlton Television) to purchase 98% of the company shares for £82 million. Carruthers was the first shareholder to receive the single page, two paragraph offer, brought directly to him by motorbike courier from London. The offer required a decision within 24 hours, but there was little argument about the proposition. Some £13 million accrued to Brittany Ferries, representing a compound annual return in excess of 70% over the period from the original investment. The transaction was completed quickly, and the money paid into the bank on 23rd December. But Gourvennec was not pleased. He wanted to know who knew about the windfall; only the three directors (Carruthers, Longden, and their alternate Stephen Shaw) were involved. "Keep it that way", he retorted. It did not serve his or the Company's interests to declare a substantial financial gain whilst he was still lambasting the French government's 'Franc fort' policy and seeking further central financial support. The scale of the sum of money involved could cause potential financial support from the French government to dry up. So the money was left in the bank account in Plymouth, and a UK tax bill of £3 million was paid, much to the frustration of the local directors.

The 1995-96 season ended with a further downturn in business from the peaks of 1994. Passenger carryings dropped to 2,497,105, a fall of 9% year on year and almost 18% over two years. Vehicles numbers fell to 593,705, down 13%, and freight by 9% to 168,581 units. Brittany Ferries made a trading loss of FF16.21 million in the financial year, a significant improvement on the FF80.26 million loss made in 1994-95. The turnover of FF1.48 billion was down 12% from the previous year, which in itself was already down by over 10% on the previous twelve months. Gourvennec cited strong British competition from P&O European Ferries and the impact of the continued weakness of sterling as the key factors behind the deficit. "We expected to be subjected to waves. There was a tsunami that completely destabilised the market" Michielini commented on the results. But Gourvennec believed that Brittany Ferries was about to turn the corner. "We have been through a period of great turbulence for the past two years," he told reporters, noting that "the fundamental rules regarding the benefits of duty-free are now respected by all cross-Channel shipping companies." The rules for purchasing these zero-rated products (tobacco and alcohol) were previously "not respected by our competitors", stressed Michielini. "Now," added Gourvennec, "the clouds have cleared and we have targeted an increase of 160,000 passengers during the fiscal year 1997-1998."

Unsurprisingly, given the weaker state of their business model, P&O European Ferries' turnover dropped by over £7 million to £85.6 million, but costs did not fall in line with this and remained high. The company moved to a loss of £15.4 million after tax, a cumulative loss of £25.5 million in just two years.

The Channel Tunnel fire gave Le Shuttle a muted end to the year, but the short-sea ferry operators enjoyed an unexpected boom in traffic in the final quarter, with three million cars travelling through Dover in 1996, 5% higher than the previous year and only slightly below the record of 1994. But these figures belied the reports of the French Tourist Board, which recorded a 20% fall in summer holiday sales from the UK, compounding similar downturns in the previous two seasons. Most of the short-sea growth was coming from day trip and short break traffic, fuelled by the highly competitive fares on offer.

Fares for the 1997 season were published in December. P&O European Ferries and Stena Line were forced to publish independent brochures following the referral of their proposed merger to the Monopolies & Mergers Commission and, with Le Shuttle distracted by the limited operation through the Channel Tunnel following the fire, Brittany Ferries led the way in setting fares for the new season. Announcing a 10% reduction in fares, which with inflation running at 3% was effectively a 13% fall in real terms, Longden noted that a merger between P&O European Ferries and Stena Line could remove the one-third of excess capacity on the English Channel. Referring to the more local merger with P&O European Ferries, Carruthers observed that "the basic principles of a deal remain but the timing has slowed down. At the moment, we are working independently."

Fares for 1997 were simplified, with the number of price bands reduced further from four to three. New Ten-Day return fares were introduced, offering a significant discount on the standard fare. A peak season Portsmouth-Caen return fare for a car and two adults would be £260, but the Ten-Day return fare brought the cost down to £196. Car fares were quoted to include the driver free, with all children under 14 also travelling without charge, and cabins were offered free on day crossings, subject to availability. Longden suggested that the 1997 fare structure would compare very favourably year on year. He stated that "1996 was a challenging year for the entire cross-Channel market with new competitors and overcapacity. We are predicting that the strengthening pound will lead to Spain and France becoming even better value, and will experience their best years from the UK for some time. In short, Brittany Ferries is focusing on the values which played such a role in making us the most popular way to cross the western Channel."

P&O European Ferries was the first of the short-sea operators to publish their 1997 prices, and offered a £99 peak season return fare on Dover-Calais for booking paid for before the end of February 1997 – a 70% reduction on the 1996 brochure fare. Stena Line undercut this fare by £1, but viewed this as positive, citing that their average fare across all customers fell from £130 in 1994 to £50 in 1996. The prospects for the short-sea ferry operators were strong, with Le Shuttle not expecting to return to the 1996 levels of market share until the end of the year because of the Channel Tunnel fire. Le Shuttle raised their standard return prices from £129 to £169, and Five-Day tickets rose from £69 to £109. Le Shuttle Managing Director Bill Dix conceded that prices were not sufficient, and suggested further rises were need in 1998, with an additional increase of up to 50% when duty-free sales opportunities were withdrawn in 1999.

The 1997 season was the first full year in which the benefits of the joint venture between Brittany Ferries and Gîtes de France could be offered to the market. With Brittany Ferries now in control, the number of properties in a new joint brochure was reduced to 1,200 with some branded as 'elite gîtes'. Prices fell by up to 47%, but Carruthers noted that the average reduction was 30% to 40%. A separate 'Holiday Homes' brochure featured homes in France owned by Britons who were members of FPOC, and this programme immediately proved popular, with bookings running 18% ahead of 1996. The Company expected gîte holidays to account for 22% of business in 1997. The new brochure was underpinned by a £350,000 advertising campaign which focused on the 'friendliness' of gîte owners and the range of properties on offer. Standards were said to have improved significantly as owners invested on their properties to stem the losses of previous years. 'Take a New Look at our France & Spain' was the theme of newspaper advertising, with brochure covers featuring prominently. Whilst the Gîtes de France logo was included in the advertising, it was not found on the brochure covers.

With a stable and comprehensive reservation system in place, Carruthers and Longden looked for ways in which management information could be improved to match the detail which they had utilised when they had been working at Hertz; they began to explore ways in which a form of yield management system could be introduced. At the time, the American team that developed the industry-standard Sabre software was active selling their system to other airlines and consideration was being given to developing a cruise line product. Carruthers and Longden wondered if there were ways in which their ferry products could be accommodated into such a system. So, they travelled over to meet the Sabre team in the USA and spent several days debating the options. Was the system capable of being adapted to handle passengers, cars, on board accommodation, and freight units? Could passengers have accommodation without booking a car? How much accommodation can you sell without cars before you frustrate later sales of car traffic? The issues were complex. It was a step too far for the Sabre team; this was not going to be an easy development project.

Carruthers and Longden returned without a deal. At the same time contacts within TT-Line indicated that they too were looking to build a yield management system. The two companies were not in any form of competition, so here was an opportunity to pool resources and share the considerable cost of developing a joint system. A full day meeting explored the options, but it became clear that it would be very difficult for the two parties to work together. Development would be easy when there was common agreement on elements of the software design, but where the two companies' interests diverged, the resultant compromise would lead to a sub-optimal solution for both. This was not the right way forward.

The pair were approached by a team that had left the Sabre software team to set up their own cruise reservation software system. They were interested in building a bespoke ferry industry yield management solution and needed to trial their software. They offered to build a system for Brittany Ferries at cost, with the proviso that it could then be sold on to other ferry operators. The initial investment was modest and could be accommodated within existing budgets. For the first year the new software was trialled on the Portsmouth-St Malo route, and the team settled in to see how sales could be optimised and yields improved by utilising a different approach. The results were outstanding. Revenues improved by 10% in this first season through better rates generated by managing inventory and implementing dynamic pricing; this represented a £3.5 million improvement to the revenue line.

The results were clear to but convincing the French management team that further implementation of the policy was the right course of action proved to be a challenge. The French were unconvinced, believing that this new-fangled wizardry had the potential to put the entire Brittany Ferries operation at risk. There was a strong reaction to the perception that prices had risen, often based on single-case examples at the peak, where prices could rise to reflect last minute demand. Gourvennec and Michielini sided with the gîte owners who readily brought these examples to their attention. The fact that many of the prices on off-peak sailings in the inventory were reduced to stimulate demand was usually overlooked.

Christophe Mathieu, who studied European Studies at University and had a Masters degree in Tourism & Business Management from Paris 1 University, joined the Plymouth team in 1997. Mathieu was given the task of developing the yield management system for the Company and worked closely with Longden on the project. He was later appointed as the Group CEO in March 2016.

On 21st January 1997 the Brittany Regional Council approved the plan to rescue Brittany Ferries in line with the arrangements previously published in December 1996. As the primary shareholder in Sabemen, the Regional Council agreed to subscribe FF90 million of the FF150 million capital increase of the SEM over a three-year period. The other shareholders - the four general councils of Brittany -agreed to contribute the remaining FF60 million. The Lower Normandy communities also agreed to invest FF100 million in Senacal and Senamanche. These capital increases allowed the SEMs to delay the repayment of loans by forgoing the payment of rents owed by Brittany Ferries until the Company's circumstances improved. The state contribution of a FF300 million reduction in payroll and port taxes would also be applied over three years. The internal restructuring plan now envisaged annual savings of between FF111 and FF116 million, including the withdrawal of the *Normandie Shipper* and the *Duchess Anne*. The 1,770-employee payroll would decrease by FF8.5 million each year following the elimination of 88 positions. Brittany Ferries expected business to grow by 150,000 passengers in 1997, in a full year of operation of the UK joint venture with Gîtes de France. The Company was hopeful that the price war on the English Channel would stabilise, with the potential for small rises in fares helping sales to rise by 8.6% between 1997 and 1999. Ernst and Young, the Company's auditors, estimated that it will be possible to return to break-even by 2000.

With the rescue plan fully ratified and a clear path to financial recovery in place, it was an appropriate time for Michielini to retire after more than 20 years leading the Company. This was the end of an era. His tenure was marked by the successful professionalisation of the business and a sustained period of route expansion and fleet acquisition. On board services had been transformed to become widely recognised as market-leading in quality and service. The fleet now comprised the youngest of any ferry company operating on the English Channel. Financial stability had been enhanced by the incorporation of the SEMs into the business. And the Company held the predominant market share of business on the western Channel. He left a secure and stable company on the way to recovery after the most bruising price war ever seen in the cross-Channel market.

Michielini acted as the bridge across the English Channel, giving Carruthers and Longden the commercial freedom to devise their strategy to expand and build the business, whilst managing the aspirations of the French shareholders and delivering the French transformation of fleet quality. Arguably only a 'foreigner' with a half-Basque parentage could have had a foot in camps on both sides of the English Channel. His key strength was finding the right people, retaining and developing them, and building their loyalty to the cause and himself. The ships' captains felt they worked for 'Micky' who worked hard at building a rapport with crews, being a frequent visitor on board as vessels berthed in port. Michielini was a charismatic leader who became upset if anyone by-passed him and went straight to Gourvennec, but this situation was rare. Gourvennec could be relied upon to win the political and physical battles necessary to achieve Brittany Ferries' objectives, but he retained considerable farming interests outside the Company, developing the largest pig farm in Europe. Brittany Ferries quickly grew beyond Gourvennec's personal control and he could no longer set the agenda and strategy. The British team were left to achieve their objectives. Michielini trusted their abilities and backed their judgement.

Michielini left the Company on 30th April 1997; his ambitions to retire to buy land and breed horses were not fully realised and his planned years of retirement were to be prematurely cut short. His relationship with Gourvennec had soured in later years and his contribution to the success of the Brittany Ferries went largely unrecognised.

Michielini was replaced by the external appointment of 47-year-old Claude Geronimi, which was announced at the beginning of February; he joined the company the following month to shadow Michielini until he retired. Geronimi came with 23 years' experience in the oil and gas industry, the last 15 of which were with Elf Petroleum managing projects on the West Coast of Africa, in Tunisia, Norway and Scotland, whilst providing expert input to other company projects in the USA and the Middle East. The choice of an 'outsider' was a surprise to many, as the corporate culture had hitherto encouraged growth and development from within the organisation. But the scale of the operation was now seen as sufficiently large to require an individual with 'big company' experience.

The 1997 season opened with strong advance bookings, and by March Brittany Ferries was able to announce levels of bookings up 15% ahead compared to 1996, driven by the growing strength of the pound, which by now had recovered to reach FF9.0.

Meanwhile, the *Normandie* and *Val de Loire* appeared in a series of four one-hour Channel 5 television 'fly on the wall' documentaries which were broadcast in May 1997. The programmes focused on life on board during crossings on the Portsmouth-Caen and Plymouth-Santander routes, with a special episode covering a freight-only sailing during the French lorry drivers' strike. They were very well received and opened up the workings

The *Normandie Shipper* at Poole, with a well loaded Truckline departure for Cherbourg. *(Miles Cowsill)*

of the Company to a national audience.

The positive news continued with bookings up by 18% by the end of June, and ahead by some 60% during the main peak season. Demand was sufficiently strong to justify the *Purbeck* being drafted in to support the multi-purpose vessels on the Portsmouth-Caen route until 14th September, so that freight space could be released to increase passenger capacity during the summer season.

On 11th June the French government announced their agreement to the short-sea merger between P&O European Ferries and Stena Line, noting that this did not eliminate competition in the sector and citing that the merger 'will allow for rationalisation of the current overcapacity of cross-channel maritime services... as well as modernisation of the fleet and the commercial services on board and ... enable the joint venture to develop the services offered, in particular the departure schedule and the speed of loading and

Above: **Christian Michielini with his business partner Pinto on a frozen salmon buying trip to Vancouver shortly before he joined Brittany Ferries.** *(Michielini family collection)*

Right: **Maurice Chollet joins Christian Michielini aboard the** *Bretagne.* *(Michielini Family Collection)*

Below left: **Christian Michielini modelling the latest in Brittany Ferries apparel in Northern Ireland.** *(Michielini Family Collection)*

Below right: **Panos Marangopoulos, Christian Michielini and Jim Mason enact a well known saying.** *(Michielini Family Collection)*

Above left: **Cake presented to Christian Michielini on his retirement.** *(Michielini Family Collection)*

Above right top: **Christian Michielini with Paul Burns.** *(Michielini Family Collection)*

Above right: **Christina Michielini entertains Prince Charles on board the** *Prince of Brittany.* *(Michielini Family Collection)*

Below: **Jim Mason, Capt. Ivan Claireaux, Jean-Raymond Thomas, Alexis Gourvennec and Christian Michielini on board the** *Bretagne.* *(Michielini Family Collection)*

unloading'. The merger remained under consideration by the European Commission and the UK competition authorities and was eventually to be approved by both, with British approval coming in November 1997.

One consequence of this decision was that P&O European Ferries' western Channel operations were required to stand-alone from the new joint venture company in 1998, which matched the preferred outcome submitted by the Brittany Ferries team. This conclusion required the Portsmouth company to establish an independent identity from P&O Stena Line, build a new brand (which became P&O Portsmouth in an attempt to distinguish itself from the short-sea routes), and build an independent reservations system. From a Brittany Ferries perspective, this took the Portsmouth operation away from centralised support, leaving it weaker, but it also allowed P&O's local management to begin to develop strategies more suited and consistent with the characteristics of the western Channel market, and adapt the business model to accommodate the lessons learned from the earlier discussions with Brittany Ferries.

The *Quiberon* proved to be a valuable workhorse for Brittany Ferries. *(Miles Cowsill)*

Both companies experienced an increase in traffic across the year.

With the pound approaching an exchange rate of FF10 by mid-July, Brittany Ferries was almost fully booked for summer vehicle traffic on the Portsmouth-St Malo route, with no outbound availability for new bookings until mid-August and return crossings full until 1st September. There was limited availability of the Portsmouth-Caen service and the holiday home business was almost completely sold out until 26th August. Passenger traffic through Portsmouth Continental Ferry Terminal grew 15% during the summer quarter between June and August, whilst car traffic was up by 16%.

The revitalised gîte business was able to boast bookings 71% ahead of 1996, with Schouller stating that "this success answers all of the gloomy reports of last year that the gîte was dead as a holiday concept." VFB Holidays had 'never experienced a more positive climate for large bookings' and the Caravan Club found demand 'unprecedented'. The holiday market from Britain was expected to grow by two million based on the strength of the currency, despite a survey from the Paris Chamber of Commerce finding that the French were perceived by the British to be 'chronically rude, dirty, idle, and disorganised'.

In the autumn Brittany Ferries made a more aggressive venture into the excursion market with a £9.95 24-hour excursion fare on the Poole-Cherbourg service, which was extended to all routes from 15th September. Finance Director Shaw explained the logic. "What we had to do with the longer routes was to make the experience more pleasurable. Instead of charging down the autoroute, people could relax with a glass of wine. We are now offering a lot of mini cruises, which appeal to people who simply want to go there and back. It has become a recognised product." With competition from P&O Portsmouth's cruise ferries on the Portsmouth-Le Havre route, the market had become significantly more cut-throat.

Growing restrictions on freight vehicle movements on French roads at weekends created significant difficulties for hauliers, and there were prospects of frequent road blockades in protest. This created an opportunity to test the market for winter freight movements from Spain, particularly if the volumes of traffic shipped through the French ports was reduced. The *Barfleur* was allocated to a new Poole-Santander 'ByPass' service between 28th November 1997 and 15th March 1998, replacing the *Bretagne's* winter service from Portsmouth and offering a reduced 29-hour passage time. The *Barfleur's* passenger certificate was reduced to 200 to allow for passenger comfort and reduce operating costs with lower crewing levels. She sailed from Poole at 18:30 on Fridays and returned from Santander at 12:00 on Sundays

Autumn breaks brochure. *(Rook Dunning)*

to arrive in Poole each Monday afternoon and take up her normal Poole-Cherbourg rotations for the remainder of the week. The emphasis was primarily on freight traffic, but the service was also offered to passengers, with fares from £213 for a car and two passengers. UK Freight Director Jon Clarke noted that "responding to customer demand had been foremost in our minds when devising a solution to enable our customers to carry on their legitimate business – even when faced with outside constraints." He emphasised that the enhanced Portsmouth-St Malo service offered the opportunity for a full nine-hour rest period to address the increased levels of enforcement of drivers' hours legislation.

Some financial recovery was evident in the 1996-97 results. At the Annual General Meeting, Gourvennec reported a healthy increase in turnover and profits as well as passenger and vehicle carryings for the 1996/7 financial year. The corporate recovery plan and an upturn in the French holiday economy were cited as the drivers for this

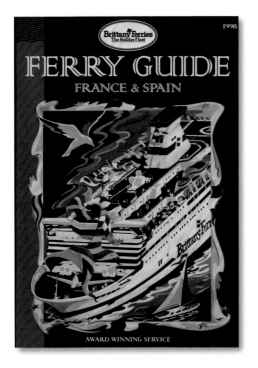

Suite of brochures for the 1998 season. *(Rook Dunning)*

improvement. Brittany Ferries planned to re-start the fleet investment programme following the achievement of these better financial returns. The Company's turnover rose by 14.5% to reach FF1,694 million, with profit after tax reaching FF84.5 million. Brittany Ferries' share of the western Channel market rose by 6.6% to 49%, with car traffic reaching 53%, and freight carryings rose by 8% to achieve a 49% market share. Passenger carryings reached 2,635,119, with 722,813 cars and 186,205 freight vehicles also being carried.

Carruthers noted that it was "encouraging to see the strength of the company's general recovery after a particularly difficult period during which increased competition and over capacity lead to a downward spiralling of fares. This, coupled with the weak pound making France less attractive to the British holidaymaker, led to an awkward trading period for the company. Now there has been some rationalisation in services and fares and the pound has recovered strongly. It is particularly heartening that we have achieved the increased carrions with one less ship which was sold the previous year after the closure of the Poole-St Malo service. The Company's recovery plan put in place in 1996 has paid dividends, and we are now actively considering our fleet needs as we approach the year 2000 and the new millennium."

The Portsmouth-St Malo route had an enhanced winter weekend service featuring the *Quiberon* and the *Bretagne*. The *Quiberon* schedule was based around positioning runs from Plymouth at 12:00 on Friday, which returned at 11:00 on Sunday. The *Bretagne* covered the Santander route from Portsmouth during the *Barfleur's* refit.

Portsmouth Port announced plans on 27th October for a new scheme to improve traffic flows, including a new link road to connect directly from the port to the M275. The following month the port won European Community funding to examine the options for a fifth berth at the port on the north side of the existing development. A new £4 million multi-storey car park was planned to be completed within three years.

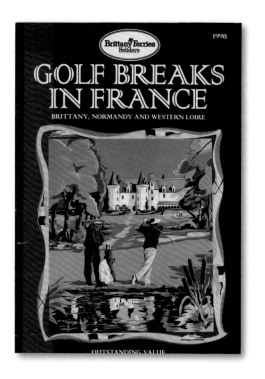

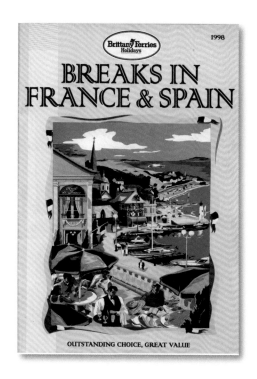

The Company's new Directeur Générale Geronimi left the Company in December 1997, after less than nine months in the role. His 'big company' background had not fitted well with the scale of operation, culture and ambitions of Brittany Ferries. Geronimi had developed plans to reorganise the management structure of the Company and build a long-term strategy, which included ambitions to enter the cruise sector, but this did not find favour with Gourvennec or the shareholders, who frequently relied on the Chairman for their direction. In a Company that did not willingly 'hire and fire', Geronimi's departure was an unusual development. He returned to Elf Petroleum as assistant to the Middle East vice president. The search began for his replacement.

The 1998 brochures featured the now familiar style of artistic covers, continued from previous years, with a bright, colourful presentation. The portfolio of holiday products now required supporting with brochures for Holiday Homes and Hotels, Short Breaks, Golf, Gîtes, and Mobile Homes, offered in conjunction with Eurocamp. Early booking discounts were used to tempt each market. The gîte programme was extended further for the 1998 season, with properties added in Burgundy, the Loire and Bordeaux. Prices were frozen from 1997, with customers offered a free night's hotel accommodation on their outward or return journey for those staying a long drive away from the western Channel ports. A week at a typical gîte near Bergerac in Aquitaine started from £55.30 per person for four passengers travelling in a car, including the ferry crossing.

With the prospect of the withdrawal of duty-free sales on the horizon for 1999, Carruthers publicised Brittany Ferries' stance by suggesting that the Company believed it would still be able to engage in the trade in international waters, outside twelve miles off the British coast and six miles from France. He described the current state of affairs as the 'chaos syndrome' because there was a total lack of clarity to how rules would be applied after 30th June 1999. "Until it is proven otherwise, we believe we can sell in international waters", he said. The Duty Free Confederation backed the Company's position, suggesting it would be foolish in the extreme if the ban was to go ahead. A typical crossing between Poole and Santander was used to illustrate the problem. UK duty and UK VAT would apply within UK waters, then UK VAT would be applied to duty-free sales in international waters; French duty and UK VAT would apply whilst the ship sailed through French waters, and Spanish duty and UK VAT when she reached Spanish waters. On the return journey, Spanish VAT would be applied instead of UK VAT, as rates charged were based on the country from which the vessel sailed.

The *Barfleur* appeared on the Portsmouth-Caen service in the early New Year following cancellation of services between Poole and Spain. The Poole-Santander service

The *Val de Loire* alongside at Ringaskiddy, Cork. *(Ferry Publications Library)*

re-opened on 20th February for a fortnight, before the *Barfleur* returned to full operation on the Poole-Cherbourg service.

The replacement for Geronimi was named on 28th February 1998 as 49-year old Jean-Michel Masson. An economics graduate, he spent most of his career with the Air France group, which he joined in 1973. After holding several management positions abroad, including periods in Japan and Britain, he joined the head office team as commercial director and later, director of strategy. In 1992, he led the merger of UTA with Air France, and was appointed Asia-Pacific General Manager, and helped turnaround the fortunes of the national airline whilst being a director of various tourism, air and service subsidiaries.

The Times diary headlined his appointment as 'Ferry Fishy' in an article which suggested that he could be the last captain on the bridge of Brittany Ferries, as a team of accountants was going through the books to determine if the Company was viable without government subsidy. Reflecting the common misconception of the time, the diarist suggested that 'Brittany Ferries had been propped up for as long as anyone can remember, despite Brussels rules on state aid and to the distress of our own P&O service'. Minister of Transport Claude Gayssot had determined that there should be no more government money, the article went on, and Brittany Ferries was facing the loss of duty-free, so the business could be scuttled before the high season.

Carruthers responded strongly to the article, and the following day the diarist pointed out that Masson had previously interviewed for the role and lost out to Geronimi. He noted that he had been taken to task and conceded that financial support for Brittany

Crowds gather on the bow of the *Bretagne* as she arrives in Portsmouth. *(Miles Cowsill)*

Ferries countered the country's 'daft' social costs. Carruthers had assured the writer that the Company was 'murdering P&O' on the Portsmouth run, and the diarist accepted that, having travelled on Brittany Ferries, it was a cut above the rest. Long may they run, he concluded.

The French Tourist Office (FTO) opened a £600,000 French Travel Centre in Piccadilly, London in February. The new one-stop travel and information office included a bank, travel agent, bookshop, tourist office desk, and offices for Brittany Ferries, SeaFrance and Air France, designed to cater for up to 200,000 office visitors each year. The two ferry companies had a monopoly of sales from the site. The FTO expected a 10% increase in visitors to the country in 1998, fuelled by an improved exchange rate for the pound and the World Cup, which was being hosted by France between 10th June and 12th July.

On 26th March P&O Portsmouth announced the charter of the fast craft *Superstar*

Express from Star Cruises to supplement their existing services on the Portsmouth-Cherbourg route from mid-May until September. This was their first venture into operation of fast craft and the *Superstar Express* was introduced for an experimental season to examine both performance and commercial potential, prior to a decision being made on whether to bring her back in 1999. The proposed journey time with the *Superstar Express* was two hours and 45 minutes at a service speed of 38 knots, although the lengthy slow approach to Portsmouth Harbour again meant that the full capabilities of the craft could not be exploited. The 82.3-metre long Austal craft could carry 872 passengers with car deck capacity for 175 cars or 70 cars and ten coaches. P&O Portsmouth also increased freight capacity on the Portsmouth-Le Havre route by chartering the *Sea Hawk*.

With both Brittany Ferries and P&O Portsmouth having decided against opening a service to south west France, the port of Bayonne opened discussions with Compagnie Viking of Le Havre about a freight service to Southampton. Both parties signed a preliminary agreement with the aim of launching a three times weekly service from as early as September. The port already had a ro-ro ramp used for the reception of motor vehicles from Portugal.

The Tour de France started in Ireland in 1998, but the contract to carry the caravan from Cork to Roscoff was awarded to Stena Line using the *Stena Challenger, Nusa Damai* and the *Koningin Beatrix*.

Brittany Ferries attracted good levels of business during the summer season especially on the Portsmouth-St Malo service, which encouraged the repeated deployment of the *Bretagne* and *Quiberon* on the route; the *Quiberon* was employed at weekends on the St Malo-Plymouth-Roscoff service. The *Val de Loire* returned to Portsmouth on 16th November to maintain the Caen service over the winter with the *Normandie*. Meanwhile the *Barfleur* was employed on the Poole-Cherbourg and Poole-Santander routes from 15th November until 12th March 1999. The Spanish service was suspended from 3rd January until 5th February during the period of the *Barfleur* refit.

At the 1997-98 annual meeting Masson reported that Brittany Ferries was starting to recover, with the first steps of the recovery plan beginning to have an impact. The company was able to report an increase of 10.7% in group turnover to FF1,875 million, generating a pre-tax profit of FF134.4 million. Prudently this profit was reduced to FF10.2 million after tax provision for repayment of French government support grant, which was still subject to European Commission approval. Masson noted that FF250 million (€38.11 million) of vessel rent had been postponed, but repayment would begin in 1999. The Company was able to record a 49.5% share of passenger movements and 50% share of freight traffic across the western Channel routes. The directors noted that Company performance had benefited from a strong sterling exchange rate during 1998, combined with a stringent management policy and the positive effects of the implementation of the new commercial plan. Brittany Ferries had carried 2,656,900 passengers (up 0.4%), 736,610 cars (up six%) and 180, 630 freight units. Carruthers was recorded as saying 'thanks to our reputation, the quality of our service and the introduction of more selective marketing strategies, we have been able to grow our turnover significantly more quickly than our traffic. We are now in a strong position to put our exciting plans in place for the new millennium later this year.'

Masson set up a new management committee, and appointed Michel Balsan, a former colleague from Air France, to take charge of the human resources team. The aim was to reassure staff, some of whom went on strike to express their concerns about the new Directeur Général's social plans, which saw the workforce reduced by 10% to 1,850 permanent staff. "The current negotiation should be successful," Masson said, "... and transform 80 seasonal positions into fixed-term contracts."

All Brittany Ferries routes were brought under the single corporate brand for the 1999 season. The independent Truckline brand had served its purpose, particularly in the early days of the Les Routiers passenger service and as a distinguishing brand for all freight operations, but more efficiency could now be achieved through a single brand identity. The *Barfleur* was repainted in Brittany Ferries delivery and marketed alongside the rest of the passenger operations in a common brochure and advertising. The Company proposed similar schedules for the fleet in 1999.

New Year's Day 1999 saw the launch of the 'Euro' across Europe, marking the end for the French Franc. However British insistence on sterling remaining outside the new common currency perpetuated the issues for Brittany Ferries of income in one currency and costs in another. The company would continue to remain vulnerable to the vagaries of exchange rate fluctuations. The pound began trading at €1.029 and was to gradually rise to €1.096 in the next twelve months

Cross-Channel operators raised their fares by up to 25% at the start of 1999 in anticipation of the withdrawal of duty-free concessions during the year. Chris Laming of P&O Stena Line noted that fares were still lower than they had been in 1994, and the company was sticking more rigidly to brochure fare levels. Eurotunnel raised the peak return fare for a car from £220 to £279, although this was compared with a rarely charged £328 price of 1996. The Brittany Ferries perspective was different. Longden observed that France was proving very popular in 1999 with bookings 10% ahead of 1998, and the gîte programme showing a 15% rise. He stated that Brittany Ferries had always been more rigid about pricing compared to competitors, although "special offers abound". It was a year of consolidation for brochure styles, with a continuation of the successful approach of previous years.

P&O Portsmouth were very satisfied with the impact of the *Superstar Express* in her first summer of operation and chartered the vessel again for the 1999 season. Fast craft offered significant time advantages for passengers, but this was not a market that Brittany Ferries had traditionally served or been concerned about. Their relative fragility did not encourage year-round operation; P&O Portsmouth overcame this issue by returning the *Superstar Express* to Malaysia for the winter, but this involved heavy repositioning costs. There were voices both for and against the concept of fast craft operation within Brittany Ferries, and many in France were supportive. The volume of abstracted business was difficult to evaluate, but the impact was sufficient to prompt a further review of the potential for fast craft operation by the Company. Carruthers decided that the best way to resolve the debate was to engage an industry expert to evaluate the opportunities, working with one of the Company's own analysts to reach a conclusion. Chris Butcher, who was a strong advocate of the fast craft concept with significant experience on ownership and operation, was brought over from Australia to share his knowledge with Richards. The pair used Brittany Ferries' internal average rate data to populate a model designed to establish if it were possible to make money by running a fast craft on any of the Company's routes. The model could not be made to work, no matter how the data was cut. The workstream concluded with a presentation to Masson and the senior team in Roscoff. Given his personal enthusiasm for the craft, Butcher had the difficult task of explaining why it would not be a good idea for Brittany Ferries to utilise one on a cross-Channel service, and the project was again put on the shelf.

The *Quiberon* left Plymouth on a regular departure to Roscoff at 23:34 on 17th March, moving astern from Millbay Docks and into Drake Channel before turning to starboard to take a south easterly heading to the west of Asia Pass. Speed was increased to the maximum 10 knots within the Harbour limits. on a clear night with the tide approaching low water. Two vessels were lying in the anchorages east of Melampus buoy so the Master of the *Quiberon* took a westerly course past the buoy to avoid them. Navigating largely by eye, he felt the vessel run aground at about 23:46 some three cables from Drake's Island. Assistance was quickly forthcoming from the tug *Faithful,* which managed to pull the *Quiberon* clear at 00:49 as the tide began to rise and finally docked at Millbay Docks at

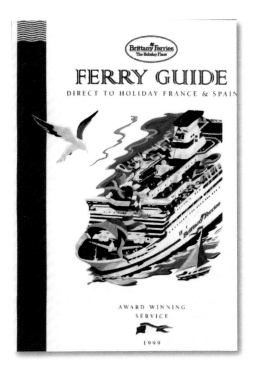 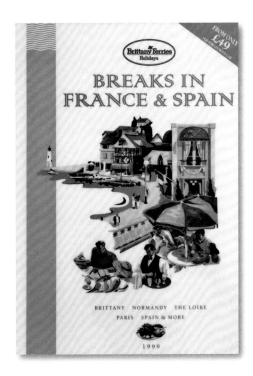

The 1999 brochures; the final season for BCB and Rook Dunning. *(Rook Dunning)*

01:15. There were no injuries and the *Quiberon* suffered minor plating damage. She was able to resume her passage at 14:30 on 18th March.

As the spring passed, there was no final clarity on the proposal to withdraw the capability to offer duty-free sales on journeys within the EU. Duty free retailers were optimistic that politicians would have a last-minute change of heart during an EU summit in Cologne at the end of May, barely a month before the proposed abolition date. The UK Foreign Secretary Robin Cook said that the duty-free issue was probably the most important item on the EU agenda as far as ordinary citizens were concerned. But reversing the decision required a unanimous vote of EU member states, and whilst Germany, Britain, and France sought to overturn the decision, a handful of member states, led by Denmark, were adamant that duty-free sales were illogical in the single European market. Danish ministers argued that duty-free sales within the EU enjoyed an annual subsidy of some €2 billion of excise duty and VAT that would otherwise be paid; some 35% of a duty-free sales operation's annual turnover were said to be accounted for by this tax advantage. This alleged subsidy amounted to state aid for ferries, airlines and airports, and distorted competition by favouring international air and sea travel over international road and rail travel. Profits from duty-free sales were said to be used to offer lower fares for freight transport, thereby distorting competition in relation to companies carrying just cargo.

UK Prime Minister Tony Blair led a campaign to permit a further 30-month extension of the facility and claimed a majority of states were in favour of retaining duty-free sales capability, but this approach did not command the unanimity required to overturn the ban. The European leaders confirmed their decision to abolish duty-free sales within the EU. From 30th June 1999, the sale of duty-free alcohol, cigarettes and other consumer goods ended for all travel within the EU. Goods sold on ferries became subject to the VAT and excise duties of the country where the journey started, although purchases for

consumption on board ferries remained duty-free.

This outcome immediately posed issues for ferry operators, with different tax regimes on sales applicable in the UK, France and Spain; how was the correct duty to be applied? More importantly the abolition of duty-free sales profits represented an immediate substantial reduction in income. This was a more significant problem for those companies – such as P&O Stena Line – which had promoted shopping opportunities through very low promotional fares with national and regional newspapers. For P&O Portsmouth this represented a substantial loss of income, but the impact was not so closely felt in Brittany Ferries, which had deliberately not ventured heavily into this market. The loss of revenue would have to be made up through a gradual increase in passenger fares; this was carefully planned to be introduced over a three-year period to soften the impact on customers.

This was just another blow to Brittany Ferries. As Carruthers put it, if you ran a management training scenario where you ran a business and your major new competitor, who needed to charge £130 to break even, decided to offer fares at £30; then your revenue is devalued by 18% due to currency fluctuations, and finally your revenue is reduced by 15% through the loss of a major income stream due to a change in fiscal policy... the game would be unmanageable. But this is just what the team was challenged with and had to overcome.

Carryings in mid-August were boosted by the solar eclipse on Wednesday 11th August, the first for 72 years, with fully sold out sailings. The blackout of the sun by the passage of the moon was visible in an arc which began over the Atlantic, a few hundred miles east of Boston, and transited the Scilly Isles and Cornwall, before crossing the English Channel to northern France and Germany. In Cornwall the impact was deadened by cloudy skies, and in parts of northern France there were downpours at the crucial moment. But in mid-Channel, as the fleet slowed and special glasses were issued to allow the phenomenon to be viewed safely, the conditions were near perfect and crowds gathered on deck to witness darkening of the sky. The best place to view the eclipse was judged to be aboard the *Quiberon* on the 08:00 sailing from Plymouth to Roscoff which was in exactly the right place when the two-minute eclipse occurred at 11:11.

The *Normandie Shipper* was sold to Adecon Shipping of the Bahamas as part of the restructuring plan in October 1999; she was registered to Bonavista Shipping Corporation and renamed the *Bonavista*.

Masson encouraged the Company to look beyond established links with advisers and suppliers to consider the advantages that might come from relationships with larger international organisations which had broader market experience. Such companies came with the 'comfort' of reputation and track record, but the intimate blend of a matched corporate culture with a series of long-standing suppliers was lost. BCB had been rebranded as CIB, with a new ownership and management structure, and when the advertising and marketing account was put up for review in 1999, Banks, Hoggins, O'Shea were selected as their replacement. The new agency was a large international group with considerable resources, which numbered Waitrose, Weetabix, the National Trust and Ferrero Rocher amongst their clients. The BCB relationship had played a key role in establishing the Brittany Ferries brand – and the Brittany Prince vegetable brand before that – and the relationship between client and agency had been one of the most enduring and productive in the advertising industry.

The winter operating pattern was repeated, with the *Val de Loire* returning to the

The *Val de Loire* makes an impressive view as she enters Portsmouth harbour from Cherbourg. *(Brian D.Smith)*

Portsmouth-Caen route alongside the *Normandie*, and the *Barfleur* covering during their refits with the *Duc de Normandie* maintaining the Poole-Cherbourg service during the *Barfleur's* absence. The *Quiberon* worked the weekend Plymouth-Roscoff service, undertaking its usual Plymouth-St Malo repositioning trip, and supporting the *Bretagne* on the Portsmouth-St Malo route during the week. The Spanish service was suspended from 16th November 1999 until mid-March 2000. In a similar move, P&O Portsmouth suspended their service to Bilbao in December and January, re-opening in February with a single weekly round trip, doubling service frequency from 21st March 2000.

A new freight-only Southampton-Bayonne service was started by Intermodal Atlantica Line, a 50:50 Joint Venture between Compagnie Viking and ships agents Naxco, in late September 1989. The *Clare* and the *Lembitu* were chartered for the operation, and the schedule featured an emphasis on weekend crossings to beat the national ban on weekend freight movements in France. The company aimed to carry up to 10% of all road freight travelling between the UK and Spain and targeted 160,000 trailers in its first year of operation. The service was suspended after just five weeks operation in October, then reduced to one round trip weekly operation with the *Clare* sailing from Southampton on Wednesdays, returning on Saturdays. The service was suspended again from 21st January 2000 after the arrest of the *Clare* on arrival in Bayonne, ironically with a full load. Traffic was said to be increasing after the initial suspension.

The fast craft *Superstar Express* had another successful seven-month season for P&O Portsmouth, carrying 325,000 passengers and 93,000 cars. This time she was laid up in Falmouth for the winter and the company announced that she would be replaced for the 2001 season by a charter of the larger *Portsmouth Express* (ex *Catalonia*) which could carry 225 cars (an increase of 50) and 920 passengers at 41 knots.

Brittany Ferries were able to report a further year of substantially improved financial results in the 1998-9 trading year, with turnover increasing by 4.1% to £195 million, despite the loss of duty-free revenues during the summer. The company recorded a profit before exceptional items of £17.2 million, an increase of 27% on the previous year. During 1998-9 Brittany Ferries carried 2,654,165 passengers, 762,650 cars and 172,950 freight vehicles giving a 52.2% share of western channel passengers (from 49.5%) and 53.7% of freight (from 50%). Over the three financial years that followed the restructuring plan, the Company had, as planned, fully reimbursed the reduced charter payments agreed by shipowner partners in 1996. This track record created the confidence for the SEMs to begin to consider investment in a new vessel.

P&O Portsmouth made a loss after tax of £9.6 million in 1999, the sixth consecutive year of deficits, but turnover broke through the £100 million level for the first time. The company exercised their option to continue the charter of *Pride of Bilbao* from Irish Continental Line at the reduced level of $35,500 per day. Until 1996 the rate had been $37,500 per day, then dropping to $36,000 per day.

Brittany Ferries planned millennium-eve trips with the *Val de Loire* to Rouen and the *Bretagne* to St Malo. The *Val de Loire's* Christmas Cruise to Santander was diverted to Rouen due to bad weather; the *Bretagne's* Christmas departure was also delayed by the weather conditions until 25th December and sailed to Cherbourg instead of St Malo.

The much heralded 'Year 2k' bug fortunately proved to be a non-event as the new millennium unfolded, with the Company well prepared to address any issues. But other changes were afoot as the New Year celebrations concluded.

Thirteen
Change in a new Millennium

B rittany Ferries' schedules for the 2000 season showed little change from 1999, but the brochure launch revealed a dramatic change in pricing policy. For the first time there were none of the familiar coloured pricing grids or tariffs, and passengers were asked to call the Company for details of sailing prices. Continued investment in reservations software had created the business intelligence and capability to employ significantly more sophisticated processes in the booking process. Ian Carruthers and David Longden held a series of lengthy and passionately argued debates about whether to risk producing a million brochures without any form of pricing in them. This was a huge gamble. But Brittany Ferries became the first travel business not to publish their prices; not even the airlines were so brave at this time. Prices were quoted 'from' a set level, and could therefore be varied to adapt to the levels of demand on specific sailings. Quotations could only be obtained by contacting the reservations offices by phone or, in a new development, through the Company's website.

The result was uproar, with the chattering classes expressing their displeasure at the change. The discussion inevitably focused on those sailings where prices were being increased, rather than the majority where lower fares were on offer. It was impossible for anyone outside the Company to fully understand how the pricing varied across all sailings, and the rate of price change that had been applied on individual departures. The team considerably under-estimated the scale of the public response, and had to overcome the initial perception that all discounted fares had been withdrawn. All the discounted fares were still there, but passengers had to trust that the computer system would undertake the necessary correct calculation. Longden appeared on Radio 4's Today programme to be interviewed about the changes by John Humphrys and James Naughtie. Whilst this was a difficult conversation to have over the sceptical airwaves, the fact that this news item was worthy of being broadcast made it clear that what Brittany Ferries did mattered; the brand was becoming of sufficient importance to be of national interest.

Variable pricing became the way forward from this time, despite this being the nascent days of the internet. Ryanair and easyJet followed the trailblazing efforts of Brittany Ferries. There were still concerns as to how the new procedure would be accepted by travel agents, who now had to call the reservations centre to price and make a booking. There was some exposure to the risk that travel agents would revert to using only those ferry operators with published prices, but the unique geographical route network of Brittany Ferries helped retain their loyalty.

Not all traffics were charged on a variable basis. The tour operator market had to be handled separately, as there was still a requirement for a Brittany Ferries rate to be published as part of the all-inclusive prices in their brochures, and this was too big a market to abandon. So, a hybrid approach was applied in the early years, with variable fares in the public market and fixed rates for tour operators. The Company's in-house holiday business also had to have a fixed price structure to allow market-competitive brochures to be published.

The new system allowed passenger and vehicle space to be allocated to the different market sectors on each sailing, with capacity re-allocated between them as appropriate.

It often felt counter-intuitive to decline bookings for a departure in a particular sector when space was available in others, but the software gave the confidence that better value traffic would materialise based on historic patterns of bookings.

Carruthers gained an insight into the public reaction by sitting in on calls in the reservation office. It took time for the new system to be effective, but it was a trail blazer for what became the norm in most transport undertakings. In the short-term it was essential that P&O Portsmouth be persuaded to adopt a similar system for their western Channel crossings. Gordon Bethune of Continental Airlines was quoted as saying "You're only as good as your dumbest competitor." It was important that both companies used the same logic to avoid fares being priced expensively when they should be cheap, and cheap when they should be expensive. This was not a discussion about market share; it was about trying to make sense of the market. If both companies adopted the same approach to fares and space allocation, then they would equally make rational decisions from similar data, whilst retaining the ability to undertake their own promotional activity. Now freed from a requirement to maintain consistency with the rest of the Group, P&O Portsmouth introduced yield management-led pricing and followed the Brittany Ferries approach.

Travel Agents and Tour Operators attempted to beat the system by creating dummy bookings on peak sailings, which gave them early access to confirmed space which could be sold on later. At this stage they did not have to pay Brittany Ferries until after the journey had been completed, so there were large sums of money at risk in the peak period. The 'ghost' bookings were quickly apparent from the repetition of dummy names. But the travel agents and tour operators were holding passengers' money and taking no risk that they would fill these spurious bookings.

There was also always the risk that these operators could be liquidated before they paid their debt to Brittany Ferries, who were usually last in the queue to secure payment. This situation rankled with Carruthers and Longden, and they determined that Brittany Ferries should become the first ferry company to insist that payment be made in full eight weeks before the departure date for a booking. This money was put into escrow and held by Brittany Ferries against future travel, paying interest where appropriate. The response from the industry was frequently hostile. Many of the larger players initially suggested that they would not go along with this approach. But Carruthers and Longden applied the sound logic that the operators were using Brittany Ferries' money to enhance their businesses, and the Company was no longer going to be the last in line to get paid. There was mutual respect between supplier and customer, space was guaranteed for passengers, and Brittany Ferries avoided future debts. It proved difficult to encourage other ferry operators to follow the initiative, as their blend of other routes with local booking characteristics placed different pressures on management.

A new advertising agency brought a new direction to brochure production and advertising from the 2000 season. The fleet was made more prominent in the brochures, whose covers adopted a simpler style using a single evocative image. The short breaks brochure was illustrated with a glass of wine and a restaurant bill; the 'Holidaying in France and Spain' brochure led with a field of lavender. The brand acquired a new strapline 'as relaxing as being there'.

On 8th December 1999 the 37,000-tonne tanker *Erika* left Dunkirk bound for Livorno, Italy with a cargo of 30,884 tonnes of heavy fuel oil. Built in 1975, she was one of eight sister ships, three of which had previously suffered major structural damage. The elderly *Erika* was an attractive vessel to operate, as tighter safety standards were forcing oil tanker charter fees upwards, and she was available at a bargain basement charter price - half that of a safer, more modern tanker.

As the *Erika* entered the Bay of Biscay, she encountered a heavy storm and soon found herself in difficulties. She began to list as the storm worsened, and by mid-afternoon on 11th December was listing by ten to twelve degrees to starboard, with water

The stricken *Erika*. *(John Batchelor)*

being taken on board and the hull beginning to split. Capt. Karun Mathur slowly lost control of his vessel. He sought assistance, but the following day the *Erika* broke her back and started to sink in about 120 metres of water, despite an unsuccessful attempt to tow her stern section further out to sea. The *Erika* was now some 30 kilometres south of the Pointe de Penmarc'h in Brittany. The crew were rescued by the French navy, but thousands of tonnes of oil leaked from the vessel's tanks. Pollution was very difficult to contain in the severe weather conditions which, coupled with high tides and currents, caused the slicks to be thrown high up on the shore. Some 400 kilometres of France's coastline was badly affected, from Brittany through the Loire Atlantique and the northern Vendée regions, to offshore islands, notably the Belle Ile. This was another environmental and ecological catastrophe, hitting wildlife, and the fishing and tourism industries.

French planes tracked oil slicks up to 15 kilometres long, but only 3% of the total spill volume was collected by the response operations at sea. The rest formed a water in oil emulsion that significantly increased the volume and viscosity of pollutant. Around 200,000 tonnes of oily waste was eventually collected and stockpiled during the clean-up operation. Almost 74,000 oiled birds were recorded on the coastline, of which around 42,000 were dead, making this the biggest ecological disaster on record for Europe's seabird population. Total, the French oil company who chartered the *Erika*, spent £85 million to seal the hull and pump out the remaining oil from the vessel's tanks.

Whilst memories of the *Amoco Cadiz* had faded, the image of oil-polluted beaches across the western shores of France was an unwelcome feature at the start of the main holiday booking period. Although the pound was trading some 5% better year on year against the Euro, by the end of May package holiday bookings to France were experiencing a 19% decline. The post duty-free abolition price rises applied to ferry crossings were clearly a factor in this drop. Brittany Ferries teamed up with the Holidaybreak Group (which comprised Eurocamp, Keycamp and Sun Sites) to launch a new website – to highlight properties available for short notice bookings. The French Tourism Minister, Michelle Demessine, declared that all Finistère beaches were oil-free, with the main remaining oil on beaches further south on the coast, in areas less frequented by British tourists.

Attempts by French investigators to trace the owner of the *Erika* were hampered by the labyrinthine nature of vessel and cargo ownership, and the vessel's Maltese flag of convenience. The paper trail led to seven different countries. Total was found guilty of failing to take into account the age of the vessel and disregarding maintenance issues and in 2008 was fined €375,000. Judge Joseph Valantin said the French company had "committed an error of negligence that is linked to the sinking" of the *Erika* and it was as a "direct consequence of the serious rust corrosion" caused by "insufficient maintenance of the ship". The French court assessed the total damages for civil parties at €192.8 million, with Total and three other parties making voluntary payments of €171.3 million to the majority of civil parties, including the French government, in addition to fines and clean-up costs. The court's decision established a legal precedent in recognising that polluters could be held responsible for damage caused to the environment.

The *Quiberon* was again employed on her complex winter schedule, including a second Jersey charter on 8th March. She returned to the Plymouth-Roscoff route a week later. The *Barfleur* returned to the full time Poole-Cherbourg service on 15th March after sailing a winter Portsmouth-Caen-Cherbourg-Poole roster.

Meanwhile, the *Superstar Express* opened the Portsmouth-Cherbourg route for P&O Portsmouth from 18th March with the larger fast craft *Portsmouth Express* taking over from 11th April.

The *Purbeck* spent the winter on the Folkestone-Boulogne route and returned to Brittany Ferries from 2nd May to support the *Normandie* and *Duc de Normandie* on the Portsmouth-Caen route. This provoked a reaction from the trade unions, who threatened to strike if she did not return as a fully French-crewed vessel. Freight Director Jon Clarke noted that 'the arrival of additional capacity on this route is in direct response to the enhanced demand from customers who recognise that Caen has recently benefited from significant improvements to the French National Route network. In operating to Caen, St Malo and Cherbourg, Truckline is providing international haulage operators – fast becoming appreciative that there are few viable alternatives – with what they want when and where they want it.'

Brittany Ferries was an early adopter in 2000 of the pilot 'Pet Passport' scheme, which applied to 22 European countries, enabling registered cats and dogs to be carried without incurring the need for any quarantine arrangements. Dogs were accommodated on all routes when travelling in cars, but only the *Bretagne* had kennels available for canines accompanying foot passengers. The same rules were applied to guide dogs.

The decision to publish brochures without detailed price grids was now replicated by both P&O Portsmouth and P&O Stena Line, but Brittany Ferries continued to come under fire for the fluid price system. One customer described this as a 'ridiculous regression to the dark ages – a sort of closed auction'. Carruthers defended the move as the Company issued guidance to FPOC members that highlighted where cheaper sailings were likely to be available. He stated that the Company would not publish prices in line with yield management systems run by other transport operators, including airlines and rail networks. "To publish 2.5 million brochures with fares set 15 months in advance is an exercise in futility" he was quoted as saying. "This will bring the ferry Industry out of the dinosaur age and give us flexibility over prices which could fall as well as rise depending on demand and availability."

Although the pound continued to exchange at an improving level against the Euro, early bookings for the 1999 season were still sluggish, with some operators reporting a 30% slump. Longden believed the downturn to be a conundrum and could not explain whether it was the millennium, foot and mouth disease, or oil on the beaches behind the change. He expressed his own view that this could be part of a fundamental change in booking trends, with the public no longer sensing the same anxiety in securing their two weeks in the summer up to twelve months in advance.

As hinted at the Annual General Meeting, the Company's financial track record in reimbursing the charter fee 'holiday' gave the SEMs the cash and the confidence to consider the next steps in fleet investment, particularly looking to finally address the imbalance in capacity between the vessels on the Portsmouth-Caen route. The Company's engineers looked with Mason at the option of securing Stena Line's *Koningin Beatrix,* visiting her at Fishguard in the New Year, and were close to agreeing a deal, but Stena held back to consider their wider fleet options on the Irish sea in the light of rising fuel costs. Brittany Ferries remained keen to secure the vessel but began to look at options for another new vessel.

This more positive outlook was reflected in the announcement on 27th April of plans for a new ship to be introduced into service by early 2002. The vessel represented an investment of £80 million in a state-of-the-art cruise ferry for the Portsmouth-Caen route, with capacity for up to 175 freight units, 600 cars and 2,000 passengers. She would be the largest ship ever planned for cross-Channel operations. Her capacity was graphically described as being the equivalent of nearly five jumbo jet loads of passengers and a mile and a half of freight vehicles. Carruthers reported that "the company is in negotiations with a number of European shipyards, but we have not yet ruled out the acquisition of nearly new and existing tonnage if it can be adapted to meet the standards and capacity required. The size of the ship, at some 36,000 tonnes, will be three and a half times larger than the vessel it will replace on the Caen route." He was quick to stress that the vessel would uphold the traditional ambience of the Brittany Ferries fleet; "We won't reflect any fads. We are constructing something for ten to 15 years. There will be areas to relax and we will have the traditional brasseries and cafeteria." The vessel was planned to displace the *Duc de Normandie* to Plymouth-Roscoff and thereby release the *Quiberon* for sale.

Bookings began to pick up as the early summer in the UK was marked by cold, wet weather in what was to become one of the wettest years on record. This domestic gloom contrasted with reports of heat waves abroad, which resulted in a surge in bookings; gîte holiday sales rose by 75% in one week, as a late boom rescued the summer trade. Meanwhile passengers drew attention to anomalies in pricing. The fare for a pair of foot passengers travelling with a cabin by day on the Portsmouth-Caen route was £111.50, but the equivalent fare for a motorbike and two passengers was £89. A Company spokesman suggested that anyone booking but not bringing a motorcycle would bizarrely be charged £22.50 extra for not taking up space on the car deck. The anomaly was corrected for the 2001 season.

All operators were affected by a French truck drivers' strike in August and yet more industrial unrest forced major disruption to services at the end of the month. French fishermen blockaded Channel ports from 29th August in protest at escalating fuel prices. Worst hit were 299 passengers on board the *Bretagne* on an overnight crossing from Portsmouth to St Malo, who found themselves back in Portsmouth after eleven hours at sea, with the vessel having been turned away from both St Malo and Cherbourg. There was little prospect of an immediate alternative crossing, which was particularly difficult for returning holidaymakers at the peak of the season. The disruption was quickly picked up in the press, and was used to highlight the growing attractions of low cost airline based holidays, which were proving increasingly popular. Eurocamp, VFB, Brittany Direct Holidays and Belle France all offered air packages for the first time in 2000. "If it's not fishermen it's lorry drivers using the British travelling public for their own ends" said a frustrated Brittany Ferries spokesman, who asked "Who will it be next? Gasmen, barmen and waitresses getting in on the act? "

With plans to secure Stena Line's *Koningin Beatrix* thwarted, the award of a contract by Senacal for the £70 million construction of a new vessel for the Portsmouth-Caen route was confirmed on 11th September. There was intense competition amongst shipyards for the contract, with strong interest from Korea and Japan, but Brittany Ferries announced that Van der Giessen de Noord of Rotterdam had been selected to build the vessel, with construction scheduled to start in March 2001. The shipyard had developed expertise in modular construction techniques, but the Brittany Ferries order required a level of quality far superior to their normal standard of output. The finished vessel would incorporate the best of the Van der Giessen de Noord construction methodology, coupled with interior designs by Deltamarin and AIA modelled on the best features of the existing fleet. All cabins would have private facilities and there would be classic Commodore Cabin suites as well as cabins designed specifically for disabled passengers. The design incorporated a choice of restaurants and bars, a club class lounge and cinemas, coupled with an Internet café and disco designed specifically for teenagers. In announcing the preliminary details of the specification, Carruthers revealed that, with the arrival of the new vessel in 2002, carrying capacity on the Portsmouth-Caen route would rise by 20% for passenger vehicles and 70% for freight, consolidating the

Company's position as the number one operator in both markets. He went on to say that "this vessel we will be the ultimate in cruise ferry design offering passengers the very best of modern sea travel and facilities and comfort. The arrival of the new ship in under two years' time will again take Brittany Ferries to new levels that our rivals will be hard pressed to compete with."

The established fast craft operation of P&O European Ferries' *SuperStar Express* and her replacement the *Portsmouth Express* could no longer be ignored as it was beginning to create a significant niche in the market. There was a need for a defensive move, as fast craft were still not a core part of the strategy and not deemed reliable enough to operate consistently throughout the year on long distance sea crossings. Carruthers and Longden looked for an approach that might allow Brittany Ferries to make a tentative entrance into the market without a major financial commitment to the concept. The solution was elegant and lay close to home. The local team already had a working relationship with Condor, following the sale of BCIF and the subsequent vessel charters and sale of the *Havelet* by Channel Island Ferries. Discussions were opened with Rob Provan of Condor on how the two parties could work together to offer a catamaran service between Poole and Cherbourg and reached a positive conclusion.

In September Brittany Ferries released details of their new joint venture with Condor for a high-speed catamaran service between Poole and Cherbourg, to operate from the 2001 season. The planned service would utilise the two catamarans *Condor Express* and *Condor Vitesse*, which would run on the route in tandem with the *Barfleur*. These Condor-owned craft would be scheduled to cross the Channel in two hours 15 minutes and would feature a new livery representing both companies. The vessels would be manned by Condor crew with Brittany Ferries catering staff on board. Carruthers told the press that "as the number one ferry operator on the western Channel we wanted to align ourselves with the best, most experienced fast craft operator in the UK. We have achieved that came with our proposed new code-share arrangement with Condor. They have a 100% reliability record on their Channel Islands service so I believe our customers who go for speed rather than classic cruise ferry crossings can look forward to an exciting new era in Brittany Ferries services." Provan responded that "the real winner will be the consumer who now has another travel option. Brittany Ferries and Condor will be working together to provide as soon as possible interlining options to both consumers and distributors on all Brittany Ferries and Condor products."

These announcements placed further pressure on P&O to consider options on their Portsmouth-Le Havre route, as the heavy charter costs of the *Pride of Portsmouth* and *Pride of Le Havre* exacerbated the continued operating losses for the company.

The *Val de Loire* experienced engine problems and was taken out of service from 9th September to head to Brest for repairs. The *Bretagne* was transferred to cover her roster from 16th September and was replaced on her Portsmouth-St Malo duties by the *Duc de Normandie*. The *Barfleur* was transferred from Poole to maintain full scheduled operations on the Portsmouth-Caen service, leaving the *Coutances* and *Purbeck* to operate back together on a freight-only operation. The *Val de Loire* resumed normal duties on 27th September. The *Purbeck* remained on the Portsmouth-Caen route for winter.

With the next stage of the fleet strategy now in the process of being delivered, the UK team turned their attention to how additional traffic could be generated to fill the expanding capacity available. Carruthers believed that the future for the holiday business would come from investment in prestige mobile homes, built and fitted out to a high standard. This idea reflected trends in the market. The partnership with Gîtes de France provided Brittany Ferries with unrivalled market knowledge and it was clear that demand had peaked, with a finite number of gîtes available in rural France. The emerging growth in the holiday market was in the mobile home business; these properties were considerably easier to add to the portfolio on specific sites, rather than going through the process of sourcing individually owned properties of a variable quality standard that required constant monitoring to ensure customer expectations were met. Carruthers considered that, if Brittany Ferries invested in a bespoke design of mobile property using the in-house skills of Bernard Bidault for the design, there would be a product consistent with the brand image with controlled quality production standards, available on specially selected sites.

Carruthers went with Xavier Schouller to the national caravan show in Paris and was impressed with the products on offer on the Beneteau stand. The well-known boat builder was adapting to a downturn in demand for their traditional fishing boat products by moving into a new market. They had reviewed the large American business in mobile homes and produced their own prototype design of mobile property which they branded the 'O'Hara'. Discussions with Beneteau suggested that an order for between 600 and 1,000 mobile homes would provide the economies of scale necessary to make this a worthwhile enterprise. This level of inventory would provide a substantial uplift in traffic by selling ferry crossings with Brittany Ferries, whilst giving the Company an asset that could, if required, be sold off at a future date. Such a project needed capital, but there were still sufficient dormant funds available from the Channel Island Ferries investment to be able to deliver this, without any requirement for French financial input. The mobile homes could be built in France by Beneteau and provide a long-term income stream for the Company.

Schouller and another VSME secondee visited holiday camp sites in France to gauge owners' appetite for the potential new product, explaining that this 'Club Class' mobile home required no capital input from the site owner; the reaction was lukewarm, as the site owners felt they would only get a limited rental income from the product. Meanwhile, the Beneteau team were impressed by their initial contact with Bidault, and the company CEO met with Alexis Gourvennec to talk through the project.

The project was approved by Directeur Général Jean-Michel Masson and worked up in detail with chief financial officer Michel Maraval; there was a common recognition that the holiday business had to expand to help provide the necessary growth in the passenger market. The gîte market could no longer be relied upon to generate growing passenger volumes, as market tastes were changing. Whilst there would need to be a financial guarantee from the parent Company, the cash was available from non-French accounts and Brittany Ferries would own a substantial asset at the end of the transaction. But Maraval became increasingly concerned that any requirement for Brittany Ferries funds would detract from the money available for fleet investment, and he believed that all the Company's access to credit was needed to sustain the ships. He disagreed with Masson about the importance of the investment and made his thoughts plain to Gourvennec.

On 5th September Masson announced that he was leaving Brittany Ferries after just over 18 months in the Directeur Général post. He had helped set the Company on the right track to overcome its financial issues and was leaving the operation in positive financial health. Explaining his departure, Masson said that "different analyses have emerged between the president and myself on certain strategic directions" for the Company. The French press reported talk of incompatibility of approach between the two men. Gourvennec was still driven by the interests of the agricultural co-operative shareholders of Finistère. Masson was popular with the UK team and his departure was much regretted. The trade unions expressed confidence about the future of the company in his absence, but a member of the Works Council noted that his resignation "comes at a time when we were to start negotiations on the application of the 35 hour week, which will unfortunately be postponed."

Masson was replaced by Maraval. Hinting at the tensions that external appointments could bring, Maraval noted in an interview that "we draw our leadership from within the company. There is a real corporate culture here, which makes it difficult for outside employees to understand."

When Maraval took the mobile home proposal to Gourvennec he was dismissive based on their earlier conversations, and repeated concerns that the project would absorb Brittany Ferries' credit with the funding banks. Furthermore, he saw the Company's ownership of mobile home properties as being in conflict with the shareholders' interest, as many of them were active participants in the gîte market. The proposal was rejected. This was a fundamental disagreement with the strategy developed by the UK team to continue to grow the business in anticipation of enhanced capacity.

Carruthers had arranged his affairs so that he could retire early, and now felt that the time was right to move on, as Gourvennec did not agree with this strategic proposal. In October, he gave a presentation to the Board on the next steps for the UK business, and after the meeting told Gourvennec of his intention to leave Brittany Ferries after 19 years driving the strategy from the UK. He proposed an orderly transition over the following three months so that he could leave in January 2001, with Longden taking over his role. His resignation was accepted by Gourvennec, and the handover arrangements were agreed as proposed. All Carruthers asked from the Company was a 'really good' party in Poole to mark his departure. This duly took place in December. He left to work with his wife Pat to develop her French property business and pursue a number of charitable interests.

Brittany Ferries made a small profit in 1999/00; this would have been significantly better if there had not been pollution from the *Erika* in December 1999. An outbreak of foot and mouth disease, which inhibited livestock movements, was another factor in the results. The Company's market share in the western Channel sector grew further to 52.6% of the passenger business and 57.7% of freight movements. Although the number of passengers carried fell slightly to 2,477,260, and there was a a similar drop in vehicle carryings to 657,404, freight shipments recovered to 175,315 units. P&O Portsmouth ended the year reporting a loss of £13.9 million, with turnover reducing by over £2 million to £98.6 million.

Longden took over the role of UK General Manager from Carruthers in January 2001. The two had long enjoyed a healthily competitive relationship, based on their mutual background as Scots and their training with both the Hertz and Heron organisations. Their joint management style encouraged debate within the UK arm of Brittany Ferries, and created an atmosphere where individual contributions were encouraged, and disagreement was not seen as career threatening. Whether they were a senior manager of the Company or marshalling vehicles on the quay, everyone had a chance to have their say. As with any company, there were often disagreements within the UK team and between the UK team and their colleagues in France, but these arguments were generally resolved without rancour to reach the right conclusion for the benefit of Brittany Ferries. The teams on both sides of the Channel were lean throughout Brittany Ferries' history, with only a comparatively small number involved in navigating and driving the Company. This enabled nimbleness of action and a clarity in local decision making that was absent in competing ferry companies.

Inevitably the character of the Company changed when Carruthers left. The creative duopoly with Longden, that saw two strong characters bounce ideas off each other and test them to destruction until the right idea became obvious, was lost. When the two came together in 1981, the Company was in deep financial trouble, nearly bankrupt with a collection of misfit vessels that could not be branded a credible fleet. They each made the commitment to make their living from the enterprise and set about putting things right. The following two decades demonstrated the effectiveness of their partnership. There was a common shared purpose as they transformed the Company from a regional cause fighting almost everyone for survival, to a holistic brand with a high-quality market-leading product. From the outset, Brittany Ferries was not a 'hire and fire' company. If someone who had been hired failed to reach their potential, then every effort would be made to help them achieve it. There was little difference in the management approaches of Carruthers and Longden. They were different personalities with complementary styles, and they made a very effective partnership. The combination of two articulate independent brains drove the strategy by eloquently putting the case for the incremental expansion of the Company. This balance changed when Carruthers left and Longden was left without a sounding board in the UK.

The structure in the UK was now well established. The Plymouth office did the UK accounting, managed information technology and ultimately, all the reservations, in the days before much of this activity transferred to the internet. The freight operations were managed from Poole, whilst the holiday business was the preserve of the Portsmouth team. Brittany Ferries did not employ a sales force; there was a strong belief that the only weapon available in a ferry company's sales force armoury was to offer to reduce prices, and this was not the way Brittany Ferries sought to transact business. Longden repeatedly told P&O's Graeme Dunlop that the biggest improvement he could make to his business was to take away the car keys from the sales force and pay them to stay at home. The Brittany Ferries marketing department was small, and the advertising agency provided much of the support work. Agencies were used to undertake tasks like placing brochure displays in travel agents. The number of staff in the UK peaked in the mid-1990s at around 500-550 people; many of these were seasonal staff as their employment could not be justified on a year-round basis.

The *Bretagne* underwent a major refit for the fitting of sponsons to her hull between 4th January and 8th March 2001 to allow her to meet new SOLAS regulations. The Plymouth-Santander route was re-started with the *Val de Loire* on 14th March, following the re-opening of the Cork-Roscoff service from 9th March.

The keel for the Company's new Portsmouth-Caen vessel was laid down at the Van der Giessen shipyard in Rotterdam on 7th June and her name was revealed to be the *Mont St Michel*, after the famous landmark in Brittany. The name of the ship had proved difficult to find. The project was initially codenamed *Normandie 2*, as the vessel would be a running mate to the *Normandie*; *Deauville* and *Honfleur* were other options considered for the name, before the team settled on the *Mont St Michel.* The design incorporated many similar aspects to the *Normandie's* general arrangement for her accommodation decks, so that the pair of vessels operating on the same route would offer similar characteristics, thereby simplifying their operation. However, learning lessons from the *Normandie's* design, the *Mont St Michel* differed in having twin funnel casings, which optimised capacity on the vehicle deck.

The role of the *Purbeck* in helping to expand freight carryings provided further justification for the impending arrival; traffic grew by 20% following the addition of the chartered vessel to the fleet in Spring 2000, at a time when the market was stagnant elsewhere. The *Mont St Michel* would bring a further 70% uplift in freight capacity, equal to the combined freight capacity of the *Duc de Normandie* and the *Normandie*. Freight Director Clarke noted that Brittany Ferries 'Central Channel services' benefited those hauliers who appreciated the increased capacity on the right route and the important mileage and fuel savings that could be made by using the services.

The *Condor Vitesse's* inaugural summer operating season ran from 22nd May to 30th September. This was a shorter season than that offered by the *Portsmouth Express*, but allowed the Company to benefit from the experience of a peak season addition to the roster. The fast craft departed from Poole at 07:30 and returned from Cherbourg at 11:30, thereby allowing her to be utilised on a return crossing from Poole to the Channel Islands for Condor in the afternoon. The return crossing from Cherbourg was timed earlier than optimal, but the combination of departures offered by the *Condor Vitesse* and *Barfleur* opened up new excursion opportunities.

In May 2001 the European Commission finally reached a decision in their investigation into the challenge by P&O European Ferries to the alleged state aid to Brittany Ferries.

The Commission found in favour of Brittany Ferries. The report noted that rental charges made by the SEMs were not below market rates. An estimate of the annual bareboat charter rates for the fleet was provided to the Commission by BRAX Shipping and Brittany Ferries. This indicated the annual charter rates to Brittany Ferries for the Sabemen vessels were $9 million for the *Val de Loire,* $7 million for the *Bretagne* and $3 million for the *Quiberon.* Senacal's *Normandie* was chartered at $8 million annually and the *Duc de Normandie* at $4 million, whilst Senamanche's *Barfleur* was chartered at $7 million per annum. In comparison, P&O Portsmouth chartered the *Pride of Bilbao* for $13.1 million annually and the *Pride of Le Havre* and *Pride of Portsmouth* for an annual charge of $9.1 million each.

Whilst P&O Portsmouth achieved record spring carryings during May – a 14.5% year

A view of Roscoff with the Brittany Ferries offices in the foreground. *(Ferry Publications Library)*

on year increase, with the Portsmouth-Bilbao route some 7.5% up - the fast craft *Portsmouth Express* had a difficult time, with a large number of technical problems disrupting sailings across May; the vessel was forced to head for dry dock repairs on two occasions. There was considerable speculation as to what the company's next moves would be, with the charter of the two 'Olau' ships on the Portsmouth-Le Havre route due to expire at the end of 2001. The *Pride of Cherbourg* and *Pride of Hampshire* on the Portsmouth-Cherbourg route also faced limited future employment as they did not meet all the SOLAS regulations which determined that the pair would have to be withdrawn at the end of October 2002 or operate with a much reduced passenger certificate.

Brittany Ferries' crews took part in industrial action over four days in May in a protracted dispute about pay and conditions. Services were further disrupted later in the year by a strike of all French Transport workers in the CGT and CFDT unions on 24th and 25th October. The *Normandie, Duc de Normandie* and *Barfleur* each lost a round trip but the *Bretagne* was unaffected.

The *Val de Loire* was amongst the potential targets being lined up by a two-man Euskadi Ta Askatasuna (ETA) terrorist bombing team that was arrested by Spanish police in Mondragon in June. Security chiefs believed the group planned to terrorise British holidaymakers by bombing the *Val de Loire* and selected popular hotels. The team had maps of Santander in their possession together with details of the sailing schedule of the *Val de Loire*, along with 35kg of dynamite. The bomb was later defused. Their alleged plan was to drive a car laden with explosives onto the *Val de Loire* and then issue a warning to

The *Mont St Michel* takes shape at the Van der Giessen de Noord shipyard in Rotterdam. *(Ferry Publications Library)*

allow the vessel to be evacuated before an explosion was triggered. A similar attack planned for a vessel sailing to Ibiza had to be abandoned when the terrorists' car broke down in the Pyrenees. Brittany Ferries' spokeswoman Sarah Hurley expressed the commonly held view that the Company was glad that the terrorists had been caught.

In September, Brittany Ferries launched a Privilege Card which could be purchased for £7 and entitled the holder to 20% discounts on hotel rooms and 10% on restaurant bills.

Passenger figures increased by 1.4% in the year to 30th September 2001 to reach 2,581,257, vehicle volumes grew to 688,215, but freight units fell to 168,536. "The return to profit was made in 2001 thanks to a drastic policy of savings and productivity improvements with the withdrawal of a ship from the fleet whilst traffic remained on the rise," explained Maraval at the AGM. The performance of the Poole-Cherbourg fast craft operation exceeded expectations, encouraging the company to retain the chartered service for the 2002 season. P&O Portsmouth grew their carryings to 1.98 million passengers but reported that their freight volumes were depressed. The company's financial performance improved marginally, but annual losses on their services still totalled £9.3 million.

Brittany Ferries was again voted Best Cross-Channel Ferry Operator in a Daily Telegraph poll of readers at the end of 2001, reflecting the Company's continued strong position in the market. The outlook for their main competitor was much worse.

The relationship with advertising agency Banks, Hoggins, O'Shea did not work out as

The launch of the *Mont St Michel* was delayed by issues at the shipyard until 15th March 1992. *(Ferry Publications Library)*

well as expected, as so much of the support activity needed by the Company in the UK involved the minutiae of brochure production, in which Rook Dunning had previously excelled, rather than glossy mainstream advertising. The culture of a large agency proved incompatible with that of an organisation the size of Brittany Ferries, and the cost were soon found to be considerably higher than those of the BCB era. The advertising account was again put up for review during the winter of 2001/2, this time including the public relations elements of the communication campaign in the UK. Toby Oliver had enjoyed a remarkable 28-year tenure with the Company and now held the title of Public Affairs Director, but the corporate desire for new blood and fresh thinking brought one of the longest standing and most productive client-consultancy relationships to an end.

This time the review focused on selecting an agency that could demonstrate cultural synergy and experience in the ferry sector. The Bournemouth-based Walker Agency was already working with the smaller budgets of Condor Ferries, and Brittany Ferries' fast craft partner was able to vouch for their competence. Walker proposed to subcontract brochure production to another specialist Bournemouth-based company – Ayleworth Fleming – to overcome the difficulties that had been experienced with Banks, Hoggins, O'Shea. This approach acknowledged the specialist expertise necessary in this area of business. The Walker Agency were selected to lead on advertising and brochure production, supported by Brighter PR, who brought Stephen Tuckwell to add communications expertise. The brief to the new agency was updated to reflect a focus on routes, experience, value, and choice, and the Walker Agency became a productive partner of the business in the UK.

The creative brief also encompassed establishing a presence on the nascent internet, the development of which held considerable attraction for the UK team, who quickly identified the opportunities that a web presence would bring. Specialist resource was brought in to handle the technicalities of web development, search engine optimisation, and all the minutiae of a strong internet site. Visibility of the website was enhanced by the gradual addition of '.COM' to the Company name branding on the fleet, although this followed extensive argument with colleagues in France, who resisted the move.

With the *Mont St Michel* project well under way, the team considered the next phase of the fleet renewal programme. The balance of capacity on the Portsmouth-Caen route would be resolved by the arrival of the new vessel, so attention turned to how other routes could be better served. A new Plymouth-based vessel for the Santander and Cork services would provide additional capacity to expand these markets whilst allowing the *Val de Loire* to be transferred to partner the *Bretagne* on the Portsmouth-St Malo route. The project was codenamed '*Bretagne 2*'.

The '*Bretagne 2*' project came to fruition on 22nd February 2002, when Brittany Ferries placed an order for the first northern European car ferry to feature cruise ship facilities including a swimming pool and cabins with either balconies or terraces. The contract for the 40,589 gross-tonne vessel was awarded to the Meyer Werft shipyard on the River Ems at Papenburg, despite pressure from trade unions in France. Alexis Gourvennec observed that Meyer Werft had been selected on their ability to meet cost and delivery date criteria, but the trade union representatives queried the €165 million ($151 million) contract price. Chantiers de l'Atlantique was unable to meet the delivery deadline, with their workload commitments to build the *Queen Mary 2* for Cunard preventing them being able to deliver a new vessel before April 2004. 25% of the cost of the new vessel was to be paid by Sabemen, with the remainder provided on the French Tax Break provisions by a banking pool, which included Crédit Agricole Indosuez, BNP Paribas, Crédit Cooperatif, Crédit Industriel de l'Ouest and Germany's KVF.

David Longden said "the arrival of two ships (including the *Mont St Michel*, which is due to into service this September) in the next 24 months will take ferry travel onto an even higher level in comfort, quality and value for money which our competitors will find it hard to match. This new building confirms Brittany Ferries' total confidence in the future of ferry travel." To be called *Pont Aven*, after the town in western Brittany, she would replace the *Val de Loire* on Spanish, French and Irish routes, allowing her to be deployed on the Portsmouth-St Malo operation. Brittany Ferries hoped that the *Pont Aven* would increase Plymouth-Roscoff carryings by up to 100,000 additional passengers each year.

The design of the vessel reflected the combined efforts of Brittany Ferries, Meyer Werft, Deltamarin and AIA to produce a distinctive answer to the challenges of operating to Santander. Maraval was heavily involved in the concept design, seeking to create a vessel that would take the quality of the Spanish route to a different level. The *Pont Aven* would feature a radical new hull form adapted to Bay of Biscay conditions, with a highly curved forward superstructure, a long and low hull and an angular stern. Her design accommodated 2,415 passengers, 650 cars or up to 85 lorries, with 650 cabins across eight different grades. With a length of 184.3 metres and a 31-metre-beam, and a service speed of 27 knots she was capable of reducing the 24-hour crossing time between Plymouth and Santander to under 20 hours from Spring 2004.

However, a fast ship of this specification would be expensive to operate, and there were internal concerns about the size of the passenger market for such a vessel and its flexibility of operation between routes. A faster and more weather-resilient crossing to Spain or France would not deliver a premium on the existing levels of fares, even though fuel and operating costs would be higher; passengers were already paying proportionately higher rates for the longer crossings. And Maraval was concerned that

The *Mont St Michel* undergoing sea trials prior to handover to Brittany Ferries. *(Ferry Publications Library)*

the innovative hull form would cause the vessel to 'squat' in shallow water, so unable to take full advantage of her speed if she was utilised in the future for a rapid daytime crossing on the Portsmouth-St Malo service.

Meanwhile, the *Mont St Michel* was launched at the Van der Giessen de Noord shipyard in Rotterdam at 07:00 on 15th March 2002, but her delivery date was slipping beyond the original planned peak season introduction date of 5th July. The shipyard had produced an over-competitive bid and encountered significant financial problems during the construction phase, requiring refinancing of the business and the installation of a new management team. The delays forced a shuffling of vessel deployment, with the *Quiberon* (which would have been laid up if the *Mont St Michel* arrived as planned) moving to Portsmouth after her first sailing from Caen on 10th July, having sailed from Plymouth to

Caen that morning. The *Duc de Normandie* made the reverse move the previous day to take up station on the Plymouth-Roscoff route and offer an increase in capacity of 15% for passengers and 17% for vehicles on the service compared to the *Quiberon*. The *Quiberon* and *Normandie* soon settled into their new sailing pattern. For the winter, the *Val de Loire* and *Bretagne* had operated on the Portsmouth-St Malo route, with the former also undertaking a St Malo-Plymouth-Cherbourg schedule. The *Duc de Normandie* remained on the Plymouth-Roscoff service. The *Quiberon* and *Normandie* were to maintain the service until the *Mont St Michel* was delivered, when it was planned that the *Quiberon* would be sold.

In an effort to resolve their problems with the *Pride of Cherbourg* and *Pride of Hampshire*, P&O Portsmouth announced the charter of the *Isle of Innisfree* from Irish Continental Line for the 2002 season, on the back of improvements in carryings of both passengers (+8.1%) and vehicles (+6.5%) on their Portsmouth-Cherbourg route in 2001. The introduction of the *Isle of Innisfree* would bring capacity for 1,650 passengers and 600 vehicles, a significant expansion on that offered by the existing Super Viking fleet. The company also extended the charter of *Pride of Bilbao* from Irish Continental Line by a further five years; the combination of the two charters was worth £70 million to Irish Continental Line. P&O Portsmouth confidently predicted a strong season for 2002.

The *Condor Vitesse* returned to Poole in May, offering a 135-minute crossing to Cherbourg, the fastest crossing on the western Channel. With schedules operating in conjunction with the *Barfleur*, passengers could take an early morning crossing aboard the *Condor Vitesse* and enjoy a full day in Cherbourg or on the Cotentin peninsula before returning to Poole on the evening sailing of the *Barfleur*.

P&O Portsmouth retained their fast craft *Portsmouth Express,* which returned to traffic on 17th April and offered up to three daily return crossings between Portsmouth and Cherbourg. On 17th June the company extended the charter of the *Pride of Le Havre* and *Pride of Portsmouth* from TT-Line by a further five years at a reduced rate. P&O Portsmouth rationalised their fleet by selling the *Pride of Hampshire* and *Pride of Cherbourg* to El Salam Maritime in advance of their replacement by the *Isle of Innisfree*, which was now renamed the *Pride of Cherbourg*. The new *Pride of Cherbourg* entered service on 12th September 2002 after an extensive refit, and became the sole vessel on the route from 1st October. The company again experienced numerous technical problems with the fast craft *Portsmouth Express,* and although she was withdrawn for crankshaft repairs in mid-July, she remained plagued by problems through the rest of the summer.

The P&O Group announced their intention to buy out Stena Line's interest in the P&O Stena Line joint venture in April 2002, some four years after the business had commenced. The transaction was completed in August and the new operation was rebranded P&O Ferries. The company moved quickly to consolidate the Group's widespread ferry interests, and on 16th October, the management of the western Channel routes was transferred from Portsmouth to Dover, with the P&O Portsmouth services rebranded as a P&O Ferries operation in line with the rest of the Group. There were significant redundancies amongst the team in Portsmouth, and the office at Peninsular House was closed.

Readers of the Daily Telegraph again voted Brittany Ferries the Best Cross-Channel operator in their annual survey. Longden said 'this is an important achievement for us as we are continually upgrading our product to meet customers' expectations. It is even more satisfactory as it is the actual travelling public, the readers of the paper, who have voted for Brittany Ferries, so our efforts are being recognised."

The *Mont St Michel* was finally handed over to Brittany Ferries on 11th December and she entered service between Caen and Portsmouth on 20th December. She could accommodate 2,140 passengers, with accommodation for 808 in cabins, together with 600 cars or 180 freight vehicles. Her interior matched the standards of her predecessors.

The central feature was a grand staircase rising through the centre of three decks. She boasted three dining options on the restaurant deck, including a gastrodôme with an à la carte restaurant and a second gourmet restaurant on the port side. The restaurant was decorated with tableaux by Cathy Banneville and Patrick Serc comprising text and images depicting imaginary sea voyages. The cafeteria was adorned with artwork by Yvonne Guégan, Aldo Paolucci, and Franch Vaucelles. Unusually the vessel featured a delicatessen selling Breton produce. At the stern Bernard Bidault created a small club library meeting room; this was truly a class apart from its competitors.

The vessel was built to an extremely high standard and fulfilled all the original design criteria. However, the difficult fit-out not only extended the delivery date for the vessel, but also contributed to severe financial difficulties for the Van der Giessen de Noord

The *Mont St Michel* arrives in Ouistreham for the first time, prior to taking up her first sailing on 20th December 2002. *(Ferry Publications Library)*

shipyard, which went into administration shortly after delivery of the *Mont St Michel*.

With the arrival of the *Mont St Michel, the* veteran *Quiberon* was now surplus to requirements, and she undertook her final Portsmouth-Caen sailing on 20th December before being laid up. She later headed to Brest for an extensive refit after being sold to Medmar/Linee Lauro; she left Brest on 14th May 2003 sailing as the *Giulia d'Abundo*.

With sales of €322.3 million and a net profit of more than €13 million achieved in 2002, Brittany Ferries was able to celebrate passenger traffic up by 4% to reach 2,670,363, with vehicles rising to 718,328 and freight units reaching 170,352. P&O Ferries saw their western Channel losses escalate to £23.4 million after tax, despite turnover rising by £24.5 million to £134.3 million.

Above: **The 'Les Romantiques' restaurant on the *Mont St Michel*.** *(Ferry Publications Library)*

Below: **The elegance of the design and fittings of the grand staircase on the *Mont St Michel* made an immediate positive impression.** *(Ferry Publications Library)*

The keel of the *Pont Aven* was laid at the Meyer Werft shipyard in Papenburg on 9th April 2003 and building proceeded quickly in anticipation of delivery in spring 2004. There were suggestions that, running at full speed, she would be capable of reducing the Plymouth-Santander passage time from 24 to 18 hours, the Plymouth-Roscoff timing by one hour and the Cork-Roscoff schedule by two hours, from 13 hours to eleven.

With the planned arrival of the *Pont Aven*, Brittany Ferries contemplated an ambitious new Portsmouth-Cherbourg route to be operated by the *Bretagne* and the *Val de Loire*, linked to their St Malo crossings. Each vessel would undertake an overnight sailing on the St Malo route, with the vessel arriving in St Malo laying over until the following evening, and the Portsmouth vessel undertaking a daytime return crossing to Cherbourg. This would capitalise on the reduction in the number of crossings offered by P&O Ferries following the introduction of the *Pride of Cherbourg*, and apply further pressure to their deteriorating finances. After planning the service and reviewing the operational consequences, it was considered that this concept stretched resources too much if operated throughout the season. Instead, the team determined that the *Bretagne* would open a new Portsmouth-Cherbourg service from 2004, in competition with P&O's *Pride of Cherbourg* and *Express*. If this route proved to be a success, there was an option to build a second *Mont St Michel* and re-allocate the *Normandie* to the Portsmouth-Cherbourg route.

The agreement with Condor for the operation of the *Condor Vitesse* on the Poole-Cherbourg service was renewed for another season, with the schedules again seeing her operate alongside the *Barfleur*.

P&O Ferries' *Express* continued to be plagued by engine problems including a cracked gearbox casing, despite undergoing an extensive refit and engine overhaul during the winter. The P&O fast craft service was suspended from late April until mid-May. Some £3 million was spent on refitting the *Pride of Bilbao* to create two new restaurants. The *P&O Express* suffered three bouts of further technical problems on the Portsmouth-Cherbourg service during the season and was withdrawn from operations earlier than planned in mid-September. The problems were said to have arisen from the intensive use of the craft during the winter months.

The *Pont Aven* was floated out at Meyer Werft on Saturday 13th September, when Gourvennec, Michel Maraval, and Henri-Jean Lebeau, jointly pressed the button to open the dock gate valves and admit 100 million litres of water into the building dock. She was then moved within the shipyard's covered building dock to be made ready for engine trials and final outfitting. Around one-third of the prefabricated cabins that were being built by G+H PreCab in Papenburg had already been installed on the ship at this time, with interior accommodation outfitting still to be completed before final delivery.

Meanwhile, the *Mont St Michel* won the prestigious 2003 Shippax award for the best restaurant. The judges' citation noted that "Themed on France's romantic authors and their literature, 'Les Romantiques' is a remarkable and diverse dining experience with a sophisticated atmosphere. Its 20-seat "table d'hotês" and "comptoir des saveurs" menu quite literally give an outstanding gastronomic first and last impression of France on the Channel crossing." This was just reward for the confidence placed by the Serestel team in delivering a quality on board product.

On 18th September plans were announced by freight operator Channel Freight Ferries to operate a new route from Southampton to RadicateI, Rouen from January 2004. New purpose-built berths would need to be to be constructed, and there were plans for the new operation to accommodate two vessels, each with capacity for 100 freight units. An overnight passage would be offered in each direction with a crossing time of nine hours. Channel Freight Ferries planned to operate day sailings from September 2004.

Brittany Ferries announced a ban on young children in reclining seat areas on board the fleet, prompted by examples of bad behaviour from uncontrolled infants. This drew criticism from parent groups but was welcomed by many passengers.

Above: **The port side arcade on the *Mont St Michel*, viewed from the upper level of the grand staircase.** *(Ferry Publications Library)*

Below: **The *Mont St Michel* quickly settled into the routine sailings of the Portsmouth-Caen route.** *(Miles Cowsill)*

Above: **The early stages of construction of the stern of the *Pont Aven* at the Meyer Werft shipyard in Germany.** *(Brian D Smith)*

Below: **The bridge section of the *Pont Aven* under construction independently from her hull.** *(Brian D Smith)*

In the final settlement of the European Commission ruling on the Brittany Ferries challenge to the support given to P&O Ferries by the district council of Vizcaya, the company was required to pay back £4.1m to return the payment made to the company when the Portsmouth-Bilbao route was set up in 1994. This one-off payment added to the losses of the western Channel operation, and the year ended with a reported loss of £11.8 million, following a £12 million drop in revenue. This continued pattern of losses did not deter the new Dover-based management team, who announced plans to operate a new fast craft service between Portsmouth and Caen (Ouistreham) from 2nd April to 30th September 2004, using the 91-metre long Incat fast craft *Max Mols*, which would be renamed the *Caen Express*.

The *Normandie Express* was Brittany Ferries first foray into the direct operation of fast craft. *(Miles Cowsill)*

The new service came as a surprise to the Brittany Ferries team, as although the Caennaise had expressed an interest in the operation of fast craft to their port, they were determined that the operator should take the risk on the service, and were not minded to provide any financial support. The initiative was seen as a response to the Brittany Ferries service to Cherbourg. The *Caen Express* had capacity for 800 passengers and 220 cars and was to be manned by Danish officers and P&O Ferries' catering staff. With a passage time of 3hrs 25mins, she would depart daily from Portsmouth at 06:45 and 15:20, and return at 12:00 and 20:30. The *Express* was renamed *Cherbourg Express* and laid over during the winter to start services from 2nd April. The *Pride of Cherbourg* underwent an extensive refit in January, but her cabin accommodation was not expanded.

The *Pont Aven* left the Papenburg shipyard for sea trials ahead of schedule on 7th

February 2004 and sailed for fitting out at Eemshaven before her handover to Brittany Ferries on 27th February. She then headed for Roscoff, pausing to call in Ouistreham during the journey, and arriving on 2nd March to undertake berthing trials, further fitting out, staff training and her christening ceremony. Her facilities quickly impressed. AIA were heavily involved with the design of her interior from the start, with Bernard Bidault, Jean-Hubert Mignot and Luc Millequant determining the appropriate décor for each of the passenger spaces on the vessel. The result was a carefully muted use of light and colour to create an ambience consistent with her deployment on the lengthy crossings to Spain. The abstract work of renowned Breton artist François Dilasser was used to decorate the vessel, with much use of natural light to create an internal feeling of spaciousness. The central feature of an atrium spanning four decks became the focal point for the passenger facilities. Cabin accommodation was spread across Deck 5, 6 and 8, with the Commodore Class accommodation on the highest level. Deck 7 hosted a range of dining opportunities from the viennoiserie 'Le Café du Festival' with views over

David Longden

the bow of the ship , to the self-service restaurant 'La Belle Angèle' with flamenco sculptures by Gérard Venturelli, the 'Fastnet' piano bar and the à la cart restaurant 'La Flora' in the stern which took full advantage of picture windows on three sides, and was decorated in Art Nouveau style. The comprehensive retail area 'La Boutique' was situated on Deck 8, with the two-deck show lounge 'Le Grand Pavois' forward of this. There were extensive outdoor areas, which included the Les Finstères swimming pool with a nautical theme, which celebrated the Breton, Spanish, British and Irish bagpipes, representing the links between the cultures of the destinations served by the *Pont Aven*.

The *Pont Aven* visited Plymouth on 17th March and commenced her service life with the 23:15 Roscoff-Plymouth sailing on 23rd March. Her first departure from Plymouth to Santander took place the following day, and her accelerated compromise of a 23-hour passage schedule commenced from 4th April. This added resilience to the service without incurring the higher fuel consumption of the dramatically quicker schedule that had initially been proposed. The power was there in reserve if needed to recover the timetable. The *Pont Aven* was presented to invited guests with a special overnight reception in Plymouth on 6th April. The new midweek Monday-Thursday schedule on the Portsmouth-Cherbourg route was inaugurated with the *Val de Loire* on 5th April. This service was fitted around the St Malo timetable, with the morning arrival in Portsmouth rescheduled to 05:30 to accommodate the additional daytime round trip in a short-term implementation of the earlier plan. The *Bretagne* took over this service during the peak season.

Early bookings for P&O Ferries' *Caen Express* proved promising, and Brittany Ferries now faced direct competition on a parallel service for the first time. The inaugural P&O Ferries' sailing from Portsmouth arrived in Ouistreham on 3rd April with 104 vehicles and 319 passengers, taking on a pilot and using the No 1 berth formerly occupied by *Duc de Normandie*. Her arrival prompted further widespread speculation about the future of the two 'Olau' vessels, but P&O Ferries pledged their commitment to the continued operation on the Portsmouth-Le Havre route, as well as that of the Portsmouth-Bilbao service. More widely, the P&O Group began a comprehensive review of its portfolio of routes and fleet.

P&O Ferries carried 8,000 passengers during the first three weeks of operation of the *Caen Express*, with 60,000 passengers transported by the end of June. Whilst this was essentially a new product in the market, there was some abstraction of traffic from Brittany Ferries evident across several routes, and the team began to consider their response.

The summer of 2004 was again noted for dramatic fare reductions on the short-sea sector. Eurotunnel reduced its lead-in return fare from £239 to £100 from 28th May, with P&O Ferries following with a drop from £282.48 to £229.68. Hoverspeed introduced a £49 one-way fare and SeaFrance, which reported losses of £1.63 million in 2003 following profits of £9.88 million in 2002, offered return Dover-Calais crossings from £95 for a car and five passengers. Brittany Ferries trimmed the Portsmouth-Caen fare slightly in response, from £554 in the Spring to £534 at the end of June.

The *Coutances* went for refit in Gdansk from 2nd to 26th August and returned in her new Brittany Ferries livery.

The *Pont Aven* lost two weeks of operation in August after a faulty valve allowed 1,200 tonnes of seawater to flood the auxiliary engine room. The incident happened at Plymouth on 10th August following completion of an inbound trip from Santander, when the sea water gate valve failed during a routine filter change. Such was the ingress of water that a marine services tug had to be summoned to pump out the affected space in the vessel. Devon Fire and Rescue also assisted with the pumping operation from the quay. Fully booked return trips to Santander and Roscoff, and the weekend sailings between Roscoff and Cork all had to be cancelled. The *Duc de Normandie* was be diverted to Poole whilst the stricken *Pont Aven* blocked her access to the linkspan in Plymouth. Losses to the Company were said to exceed £6 million following this incident, and Brittany Ferries sought compensation from Meyer Werft. The *Pont Aven* was sent across to Brest for repairs; she headed back to Plymouth from the shipyard but two of her four generators failed shortly after leaving Brest, forcing her to be sent back for further repairs. She returned to service to operate at a reduced speed, but was withdrawn again after two days for further works.

The *Pont Aven* was allocated to the Portsmouth-St Malo route for the winter and, whilst there was resistance to the switch from Plymouth, the move to Portsmouth was a good one for business. But the *Pont Aven* was forced to operate as a stern loading vessel, when further problems required her bow door to be welded shut. She was again withdrawn from service on 18th November following a further series of technical problems, and headed to Dunkirk for drydocking and replacement of her damaged alternators. The problems were resolved during her refit, which allowed the *Pont Aven* to operate normally from the New Year.

On 26th September officers and crew on the *Duc de Normandie* received notice that the vessel was to be laid up and offered for sale. She completed her last sailing on the Plymouth-Roscoff route on 30th September and sailed to Ouistreham to discharge. The *Duc de Normandie* was then laid up in Caen, before returning to Portsmouth on 17th November and then heading to the Gdansk shipyard for the fitting of a new sprinkler system, prior to a potential sale.

As the summer progressed it became increasingly obvious that P&O Ferries was still struggling to find a formula to turn around the financial performance of the two 'Olau' vessels on the Portsmouth-Le Havre route. Unlike Brittany Ferries' fleet on the Portsmouth-Caen service, the *Pride of Portsmouth* and *Pride of Le Havre* had been acquired out of necessity rather than being purpose-built for the route. Their high charter costs and general unsuitability for day crossings, coupled with the deteriorating competitive situation of the parent company on the short-sea routes, placed P&O Ferries'

Above: The *Pont Aven* heads slowly down the River Ems after leaving the Meyer Werft shipyard. *(Miles Cowsill)*

Below: The distinctive profile of the *Pont Aven* makes her ideally suited to sea conditions in the Bay of Biscay. *(FotoFlite)*

Above: **The nautically themed Les Finstères swimming pool celebrates cultural links between destinations served by the *Pont Aven*.** *(Ferry Publications Library)*

Below: **Le Grand Pavois bar on board the *Pont Aven*.** *(Ferry Publications Library)*

finances under pressure. 'The Times' reported that P&O Ferries' pricing strategy on the western Channel had been suicidal, with some crossings to Le Havre and Cherbourg being offered for £100 compared to brochure fares in excess of £500.

There was sufficient business to sustain one profitable operator on the western Channel, but competition between two companies as well against other cross-Channel sectors and Eurotunnel, and the growing business for low cost airlines was making it a tough business for both. Formal discussions were initiated with Brittany Ferries by P&O Ferries to explore options that would allow the Dover-managed company to exit the western Channel market to France. Brittany Ferries were keen to see greater price stability in the market, and recognised that the reduction in capacity would produce a more stable business. Longden considered that it might be possible to absorb the charters of the two 'Olau' vessels within the Brittany Ferries structure, supported by the transfer of crew and staff needed for their operation. They could be redeployed more effectively elsewhere within the Brittany Ferries portfolio of routes. He felt positively that this was the right way forward.

As the discussions progressed so P&O Ferries' enthusiasm for the transaction grew, and the cost of Brittany Ferries acquiring the operation fell. The two sides met for dinner in the art deco Hotel Georges V, just off the Champs-Elysees in Paris in an attempt to seal a deal. P&O Group chairman Lord Sterling flew over from London with his entourage in the corporate helicopter and proceed to try and seduce Gourvennec with a lavish meal accompanied by the finest wines the Michelin starred restaurant had to offer. Longden was concerned that the most lavish meal of his life did not end up on his expenses... This was a surreal situation for Gourvennec; his Breton enterprise, that had begun to such ridicule from established ferry operators, was now being courted by one of the biggest names in world shipping wishing to divest itself of its competing operations. The 'paper tiger' was now pulling the strings. P&O Ferries' western Channel business was eventually offered to Brittany Ferries for €1, with the costs of a further six-month charter of the two 'Olau' ships also covered. But there were still significant issues on pension obligations and the TUPE (Transfer of Undertakings Protection of Employment) legislation, which would safeguard the employment conditions of the former P&O staff, that needed to be resolved. Gourvennec remained highly enthusiastic about the transaction and a memorandum of understanding was drawn up between the parties.

Whilst the negotiations continued, P&O Ferries announced the conclusions of their detailed and wide-ranging business review on 28th September. Their proposal reduced the P&O Ferries fleet from 31 to 23 vessels, closed four of its 13 routes, and cut the workforce by 1,200 jobs, with a further 350 roles transferred within the Group. It was expected to benefit the Group operating result by £55 million a year. In the Western Channel, P&O Ferries announced plans to close the routes from Portsmouth to Le Havre, Caen and Cherbourg, and from Rosslare to Cherbourg, with the *Pride of Cherbourg*, *Cherbourg Express* and *Caen Express* withdrawn from the sector. They intended to transfer the *Pride of Portsmouth* and *Pride of Le Havre* to Brittany Ferries, together with the crews of both ships and some of the related shore staff, with a view to these vessels remaining on the Portsmouth-Le Havre route until 2007. The *Pride of Cherbourg* would close the Portsmouth-Cherbourg service on 31st December 2004, but the *Pride of Bilbao* would continue operating for P&O Ferries from Portsmouth to Bilbao. NUMAST senior national secretary Paul Moloney said "management, like rabbits in the headlights, are locked into a spiral of decline, rather than seeking imaginative and bold strategies. Over the past five years, our members have had to fight off the effects of the Channel Tunnel, the loss of duty-free sales and the emergence of low-cost airlines and now they are having to fight off the effects of incompetent management." This was not going to be an easy 'sell'.

The plan was publicly backed by comment from Brittany Ferries. Longden said "these are challenging times for the ferry industry with the Channel Tunnel, new seasonal services, increasing competition from low cost airlines and continuous price pressure, led in particular by the Dover-Calais route, resulting in downward pressure on rates. These developments will enable us to provide our customers, both passenger and freight, with the reassurance of route choice and the highest level of service. This initiative by Brittany Ferries will also help us to secure continuity and a significant number of jobs, both on shore in Portsmouth and Le Havre as well as on board the two ships involved."

In an attempt to alleviate widespread concerns about Brittany Ferries' new status as the sole operator of services to France on the western Channel, Longden pledged not to raise fares. He told 'The Times' that "there is a huge difference between being a sole operator and having a monopoly. Anyone can turn up and set sail with a fast craft or ship. It's not like Heathrow – there are plenty of openings for another company to start up." Noting that fares for the 2004 season had been frozen at the same level as 2003, he went on "we can't stand apart from the price war on the Dover-Calais routes. I don't see the western Channel as being in a market of its own. With better roads, driving between Calais and Brittany is a hell of a lot easier these days." Brittany Ferries would offer stable fares and be looking to operate fewer ships but at better times and with better prices. The future would bring a more stable business and maintain full consumer choice of routes.

The proposal envisaged that the *Pride of Portsmouth* and *Pride of Le Havre* would remain under the British flag through a management company, until they were either replaced or Brittany Ferries decided to extend the charter arrangements with their owner, TT-Line. The French press reported that the vessels were to be renamed *Etretat* and *Honfleur* to operate two round sailings per day on the Portsmouth-Le Havre route, with the option of a daytime service to Cherbourg. In the absence of any P&O staff at Portsmouth, Brittany Ferries would become responsible for managing the company's operations. A concerned Portsmouth City Council noted that P&O Ferries was committed to paying £5.2 million a year for use of the Continental Ferry Terminal until 2007.

The memorandum of understanding between P&O Ferries and Brittany Ferries was subjected to consideration by the Office of Fair Trading (OFT). The jointly prepared proposal to the OFT noted that ferry services had seen dramatic changes in the previous decade following the opening of the Channel Tunnel in 1994, the loss of duty-free revenues in 1999, changes in French excise taxes on tobacco, the rise of low cost airlines, the development of the high speed rail network in France, and the increasing competition across all modes of transport to France as a destination. The freight business was seen as a single market across the English Channel, with the short-sea sector providing strong competition for the Portsmouth-Le Havre route, a situation exacerbated by the improvement of motorway connections in France. The proposed transaction was believed to have limited impact on competition because of the ease of entry into the market, with port berth space, ramp slots and vessels for charter all readily available in both the passenger and freight markets. Customers would benefit if the Portsmouth-Le Havre route remained open, rather than being closed or replaced by an inferior service, and there would be minimal disruption to existing travel plans in a changing market. Brittany Ferries would be able to extend its network and offer more efficient sailing schedules following implementation of the proposal but would be constrained from exploiting its sole operator status by competitors in the wider cross-Channel market and the threat of new entrants.

The OFT assembled a large team of consultants and specialists, and began their investigation by spending time visiting the ports to understand the nature of the business. They were particularly interested in the relationships between Brittany Ferries and the French authorities, and the involvement of the latter in management of the business. Although the French and Spanish authorities expressed no objection to the takeover, the OFT announced on 7th December they could not give the green light to the proposals without referring them for further investigation by the Competition Commission to

P&O Ferries' *Pride of Portsmouth* was one of the twin vessels chartered from TT-Line for the Portsmouth-Le Havre service. The high charter costs led to substantial losses for the company. *(Miles Cowsill)*

examine: -

1.   Whether arrangements were in progress or in contemplation which, if carried into effect, would result in the creation of a relevant merger situation; and
2.   if so, whether the creation of that situation may be expected to result in a substantial lessening of competition within any market or markets in the UK.

The decision curtailed Brittany Ferries' immediate plans to utilise the *Pride of Le Havre* and *Pride of Portsmouth* on their schedules. Longden said "whilst we respect the views of the Office of Fair Trading unfortunately this decision prolongs the uncertainty for many employees of P&O who are hoping for some job security, as well as holidaymakers planning their trips to France next year." NUMAST assistant general secretary Mark Dickenson described the decision as extremely disappointing and said the union were going to make a robust case for the proposals to be approved at an early date.

The *Pride of Portsmouth* and *Pride of Le Havre* required significant work to prepare them to match the characteristics of the rest of the Brittany Ferries' fleet. Several options were considered for their deployment. One idea was to strengthen their forecastles and bow doors in a similar way to the modifications made to the *Val de Loire*, and utilise then on the two Spanish services, with the *Pride of Bilbao* returned to Irish Continental Line. This would create a well-balanced service, with consistent capacity. The Portsmouth-Le Havre service could then continue with less sophisticated vessels. The Portsmouth-St Malo route was seen by Longden as a more difficult deployment for the twin ships, as although there would be a very attractive overnight service, the long daytime crossing was a weaker proposition. The *Pont Aven* was the best option for this route if she undertook the daytime crossing at her service speed to minimise the duration, but the 'squat' problem and the cost in fuel and engine stress was prohibitive.

The Competition Commission met at plush premises in London. Longden led the Brittany Ferries delegation to a review session, supported by Maraval and a plethora of lawyers and economists, whose role was to apply supportive 'nudges' as the questioning proceeded. The large number of appointed Commissioners sat theatre-style opposite the Brittany Ferries' team and began the questioning and commentary. It seemed that everyone wanted to be heard so that they featured on the record and justified their presence. The focus of the debate was on pricing. "What guarantees do we have that your pricing will be fair?" the Commissioners asked. Longden responded that markets determined the prices and Brittany Ferries was constrained by the market. "Where are the guarantees?" they asked. Again, Longden replied that "All you have is my word that we wish to stay in business and the market will provide the guarantee." The team left, observing that not one of the Commissioners present had shown any concerns for the P&O Ferries jobs that would be lost if the transaction did not go ahead. The Commissioners continued to deliberate.

The scale of the problems facing P&O Ferries was evident in the company's losses for 2004, which reached £70.0 million following the inclusion of restructuring costs. The cumulative loss in the last decade of trading had reached £176.7 million. In the financial year 2003/4 Brittany Ferries suffered a 3.9% drop in passenger numbers to 2.53 million, with the tourist vehicle traffic down by 3% to 754,936. However, there was continued growth in the freight market, which saw an 8% increase in traffic to 204,291 trailers. Although turnover fell by 4.1% to €346.6 million, the Company was able to publish a consolidated net profit of €19.5 million. The company received a payment of some €15.06 million from the international oil fuel compensation fund for losses suffered as a result of the effects following the grounding of the tanker *Erika* in 2004.

The P&O Ferries fast craft operation had demonstrated that there was an additional market for this type of service which could supplement existing business on the western Channel. All the previous analysis – and the track record of P&O Ferries' operations to date - had suggested that it would be very difficult to achieve a positive financial return from the deployment of fast craft, as they were subject to mechanical breakdown, suffered in bad weather, and could not take freight traffic, whilst consuming considerable quantities of fuel. The Hoverspeed and P&O Ferries' experience, coupled with the outcome of the joint fast craft venture with Condor showed that these craft were only effective on seasonal services. The concept of a Company operated craft went against the long-established Brittany Ferries focus on offering mixed-traffic services, and it proved difficult to find a balanced schedule that could optimise the carrying of passenger business. But the growth achieved by the P&O Ferries Portsmouth-Caen service was not something to be thrown away if the utilisation of a craft could be optimised. And the operation of a fast craft would place further competitive pressure on P&O Ferries, whose operation in the western Channel was looking increasingly fragile. Thoughts turned to opening a fast craft route from Portsmouth to Cherbourg to fill the gap caused by the impending withdrawal of P&O Ferries' service, as the use of the *Bretagne* and *Val de Loire* had not yielded the expected inroads into the market, and they were better deployed on the Portsmouth-St Malo service. The proposed schedule incorporated two round trip sailings each day on the Portsmouth-Cherbourg route between Mondays and Thursdays, but at weekends the vessel could provide additional capacity on the Portsmouth-Caen route. This was the optimal solution that had been looked for.

Longden and Mason headed off to Hobart, Tasmania to meet Bob Clifford of InCat, who had an 'Evolution 10B' catamaran available for charter. The 2000-built 97-metre long vessel (Yard 057) could carry 900 passengers and 280 cars. She had been operating for Tranz Rail between Wellington and Picton in New Zealand and had been laid up in

Hobart for almost 18 months. A charter party was agreed in December 2004 and the vessel was renamed *Normandie Express* the following month.

The *Pont Aven* and *Val de Loire* were chartered to CruiseWorld over the Christmas period with the *Pont Aven* taking a special cruise to Santander on 24th December, returning again to Spain on 31st December. A planned trip to Cork was cancelled and replaced by a short special cruise. Meanwhile, the *Val de Loire* made two festive trips from Portsmouth to Rouen on 24th and 29th December.

P&O Ferries closed the Portsmouth-Cherbourg route after the final sailing of the *Pride of Cherbourg* on 2nd January 2005. This left the *Pride of Bilbao* with an imbalanced service pattern, and her schedule was amended to operate a rolling three-day rotation of sailings to Bilbao, leaving Portsmouth at 20:45 and returning from Bilbao at 13:15 two days later. Brittany Ferries covered the gap in French services with a new Portsmouth-Cherbourg route which commenced operation from 2nd January with the *Normandie*, before the *Val de Loire* later joined the route.

In January, Brittany Ferries announced that the *Barfleur* would operate a Poole-Cherbourg-Portsmouth-Cherbourg-Poole rotation to incorporate the Portsmouth route, instead of a roster of two Poole-Cherbourg sailings each day. The *Normandie* and *Mont St Michel* maintained the Portsmouth-Caen service with the *Val de Loire* running on Portsmouth-St Malo, operating overnight from Portsmouth and returning by day. The *Bretagne* replaced the *Duc de Normandie* on the Plymouth-Roscoff service, operating with the *Pont Aven*. The Cork-Roscoff route re-opened from 1st April with the *Pont Aven*. The *Pont Aven* was to suffer from further technical issues during her first full year of operation.

The *Normandie Express* sailed from Hobart on 22nd January travelling via Indonesia to deliver aid to areas devastated by the Boxing Day 2004 tsunami, in a joint aid project between Brittany Ferries, the vessel's builders Incat, the government of Tasmania, and AusAid. She carried a substantial cargo for the project, including 80 pallets of bottled drinking water, 320 multi-aid tents, 40 sewage treatment plants, several four-wheel drive vehicles including a fire truck, and medical supplies, bedding, baby food and other non-perishable items. She also brought back the yacht *Sill-et-Voilia*, which had been forced to drop out of the Vendée Globe solo round the world race after sustaining hull damage. The *Normandie Express* arrived in France at the end of her delivery voyage on 22nd February. She was re-registered in the Bahamas and manned by British officers and French catering crew in an arrangement managed by Denholm Ship Management. Longden argued that the vessel should be fully British-manned as the working day would start and end in Portsmouth, but Serestel were keen that the on board product be delivered by French crew to deliver quality standards consistent with the rest of the fleet. So, the French catering crew were based in Portsmouth and worked the same roster as the British officers on board, but they drove a hard bargain; the Company was forced to buy two properties to accommodate them in the Portsmouth area and purchase two cars to take them to and from the port.

As the Competition Commission continued their evaluation of the P&O Ferries acquisition proposal through the winter of 2004/5, and the likely publication date for their deliberations slipped towards the summer, Longden's concerns about the transaction grew. There was no sign of letting up in the competitive situation being driven by the short-sea routes, and the continued downward pressure on rates was impacting on the financial viability of the P&O Ferries project. The *Pride of Bilbao* was considered a fine ship, but her charter rates were too expensive to enable her to operate profitably if she was absorbed into the Brittany Ferries fleet. The ongoing examination of the options for utilising the *Pride of Portsmouth* and *Pride of Le Havre* within a combined route structure repeatedly concluded that Brittany Ferries could only 'draw or lose' under the new arrangements. There was no upside that could be seen to be made to work; the P&O Ferries fleet was simply the wrong ships for the wrong routes, and their financial performance was dire. With additional evidence becoming available from the five months of trading since the submission of the proposal, it became clear from the trends in traffic volume and revenue yields that the proposal now had no commercial logic.

The Brittany Ferries Board met to consider the situation and concluded that the Company should continue to take the long-term view and implement their own plan to overcome the challenge of competition from the short-sea sector. They could find their own solution to address the absence of P&O Ferries' services from the market, so it was time to abandon the acquisition proposal. Longden faced the long drive from Plymouth to Dover to meet with Russ Peters of P&O Ferries and advise him of the outcome. Understandably, the decision was not well received. There were serious financial consequences for P&O Ferries and Lord Sterling rang Gourvennec to try and persuade him to change the Board's position, but the call could not alter the logic of the decision. Meanwhile, Longden had an equally difficult conversation with Portsmouth South MP Mike Hancock, who had been supportive of the proposal and was concerned at the loss of jobs in the community.

Subsequent history was to demonstrate that the decision to withdraw from the transaction was the right one. The Competition Commission cancelled their Inquiry on 4th March having received assurances from Brittany Ferries that the proposed acquisition had been abandoned.

The *Normandie Express* began her maiden season on the Portsmouth-Cherbourg/Caen service on 16th March. The fast craft was employed on a daily two round trip sailing schedule, employed on the Portsmouth-Cherbourg operation during the week, and serving the Portsmouth-Caen route on Fridays, Saturdays and Sundays, with a season that continued until 10th November. Longden said "these new high-speed crossings from Portsmouth will complement our existing Poole to Cherbourg fast ferry operation. We recognise that some wish to get to their destination as quick as possible, whereas others seek relaxation and a good French meal that can be enjoyed on one of our more leisurely crossings either by day all night on our luxury cruise ferry services. The important thing for us is to provide a market with the widest possible choice." The *Normandie Express* operated consistently across the summer with no interruptions to service. She provided valuable addition capacity on the Portsmouth-Caen route during peak weekends and achieved good levels of business on both routes. The *Val de Loire* reverted to full operation on the Portsmouth-St Malo route alongside the *Bretagne*.

Meanwhile the *Duc de Normandie* was sold to Trans Europa Ferries in March 2005. She arrived in Ostend on 14th March and was renamed the *Wisteria* before heading to the Mediterranean to operate on the Almeria-Nador route.

On 3rd August news broke of the departure of Maraval, following a strong difference of opinion with Gourvennec about the commercial direction of the Company. The press reported that, with a heavy dependence on the 85% of traffic which came from the British market, the Company needed to develop traffic at a time when France was proving less popular, and low-cost airlines were becoming an increasing threat to the business. Maraval joined the Veolia Group to take charge of their maritime and ferry interests. Sadly, his tenure with Veolia was short, and Maraval died of cancer in 2009 at the age of 55. He left a strong legacy in the Brittany Ferries fleet from the design of the *Bretagne* in 1989 to the *Pont Aven* of 2004; his work on the *Pont Aven* merited the receipt of the ShipPax 'Ferry Concept' award in 2005 'for the overall design and service approach reflecting a unique sense of sophisticated modern European hospitality architecture throughout the public areas and accommodations'.

Gourvennec became ill with cancer in late 2004, and gradually reduced his day to day responsibilities in Brittany Ferries. He appointed Jean-Michel Giguet as Maraval's replacement, promoting him from his responsibilities with Serestel. Martine Nicolas moved from being administrative and finance director to take on the responsibilities of Deputy Director. Recognising the need for a succession, Gourvennec amended the

Company management structure to create a directoire comprising of Giguet, Nicolas and Longden. This group became responsible for directing the entire business. Nicolas looked after the finances, Giguet assumed accountability for all on board services and to a lesser extent the crew, and Longden was responsible for everything else across the business. The structure began to create a single management team, irrespective of geography, and broke down barriers across the Channel. As a consequence, Longden was to spend much of his time in France. It was a new experience for many of the French team to take direction from a Briton.

On the day after the public reports of Maraval's departure, Brittany Ferries announced that agreement had been reached for the construction of a new vessel for the Plymouth-Roscoff route by the Aker yards in Helsinki. The new vessel, given the project name 'Coutances 2', after the vessel which she would replace, was scheduled for delivery in 2007. She would measure 165 metres in length, with a beam of 26.8 metres, and boast deck capacity of 2,200 lane-metres with accommodation comprising of 120 cabins. The contract price totalled €80 million, with an option for a second vessel. The purchase was supported by Senamanche, with Brittany Ferries agreeing to lease the vessel for 25 years.

P&O Ferries closed their Portsmouth-Le Havre route on 30th September, with their final sailing leaving the French port at 16:30. But this was not the end of competition on the route for Brittany Ferries. Within three days the service had been taken up by a new company, LD Lines, a subsidiary of the Louis Dreyfus Armateurs shipping and logistics group. LD Lines initially chartered, then later purchased, a former P&O Ferries vessel, the *Pride of Aquitaine*, which was renamed *Norman Spirit*. LD Lines commenced operations on the Portsmouth-Le Havre route on 3rd October; the *Norman Spirit* was employed on a single round trip sailing each day, operating overnight from Portsmouth with a long lay over in Le Havre prior to her return sailing in the afternoon. The company had ambitious plans to carry one million passengers and 70,000 lorries during the first year of operation, but it was quickly pointed out that this was greater than the capacity of the ship. LD lines positioned itself as a 'no frills' alternative to Brittany Ferries and was to carry 260,000 passengers, 90,000 cars and 36,000 freight units in the first twelve months of operation.

DFDS had long expressed an interest in acquiring the *Val de Loire* from Brittany Ferries, and they made several attempts to interest the Company over a two-year period. Maraval had repeatedly rebuffed the approaches, but with his departure DFDS tried again. Although the *Val de Loire* had been heavily modified to suit her original role before entering service on the Plymouth-Santander route, she did not prove to be a good ship in bad weather. There was a limited opportunity to dispose of her and consider other options for the future. Gourvennec listened to the case and agreed to the transaction. DFDS had a surplus vessel within their fleet that might act as a stop gap until a new vessel could be made available for the route. The *Dana Anglia* was not the most appropriate of vessels but would be a suitable, if short-term, charter. A three-year deal would give time for Brittany Ferries to build another ship for the route. The transaction was completed on 25th November, and the vessel named *Pont l'Abbé* after the capital of Pays Bigouden in Finistère.

It did not take long for Brittany Ferries to announce their plans for a vessel to replace the *Pont l'Abbé*. The 'Armorique 2' project would build a new ship to be modelled on the successful *Mont St Michel* design, and be built by the Aker shipyard in Helsinki. With delivery planned for 2008, she would replace the charter of the *Pont l'Abbé* on the Plymouth-Roscoff route. The ship's specification provoked a lengthy internal debate. Longden wanted her to provide a small restaurant as a 'halo' facility, but the accountants wanted the catering to be profitable, and there was little prospect of a financial return from such a feature. They argued that the *Duc de Normandie*, operated on the route, the restaurant was much admired but little used, largely due to the timing of the sailings. The Company's success had been built on restricting the accountants' influence to reporting

The *Pont l'Abbe* provided a short term capacity substitute after the *Val de Loire* was sold to DFDS. She was replaced by the '*Armorique 2*' project. *(Miles Cowsill)*

on what had happened, rather than what would happen; that was the role of the marketing team. On this occasion the accountants won the argument, and the vessel was planned without a restaurant. This drew much criticism when the ship entered service, but when asked if they would have used a restaurant, critics would respond "No, but I might have..."

The *Val de Loire* made her final sailing on the Portsmouth-Cherbourg route on 20th February 2006, before being handed over to DFDS as the *King of Scandinavia*. The *Pont l'Abbe* took up the Portsmouth-Cherbourg service on 6th March 2006 and transferred to the Plymouth-Roscoff service on 31st March, allowing the *Bretagne* to transfer back to Portsmouth-St Malo. The *Pont l'Abbe* showed a different side to the general perceptions about Scandinavian quality...

The 2004-5 season was another successful one for Brittany Ferries, helped by the demise of P&O Ferries' western Channel services. Passenger numbers grew by 8.8% to reach 2.46 million and freight carryings rose by 10.1% to 232,723 units.

The end of the season marked a watershed for Brittany Ferries. The closure of P&O Ferries' French routes represented the completion of a cycle which had begun back in 1973 when the *Kerisnel* began to challenge the established order of ferry operations. The Company had its roots in the sense of mission shared by the Breton farming community, rather than a commercial group with any desire to be a ferry operator. The service had to remain operational even if not financially viable, as it was required to fulfil the farmers' need to get produce to market ahead of their agricultural competitors. From its earliest days, Brittany Ferries had a unique desire to 'survive'; the aspirations of the Breton funders were modest, and their ambitions were driven by the long-standing Celtic 'cause' and a desire to control their destiny by building an export market to sister regions.

Townsend Thoresen and Sealink were not alone in dismissing the new operation, with a multitude of hurdles erected by authorities in Britain to hinder the fledgling business.

They reckoned without Gourvennec and his colleagues, and the passion and commitment with which they met the multitude of challenges thrown at them. Brittany Ferries could have gone under on several occasions during the first three decades of existence, but each time it faced oblivion, resources were marshalled to overcome the issues and take the business to another level.

The appointment of Christian Michielini and the freedom given to professional management in the UK, the introduction of SEM funding and the long-term perspective this engendered, the creation of Serestel and transformation of the on board product, and the detailed understanding enabled by investment in systems, were all milestones in building a formidable business. The Anglo-French management structure created clear

Old and new. The *Duc de Normandie* is passed by the *Pont Aven* at Roscoff. *(Ferry Publications Library)*

responsibilities according to respective strengths and brought out the best from both nationalities. This was a true multi-national enterprise. Loyal British colleagues embraced the Breton cause and proved equally committed and passionate as their French counterparts to the achievement of success. There were good years and bad years, but the Company and its funding partners consistently took the long-term view and invested for the future. Brittany Ferries remains French-owned in 2020 and has the same shareholders today as it had back when the services opened in 1973, a fact which the Breton community remains very proud of.

A high proportion of the early employees spent their working lives with the Company, exhibiting a strong degree of loyalty and commitment to the cause. Many others joined later in the story, absorbed 'l'esprit de Brittany Ferries', and progressed to become the senior team of today. The Brittany Ferries culture was summarised well in this description.

Employees did not work by badges of rank. There were some people in suits and there were others in boiler suits, but there was an equality for all based around a common purpose, which helped distinguish the Company from its competitors.

Other ferry companies were more conventional commercially-driven enterprises, that had the comparative freedom to adapt their route structure as the financial demands of the balance sheet dictated. They did not share the degree of commitment shown by Brittany Ferries to the regional market of the western Channel and the Spanish routes, and the 'short-termism' of their fleet strategies often helped rather than hinder the Company. But this wider focus also led to the adoption of pricing strategies that supported the commercial interests of the short-sea routes rather than the longer crossings in their portfolios. Ultimately the long-term perspective and regional focus of Brittany Ferries trumped the shorter term demands of competitors' shareholders, and the French business model proved the most resilient.

The buccaneering early days of Brittany Ferries were a necessary phase in building a new and different approach, and tackle the adversity that features so prominently in this story. The Company gradually matured into an organisation that brought consistency of quality and a professional approach across the business, whilst delivering a long-term fleet investment plan. With an industry-leading holiday business and award-winning vessels at sea, Brittany Ferries was well positioned to become the sole operator of cruise ferry services from Britain and Ireland to both France and Spain. The Cause had truly become a Brand.

Fourteen
Postscript

Sharon Alexander, who joined Brittany Ferries in 1976 and compiled the reservation charts for the first *Armorique*, stands in front of the second *Armorique* at Plymouth. She is still working for Brittany Ferries in 2020, some 43 years after joining the Company. *(Paul Burns collection)*

Sadly, neither Christian Michielini or Alexis Gourvennec were able to enjoy the long healthy retirement that their contribution to Brittany Ferries' success richly deserved. Gourvennec died on 19th February 2007 and Michielini followed less than a year later on 30th January 2008.

Competition on western Channel ferry services remained limited after the withdrawal of P&O Ferries' French routes from Portsmouth. The Portsmouth-Bilbao route continued until the charter of the *Pride of Bilbao* was completed, and the service closed on 28th September 2010. The LD lines operation between Portsmouth and Le Havre continued as a one ship service, and was transferred to DFDS Seaways France in 2013 before being closed by them at the end of the following year.

Meanwhile, Brittany Ferries continued their programme of fleet investment. The *Cotentin* was completed in 2007 at the Aker Finnyard in Helsinki for the Poole-Cherbourg route, and opened a new link from Poole to Santander. The second *Armorique* was launched in Finland in 2008 and was joined in 2010 by the acquisition of the *Cap Finistère*, the former *Superfast V*. She was utilised to offer a replacement for the withdrawn P&O Ferries service from Portsmouth to Bilbao, which helped up the number of weekly sailings to Spain to five. The 40th anniversary of the inaugural sailing as celebrated in 2013 in difficult financial conditions, and the *Cotentin* was withdrawn from operation at the end of the summer. The problems were short lived, and Brittany Ferries bounced back to record carryings in 2014, helped by the charter of the *Etretat* and the introduction of 'économie' sailings from Portsmouth to Le Havre and Santander to offer strong competition to low cost airlines. This success encouraged the charter of the *Baie de Seine* to bolster the Spanish services and release the *Etretat* to grow the Portsmouth-Le Havre route.

Expanding freight volumes resulted in the charter of the *Pelican* from 2016, in a year in which the Company saw further expansion of passenger and car carryings, with a record 21,900 passengers carried on 14th August 2016. At the end of the year, Brittany Ferries signed a letter of intent with the FSG shipyard in Germany for a new vessel for the Portsmouth-Caen service to be called the *Honfleur* for introduction in summer 2019, although protracted delays at the builders ultimately led to the cancellation of the order in 2020. However, contracts were signed with Stena Ro-Ro in 2018 for two E-Flexer vessels for the Spanish services, later joined by a third order, which will bring a degree of homogeneity to the fleet for the first time.

A new generation of management has brought fresh direction to the Company, which now operates on a scale undreamt of when the *Kerisnel* left Roscoff for the first time in 1973.

Brittany Ferries is still owned by the original Breton agricultural co-operative shareholders in 2020. The Company has grown to a turnover of around €444.2m each year and provides employment for up to 3,100 people at the peak, including 1,700 seafarers and 360 in the UK. The services have expanded to embrace the ports of Portsmouth, Poole, Plymouth, Cork, Rosslare, Caen, Cherbourg, Le Havre, St Malo, Roscoff, Bilbao, and Santander, served by a fleet of twelve ships. Between 2.5 and 2.7 million passengers are carried in a 'normal' year, accompanied by 900,000 cars and 210,000 freight units. Although the Covid-19 virus hit traffic hard in 2020, Brittany Ferries opened new routes from Rosslare to Bilbao and Roscoff, with the latter service due to switch to Cherbourg in 2021. The Company continues to invest in modern, innovative and environmentally friendly ships as part of an ongoing fleet renewal strategy, with three new vessels programmed to join the fleet by 2023. Brittany Ferries retains its position as France's leading maritime transport operator, with an award-winning reputation for service, and continues to demonstrate its resilience in the face of challenging external events. A long-term perspective and a consistent investment in quality continues to serve Brittany Ferries well as the Company approaches its half century of operation.

Long may it continue to do so.

The Fleet 1973-2005

BRITTANY FERRIES FLEET

	Built	GT	Pass	Cars	Freight	Brittany Ferries service
Ailsa Princess	1971	3,715	1,800	190		1982
Armorique	1972	5,732	700	170		1976-1993
Barfleur	1992	20,133	1,212	550	1,530	1992 to date
Beaverdale	1977	5,669	12	-	780	1987, 1989
Bénodet	1970	4,238	1,200	260		1983-1984
Bonanza	1972	2,718	750	200	1976	
Breizh-Izel	1970	2,769	12		65 tlr	1980-1987
Bretagne	1989	24,534	2,056	580	735	1989 to date
Celtic Pride	1972	7,801	1,000	170		1987-1988
Condor Vitesse	1997	5,007	800	200	-	2001-2007
Cornouailles	1977	3,383	550	205	450	1977-1989
Coutances	1978	2,736	58		800	1986-2007
Dania	1972	722	12		480	1979
Duc de Normandie	1978	13,505	1,500	320	528	1986-2005
Duchesse Anne	1979	9,796	1,500	332		1989-1996
Faraday	1980	2,932	12		1,230	1980
Gabrielle Wehr	1978	1,599	12	-	1,148	1988
Goelo	1967	5,073	1,170	210	-	1980-1982
Gotland	1973	6,642	1,670	300	-	1988
Kerisnel	1972	3,395	12	-	540	1972-1974
Miseva	1972	6,057	12	-	552	1987
Mont St Michel	2002	35,592	2,120	874	2,250	2002 to date
Munster	1968	4,067	1,000	220	-	1979
Normandia	1970	2,312	12	-	636	1979
Normandie	1992	27,541	2,160	648	1,720	1992 to date
Normandie Express	2000	6,581	900	260		2005 to date
Normandie Shipper	1973	4,078	36	-	1,050	1989-1999
Olau West	1963	3,061	1,500	180		1976
Penn-Ar-Bed	1974	2,891	250	235		1974-1984
Pont Aven	2004	41,589	2,400	650		2004 to date
Poseidon	1964	1,358	805	-	-	1973
Prince de Bretagne	1975	2,424	346	250		1975
Prince of Brittany	1970	5,464	1,020	210	20 tlr	1978-1989
(Reine Mathilde)						1989-1991
Purbeck	1978	6,507	58	-	60 tlr	1986-1994, 1997, 2000-2003

Quiberon	1975	7,927	1,140	252	540	1982-2002
Regina	1972	8,020	1,000	170	-	1979
Skarvøy	1974	3,710	12	-	695	1990
Stena Searider	1973	3,209	12	-	1,000	1985-1986
Trégastel	1971	3,998	1,500	370		1985-1991
Val de Loire	1987	31,360	2,280	570	1,250	1993-2006
Valérie	1972	3,390				1974
Viking 1	1970	4,485	1,200	260		1982

Brittany Ferries owned vessels in bold, chartered ships in italics.

CHANNEL ISLAND FERRIES FLEET

	Built	GT	Pass	Cars	Freight	CIF/BCIF service
Beauport (BCIF)	1970	5,464	1,020	210	-	1989, 1992-1993
Breizh-Izel (BCIF)	1970	2,769	12	-	65 tlr	1986-1988
Corbière	1970	4,238	1,200	260	-	1985-1988
Havelet (BCIF)	1976	6,918	500	205	-	1986, 1987, 1989-1994
Portelet (BCIF)	1967	6,280	1,200	170	-	1987-1988
Rozel (BCIF)	1973	8,987	1,300	296	-	1989-1992
Sylbe (BCIF)	1971	982	-	-	-	1990-1993

BRITTANY FERRIES FLEET BY YEAR

1972   *Kerisnel*

1973   *Kerisnel, (Poseidon)*

1974   *Kerisnel, Penn-Ar-Bed, Valérie*

1975   *Prince de Bretagne, Penn-Ar-Bed*

1976   *Armorique, Bonanza, Olau West, Penn-Ar-Bed*

1977   *Armorique, Cornouailles, Penn-Ar-Bed*

1978   *Armorique, Cornouailles, Penn-Ar-Bed, Prince of Brittany*

1979   *Armorique, Cornouailles, Dania, Munster, Normandia, Penn-Ar-Bed, Prince of Brittany,   Regina*

1980   *Armorique, Breizh-Izel, Cornouailles, Faraday, Goelo, Penn-Ar-Bed, Prince of Brittany*

1981   *Armorique, Breizh-Izel, Cornouailles, Goelo, Penn-Ar-Bed, Prince of Brittany*

1982   *Ailsa Princess, Armorique, Breizh-Izel, Cornouailles, Goelo, Penn-Ar-Bed, Prince of Brittany, Quiberon, Viking 1*

1983   *Armorique, Bénodet, Breizh-Izel, Cornouailles, Penn-Ar-Bed, Prince of Brittany, Quiberon*

1984   *Armorique, Bénodet, Breizh-Izel, Cornouailles, Penn-Ar-Bed, Prince of Brittany, Quiberon*

1985   *Armorique, Breizh-Izel, Cornouailles, Prince of Brittany, Quiberon, Stena Searider, Trégastel*

1986   *Armorique, Breizh-Izel, Cornouailles, Coutances, Duc de Normandie, Prince of Brittany, Purbeck, Quiberon, Stena Searider, Trégastel*

1987	*Armorique, Beaverdale, Breizh-Izel, Celtic Pride, Cornouailles, Coutances, Duc de Normandie, Miseva, Prince of Brittany, Purbeck, Quiberon, Trégastel*
1988	*Armorique, Celtic Pride, Cornouailles, Coutances, Duc de Normandie, Gabrielle Wehr, Gotland, Prince of Brittany, Purbeck, Quiberon, Trégastel*
1989	*Armorique, Beaverdale, Bretagne, Cornouailles, Coutances, Duc de Normandie, Duchesse Anne, Normandie Shipper, Reine Mathilde, Purbeck, Quiberon, Trégastel*
1990	*Armorique, Bretagne, Coutances, Duc de Normandie, Duchesse Anne, Normandie Shipper, Reine Mathilde, Purbeck, Quiberon, Skarvøy, Trégastel*
1991	*Armorique, Bretagne, Coutances, Duc de Normandie, Duchesse Anne, Normandie Shipper, Reine Mathilde, Purbeck, Quiberon, Trégastel*
1992	*Armorique, Barfleur, Bretagne, Coutances, Duc de Normandie, Duchesse Anne, Normandie, Normandie Shipper, Purbeck, Quiberon*
1993	*Armorique, Barfleur, Bretagne, Coutances, Duc de Normandie, Duchesse Anne, Normandie, Normandie Shipper, Purbeck, Quiberon, Val de Loire*
1994	*Barfleur, Bretagne, Coutances, Duc de Normandie, Duchesse Anne, Normandie, Normandie Shipper, Quiberon, Val de Loire*
1995	*Barfleur, Bretagne, Coutances, Duc de Normandie, Duchesse Anne, Normandie, Normandie Shipper, Quiberon, Val de Loire*
1996	*Barfleur, Bretagne, Coutances, Duc de Normandie, Duchesse Anne, Normandie, Normandie Shipper, Quiberon, Val de Loire*
1997	*Barfleur, Bretagne, Coutances, Duc de Normandie, Normandie, Normandie Shipper, Purbeck, Quiberon, Val de Loire*
1998	*Barfleur, Bretagne, Coutances, Duc de Normandie, Normandie, Normandie Shipper, Quiberon, Val de Loire*
1999	*Barfleur, Bretagne, Coutances, Duc de Normandie, Normandie, Normandie Shipper, Quiberon, Val de Loire*
2000	*Barfleur, Bretagne, Coutances, Duc de Normandie, Normandie, Purbeck, Quiberon, Val de Loire*
2001	*Barfleur, Bretagne, Condor Vitesse, Coutances, Duc de Normandie, Normandie, Purbeck, Quiberon, Val de Loire*
2002	*Barfleur, Bretagne, Condor Vitesse, Coutances, Duc de Normandie, Mont St Michel, Normandie, Purbeck, Quiberon. Val de Loire*
2003	*Barfleur, Bretagne, Condor Vitesse, Coutances, Duc de Normandie, Mont St Michel, Normandie, Purbeck, Val de Loire*
2004	*Barfleur, Bretagne, Condor Vitesse, Coutances, Duc de Normandie, Mont St Michel, Normandie, Pont Aven, Val de Loire*
2005	*Barfleur, Bretagne, Condor Vitesse, Coutances, Duc de Normandie, Mont St Michel, Normandie, Normandie Express, Pont Aven, Val de Loire*

Abbreviations and Bibliography

AA: Automobile Association
ACAS: Advisory, Conciliation and Arbitration Service
ABP: Associated British Ports
AIA: Architectes Ingénieurs Associés
BAI: Bretagne Angleterre Irlande
BCB: Bryan, Constantinidi & Brightwell
BCIF: British Channel Island Ferries
BTDB: British Transport Docks Board
Cerafel: Comité Économique Régional Agricole Fruits et Légumes de Bretagne
CFDT: Confédération Française Démocratique du Travail
CGT: Confédération Générale du Travail
CIÉ: Córas Iompair Éireann
EEC: European Economic Community
EIG: Economic Interest Group
ERM: Exchange Rate Mechanism
ETA: Euskadi Ta Askatasuna
EU: European Union
FCB: Foote, Cone and Belding
FGTO: French Government Tourist Office
FPOC: French Property Owners Club
FTO: French Tourist Office
HSS: High Speed Sea Service
ITX: Inclusive Tour fare
lo-lo: lift-on lift-off
L&SWR: London & South Western Railway
MMD: Mainland Market Deliveries
NUMAST: National Union of Marine, Aviation and Shipping Transport Officers
NUR: National Union of Railwaymen
NUS: National Union of Seamen
OFT: Office of Fair Trading
OPEC: Organisation of Petroleum Exporting Countries
POLMAR: POLlution MARitime
QHM: Queen's Harbour Master
RAC: Royal Automobile Club
ro-ro: roll-on roll-off
RMT: National Union of Rail, Maritime and Transport Workers
RSPCA: Royal Society for the Prevention of Cruelty to Animals
Sabemen: Société Anonyme Bretonne d'Économie Mixte d'Équipement Naval
SAGA: Société Anonyme de Gérance et d'Armement
SEM: Société d'Économie Mixte
Senacal: Société d'Équipement Naval du Calvados

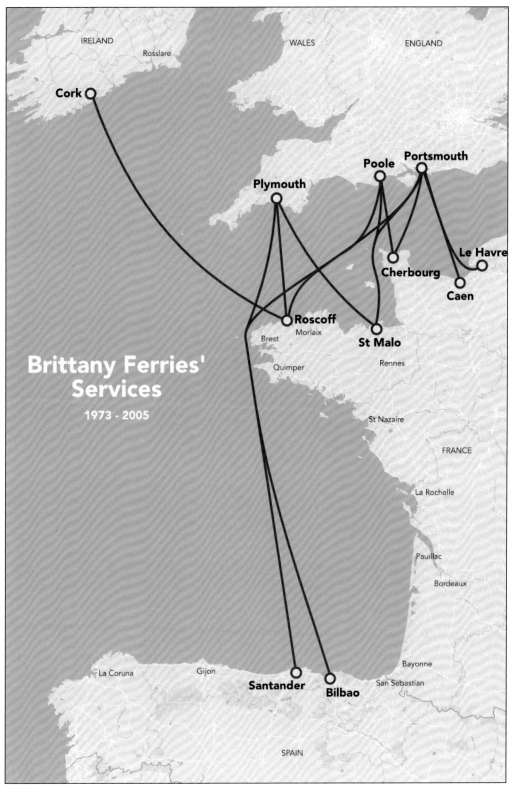

Brittany Ferries'
Services

1973 - 2005

Senamanche: Société d'Équipement Naval de la Manche
Serestel: Société De Services De Restauration et D'Hotellerie
SICA: Société d'Intérêt Collectif Agricole
SMZ: Stoomvart Maatschappijby Zeeland
SNAT: Société Nationale d' Armement Transmanche
SNCF: Société Nationale des Chemins de fer Français
SOLAS: Safety of Life at Sea
TGWU: Transport & General Workers Union
THF: Trust House Forte

Bibliography

Atkins Tony (2014): Great Western Docks and Marine
Baudoin Alain & Dautriat Louis (1977): Alexis Gourvennec, Paysan-Directeur General
Bell B (1994): Insight Guide Brittany
Cowsill Miles & Hendy John (1988): The Townsend Thoresen Years
Cowsill Miles (1989): Only Brittany Ferries
Cowsill Miles (1993): Brittany Ferries, de la terre a la mer
Cowsill Miles (1995): Ferries of Portsmouth and the Solent
Cowsill Miles (2007): Brittany Ferries 1973-2007
Cowsill Miles & Merrigan Justin (2013): Irish Ferries an ambitious voyage
Cowsill Miles & Bombail Marc-Antoine (2018): Brittany Ferries, The Fleet Book
Fairhall David & Jordan Philip (1980): Black Tide Rising: The wreck of the Amoco Cadiz
Faulkner JN & Williams RA (1988): The LSWR in the twentieth century
Geli Helene (2003): L'epopee d'un armement paysan
Genicot Christian (Ed): Brittany Ferries Story 1973-1993
Hendy John (2009): Dover-Calais, the short sea route
Hendy John, Merrigan Justin & Peter Bruce (2015): Sealink and before
Holland George (2016): The LD Lines Story
Kirkman Richard (2013): Battle for the passenger (in Ferry & Cruise 2014)
Kirkman Richard (2018): By Sea to the Channel Islands
Lucking JH (1971): The Great Western at Weymouth
Merrigan Justin (2004): Car Ferries of the Irish Sea 1954-2004
Murtland Matthew & Seville Richard (2015): Sealink and beyond
Ortel K (2014): TT Line through five decades
Peter Bruce & Dawson Philip (2010): The Ferry: a drive through history
Peter Bruce (2012): Knud E. Hansen A/S: 75 years of ship design
Piette Gwenno (2008): A concise history of Brittany
Le Scelleur Kevin (1997): Commodore Shipping - The First Half Century 1947-1997
Sibiril Alain, Sibiril Monique & James Trevor (2009): Rendezvous in Princetown
Wilson Jeremy & Spick Jerome (1994): Eurotunnel – the illustrated journey

Acknowledgements

The *Normandie* leaves Portsmouth for Caen prior to her scrubber work. *(Brian D. Smith)*

The inspiration for this volume came from a meeting with Ian Carruthers, during which he recounted stories of the early buccaneering years of Brittany Ferries; it was clear there was an epic saga to be told. The author spent part of his career with BCIF, and later was one who monitored the progress of Brittany Ferries from the perspective of being a competitor in P&O European Ferries. It has been illuminating to see the inside story revealed. He is grateful to Lainson Publishing for bringing this project to fruition.

Compilation of this book would not have been possible without the significant contributions from a large number of individuals who gave generously of their time and helped research detail from their own and other archives of material. Much personal information and many anecdotes are published for the first time and I thank all those who agreed to having their recollections published.

The project was initiated with a series of extensive and lively interviews and round table discussions involving Paul Burns, Ian Carruthers, Miles Cowsill, David Longden, Jim Mason, and Toby Oliver, which not only provided colour for the narrative, but reinvigorated the passion and drive that characterised the early years of the Company. Richard Dunning told the advertising tale from the perspective of Rook Dunning; sadly, Bill Rook and Derek Brightwell died many years ago and Michael Constantinidi passed away during the preparation of the manuscript. Julie Burrows, Phil Bowditch, and Jim Butler, remembered their time with the UK Company; Modesto Piñeiro Jnr recalled his father's and his own time with the Spanish Company, Anne Murphy (nee Upton) and Trish Murphy, their time with the Irish Company. All provided helpful anecdotes, and several members of the current Brittany Ferries team added their own perspective. Few companies can have such a strong track record of recruiting and retaining such loyal employees, who went on to spend the bulk of their careers embracing a common cause and brand.

Dr. Bruno Michielini, son of Christian, supported by Marie-Jo Véron, who spent many years as personal assistant to Michielini, sourced material from the family collection and helped portray the humour that was so much part of his father's life. Modesto Pinheiro Jr. brought a Spanish perspective to the story and went through the family archives in Santander to help illustrate his father and grandfather's productive relationship with Brittany Ferries. Alain Sibiril gave a unique view of the start of the Company told from, what is believed to be, the perspective of the Company's first customer and graciously made available a number of invaluable items from his collection of memorabilia. Lindsay Clarke provided valuable insight into the life of her aunt, Josee Dyer. Mick Gilbert researched and provided material from the Rook Dunning archive, producing a comprehensive selection of brochures and advertising material from the collection to support the narrative.

John Hendy, Bruno Michielini, Modesto Pinheiro Jr and Brian D Smith trawled their photographic collections to source images to enhance the book, and further images were provided by Miles Cowsill, the Ferry Publications Library, FotoFlite, Lachlan Goudie, Dave Hoquard, Robert Le Maistre, Sara Mackeown (Port of Cork) and the Plymouth Herald.

Miles Cowsill applied his consummate skill and flair to the book design, and was hugely encouraging throughout the project.

The books listed in the Bibliography have each added different details to the narrative. Further background material was sourced from the British Newspaper archive, The Times and Sunday Times archive, the Guardian and Observer archives, and the archives of Ouest France, Le Journal de la Marine Marchande and Le Télégramme. British Ferry Scene, which later expanded to become British & European Ferry Scene and now Ferry & Cruise Review (of which the author is editor), has consistently provided an invaluable quarterly review of vessel deployments, news and competitor activity.

The biggest thanks go to my loving wife Christina, who graciously tolerated her husband's all too frequent disappearances to 'work on the book'. I hope this book justifies her patience.

Richard Kirkman
Seaford, East Sussex
August 2020